Kay L. Gorman
January 1998

PREFACE.

In presenting to the public THE ANNALS OF THE WAR, the publishers do not assume to offer only that which is thoroughly reliable as chapters in the history of the most thrilling and bloody drama of the century, but it is assumed that in no way can the truth of history be so nearly ascertained as by the statements of the leading actors themselves. The series of contributions contained in this volume were furnished as special articles for THE PHILADELPHIA WEEKLY TIMES, with the view of correcting many of the grave errors of the hastily compiled, heedlessly imperfect, and strongly partisan histories which appeared during and soon after the close of the war.

The fierce passions which attend civil war are unequaled in any conflicts between separate peoples, and the advanced intelligence, the community of interest, the common pride of past achievements, and the long maintained brotherhood through generations, all intensified the bitterness of our internecine strife. A war so gigantic, enduring for four long years, so costly in blood and treasure, and reaching almost every household with its sore bereavements, could not but inflame the bitterest passions and resentments, obliterate recollections of virtue in each other's foes, and direct all the agencies of power to color the causes and events of the war to harmonize with the prejudices which ruled North and South.

It was to correct as far as possible the pages of the future history of the war of the late rebellion, that the contributions herein given were solicited, and they have all been *written with the view of attaining that purpose. Already many of the leading actors of the war have passed away. Lincoln fell by the assassin's hand just when he had achieved the final victory for the Union, lamented by those who were then his foes as keenly as by the loyal men who so bravely sustained him; and of his original cabinet but two members survive. Stanton, the great War Minister, has gone to his final account; Mead and Lee, who met the shock of decisive battle at Gettysburg, now sleep in the "City of the Silent;" and hundreds of others, who were conspicuous in civil councils and on the sanguinary field, are in their eternal rest. Official sources of reliable information have perished in a multitude of instances, and the country is to-day without a single trustworthy history of the greatest struggle in the records of any modern civilization.*

The Annals of the War furnish the most valuable contributions to the future historian which have yet been given to the world. They are far from being perfect; but they have elicited the truth to a degree that no other means could have accomplished. They are from the pens of a number of the most honored, intelligent and impartial of the immediate actors in the scenes they portray. They embrace in the list of authors men of high rank in military circles on both sides, and statesmen and historians of great trust and attainments, who favored the cause of both the Blue and the Gray. That they are entirely free from prejudice or from the coloring that all must accept in describing momentous events with which they were interwoven by every inspiration of devotion and ambition, is not to be pretended; but that they are written in integrity of purpose, and that they give the substance of the truth, can be justly claimed for them. Coming as they do from soldiers and civilians of both sides, presenting the same battles and the same results from entirely different standpoints, they, of necessity, often proffer antagonistic conclusions; but the freedom of expression from the opposing heroes, has enabled the intelligent and impartial student to arrive as nearly at the exact truth as history can ever attain. The Confederate story of the battle of Gettysburg has never been accurately given to the world until it was done by the various contributions to THE PHILADELPHIA WEEKLY TIMES, and now herein reproduced, commencing with the exhaustive narrative of General Longstreet. That publication has led to a multitude of explanatory articles from the highest Southern military authorities, until the whole truth is now, for the first time, presented for the future historian of the war.

Nor do THE ANNALS OF THE WAR limit their interest to the details of military history, the manœuvres of armies, or the mere achievements of the sword. They present the most entertaining and instructive chapters of many of the countless incidents of a great war, which will be gratefully preserved by a people justly proud of their heroism in their homes, at their altars, and in their multitude of trials outside of the flame of battle. Of the many narratives gathered in this volume, none will be of more enduring interest and profit to the general reader, North and South, than the records of social life, the individual and untitled heroism displayed by men, women and children in the sad drama that yet lingers in every memory. Not only in the great conflicts of armies, but in all the efforts summoned by the necessities of desolating strife, there are chapters of history herein given which tell of the grandeur of the whole American people; of their courage in war; of their beneficence in peace; of their devotion to home and country; of their completed circle of attributes, which united again under one constitution, one supreme national authority, and looking to one destiny, make them the noblest people of the earth.

The sword has been sheathed between the North and the South; the banners of the Blue and of the Gray have been furled; the dead of the conflict have sacred sepulchre; flowers bloom for the now peaceful warriors as they sleep side by side in their mingled dust; monuments dot the hillsides and plains where the battle once raged, telling of the matchless heroism of American soldiers. Federal and Confederate chieftains sit in the same Senate and House as national law-makers; in the same cabinet of Presidential advisers, and heroes of both armies represent the reunited Republic in foreign lands. Peace has spread her silver wings over the desolation and bereavements of the terrible conflict, and Liberty and Law are the declared attributes of free government for all classes, conditions and races amongst us. Of such a country and such a people the truth of history must be the grandest eulogy, and THE ANNALS OF THE WAR will be the most welcome of eulogiums, because the most faithful record of their achievements.

A. K. M.

PHILADELPHIA, *January, 1879.*

CONTENTS.

WITH ILLUSTRATIONS.

THE ANNALS OF THE WAR.

THE FIRST IRON-CLAD MONITOR.

BY HON. GIDEON WELLES.

THE Navy of the United States, at the commencement of Mr. Lincoln's administration, was feeble, and in no condition for belligerent operations. Most of the vessels in commission were on foreign service; only three or four, and they of an inferior class, were available for active duty. Neither the retiring administration nor Congress seemed to have been aware of the actual condition of public affairs, or to have apprehended serious difficulty. No preparations had been made for portentous coming events. The assault upon Sumter, followed by proclamations to blockade the whole coast, from the Chesapeake to the Rio Grande, a distance of more than three thousand miles, necessitated prompt and energetic action by the Navy Department, to make the blockade effectual. Steps were immediately taken to fit out and put in commission every naval vessel, and to secure and arm every suitable vessel that could be procured from the merchant service. Commerce and the shipping interest were, for a time, so paralyzed by the war that a large number of excellent vessels were purchased on terms highly advantageous to the government. There was, in fact, an extraordinary pressure, by owners, to induce the Navy Department to take not only good, but old vessels, such as were not, from their size or defects, adapted to the service required. Large and expensive steamers, thrown out of employment, were tendered, at almost any price, by parties in interest, who, desirous to assist the government in that emergency, as well as to get rid of their steamers, were actuated by patriotic as well as interested motives. The Vanderbilt, the Baltic, the Illinois, and

2

other steamers of immense tonnage, costing a large amount to purchase, in the first instance, and which would have been a great expense to move and keep afloat. Vessels wholly unfit, from their great draught, to perform blockade duty on our shallow coast, were urged upon the Department, which declined to purchase them, and was soundly berated for declining. Economy and efficiency required a smaller and different class of vessels. The Secretary of the Navy was compelled to act without legislative authority or appropriation, and without funds, he, on his own responsibility, entered into contract for thirty gunboats, each of about five hundred tons.

The Government was wholly destitute of iron-clad steamers or floating batteries; little interest had been given the subject, but the attention of Congress was invited thereto, at the extra session in July. The suggestions of the Secretary were approved, and an act was passed on the third of August, placing at the disposal of the Navy Department one and a-half millions of dollars, to carry his recommendation into effect. On the seventh of August an advertisement was issued, inviting plans and proposals for armed vessels. On the next day, the eighth of August, a board of naval officers was appointed to receive and report upon the plans which might be submitted within twenty-five days.

Commodore Joseph Smith, Chief of the Bureau of Yards and Docks, was the senior officer and chairman of this Board, and with him were associated Commodore Hiram Paulding and Captain Charles H. Davis. All were officers of merit, but Commodore Smith, in addition to great nautical and civil experience, possessed a singularly mechanical and practical mind. On him devolved, ultimately, the chief responsibility and supervision of the execution of the plans adopted. My personal relations and acquaintance with him were not only friendly, but I may say intimate. We were each made Chief of a Naval Bureau, in the spring of 1846, and from the acquaintance then first commenced, I had confidence in his ability and intelligence, which was increased when, fifteen years later, I was called to preside over the Navy Department, where he had remained on continuous duty. I had, therefore, whenever required, the benefit of his counsel and judgment.

Before the limit of twenty-five days for receiving proposals for iron-clads expired, I went to Hartford, which place I had not revisited after leaving, in February, on Mr. Lincoln's invitation to become a member of his Cabinet. While at Hartford, Mr. Cornelius S. Bushnell laid before me a model, invented by John Ericsson, for a turreted vessel, or floating battery, which impressed me favorably, as possessing some extraordinary and valuable features, tending to the development of certain principles, then being studied, for our coast and river blockade, involving a revolution in naval warfare. The twenty-five days for receiving proposals had, I think, expired; but I was so interested in this novel proposition that I directed Mr. Bushnell to proceed immediately to Washington, and submit the model to the Board for examination and report. But, deeming the subject of great importance, and fearing the Board would be restrained by the limit of twenty-five days, I immediately followed, and arrived in Washington almost as soon as Mr. Bushnell with the model.

Seventeen plans for armored vessels were submitted, and propositions made, by different parties, for their construction. Three of them received a favorable report, among them Ericsson's turret vessel, with guns of immense calibre, which, when built, was called, by his request, the "Monitor."

A contract for this vessel was made and signed on the fourth of October, 1861. It was stipulated that she should be complete in all her parts and appurtenances; should have a speed of eight knots per hour, with security or successful working of the turret and guns, with safety to the vessel and the men in the turrets, and "that said vessel and equipments, in all respects, shall be completed and ready for sea in one hundred days from the date of this indenture." It was agreed by the Navy Department, that the Government should pay therefor $275,000, in payments of $50,000, with the usual reservation of 25 per cent. as the work progressed, and that the final payment should be made after tests, satisfactory to the Navy Department, but which tests should be within ninety days after she was turned over to the Government.

Unfortunately for the design of the Navy Department, and, perhaps, for the country, there was delay on the part of the contractors. Instead of completing and delivering the vessel as stipulated, in one hundred days, which would have been in January, she was not turned over to the Government until the third of March—forty days later than was agreed upon and expected. This delay of forty days defeated an arrangement which the Navy Department originally designed, if successful, should be a satisfactory test of the capabilities of this extraordinary vessel. That test may now be stated.

The steamship "Merrimac," a naval vessel, which the rebels scuttled and sunk the day previous to the abandonment of the Navy Yard at Norfolk, they subsequently raised and took into the dry-dock, where she was being repaired and clothed with iron armor, when the contract for the "Monitor" was made. We, of course, felt great solicitude in regard to this proceeding of the rebels, not lessened by the fact that extraordinary pains were taken by them to keep secret from us their labors and purposes. Their efforts to withhold information, though rigid, were not wholly successful, for we contrived to get occasional vague intelligence of the work as it progressed. When the contract for the "Monitor" was made, in October, with a primary condition that she should be ready for sea in one hundred days, the Navy Department intended that the battery should, immediately after reaching Hampton Roads, proceed up Elizabeth river to the Navy Yard at Norfolk, place herself opposite the dry-dock, and with her heavy guns destroy both the dock and the "Merrimac." This was our secret. The "Monitor" could easily have done what was required, for her appearance at Norfolk would have been a surprise. But the hundred days expired, weeks passed on, and the "Monitor" was not ready.

Late in February, a negro woman, who resided in Norfolk, came to the Navy Department and desired a private interview with me. She and others had closely watched the work upon the "Merrimac," and she, by their request, had come to report that the ship was nearly finished, had come out of the dock, and was about receiving her armament. The woman had passed through the lines, at great risk to herself, to bring me the information, and, in confirmation of her statement, she took from the bosom of her dress a letter from a Union man, a mechanic in the Navy Yard, giving briefly the facts as stated by her. This news, of course, put an end to the test, which had been originally designed, of destroying the "Merrimac" in the dry-dock; but made us not less anxious for the speedy completion of the battery.

The capitalists who were associated with Mr. Ericsson in the contract for the "Monitor," even though delinquent as to time, are entitled to great credit for what they did, although, in addition to patriotic impulses, it was with them a business transaction, for which they claimed and received consideration in subsequent contracts. But, while acknowledging their merits, injustice should not be done to others.

The "Monitor" was one of the early, and, it may be said, one of the most prominent practical developments of what may be called the American idea evolved by our civil war, which has wrought a change in naval warfare—that of concentrating the weight of metal in the smallest possible compass, and presenting the slightest possible target to an enemy. In the single shot of a fifteen-inch gun is compressed a weight of metal equal to a whole broadside of our old wooden ships, which, with their lofty bulwarks standing many feet out of water, presented a magnificent mark for the heavy ordnance of a floating and almost submerged "Monitor" battery to perforate. Whatever patriotic or money-making motives may have actuated or influenced the contractors, they were but the agents or instruments of the Navy Department in developing certain principles relative to ordnance and armament—assault and resistance—which it had a purpose to accomplish.

In Ericsson's invention there was an advance made, an incipient step taken toward the great object which naval intelligence and naval experts were studying in the early days of our civil war. The inventive genius and skill of our countrymen made rapid and great proficiency in the work before them. Their improved ordnance and their turret vessels compelled a change in naval tactics, and wrought such a revolution in naval operations as has added greatly to the security of our coast defences, and probably put an end to ocean conflicts between immense squadrons like those of Trafalgar and the Nile. No large fleet of armored steamers will cross the sea to attack us, and a single "Monitor," with its fifteen-inch guns, would make havoc with a squadron of wooden ships under canvas. But the Navy Department and its experts, who took the responsibility of these innovations, encountered opposition until their innovations proved successful; when contractors who had been employed, and party politicians who had ends to subserve, sought to appropriate to themselves the credit, denied the Department any merit, and utterly ignored its ingenious and scientific assistants.

It was asserted on the floor of Congress, as late as 1868, by General Benjamin F. Butler, one of the leading and most influential politicians of that day: " I desire to say here, that the country is under the greatest obligations to a member of this House, a member from New York, who advanced the money and paid the entire expenses out of his own funds in order to get the "Monitor" built, which met the "Merrimac" in Hampton Roads."

Mr. John A. Griswold, the gentleman alluded to, a wealthy ironmaster, and one of the contractors for the "Monitor," was then a member, and at the time this declaration was made was a candidate for the office of Governor of New York. He not only quietly listened, without any attempt to correct what he knew to be the misstatement of General Butler, but a paper published at his place of residence, and of which I was informed he was a part owner, repeated many times the averment, and asserted that Mr. Griswold and his associates "built the original "Monitor" at their own risk, having agreed not to call upon the Government for remuneration until the vessel had been tested in action. Strong in faith, receiving but a negative support from the Navy Department, they completed the "Monitor" at their own cost."

These misstatements, repeated and exaggerated by others, in newspaper paragraphs and sensational lectures, to miscellaneous crowds, as well by extreme partisans in Congress and out, found listeners and readers. They served to create false impressions and to make false history. Truth and justice to others demand correction.

The project of attempting in this country the construction of iron-clad vessels and heavy ordnance originated in the Navy Department in 1861, and the "Monitor" plan, invented by Ericsson, was adopted by naval officers, with the approval of the Navy Department, within three months after the first recommendation of the Department was made. This was before the ironmaster and capitalists who contracted for the battery were known to the Department that awarded the contract.

Instead of advancing the money and paying the entire expense out of his own funds, as stated by General Butler, payments were promptly made by the Navy Department to Mr. Griswold and his associates, as rapidly, at least, as the work progressed, and was certified to by the supervising agent of the Department; there being an interval of only fifteen or twenty days between each payment, as will be seen by the following from the official record:

1861.—November 15, first payment, $50,000, less 25 per cent. $37,500
          December 3, second payment, $50,000, less 25 per cent. 37,500
          December 17, third payment, $50,000, less 25 per cent. 37,500
1862.—January 3, fourth payment, $50,000, less 25 per cent. 37,500
          February 6, fifth payment, $50,000, less 25 cent. 37,500
          March 3, sixth payment, $25,000, less 25 per cent. 18,750
          March 14, last payment, reservations 68,750

        Total $275,000

Save reservations, which were made in all cases of vessels built by contract, the last payment, on the completion of the battery, was on the 3d of March, and, as time was precious and pressing, she was hastily commissioned, officered, manned, supplied, and left New York for Hampton Roads three days after, on the 6th of March.

Intense anxiety was naturally felt by the officials in the Navy Department, who knew and appreciated the importance of the occasion, and the responsibility depending on them for the success of this vessel in her voyage, and in her power and fighting qualities after she should reach her destination. Many naval officers hesitated to give the experiment their indorsement. Some of the best engineers and naval constructors in the service expressed their want of confidence in the craft, and declared it would prove a failure. It was predicted that she could not float, that she would plunge to the bottom when launched, and that to send her to Hampton Roads would be reckless- ness amounting to crime. As mentioned by me on another occasion, it was the misfortune of the Navy Department to encounter hostility and forebodings of failure with every improvement made during the war, and often from those of whom encouragement and support might have reasonably been expected. A constant succession of struggles against prejudices, ignorance and fixed habits and opinions was the fate of the Department at every step which was taken in the extraor- dinary exigencies of the war, and the voyage and fighting qualities of the "Monitor" were now to be proved.

Full confidence was felt in her commander, Worden—who had just returned from a captivity of several months at Montgomery—his subordinates, and the small but selected and gallant crew who were embarked in this experiment. So great was the interest that the Assistant Secretary, Mr. Fox, Lieutenant Wise, of the Ordnance Bureau, and some members of my family, left Washington on Satur- day, the 8th of March, for Fortress Monroe, to meet and greet the "Monitor" on her arrival. Doubts were entertained and freely ex- pressed whether the battery could perform the voyage.

On Sunday morning, the 9th of March, while at the Navy Department, examining the dispatches received, Mr. Watson, Assist- ant Secretary of War, hastily entered with a telegram from General Wool, at Fortress Monroe, stating that the "Merrimac" had come down from Norfolk the preceding day, attacked the fleet in Hampton Roads, and destroyed the "Cumberland" and "Congress." Appre- hensions were expressed by General Wool that the remaining vessels would be made victims the following day, and that the Fortress itself was in danger, for the "Merrimac" was impenetrable, and could take what position she pleased for assault. I had scarcely read the telegram when a message from the President requested my immediate attend- ance at the Executive Mansion. The Secretary of War, on receiving General Wool's telegram, had gone instantly to the President, and at the same time sent messages to the other Cabinet officers, while the Assistant Secretary came to me. I went at once to the White House. Mr. Seward and Mr. Chase, with Mr. Stanton, were already there, had read the telegram, and were discussing the intelligence in much alarm. Each inquired what had been, and what could be done, to meet and check this formidable monster, which in a single brief visit had made such devastation, and would, herself uninjured,

repeat her destructive visit with still greater havoc, probably, while
we were in council.

I stated that I knew of no immediate steps that could be taken;
that Commodore Goldsborough, who was in command of the North
Atlantic Squadron, had reputation for ability and skill; but that he,
on whom we relied, was not at Hampton Roads at this critical juncture, but in the sounds of North Carolina. There were, however,
other and perhaps as capable officers as Goldsborough on the station,
with some of the best and most powerful vessels in the navy, but
judging from the dispatch of General Wool, they could be of little
avail against this impregnable antagonist. I had expected that our
new iron-clad battery, which left New York on Thursday, would
have reached the Roads on Saturday, and my main reliance was
upon her. We had, however, no information, as yet, of her arrival.
General Wool made no allusion to her in his telegram, which, it
happened, was the first received over the line that had been completed from Fortress Monroe only the preceding evening, but as we
now had telegraphic communication, I momentarily expected a
dispatch from Mr. Fox, or the senior naval officer on the station.

Mr. Stanton, impulsive, and always a sensationalist, was terribly
excited, walked the room in great agitation, and gave brusque utterances, and deprecatory answers to all that was said, and censured
everything that had been done or was omitted to be done. Mr.
Seward, usually buoyant and self-reliant, overwhelmed with the intelligence, listened in responsive sympathy to Stanton, and was greatly
depressed, as, indeed, were all the members, who, in the meantime,
had arrived, with the exception of Mr. Blair, as well as one or two
others—naval and military officers—among them, Commander Dahlgren and Colonel Meigs.

"The 'Merrimac,'" said Stanton, who was vehement, and did
most of the talking, "will change the whole character of the war; she
will destroy, seriatim, every naval vessel; she will lay all the cities on
the seaboard under contribution. I shall immediately recall Burnside; Port Royal must be abandoned. I will notify the Governors and
municipal authorities in the North to take instant measures to protect
their harbors." It is difficult to repeat his language, which was
broken and denunciatory, or to characterize his manner, or the panic
under which he labored, and which added to the apprehension of
others. He had no doubt, he said, that the monster was at this moment on her way to Washington, and, looking out of the window,
which commanded a view of the Potomac for many miles, "not
unlikely we shall have a shell or cannon-ball from one of her guns

in the White House before we leave this room." Most of Stanton's complaints were directed to me, and to me the others turned—not complainingly, but naturally for information or suggestion that might give relief. I had little to impart, except my faith in the untried "Monitor" experiment, which we had prepared for the emergency; an assurance that the "Merrimac," with her draught, and loaded with iron, could not pass Kettle Bottom Shoals, in the Potomac, and ascend the river and surprise us with a cannon-ball; and advised that, instead of adding to the general panic, it would better become us to calmly consider the situation, and inspire confidence by acting, so far as we could, intelligently, and with discretion and judgment. Mr. Chase approved the suggestion, but thought it might be well to telegraph Governor Morgan and Mayor Opdyke, at New York, that they might be on their guard. Stanton said he should warn the authorities in all the chief cities. I questioned the propriety of sending abroad panic missives, or adding to the alarm that would naturally be felt, and said it was doubtful whether the vessel, so cut down and loaded with armor, would venture outside of the Capes; certainly, she could not, with her draught of water, get into the sounds of North Carolina to disturb Burnside and our forces there; nor was she omnipresent, to make general destruction at New York, Boston, Port Royal, etc., at the same time; that there would be general alarm created; and repeated that my dependence was on the "Monitor," and my confidence in her great. "What," asked Stanton, "is the size and strength of this "Monitor?" How many guns does she carry?" When I replied two, but of large calibre, he turned away with a look of mingled amazement, contempt, and distress, that was painfully ludicrous. Mr. Seward said that my remark concerning the draught of water which the "Merrimac" drew, and the assurance that it was impossible for her to get at our forces under Burnside, afforded him the first moment of relief and real comfort he had received. It was his sensitive nature to be easily depressed, but yet to promptly rally and catch at hope. Turning to Stanton, he said we had, perhaps, given away too much to our apprehensions. He saw no alternative but to wait and hear what our new battery might accomplish.

Stanton left abruptly after Seward's remark. The President ordered his carriage, and went to the Navy Yard to see what might be the views of the naval officers.

Returning to my house a little before twelve o'clock, I stopped at St. John's Church, and called out Commodore Smith, to whom I communicated the tidings we had received, and that the "Congress," commanded by his son, Commander Joseph Smith, had been sunk.

"The 'Congress' sunk!" he exclaimed, at the same time buttoning up his coat, and looking me calmly and steadily in the face; "then Joe is dead." I told him this did not follow; the officers and crew doubt-less escaped, for the shore was not distant. "You don't know Joe," said the veteran father, "as well as I do; he would not survive his ship." And he did not; but, mortally wounded, perished with her.

Most of the Cabinet met again that sad Sunday at the White House, but not by appointment. A little time and reflection had brought a more calm and resolute feeling. Stanton, whose alarm had not subsided, said he had telegraphed to the North to take care of themselves; asked what I proposed to do to check the "Merri-mac," and prevent her from reaching Washington. I replied, nothing more till I knew more. I told him she could not get over Kettle Bottom Shoals and come to Washington; thought we ought not to be frightened; not to make a general panic, but act deliberately, and with a knowledge of what was best.

He spoke out with some fierceness, as if he thought my remarks were intended for him, and said he had no expectation of any formi-dable resistance from any little vessel of two guns against a frigate clothed with iron, nor much confidence in naval officers for such a crisis. If not old fogies, their training was not for this state of things. He would soon have good sailors from the merchant service, and had sent for Vanderbilt to come to Washington, and intended to consult him. Vanderbilt, he said, had large steamers, was a man of resources and great energy, and his opinion would be more valuable than that of any other person. He also proposed to make preparations to put a stop to the "Merrimac's" coming to Washington by obstruct-ing the channel of the river, and wished that he might have Dahlgren, who was in command of the Navy Yard, to consult with. To this I assented, but objected to any obstructions to navigation.

At a late hour, I received a telegram from Mr. Fox, stating that the "Monitor" had reached Hampton Roads a little before midnight of the 8th, and had encountered and driven off the "Merrimac." The submerged telegraph cable, which had been completed from Fortress Monroe to Cherrystone the preceding evening, parted on Sunday evening, and further communication ceased at this highly interesting crisis until the arrival of the mail, via Baltimore, on Monday.

It is not my purpose to narrate the particulars of the conflict, which has been so well and accurately detailed in the official reports of the officers, and are matters of record, and were published in the day and time of that remarkable encounter. Other and generally unpublished facts and incidents are here mentioned.

On the evening of that memorable Sunday, I received from Dahlgren, who was in command of the Navy Yard, a message, stating that he, and all the force he could command, were employed in loading and preparing the boats which had been sent to the yard. He supposed by my order and with my approval, although he had received no word from me. I replied that I had purchased no boats, given no orders, and that if I, rightly apprehended the object and intention of the work in which he was engaged, I did not approve it. When I called on the President the next morning, Stanton was already there, stating some grievance, and, as I entered, he turned to me and inquired my reason for countermanding his orders. He proceeded to state that he had directed the purchase of all the boats that could be procured in Washington, Georgetown and Alexandria, which were being laden with stone and earth, under the direction of Colonel Meigs and Dahlgren, with a view of sinking them at Kettle Bottom Shoals, some fifty miles or more below, in order to prevent the ascension of the "Merrimac." That while the officers whom he had detailed, he supposed with my approval, were actively engaged, they had been suddenly stopped by an order from me to Dahlgren. He was still complaining when Dahlgren, and I believe Meigs also, came in, and I then learned that great preparations had been made to procure a fleet of boats, which were to be sunk at Kettle Bottom, to protect Washington. I objected, and said I would rather expend money to remove obstacles than to impede navigation; that the navy had labored through the fall and winter to keep open this avenue to the ocean; that the army had not driven the rebels from the Virginia shore, nor assisted us in this work, though they had been greatly benefited by our efforts in the transportation of their supplies, forage, etc.; that to our shame there was but a single railroad track to the Capital, though we had here an army of more than one hundred thousand to feed, and that I should not consent to take any of the naval appropriation to cut off water communication, unless so ordered by the President; but should protest against obstructing the channel of the river. Our conversation was very earnest, and the President attentively listened, but with an evident inclination to guard in every way against the "Merrimac," but yet unwilling to interrupt ocean communication, so essential to Washington. Giving the interview a pleasant turn, he said that it was evident that Mars not only wanted exclusive control of military operations, (Stanton had manifested much dissatisfaction with McClellan as General-in-Chief,) but that he wanted a navy, and had begun to improvise one. Having already got his fleet, the President thought he might as well be permitted to

finish his work, but he must not destroy communication on the
Potomac, or cripple Neptune. The boats purchased might be loaded
and sent down the river, but not sunk in the channel until it was
known that the "Merrimac" had entered the river, or was on its way
hither. Whatever expense was incurred must be defrayed by the
War Department. With this understanding, Dahlgren was authorized to supervise and assist Stanton's squadron.

In addition to his fleet of canalboats, scowboats and other
craft, Cornelius Vanderbilt, who owned several large steamers, a
man of well-known energy and enterprise, was invited by Stanton to
Washington for consultation and advice. He was informed that the
egress of the "Merrimac" must be prevented, and the vessel destroyed
whenever she appeared; that the War Department did not rely
upon the "Monitor," but proposed to stop and destroy her independent
of the navy, and that he had more confidence in the capability, suggestions and prowess of individuals like Vanderbilt, who depended
on their own resources, than on naval officers, who were circum-
scribed by their education, and trained to a particular service. He
concluded by asking the great steamboat chief if he could, in any
way, destroy or overcome the "Merrimac."

Gratified with the summons, and complimented by the confidence expressed in his superior ability by the Secretary of War,
Vanderbilt responded that he could destroy the "Merrimac," and was
ready to do so, but he wanted the "Monitor" out of the way, and must
be permitted to do the work subject to no control of naval officers,
or any interference from them, or from naval vessels. If they
would all get out of the way, he would run down the "Merrimac"
with his big ship Vanderbilt. The employment of this great ship
corresponded with Stanton's ideas of power and force. He was
delighted, and went with Vanderbilt to the President, who assented
to the scheme, but was unwilling to dispense with the "Monitor,"
which had done so well, and suggested that an encounter of the
large wooden steamer with the armored ship might result in the
destruction of the Vanderbilt instead of the "Merrimac." In that
event a good sale would be made of the Vanderbilt, and the Government might be compelled to pay largely for the experiment, without
being benefited. Vanderbilt replied that he would take the risk;
that he was anxious to assist the Government; that he had already
offered his vessel to the Secretary of the Navy on his own terms, and
would have given her to him, but the Secretary wouldn't take her;
he would make a present of her to the President, requiring, however, that the engineers and employes on board should be retained

at present wages. Pleased with the suggestion that the "Merrimac" might be run down, and thus a double security provided against her, not only the Vanderbilt, but the Baltic, and one or two other large merchant steamers were chartered, and stationed in Hampton Roads.

These immense vessels, lofty and grand, were anchored near Fortress Monroe, where they remained for two months, at no small expense, awaiting the appearance of the "Merrimac," but no opportunity occurred to run her down. That vessel in her conflict with the "Monitor" sustained serious injury, and her officers, dreading more the novel craft which she had encountered on the 9th of March than the large wooden steamers, never again descended Elizabeth river to the Roads.

In the early part of May, the President, accompanied by Secretaries Chase and Stanton, took a steamer to visit Fortress Monroe and the army under McClellan, then on the York peninsula.

While descending the Potomac the attention of the party was directed to a string of boats nearly a mile in length on the Maryland shore, some fifty miles below Washington. Inquiry was made as to the object of such an immense collection of miscellaneous water craft. The pilot said he believed they were put there to oppose the "Merrimac," but the little "Monitor" had taken care of her. "Oh!" said the President, pointing to the boats which lined the shore, "that is Stanton's navy; that is the squadron that Welles would have nothing to do with, and about which he and Stanton had the dispute. It was finally decided, I believe, that the War Department might have a fleet of its own to fight the "Merrimac," and there it is. We were all a little scared at that time. Mr. Welles felt bad enough, but was not enough scared to listen to Stanton's scheme of blockading the river; said the fleet of boats would be useless, and, if used, worse than useless."

Stanton, who was a little disconcerted by the President's levity, said he had believed it was best to provide for an emergency, and should the "Merrimac" now attempt to come up the river, the boats which he had procured and loaded might be found to answer a useful purpose in protecting Washington.

"Your emergency," said Mr. Lincoln, "reminds me of a circumstance which took place in Illinois. We had on our circuit a respectable lawyer named B——, noted for a remarkable development of his breast, the glands being enormous, more protuberent than those of many females. In a conversation which took place among the lawyers at one of the hotels, there was a discussion regarding the singular development which, in a man, was almost a deformity, and could be of no possible use. B—— controverted this, and said that, supposing he were to be cast away upon an uninhabited island, with no other human being but a nursing infant, for which he would have to provide. In such an emergency, he had no doubt Providence would furnish, through him, nourishment for the child." This he said, remarked the President, " with as much apparent sincerity as Stanton showed when he urged a navy composed of canalboats to stop the "Merrimac." I think B——'s paps to nurse an infant will be as serviceable, and required about as soon, as Stanton's fleet to fight and keep back an iron frigate. The preparation for an anticipated emergency, which is about as likely to occur in one case as the other, is very striking."

Mr. Chase related to me this incident, which was afterwards, at his request, repeated by the President in the presence of others, to the great annoyance of Mr. Stanton, who never enjoyed the anecdotical humors of the President if at his expense.

The "Merrimac" was, a few days thereafter—on the 10th of May, while the President and party were at Fortress Monroe—abandoned and destroyed by the rebels themselves. The large steamers that had awaited her advent, at an expense of several hundred thousand dollars, were discharged, with the exception of the Vanderbilt, which remained a white elephant in the hands of the War Department. Eventually, she was turned over to the navy, that had declined to purchase and did not want her. She was too large for blockade service, but, as she was to be employed, the Navy Department sent her off on an unsuccessful cruise for the "Alabama," under a very capable commander, at a cost to the Government of more than one thousand dollars per day, without result. The War Department had paid two thousand dollars per day to her owner for her use.

In giving this magnificent vessel to the Government, Mr. Vanderbilt performed a magnificent and patriotic act, for which he received and deserved the thanks of Congress; but it was to the Government a costly present. The Quartermaster General, on a call from Congress in 1865, reported that "previous to her presentation to the government," the War Department had paid for her services three hundred and three thousand five hundred and eighty-nine dollars and ten cents ($303,589.10). The Secretary of the Navy, on a similar call from Congress in 1868, reported that the Navy Department had expended over four hundred thousand dollars ($400,000) in repairing the Vanderbilt, and that a further outlay of, at least, half a million dollars would be then required to fit her for service; that she was at Mare Island, used for berthing and messing the men detailed to take care of the ships in ordinary. So that this ship, donated to the Government to run down the "Merrimac," if the "Monitor" would get out of the way, was, without accomplishing that object, an expense to the Government of three times the original cost of the "Monitor."

I mention these facts, not to detract from the merit of Cornelius Vanderbilt's patriotic gift, but to exemplify the greater value of the little "Monitor" of John Ericsson for naval purposes, and the reason why the Navy Department declined to purchase the Vanderbilt, Illinois, and other immense steamers that were pressed, by influential persons, by the press, and by interested parties, upon the Navy Department and the Government. The War Department, taking a different view, bought the Illinois for four hundred thousand dollars ($400,000). The Illinois, by the way, has never had a day's sea-service since the War Department purchased her, and will never pass Sandy Hook.

The "Monitor," which rendered such gallant service to the country, and was the progenitor of a class of vessels that is to be found in the navy of almost every maritime nation, was foundered on the 30th of December, 1862, in a storm off Cape Hatteras.

THE EXCHANGE OF PRISONERS.

BY JUDGE ROBERT OULD.

I KNOW it is a very difficult matter for one who was an active participant in any of the affairs of our late war, to divest himself of prejudice or partisanship in giving an account or history of the same. Perhaps I am as liable as most men to these disturbing influences; but I hope not to the extent of causing me to distort and, still less, to falsify the facts of the case. While in this communication I have presented the matter of the exchange of prisoners. and the troubles attendant thereon, from a Confederate standpoint, I have yet sought to be accurate. I trust I have not been unfair. I think I can safely say that I can support everything herein stated as a fact by abundant testimony, Federal as well as Confederate. As to the conclusions, which I have drawn from these facts, I submit them to the impartial judgment of your readers, hoping that the lapse of years has been sufficient to enable them to be in that frame of mind.

Previous to July, 1862, no formal or permanent cartel of exchange had been adopted by the belligerent parties to our great civil war. Before that time it is true that there had been many captures by either side; but the prisoners had either been exchanged man for man or officer for officer of equal grade, or had been released on parole by the respective governments, or by commanders in the field.

On the 22d of July, 1862, a cartel of exchange was drawn up and signed by General John A. Dix and General D. H. Hill, representing the respective belligerents. By its terms, "all prisoners of war were to be discharged on parole in ten days after their

(32)

capture, and the prisoners then held, and those thereafter taken, were to be transported to the points mutually agreed upon, at the expense of the capturing party. The surplus prisoners on one side or the other, who were not exchanged, were not to be permitted to take up arms until they were exchanged under the provisions of the cartel. Each party, upon the discharge of prisoners of the other party, was authorized to discharge an equal number of their own officers and men from parole, furnishing, at the same time to the other party, a list of their prisoners discharged, and of their own officers and men relieved from parole; thus enabling each party to relieve from parole such of their own officers and men as the party might choose." The cartel provided that its stipulations and provisions should be "of binding obligation during the continuance of the war, it matters not which party may have the surplus of prisoners." Its ninth and closing article was in these words: "And in case any misunderstanding shall arise in regard to any clause or stipulation in the foregoing articles, it is mutually agreed that such misunderstanding shall not interrupt the release of prisoners on parole, as herein provided, but shall be made the subject of friendly explanation, in order that the object of this agreement may neither be defeated or postponed."

The cardinal idea of the cartel was that all prisoners should be *delivered* within ten days after capture, and if the adversary party had an equal number in its hands, then an *exchange* as to such should take place, so that each set could at once take up arms. If one side held an excess of prisoners, they were still to be delivered within ten days after capture, but that excess was to be considered as being on parole, and not to be returned to military duty until their equivalents were given, and they thereby declared exchanged. Thus the cartel required all prisoners to be released, though they were not exchanged. Exchanges could never take place except upon equivalents; releases or deliveries on parole could. When one of the belligerents could not furnish equivalents for all the officers and men delivered, the excess remained on parole, and could not take up arms until the debt was paid. As discharged and released men were not necessarily exchanged, the cartel provided that declarations of exchange might be made from time to time, and reserved to each side the right of making such declarations, whenever it released from captivity or parole, an equal number of the adversary's officers and men. It is important, also, to observe that there were two kinds of paroles—those given on the battle-field, when the parties were there released, and those given by the parties who were delivered at the points designated in the cartel.

3

I have been thus particular in these explanations, that the nomenclature herein used may be fully understood. Aiken's Landing, on James river, a place about thirty miles distant by water from Richmond, and Vicksburg, were the first places selected for the delivery of the prisoners of both belligerents. At the former place I met General Lorenzo Thomas, the first Federal agent of exchange, in August, 1862. Not appreciating the magnitude of the work before us, we began to exchange officers by name, one for another. That method was, however, very soon abandoned for the more expeditious one of exchange by grade, or by equivalent in mass. Our first duty was to compute the paroles held by each side, and to declare exchanges so far as equivalents could be furnished. That computation left quite a balance of paroles in Confederate hands—that is, after all the Confederates, who had been captured and paroled, were declared exchanged, it was found there was an excess of Federal prisoners, for whom the United States could furnish no equivalents. Of course that excess continued to remain on parole until, from time to time, equivalents were furnished. This state of affairs, so far as captures and paroles were concerned, continued until July, 1863, when the disasters at Gettysburg and Vicksburg occurred. Yet, during that time, deliveries of Federal prisoners were made as fast as transportation was furnished. Indeed, more than once the United States authorities were urged to forward greater facilities for their removal.

After Vicksburg and Gettysburg the situation became changed, and the excess was thrown on the Federal side. From that day began the serious troubles of the exchange question, ending finally in the cessation of all deliveries, except in special cases. It is true that differences of interpretation of the cartel had existed before that time, and it is also true that there had been mutual complaints and charges of bad faith—such as refusing to deliver officers and men who had been declared exchanged. I had frequently complained that Confederate officers and men had been detained, sometimes in irons and close confinement under false or frivolous charges; that enlisted men had been treated as guerrillas or bushwhackers, and that recruiting officers, regularly commissioned and in uniform, had been executed as spies; yet exchanges up to that time went on without very serious difficulty. Complications of these kinds could generally be managed by threatened retaliation.

The practice of the agents of exchange up to May, 1863, had been to recognize paroles taken upon the battle-field, even though the parties thereto were not kept for some time in the possession of the capturing party, or delivered at the points designated in the cartel. In that month, however, I was notified that a new rule had been adopted by the Federal authorities, contained in their General Orders Nos. 59 and 100 of the year 1863, which provided that no paroles, unaccompanied by continued possession and actual delivery at the points designated in the cartel, would be recognized. An exception was made where paroles were taken in pursuance of an agreement between the commanders of two opposing armies. But while these general orders invalidated all paroles not coming within the description, they distinctly declared that if a parole should be given under different circumstances, and the United States did not approve of the same, "the paroled officer must return into captivity."

On the 7th of July, 1863, I was notified of another General Order, No. 207, dated July 3, 1863, declaring that "all captures must be reduced to actual possession, and all prisoners of war must be delivered at the place designated, there to be exchanged or paroled until exchange can be effected." This general order, however, did not contain the provision of the others, that the paroled officer, if he gave an unauthorized parole, should return into captivity. All three of these general orders, however, purported to be declarations of the laws of war, inconsistent as they were with each other. The civilians of the War Department seem to have been under the belief that they could make and unmake the laws of war to suit emergencies.

The application of these general orders to the facts connected with exchanges produced the first serious difficulty. It may be that the position taken by the United States authorities in these general orders was strongly supported by the language of the cartel, which required "all prisoners of war to be discharged on parole in ten days after their capture, and the prisoners now held, and those hereafter taken, to be transported to the points mutually agreed upon, at the expense of the capturing party." But the practice of both sides, from the beginning of the war up to May, 1863, had been otherwise. Each had claimed paroles which had been given where the persons captured had been set at liberty at once. Each had recognized the validity of such paroles held by the adverse party. Moreover, it was contended by me that the cartel did not touch in any way the question of the validity of paroles; that it was designed to apply, so far as delivery was concerned, only to such prisoners as were in captivity, or "held" by either party, to such as were in military depots and prisons, to such as had been removed from the battle-field or place of capture, and reduced into actual possession—

that it left the force and effect of military paroles, and the respect which should be paid to them, to be determined by the usages of war, and that it did not prevent a wounded officer or man from entering into a stipulation not to take up arms until unchanged, as a condition of his release, when it might be his life would be at serious risk if he did not make the contract. I contended that the cartel nowhere denied the right of any soldier, whether wounded or not, to bind his government by his military obligation, when he was in the hands of the enemy. I will give one of a large number, as a specimen of the military paroles to which I refer. It is that of Colonel Roy Stone, of the One Hundred and Forty-ninth Pennsylvania Volunteers, captured at Gettysburg:

"I, the subscriber, a prisoner of war, captured near Gettysburg, Pa., do give my parole of honor not to take up arms against the Confederate States, or to do any military duty whatever, or to give any information that may be prejudicial to the interests of the same, until regularly exchanged. This parole is unconditional, and extended to a wounded officer for the sake of humanity, to save a painful and tedious journey to the rear.   ROY STONE,
"Colonel 149th Pennsylvania Volunteers."

Other paroles declared that if they were not recognized by the Federal authorities, the parties would report at Richmond as prisoners of war within a certain number of days, or that they would not take up arms until exchanged, even if they were required to do so by their government.

While the views of the Confederate Government were such as I have represented, it was not disposed to risk the continuance of the cartel by insisting upon them. It agreed to ignore the previous practice as a rule for the future, insisting, however, that the paroles which had been given on both sides previous to the date of the communication of the general orders to me, to wit, 23d of May, 1863, should be held to be valid. Accordingly, on the 24th of August, 1863, I made the following proposal to the Federal agent: "I propose that all paroles on both sides heretofore given, shall be determined by the general orders issued by the War Department of the United States, to wit: No. 49, No. 100, and No. 207, of this year, according to their respective dates, and in conformity to Paragraph 131 of General Order 100, so long as said paragraph was in force. If this proposition is not acceptable, I propose that the practice heretofore adopted respecting paroles and exchanges be continued. In other words, I propose that the whole question of paroles be determined by the general orders of the United States, according to dates, or that it be decided by former practice."

It will be observed that the matter of the dates of the respective general orders was very material, because General Orders No. 49 and No. 100 declared that if a parole was not approved, the party giving it was bound to return and surrender himself as a prisoner of war. General Order No. 49 contained also this language, to wit: "His own government cannot at the same time disown his own engagement, and refuse his return as a prisoner." I then thought and still think these were honest words. The date of General Order No. 49 was February 28th, 1863, that of General Order No. 100 was April 24th, 1863, and that of General Order No. 207 was July 3d, 1863.

It thus appears that the Confederate Government was willing to recede from former practice, and only insisted that the matter of paroles on both sides should be determined by the United States general order in force when the paroles were given. Was not this fair? Ought it not to have been acceptable to the United States? Yet they did not consent. It may be asked why? It was because, according to the express provision of General Orders Nos. 49 and 100, it became the duty of the parties who had been paroled while these orders were in force, to return into captivity if their government disapproved of their paroles. To avoid that result, the Federal agent insisted that General Order 207, dated July 3d, 1863, should be deemed to be retroactive, and control paroles which were given before it was in existence. The Confederates had captured and paroled a large number of prisoners in the months of March, April, May and June, and, by virtue of general orders in force at those dates, if the paroles were not recognized, it became the duty of the paroled parties to return into captivity. I knew very well that there would be no such return, and that the Federal Government would recognize the validity of their paroles, rather than send its officers and men back into captivity. To escape the dilemma of recognizing the paroles, or sending the officers and men back into captivity, neither of which the Federal authorities intended to do, they were forced into the absurd position that General Order No. 207, which recognized neither paroles or a return into captivity, should be deemed to be in force before it had any existence.

As an illustration in this connection of what strange things are done in time of war, I refer to a Court of Inquiry, the official proceedings of which are found in the *Army and Navy Official Gazette*, under date of July 14th, 1863. The court was convened on June 30th, 1863, to determine whether Major Duane and Captain Michler, who had been captured and paroled on the 28th of June, 1863, by General Stuart, should be placed on duty without exchange, or be returned to the enemy as prisoners of war. The general order then in force, in its 131st paragraph, declared that "if the government does not approve of the parole, the paroled officer must return into captivity." Yet the court found that the government was free to place those officers on duty without having been exchanged, and gave as its reason that I had been notified that such paroles would not be recognized. But the court forgot to state that along with that notification came another, that "the paroled officer must return into captivity," and that the United States Government could not "at the same time disown his (the officer's) engagement, and refuse his return as a prisoner."

While I am dealing with incidents, I will give another. On March 9th, 1863, that terrible soldier, General Robert Schenck, issued a General Order No. 15, requiring all officers and men who who had been captured and released on parole in his department, and particularly in the Shenandoah Valley, but who had not been declared exchanged, to return to duty on penalty of being considered deserters. The general order of the United States then in force was No. 49, to the provisions of which I have already referred. At the time of Schenck's order and afterward, the Federal agent was charging against me and receiving credit for captures and paroles similar to those thus repudiated. It is due to Colonel Ludlow, Agent of Exchange at the time, to say that when this matter was brought to his attention, he declared that Schenck's action was without proper authority, and that I should have credit for such as reported for duty under the order. But it is just as true that I was never informed of any who did return, nor was I given any credit on that account.

It is hardly necessary for me to state that I utterly refused to agree to any arrangement by which a general order of the United States War Department should be construed as being in force before it was issued, or that paroles given in May or June should be determined by an order made in the following July. I thought I had conceded enough when I agreed to reverse a practice followed by both sides since the beginning of the war without objection, and abide by the orders made by the adversary, according to their date.

As soon as I discovered the purpose of the Federal agent in respect to the paroles held by me, I notified him that so long as he refused to recognize the validity of the paroles held by the Confederate authorities, and especially the paroles given in Tennessee and Kentucky shortly after the adoption of the cartel and before the date of the general orders, that he need not send any officers with the expectation of receiving as equivalents only those who were in captivity. I closed my letter to him in these words: "If captivity, privation and misery are to be the fate of officers on both sides hereafter, let God judge between us. I have struggled in this matter as if it had been a matter of life and death to me. I am heartsick at the termination; but I have no self-reproaches."

The inevitable effect of the new rule insisted upon by the Federal agent, besides ignoring the tens of thousands of valid paroles held by the Confederates, would have been to confine exchanges to the officers and men who were in captivity, leaving the excess in prison. Even if the Confederates had not have had any paroles to offer as equivalents for deliveries, it was the duty of the adverse party, under the cartel, to make the deliveries and wait for equivalents. But, in addition to this violation, the course of the Federal agent in refusing to accept valid paroles as equivalents made a case of aggravation which could not to be tolerated. So resolute were the Confederate authorities in this respect that when some of their officers were sent to City Point to be exchanged only for officers who were in confinement, they refused to receive them on such condition, and they were carried back to Fortress Monroe.

I have said that I believe that the course pursued by the Federal authorities in relation to the paroles held by the Confederates was the chief and special cause of the suspension of the cartel. It was not a case for retaliation. The difficulty could not be obviated or cured even by that violent remedy. I know there were other hindrances in the way of a full observance of the cartel; but these, singly or altogether, were trivial in comparison. General Hitchcock, Commissioner of Exchange, in his report to Mr. Stanton, in November, 1865, lays stress on the action of Mr. Davis and the Confederate Congress in relation to officers in command of negro troops, and cites that as the chief cause of the disruption of the cartel. But no officer of the Federal army, during the progress of the war, was ever punished in any way for commanding or leading negro troops, though the Confederates had in captivity many such. They were always treated as other Federal officers, and, like them, delivered for exchange or released on parole. The Confederate law which authorized the delivery of negro soldiers to the authorities of the State in which they were captured was never enforced, and was, even in those days, considered as legislation *in terrorem.* It did not present any practical difficulty, though, doubtless, it would if it had been executed. General Hitchcock and others made very good use of this Confederate legislation in continually thrusting it forward as an excuse for Federal breaches of the cartel. It was the theme for not a little "high

rhetoric." Another reason given by General Hitchcock for the
failure on the part of the Federal authorities to deliver prisoners
according to the terms of the cartel, was that I had unduly and
improperly declared to be exchanged Confederate soldiers who had
been released on parole, but not exchanged. Nothing could be more
untrue. In the first place, the difficulty in the way of delivery and
exchange of prisoners had occurred long before any alleged obnoxious
notice of exchange on my part had ever appeared. The ground
taken by the Federal authorities in relation to paroles, and under
which deliveries would only be made where equivalents of officers
and men in actual confinement would be furnished, was long anterior
to any declaration of exchange on my part to which exception was
ever taken. General Hitchcock and others had certain purposes in
view, and he and they used my notes of exchange just as they
employed the Federal general orders. They also were made to be
retroactive, and were held up as the proximate cause of occurrences
which happened long before their birth.

It would be a curious matter to trace the history of the notices
of exchange which each side issued during the progress of the war.
I wish I had the space to do so. I can only notice one calumny of
many in this connection. General Hitchcock, in his before-men-
tioned report, charges that I made a declaration of exchange
with a view to the coming battles of Chickamauga and Chattanooga, and that many of the prisoners paroled by General
Grant and General Banks, at Vicksburg and Port Hudson, participated in said battles without having been duly exchanged. It
would be difficult to crowd more untruths in one sentence. The
declaration of exchange to which General Hitchcock refers, was
fairly, honestly and properly made. The cartel, by its express
terms, gave me authority to make it. I had, in my possession at
the time, more valid paroles of Federal officers and men than were
an equivalent for the exchange which I then declared. Moreover,
between that declaration of exchange and the preceding one, I had
delivered at City Point, then the agreed point of delivery, some ten
or twelve thousand Federal prisoners. The declaration was not
only expressly authorized by the cartel, but was in the strictest
accordance with the common practice of the Federal Agent of
Exchange. Besides, not one of the officers or men declared to be
exchanged at that time was in the battles to which General Hitchcock refers; though if they had been, they would have been there
rightfully.

It has been frequently stated as an excuse for the refusal of the

Federal authorities to deliver all prisoners of war held by them, and that if it had been done, when they had the surplus, the excess would have been put in the field by the Confederates. This is another of General Hitchcock's imputations. Nothing could be more untrue, either as to intention or fact. There was no more reason for such a stigma than there was for a similar charge against the United States when the excess of prisoners was held by the Confederates. Yet the fear that such a course might be pursued did not restrain the Confederate authorities from delivering all prisoners in their hands when they held an excess; and that, too, after they were informed of General Schenck's aforesaid general order.

It was the practice of my office to make a careful computation of paroles and deliveries, and on that basis to declare exchanges. In no one instance, from the beginning of the war to its close, was any declaration of exchange made which was not just in every particular, and fully warranted by the facts. In no one case did I ever discharge Confederates from their parole until I had offered valid equivalents to the United States.

After deliveries were broken off, I did not abandon the hope that there would be a return to the main features of the cartel. From that time I kept the offer open that officers and men should be released, the excess on one side or the other to be on parole, and that the validity of all paroles should be determined by the general orders of the United States War Department, according to dates. The Confederate Government stood ready and indeed anxious at all times to accept these terms. Whenever I pressed them upon the Federal agents, and that was very frequently, I was met with homilies on Mr. Davis' message and my unjustifiable (so-called) declarations of exchange.

At length I was forced into the conviction that the persons who had the control of the matter did not desire exchanges or mutual deliveries of prisoners on any terms—that they believed that such deliveries were unwise in a military point of view—that they had come to the conclusion that a soldier was more valuable to the Confederacy than he was to the United States. I do not mean by that to say that they or anybody else thought that a Confederate soldier was better or braver than a Union soldier, but simply that in the then condition of affairs the United States could better afford the absence of a soldier from the field than the Confederacy. Perhaps, also, some of these persons thought it would not be an unwise military expedient to quarter fifty thousand men upon

States drifting into actual want. Perhaps, too, some of them thought that the story, real or exaggerated, of the sufferings of the prisoners would "fire the Northern heart." Be all this as it may, I suppose no one is prepared to challenge the suspension of the cartel as an unwise military expedient in a Federal point of view. In other aspects of the case it was not quite so clever.

In the early spring of 1864, still desirous of restoring the cartel, even with modifications if they were pressed, I determined to invoke the aid of General B. F. Butler, having learned that it would not be disagreeable to him to have an interview. General Butler some months before that time had been appointed Federal Agent of Exchange. The Confederate Government very unwisely, as I then thought, and now think, had refused to recognize him as an agent of exchange, or to hold any intercourse with him as such. About the time of his appointment he sent a detachment of prisoners, requiring, however, a return delivery of a like number of such as were in confinement. Lest the United States Government might suppose from the refusal of the Confederate authorities to recognize General Butler as an agent of exchange, that they did not desire the full restoration of the cartel, I expressed in writing to General Mulford their readiness to resume and to deliver all prisoners, the excess to be on parole; but refusing any other arrangement, and notifying him that unless this was the distinct understanding, no deliveries would be made. I delivered at the same time to General Mulford more prisoners than he brought, notifying him that I accepted his delivery as in earnest that such was the understanding of the Federal Government. I concluded my letter to him by saying, that "in no event can we consent that the general release of prisoners, so distinctly required by the cartel, shall be evaded by partial deliveries. Accepting the present delivery as a step toward a general exchange on the principles of the cartel, I trust I may be permitted to express the hope that deliveries on the basis above indicated, will be continued until all the troops in confinement on both sides are released."

The date of this letter was December 27th, 1863. Some two or three months afterward, I had a reason to believe that General Butler held views favorable to the restoration of the cartel, though in the interval of these dates very few deliveries were made, and I had no official information that a general release would take place. But I was confident that General Butler and I could discuss controverted questions in better temper than General Meredith, the Federal Agent of Exchange, and myself had manifested. Moreover, the information which I had from time to time received as to his interference in behalf of prisoners confined at Point Lookout, still more emboldened me. I then believed, and now believe, that Point Lookout was more humanely governed than any other prison depot from Fort Warren to Western Missouri. It may perhaps astonish some people when I say that of all the persons having control of matters pertaining to exchanges whom I encountered, he was the fairest and the most truthful. The distance between him and Hitchcock in these respects was almost infinite.

I went to Fortress Monroe on a flag-of-truce steamer, and was received by General Butler with great courtesy. I remained there three days, during which we had protracted discussions. He expressed himself in the general in favor of the cartel, though in a mere military point of view he thought it was a disadvantage to the United States. To some of the provisions of the cartel he expressed very decided objections. We mutually yielded our opposing views, and at length there remained but one matter upon which we could not agree, and that was negro slaves. There was no difference between us as to Northern negro soldiers or even the free negro soldier of the South. I agreed that both of these classes should be deemed proper subjects of exchange. But I contended if Southern soldiers recaptured their former slaves that, under the *just postliminii*, they had the right to hold them in their former state; that under our Constitutions, Confederate and State, slaves were recognized as property, and on recapture followed the rule of all property, and reverted to their former condition. I held that an edict of emancipation promulgated by a hostile power did not defeat the rights of the owner, when the slave came back into his possession by recapture. General Butler, on the other hand, while admitting that under the Constitution and laws of the Southern States, slaves were property while under the dominion of their masters, contended that if they fled from them and sought the protection of the United States, and were then clothed with freedom, that then if recaptured by their masters, they were taken as freemen, and not as slaves. Availing myself of his admission that slaves were property under our Constitutions and laws, I asked him whether, if he emancipated Confederate horses and declared that their backs should never again be desecrated by saddle or harness, such an edict would extinguish the former owner's rights on recapture. He did not answer the question. Perhaps he did not find it easy.

I wish I had space to give the discussion more at length. In the course of it, General Butler let fly a good many expressions which certainly did not lack vigor, if they were objectionable on other grounds. I soon found that we could not agree upon the topic; and, therefore, I sought to flank the difficulty. I suggested that it was very unwise for us to reject the paper about which we had agreed in every other respect, because we disagreed about one item—that the new cartel might be silent as to recaptured slaves, leaving to the United States the right to resort to such measures of retaliation, if they were not released, as was practiced in the case of white soldiers, when they were improperly detained. I urged that a difficulty about the release of slaves, who did not form one-fiftieth part of the prisoners, should not prevent the exchange of others— that when Streight's men were detained on our side, or Morgan's men on his, exchanges were not stopped thereby, and that it was hardly fair to have one rule for the white man and a better one for the black. At length, General Butler assented to this view, and so we constructed a new cartel, which settled the old points of dispute, but was silent as to such soldiers as were slaves at the outbreak of the war. The position which I had all along maintained in relation to paroles was unhesitatingly accepted by General Butler.

When the paper was prepared, I suggested that it be signed by us, signifying that I was authorized to do so on the part of the Confederate Government. But General Butler said he was not authorized to do so, and would be compelled to send it to the War Department, at Washington, for approval, which he hoped and believed it would receive. When I expressed my readiness to sign the paper, he pleasantly observed that the Confederate authorities had always shown their good sense in leaving measures to the judgment of those who knew most about them; but that though he was the commander of a department, he had not the power to bind the United States to the instrument, strange as that might appear. I have reason to believe that General Butler urged the adoption of the new cartel with good faith and zeal. It was transmitted by the War Department to General Grant, then in front of Petersburg, for his approval or rejection. It is well known to the country what his action was. General Butler, in his report to the Committee on the Conduct of the War, states that General Grant communicated his rejection to him, giving in substance as his reason that Sherman would be overwhelmed and his own position on the James endangered. Over one hundred thousand officers and men were, at or about that time, in confinement on both sides, the United States holding quite a large majority.

When this effort to renew exchanges failed, so anxious were the Confederate authorities to have some plan of relief adopted, that they instructed me to abate our just demands and accede to the offer more than once made by the Federal Agent of Exchange, to exchange officer for officer, and man for man. As the United States held the majority, this plan of operation would have released all the Federal prisoners, while a large number of Confederates would still have remained in captivity.

Accordingly, on the 10th of August, 1864, I addressed the following letter to General Mulford, Assistant Agent of Exchange:

"You have several times proposed to me to exchange the prisoners respectively held by the two belligerents, officer for officer, and man for man. The same offer has also been made by other officials having charge of matters connected with the exchange of prisoners. This proposal has heretofore been declined by the Confederate authorities, they insisting upon the terms of the cartel, which required the delivery of the excess on either side on parole. In view, however, of the very large number of prisoners now held by each party, and the suffering consequent upon their continued confinement, I now consent to the above proposal, and agree to deliver to you the prisoners held in captivity by the Confederate authorities, provided you agree to deliver an equal number of Confederate officers and men. As equal numbers are delivered from time to time, they will be declared exchanged. This proposal is made with the understanding that the officers and men on both sides who have been longest in captivity will be first delivered, where it is practicable.

"I shall be happy to hear from you as speedily as possible, whether this arrangement can be carried out."

The delivery of this letter was accompanied with a statement of the mortality which was hurrying so many Federal prisoners at Andersonville to the grave.

On the 22d of August following, not having heard anything in response, I addressed a communication to General Hitchcock, United States Commissioner of Exchange, covering a copy of the foregoing letter to General Mulford, and requesting an acceptance of my proposal. No answer was received to either of these letters, nor were they ever noticed, except that General Mulford, on the 31st of August of the same year, informed me in writing that he had no communication on the subject from the United States authorities, and that he was not authorized to make *any* answer.

General Butler, in his speech at Hamilton, Ohio, after the close of the war, as it is reported in the newspapers, in referring to this offer of mine to exchange officer for officer, and man for man, thus leaving a large excess in Federal hands, said: "I wrote an argument, offensively put, to the Confederate Commissioner, so that he could stop all further offers of the exchange. I say nothing about the policy of this course; I offer no criticism of it whatever; I only say that whether it be a good or a bad policy, it was not mine, and that my part of it was wholly in obedience to orders from my commanding officer, the lieutenant general." So that it seems that even *offers* of exchange from the Confederates had become disagreeable and annoying, and were met *offensively* to put a stop to them.

This statement of General Butler is substantially repeated by him in his report to the Committee on the Conduct of the War, which he concludes by saying, that he was compelled to make the exposition "so that it might be seen that these lives were spent as a part of the system of attack upon the rebellion, devised by the wisdom of the general-in-chief of the armies to destroy it by depletion, depending upon our superior numbers to win the victory at last." Nor were these the only statements made by General Butler in relation to these matters. In his speech at Lowell on the 28th of January, 1865, after referring to the conference held at Fortress Monroe between himself and me, he said: "I reported the points of agreement between myself and the rebel agent to the Secretary of War, and asked for power to adjust the other questions of difference, so as to have the question of enslaving negro soldiers stand alone, to be dealt with by itself; and that the whole power of the United States should be exerted to do justice to those who had fought the battles of the country, and been captured in its service. The whole subject was referred by the Secretary of War to the lieutenant general commanding, who telegraphed me on the 14th of April, 1864, in substance: ʹ'Break off all negotiations on the subject of exchange till further orders.' And, therefore, all negotiations were broken off, save that a special exchange of sick and wounded on either side went on. On the 20th of April I received another telegram of General Grant, ordering 'not another man to be given to the rebels.' To that I answered on the same day: 'Lieutenant General Grant's instructions shall be implicitly obeyed. I assume that you do not mean to stop the special exchange of the sick and wounded now going on.' To this I received a reply in substance: 'Do not give the rebels a single able-bodied man.' From that hour, so long as I remained in the department, exchanges of prisoners stopped under that order, because I could not give the rebels any of their able-bodied soldiers in exchange. By sending the sick and wounded forward, however, some twelve thousand of our suffering soldiers were relieved, being upwards of eight thousand more than we gave the rebels. In August last, Mr. Ould, finding negotiations were broken off, and that no exchanges were made, wrote to General Hitchcock, the Commissioner, at Washington, that the rebels were ready to exchange, man for man, all the prisoners held by them, as I had proposed in December. Under the instructions of the lieutenant general I wrote to Mr. Ould, a letter, which has been published, saying: 'Do you mean to give up all your action, and revoke all your laws about black men employed as soldiers?' These questions were therein argued justly, as I think, not diplomatically, but obtrusively and demonstratively, not for the purpose of furthering exchange of prisoners, but for the purpose of preventing and stopping the exchange, and furnishing a ground on which we could fairly stand. I am now at liberty to state these facts, because they appear in the correspondence on the subject of exchange, now on the public files of Congress, furnished by the War Department upon resolution. I am not at liberty to state my opinions as to the correctness and propriety of this course of action of the lieutenant general in relation to exchanges, because, as it is not proper to utter a word of condemnation of any act of my superiors, I may not even applaud where I think them right, lest, not applauding in other instances, such acts as I may mention would imply censure. I only desire that the responsibility of stopping exchanges of prisoners, be it wise or unwise, should rest upon the lieutenant general commanding, and not on me. I have carried the weight of so grave a matter for nine months, and now propose, as the facts are laid before Congress and the country, not to carry any longer any more of it than belongs to me."

It would be a curious study to compare these statements of a Federal general with General Hitchcock's report of the same matters. I have not the space to do so here, and must content myself in using General Butler as my proof that the reason why my aforesaid letter to General Hitchcock was not answered was not that it was not received or not considered, but that policy prevented it. But, as the same policy would not allow a direct refusal to accede to such terms, my letter, instead of receiving a reply, was met by an "argument offensively put," from another person, who, doubtless, was much more capable of making it than General Hitchcock. Silence covered Hitchcock, while General Butler, in obedience to the orders of the lieutenant general, fulminated "obtrusively and demonstratively— not for the purpose of furthering exchange of prisoners, but for the purpose of preventing and stopping the exchange." Heaven knows that Hitchcock had virus enough to perform that service "offensively" to the last degree; but the managers seem to have thought, and, doubtless, correctly, he had a lack of other essential qualifications. There is another noteworthy fact disclosed in this confession of General Butler. It appears that these maligned Confederates delivered eight thousand more sick and wounded prisoners to him than they received. Is it necessary to go behind this pregnant fact to show any other proof that the Confederates were ready to agree to any fair system of exchange? Even upon a plan injurious to them and violative of the terms of the cartel, they delivered an excess of eight thousand prisoners in a comparatively short space of time. Indeed, the whole operation had become so monstrously wrong that General Butler, under the instincts of self-preservation, proposed to "stand from under," and declined to carry the burden any longer. Before, however, he came to that conclusion, it began to be seriously feared that the Confederates, in their anxiety to secure exchanges on any terms, would agree to the Federal demand about the delivery and exchange of their own slaves, and, in apprehension of that result, we have it on the authority of General Butler himself that he and General Grant conferred together as to how exchanges were to be prevented in that event. What result their ingenuity reached we are not informed. The Confederates never gave an opportunity for disclosure, as they maintained their position on the slave question to the end.

Not having been able to obtain any answer to my letter to General Hitchcock, I made another move in August, 1864, the actual result of which staggers belief. Under the instructions of the Confederate authorities, I offered to the United States their sick and wounded *without requiring any equivalents.* I tendered ten or fifteen thousand of this class, to be delivered at the mouth of the Savannah river, assuring the Federal agent that if the number for which he might send transportation could not be readily made up from the sick and wounded at Andersonville and elsewhere, I would supply the deficiency with well men. Although this offer was made in the summer of 1864, transportation was not sent to the Savannah river until about the middle or last of November, and then I delivered as many prisoners as could be transported with the means at hand, some thirteen thousand in number, among whom were more than five thousand well men. It has been asserted that no such offer was made in August, 1864, and that the first proposal, looking to anything like a general delivery of the sick and wounded, was first made by the United States, in October, 1864, and that the delivery at Savannah was in consequence of this last-mentioned movement. General Butler so asserted on the floor of the House of Representatives, on the 17th of July, 1867, when the question of an inquiry into the treatment of Confederate soldiers in Northern prisons was under discussion. He is mistaken. The offer in August was made to General Mulford, and by him communicated to the Federal authorities. If anybody disputes it, I appeal to him for proof.

More than once I urged the mortality at Andersonville as a reason for haste, yet there was delay from August until November in sending transportation for the sick and wounded, for whom no equivalents were asked. It was during that interval that the largest proportionate mortality occurred at Andersonville. Although the terms of my offer did not require the Federal authorities to deliver any equivalents for the ten or fifteen thousand I promised, yet some thirty-five hundred sick and wounded Confederate prisoners were delivered at that time. I can call upon every Federal and Confederate officer and man who saw that cargo of living death, and who is familar with the character of the deliveries made by the Confederate authorities, to bear witness that none such was ever made by the latter, even when the very sick and desperately wounded alone were requested. For on two occasions at least in 1864, such men were specially asked for, hospital boats were sent, and particular request was made for those who were so desperately sick that it would be doubtful whether they would survive a removal a few miles down James river. Accordingly, Confederate hospitals in Richmond were searched for the worst cases, and after they were delivered they were taken to Annapolis, Congress was invited to inspect them, and for the benefit of those who did not see them they were photographed as specimens of Confederate barbarity, and illustrations of the manner in which Union soldiers were treated in the ordinary Southern prisons. The photographs of the sick and diseased men at Annapolis were terrible indeed, but the misery they portrayed was surpassed at Savannah.

In the winter of 1864–65, General Grant took control of matters relating to exchanges, and my correspondence on that subject took place with him. The result was the delivery of a large number of prisoners on both sides, chiefly during the months of February and March, 1865, too late for the returned Confederate soldiers to be of any service to a cause which, even before those dates, had become desperate. These deliveries were officer for officer according to grade, and man for man, the excess remaining in captivity. The deliveries made by the Confederates were made at several points, east and west, as fast as possible, and their equivalents were received in James river. In carrying out his agreements and arrangements with me, I found General Grant to be scrupulously correct. He never deviated in the slightest from his contracts.

On the occupation of Richmond I followed General Lee's army

4

to Appomatox Court House, and was there at the surrender. I offered my parole to General Grant who generously declined to subject me even to parole, saying that he did not consider an officer of the Exchange Bureau subject to capture. He gave me a passport and escort to Richmond, when he learned it was my purpose to return to that place. Upon my return to Richmond I set about closing up the affairs of the Exchange Bureau, knowing that the end had come. At the expiration of about ten days, while thus engaged, I was arrested by order of Mr. Secretary Stanton and thrown into prison. His order was special that I should be put in close confinement. Seven years before that I had a professional collision with Mr. Stanton in the trial of Daniel E. Sickles for the murder of Philip Barton Key. I was then United States District Attorney for the District of Columbia, and he was one of the defendant's counsel. I had occasion during the course of the trial, after gross and repeated provocation, to denounce his conduct, and to charge that he had been imported into the case to play the part of a bully and a bruiser. He had not forgotten this occurrence, even after the lapse of so many years, and took his revenge in the manner indicated. Of the hundreds of thousands engaged in the war on the Confederate side, I was the only one who held an office by the express consent of the United States. The cartel provided that each side should appoint an Agent of Exchange. I was not only thrown into prison, but was indicted for treason in Underwood's court—treason in filling an office to which, and to the incumbency of which by myself, the United States had assented. All my official papers, including those delivered to me by the Federal Agents of Exchange, were seized and taken away. I did save my letter-book alone, which I prize very highly, if for no other purpose than to show the malignant falsehoods of certain publications, some of them official, which purport to give the correspondence of my office. I include in this list House Document No. 32, Second Session, Thirty-eighth Congress, which pretends to show the correspondence of the Agents of Exchange on both sides, but which does not rise even to the dignity of a travesty. My house was also searched, and my private papers taken. A military commission sat on me to find out whether any charges could be brought against me, or sustained, if brought. After two weeks' incubation, during which they examined witnesses against me, while I was not allowed to be present, the commission reported that they could find nothing against me, but much to my credit; and thereupon, after two months' confinement, I was released.

I have thus given the more prominent incidents connected with the exchange question, and especially the matters that led to a suspension of the cartel. In narrating them, I have, as far as I well could, presented them in chronological order, that they might be better grasped. There are some other matters connected with exchanges which, though minor in importance, may be of interest.

One of the earliest difficulties connected with the cartel was the matter of the arrest and detention of non-combatants. General Pope, who proclaimed that his *headquarters* were in the saddle, a thing which most people would have believed without that information from him, on the 23d of July, 1862, one day after the adoption of the cartel, issued a general order directing the arrest of all disloyal male citizens within the Federal lines, or within their reach in the rear. Those who would take the oath of allegiance to the United States, and furnish sufficient security for its observance, could remain unmolested; but those who refused were to be removed from their homes, and if found again within the lines, or at any point in the rear, they were to be "considered spies and subjected to the extreme rigor of military law." In pursuance of this and other orders, peaceable, non-combatant citizens of the Confederate States, especially men of mature age, engaged in the pursuit of their ordinary avocations, were arrested and thrown into prison or sent from their homes. This was frequently done during the march of the Federal forces through the Confederate States, and, it may be, in some cases under circumstances which justified the arrest. But our complaint, prolonged through the war, was loud that when the invading army retired from the neighborhood where the arrest was made, the non-combatants were not released from imprisonment. This practice forced upon the Confederates a partial system of retaliation, and accordingly, upon the invasion of Pennsylvania by General Lee, some fifty non-combatants of that State and Maryland were captured and brought to Richmond. Moreover, some persons of well-known Union sentiments within the Confederate States were arrested and confined in Castle Thunder. These circumstances provoked a long correspondence between the respective Agents of Exchange. I sought as earnestly as I could to establish a rule which would prevent the arrest or incarceration of civilians on either side. I maintained that the capture of non-combatants in the general was illegal and contrary to the usages of civilized warfare, and only excused the arrest of the Pennsylvanians on the ground of retaliation, after the failure of all other means of prevention. To show clearly and officially what were the actual views of the Confederate Government in this matter, I quote the material part of a letter which, on the 31st of October, 1863, I addressed to General S. A. Meredith:

"More than a year ago, recognizing the injustice of the arrest of non-combatants, I submitted the following proposition to the Federal authorities, to wit: That peaceable, non-combatant citizens, of both the United States and the Confederate States, who are not connected with any military organization, shall not be arrested by either the United States or Confederate armies within the territory of the adverse party. If this proposition is too broad, let the only exception be the case of a temporary arrest of parties within army lines, where the arresting party has good reason to believe that their presence is dangerous to the safety of the army, from the opportunity afforded of giving intelligence to the enemy. It is to be understood, however, in the latter case, the arrest is to cease as soon as the reason for making it ceases, in the withdrawal of the army, or for any other cause. This proposal is understood to include such arrests and imprisonments as are already in force. Although this proposition, so reasonable and humane in its terms, has been before your Government for more than a year, it has never been accepted. I now again invite your attention to it. If it does not suit you, I will thank you to suggest any modification. I am willing to adopt any fair and reciprocal rule that will settle this matter on principle. It must, however, be settled by rule. It cannot, with any safety, be determined by 'special cases.'"

The Federal authorities never did accede to these terms, or agree to the adoption of any common rule on the subject. And yet General Hitchcock, in his report, says that "the rebels inaugurated a system of seizing unoffending citizens of the United States and subjecting them to maltreatment in various ways, in order to effect a particular object, which became apparent when a demand was made for their release;" and asserts that the aforesaid agreement on the subject, which the Confederates sought to obtain, "would have been a virtual acknowledgment of the independence of the rebel government, and would have foreclosed all proceedings of the United States against all persons whomsoever engaged in the crime of treason and rebellion." General Hitchcock, it seems, did not stop to inquire whether the same argument, if there was any force in it, could not just as easily have been urged against the adoption of any cartel. But the pretension that the rebels "inaugurated" the system of seizing unoffending citizens is too bald for anybody's credence. This extract from Hitchcock's report, however, discloses one thing, which was really the prime cause of all the difficulties connected with the detention and exchange of prisoners, civil and military, to wit: an unwillingness to recognize the equality of the belligerents. Pray, how, upon any other theory than that of equality, can a cartel be framed or executed?

On the 26th of July, 1863, General John H. Morgan and his command were captured. They were carried to Cincinnati, and from thence, by General Burnside's order, he and twenty-eight of his officers were sent to the penitentiary at Columbus, where they were shaved and their hair cut very close by a negro convict. They were then marched to the bath-room and scrubbed, and thence to their cells. Seven days afterward forty-two more of General Morgan's officers were sent from Johnson's Island to the penitentiary, and subjected to the same indignities. On the 30th of July, 1863, I was informed by the Federal agent of exchange, General Meredith, "that General John H. Morgan and his officers will be placed in close confinement, and held as hostages for the members of Colonel Streight's command." I replied, on the 1st of August, that Colonel Streight's command was treated exactly as were other officers. On the 28th of August I wrote another letter, asking the Federal Agent whether he wished Colonel Streight to be shaved and put in a felon's cell, and suggesting, if he did, that the Federal authorities were pursuing exactly the course to secure that result. To that letter I received the following reply, which I will give entire, as something of a portrait of the man I was dealing with:

FORTRESS MONROE, September 30th, 1863.

Hon. Robert Ould, Agent of Exchange, Richmond, Va.:

SIR:—Had I succeeded, after waiting thirty hours, in obtaining an interview with you, when I was last at City Point, I had intended to explain to you that the United States authorities had nothing to do with the treatment that General Morgan and his command received when imprisoned at Columbus. Such treatment was wholly unauthorized.

Very respectfully, your obedient servant,

S. A. MEREDITH,
Brigadier General and Commissioner for Exchange.

A few days after the receipt of this letter, General Meredith informed me that General Morgan and his officers were held for others than "the members of Colonel Streight's command." He showed me a letter from General Hitchcock, in which the same statement was made. Thus it appears that I was first notified that General Morgan and his officers would be placed in close confinement for the members of Streight's command—then two months afterward I was informed that the United States had nothing to do with the treatment that General Morgan and his command received —and then I was told that General Morgan and his officers were not held for the members of Colonel Streight's command. Yet, during all this time, and for a long time afterward, General Morgan and his officers were continued in the penitentiary, and compelled to suffer all the indignities of felon life. It taxes credulity too much to believe that the United States were not responsible for the treatment they received, sent there as they were by General Burnside, and kept there by the United States War Department.

While on the subject of Morgan's command, it may not be inappropriate to relate an incident which furnishes a dark chapter in the history of paroles, and serves to show the times upon which the country had then fallen My authority is a letter from Lieutenant Colonel Alston, of Morgan's command, to the Confederate Secretary of War. On the 5th of July, 1863, General Morgan captured the command of Lieutenant Colonel Charles H. Hanson, at Lebanon, Kentucky. The latter requested that he and his command be paroled, pledging his personal honor that he not only would observe it, but would see that every other one to whom the privilege was extended should observe it; and further, that if he should be ordered back into service, he would report to General Morgan at some point within the Confederate lines. Colonel Hanson and his command were paroled, and as a return for this favor, three days after, a portion of his command thus paroled actually captured a part of General Morgan's force. Lietenant Colonel Hanson himself, a few days after his capture under the circumstances detailed, was ordered to Louisville to do provost duty. It would be difficult to find in the annals of war a parallel to this.

Colonel Streight and his officers were detained in Richmond, on allegations from the highest authority in Alabama, charging him and his officers with grave offenses as well against the laws of that State as the usages of civilized warfare. I informed the Federal Agent, in response to an inquiry from him, that they were detained "until proper inquiries can be made and the facts ascertained, when a determination will be made by the Confederate Government whether they come within the obligations of the cartel as prisoners of war, or are to be dealt with as criminals against the laws of war and the State." The right of the Confederate Government to detain and try Colonel Streight and his officers was distinctly recognized by the United States in their General Order, No. 100. The 59th paragraph of that order declared that "a prisoner of war remains answerable for his crimes committed against the captor's army or people, committed before he was captured, and for which he has not been punished by his own authorities." Moreover, the United States had claimed and exercised the right of holding many Confederate officers on the merest suspicion, without trial or proceedings of any sort against them. Yet, when the Confederates retained Colonel Streight and his officers, on charges preferred by the highest authority in Alabama, and in accordance with Federal practice and general order, a great outcry was made.

Frequent applications were made for special exchange—that is, for the exchange of a particular officer for another particularly named. I set my face against this system from the beginning, whether the application came from one side or the other. Fathers and mothers and sisters frequently besought me with tears to give their kindred the benefit of a special exchange; but I was obdurate to the last. Sometimes they would appreciate my reason, and go away satisfied, but in the large majority of cases, knowing only the bitterness of their own hearts, they thought hardly of me. There were many objections to special exchanges. The system at best, was favoritism. It was not right or fair to pursue a policy, which would put one prisoner in a more favorable position than another of equal merit. Moreover, it gave the opportunity to the belligerent proposing such an exchange, to select a valuable officer in the enemy's hands, and give for him one very worthless, or what was worse, one who had been tampered with. But my chief objection was, that if all those whom the United States particularly desired were specially exchanged, the Confederate Government would have none in captivity who could bring any pressure to bear in favor of a general exchange. So resolute was I in this matter that, with the approval of the Confederate Government, in one case I sent back a Confederate officer who came to secure a special exchange, and in other cases I refused to send the designated Federal officers, and gave other equivalents.

The prisoners on both sides, when delivered, were always welcomed to their respective flags with almost wild delight; but otherwise it was not often that anything happened to break the common routine. The Federal prisoners were generally put on board a steamer at Richmond, and then carried some thirty miles down the James river and transferred to the flag-of-truce boat "New York." Once or twice they were marched a shorter distance. They would generally meet a returning body of Confederate prisoners; and from the manner in which the two parties met and fraternized, no one would have supposed that they were enemies, or believed in the doctrine of prize cases. Sometimes they sang, in turn, their respective camp songs, and both sides would greet any good hit with uproarious merriment. I recollect one occasion when this amusement was kept up for hours, to the delight of all, each set of prisoners having several capital voices, with an apparently exhaustless variety of songs, in which the names of all the notables of both armies, and especially Stonewall Jackson's, figured.

There was one incident in the course of deliveries which was quite dramatic, though very painful to one of the parties—a Pennsylvania colonel. In the beginning of the war, surgeons were regarded as non-combatants, and not subject to detention on either side. A difficulty, however, arose between the two governments about one Dr. Rucker, who was held in confinement on the charge of murder, and other high crimes. The United States demanded his release, and failing to secure it, put Dr. Green, a Confederate surgeon, in confinement in retaliation. This led to the detention of all surgeons on both sides. I made vigorous efforts to restore the old practice, and at length succeeded. Accordingly, a day was fixed for the delivery of all surgeons on both sides at City Point, and all the Federal surgeons were directed to be sent from the Libby and put on board the flag-of-truce steamer. I accompanied the party. When we were nearing the steamer "New York," I perceived that a signal was flying for me to come to the shore with my boat. I did so, and found there a communication stating that Colonel Harry White, commanding one of the Pennsylvania regiments, had disguised himself as a surgeon and was then on board my boat. I immediately directed the prisoners to be drawn up in line on the shore and made them an address, in which I recounted the efforts I had made to secure the immunity of their class, and stated that an officer of the line, not entitled to exchange or release, was among them, disguised as a surgeon. I then raised my voice and shouted: "Colonel Harry White, come forth." He stepped in front at once, and in a few words claimed that he had the right to resort to any stratagem to effect his release. I replied that I was not there to dispute or affirm what he said, but that he must return to Richmond under arrest. It was a heavy blow to him, struck at the moment when he was sanguine of his liberty. Two minutes more would have placed him on the "New York," where he would have been safe, even if his disguise had been there detected. He had been a long time in captivity, and extraordinary efforts had been made to secure for him a special exchange. He had been elected as a Republican to the Pennsylvania Senate, which, without him, was equally divided between the war and anti-war parties. His presence was needed to effect an organization and working majority in that body. I had learned these facts from more than one quarter, and was not disposed to assist in giving aid and comfort to the war party. I was under no duty to release Colonel White, as the exchange of officers had ceased. So obstinate was I, that when the Federal Agent offered me a major general and several officers of lower grade for him, I declined to accept. I might have speculated to great advantage on him if I had been so disposed, and the situation in Pennsylvania would have warranted it. If every officer and man had been a Harry White, there never would have been any difficulty about exchanges. Indeed, if the anxiety manifested about him had been distributed, instead of making him the reservoir of all, it would have been better for a good many people. "Great is Diana of the Ephesians."

Colonel White's was by no means the only case of false personation during the war. The late Secretary of War was exchanged as a private or non-commissioned officer, there being a difficulty about the exchange of officers at the time of his capture. Once when a body of Confederate chaplains was to be delivered, an army officer assumed the name of one who was on the list, but who was too sick to be sent, and came with the parsons as one of them to Fortress Monroe. They were put on board the "New York," early in the morning, to be brought up the James river. General Mulford, the courteous flag-of-truce officer, knowing the cloth of his prisoners and supposing that they would desire to have prayers before breakfast, offered for that purpose a Bible to one of the party, and, as accident would have it, gave the book to our army friend, who was the only bogus chaplain in the lot. To have declined would have exposed him to suspicion, if not detection. Although not a professor of religion he boldly took the book and read a chapter. Then kneeling with his comrades he began the Lord's Prayer, and, as the story goes, broke down in the middle!

I have named the person with whom I was brought in contact as Confederate Agent of Exchange. I found Colonel Ludlow to be courteous and just when he was allowed to follow his own instincts or judgment. I believe he was removed because he desired to be just, and I paid him officially that compliment when he was relieved to give place to a supple tool. General Mulford was a flower of chivalry and standing toast with Confederate prisoners, officers and men. From the date of the cartel to the close of the war he discharged the responsible duties of flag-of-truce officer and Assistant Agent of Exchange with consummate address and always with a courteous spirit. He was a genuine lover of fair play. He never told me a lie, or told one on me. I wish in my heart I could say the same as to all the others. He was as kind to our prisoners as if he had been a natural brother to each one of them. If he could have had the power to adjust and settle, there never would have been any trouble. He was tied by others who did not feel as he did. I hope I will do him no harm by this inadequate testimonial to his virtues.

General Sullivan A. Meredith, of Philadelphia, followed Colonel Ludlow as Federal agent of exchange. At my first interview with him I strongly suspected that he had been sent to break off exchanges, instead of furthering them. I was convinced of it afterward. He abounded in all the qualities which would make him useful on just such a service. He was coarse, rude, arrogant, and so unacquainted with the matters committed to his charge, that it was difficult to transact any business with him.

General Hitchcock, whom I never saw during the war, had his headquarters at Washington. He styled himself "Commissioner for the Exchange of Prisoners." What his precise function was I never was able to learn; for while he was Commissioner at Washington, there was always a Federal Agent of Exchange somewhere else. How far the authority of each extended, or how far one was subordinate to the other, or how far one could refuse what the other allowed, or deny what the other said, never clearly appeared. I suppose that both could be put to valuable uses, "each after his kind." As far as I could gather, Hitchcock seems to have been a sort of Tycoon of exchanges, solemnly sitting in Washington to superintend matters about which he knew little or nothing, if his report is to be believed. He never condescended to write to me, though I did more than once to him, not having any special fear of his august sacredness. One of these letters, which he ought to have answered, and for his failure so to do, he deserves to be impaled upon the wrath of mankind, I will give. Oh! what weltering woe and wretchedness it would have saved.

RICHMOND, VA., January 24th, 1864.

Major General E. A. Hitchcock, Agent of Exchange:

SIR:—In view of the present difficulties attending the exchange and release of prisoners, I propose that all such, on each side, shall be attended by a proper number of their own surgeons, who, under rules to be established, shall be permitted to take charge of their health and comfort.

I also propose that these surgeons shall act as commissaries, with power to receive and distribute such contributions of money, food, clothing and medicines as may be forwarded for the relief of prisoners. I further propose that these surgeons be selected by their own governments, and that they shall have full liberty at any and all times, through the Agents of Exchange, to make reports not only of their own acts, but of any matters relating to the welfare of the prisoners.

Respectfully, your obedient servant,

ROBERT OULD,
Agent of Exchange.

It gives me no pleasure to write these things; nor do I seek to bring myself unduly forward in this matter. I wish the cup could pass from me. But the official position I occupied during the war seems to require that I should step to the front to vindicate the truth of history, when false statements, official and unofficial, are so rife. It is not done in the interest of hate, nor to revive sectional controversy, nor to inflame the now subsiding passions of war. Least of all do I desire to put any stigma upon the people of the North. The sins which were committed were those of individuals, and they were few in number. I believe a true understanding of the facts in connection with the exchange of prisoners and their treatment, instead of increasing any feeling of hate between the North and South would tend to allay it. It would then be seen that the sections were not to be blamed—that the people on both sides were not justly amenable to reproach—that honor, integrity, and Christian civilization reigned North and South, and that our civil war, though necessarily harsh and cruel in its general aspect, was illustrated by high and shining examples of moderation, kindness, good faith, generosity, and knightly courtesy.

GENERAL REYNOLDS' LAST BATTLE.

BY MAJOR JOSEPH G. ROSENGARTEN.

GETTYSBURG has become a consecrated name, and among all the long array of those who fell there, John Fulton Reynolds will forever stand out foremost. A soldier by profession, he won a reputation that gave promise of achievement, not fully realized by reason of his early death. A native of Pennsylvania, it was eminently fitting that he should lead the van of the Army of the Potomac, when it hurried to the defense of the State in which he was born. Singularly beloved by his comrades in the army, from his West Point days, through his campaigns in Florida, his services on the frontier, his life upon the Plains, he was admired by his volunteer soldiers, and by the great number of civilians with whom he was brought into intimate relationship in the two campaigns in Pennsylvania and Maryland, in which he was prominently engaged. Free from any personal ambition, he devoted himself to his duty in every post in which he was placed, and he won the confidence alike of subordinates and superiors, so that his name was constantly suggested for the very highest command. His modest preference for Meade as the chief of the Army of the Potomac, when Hooker was relieved, no doubt brought Reynolds to the spot where he found his death; but it was characteristic of his life, and he undoubtedly preferred to serve in the immediate command of the lesser body of troops, that he might inspire them with his own example of courage, rather than to take upon himself responsibilities without adequate power. Impetuous without rashness, rapid without haste, ready without heedlessness, he liked better to be at the head of a compact corps than to command a scattered army.

In no instance of the many supplied by West Point, was there a better example than that of Reynolds of the wonderful effects of a West Point training upon a characteristic American mind. Here was a lad taken from a modest family, brought up in a country town, grown into manhood at West Point, sent to Florida, then from point to point through the West, slowly earning his promotion, recognized as a good soldier, and so good a disciplinarian, that even at the outbreak of the war he was appointed to duty at West Point, and soon after assigned to the slow business of organizing one of the new regular regiments, then given a brigade of the Pennsylvania Reserves, and from that moment showing himself master of the art of war, and rapidly rising to the height of every new command, of every novel duty, of every fresh demand upon his military skill and resources. It was his brigade that first smelled powder at Draines-ville; it was his division that made the stoutest resistance on the Peninsula, and his imprisonment at Richmond after his capture, ended only in time to find him sent to Pennsylvania to organize and command the hasty levies of militiamen, brought together to resist the raid of 1862. He thoroughly inspired his subordinates with his own zeal, and the men who served under him felt that unconscious and irresistible strength, which comes from a commander fully competent to his work, ready to do it with whatever forces are given him, and able to command success from every opportunity. That task done, he led the division which, at the second Bull Run, held its own against overwhelming odds, and helped to save the army. His corps won the only success at Fredericksburg, and in the operations that ended so disastrously at Chancellorsville, Reynolds took a leading and always prominent part. In all the intrigues of the army, and the interference of the politicians in its management, he silently set aside the tempting offers to take part, and served his successive commanders with unswerving loyalty and zeal and faith.

When the Gettysburg campaign was inaugurated, he was as-signed to the command of the three corps, his own, the First, Sickles' Third and Howard's Eleventh, and led the left wing in its rapid passage through the country that lay in front of Washington, pro-tecting it from the armies that moved up in the sheltered valleys, feeling them through the gaps, offering them battle, crossing the Potomac and following and seeking to engage Lee's forces wherever they could be found. In the midst of this energetic and unceasing action, came the sudden order relieving Hooker from the command of the Army of the Potomac, and it is a tradition of Reynolds' Corps that the post was offered to him, that he made the accepting of it conditional upon being left absolutely free and untrammeled from any interference or supervision from Washington; that being denied, he was asked who ought to have the command, and said that Meade was the man, and it was to his persuasion and the promise of his aid, that Meade yielded. He was with Meade at Frederick when the order assigning Meade to the command of the Army of the Potomac came, and during the brief hours of that summer night he aided Meade in working out the plan which ended in Gettysburg. It was characteristic of the man that from that momentous interview, he rushed to the front and swooped down on a poor German cavalry general, safely ensconced in a Maryland border village, sending in as dispatches from his scouts and his own observations reports made up of the rumors published in the newspapers. The poor German was soon sent to the rear, never more to be heard of, and a trusty soldier put in his place, while Reynolds hurried on to concentrate his forces and secure the combined strength of the Army of the Potomac for the great struggle that was at hand.

Reynolds knew Buford thoroughly, and knowing him and the value of cavalry under such a leader, sent them through the mountain passes beyond Gettysburg to find and feel the enemy. The old rule would have been to keep them back near the infantry, but Reynolds sent Buford on, and Buford went on, knowing that wherever Reynolds sent him, he was sure to be supported, followed, and secure. It was Buford who first attracted Reynolds' attention to the concentration of roads that gave Gettysburg its strategic importance, and it was Reynolds who first appreciated the strength and value of Cemetery Hill, and the plateau between that point and Round Top, as the stronghold to be secured for the concentration of the scattered corps and as the place where Meade could put his army to meet and overthrow the larger body he was pursuing. Together they found Gettysburg and made it the spot upon which the Union forces won a victory that was bought with his among the precious lives lost there. Buford and Reynolds were soldiers of the same order, and each found in the other just the qualities that were most needed to perfect and complete the task intrusted to them. The brilliant achievement of Buford, with his small body of cavalry, up to that time hardly appreciated as to the right use to be made of them, is but too little considered in the history of the battle of Gettysburg. It was his foresight and energy, his pluck and self-reliance, in thrusting forward his forces and pushing the enemy, and thus inviting, almost compelling their return, that brought on the engagement of the first of July.

Buford counted on Reynolds' support, and he had it fully, faithfully, and energetically. Reynolds counted in turn on having within his reach and at his immediate service at least the three corps that belonged to him, and there can be little question that if they had been up as promptly as he was in answer to Buford's call, the line he had marked out would have been fully manned and firmly held, while Meade's concentration behind Gettysburg would have gone on easily, and the whole of the Army of the Potomac would have done briefly and effectually what was gained only at the end of three days of hard fighting, with varying successes that more than once threatened to turn against ns, and the loss on our side would have been so much less that the pursuit of Lee's forces could have been made promptly and irresistibly. It is not, however, given to all men to be of the same spirit, and the three corps that were under Reynolds followed his orders in a very different way from that in which he always did his work. When he got Buford's demand for infantry support on the morning of the first, it was just what Reynolds expected, and with characteristic energy, he went forward, saw Buford, accepted at once the responsibility, and returning to find the leading division of the First Corps (Wadsworth's), took it in hand, brought it to the front, put it in position, renewed his orders for the rest of the corps, assigned the positions for the other divisions, sent for his other corps, urged their coming with the greatest speed, directed the point to be held by the reserve, renewed his report to Meade that Buford had found the place for a battle, and that he had begun it, then calmly and coolly hurried some fresh troops forward to fill a gap in his lengthening lines, and as he returned to find fresh divisions, fell at the first onset.

The suddenness of the shock was in itself, perhaps, a relief to those who were nearest to Reynolds. In the full flush of life and health, vigorously leading on the troops in hand, and energetically summoning up the rest of his command, watching and even leading the attack of a comparatively small body, a glorious picture of the best type of military leader, superbly mounted, and horse and man sharing in the excitement of the shock of battle, Reynolds was, of course, a shining mark to the enemy's sharpshooters. He had taken his troops into a heavy growth of timber on the slope of a hill-side, and, under their regimental and brigade commanders, the men did their work well and promptly. Returning to join the expected divisions, he was struck by a Minnie ball, fired by a sharpshooter hidden in the branches of a tree amost overhead, and killed at once ; his horse bore him to the little clump of trees, where a cairn of stones and a rude mark on the bark, now almost overgrown, still tells the fatal spot. The battle went on in varying fortune, and so long as the influence of his orders that had inspired men and officers could still be felt, all went well; but when the command had been changed by the successive arrival of generals who outranked each other, what there was of plan could hardly be made out, and the troops of the First Corps, without reinforcements and worn out and outnumbered, fell back at first with some show of order, and then as best they could, to find shelter in the lines pointed out by Reynolds for the concentration of his fresh troops. Thus even after his death, his military foresight had provided for the temporary defeat, which prepared the way for the great victory.

It is a striking proof of the discipline he had taught his own corps, that the news of the death, although it spread rapidly and that at a time when the inequality of numbers became apparent, produced no ill effect, led to no disorder, changed no disposition that he had directed, and in itself made the men only the more eager to carry out his orders. At the moment that his body was taken to the rear, for his death was instantaneous, two of his most gallant staff officers, Captain Riddle and Captain Wadsworth, in pursuance of his directions, effected a slight movement which made prisoners of Archer's Brigade, so that the rebel prisoners went to the rear almost at the same time, and their respectful conduct was in itself the highest tribute they could pay to him who had thus fallen. While his body lay in the little house on the Emmetsburg road, which he had passed in such full life only a few short hours before, Major Baird, his Assistant Adjutant General, was practically carrying out his orders in the disposition of the troops as they came up, and General Hofmann, whose Fifty-sixth Pennsylvania had made the first onset, was supported by Wadsworth, himself in the far front, until other regiments could be deployed and the line taken. From the extreme left, where Colonel Chapman Biddle, in charge of the brigade, and Colonel Alexander Biddle, in immediate command of the One Hundred and Twenty-first Pennsylvania, which withstood the shock of attack quite without support and literally in air, that is, with no troops or even natural or artificial cover to protect their exposed flank, to the extreme right, where the Eleventh Corps was at last put in position, the First Corps was deployed in thin ranks. Reynolds had counted on having the Third Corps well in hand to extend his line to the left, but it was late in starting, late in moving, lost its way and got far out into the hostile lines, and got back only by Humphrey's skill and readiness, and long before they were on the field, Reynolds' dead body was on its way to a place of safety.

While the battle waged in the woods in front of the Seminary, and the overwhelming forces came out from behind the ridges that had sheltered them from sight, Reynolds' aides and messengers were busy bringing to Meade news of the conflict, looking for Howard to urge forward his corps, and hunting up Sickles to put him on the right road. Buford was busy, too, in making his little cavalry force, with its few batteries of horse artillery, serve to support in turn the infantry, which had come forward at his demand, and thus lengthening out the hours of the battle before the troops came up. It was Reynolds who had pointed out Cemetery Hill as the key of the position, on which he saw that Meade must fight to win, and while some of the horse batteries, shattered and badly used up, went into position there, his body lay dead and stark in a little house at the foot of the hill. It was only after the arrival of the head of Howard's command that Schurz took his division out to support the right of the First Corps, and the other division took its place as a reserve on Cemetery Hill, and after Reynolds' staff had communicated his last orders to Doubleday and Howard, who in turn succeeded to the command, that the necessity arose of providing a safe and suitable place for the care of the sacred dust. In the midst of the turning tide, when it was feared that the day was lost, the positions turned, and stragglers began to pour in from the front, an ambulance started off with Reynolds' body, in charge of his faithful and gallant orderly, and one or two others. Soon after leaving the town behind, Hancock met the little cortège, and it was stopped to give him the last news of the day, while on the arrival at Meade's headquarters, in the midst of sincere expressions of deep sorrow and an overwhelming loss, time was taken to explain to Meade, and Warren, and Hunt, and Williams, and Tyler, all that could serve to explain the actual condition of affairs, the real state of the case, the advantages of the position, the need of troops and the necessity of moving immediately to the front.

As Meade went off in that direction, the little group carried on their sacred burden until the railroad was reached. From that point to Baltimore was a comparatively easy journey, and then came the sad, slow move to Philadelphia and Lancaster, where, at last, on the Fourth of July, when the army of the Potomac had been declared the victor on the field of Gettysburg, Reynolds was buried in the tranquil cemetery, where he lies in the midst of his family, near the scenes of his own childhood, and on the soil of his native State, in whose defense, and in the service of the cause of the Union, he had given up his life. The record of his career

5

would not be complete without an expression of regret that due justice was not done his services and his memory by those who best knew both—his immediate commander, and those in authority at Washington.   Yet, in spite of the brief and imperfect record that has been made, his name is still affectionately cherished by his old comrades of the regular army; by all who served with him in his successive commands; by the veterans of his own First Corps; by the volunteers and militia who felt his force and will and military qualities, even in their brief term of service under him.   To their united loyal efforts and assistance, and to the persistent energy of a few of his old officers, is due the statue of Reynolds; noble it stands on Cemetery Hill, looking over Gettysburg, and out beyond to the long line of wooded country through which he moved with his troops, and to the little knoll where he fell in the very front, and almost at the first onset.   It is right that his memorial should thus command the field, for his influence made itself felt through the long days of that great battle, and its final success was largely due to the plans he had made and the operations he had conducted.

The history of Gettysburg yet remains to be written.   So barren is the official record that a very gallant officer of the old First Corps said once that he often wondered if he had really been there, for he looked in vain at the official reports for any mention of his command, and yet Dick Coulter was never in action without leaving his mark.   There have been hot and angry disputes, and an amount of angry recrimination and plain talk between very prominent general officers as to their respective shares in the credit of the battle, and there have been learned essays on the strategy and grand tactics of the operations that made part of the campaign of Gettysburg, by men who never set a squadron in the field, but the whole story still remains to be told.   Perhaps the Count of Paris may put the record straight, for his history of our great civil war seems likely to be the best, and to serve as the last resort, beyond which there will be no appeal.   Be that as it may, the subject is one that ought to be properly and exhaustively treated, and it would be well if the entire and complete set of official reports from officers of all grades and arms of service engaged in the battle, could be published from the archives at Washington.   If we cannot get an official history of the war, such as the German and French staff have already supplied for their campaign, let us have at least the sources of history, the reports that give the story as it was told at the time.   Reynolds is in no need of posthumous fame, but the country ought to know what such a man did, and then it could the better judge of what it lost in a life so prematurely cut short in its service.

THE LAST CONFEDERATE SURRENDER.

BY LIEUTENANT GENERAL RICHARD TAYLOR.

To WRITE an impartial and unprejudiced account of exciting contemporary events has always been a difficult task. More especially is this true of civil strife, which, like all "family jars," evolves a peculiar flavor of bitterness. But slight sketches of minor incidents, by actors and eye-witnesses, may prove of service to the future writer, who undertakes the more ambitious and severe duty of historian. The following *memoir pour servir* has this object.

In the summer of 1864, after the close of the Red river campaign, I was ordered to cross the Mississippi, and report my arrival on the east bank by telegraph to Richmond. All the fortified posts on the river were held by the Federals, and the intermediate portions of the stream closely guarded by gunboats to impede and, as far as possible, prevent passage. This delayed the transmission of the order above-mentioned until August, when I crossed at a point just above the mouth of the Red river. On a dark night, in a small canoe, with horses swimming alongside, I got over without attracting the attention of a gunboat, anchored a short distance below. Woodville, Wilkinson county, Mississippi, was the nearest place in telegraphic communication with Richmond. Here, in reply to a dispatch to Richmond, I was directed to assume command of the Department of Alabama, Mississippi, etc., with headquarters at Meridian, Mississippi, and informed that President Davis would, at an early day, meet me at Montgomery, Alabama. The military situation was as follows: Sherman occupied Atlanta, Hood lying some distance to the southwest; Farragut had forced the defenses of

(67)

Mobile bay, capturing Fort Morgan, etc., and the Federals held Pensacola, but had made no movements into the interior.

Major General Maury commanded the Confederate forces garrisoning Mobile and adjacent works, with Commodore Farrand, Confederate Navy, in charge of several armed vessels. Small bodies of troops were stationed at different points through the department, and Major General Forrest, with his division of cavalry, was in the Northeast Mississippi. Directing this latter officer to move his command across the Tennessee river, and use every effort to interrupt Sherman's communications south of Nashville, I proceeded to Mobile to inspect the fortifications; thence to Montgomery, to meet President Davis. The interview extended over many hours, and the military situation was freely discussed. Our next meeting was at Fortress Monroe, where, during his confinement, I obtained permission to visit him. The closing scenes of the great drama succeeded each other with startling rapidity. Sherman marched, unopposed, to the sea. Hood was driven from Nashville across the Tennessee, and asked to be relieved. Assigned to this duty I met him near Tupelo, North Mississippi, and witnessed the melancholy spectacle presented by a retreating army. Guns, small-arms and accoutrements lost, men without shoes or blankets, and this in a winter of unusual severity for that latitude. Making every effort to re-equip this force, I suggested to General Lee, then commanding all the armies of the Confederacy, that it should be moved to the Carolinas, to interpose between Sherman's advance and his (Lee's) lines of supply, and, in the last necessity, of retreat. The suggestion was adopted, and this force so moved. General Wilson, with a well-appointed and ably-led command of Federal cavalry, moved rapidly through North Alabama, seized Selma, and, turning east to Montgomery, continued into Georgia.

General Canby, commanding the Union armies in the South-west, advanced up the eastern shore of Mobile bay and invested Spanish Fort and Blakely, important Confederate works in that quarter. After repulsing an assault, General Maury, in accordance with instructions, withdrew his garrisons, in the night, to Mobile, and then evacuated the city, falling back to Meridian, on the line of the Mobile and Ohio Railway. General Forrest was drawn in to the same point, and the little army, less than eight thousand of all arms, held in readiness to discharge such duties as the waning fortunes of the "cause" and the honor of its arms might demand.

Intelligence of Lee's surrender reached us. Staff officers from Johnston and Sherman came across the country to inform Canby and myself of their "convention." Whereupon an interview was arranged between us to determine a course of action, and a place selected ten miles north of Mobile, near the railway. Accompanied by a staff officer, Colonel William M. Levy (now a member of Congress from Louisiana), and making use of a "hand car," I reached the appointed spot, and found General Canby with a large escort, and many staff and other officers. Among these I recognized some old friends, notably General Canby himself and Admiral James Palmer. All extended cordial greetings. A few moments of private conversation with Canby led to the establishment of a truce, to await further intelligence from the North. Forty-eight hours' notice was to be given by the party desiring to terminate the truce. We then joined the throng of officers, and although every one present felt a deep conviction that the last hour of the sad struggle approached, no allusion was made to it. Subjects awakening memories of the past, when all were sons of a loved, united country, were, as by the natural selection of good breeding, chosen. A bountiful luncheon was soon spread, and I was invited to partake of patis, champagne-frappe, and other "delights," which, to me, had long been as lost arts. As we took our seats at the table, a military band in attendance commenced playing "Hail Columbia." Excusing himself, General Canby walked to the door. The music ceased for a moment, and then the strain of "Dixie" was heard. Old Froissart records no gentler act of "courtesie." Warmly thanking General Canby for his delicate consideration, I asked for "Hail Columbia," and proposed we should unite in the hope that our Columbia would soon be, once more, a happy land. This and other kindred sentiments were duly honored in "frappe," and, after much pleasant intercourse, the party separated.

The succeeding hours were filled with a grave responsibility, which could not be evaded or shared. Circumstances had appointed me to watch the dying agonies of a cause that had fixed the attention of the world. To my camp, as the last refuge in the storm, came many members of the Confederate Congress. These gentlemen were urged to go at once to their respective homes, and, by precept and example, teach the people to submit to the inevitable, obey the laws, and resume the peaceful occupations on which society depends. This advice was followed, and with excellent effect on public tranquility.

General Canby dispatched that his government disavowed the Johnston-Sherman convention, and it would be his duty to resume hostilities. Almost at the same instant came the news of Johnston's surrender. There was no room for hesitancy. Folly and madness combined would not have justified an attempt to prolong a hopeless contest.

General Canby was informed that I desired to meet him for the purpose of negotiating a *surrender* of my forces, and that Commodore Farrand, commanding the armed vessels in the Alabama river, desired to meet Rear Admiral Thatcher for a similar purpose. Citronville, some forty miles north of Mobile, was the appointed place; and there, in the early days of May, 1865, the great war virtually ended.

After this, no hostile gun was fired, and the authority of the United States was supreme in the land. Conditions of surrender were speedily determined, and of a character to soothe the pride of the vanquished—officers to retain side-arms, troops to turn in arms and equipments to their own ordnance officers, so of the quartermaster and commissary stores; the Confederate cotton agent for Alabama and Mississippi to settle his accounts with the Treasury Agent of the United States; muster-rolls to be prepared, etc.; transportation to be provided for the men. All this under my control and supervision. Here a curious incident may be mentioned. At an early period of the war, when Colonel Albert Sidney Johnston retired to the south of the Tennessee river, Isham G. Harris, Governor of Tennessee, accompanied him, taking, at the same time, the coin from the vaults of the State Bank of Tennessee, at Nashville. This coin, in the immediate charge of a bonded officer of the bank, had occasioned much solicitude to the Governor in his many wanderings. He appealed to me to assist in the restoration of the coin to the bank. At my request, General Canby detailed an officer and escort, and the money reached the bank intact.

The condition of the people of Alabama and Mississippi was at this time deplorable. The waste of war had stripped large areas of the necessaries of life. In view of this, I suggested to General Canby that his troops, sent to the interior, should be limited to the number required for the preservation of order, and be stationed at points where supplies were more abundant. That trade would soon be established between soldiers and people—furnishing the latter with currency, of which they were destitute—and friendly relations promoted. These suggestions were adopted, and a day or two thereafter, at Meridian, a note was received from General Canby, inclosing copies of orders to Generals Granger and Steele, commanding army corps, by which it appeared these officers were directed to call on me for, and conform to, advice relative to movements of their troops.

Strange, indeed, must such confidence appear to statesmen of the "bloody-shirt" persuasion. In due time, Federal staff-officers reached my camp. The men were paroled and sent home. Public property was turned over and receipted for, and this as orderly and quietly as in time of peace between officers of the same service.

What years of discord, bitterness, injustice and loss would not our country have been spared, had the wounds of war healed "by first intention" under the tender ministrations of the hands that fought the battles? But the task was allotted to ambitious partisians, most of whom had not heard the sound of a gun. As of old, the Lion and the Bear fight openly and sturdily—the stealthy Fox carries off the prize.

THE FIRST GREAT CRIME OF THE WAR.

BY MAJOR GENERAL W. B. FRANKLIN.

NEARLY sixteen years ago the country was wrenched to its centre by the battle of Bull Run. This battle was the climax of a campaign, undertaken at the dictation of a clique in the press led by the New York *Tribune*, and in the then excited state of public feeling, the spirit awakened against the apparent inaction at Washington was enough to override the President, the Secretaries, and the General - in - Chief. The facts that 75,000 militia should have been called out nearly three months before, and that a large number of them were encamped near Washington, that they had, so far, struck no blow for its defense (although their presence alone was ample defense), that few, if any, had been killed, and that the rebels were in force at Manassas, defying these defenders to come forward, were so flagrant and preposterous, that their mere presentation broke down all military caution and conservatism, and the "On to Richmond" cry forced the Bull Run campaign on the country, with all its sequence of disaster and depression, and the mixed feelings of shame, and grief, and rage, which swept over the country like a whirlwind. The Bull Run fight had one good result for our side, and, so far as I am aware, only one. It taught our people to be a little patient, and not to expect the army to be ready to move next week. The disaster which came upon us in July, when thirty thousand three months' men, whose terms of enlistment would expire in a few days, commanded by general officers, not one of whom had been in action in a grade higher than that of captain, were hurried forward to defeat, would certainly have come upon us in September,

(72)

when hundreds of thousands of recruits would have begun to gather in the Eastern and Western camps of instruction, which General Scott had intended to form. The same feelings that urged us on to Bull Run in July would have sent forward a larger and quite an undisciplined an army at a later day, and the outcry would have been all the louder, as the force was greater in number, no matter if they were only enlisted yesterday. So I have no doubt that Bull Run was not an unmixed evil, but that Providence may have so overruled in our favor that the infliction of this defeat of a small army, depressing as it was, may have saved us from severer defeat two months afterward. No thanks, however, to those who brought on the campaign. In any event, the people were more patient, and afterward bore delays, which they could not understand, with a noble and self-sacrificing spirit.

So it happened that the first step taken by the dazed administration, after the battle of Bull Run, was to order to Washington, in command of the Army of the Potomac, the young General McClellan, who had been so far the only general upon whose banners victory for the cause had perched. He at once began a system of organization and distribution of troops, of purchase of material of war, of recommendations of generals to important commands East, West and South, of the erection of field fortifications, which to complete involved a long time, longer far than was suspected by the administration or the people. He and his subordinates worked day and night to perfect his system, and worked ably and with good effect. One day in August, shortly after his arrival at Washington, he, General Blair, and myself were together in a room in the seven buildings then occupied, I believe, as the headquarter offices. General McClellan stated to General Blair, who was Chairman of the Committee on Military Affairs in the House of Representatives, certain matters upon which he was anxious that the committee should act favorably and speedily. General Blair promised that the matter should be settled at once as General McClellan wished to have it, and then said in effect, "General, anything that you indicate as necessary shall always be acted upon favorably by our committee, and if you do not feel that you are to-day king of this country, you do not appreciate your position." Although the saying was impulsive and extravagant, it nevertheless indicated the honest feelings of the speaker, and was a type of the sentiments of a great number of people then gathered in Washington. But the fall wore away, and no movement of the great army collected in front and rear of Washington was made.

About the 1st of November, the country again began to get impatient that no forward movement was begun by any of the armies, but in the East this impatience was intensified against the Army of the Potomac. Bull Run was forgotten, and the facts that the enemy had once made his appearance on Munson's Hill, that the Potomac was virtually closed, and that we had met with a disaster at Ball's Bluff, were always present. But the great fact of all was, there were more than one hundred thousand soldiers about Washington. Although these men were generally raw troops who had never heard a hostile gun, and were daily improving in drill and discipline and physique, there was a feeling in Washington and in the country generally that they ought to be pushed forward into Virginia at all hazards. This feeling, considering the small amount of military knowledge among the people and the enormous expenditure then going on, was not singular, but it was nevertheless one that did harm, and was used by a set of politicians who had just come up, and who have remained up ever since, to excite the administration and the country against the management of the army.

In the latter part of the fall Lieutenant General Scott asked to be retired, and his request was granted. General McClellan was then made Commander-in-Chief of the army, and at once became responsible for the movements and organization of all of the forces East and West. He determined, therefore, to carry out a plan as to the movement of the Army of the Potomac, which he had studied long, and which, independent of political and financial considerations, commends itself to every military mind as the very best for making a campaign against Richmond at that time. After events demonstrated the wisdom of this plan. In few words, the plan was to move the whole Army of the Potomac, except a force sufficient for the defense of Washington to the vicinity of a place named Urbana, on the Rappahannock, and from this point as a base, to advance upon Richmond. But this involved a delay until spring, and as soon as it became generally known that there was to be this delay, as its cause was not known, the most strenuous efforts were made by Congress and the press to find out what was contemplated. Generals commanding divisions who were known to be in General McClellan's confidence, were examined by Congressional committees for the sole purpose of finding out what he intended to do. On one occasion, in December, I think, I was examined before the Committee on the Conduct of the War. I was asked whether I knew General McClellan's plans, and I answered in the affirmative. I was then asked to divulge them, and replied that I would prefer to wait until

I could confer with him, he being then dangerously ill, and that my information was confidential. The committee then lost all interest in me, and the remainder of the time was taken up by Hon. Andrew Johnson, then a member of the committee, who demonstrated that a force of 50,000 men ought to be detached from the Army of the Potomac, marched through Leesburg, thence southwest through West Virginia, so as to reach and set free from the rebels East Tennessee. The matter of transportation and provisions in a march through such a country was below the attention of the committee, and any suggestion looking to difficulty in that direction was considered as an indication of Fabian policy.

General McClellan's position during this period was one of great difficulty and delicacy. He had determined upon a plan of campaign which involved a delay of movement of the armies until spring. The delay being misunderstood, his enemies, who, in some noted cases, pretended to be his best friends, quietly insinuated that he was not the man for the position. The duties of his command were excessively harassing, and the undercurrent of detraction began to come to the surface, and make itself felt in the administration. He attended the funeral of General Lander, who died in March, and was buried in Washington. Telling me about the funeral on the next day, he said that when he saw Lander's face in the coffin, looking so calm and peaceful, and thought of the troubles he was then having, and was to have thereafter, he regretted that he was not lying there instead of Lander. These were the defiant and insubordinate feelings of the General-in-Chief.

At length he was taken sick with typhoid fever, and for a long time he was on the border of death. His sickness gave his enemies an opportunity which they were not slow to embrace; and vilification and detraction increased, so that, at last, the President even began to think that something ought to be done to conciliate public opinion, by making an effort to start the Army of the Potomac, even if it had to move without the commanding general. During this time the troops lay quietly in camp. They were well clothed and fed, and, in general, enjoyed the life. The weather and ground were not fit for drill, and the roads were too bad for marching. At long intervals, and until General McClellan was taken sick, large reviews broke the monotony of the life; but it was, nevertheless, very dull. The discipline improved visibly, and the long quiet fostered the feeling of comradeship and reliance upon each other, which, to a great extent, makes the difference between the recruit and the old soldier. Glee and minstrel and amateur theatrical clubs were formed, and performances were given by the men, and the army on the south side of the Potomac lived its own life as if it were hundreds of miles away from Washington, as many of its members devoutly wished it was. The men learned many old-soldier tricks. One of these was reported to me by a colonel of my division, with an air of great disgust. Some of his companies lived in huts built by themselves. The huts were two in number, on both sides of the company parade ground—half of the company sleeping in each hut. At reveille some dozen of the men would turn out, and when the roll was called the remainder would answer to their names from their beds in the huts, and stay in bed until breakfast time. But, although the army was improving, the nervousness of the administration and Congress, caused by the delay and the alarming sickness of General McClellan, continually increased.

On Friday evening, January 10th, 1862, I received a dispatch from the Assistant Secretary of War, informing me that the President wished to see me at eight o'clock that evening, if I could safely leave my command. I went to Washington, and arrived at the White House at eight o'clock. I was received in a small room in the northeast corner of the house, and found the President, Secretaries Seward and Chase, the Assistant Secretary of War, and General McDowell. The President was in great distress over the condition of the country. He complained that he was abused in Congress for the military inaction; that, notwithstanding the enormous amount of money which had been spent, nothing was doing East or West; that there was a general feeling of depression on account of the inaction; and that, as he expressed it, the bottom appeared to be falling out of everything. He was exceedingly sorry for the sickness of General McClellan. He was not allowed to see him to talk over military matters, and he wanted to produce some concerted action between Generals Halleck and Buell, who did not appear to pull together. He could, of course, do nothing with the Western armies; they were out of his reach; but he thought that he could, in a very short time, do something with the Army of the Potomac, if he were allowed to have his own way, and had sent for General McDowell and me so that he might have somebody to talk to on the subject. In fact, he wanted, he said, to *borrow* the Army of the Potomac from General McClellan for a few weeks, and wanted us to help him as to how to do it. He complained of the rise of gold, of the unreasonableness of Congress, of the virulence of the press, and, in general, told us all that depressed him, in a plain, blunt way that was touching to a degree. Mr. Seward told us that an

Englishman whom he had sent into the enemy's lines had returned, giving him information of the number of rebel troops at Centreville, Richmond, Norfolk, etc.; and I inferred that Johnston, who commanded at Centreville, could have raised about 75,000 men to meet any attack which we might make within a moderate time.

Mr. Chase said very little, but what he did say left it plainly to be inferred that he thought that the army ought to be moved at once. General McDowell said that, in his opinion, the army ought to be formed into army corps, and that a vigorous movement in the direction of Centreville would enable us, he thought, to get into position by which we could cut the enemy's lines of communication, and that by the use of the railroad from Alexandria, and the connection of the Baltimore and Ohio Road with those south of the river by a railroad over the Long Bridge, large wagon trains would be avoided. He, however, did not know how long a time would be required to get ready to make the movement which he advocated. I said that I was ignorant of the things necessary to enable me to form a judgment on the subject, only knowing my own division, which was ready for the field. That I thought that the proper disposition to make of the Army of the Potomac was to transport it by the easiest and quickest route to York river, to operate against Richmond, leaving force enough to prevent any danger to Washington.

The Assistant Secretary of War thought that the transportation of this force in a reasonable time would be a very difficult work. As General McDowell and I both felt too ignorant of the proper state of the supply departments to justify us in speaking any more definitely, it was determined by the President that the same party should meet on the next evening at the same time, and that General McDowell and I should in the meantime get all the information from the chiefs of the various staff departments of the Army of the Potomac, as to their status with regard to a movement of the army within a short time. So on Saturday we met in the morning, and went to all of the chiefs of the staff departments, and obtained from them such information as to their departments as they could give us. We learned from Mr. Chase the destination of Burnside's expedition, which, until then, had been unknown to us, and he relieved our minds as to the apparent impropriety of our obtaining information from the chiefs of the staff departments without the authority of the commanding general, by reminding us that as we were acting by the direct orders of the President, we ought to execute those orders. He also told us what was McClellan's plan of operations for the Army of the Potomac. In the evening we again met at the White House. The party of the evening before were there with the addition of Judge Blair, the Postmaster General. General McDowell read a paper embodying our joint views, which were in substance, that if the Army of the Potomac was to be moved *at once*, it would be better to march it into Virginia than to transport it by vessels. General McDowell was, however, in favor of the immediate movement into Virginia. I was not. Just here the presence of Judge Blair was felt. He strongly opposed any movement toward Centreville at that time, denounced it as bad strategy, said that a second Bull Run would occur, and strenuously and ably advocated the movement to the Peninsula by transports. Mr. Seward and Judge Chase were of opinion that a victory over the enemy was what was required, whether gained in front of Washington or further South, and that our difficulties would probably be as great on the Peninsula as they would be at Centreville. I thought that the President, who said little, was much impressed by what Judge Blair said, and he adjourned the meeting until three o'clock the next day, directing General McDowell and myself to see the Quartermaster General in the meantime as to water transportation for the army.

On Sunday General McDowell and I saw General Meigs, the Quartermaster General. He thought that a month or six weeks would be required to collect the water transportation necessary for the movement of the army. Some of us were gathered at three o'clock for the ordered meeting. Suddenly Mr. Seward hurried in, threw down his hat in great excitement, and exclaimed, "Gentlemen, I have seen General McClellan, and *he is a well man*. I think that this meeting would better adjourn." A general discussion was entered upon as to what was the best course to pursue with regard to the army, and it was understood that we would meet again on Monday, at one o'clock, when General McClellan would be present. On Monday, January 13th, at one o'clock, the same party was gathered at the President's. General McClellan shortly afterward appeared, looking exceedingly pale and weak. The President explained, in an apologetic way, why he had called General McDowell and me to these conferences, and asked General McDowell to explain the proposed plan of operations. General McDowell did so, he and I differing slightly as to the time of commencement of the movement from our front. In answer to some statement from General McDowell as to the delicate position in which we were placed, General McClellan stated that we were, of course, entitled to our opinions. I stated that in giving my opinion as to the Peninsula movement, I knew that my judgment coincided with General

McClellan's. General McDowell stated that he was in ignorance of any plan of General McClellan's. The President went over the subject of discussion in a general way, and then there was a silence. It was broken by Governor Chase, who asked General McClellan if he had any objection to telling the persons there assembled what his plan for the movement of the Army of the Potomac was. After a long silence the General made a few general remarks, and ended by saying to the President that he knew when his plans had hitherto been told to the Cabinet that they had leaked out, and he would therefore decline to divulge them now, unless the President would order him so to do. Then there was another long silence, and the President broke it by asking the General if he had matured a plan for the movement of the Army of the Potomac. The General answered that he had. After another silence the President said, " Then, General, I shall not order you to give it." During this time Governor Chase, General McDowell and I were standing in one of the window embrasures. When General McClellan declined to give his plans to the meeting, Governor Chase * said to us, "Well, if that is Mac's decision, he is a ruined man." The President then adjourned the meeting, and this episode was over. About a fortnight after this time the President ordered the Army of the Potomac to move forward on or before February 22d, to take Manassas. This order was countermanded early in February, and toward the end of the month orders were given to collect the transportation necessary to move the army by water.

On the 8th of March I was ordered to repair to headquarters. Assembled there were the General-in-chief, the Engineer of the Army of the Potomac, and all of the division commanders, except General Hooker, who was represented by General Naglee. General McClellan submitted to us his plan for the movement of the army, and then left us to ourselves. Upon the question of approval of his plan the vote was, I think, nine for approval to three against it, although it has been reported as eight to four. I believed then, and still believe, that the main object of the meeting was to obtain a condemnation of the plan by the subordinate generals. Immediately after this meeting we were informed that the President wished to see us. We went to the White House, and found there the President and Secretary of War. They knew the result of our meeting.

---

* In thinking over this matter, I find that I cannot be positive whether it was Governor Chase or Judge Blair who was with General McDowell and me, and made this remark. It was one of them, however.

Each one of us was asked in turn by the Secretary of War our opinion of the time required to transfer the army to its new base. The general opinion was that a month would be required, and each was asked by the Secretary whether he was willing to have this suffering country wait a month longer before a blow was inflicted upon the enemy. We were then asked in turn whether we thought the army ought to be organized into army corps or not. We unanimously answered that we thought it ought to be so organized. The President then informed us that he deferred his opinion as to the proper method of moving the army to ours. He asked us to use all our energies to help the country out of its great dangers, and ended by saying to us, "If you are faithful to me, I, on my part, will be faithful to you." He then said that he should form the Army of the Potomac into four army corps, and knowing but little of the capacities of the generals suitable for the command of these corps, should assign the commands according to rank. The meeting was then dismissed.

General Johnston having evacuated his position at Centreville on the 8th of March, the army was immediately moved to Fairfax Court-House. Here the assignment to corps was made, and my division was assigned to General McDowell's corps. Shortly afterward, about the middle of March, we returned to a position in front of Alexandria to await transportation. It was determined that the bulk of the army should be landed at Fortress Monroe, and move up the Peninsula between the York and James rivers, and that General McDowell's corps should land on the north side of the York river. By this plan a force of over 80,000 men would have been on the Peninsula, and a corps of nearly 30,000 men would have been on the north side of the York river, in position to turn Yorktown. The result of carrying out this plan would have been that Yorktown would have been evacuated without a siege, the Williamsburg battle would not have taken place, and the whole army would have concentrated in front of Richmond in a few days after McDowell's corps would have joined—without serious loss. Communication would have easily been kept up between the two banks of the river by the squadron under Captain Missroon, which was then in the river. This arrangement required that General McDowell's corps should move last, and General McClellan, with his headquarters, left Alexandria on April 1st, he supposing that nothing could occur to change that arrangement.

On the 3d of April I was ordered to embark my division. About eleven o'clock in the evening I received orders to move part of the division on the next day, and to call at headquarters for further instructions. Going at once to the War Department I found General McDowell and General Wadsworth there. General McDowell informed me that the Secretary of War had told him about an hour before that General McClellan intended to work by strategy and not by fighting, and that he should not have another man from his department; that all of the enemies of the administration centred around him, and the Secretary accused him of having political aspirations. Also, that he had not left the number of troops to defend Washington that the President required—in other words, that he had disobeyed the President's orders. General McDowell remonstrated against the step which was about to be taken, arguing that if General McClellan had political aspirations they would be forwarded by the very course which the administration was taking in this case. He used all of the arguments which he could bring to bear, to convince the Secretary that he was making a mistake in ordering the detachment of his corps. The result was, General McDowell's corps was detached from the Army of the Potomac, and was marched to Catlett's Station, on the Orange and Alexandria Railroad, where it could do no possible good. General McClellan's plan of turning Yorktown, by the movement of McDowell's corps on the north bank of the York river, was utterly destroyed. The Army of the Potomac was forced to stay a whole month on the Peninsula uselessly, to make the expensive and abortive siege of Yorktown, to fight the bloody battle of Williamsburg; and the capture of Richmond, which in all human probability would have been made in the month of May, had General McClellan's plan been carried out, was deferred for three years.

Thus was consummated the first great crime of the war. An army of nearly one hundred thousand men which had been in preparation for more than six months, was despatched to deal the enemy a deadly blow, under the general who had organized it, and was beloved by it, and who was unanimously recognized by soldiers and civilians as its proper commander. Before he had been absent forty-eight hours, his largest corps, commanded by his second in command, containing more than one-fourth of his army, assigned to a service which was vital to the success of his campaign, was detached from his command, without consultation with him and without his knowledge. I do not know whether the perpetrators of this crime were punished for it in this life; but the ghastly account of bloodshed in Virginia for the next three years shows that the innocent country was punished, in a way that will be remembered by widows and orphans for a generation.

LEE'S WEST VIRGINIA CAMPAIGN.

BY GENERAL A. L. LONG.

BEFORE proceeding with the operations in Northwestern Virginia, it will be necessary to glance at the condition of that section, and the previous military operations that had been carried on within its limits. This section of Virginia did not cordially coincide in the ordinance of secession that had been passed by the State Convention, inasmuch as a considerable part of its inhabitants were opposed to secession, or, in other words, were Unionists. A large number, however, of its most influential citizens were ardent Southern supporters; and there was, also, an intermediate class, indifferent to politics, which was ready to join the party which might prove the strongest. Besides, it soon became apparent that the Baltimore and Ohio Railroad was destined to exercise an important influence on military movements; therefore, this section became an object of interest to both sides. At first, the Confederate Colonel Porterfield was sent with a few companies to operate on the Baltimore and Ohio Railroad; but this force was too small, and illy provided with the essentials for service, so that it could effect nothing. Shortly afterward, General Robert Garnett was sent by the Confederate authorities to seize the Baltimore and Ohio Railroad, and to confirm the Northwestern Virginians in their allegiance to the State. Garnett, with a force of about five thousand men, reached the railroad in June, and occupied Laurel Hill. About the same time, General McClellan crossed the Ohio into Northwestern Virginia, with the view of gaining the adherence of its inhabitants to the Federal Government, and to protect the Baltimore and Ohio

Railroad. Having a greatly superior force, he made it his first object to attack Garnett before that general could be reinforced (Colonel Pegram, with a considerable detachment, being defeated by General Rosecrans, with a part of McClellan's force), and was obliged to retreat, in order to save the rest of his little army. McClellan pursued, and overtaking the rear guard at Carrick's Ford, a skirmish ensued, in which Garnett was killed. Colonel Starke, aide-de-camp, relates that, soon after Garnett fell, McClellan arrived on the ground, and recognizing in the prostrate form of his adversary an old acquaintance, he dismounted, and, with the true heart of a soldier, bending over the body of a comrade and friend of better days, he did not attempt to conceal his emotion. "Poor Garnett!" he exclaimed, "has it come to this?" Every facility was allowed for the proper disposition of the body.

McClellan was always distinguished for courtesy and kindness to those whom the chances of war placed in his power. The Adjutant General, Captain Corley, assisted by other members of Garnett's staff, safely continued the retreat, and was mainly instrumental in placing the army in safety. I will here relate an adventure of De Lagrel, connected with Garnett's defeat, which exhibited great courage, endurance and address. De Lagrel was an old army officer, and commanded the artillery of Pegram's detachment. When attacked by Rosecrans at Rich Mountain, he fought his guns with great gallantry and effect. His men behaved well until the enemy began to close in upon them; they then fled, leaving De Lagrel almost alone. Undaunted by the desertion of his men, he served a gun himself until disabled by a.severe wound. Then, amid the confusion of a defeat, he escaped to a laurel thicket near by, in which he concealed himself until the enemy had disappeared. He then found shelter under the roof of a friendly mountaineer. His kind host and hostess concealed and attended him until his wound was healed and his strength restored. He then determined to join the Confederate forces, which had again entered Northwestern Virginia; but to do so it was necessary to pass through the Federal liness. To accomplish this, he concluded to assume the character of a mountaineer, being supplied by his host with a herder's garb, with the exception of shoes. Then, with a well-filled wallet over his shoulder and a staff in his hand, he bid adieu to his kind friends and launched forth into the mountains. After wandering among them for several days, he fell in with the Federal pickets. On being questioned by them, he so well sustained the character he had assumed that all the pickets were easily passed, until he reached the last outpost that separated him from his friends. Here he was more strictly examined than he had hitherto been, but by his wit fully sustained the character he had adopted, and was told to continue his way; but, just as he was about to depart, one of the guards observed his boots, which, though soiled and worn, still exhibited signs of a fashionable make. Upon this the examination was renewed, and, with all his ingenuity, he could not escape detection; his boots had betrayed him. These traitors were drawn off, and in the leg of one the name of "De Lagrel" was found, and he was at once recognized as the officer whose disappearance at Rich Mountain had led to so much inquiry. He was sent a prisoner of war to the Federal headquarters, where he was courteously received.

The defeat of General Garnett left McClellan in undisputed possession of all Northwestern Virginia. In order to secure his acquisition he strongly occupied some of the principal mountain passes, and took other measures for its permanent occupation. A few days later the total defeat of McDowell at Bull Run considerably changed the order of things. McClellan was called to take the command of the Army of the Potomac, and the greater part of his forces was withdrawn, leaving only a few thousand men to hold Northwestern Virginia. The result of McClellan's success in that quarter proved to be of much greater importance than was at first apprehended, by disheartening its loyal inhabitants and encouraging the doubtful or indifferent to give their adhesion to the Federal Government. The Confederate authorities, being aware of the importance of Western Virginia at that time, both in a political and military point of view, determined to send them a force sufficiently strong to re-occupy and retain possession of it. There had been assembled in the neighborhood of Staunton five or six thousand men for the purpose of reinforcing General Garnett. These troops were ordered to advance, on the 15th of July, under the command of General Henry R. Jackson, on the Parkersburg turnpike, to re-enter Western Virginia, and to occupy some convenient position until the remainder of the forces intended to operate in that quarter should arrive. Loring, whom we have seen assigned to the command of the Army of Northwestern Virginia, was an officer of considerable reputation. He had served with distinction in the Mexican war, had subsequently become colonel of a regiment of mounted rifles, and for several years prior to his resignation had commanded the Department of New Mexico, where he acquired an experience in mountain service. His appointment, therefore, gave general satisfaction. His staff was composed chiefly of experienced officers—Colonel Carter Stevenson,

Adjutant General; Major A. L. Long, Chief of Artillery; Captain Corley, Chief Quartermaster; Captain Cole, Chief Commissary; Lieutenant Matthews, Aide-de-camp, and Colonel Starks, volunteer Aide-de-camp; and, as the country was full of enthusiasm on account of the recent victory at Manassas, he was about to enter upon his new field of operations under the most favorable auspices.

General Loring, accompanied by his staff, left Richmond on the 22d of July, the day after the battle and victory of Manassas. On the 24th he arrived at Monterey, a small village about sixty miles west of Staunton; there he found Jackson, who informed him that on arriving at the Greenbrier river he had found Cheat Mountain Pass so strongly occupied by Federals that he deemed it inadvisable to attempt to carry it by a direct attack. So he retired, leaving Colonel Edward Johnston, with the Twelfth Georgia Regiment and Anderson's Battery to occupy the Alleghany Mountain Pass, and posting Rust's Arkansas Regiment and Baldwin's Virginia Regiment in convenient supporting distance of Johnston, established himself at Monterey, with Fulkerson's and Scott's Virginia Regiments, the First Georgia Regiment (Colonel Ramsey's), Major Jackson's Cavalry, and Shoemaker's Battery. Having heard of a Pass about forty miles west, near Huntersville, by which Cheat Mountain might be turned, he sent Colonel Gilliam, with his own Virginia Regiment and Colonel Lee's Sixth North Carolina Regiment, being a force of about two thousand men, to occupy this Pass, and had ordered the remaining troops intended for the Army of Northwestern Virginia to proceed direct from Staunton to Huntersville. This was the condition of affairs when General Loring arrived at Monterey and assumed command. He remained several days in the neighborhood of Monterey, examining the condition of the troops and reconnoitering the position of the enemy on Cheat Mountain. Cheat Mountain Pass is a narrow gap near the top of the mountain, whose natural strength had been greatly increased by the art of engineers since its occupation by the Federals. It was approachable from the east only by the Parkersburg turnpike, which, ascending the rugged side of the mountain, enters this narrow defile and winds its way through it for nearly a mile before it begins the western descent.

The Federals finding this Pass unoccupied, and foreseeing the importance the Parkersburg turnpike would be to the Confederates in their attempt to re-occupy West Virginia, seized it and fortified it, and now held it with a force of about twenty-five hundred men; the remainder of the Federal force was in the vicinity of Beverly, a village a few miles west of Cheat river. General Loring, having satisfied himself that a direct attack on Cheat Mountain Pass was impracticable, and that there was no force of the enemy near the west base of the Cheat Mountain except that at Beverly, determined to take command of the force which had been ordered to rendezvous at Huntersville, and advance by the Pass that Colonel Gilliam had been directed to occupy, to the rear of the enemy's position on Cheat Mountain. He therefore directed General Jackson to advance his whole force, which at this time amounted to six thousand men, to the Greenbrier river and hold himself in readiness to co-operate when the advance was made from Huntersville, and then proceeded to that place to make arrangements for the proposed movement. When General Loring arrived at Huntersville, about the 1st of August, he found already there Maney's, Hatten's, and Savage's Tennessee Regiments, Campbell's Virginia Regiment, a battalion of Virginia regulars, four hundred strong, commanded by Colonel Munford, Major W. H. F. Lee's squadron of cavalry, and Marye's and Stanley's batteries of artillery. Colonel Gilliam was at Valley Mountain Pass, fifteen miles west of Huntersville, with two regiments, and two other regiments. Burk's Virginia and Colonel ——'s Georgia Regiment were en route from Staunton. The force of Loring on the Huntersville line amounted in round numbers to eight thousand five hundred effective men. The General's staff were particularly active in their efforts to prepare for a speedy advance. Colonel Stevenson, Adjutant General, and Captains Corley and Cole, Chief Quartermaster and Commissary, being experienced officers, rendered valuable service in organizing the troops and in collecting transportation and supplies. Major A. L. Long, in addition to his duties as Chief of Artillery, had assigned him those of Inspector General. The troops were well armed and equipped, all of them were accustomed to the use of arms, and many were expert marksmen, and a large proportion had received military instruction in the various volunteer companies of which they had been members. The troops were in fine spirits, and desired nothing more than to be led against the enemy. It was obvious to all those about the General that the success of the proposed movement depended upon its speedy execution. It was impossible that the occupation of Valley Mountain by a force as large as that of Gilliam could escape the observation of the Federals, and its position would expose the design of the Confederates. Delay would enable the Federals to seize all the important Passes on the route, and fortify them so strongly that they would effectually arrest the advance of any force. Notwithstanding the great value of time in the execution of the movement contemplated by General Loring, he seemed to regard the formation of a depot of supplies at Huntersville, and the organization of a supply train, as a matter of first importance. He appeared to overlook the fact that the line from Huntersville to Beverly, only forty miles long, was to be only temporary; for so soon as Cheat Mountain Pass was opened he would draw his supplies from Staunton over the Parkersburg turnpike, and also, that the country along his line abounded in beef and grain.

While General Loring was preparing to advance, we will take a view of affairs in other quarters. After the withdrawal of McClellan, General Rosecrans was assigned to the command of the Department of Western Virginia. At the same time a large portion of the troops in that department were withdrawn for the defense of the capital. The Federal force in Western Virginia, at the time General Loring assumed command of the Army of Northwestern Virginia, was only about six or seven thousand men; about half of which, under the command of General Reynolds, occupying the Cheat Mountain Pass. The other portion, commanded by General Cox, was designed for operations on the line of the Kanawha. General Rosecrans was one of the most energetic and skilful of the Federal commanders. As soon as he found himself in command of the Department of Western Virginia he set about increasing his force and strengthening his position. General Rosecrans, taking advantage of the political disaffection among the Western Virginians, obtained many recruits, which, with recruits from other quarters rapidly increased his force. The Confederate authorities in the meantime being informed of the advance of General Cox to the Kanawha, sent a force of about five thousand men to oppose him, under the command of General Floyd, and appointed General Robert E. Lee to the command of the Department of Western Virginia. He had displayed such remarkable administrative ability in the organization of the Virginia troops that he was retained at the head of the Confederate Military Bureau to the time of his appointment to the command of the Department of Western Virginia. Although aware of the difficulties to be met with in a country like Western Virginia, whose mountains, and more than half of whose inhabitants were in hostile array on the side of a powerful adversary, he unflinchingly accepted it, and entered upon his arduous task with no other feelings than those for the good of his country. When General Lee arrived at Huntersville he found General Loring busily engaged forming his depot of supplies and organizing his transportation train. Several days had already elapsed, and several days more would be necessary before he could complete his preparations for an advance. The arrival of General Lee at Huntersville, as commander of the department, took General Loring by surprise. Having been his superior in rank in the old army, he could not suppress a feeling of jealousy. General Lee was accompanied by his aides-de-camp, Colonel John A. Washington and Captain Walter H. Taylor. After remaining several days at Huntersville without gaining any positive information from General Loring in regard to the time of his probable advance, he proceeded to join Colonel Gilliam at Valley Mountain. He took with him Major Lee's cavalry, not as an escort, but for the purpose of scouting and reconnoitering. It had now been eight or ten days since Colonel Gilliam first arrived at Valley Mountain Pass. At that time he learned from the inhabitants and his scouts that the road to Beverly was unoccupied. But within the last day or two, a force of the Federals had advanced within less than a mile of his front, and then retired. General Lee at once busied himself about gaining information respecting the position of the enemy. He soon learned that the Federals had taken possession of a strong Pass, ten miles in front of Valley Mountain, and were actively engaged in fortifying it. When General Loring arrived, about the 12th of August, the Federals had been reinforced, and this position had been so greatly strengthened that General Lee deemed it unadvisable to attempt a direct attack, so the only course now to be pursued was to gain the Federal flank or rear, and strike them when they least expected an attack.

General Lee had been distinguished in the Mexican war as a reconnoitering officer, and General Scott had been mainly indebted to his bold reconnoissance for the brilliant success of his Mexican campaigns. Rank and age had not impaired the qualities that had formerly rendered him so distinguished. He brought them with him to the mountains of Virginia. There was not a day when it was possible for him to be out, that the General, with either Colonel Washington or Captain Taylor, might not be seen crossing the mountains, climbing over rocks and crags, to get a view of the Federal position. Ever mindful of the safety of his men, he would never spare himself toil or fatigue when seeking the means to prevent unnecessary loss of life. By way of illustrating his boldness as a reconnoitering officer, I will relate an anecdote told me by Captain Preston, Adjutant of the Forty-eighth Virginia Regiment (Colonel Campbell's). The regiment being on picket, seeing three men on an elevated point about half a mile in advance of the line of pickets, and believing them to be Yankees, he asked his colonel to let him capture them. Permission being obtained, and selecting two men from a number of volunteers who had offered to accompany him, he set forth to capture the Federal scouts. Dashing through the brush-wood, and over the rocks, he suddenly burst upon the unsuspecting trio, when lo! to his amazement, General Lee stood before him.

To add to the difficulties of a campaign in the mountains, the rainy season set in; it began to rain about the middle of August, and continued without much cessation for several weeks; in the meantime, the narrow mountain roads became saturated and softened, so that the passage of heavy trains of wagons soon rendered them almost impassable; while the wet weather lasted, any movement was simply impossible. The troops being new, and unaccustomed to camp life, began to suffer from all the camp diseases. Typhoid fever, measles, and homesickness began to spread among them, so that in the course of a few weeks nearly one-third of the army was rendered *hors de combat* by sickness. Amid this accumulation of difficulties General Lee preserved his equanimity and cheerfulness; his chief aim now was to ameliorate, as much as possible, the sufferings of his men. During this period of inactivity General Lee was exerting himself to find a practicable route leading to the rear of Cheat Mountain Pass, the route by which General Loring proposed to reach it being now effectually closed. The possession of the Pass was of great importance to the Confederates, as the Parkersburg turnpike was the principal line over which operations could be successfully carried on in Northwestern Virginia. Individual scouts were employed, both from among the well-affected inhabitants and the enterprising young soldiers of the army; Lieutenant Lewis Randolph, of the Virginia State Regulars, was particularly distinguished for the boldness of his reconnoissances. About the 25th of September, General Jackson reported to General Loring that Colonel Rust had made a reconnoissance to the rear of Cheat Mountain Pass, and had discovered a route, though difficult, by which infantry could be led. Soon after, Colonel Rust reported in person and informed General Lee of the practicability of reaching the rear of the enemy's position on Cheat Mountain, from which a favorable attack could be made, and requested the General that, in case his information was favorably considered, to be allowed to lead the attacking column, to consist of his regiment and such other troops as the General might designate. Another route was, in the meantime, discovered, leading along the western side of Cheat Mountain, by which troops could be conducted to a point on the Parkersburg turnpike, about two miles below the Federal position in the Pass. This being the information that General Lee had been most desirous of obtaining, he determined to attack the enemy without further delay. The opposing forces were at this time about equal in numbers. Loring's force was now six thousand, General Jackson's about five thousand strong. General Reynold's force had been increased to about eleven thousand men; of these, two thousand were on Cheat Mountain, about five thousand in position on the Lewisburg road in front of General Loring. The remainder of General Reynold's force was held in reserve near the junction of the Parkersburg turnpike and the Lewisburg road.

General Lee determined to attack on the morning of the 28th of September. The plan was that Colonel Rust should gain the rear of the Federal position by early dawn, and begin the attack. General Anderson, with two Tennessee regiments from Loring's command, was to support him; while General Jackson was to make a diverson in front. Cheat Mountain Pass being carried, General Jackson, with his whole force, was to sweep down the mountain and fall upon the rear of the other Federal position; General Donaldson, with two regiments, was to gain a favorable position for attacking the enemy on the Lewisburg road, in flank or rear; and Loring was to advance, by the main road, on the Federal front. In case of failure, Anderson and Donaldson were to rejoin Loring, and Rust was to find his way back to Jackson. The troops gained their designated positions with remarkable promptness and accuracy in point of time, considering the distance and the difficulties to be overcome. Colonel Rust's attack on Cheat Mountain was to be the signal for the general advance of all the troops. It was anxiously expected, from early dawn, throughout the day. On every side was continuously heard, "What has become of Rust?" "Why don't he attack?" "Rust must have lost his way." The Tennesseeans, under Anderson, became so impatient that they requested to be led to the attack without waiting for Rust; but General Anderson thought that he must be governed by the letter of his instructions, and declined granting the request of his men. Thus we see a plan that offered every prospect of success come to naught by the failure of a subordinate officer to come up to the expectations of his commander. Anderson and Donaldson, finding that their situation was becoming critical—being liable to discovery, and being between two superior forces—rejoined General Loring on the 29th. On the same day, Colonel Rust reported in person his operations, which amounted to this: he heard nothing of General Anderson; his heart failed him; he passed the day watching the Federals, and then retired. When Colonel Rust rendered his report, General Lee, perceiving the deep mortification he felt at the great blunder he had committed, permitted him to rejoin his regiment. A council of war was then held, in which it was decided that the position of the Federals was too strong to be attacked in front with any reasonable prospect of success, and that a flank attack was now out of the question, inasmuch as the Federals had been aroused by the discovery of the danger which had so recently threatened them; so the troops were ordered to resume their former positions. During the operations just related, there had been but little skirmishing, and the Confederate loss had been slight. One circumstance, however, occurred which cast a gloom over the whole army. Colonel J. A. Washington, while making a reconnoissance, fell into an ambuscade, and was killed. He had, by his soldierly qualities and high gentlemanly bearing, gained the esteem of all. Too much praise cannot be bestowed upon the troops for their courage and patient endurance in this campaign; and Colonels Burk, Gilliam, Campbell, Lee, Munford, Maney, Hatten and Savage were worthy of the gallant fellows that it had fallen to their lot to command.

We will now examine into the condition of affairs on the line of the Kanawha. General Floyd entered the Kanawha Valley in August. General Cox was then near Charleston. After some maneuvring, Floyd fell back to the junction of the New river and the Gauley, where he was joined by General Wise. Floyd's force now numbered between eight and ten thousand men. Being uncertain whether Cox would advance up the New river line or upon that of the Gauley, he posted a force, under Wise, on the New river line, while he occupied a favorable position on the Gauley. At Carnifax's Ferry, Floyd and Wise were in easy supporting distance of each other; but there was no cordiality between them. About the 15th of September, General Floyd, seeing that it was the evident intention of Rosecrans to attack him, ordered Wise to his support, which order Wise failed to obey, and Floyd was left to receive alone the attack of a greatly superior force, which, however, he succeeded in repulsing with considerable loss; but, being still unsupported by Wise, he was obliged to retire. Among the casualties on the side of the Confederates, General Floyd received a painful wound in the arm. General Wise having finally joined Floyd, they fell back to a position on the James river and Kanawha turnpike, near the Hawk's Nest.

About the last of September General Rosecrans, having reinforced Cox, took command in person and advanced on the James River and Kanawha turnpike, gradually pushing back Floyd and Wise in the direction of Lewisburg, it being his intention to turn the Confederate position on Valley Mountain and the Greenbrier river. Such was the condition of affairs on the line of the Kanawha at the close of the Valley Mountain campaign. General Lee, perceiving that the operations on the Kanawha were not progressing favorably, determined to take control of affairs in that quarter himself. He, therefore, directed Loring to detach Gilliam with his own regiment (the battalion of State Regulars) and a section of artillery to occupy Valley Mountain Pass, and proceed with the remainder of his force to reinforce General Floyd. General Lee arrived at Meadow Bluff about the 7th of October, where he found Floyd. Meadow Bluff is a small village near the eastern base of Sewell Mountain. Floyd had proposed making a stand there, but Wise had halted on the top of the mountain, five miles in rear, where he had determined to fight. The hostility that had previously existed between the two generals had not been diminished by the affair at Carnifax's Ferry; the arrival of General Lee was, therefore, fortunate, as it most probably prevented a disaster, since Rosecrans was advancing, and would have been able to strike both Wise and Floyd in detail. General Lee found General Wise occupying the eastern crest of Sewell Mountain; being satisfied with the position, he determined to hold it, and give battle to Rosecrans if he persisted in advancing. So he ordered Floyd to return and support Wise. General Lee had barely time to complete his arrangements when Rosecrans appeared on the opposite crest. Each army now occupied a mountain crest nearly parallel, separated by a gap or depression forming a notch in the mountain about a mile wide, over which it was difficult to pass except by the James River and Kanawha turnpike, which crosses it. Both positions were naturally very strong. The Confederate force being greatly inferior to that of the Federals, and General Rosecrans having assumed the offensive, General Lee naturally expected to be attacked before Loring could come up; he, therefore, actively employed his skill as an engineer in adding to the natural strength of his position. Rosecrans, discovering the formidable preparations of the Confederates, prudently forebore attacking them. The arrival of General Loring, on the 9th, placed General Lee's force almost on an equality with that of the Federals.

The force of General Lee now amounted to about fifteen thousand men. The troops were in fine spirits, and anxious to be led to the attack; but the General, ever mindful of the safety of his men, restrained their ardor. On one occasion, when several of the commanders were urging an attack, he remarked: "I know, gentlemen, you could carry the enemy's lines; but we cannot spare the brave men who would lose their lives in doing it. If General Rosecrans does not attack us, we will find a way to reach him that will not cost us so dearly." After waiting several days for General Rosecrans to attack, he began to make preparations for a flank movement to gain Rosecrans' rear, who no longer manifested a disposition to continue the aggressive. General Floyd and others, who had a good knowledge of the routes in the vicinity of Sewell Mountain, reported to General Lee a practicable route for artillery and infantry leading about ten miles to the rear of the Federal position. Upon this information, he conceived the plan of sending a column of five thousand men by this route at night, and at dawn to fall upon the Federals' rear while a strong demonstration was being made in front. Had this plan been executed, it would most likely have been successful; but General Rosecrans escaped the trap by a night retreat. Great was the disappointment of the troops when they discovered that the Federals had retired, and the prospects of a battle had vanished. As soon as the retreat of the Federals was discovered, pursuit was ordered; but General Lee soon perceived that it would be impossible to overtake General Rosecrans and bring him to a successful engagement in the rough, mountainous country through which he was retreating; and, not wishing to harass his troops unnecessarily, ordered them to return to their several positions, and Rosecrans was allowed to pursue his retreat unmolested to the Kanawha. General Lee knew that, with the bravery of his troops, and the strength of his position, he could repel any attack that the Federals could make; while, on the other hand, if he attacked them in their position, the result, even if successful, would be attended with great loss. He, therefore, determined to give Rosecrans every opportunity to attack before taking the offensive himself, which, as we have seen, Rosecrans prevented by abandoning his own plans and retreating.

The season was now so far advanced that it was impossible to continue active operations in Western Virginia. Snow had already fallen, and the roads had become almost impassable. General Lee therefore determined to withdraw the troops from Sewell Mountain. About the 1st of November the different columns were sent to their various destinations. The campaign had been pronounced a failure. The press and the public were clamorous against him. No one stopped to inquire the cause or examine into the difficulties that surrounded him. Upon him alone were heaped the impracticability of mountains, the hostility of the elements, and the inefficiency and captiousness of subordinate commanders. The difficulties to be encountered in Western Virginia were so great, and the chances of success so doubtful (as had been shown by the recent operations in that quarter), that the Confederate authorities abandoned the idea of its further occupation. Therefore, the greater part of the troops that had been serving in Western Virginia were ordered where their services would be more available, and General Lee was assigned to the command of the Department of South Carolina, Georgia and Florida. While the operations on Big Sewell were in progress, General Reynolds made a descent from Cheat Mountain and attacked the Confederate position on the Greenbrier. This attack was promptly met by General H. R. Jackson, and repulsed with considerable loss. Soon after his return to Huntersville, General Loring was instructed to report to General T. J. Jackson (Stonewall Jackson), then commanding in the Shenandoah Valley, to participate in a contemplated winter campaign. About the same time I received orders from the War Office to report to General Lee in the Department of South Carolina, Georgia and Florida.

THE SIEGE OF MORRIS ISLAND.

BY GENERAL W. W. H. DAVIS.

THE siege of Morris Island has passed into history. The wearisome day and nights in the trenches, with shovel and rifle, under the plunging fire of the enemy's batteries, and the repeated assaults of almost impregnable earthworks, are numbered among the past events of our late wonderful war. Morris Island is a sandy waif of the sea, lying on the west side of the outer harbor of Charleston, and stretching three miles from north to south. It varies in width from two or three hundred yards to a few feet at the narrowest part. A ridge of sand-hills run parallel with the beach, just out of reach of the tidal-line on the east; while on the west it slopes into marshes, two miles wide, and intersected by a labyrinth of water-courses, which separates it from James Island. At a few points the tide breaks entirely across it. It is an island of fine white sand.

A watchful enemy had carefully guarded this approach to Charleston, where the late rebellion had its birth. A strong earth-work, known as Battery Gregg, had been erected on Cumming's Point, at the north end of the island, mounting four ten-inch columbiads and one ten-inch mortar. This battery had been used in the siege of Fort Sumter, in April, 1861; but the work had been altered and strengthened, and some of its guns now pointed down the island. About the narrowest part of the island, where Vincent's creek approaches the sea, was erected Battery Wagner, on which were mounted sixteen guns and mortars, most of them of heavy calibre. This was one of the strongest earthworks ever built, and gave evidence of the highest order of engineering ability. The bomb-proof would accomodate a garrison of fourteen hundred men, and was strong enough to resist the heaviest shot and shell. It was flanked on the west by Vincent's creek and the marshes, on the east by the sea, and had a wet ditch. It could only be approached in front over ground that was completely swept by its guns. The guns of Gregg took it in reverse, while those of the enemy's batteries on James and Sullivan's Islands took it both in reverse and flank. The barbette guns of Sumter commanded it by a plunging fire, and threw shells a mile beyond. The operations were carried on along a narrow strip of land less than one-half the front of the work, a thing of rare occurrence in besieging a strong work; while it differed from most operations of the kind, in the fact that both parties had communication with the sea. A more difficult problem than the reduction of Battery Wagner has seldom been presented to the engineer for solution. The enemy had also constructed detached batteries in the sand-hills lower down the island, which, with those previously mentioned, commanded the approaches to it from all quarters. On the south end of the island was a long rifle-pit to guard against a landing from boats. Directly south of Morris lies Folly Island, separated from it by an inlet of the sea three hundred yards wide. Its general features are the same, except that it is covered by a heavy growth of timber, well calculated to conceal preliminary operations. On the west Folly Island is separated from James Island by a narrow stream and a continuation of the marshes that bound Morris Island on that side.

After the failure of the attack on Fort Sumter, in April, the government determined to place Brigadier General Quincy A. Gillmore in charge of the operations about to be renewed against the defenses before Charleston. At the time he was at the head of a division in the field in Kentucky. He was called to Washington. After listening to the views of the administration and fully understanding their wishes, he agreed to accomplish three things, if placed in command of the land operations, viz.: possess and hold the south end of Morris Island, reduce Fort Wagner, and destroy Sumter for offensive purposes. The Secretary of the Navy gave him to understand that if these things were accomplished, the iron-clads would go in and finish what remained to be done in the capture of Charleston.

General Gillmore reached Hilton Head on the 12th of June, 1863, at which time we had a small force on Folly Island, holding it as a base of future operations. The General immediately proceeded hither to examine the situation. From the jungles on the north end of the island he looked across the inlet on to the sand-hills of

Morris, crowned with Confederate guns. From where he stood Sumter was in plain view. He saw everything with the eye of a practical engineer, and decided at a glance where to erect his batteries, and the use he would make of them. Necessity compelled their erection within a few hundred yards of a vigilant enemy; discovery would defeat the enterprise. The engineers were immediately set to work, and a dense thicket served to conceal our operations. The laborers, materials, guns, and, in fact, everything used in constructing the batteries, were taken to the front at night. The greater part of the work was done under fire, for the enemy suspected we had a force at the head of the island, and they shelled it continually. Troops were landed under cover of the darkness, and before the morning dawned they were concealed in the timber and bushes, and the transports that brought them were sent to sea again. The island was carefully picketed to prevent the enemy's spies landing to discover what we were doing.

In twenty days the batteries were finished, mounting forty-eight guns and mortars, with all the appliances of bomb-proofs, magazines, etc., and each piece supplied with two hundred rounds of ammunition. So well had all our movements been concealed from the enemy that he did not dream of the existence of our batteries until they opened fire upon him. The assault was made on Morris Island the morning of the 10th of July. It was a combined attack by infantry in boats, consisting of General Strong's Brigade, and a heavy cannonade from our batteries. The infantry embarked during the night of the 9th, on Folly river, and at daylight in the morning lay in Light House Inlet, off the southwestern point of the island. General Truman B. Seymour came into the batteries just before daylight, impatient for the bombardment to open. The night before, the brush in front of the batteries had been cut away, and the embrasures opened. Seymour asked the officer in command of the three thirty-pounder Parrotts on the right if he could see a certain gun of the enemy mounted among the sand-hills distinctly enough to take aim at it On the officer replying in the negative the General called a party of engineers to shovel the sand away from the embrasure Day broke before they had finished, and the General remarking, "It will never do to let them get the first fire," called in the engineers, and directed the officer to "blaze away." Immediately the quiet of the morning was broken by the roar of artillery. The infantry moved up about the same time, and in a little while effected a landing, and carried the enemy's rifle-pits. General Strong, in his anxiety to land, stepped overboard in seven feet of water; but this mishap did not prevent him mounting a Confederate horse, without saddle, and barefooted, and join in the pursuit of the foe. His patriotism received the double baptism of fire and water. The reveille had just sounded in the enemy's camp, and they had turned out for roll-call, when our shot and shell went tearing through their ranks. Officers and men were killed before they had time to dress. The iron-clads crossed the bar at daylight, and after we had effected a landing, they moved up and rolled their ponderous shells over the island. At the Beacon House our troops came within reach of the guns of Wagner, when a halt was made, and some intrenchments thrown up. The day was intensely hot, and the troops were completely prostrated. Our loss was small. Thus had General Gillmore redeemed his first pledge. At this period in the operations a fatal mistake was made. Fort Wagner should have been immediately assailed, and would then have fallen into our hands without much opposition. The assault was delayed until the next day, when we were repulsed with considerable loss. While these operations were going on, a division of troops was sent over to James Island to engage the enemy's attention in that direction, where a spirited action was fought on the 16th of July, in which the Federal forces were victorious.

The failure of the attack on the 11th satisfied General Gillmore that siege operations must be commenced against Wagner. Ground was broken on the night of the 13th, and the work was pushed with such vigor that the first parallel, at the distance of thirteen hundred and fifty yards, was completed on the 17th. It mounted twenty-five rifled guns and mortars. An assault was arranged for twilight the next evening, and two additional brigades were added to our forces. During the day our batteries, in conjunction with the navy, kept up a warm cannonade on the fort, and by 4 P. M. the enemy's guns were silenced. The troops chosen for the assault were the brigades of Seymour, Strong and Putnam, the whole under the command of General Seymour. They moved up the beach about sundown, and advanced upon the work in deployed lines. At the distance of nearly a mile, the enemy opened upon them with shot and shell, which they changed to grape, canister and musketry at closer range. The troops steadily advanced in spite of this iron and leaden hail, with scores of men falling, killed and wounded, at every step. A portion of them reached the ditch and mounted the parapet, and seized and held that part of the work near the salient for some time, but, after a fierce struggle for the mastery, were compelled to retire, leaving the killed and wounded in the hands of the enemy. The assault was bravely made, and the repulse bloody. Our loss footed up 1,517. The attack was a direct one, the situation of the work being such that no feint or diversion could be made. The guns of the enemy swept every foot of the ground our men marched over. When they left the ditch for the parapet they were met by the bayonet, and nearly every other missile and weapon that is used on such occasions. The gunners were driven from the curtain, and many of the garrison sought safety in the bomb-proof. The fort was within an ace of being ours; but we were driven back. There comes the old story that somebody failed to support the advance at the proper time; but here the responsibility ends.

This repulse caused a modification in the plan of operations. By possessing Wagner the works on Cumming's Point would have fallen of their own weight; whence it would be an easy matter to bombard Sumter. General Gillmore was now convinced that Wagner was too strong to be taken by assault, and could only be reduced by regular siege. As the guns of Sumter would be a great annoyance to the men in the trenches, commanding them by a plunging fire, he determined to destroy that fortress over the head of Wagner. This was contrary to the usual course of military engineering, but necessity compelled its adoption. The distance at which the breaching batteries had to be erected was unprecedented, and the task was pronounced impracticable. None but the boldest engineer would have undertaken the work. Beauregard assured his troops that Sumter could not be breached until after Wagner had been reduced; but Gillmore thought differently, and bent all his energies to make good the faith that was in him.

The engineers commenced work on the night of the 25th of July, and by the 16th of August the batteries were completed. They were eight in number—the nearest one being thirty-four hundred yards from Sumter, and the farthest forty-two hundred and thirty-five yards. Seven of these batteries bore the distinctive names of Brown, Rosecrans, Meade, Hayes, Reno, Stevens, and Strong, mounting the following guns, viz.: one three-hundred-pounder, six two-hundred-pounders, nine one-hundred-pounders, two eighty-four-pounder Whitworth, two thirty and four twenty-pounders; all Parrotts except two guns, and the whole of them rifled. Never before had such a weight of metal been directed against any fortress in one attack since the art of war began. Those who have not engaged in such operations can have only a faint idea of the labor and fatigue attending the construction of the batteries and mounting the guns. The three-hundred-pounder gave great trouble before it was got into position. It was transported more than a mile from the dock, through deep sands, and across semi-marsh overflowed by the tide. It broke down three sling-carts. It was about a week on the way, and in the daytime it was covered with brush and weeds to conceal it from the enemy. Not only were the batteries mostly built, but all the guns were mounted, at night. Most of the work was done under fire.

At this period there sprang into existence a battery built in the marsh between Morris and James Islands, which has become famous as the "Swamp Angel," and as such will go down to history. Its construction was early determined upon, and the suggestion, we believe, was that of Colonel Serrell, commanding the New York Volunteer Engineers. It was expected that shells thrown from it would reach the city and probably cause the enemy to evacuate. The spot chosen was almost a mile from Morris Island, and nearly on a line between what were known as the "left batteries" and Charleston, on the edge of a deep creek that served as a wet ditch. On reconnoitering the locality it was found that a pole could be run down sixteen feet anywhere thereabouts before coming to bottom. The active part of the work was assigned to a lieutenant of engineers who, when shown where the battery was to be built, pronounced the thing impracticable. The colonel replied that the project was practicable, and the battery must be built on the spot selected. The officer was directed to call for anything he might deem necessary for the work. The next day he made a requisition on the quartermaster for one hundred men, eighteen feet high, to wade through mud sixteen feet deep, and immediately called on the surgeon of his regiment and inquired if he could splice the men if furnished. This piece of pleasantry cost the lieutenant his arrest, and the battery was built by men of ordinary stature. A heavy foundation of pine logs was laid in the mud, on which the battery was built entirely of sand-bags. The timber was hauled several miles from Folly Island. The bags were filled with sand on the island and taken to the battery in boats. All the work was done at night, for the eyes of a watchful enemy were upon all our movements. They knew we were at some mischief so far out on the marsh, but did not realize the truth until they looked across one bright morning and saw that, like Jonah's gourd, a battery had grown up in the night. It was commenced on the 4th and completed on the 19th of August. The sand-bags cost five thousand dollars. The battery was mounted with a two hundred-pounder Parrott, and great labor was required to put it in position. It was hauled to the edge of the marsh, where it was embarked on a raft in the creek, and thus floated down to the battery. The distance from Charleston was eight thousand eight hundred yards, and the gun was fired at an elevation of thirty-five degrees. The strain on it was such that it burst at the thirty-fourth discharge.

The "Greek fire," of which so much was said, was one of the great humbugs of the war. Nothing of the kind was used during the siege. Three shells filled with pieces of ordinary port-fire were fired into the city of Charleston; but everything beyond this was due to the fancy of newspaper correspondents. The distinctive name of "Swamp Angel" is said to have been suggested by Sergeant Feller, of the New York Volunteer Engineers.

Meanwhile, the enemy had not been idle. We contended against a foe as brave and vigilant as ourselves, and they taxed every resource of the profession to repel us. They erected new batteries on James Island to take us in flank, and strengthened those on Sullivan. They mounted new guns to match our superior weight of metal as far as possible. The range of one of our guns was tried on Sumter on the 12th of August. The shell struck the parapet and knocked down a quantity of bricks, which fell on a steamer lying alongside, and broke off her smoke-stack.

The regular bombardment was opened on Sumter at sunrise on the 17th, and continued without cessation, from day to day, until the 23d. At the same time the iron-clads moved up and took part ; the monitor batteries "Passaic" and "Patapsco" directing their fire at the fort, while the others engaged Wagner. When the firing ceased on the 23d, the fort was practically destroyed for all offensive purposes. The barbette guns were dismounted and buried up in the debris. The gorge-wall and sea-face were so badly breached that in many places the arches of the casemates were exposed. The lines were entirely destroyed, and it appeared a shapeless mass of brick and mortar. Our batteries were occasionally reopened until the 1st of September, when the first bombardment terminated. In this time we threw six thousand two hundred and fifty projectiles, of which two thousand one hundred and sixty-five were solid shot and four thousand and eighty-five percussion shell. They were of the calibre of one, two and three hundred-pounders. The enemy replied feebly to our fire, and did but little damage. The sight was a fine one; the artillery practice as good as ever was seen. The scream of the shot and shell, as they took their course to the devoted fortress was fearful, and every hit was followed by a cloud of brick and dust thrown into the air. The fire of the land batteries was continuous, with reliefs of artillerists for the guns. On the last day of the bombardment the "Ironsides" and monitors took an active part. The correspondent of the Mobile *Tribune* gave an interesting account of the situation of the garrison of Sumter at this period. He said:

The "Ironsides" and monitors commenced a terrific bombardment. A fog protected them from the guns of Moultrie. Sumter, having only two ten-inch and one eleven-inch gun left on barbette, could only fire an occasional shot to show life. For seven hours, at close range, the fleet hurled shot and shell into the work. Striking the wall near the parapet, loose bricks were thrown up in columns, and fell in showers around the gunners and around the work. Walls were ploughed through, casemates filled with sand, and the shells passed across the parade, striking the interior wall of the west magazine, containing powder enough to destroy the fort and garrison. One shell struck the ventilator and exploded. It filled the magazine with smoke. Another more successful shot and all would have been lost. It was an anxious moment, but the fort was held. Gradually the morning dawned. The fog lifted, and Fort Moultrie opened fire on the ships. *Instead of continuing their fire at this critical period the fleet withdrew, and the danger was removed.* The object was now, in the unsafe condition of the fort, to get rid of the powder. *It depended on time and the movements of the fleet. Had the fleet renewed the attack the business might have been done. The fleet delayed!* Night after night the powder, ten thousand pounds, was moved in barrels, under the enemy's guns. Only eight hundred pounds were left; *the crisis was passed.*

While the batteries were being erected and their guns directed against Sumter, the engineers pushed operations against Wagner, which they approached with steady and toilsome pace. On the night of the 23d of July the second parallel was opened six hundred yards nearer the fort. Here was our strongest position, defensive as well as offensive. In this parallel, it will be remembered, was mounted some of the guns that breached Sumter, and batteries were erected there mounting fifteen other guns and mortars. Here was built a store magazine that contained a supply of powder for all the contiguous batteries, and a small splinter-proof contained an army telegraph instrument to communicate with headquarters. Here was the "headquarters" of the trenches, where the general and field officer of the day remained when on duty at the front; and from this point the details for guards and fatigue in the trenches were sent to their respective localities. On the top of the magazine a soldier was stationed to watch the firing of the enemy's batteries, and when he pronounced the significant words, "Johnson, cover!" or "Simpkins, cover!" every one sought the friendly shelter of the neighboring sand-bags. In front of the parallel was constructed a wire entanglement to trip up assailing parties in the dark. Firing was resumed between the enemy's batteries and our own on the 25th, and there were numerous casualties. On the night of the 26th a shell from James Island burst amid a fatigue party mounting a gun, and wounded twenty-one men.

The third parallel, four hundred and fifty yards from Wagner, was opened on the 9th of August. The approaches were pushed forward as rapidly as possible, sometimes by the full, and at other times by the flying, sap. The fourth parallel was opened on the 22d within three hundred yards of the fort. Immediately in front was a sand ridge where the enemy's sharpshooters were stationed, from which they constantly annoyed our men in the trenches. To take it was a necessity, for while they held it the approaches could not be advanced. On the night of the 26th a dash was made at it with the bayonet, when it was taken, with seventy prisoners. The alarm opened the guns of Wagner, and brought a shower of grape, which killed and wounded a few of our men. Shovels were placed in the hands of the prisoners, who were obliged to dig for shelter from their own people. The fifth parallel was opened the same night, within two hundred yards of Wagner. This was the most advanced parallel. Beyond this point the approaches were simply zig-zags, making sharp angles with each other, and thus the engineers crept gradually up to the work until the counterscarp was crowned on the night of the 6th of September.

The next day after the ridge was taken the enemy made one of those fatal shots sometimes witnessed in siege operations. The Eighty-fifth Pennsylvania Regiment was the guard in the trenches. There had not been much firing during the day, and in consequence the men became careless. Nine soldiers of this regiment were sitting in a little area, without the cover of the trenches, when toward evening a single mortar shell was fired from James Island. Slowly it described the usual curve of such projectiles, and coming to the earth, fell and exploded in the midst of the party. Seven were killed outright, and the two others so badly wounded that they died in a short time. The members of their bodies, clothing, equipments and broken guns were scattered in all directions. The nearer the approach to the fort the more difficult and dangerous became the operations. The enemy kept up an incessant fire day and night, and the low trenches afforded poor shelter to the troops guarding them. The engineers and fatigue parties were almost entirely without protection. The enemy had planted the ground immediately in front of the fort with torpedoes, which increased the danger; a number were digged up and destroyed, while others exploded with fatal effect to our men. The ground was literally sown with them; they were buried just beneath the surface, and so arranged with a plunger that they would explode on being trod upon. Their presence was rather turned to our advantage, for they prevented a sortie from the enemy.

Immediately we had secured a lodgment on Morris Island, a party of boat infantry was organized to patrol the creeks and watercourses that lie between this island and James, to prevent the landing of the spies and scouts of the enemy. The enemy employed a similar force, and occasionally these boat pickets had an encounter upon the water. Two attempts were made to surprise Battery Gregg, by a night attack in boats, which, if successful, would compel the garrison of Wagner to surrender. The enemy discovered the approach of our boats, and both attempts were failures. In one of these the commanding officer of the expedition called for a volunteer to blow up the magazine—one who "feared neither man nor devil" —when Sergeant Rosenberger, a fine young soldier of the One Hundred and Fourth Pennsylvania Regiment, stepped forward and offered to apply the match.

Sumter out of the question, every energy was directed to the reduction of Wagner, which alone stood in the way of our possessing the whole of Morris Island. The siege operations dragged their slow length along. Day after day and night after night our brave men digged and guarded in the trenches, subject to a galling fire. The enemy clung to their stronghold with great tenacity, for it was then considered the gateway to Charleston. They met us with a sternness and courage worthy of a better cause. It was Greek pitted against Greek. The extreme heat of the weather and the excessive fatigue were rapidly wearing down the men, while their constant exposure to death in the trenches was more dreaded than open combat. Only those who have experienced it know how it tries the nerves of men to lie in a narrow trench with the thermometer at 120 degrees, exposed to a heavy fire, or, while thus situated, to ply the shovel. The casualties were numerous; the sick list was largely on the increase—some of the regiments having more than half their men unfit for duty. We had already lost three thousand of our brave fellows on that narrow sand bank. The burial of the dead was constantly going on, and at last became so frequent that music was prohibited at soldiers' funerals. At this period the medical inspector of the department reported that unless Wagner should soon fall the troops would not be in a condition to further prosecute the siege; and that a third assault would be more economical of life than a continuance of the present operations.

The night attack in boats on Battery Gregg having failed, it became evident that Wagner must be stormed, if taken at all, and this was resolved upon. The time fixed for the assault was Monday morning, the 7th of September. Operations were pushed against the enemy as vigorously as possible. The garrison was harassed day and night. To prevent them repairing damages at night a powerful calcium light was turned upon the ramparts, which made them as light as day—thus blinding the enemy, while it enabled our men to see what was going on. Our sharpshooters were so numerous and so close to the fort, that the enemy were kept from their guns. Our trenches were widened and deepened to hold the troops for the assault, and the light mortars were taken forward and mounted on the advanced parallels. The final bombardment was opened on the fort on the morning of the 5th of September, and continued more than forty hours without cessation. At the same time the iron-clad frigate "New Ironsides" moved up within a thousand yards, and opened upon it with her heavy broadsides. The air was filled with shells bursting in and over the fort, which drove every living thing from sight. The garrison was compelled to seek shelter beneath their impenetrable bomb-proofs. The island and the sea fairly trembled under the discharge of artillery. At night the spectacle was grand, for the heavens seemed alive with the fiery projectiles as they flew to their destination. During the last thirty-six hours of the bombardment the admitted loss of the enemy was one hundred and twenty-five, in spite of all their means of protection.

At eight o'clock on the evening of the 6th of September the commander of the troops selected for the assault of the next morning met General Gillmore in council. The troops chosen consisted of two brigades and two regiments. The two regiments were to assail the sea bastion from the trenches, spike the guns that swept the beach, and secure the entrance to the bomb-proofs. The two brigades were to pass the sea bastions, and, while one was to assault the fort in the rear, the other was to form across the island, to prevent reinforcements coming down. The troops were to be concealed in the trenches; the signal of the attack was to be the raising of the American flag on the surf battery, when they were to rush out by the nearest parallel to the assault. The batteries were to continue their fire to the latest moment. Our final instructions arrived at midnight, and each regimental and brigade commander was furnished with a drawing of the fort. The troops were to be under arms at half-past one o'clock, so as to take their place in the trenches before daylight. The hour of assault was fixed at nine o'clock A. M. Brigadier General Terry was placed in command of the troops, and had charge of the assault.

The night was an anxious one to all who were to participate in the work of the morrow. Many important, but unpleasant, offices have to be performed before one is prepared to enter the "eminent deadly breach," and there was but little time allowed for them. The troops were aroused soon after midnight, and by the hour designated were under arms on the beach. The men carried a canteen of water each, and a few crackers in their haversacks. Two hundred men carried shovels in addition to their arms and equipments. The regiments report at the place of rendezvous, and the column is soon formed. Although a mile and a half from the enemy, everything was done in the quietest manner. The commands were given in that low tone of voice that marks the approach of danger. The morning was bright with moonlight; there was hardly a breath of air stirring, and the quieted sea broke in gentle murmurs on the sandy shore. In view of what was to come, a marked solemnity impressed everything. While waiting to move forward an undefined rumor reached us that a deserter had come in and stated that the fort had been evacuated; but as it could not be traced to any reliable source it was considered a camp story. At two o'clock we moved up to what was thought to be a bloody morning's work. At the Beacon House a halt was ordered. After waiting some time we were joined by General Terry, who announced that the fort had been evacuated between nine and ten the night before, and that we were marching to a bloodless victory. The enemy retired by way of Cumming's Point in boats, a few of them only falling into the hands of our boat infantry. Captain Walker, of the New York Volunteer Engineers, pulled up some of the pallisading around the fort about ten o'clock, most likely while the evacuation was going on. The first man to enter the work was a sergeant of the Thirty-ninth Illinois, who is said to have volunteered to go in alone to see if the enemy had gone. Upon his return a few troops entered and took undisputed possession.

The announcement that the enemy had left was received with satisfaction. Three thousand hearts beat happier. However ardent a soldier may be in the cause he fights for, he feels no chagrin and mortification when the enemy yields him a triumph not purchased by blood. The pen of the romancer may write about the disappointment because there were no enemy to fight, and the untried soldier imagine it, but he who breasts the bullets and the storm does not participate in this unnatural feeling. The troops marched up to the head of the island under a cross-fire from the batteries on James and Sullivan's Islands. On the return I went into Wagner, and never before saw a place in such universal ruin. Everything but the sand was knocked to pieces; guns dismounted, carriages broken, and wagons smashed up. The commissary building was literally reduced to splinters. The impenetrable bomb-proof was the salvation of the garrison. The filth was in keeping with the ruin that prevailed; and the heap of unburied dead without the sally-port showed how hasty had been the flight of the enemy. The troops returned to their camp about sunrise. The night of the 7th Admiral Dahlgren made an attack upon Sumter in boats manned by sailors and marines from the fleet. It was anticipated and repulsed. The next day an action took place between the iron-clad fleet and the enemy's batteries on Sullivan's Island, which was, probably, the severest naval engagement that ever took place in America. The enemy opened with a hundred guns of heavy calibre, but before the day was closed they had all been silenced. The "New Ironsides," commanded by that noble old sailor, Commodore Rowan, played a giant's part in the fight. Another bombardment would have given us the island, but the Commodore was not permitted to renew the action in the morning, and the time given the enemy to strengthen his batteries rendered them quite impregnable.

The engineers were immediately set to work erecting strong batteries at the head of Morris Island for offensive and defensive purposes. Our guns at Cumming's Point were a mile and a half from Forts Johnston and Moultrie, and within less than a mile of Sumter; and from Charleston, as the bird flies, more than three miles. By the 17th of November our batteries erected against the city were in such state of completeness that fire was opened and thirteen shells were thrown into Charleston from a thirty-pounder Parrott. The next day a one hundred-pounder was opened from near the same point, which threw fourteen shells into the city. From that hour to its surrender the firing was continued on this doomed city; at periods of several nights in succession a shell was dropped into it every five minutes. One of the thirty-pounders had a remarkable life. It was one of the two first that opened upon the city, and was fired at an elevation of forty-two degrees. Day and night it continued to hurl the missiles of destruction until the night of the 19th of March, when it gave up the ghost at the four thousand six hundred and fifteenth round. This was the first gun of this class and calibre that had been known to burst, and I challenge the history of artillery to show equal endurance in any other gun. There were fired from it one hundred and thirty-eight thousand four hundred and fifty pounds of iron, and it burned one-sixth as much powder. Down to the time of which I write, the 19th of March, there had burst in our operations twenty-three heavy guns, of which one was a three hundred-pounder, five were two hundred-pounders, and seventeen one hundred-pounders, and in only a single instance was injury done to the artillerists. The amount of labor performed during the siege operations was enormous. I have no means of giving that done by the whole army, and can only speak of my own immediate command. The little brigade which I had the honor to command, and which never had much over one thousand men for detail, performed nearly an hundred thousand days and nights of duty. The trenches, parallels, splinter-proofs and batteries constructed measured about eight miles in length. Think of the days and nights of toil, and labor, and danger, that fashioned these eight miles of moving sand into strong defenses, and how often their earthen walls were bathed in the blood of the trusty soldier!

Numerous interesting incidents happened during the siege. The night we broke ground to erect a heavy battery between Wagner and Gregg there occurred an event which seemed to be a Providential punishment of those who avoided their duty. The working party was in charge of Captain Pratt, of the Fifty-fifth Massachusetts Volunteers. After he had placed the first relief on duty he walked out to the beach; he saw there two soldiers sitting in a large hole made by one of the enemy's shells. Upon being asked who they were, they replied that they belonged to the second relief. He suspected they were shirking duty, and kept them in mind. The Captain again walked out to the beach, after the second relief had been placed on duty, and found the same men sitting in the shell hole, who failed to recognize him in the dark. He repeated his inquiry, and was told they belonged to the first relief that had just come off duty. Almost at the same moment he looked across the harbor toward Fort Moultrie, for he was on the beach facing it, and saw a mortar shell rise from the fort. Knowing the range was taken for his working party, he stepped to one side and watched the flight of this messenger of death. He saw it rise high in the air; the fuse twinkling like a moving star; describe the usual curve, and fall to the earth a short distance from him. Upon going to the spot he found that it had fallen into the hole where the two were sitting and killed them both. They died shirking their duty, with a lie on their lips.

Soon after we took Battery Gregg there happened a very sad accident. A captain of a Maine regiment, who was a member of a court-martial, and not engaged in the operations, went to the front one afternoon to have a good view of Charleston. He stood alone on the top of the bomb-proof at Gregg, in plain sight of the enemy's batteries on James Island, a mile and a half distant. A rebel gunner in Fort Johnston trained a gun on him and fired. The aim was unerring, and the shell cut him in two.

About the same time, while a party of the One Hundred and Fourth Pennsylvania Volunteers were asleep at night in the bomb-proof of Gregg, a shell fired from James Island entered the door and exploded, killing and wounding seven. Many things likewise occurred that were amusing. One day a small negro boy was leading a horse, hitched to a cart, up to the head of the island; Moultrie paid her respects to the young African, and, a large shell bursting near him, killed his horse, knocking the head off of it, leaving the boy unharmed, with the bridle in his hand.

The siege of Morris Island, or, as it will be known in history, "The operations against the defenses before Charleston," is, in many respects, one of the most wonderful in military annals. In the future the student of military science will study it with marked attention and interest. Here was first developed the power of the modern long-range gun, and the experiments proved the Parrott rifled projectile to be superior to any other in the world. Instead of battering down walls of masonry at the distance of a few hundred yards, Gillmore taught the world that American guns could do it nearly three miles. Whoever before heard of a first-class fortification being destroyed over the head of intermediate works, two miles removed from it? And where do we find a city bombarded from a battery that was five miles distant? This was the first operation in modern times, on land, where guns of a heavier calibre than the one hundred-pounder were used to any extent. It introduced the two hundred and three hundred-pounder rifle, never before used in siege operations, and demonstrated their great superiority over every other arm in use. It was all that was required to make the United States the first nation in the world in all things that pertain to the art of war.

That part of the operations devoted to Sumter opened a new chapter in military engineering. Hitherto batteries to breach walls of masonry had seldom, if ever, been erected one mile from the place to be battered down, and a gun that carried a projectile that weighed sixty-four pounds was the heaviest metal used. In the days of Vauban, in his time the first military engineer in the world, and almost the father of the present system of permanent fortification, as well as the system of attack and defense of fortified places, it was laid down as a rule that the first parallel should not be opened at a greater distance than six hundred yards from the salient angle of the covered way. With him it was customary to establish breaching batteries on the glacie. General Gillmore overturned the theories and practice of the schools, and set at naught the teachings of the oldest masters. He erected his breaching batteries miles away from the point of attack, and under the most favorable circumstances did not wish to approach nearer than a mile before he let the enemy feel the weight of his metal. He looked upon the old forty-twos and sixty-fours as discarded engines of war, fit to be laid up as "bruised monuments," but no longer to figure in war's active operations. He chose instead the new projectiles of Parrott, and hurled at this proud fortress of the sea shot and shell that weighed two and three hundred pounds each. His operations astonished both friend and foe. Then, again, Wagner was approached over ground much less in width than the front of the work, a thing very unusual, if not almost entirely unknown. A narrow sand ridge, bounded on each side by the sea, and only a few hundred feet across in its widest part, was all the space to develop the trenches and parallels. There was another peculiarity in these operations; the communications of both parties were open to the rear, and could not be interfered with. When the history of the war comes to be written, General Gillmore will be pronounced its foremost engineer, and his operations on Morris Island considered one of its most creditable performances.

VICKSBURG DURING THE SIEGE.

BY EDWARD S. GREGORY.

On January 24th, 1862, a fleet bearing the united forces of Generals Grant and Sherman, descending the Mississippi from Memphis, appeared before the "terraced city of the hills"—the name given Vicksburg, according to local tradition, by Daniel Webster. The disastrous experiment made in the previous December by General Sherman—of approaching the town on the Yazoo line—was not repeated. The troops were disembarked on the west bank of the river, and began to dig a canal across the isthmus which the great bend of the river opposite Vicksburg makes; the original idea of which scheme of isolation had occurred to General Williams the year before. Demonstrations in other directions were not neglected, meanwhile. Nine gunboats, carrying 4,000 men, in March made a move down the Tallahatchie, but were repulsed by General Loring at Fort Pemberton. General Pemberton, in command of the Department of Mississippi, was induced for a while to think that the city was in no immediate danger, and that a large part of General Grant's army had been sent to join Rosecrans. He soon had occasion to alter his mind in this connection, and the troops which he had dispatched to General Bragg, at Chattanooga, were promptly withdrawn.

Early in April, a new plan of campaign was adopted by General Grant. He struck work on the canal. His new scheme was to march his troops down on the west bank of the river to some suitable point below Vicksburg, and throw them over in transports that were to pass the batteries under veil of night. Already, in March, the

"Hartford" and "Albatross," of Farragut's squadron, had passed the Port Hudson guns. On the night of April 16th, a Federal fleet of gunboats and three transports, towing barges, ran by the batteries at Vicksburg and moored at Hard Times, La. (thirty miles, say, below the city), where the forces had arrived. On the night of the 22d six more transports and barges followed. The damage done by the Confederate artillerists on these two occasions summed up as follows: One transport sunk, one burned, six barges rendered unserviceable. We shall hear more fully of these feats hereafter. The rigor of the game began when, on the 29th of April, Admiral Porter opened the guns of his ships on the Confederate intrenchments at Grand Gulf, the Thirteenth Corps (McClernand's) being held in readiness to cross over when these were silenced. At sunset the guns were still vocal, and General Grant determined to land at Bruinsburg, which was ten or twelve miles lower down. Gunboats and transports gave the batteries the slip at night in numbers sufficient to ferry over a division at a time. More than twenty vessels of different descriptions had then passed the Confederate fortifications.

On April 30th the four divisions of McClernand's corps crossed, and on the 1st of May moved, and in brief time encountered the Confederate command of General Bowen, consisting of the brigades of Green and Tracy, four miles from Port Gibson. The Confederates were choice men, and fought gallantly against great odds; but on the next day General Bowen was forced out of Port Gibson, and retired across the suspension bridge of the Bayou Pierre to Grand Gulf. His stay here was transient, seeing that his flank was almost immediately turned. On the 3d he marched to Hankinson's Ferry, on the Big Black, and there met Loring and his division, sent from Jackson by Pemberton, whose headquarters were at Edwards' Depot. On the 30th of April, General Sherman, commanding the Fifteenth Corps, after a slight feint on Haines' Bluff, on the Yazoo, returned to Milliken's Bend and proceeded to the main body. On the 8th, the three corps met at Willow Spring, where McClernand and McPherson (commanding the Seventeenth Corps) had been waiting since the 3d. On the same day they advanced, on parallel roads, northeast; but the Thirteenth shortly turned off toward Edwards' Depot; while the Seventeenth, followed by the Fifteenth, kept their faces toward Jackson. The latter column, on the 12th, encountered the single brigade of Gregg at Raymond and drove it away—not till after a stout resistance. McPherson then moved on Clinton—a station on the railroad ten miles west of Jackson—interposing between Vicksburg and General Joseph E. Johnston (who had arrived in Jackson on the 13th and assumed command), and breaking the line of Confederate coummunications.

Prior to his departure from Tullahoma for the scene of war, General Johnston had sent an order to General Pemberton in these words: "If Grant's army crosses [the Mississippi], unite all your forces to beat him. Success will give you back what you abandoned to win it." One dispatch had been received from General Pemberton, bearing date the 12th, and beginning: "The enemy is apparently moving in heavy force toward Edwards' Depot, on Southern Railroad." The "movable army" of Pemberton, consisting of the divisions of Bowen and Loring, which had come up from Grand Gulf, and Stevenson, who was detached from the garrison of Vicksburg, leaving the two divisions of Forney and M. L. Smith *in loco*, was now at Edwards' Depot, eighteen miles east of Vicksburg; and headquarters were at Bovina, a station some four miles west.

On the 13th, General Johnston sent a dispatch to the War Department in these words: "I arrived this evening, finding the enemy in force between this place and General Pemberton. *I am too late.*" These were ominous words. Through Captain Yerger he dispatched that order to General Pemberton which has been the bone of contention in all the subsequent discussions on the responsibility of failure. It directed the latter to come up, if practicable, on the rear of McPherson at Clinton at once. "All the strength you can quickly assemble should be brought. Time is all important." This was put into Pemberton's hands at 7 o'clock on the morning of the 14th. He answered at once, signifying his purpose to obey, though he did not think his force justified attacking. But immediately he summoned a council of war, to which the question was submitted for discussion, and a majority of the major generals present sustained the execution of the order; others said "nay." General Pemberton concluded that he would obey the order in this wise: He would set off for Clinton, which was twelve miles east, by moving on Dillon's, which was eight miles south. By this route he might break the communications of the enemy, and force them to attack. If his luck was good, he might proceed to Clinton, or else take advantage of any improved posture of affairs that the movement might bring about. On the morning of the 15th, the three divisions set out on their march, being compelled to make a tedious detour because of the destruction by flood of a bridge over Baker's creek, which runs a little east of Edwards' Depot, in a southwesterly

8

course, to the Big Black river. That such was to be his mode of obeying the order, General Pemberton had written General Johnston, in a note dated the 14th, at 5 P.M.; which contained, however, no reference to the council of war. It was part of the tragedy of errors which the whole campaign illustrated, that this answer reached General Johnston before the note previously sent.

Meanwhile, no grass was growing under Sherman's feet. On the 14th, Johnston, hearing that the Fifteenth Corps was twelve miles from Jackson, on the Raymond road, and that both it and McPherson were moving on Jackson, sent out one brigade to meet each corps, and evacuated the city, which was promptly entered. McClernand, who had been near Edwards' Depot, having received orders to that effect, joined the main body in the neighborhood of Jackson, out of which General Johnston had marched with his little army, then 6,000 at most, toward Clinton, twenty odd miles north. Ascertaining the Federal concentration, he dispatched an order to Pemberton on the same day, informing him of the situation of affairs and the disposition of forces, and asking if he could not close their communications with the river, and above all beat them if for want of supplies they were compelled to fall back. It was part the second of this tragedy of errors that Pemberton received this communication not till after the battle of Baker's creek, when too late to affect his action.

The battle of Baker's creek happened in this wise : When General Johnston, on the 15th, received General Pemberton's second note of the day before, disclosing his designs on Dillon's, Johnston instantly replied that "the only mode by which we could unite was his [Pemberton's] moving directly to Clinton and informing me [Johnston], that I might meet him there with 6,000 men." Hardly had Pemberton got well clear of Baker's creek when this order reached him. He reversed his columns and prepared to obey it promptly, and dispatched a courier so to inform General Johnston. Just at this point a new factor appears, in the shape of Grant, who had heard in Jackson of Pemberton's designs to attack him piecemeal, and who had conceived the design of reversing the operation. McPherson, McClernand, Blair and Hovey were ordered on the 15th to march to Bolton's Depot, eight miles east of Edwards' Depot. Returning to Edwards' Depot, General Pemberton formed his line of battle—remaining, General Johnston contends, for five hours in front of a single Federal division, which he might have crushed. Battle was delivered by Grant on the 16th, with all his force. The Confederate resistance was spirited, but unavailing. General Pemberton lays the blame of defeat on Loring, who declined to reinforce the Confederate left. For this same inaction General Loring is equally praised by Johnston. The field was lost, and Loring, after guarding the retreat of the army across the creek, and seeing the bridge burned, moved out by a wide detour and joined General Johnston with his division. Next day the Federals, crossing Baker's creek on pontoon bridges, renewed the battle at the Big Black river, east of which Pemberton had stationed Bowen, while Stevenson was bivouacked on the other side. The Confederates were disheartened and divided, and the fight soon became a flight. Eighteen Confederate cannon were captured. The remnant of Bowen's command was conducted from the field by Stevenson. Grant followed swiftly, and the pickets of the advance were before Vicksburg on the 18th. On the next day the investment was complete.

On the 17th, Johnston, marching his two brigades on the road from Livingston to Edwards' received Pemberton's account of events, including the council of war on the 14th, and the battle at Baker's creek. The action at the river was progressing at the moment of General Pemberton's latest communication. Hearing immediately afterward of the abandonment of the Big Black, General Johnston orders Pemberton: "If Haines' Bluff is untenable, Vicksburg is of no value and cannot be held. * * * Evacuate Vicksburg, if not too late, retreating to the northeast." Expecting that this order was obeyed, Johnston marches to the northwest to meet the garrison. On the 18th he received a dispatch from Pemberton, at Vicksburg, announcing his retreat into the intrenchments, and adding that the order of evacuation had been submitted to a council of war, and while it was holding the enemy's guns opened. "I have decided to hold Vicksburg as long as possible. I still conceive it to be the most important point in the Confederacy." Johnston answers Pemberton encouraging him to hold out—"I am trying to get together a force to help you"—and orders Gardner to evacuate Port Hudson. Before this order could be repeated Port Hudson was invested by the whole force from Baton Rouge. Thus far the preliminary narrative, which has been condensed to the exclusion of many important points— among them the discussion between General Johnston and the administration as to the authority of the former over the army in Tennessee to order reinforcements from it to Mississippi. How far results were affected and responsibility fixed by these disagreements, and that between the generals in the field, may be considered on a later page.

It may be well credited that the garrison and the populace had not been indifferent while these great actions sped. That a crisis impended, every man and woman felt; and that the odds were greatly against us was equally evident. Still the people would not harbor the thought of defeat, and they were equally unprepared for the siege. The city had been bombarded once before; an ordeal invoked by the defiant reply of the mayor speaking for the citizens, when S. P. Lee demanded their surrender after the fall of New Orleans. When, therefore, the sudden unfolding of a ball of dense white smoke in the sky above them gave sign on the 18th that the enemy had arrived, the fact did not frighten the brave community, however much it may have surprised them. At first the depressing shadow of exclusion, with constant peril of death and the corrosion of anxiety and of imminent famine, was relieved by the excitement of battle; for on the 19th and 20th sharp attacks were made on the lines, which were repulsed with great slaughter of the Federal column. The novelty of the situation sustained the spirits of the people still longer, and their courage was never dimmed. But the sickness of hope deferred was of gradual growth, while the sordid conditions of life, made necessary by the exigencies and exposure which were incident to the siege, had their own sad effects of steady and hard attrition. Just how and by what distinct stages a " city full of stirs—a tumult-uous city—a joyous city," such as the Jerusalem of the prophet's vision, takes on itself the aspect of a camp or a trench, devoid of the attendants of home and ease, and marked by every feature of war's worst exactions and destructions, nothing short of a diary of contem-poraneous experience could describe. It answers the purpose of a picture to select any period when the siege was well advanced and distinctly charactered; when the life of the people had become adapted to it, and when the full consequences of such abnormal influences were developed.

I have spoken of the element of danger. The Federals fought the garrison in part, but the city mainly. Even the fire on the lines was not confined to them in its effects, for hardly any part of the city was outside the range of the enemy's artillery from any direction except the south. Shot from opposite quarters might have collided above the city. But the city was a target in itself, and was hit every time. Just across the Mississippi, a few days after the lines were closed, seven eleven- and thirteen-inch mortars were put in position and trained directly on the homes of the people; and if any one of them was silent from that time till the white flag was raised any longer than was necessary to cool and load it, I fail to recall the occasion. Twenty-four hours of each day these preachers of the Union made their touching remarks to the town. All night long their deadly hail of iron dropped through roofs and tore up the deserted and denuded streets. It was a feature of their practice that early in the night their favors would be addressed to one part of the city, and afterward changed so as to reach the cases of persons in other parts who had gone to bed in fancied security. Those who could forget the deadly design and properties of these missiles might admire every night the trail which they made across the western heavens; rising steadily and shiningly in great parabolic curves, descending with ever-increasing swiftness, and falling with deafening shriek and explosion; hurling in many a radius their ponderous fragments. It is believed by the expert that a mortar shell is the most demoralizing agency of war. Throughout the war the Confederates had the same horror of them that the other side felt for masked batteries and Black Horse cavalry. For forty days and nights, without interval, the women and children of Vicksburg took calmly and bravely the iron storm which, in less volume and in a few minutes, turned back the victorious column of Beauregard from Pittsburg Landing. They wreaked their worst and utmost on the town, bringing out the most vicious of all war's aspects. That the ordinary atmosphere of life, the course of conversation, the thread of every human existence took in for nearly two months the momently contingency of these messengers of thunder and murder, is past ordinary comprehension. How many of them came and burst, nobody can have the least idea. An account says that on June 22d 150,000 shells fell inside of the city; but this was probably an exaggeration. They became at last such an ordinary occurrence of daily life that I have seen ladies walk quietly along the streets while the shells burst above them, their heads protected meanwhile by a parasol held between them and the sun.

Nothing was spared by the shells. The churches fared especially severely, and the reverend clergy had narrow escapes. The libraries of the Rev. Dr. Lord, of the Episcopalian, and of Rev. Dr. Rutherford, of the Presbyterian church, were both invaded and badly worsted. One Baptist church had been rendered useless for purposes of worship by the previous shelling. But what mattered churches, or any sacred place, or sacred exercise at such a time? There was nothing more striking about the interior of the siege than the breaking down of the ordinary partition between the days of the week, as well as the walls which make safe and sacred domestic life. During those long weeks there was no sound or summon of bell to prayer. There was no song of praise.* The mortars had no almanac, and the mortars kept at home a perpetual service of fast and humiliation.

I have spoken of the wretched expedients to which families resorted in the hope of safety. Vicksburg hangs on the side of a hill, whose name is poetical—the Sky Parlor. On it thousands of people assembled to see the great sight when the Federal ships went by on the night of the 16th of April; at which time the houses of De Soto were kindled on the other side, lending a lurid background to the dark shadows of the boats, while the fire of the batteries made the river a mirror of flame! But the Sky Parlor was reserved for other uses. Its soil was light and friable, and yet sufficiently stiff to answer the purpose of excavation. Wherever the passage of a street left the face of the hill exposed, into it and under it the people burrowed, making long ranges and systems of chambers and arches within which the women and young took shelter. In them all the offices of life had to be discharged, except that generally the cooking-stove stood near the entrance, opportunity to perform upon it being seized and improved during the shells' diversions in other quarters. Sometimes the caves were strengthened by pillars and wooden joists, and beds and furniture were crowded in them. Whether they were really effective as against the largest shells dropped directly above, I cannot tell. Stories were told, more than once during the siege, of people who had been buried alive by the collapse of caves; but they probably were not true. They made good shelter against the flying fragments of the bombs, and this was no small matter. It was rather a point of honor among men not to hide in these places, which were reserved for the women and children. Under all circumstances of difficulty, the modesty of these was supported in the half-exposed life of the caves with a pathos which affected me more deeply than any other circumstance of the siege. Another refuge of a few young ladies in the neighborhood of General Smith's headquarters, which had been a bank, was a vault in its cellar. One night, when more than a dozen of them were huddled in it, a shell struck the brick arch squarely and burst the same moment. None of the pieces penetrated; but would the whole bomb have gone through, was the question. And suppose it had, and had then burst? I believe the vault was never again occupied by the ladies. Considering the constant danger and the many narrow escapes, it is a great wonder that the casualties among the non-combatants were so

* Rev. Dr. Lord states that there were regular Sunday morning services at the Episcopal and Catholic churches during the siege.

few.   I know of but one, and that was not fatal; the loss of an arm
by Mrs. Major Reid, while bringing her children under shelter from
a sudden storm of shells.   There were doubtless others, but I have
sought in vain to obtain the facts and names.   Inside and outside
the lines there were many exaggerated stories in this connection.
One of the mortalities published was that of Mrs. General Pemberton,
who was at Gainesville, Alabama, the while.

How these people subsisted was another wonder.   The straits
to which the garrison were reduced are known, in part.   "After the
tenth day of the siege," says the report of General Stephen D. Lee,
"the men lived on about half rations, and less than that toward the
close."   The ration has been described to consist of one-quarter
pound of bacon, one-half pound of beef, five-eighths quart of meal,
beside an allowance of peas, rice, sugar, and molasses.   Of this, anon.
The citizens must have had less; and where they got that from was a
mystery.   Business, of course, was suspended.   There were some
stores that had supplies, and at these prices climbed steadily in a
manner suggestive of the prophecy of Jerusalem's undoing.   A barrel
of flour at last came to sell for one thousand dollars—an immense
figure then; but worse than the figure were the two later facts—that
nobody had the money and then nobody had the flour.   Some people
eked out their supplies by cooking the tender sprouts of the common
cane, of which there was an immense "brake" just below Vicksburg.
I have reason to believe that few applications, and these only by the
poorest people, were made to the military powers for help throughout
all this trial.   Sympathy and patriotism must have improvised a
practical communism.   The cruise and barrel had a little dust and
unction to the last.

How about the mule meat? everybody will inquire, while rations
are being treated.   Both horse and mule meat were extensively sam-
pled during the siege, though not in the way that by many may be
imagined.   On account of the want of provender nearly all the horses
of the garrison were turned out of the lines, and as the other side
could not safely take them unless they strayed within reach, many of
them were killed by the cross-fire.   Early in the siege, when some
of the men complained of the scanty ration, General M. L. Smith, I
believe, who had seen the thing done on the Plains, issued a circular
to his brigades, recommending that the experiment of horse meat be
tried to piece out supplies.   I was on hand that very evening, when
somebody, waiting till dark, slid over the works and cut a steak out
of a horse that had been shot that day beneath them.   It was cooked
at General Vaughn's fire, and everybody tasted a little; but the flesh

was coarse and nobody hungered for any more. Some of the soldiers did like it and eat it; not to speak of rats and other small deer which the Louisianians, being Frenchmen, were said to prepare in many elegant styles for the table. When Pemberton was thinking about forcing his way out, he had half a dozen fellows, men who looked like Mexicans or Indians, cutting mule meat at the old depot of the Southern Railroad, and jerking it over slow fires to make it handy and lasting. One morning, for trial, I bought a pound of mule meat at this market, and had it served at breakfast for the mess. There was no need to try again. On the day of the surrender, and only then, a ration of mule meat was actually issued; but nobody need eat it, as General Grant issued abundant supplies of the best that his army had.

Another expedient, amiably intended by General Pemberton to reinforce his commissariat, became unhappily famous at the time by the name of pea bread. It has been mentioned that part of the siege ration was the common stock pea. It occurred to the General, or to some profound commissary, that this could be ground up and mixed with meal and issued as the "staff of life." But the scheme did not succeed for the best of reasons, to wit: that the meal part was cooked an hour or so before the pea part got well warmed. The effects on the human system of a hash composed of corn bread and rare pea bread combined, may probably be imagined, without any inquiry of the doctors. From that time the soldiers had their peas and meal served them at separate courses.

One great trouble in the trenches, not so great in the town, was the scarcity and bad quality of the water. The use of the cisterns, on which the people in that country have to rely, was confined to the citizens necessarily; and the drink of the soldiers had to be hauled in barrels from the river. It was muddy and warm, and not wholesome for many reasons, and caused many of the disorders which prevailed with effects so fatal. As to spirituous drinks, I believe the city was as bare of them as Murphy himself could wish. Even Louisiana rum, the poison that had once been so abundant, withdrew its consolations from the beleaguered city. Of ice, also, there was never a pound in the city during all the war.

A state of siege fulfils, in more ways than would be imagined by the uninitiated, all that is involved in the suspension of civilization. Its influences survive; its appliances vanish. The broader lines of the picture have been drawn; the instant danger, the hovering death, the troglodyte existence, the discomfort, hunger, exposure. These are things which affect the needs of life; but to them men become more easily habituated than to the absence of many really dispensable comforts and pleasures. I have said all partitions were broken down—as completely as in that valley residence of a Revolutionary general of Virginia, in which the apartments assigned to his guests were indicated by chalk lines upon the floor. Home was a den shared with others, perhaps with strangers. All of the invasions into normal restraints and sanctities that this implied was known, perhaps, only to those who could not undress to rest or change their clothing except by arrangement. That people had to wait on themselves was a matter of course, and by comparison a minor hardship. It has been said there was no business, no mails, no open stores, no hotels, or places of congregation and discourse; no passage of vehicles, no social pastimes, no newspapers, no voice of the Sabbath bell. When the weight of anxiety that rested on the hearts of the people is duly reckoned, and with it the total lack of all means by which anxiety is usually diverted and the tension of thought relieved, it is a great wonder that many did not become insane. That they did not, gives another proof of the heroic texture of the beleaguered population.

It is not quite true that there were no papers. Three copies of the *Citizen* were published by Mr. John J. Shannon, an old gentleman, in whom, however, there was no lack of ardor and courage. The *Whig* office was burned just before the siege, and the *Citizen's* quarters were struck by the shells time and again, its type scattered, its floors flindered; but the semi-occasional issue was continued to the last. It was printed on the back of wall-paper, and its circulation was limited. Sometimes papers were handed across the lines and sent to headquarters and afterward, by regular grade, through the circle of headquarter attaches. Every one was worn to a frazzle, though the news it contained was not generally of a kind to encourage perusal. In this state of suspended animation, it is really wonderful how people continued to drag out their endurance from one hopeless day to another. Perhaps the very vigilance they had to exercise against the shells and the activity necessary to avoid them, kept the besieged alive. Every day, too, somebody would start or speed a new story of deliverance from without, that stirred up, although for a fitful season only, the hearts bowed down by deep despair. Now it was E. Kirby Smith, and now Joe Johnston, who was at the gates. The faith that something would and *must* be done to save the city was desperately clung to till the last. It probably never had deep roots in the reason of the generals, the men in the lines, or the people. But at such times men do not reason. The hand of Fate seems to rest upon them. Powerless to resist the tide of events, their only refuge is in the indulgence of a desperate hope, whose alternative is despair and madness.

There were, it is true, occasional breaks in the heavy monotone of time and things. One of these was the sinking of the gunboat "Cincinnati," on May 26th. With notable audacity this vessel attempted to run suddenly upon and close with the batteries at the north end of the city, which were manned by a gallant command of Tennesseeans, and constituted the protection of the garrison's extreme left wing. As soon as she began steaming down the river, and even before she had passed the bend, the "Cincinnati" became the target of a concentrated and powerful cannonade, which was made none the less steady and effective by the Federals' own heavy fire. Before she reached the middle of the stream it was evident that her vitals were wounded. Reversing her course, she steamed heavily up the current, but only succeeded in running ashore on the west bank, a little above the extremity of the isthmus. Forty of her people had been killed or hurt. The glory of this victory was short-lived, seeing that the heavy rifled-guns of the steamer were promptly removed from her decks and remounted near the spot of the wreck. They were her avenging spirits; if not doing more damage, certainly causing more fear, by the intense and hideous hiss of their conical balls' passage and explosion than even the heaviest of the smooth-bore mortars effected.

A great fire broke out on the night of June 6th—the Federal accounts say caused by the explosion of their shells. There was nothing to do except to remove the articles of value from the houses within its range. A great crowd collected, notwsthstanding the concentration of the mortar fire; and yet there were no remembered casualties. The whole block was burned, of course, and the wonder is only one.

On the 21st of June, a mine constructed in McPherson's front was sprung under that part of the Confederate line occupied by Hebert's Brigade of Louisianians—immediately under the Thirty-first Regiment, I believe. The mine was a failure, and the truthful chroniclers of the time report did more harm to the diggers than the under-dug. Hebert's men had their revenge, too, on the troops that had been moved up close to take advantage of the panic that did not ensue; among other things, rolling down on their heads boombs with fuses cut short, which barely had time to leave the Confederates' hands before they burst.

A Lynchburg man performed, late in the siege, a feat never heretofore recorded, and of courage worthy of the honest Irish blood that flowed in his veins. Major Mike Connell, having resigned his commission in a Memphis regiment as having passed the age of service, undertook to convoy a large purchase of sugar from somewhere in Louisiana to its owner in Virginia. He had maneuvred it as far as Vicksburg, and there the siege settled on it. After awaiting its issue from week to week, being satisfied that he could accomplish no good by remaining, and was only one more mouth to be fed out of next to nothing, Major Connell decided to make his escape. He intimated his purpose to the numerous Virginians in the city, and to other friends, and received from these a great budget of letters, which was all his load. Waiting for a stormy night, he laid himself flat in the bottom of a dug-out, just large enough to hold him, and was pushed out to take the chances of the Mississippi's arrowy current. He drifted, by good luck, between the gunboats and the guard-boats around them, and late next day was swept by a turn of the stream to the east bank near Rodney, and struggled through swamps and across bayous to *terra firma*. Borrowing somebody's mule (on what terms history is silent), he made his way painfully across the country to the nearest station on the Mobile and Ohio Railroad, whence he took cars for Mobile. His letters were mailed, and a six weeks' brain fever was the penalty paid for his hardihood. Not many letters have seemed to come so nearly out of the grave as did these missives to their astonished recipients.

Other people went and came between the garrison and the world outside. Others started who never reached their destination; some were captured and some deserted. General Johnston had ten dispatches from Pemberton during the siege, but the number received from him was smaller. How these messengers made their way in and out I have no means of knowing; perhaps through the woods, and between the intricate system of hills and vales that surround the city, and perhaps in disguise as citizens of the country. One of the deserters was a youth named Douglass, a native of Illinois, who had lived several years in Texas, and was supposed to be "loyal"—our way. It was he who refreshed the correspondents with the news that Mrs. Pemberton (in Alabama) had been killed by a mortar shell. There were reports from time to time of the flitting of Lamar Fontaine, one of the numerous poets for whom the authorship of "All Quiet Along the Potomac To-Night" is claimed, between the garrison and the outside world. I do not know if they were true or not.

Once in a while authentic information, from official sources, of the enemy's proceedings reached General Pemberton in a way they did not suspect. Just prior to the siege the alphabet of the Federal Signal Corps was communicated to Captain Maxwell T. Davidson, the very valuable officer in command of the Signal Corps of M. L. Smith's Division, from the Bureau at Richmond, and was required to be committed to memory by his men. It may be said, *apropos*, that we always had the Federal alphabet during the war; and I suppose they had ours. The Confederate signal station on the Devil's Backbone, a high hill running along the river to the north of the city, commanded a Federal signal station on the isthmus, and every motion of its flags and lamps was readily seen by the officer in charge of the former—an alert and intelligent Creole named Mathew H. Asbury. Asbury made the watching of the Federal flags the business of his life, and hardly every missed a communication of those exchanged between General Grant and Admiral Porter. By this means the first intelligence of Banks' attack upon and repulse from the works of Port Hudson was received and communicated to headquarters. A more noticeable feat remained to be achieved by the gallant Louisianian. After Pemberton's last proposition was submitted to Grant, there elapsed an interval during which its fate was uncertain. The bombardment was still suspended. This was the night of July 3d, and an ominous and awful quiet reigned over all the scene—less welcome, no doubt, to the hearts of many than the utmost fury of the bombardment. Suddenly the lamps flashed, and then began swinging, and their message was traced letter by letter and word by word—not only by the eyes for which it was designed, but by others, if possible, more keen and eager. It said, in effect, to Admiral Porter (being sent by the general in command), that a council of the generals was, in the main, opposed to the paroling of the surrendered garrison, and thought it would be better to send the whole party North; but that he, General Grant, had ruled otherwise, on the principle that the garrison was probably demoralized enough to spread the same feeling wherever they went in the South; and that he could not spare sufficient guards and transports to send them to Northern prisons, because their absence would interfere with his proposed advance into the country. (I do not pretend to give the words.) Asbury mounted a horse and dashed into town, and found a grave council of generals in silent session at Pemberton's headquarters, awaiting the verdict. With intense feeling he laid before them the intercepted dispatch which fulfilled their hopes or their fears. With never a word more the council of war broke up—

the stroke had fallen. When the garrison marched out, Captain Davidson concealed the sheets containing all the dispatches intercepted during the siege between his cap and its lining, but lost them in after years, and was unable to respond to my desire to have their very language for this paper.

The Signal Corps headquarters in the city was a room in the court-house, and its station was the cupola of the same. The court-house was set on the highest point of the town, and the cupola formed the most prominent feature of its river *facade*, except, perhaps, the soaring light spire and gold cross of the Catholic church, which was, I believe, never defaced by the fire of the enemy. Whether this was chance or intention is another study. I suspect Porter's Pats and Mikes didn't want to hurt it. Far otherwise with the Temple of Justice. The Federal papers say it was the general centre of their fire, and so say I, who was in it. The building and grounds were struck twenty-four times or more, and yet but one shell was fatal in its effects. *That* came at midnight, crushing through the roof, and, passing below to the marble pavement of the ground floor, exploded and flung two poor fellows against the wall with such mutilation that their mothers would not have known their dead darlings. They were Mississippi militiamen. Their comrades above suffered only less cruelly. The heavy shell passing through the court-room, which was packed with sleeping men, struck squarely a massive iron railing that inclosed the seats of the lawyers and witnesses, and scattered its fragments on every hand. Legs were broken, heads crushed—all manner of injury inflicted. This one shell killed and disabled fourteen men; and, by strange fatality, two more men of those who went out to bury the two first killed, lost their lives on their way to the graveyard. This inclosure, also—the beautiful City Cemetery—was riddled by the plunging shot. That was, doubtless, an accident of war. It was charged that the Federals did fire on the Marine Hospital, which was full of wounded men, and over which the yellow flag was hoisted. It was struck frequently, and wounded men wounded anew; but whether by aim or accident I do not know.

No history of the siege would be complete without some detailed allusion to the ceaseless generation of sensational reports within and without the city, both North and South. Considering the fertility of inventions then displayed, it is a wonder that the coming American novel has never come. There may have been something in the sulphurous atmosphere more favorable to the stimulation of genius than belongs to the ordinary environment. Munchausen was prosaic to the fellows who wrote and talked and were believed at that time.

The Richmond papers pathetically complained of the "telegraphic genius at Jackson." The telegraphic geniuses at Young's Point and Milliken's Bend were far greater masters of the art of fiction. I will mention a case that preceded the investment. On the 3d of May, the tug Sturgis, with two barges, loaded with 400,000 rations and medical supplies, was ordered to pass the batteries, and tried to do so, carrying a picked guard. The late A. D. Richardson, representing the New York *Tribune*, Junius Henri Browne, of the *Times*, and somebody else of the *World*, volunteered for the passage. At 12.45 the tug was exploded by the batteries' fire, several men killed, others drowned, and the Scribes and Pharisees, clinging to bales of hay, with which the barges were fortified, drifted to land, were picked up and conveyed to a room in the court-house with other victims. They were treated as handsomely as circumstances allowed, and Richardson, in particular, a hearty fellow, made almost too good an impression, for he was so thoroughly full of faith in the resources of the Union and in the approaching downfall of Jeff Davis, that he cast a shadow of doubt over some young Confederates' breasts. They were all soon exchanged, going home by way of Richmond. They saw a few things from the windows of jails and cars, and wrote to their papers from Fortress Monroe most astonishing letters, containing revelations which they could hardly have been possessed of, unless they were members of the Cabinet of Mr. Davis.

Another correspondent of the *Tribune* essayed to describe the passage of eight gunboats on the 16th. He was evidently not so venturesome as Richardson, and his picture reads as those pictures look of shipwrecks, which no soul survives, in the illustrated papers, "by our special artist." His coquetry with truth consisted in describing, as a mysterious and dreadful beacon that rose out of the earth at Vicksburg, the homely burning of some shanties in De Soto, which were set on fire to assist the aim of the artillery. The scene was terrific, and, no wonder, took on it for this correspondent a supernatural expression. But the war maps that were published were the greatest feats—quite distancing the creations of Ptolemy and Psalmanazar. The *Herald* had one representing "rebel batteries in the streets," "rebel redoubts" on the same, "masked batteries" lying around loose, a tall signal station whose architect was the artist, and the Marine Hospital at the wrong end of the town. And every day some new version of victory thrilled across the wires. One hundred women were killed the first day, was one statement; a woman and two children fell at the first fire, said another. General C. C. Auger telegraphed, on the 23d of May, that "deserters report that General Pemberton has been hanged by his own men!" 3,600 shells lodged in the town in one hour, said somebody else. One paper gave a detailed statement of the amputation of General Sherman's leg. Another said "the citizens demand the surrender of Vicksburg, and Pemberton refuses!" Another said Pemberton had answered with profane violence the charge of his men shooting poisoned balls. In the city the reports took shape mainly with reference to the supposed movements of Johnston and E. K. Smith. One day the forces had gone to Memphis, to cut Grant off from his supplies, a report that provoked a poem from a gallant, gay boy named Cannon (afterward killed), which had this refrain:

> "Damn Memphis and strategy—Vicksburg's the place,
> And I am, dear Joseph, your Cannon, in haste."

Next time it was Milliken's Bend that had been captured (there was a fight there). And then Kirby Smith had crossed the river at Natchez, and had a division at Young's Point. And so on, over and over, like the dreams of fever. General Johnston appears, from his dispatches, to have really believed that assistance could be expected from the Trans-Mississippi Department; a strange delusion which might even appear, in the minds of the prejudiced, an attempt to transfer the responsibility of events. One of the rumors that somehow reached us in Vicksburg was that Virginia had elected a Union State ticket, and was making ready to desert the Confederate cause. The joke of this story consists in the circumstance that Governor William Smith, known as "Extra Billy," bravest of soldiers and staunchest of rebels, headed the ticket described as "Union."

In order that the circumstances under which the surrender was finally made, and the train of events which served to make it inevitable may be fairly judged, I condense the dispatches exchanged between Generals Johnston and Pemberton after the siege began. The first of the series has been given. On May 25th, General Johnston wrote that he was coming, and asked Pemberton what route he ought to take. On the 29th he wrote that he was too late to save Vicksburg, but would assist in saving the garrison. On June 3d, Pemberton wrote that he had heard nothing from Johnston since May 29th; that the man bringing musket-caps had been captured, and that he hopes General Johnston will move on the north of Jackson road. On the 7th, Johnston again wants to know how co-operation can be effected. On the same day Pemberton writes of the enemy's intrenching, the good spirits of the men, and that he had twenty days' provisions. On the 10th, Pemberton says the enemy is bombarding night and day with seven mortars and artillery, and that he is losing many officers and men. He will hold out while he has anything to eat. Activity is urged by General Pemberton in a dispatch of the 15th.

On June 14th and 15th, General Johnston writes Pemberton that he can only hope to save the garrison, and asks for the details of a plan of co-operation. He also holds out the hope of General Dick Taylor's reinforcing the outside army with 8,000 men from Richmond, La. On the 21st, Pemberton suggested as his plan that Johnston should move at night to the north of the railroad while he marched by the Warrenton road, by Hankinson's ferry, to which Johnston was to send two brigades of cavalry and two batteries. Snyder's Bluff was also suggested as his objective point. By verbal message General Pemberton said the army for his relief ought not to be less than 40,000 men. General Johnston asserts that his force never amounted to more than two-thirds of this minimum. On the 22d, however, he still engages to make a trial, but recommends that General Pemberton cross the Mississippi river rather than surrender. On that date, General Pemberton asked General Johnston to treat with Grant for the surrender of the place without the troops. On the 27th, General Johnston declines to negotiate, and makes another flourish of Kirby Smith. No other dispatches were received. After dispatching Pemberton that he would advance to see what could be done on the 7th of July, he examines the country to the north of the railroad, and is satisfied that nothing can be effected. When he has just begun the like examination of the southern line, he hears on the 4th of the surrender of the town and its defenders. General Johnston was again too late.

On the 3d, the white flag went up for a parley. The first proposition of General Pemberton, which was delivered by Major General Bowen and Colonel Montgomery, suggested that the terms of surrender should be left for decision to three commissioners on either side. General Grant, courteously receiving the flag-of-truce, made answer, rejecting the proposal of commissioners as unnecessary, and suggesting a personal conference with the general of the defense, whose gallantry and stubbornness he highly lauded. At three o'clock P. M. the two commanders met in what is described by some correspondent, who, perhaps, never saw the place, as "a small vale, where the apricots and fig-trees had bloomed in happier times." The same correspondent says the two men had been personal friends in the same "happier times." Certainly the bearing of General Grant was all that magnanimity and the sympathy of the brave could inspire.

General Pemberton's proposition, however, that the men should march out, was met with the blunt qualification, "not except as prisoners of war." After the conference between the generals, Grant's ultimatum was sent by General Logan and Lieutenant Colonel Wilson. Pemberton's proposed amendments were that the men should stack arms and march out, and that the rights of the citizens should be guaranteed. Grant rejected the amendments, contending that every officer and man should be paroled over his own signature, and he would not be restricted with respect to the citizens. He allowed each soldier, however, to carry his private kit, the officers their side-arms, and the field officers their horses. These terms were accepted, and the white flag remained on the works.

The suspension of the firing had prepared the minds of the men and citizens for the event which many had long perceived to be written in the book of Fate. Yet was there great reaction and great sorrow when the iron crown of the Mississippi, a fortress maiden as Namur and defiant as Ghazi Schumla, became the enemy's prize. During the night many officers went wandering sadly around the town, taking a last look at its honorably scarred homes and ploughed streets, and making farewell to the heroic citizens whom they knew. A load was no doubt lifted from the hearts of the surrendered; but a new load, that seemed even heavier, was deposited in its place. What feeling the people had, made no public demonstration; for they prudently returned to their homes, and made the best shift that the time allowed, reserving their sorrow for their own home-circles. When the poor wasted garrison rose out of the long imprisonment of the trenches to stack the weapons they had used so well, many reeled and staggered like drunken men from emaciation and from emotion, and wept like children that all their long sacrifice was unavailing.

To Logan's Division was assigned the duty of taking possession of the captured town. The boys in blue entered by the north end of Cherry street, and made a grand procession as they stepped by in extended line, their flags waving, their officers glittering in full uniform, and the air torn with the glad shouts that went up from victorious throats. Logan himself stood on the east portico of the court-house and looked with swelling pride and profound gratification on the scene so picturesque and historic. He dropped some emphatic exclamations as to the joy it gave him to hear the boys cheer. By-the-by, the fact has never been published, but is no less true, that a company of Illinois soldiers, *on the Southern side*, once constituted part of the Vicksburg garrison, though it went to pieces

9

long before the siege. Some of their unassigned officers—I well recollect one named Parker—may still have been there.

In the main, nay, almost without exception, during the five days occupied by the paroling of the garrison, the Federal army of possession conducted itself in an exemplary manner. The men who had leave to go over the city expressed the greatest curiosity as to the caves and other objects of interest, and were mad to lay hands on relics. The wall-paper copies of the *Citizen* were in great demand. A general officer, who, I think, was Grant, accompanied by a full suite, some of whom were full of other exhilerations than success, went up to the cupola of the court-house, and when they came back, the staff were vociferously chanting the "Star Spangled Banner," and brandishing as a trophy an old signal flag that had been carelessly left there. I well remember the silent general in the midst of them, who *must* have been Grant. During all this time I heard but two phrases of offense to the Confederates, and one of these offenders was a drunken newsboy, selling copies of *Harper's Weekly*, whose front page was garnished with a picture of Beall's execution. The other, an officer, walking up the iron stairway of the court-house, and, noticing the name of the Cincinnati maker moulded on it, damned the impudence of the people who thought they could whip the United States when they couldn't even make their own staircases.

The paroling of the men in duplicate was rapidly effected by means of printed forms and a full staff of clerks, who filled in the names and commands of the soldiers and officers. One of these duplicates was retained by the prisoner, the other for the government by the paroling officials. The examination of knapsacks made on the lines was carelessly done, and with many apologies, by officers who seemed to be ashamed of the service. During the five days full rations had been issued by the commissaries of General Grant to the whole garrison, sick and well, the whole amounting to thirty-one thousand people, of whom but eighteen thousand were effective. They consisted mainly of hard-tack and rich Western bacon; and many a Confederate can say, on the conscience of his stomach, that he never ate anything that tasted better.

The armies parted with mutual good will, as is the case with foemen who are worthy of each others' steel. But the discontent of the disarmed captives began to gather volume, and to speak in no bated breath, very soon after the lines were passed. The march, owing to the feeble state of the men, was very painful and tedious. Jackson was left to the north, and the column's first sight of streets

was when, after four days, the town of Brandon, ten miles east of
Jackson, was reached. It had been generally supposed by the men
that their paroles gave them the right to go home as soon as they
could get there, and without restrictions. Many had already deserted
to the Trans-Mississippi, despite the aid of Federal guard-boats to
check the stream. But when, at Brandon, it was learned that the
cars would not receive them to take them home, and that they were
to march to Enterprise, and there go into parole camp, their indignation burst all bounds. Efforts were made, by moving the switch, to
throw the trains, on which General Johnston was removing supplies
from Jackson, from the track; and the officers had to draw and
threaten to use their side-arms before the mob could be subdued.
One man got up in the plaza of Brandon and offered to be one of
fifty to go and hang Pemberton, the traitor. What further befell
these mad patriots I cannot, as a spectator, narrate, for a sick leave
enabled me to depart on the last train from Jackson that went east—
riding to Enterprise on the top of a freight car, at the end of a long
train, and exposed to worse risk, I believe, for those forty miles than
even in the Vicksburg court-house. I ought to remark that one
pleasing feature of the march through Mississippi was the habit
which women and children had of coming out to the fences and
inquiring what made us surrender Vicksburg.

The demoralization of the garrison extended beyond the State.
At Demopolis the guard of the provost marshal came down to the
wharf to stop the prisoners who had gotten so far, and to put them
in parole camp at that point. The prisoners attacked them, broke
through the line, and flung some of them into the gutter. They
soon yielded to reason, however, and surrendered their paroles to
the provost marshal. And this was the last I saw of the ill-starved
garrison until, at Enterprise, Mr. Davis told them that Bragg would
pave Rosecrans' way in gold if he (Bragg) could get the Federal
general to attack him on Lookout Mountain—with more of the same
sort; and where Johnston, following, spoke more to the point, in
saying: "Soldiers! I hope to see you soon, with arms in your hands,
in the presence of the enemy!"

Who was to blame? The answer is, everybody—nobody. There
were great adverse odds to begin with. General Grant, according to
Badeau, had 130,000 men at his disposal with which to effect the
reduction of Vicksburg; while the effectives of Johnston and Pemberton combined—and they were never combined—never reached one-
third that number. General Johnston was too sick when he arrived
at Jackson to take command in the field ("Narrative," page 187), an

illness which "infected the very life-blood of our enterprise," like the Earl of Northumberland's. General Johnston covers the whole ground in saying of General Pemberton, "His design and objects and mine are founded on exactly opposite military principles." General Johnston was not in accord with the Richmond government, and General Pemberton was not in accord with General Johnston. Those whom God had put asunder, man had joined together. Mistaking and mistrusting each other, neither one did as well as he might have done without the other. General Pemberton thought the objective of the campaign was to save Vicksburg, or make a fight for it, and in this was supported by the administration. General Johnston thought the safety of the army was the first consideration, that the enemy might still be confronted, no matter what position he might gain. Each accuses the other of slowness, and each, probably, is right. General Pemberton, brave man, stout fighter, doubtless, and faithful to the South as any native son—a fidelity never doubted by the intelligent among his men—was deliberate, slow of assuming responsibilities, perhaps not equal to the movement and management of large bodies, and utterly devoid of personal magnetism. What character General Johnston has as a soldier, history has already, in part, decided. In military resources perhaps no captain of the South excelled him; but at Jackson he was flustered by a responsibility suddenly assumed, and for which his mind was not schooled; between which and the discharge of duties well grasped in advance, there is the same difference as between "two o'clock in the morning courage," and the ordinary daring of the soldier who obeys orders and feels the contact of his comrade's elbow.

General Pemberton is said to have felt keenly the injustice done him with respect to the fall of Vicksburg. At one time during the siege, when some exaggerated victory was reported in Richmond, the press almost smothered him with laurels. The *Dispatch* said that Beauregard and Lee had both urged his promotion, and that Johnston had fairly begged for him to be his chief-of-staff! But public sentiment told a different tale when failure befel his army. Assigned to command of the artillery around Richmond, he was greeted with jeers by the men as he rode down the lines. Ever since the war General Pemberton is said to have felt most deeply the odium attaching to him as the man who surrendered Vicksburg and sundered the South. It is a curious fact that no portrait of him appears among Confederate collections. I never saw him in person, but I do him the bare justice of recording my own conviction that his fealty to the cause which he espoused was beyond all peradventure of suspicion; that he did the very best he could; that he acted in accordance with his orders from Richmond; and that he departed no further from his immediate orders than did General Loring from *his* at Edwards' Depot, an act of independence for which General Johnston warmly lauds the latter.

The effect of the surrender, North and South, was immense. At Washington Mr. Seward, in response to a serenade, was ready to swear that even old Virginia would soon be asking forgiveness on her knees. He never saw Virginia in that posture; but it may be doubted whether, after Vicksburg and the twin tragedy of Gettysburg, there was ever any vital hope in the Southern heart except among the soldiers. The army kept its high crest and stern front to the last, and died only with annihilation; but many a Vicksburg prisoner, gone home, spread the tale of disaster and the influence of dismay among simple folk whose faith never rallied. There were desperate battles afterward, and occasional victories, but their light only rendered deeper the advancing and impending shadow of ultimate failure. The world is familiar with the story. Magnifying, as they deserve to be, the heroism of the garrison, and the community of Vicksburg, and the "vindictive tenacity" with which Pemberton held it till the last spark of hope had faded, I believe that the surrender was the stab to the Confederacy from which it never recovered; and that no rational chance of its triumph remained after the white flag flew on the ramparts of the terraced city, and the dumb guns around it no longer spoke defiance to its foes.

THE BATTLE OF BEVERLY FORD.

BY COLONEL F. C. NEWHALL.

THE interest excited by General D. McM. Gregg's narrative of the operations of the Union cavalry in the Gettysburg campaign, has been stimulated by the narrative of Major McClellan, the Adjutant General of the Cavalry of the Army of Northern Virginia; and this latter account, as a pendant to the former, affords an opportunity to emphasize the fact that the Gettysburg campaign was opened actively in Virginia, when General Pleasonton's command crossed the Rappahannock river, on the morning of the 9th of June, 1863, at Kelly's and Beverly fords, and engaged the command of General J. E. B. Stuart. The influence of that day's encounter on the great campaign which it inaugurated, has never been fully understood or appreciated by the public, and Major McClellan has done well to draw renewed attention to this eventful action. It is proper to recognize and applaud the magnanimous and soldierly vein pervading his narrative, where all the merit is awarded to the Northern cavalry which the most enthusiastic trooper among them could possibly lay claim to, and one could not reasonably expect from a Southern source such hearty and striking commendation. What he says of the causes of the decline of the Southern cavalry in numbers and efficiency, is deserving of generous consideration, and to his excuses in their behalf may well be added—what he refrains from saying—that laboring under many disadvantages, unknown to our more favored soldiers, their efforts to maintain themselves in the field were in keeping with the patient courage and self-sacrificing spirit which marked the conduct of the Southern troops, meriting, in a military sense, the admiration of the world.

(134)

Before passing to the field to which Major McClellan has mainly confined himself, I may, for historical purposes, be allowed to say, in reply to one of his preliminary remarks, that, however it may have been on his side, the entire strength of the cavalry of the Army of the Potomac was not concentrated at Trevilian Station, Virginia, in June, 1864. We had but two divisions there (Torbert's and Gregg's), Wilson's having remained with the Army of the Potomac near James river. Fair-minded troopers on our side call the fierce engagement between Sheridan and Wade Hampton at Trevilian a drawn battle. It was fought in a densely-wooded country, very remote from our main army and from any base of supply. The object of our expedition was to effect a junction with Hunter near Gordonsville; but Hunter was not at Gordonsville, nor near there, when we reached Trevilian Station, and no tidings could be had of him. He was over the hills and far away, marching directly from us instead of to a junction with us, and as we had no plans independent of him, we had no alternative but to rejoin the Army of the Potomac when he could not be found. A crow could scarcely find subsistence in the country about Trevilian Station; we were encumbered, after two days' hard fighting, with many wounded and prisoners; we were far from our base, with ammunition and rations nearly expended. We voluntarily withdrew from Hampton's front, and withdrew at night as a matter of common discretion; but we remained within easy reach of his lines the next day, and went comfortably into camp. Day after day, through the heat and dust, camping regularly at night, we continued our long march to James river, hampered with weary and foot-sore prisoners, and a long train of wagons and carts, mostly filled with wounded; but we went unvexed by General Hampton until he came again close under the wing of Lee's army. We regard the two days' fight as a drawn battle, and we think there is something rather fine in the aspect of our troopers stalking through so many miles of hostile territory directly afterward, unimpeded by the enemy's cavalry, who were close at hand, and had us somewhat at a disadvantage. But we freely admit anything that anybody can say of the expedition, as to its futility, barrenness and general worthlessness, of which we were conscious and heartily tired long before we saw the end of it.

The battle of Beverly Ford, as we call it, or of Fleetwood, as General Stuart styled it, is interesting in the first place, because it was the first occasion when the cavalry of the Army of the Potomac went into action as a body. The cavalry had been organized by General Hooker into a corps under Stoneman during the winter of

1862–63, and Stoneman had commanded the greater part of it as a unit in the field during his celebrated but entirely fruitless raid in the Chancellorsville campaign; but there had been no fighting— simply long marches in rain and mud, and much loss of sleep. General Stoneman, naturally of an anxious habit of mind, was unfitted by temperament, as well as by bodily suffering, for independent operations remote from the main army. After the return from the raid he was unjustly held to blame for a share in the Chancellorsville failure, and General Pleasonton succeeded to the command of the cavalry corps. Since the opening of the war there had been more or less fighting, scouting and picketing, by our cavalry, in which the men had borne themselves well, although, acting as they did for the most part in small detachments, no material results were impressed on the public mind; but the good effects of the experience already had by the regiments in their isolated service were at once apparent when the corps was called together. General Stoneman, and then General Pleasonton, on assuming command of the whole, found an efficient body of troops ready to hand, and not a mass of crude material to be moulded into form before it should be fit for the field. Neither Stoneman, Pleasonton, nor Sheridan, is entitled to a very large share of credit for the excellent material which the cavalry corps afforded and the excellent work it was able to do. No one man can fairly lay claim to a chief share in its development; it was self-developed, in a difficult country of woods, marshes and stone walls, where each regiment's daily experience was a daily lesson learned and improved, and to name all who contributed to the efficiency of the corps would be to name not only all those from time to time in high command, but also many brave and intelligent regimental field officers, company commanders and enlisted men. "Sheridan's Cavalry," which broke on the world with the results of the final campaign against Lee, was just as good cavalry before Sheridan became connected with it. To give no other example, when the service rendered by General Buford on the first day of Gettysburg comes to be understood and appreciated, it will be seen that he and his command had then but little to learn of skill, courage and adaptability; and all the earlier operations of the Gettysburg campaign, beginning, as I have said, with the battle of Beverly Ford, and continuing along the east flank of the Blue Ridge to the Potomac, were quite as creditable to the spirit and capacity of our cavalry as the world-famous campaign from Petersburg through Dinwiddie Court-House, Five Forks and Sailors' Creek to Appomattox. The success of Sheridan's cavalry in the latter campaign created a revolution in the ideas of European officers, who recognized a new feature in war. But it is not to the point that our fame is less in the former than in the latter campaign, and it should not be lost sight of that, on the 9th of June, 1863, the cavalry of Lee's army was in its prime; it was never seen afterward in equal glory.

Pleasonton's movement across the Rappahannock that day was in fact a reconnoissance in force to ascertain for General Hooker's information to what extent the rumors were true that Lee was en route across the Blue Ridge to the Shenandoah Valley, and so no doubt to the Potomac and beyond. Hooker's army was in the old camps opposite Fredericksburg, to which he had retired after the *fiasco* of Chancellorsville. Lee's troops had been encamped behind Culpepper Court-House, along the Rapidan, as well as in the neighborhood of Fredericksburg; but it was now known that a part of his army was already in motion in a dangerous direction, and it was also known that Stuart was accumulating his cavalry at Culpepper Court-House, if he had not already set out in advance of Lee's infantry. Culpepper Court-House is some ten miles south of the river, and there was no expectation on General Pleasonton's part of encountering Stuart's troopers immediately on crossing the fords of the Rappahannock. Indeed, as Major McClellan states, Stuart's advance to the river was simultaneous with our own. As we silently encamped on the north bank on the pleasant evening of the 8th of June, and had to be content with cold suppers, because General Pleasonton would permit no camp-fires to be lighted, Stuart's men made their bold bivouac on the southern shore of the river so confidently that, as Major McClellan informs us, there was nothing but a picket between Beverly ford, and four batteries of horse artillery parked but a short distance in the rear. General Pleasonton, having no reason to expect the presence of the enemy in force this side of Culpepper Court-House, his plan contemplated a movement of at least two columns on Brandy Station, an intermediate point on the Orange and Alexandria Railroad, between Culpepper and the Rappahannock. The Orange and Alexandria Railroad crosses the river at Rappahannock Station. Beverly ford is, perhaps, a mile and a half above, and Kelly's ford some four miles below the railroad, and for the purposes of his reconnoissance General Pleasonton determined to pass his troops over both these fords. The consequences of this plan proved to be to some extent unfortunate, because, when the river was crossed on the morning of the 9th, and the troops became engaged, the operations of the widely-severed connections were independent of each other, and could not, at that distance, in a wooded and irregular country, be brought promptly into harmony. This state of affairs, purely accidental and unexpected as it was, reflects no blame on General Pleasonton; but it is noteworthy how often, in war, operations from a common centre outward are better advised than by the contrary method. Concentration of troops is often so difficult of attainment when the links of connection are once lost. A conspicuous example of this truth has been lately brought to mind by Dr. Lambdin's admirable narrative read at the Centennial celebration of the battle of Germantown, and even now one can but feel sorry for General Washington as a soldier—thinking of him in the fog before Chew's house, with Sullivan and Wayne groping in front, and no tidings as yet of Greene on the Limekiln road, and Armstrong at the mouth of the Wissahickon. If he had spread his battle-fan outward from his centre on the turnpike, unfolding it as he advanced, perhaps no one would have inquired a century after why the good people of Germantown wished to commemorate a defeat. Be that as it may, General Pleasonton was destined to reap some of the occasional disadvantages of a broken military chain. The force dispatched to Kelly's ford was composed of Gregg's and Duffie's cavalry, and a small brigade of infantry, perhaps fifteen hundred men, commanded by the gallant General David Russell, who was subsequently killed in the battle of the Opequan, in the Shenandoah Valley. The force to cross at Beverly ford was accompanied by General Pleasonton in person, and was composed of Buford's cavalry and a small brigade of infantry, commanded by General Adelbert Ames, afterward greatly distinguished in leading the successful assault on Fort Fisher, and notorious later on as the "carpet-bag" Governor of Mississippi. To effect the contemplated junction near Brandy Station, the Beverly ford column would bear to the left, the Kelly's ford column to the right—the Orange and Alexandria Railroad lying between them as they marched. As an aide-de-camp to General Pleasonton, it was my fortune to be thrown with the Beverly ford column, and all that I saw of what occurred after the crossing of the river, on the morning of the 9th, was connected with the operations on the right.

It was not yet dawn when General Pleasonton rode to the river bank at Beverly ford. The atmosphere at that hour was very hazy, and the group of officers assembled near the General were half hidden from each other by the mist. General Buford was there, with his usual smile. He rode a gray horse, at a slow walk generally, and smoked a pipe, no matter what was going on around him, and it was always reassuring to see him in the saddle when there was any chance of a fight. General Pleasonton's staff was partly composed of men who became distinguished. The Adjutant General was A. J. Alexander, of Kentucky, a very handsome fellow, who was afterward a brigadier general with Thomas in the West. Among the aides was Captain Farnsworth, Eighth Illinois Cavalry, who so distinguished himself in the coming battle, and in the subsequent operations south of the Potomac, that he was made a brigadier general, and with that rank fell at Gettysburg at the head of a brigade of cavalry which he had commanded but a few days. Another aide was the brilliant Custer, then a lieutenant, whose career and lamented death there is no need to recall. Another was Lieutenant R. S. McKenzie, of the engineers, now General McKenzie of well-won fame—the youngest colonel of the regular army; and still another was Ulric Dahlgren. General Pleasonton had certainly no lack of intelligence, dash and hard-riding to rely on in those about him. Colonel B. F. Davis, Eighth New York Cavalry, in advance, led his brigade across the river while the light was still dim. He fell in a moment, mortally wounded, on the further bank, and should be remembered with special honor, for he was a Southern man, and a graduate of West Point. He was called "Grimes" Davis by all his army friends, and was the beau ideal of a cavalry officer. His most famous exploit was his escape with his command from Harper's Ferry, when Miles, led on by treason or infatuation, abandoned all the grand surrounding hills to the enemy, without a struggle, and awaited his own inevitable surrender in the basin below, although it was written before him, in characters mountain-high, that Harper's Ferry cannot be defended except on Bolivar, Loudon and Maryland Heights.

Colonel Davis' troops had now no sooner emerged from the river at Beverly ford, where the water was scarcely stirrup-deep, than they encountered the enemy's pickets, to whom they were, doubtless, an astounding apparition from the fog. Piff! paff! went the carbines, and our troops on this side pressed on faster, the narrowness of the ford road and of the ford itself compelling them to move in column of fours. Major McClellan describes the alarm and confusion existing among Stuart's exposed artillery and trains while Colonel Davis pushed his advance rapidly toward their camp. In his eagerness to profit by the surprise, he rashly rode with his skirmishers, if not in front of them, and was shot by a soldier on foot, who sprang from behind a tree in the edge of the first wood. He was borne back in a blanket just as General Pleasonton gained

the southern bank of the river; and in a moment more we met
some men carrying Captain George A. Forsyth, Eighth Illinois
Cavalry, who was shot through the thigh. This able and daring
officer has since become renowned as an aide-de-camp of General
Sheridan throughout his campaigns in Virginia, and as the hero of
the most remarkable fight with Indians on the plains of which there
is any record. Forsyth reported a sharp fight at the front, and
expressed great regret that he had not been wounded at sundown
instead of at sunrise. Meantime the reserve brigade of cavalry had
passed on to join in the melee, the sounds of which were now
formidable in front, while shells came flying from our right and
demanded attention. The reserve brigade, which included the
regular regiments and the Sixth Pennsylvania Cavalry, was soon
hotly engaged charging the enemy's line, which had taken position
near St. James' Church, as described by Major McClellan. St.
James' Church was a modest sanctuary, suggesting the time when
"the woods were the first churches," and it lay directly on the road
toward Brandy Station, our rendezvous with the Kelly's ford
column. The Sixth Pennsylvania Cavalry, attacking the enemy's
troopers on the plateau near the church, met with a tremendous fire
from artillery on the flank, and was compelled to fall back with
heavy loss of officers and men, including Major Robert Morris, in
command of the regiment, whose horse fell with him, and he was
taken prisoner. The regulars, part of whom charged at the same
time, or a moment later, fared better, on the whole, but were brought
to a stand still; and meantime our right, nearer to the river, was
seriously threatened, endangering our possession of Beverly ford.
Ames' infantry was ordered to replace the reserve brigade in the
woods below St. James' Church, which they did without any serious
fighting, and the reserve brigade was sent to the open fields on our
right, where the enemy, dismounted, had secured a line of stone
walls, with artillery on the higher ground behind them. Some guns
of ours were unlimbered on a knoll a short distance from the ford,
commanding the fields into which the reserve brigade was moving,
and a lively duel was immediately begun with the opposing artillery,
while General Pleasonton took to the knoll for a post of observation,
regardless of the enemy's shells, which flew like a flock of pigeons
past our battery. On the lower ground in front very sharp skirmishing ensued, our men in turn adopting the stone-wall manœuvre.
There was no word as yet of the Kelly's ford column, and our
own progress toward Brandy Station had been greatly delayed; but
nothing could be done to get on faster until our right was relieved
from the pressure of the enemy toward Beverly ford.

As soon, therefore, as General Buford had everything arranged
to his satisfaction, he ordered the reserve brigade to advance, and
ground was quickly gained on our right from wall to wall, and from
knoll to knoll, the enemy abandoning all their positions threatening
the ford, and retiring up the open fields beyond the woods, on a line
parallel with the position of their troops at St. James' Church. The
ground over which they passed is rolling, and admirably adapted for
cavalry movements. A conspicuous object in landscape was a large
brick house, to which the whirligig of war brought us for a headquarters in the following winter, and on reaching this house, to
follow the direction of the enemy's retreat, our men bore to the left,
and still advanced through open country, a ridge of high open ground
on their right, and woods for the most part on their left. Leaving
General Buford to push on as rapidly as possible, General Pleasonton
now rode to St. James' Church, where all was quiet, with no enemy
in sight. Toward Brandy Station a high hill confronted us, shutting
off all view in that direction, but Buford's success now made it possible to resume the march, which was about to be done, when General
Gregg rode into our lines from the left, reporting the results of the
operations of the Kelly's ford column, so far as he was himself aware
of them. I have no reason to question the entire accuracy of Major
McClellan's spirited account of these, and it is confirmed from various
other trustworthy sources. Before reaching Brandy Station, Colonel
Duffie had turned to his left, hoping to accomplish something in the
enemy's rear. Near Stevensburg he encountered a force of cavalry,
which was charged—the First Massachusetts and Third Pennsylvania
Cavalry in advance—and driven through and beyond Stevensburg in
disorder, as Major McClellan himself avows, with all possible candor.
Here Colonel Duffie paused, distrusting, no doubt, his isolation from
the main body of the Kelly's ford column. General Gregg had
advanced directly upon Brandy Station without opposition, and
thence to the "Fleetwood hill," where Stuart made hasty preparations to receive him. Fleetwood hill is a ridge of ground, half a
mile from Brandy Station, toward the Rappahannock, and west of
the railroad. St. James' Church is on the river side of the hill, and
Buford was now working his way up to it from that side also ; hence
while the Beverly ford column was approaching it from one side,
Gregg had been moving on it from the other, neither column having
knowledge, however, of the other's movements, whereby Stuart
escaped the consequences supposed to arise from being between two
fires. The disadvantage of operations from without inward, to
which I have alluded, is here made manifest on our side, while Stuart

by his own position and the nature of our disjointed attack, was enabled to concentrate his force within a very limited field on and near Fleetwood hill, permitting a swift reinforcement of the most endangered points, his men fighting, as it were, back to back, while ours were so widely scattered. Gregg gained this hill and the house that surmounted it, and a fierce fight was brought on, with charges and counter-charges, at the end of which Gregg found himself overmatched, and withdrew to the low ground again, losing as he fell back three pieces of artillery, after a desperate effort to save them, as Major McClellan describes.

It would, perhaps, have been better if General Gregg, postponing his attack, had borne to his right from Brandy Station until he came into connection with the Beverly ford column, but he could not certainly know this at the time, and seeing an opportunity to attack the enemy in front of him he availed himself of it like the good soldier that he was. It was after his own repulse that he was rejoined by Colonel Duffie, and meantime the enemy were pouring infantry into Brandy Station by railroad from Culpepper Court-House, introducing a new but not unexpected element to General Pleasonton's consideration. When Gregg reported all this to General Pleasonton at St. James' Church, all that was necessary to the purposes of General Hooker had been fully accomplished; the information required had been secured with unmistakable accuracy from personal observation and from the official documents captured on the field, as related by Major McClellan. There was nothing to demand any further effort on General Pleasonton's part, and in view of the approach of the enemy's infantry he determined to recross the river without further delay. He ordered General Gregg to retire by way of Rappahannock Station with the whole of the Kelly's ford column, thus bringing those troops within supporting distance of the other column on its return to Beverly ford. General Gregg left us to comply with this order, and it is only necessary to say further in regard to his column that it was not molested on its march to Rappahannock Station, and that it crossed the river there in safety, accompanied by Russell's Brigade of Infantry, which, as a precautionary measure to protect the lower fords, had hugged the river bank all day, and so far as I know had not exchanged shots with the enemy at all. General Pleasonton at the same time began the withdrawal of the cavalry and infantry from St. James' Church, and as it happened that I was dispatched by him with orders to General Buford to give up his attack and retire to Beverly ford, I am able to speak positively as to the last events of the day on our right.

When I had been last with General Buford, he had just passed the brick house which I spoke of as being a landmark in the open fields above Beverly ford, on our right, and bearing then to his left, was advancing. The ground in front of him was open for a long distance, as I have described, and had the appearance of a valley, flanked as it was by a ridge on one hand and woods on the other. On arriving now at the brick house, I saw Buford's troops engaged on high ground at the extreme end of the valley, in the edge of a wood, and I should say some two miles or more from the river. He was entirely isolated from the rest of the command with Pleasonton and Gregg; but paying no undue attention to that fact, was fighting straight on. As I rode rapidly up the valley, I met with a stream of wounded men flowing to the rear, and the rattle of carbines in front was incessant. On reaching the plateau at the end of the valley, I found the Fifth and Sixth Regulars massed in column, mounted, on the open hillside, suffering somewhat from the enemy's fire from the woods at the top of the hill on their front and right, but not replying. They were perfectly firm and steady in the ranks, and under no pressure whatever, waiting apparently for orders to advance. I inquired for General Buford, but could not learn where he was, and though it seemed hardly possible that he should be in the midst of the fierce, almost hand-to-hand fight, which was raging in the edge of the woods, he had to be found, and I could see neither him nor any of his staff in the open. It was but a few yards up the hill to the troops who were actually engaged, and as I rode among them I found myself with my own regiment, the Sixth Pennsylvania Cavalry, and at that moment the adjutant, Lieutenant Rudolph Ellis, was severely wounded, and turned his horse down the hill. I said a word to him, and was then immediately confronted by Captain Wesley Merritt, commanding the Second Regulars, who was dashing through the woods without a hat, having just lost it by a sabre cut. He was rewarded for his conspicuous gallantry on this day, and soon became a brigadier general; then, like Custer, a major general in good time, and one of the ablest and best of our cavalry commanders to the end of the war.

Of Merritt and Ellis and a dozen more, I inquired in vain for General Buford. No one knew anything of him, but the fight went on briskly all the same. Hurrying back then to the troops in the open, I reported to Major Whiting, of the Second Regulars, the senior officer present with the brigade, that I had a pressing order from General Pleasonton for General Buford to retire at once, but he could not be found, and I asked Major Whiting if he would accept the order and act on it. This he declined to do; but at that moment I caught sight of a group of officers on a bare hill to the left and in front of Major Whiting's position, and galloping there, found General Buford with his staff. I informed him of General Pleasonton's order, and as he proceeded to carry it into effect, I remained with him long enough to see that he had no difficulty in withdrawing, and that as his troops fell back they were permitted to go in peace. On returning to General Pleasonton, who was en route to Beverly ford with the troops from St. James' Church, and no enemy in pursuit, I was ordered to post a regiment of Ames' infantry on the skirt of the woods below the red brick house, in case of need for Buford's support; but Buford came along serenely at a moderate walk, and this infantry regiment had no occasion to fire a shot, the pursuit of Buford by the enemy being a mere following, as if for observation. The greater part of the troops from St. James' Church were by this time safely recrossed at Beverly ford to the north bank of the Rappahannock, and the head of Buford's column had nearly reached the river; a few moments later, when the First Regulars, who had been absent all day from the fight on some detached duty, came plunging through the ford from the northern side to offer their services if needed. General Pleasonton ordered Captain Lord, commanding the regiment, to cover the ford until Buford's column and the last of the infantry had passed the river; and in obedience to this order, Captain Lord deployed his whole regiment as mounted skirmishers on a long line, which had for its centre the knoll where our artillery had been posted in the morning. The sun had now set, but there was a mellow light on the fields, and the figures of Lord's troopers stood boldly out against the background of yellow sky above the horizon. Occasionally the dust would fly from the ground between the horses where a bullet struck, and there was a scattering fire kept up by Lord's regiment, but he did not lose a man. Meantime our guns were unlimbered on the bluff on the north bank of the river, awaiting the enemy's appearance, and at this commanding point a large group of officers was gathered, including General Pleasonton and all his staff, who watched with interest the closing scene of the long day's action of Beverly ford. There could not be a prettier sight, and it was often recalled among us. The river flowed beneath us; as far as we could see to right and left on the southern bank no living object was visible; the plain and woods in front of us were growing misty, but the burnished and glowing horizon threw everything on high ground into wonderful relief. Where the skirmishers of Lord's undulating line rose to the crest of the knoll, we could see even their features when turned in profile. The commands were all by bugle, and the notes came to us distinctly from the skirmish line until, no other troops of ours remaining on that side, the rally was sounded, and then the retreat, and the regiment trotted down to the ford and crossed it, entirely unmolested by the enemy, who, if they advanced to the river at all, were lost to us in the twilight and darkness which soon came on. Considering the distance from the river to which our troops had penetrated, and that the various columns, widely separated though they were, withdrew from their advanced positions and recrossed the Rappahannock without the slightest interruption from the enemy, I feel justified in denying that we were "driven across the river," although it was so reported by General Lee to the authorities at Richmond.

I have not attempted to dispute with Major McClellan as to the numbers in action, for such an argument is always unprofitable. We had all our available cavalry, and so had Stuart; and no doubt the numbers opposed were very nearly equal, though on neither side was the full force seriously engaged at one time, while on both sides the moral effect of infantry supports was the principal benefit derived from that source. There is no question that the action began in mutual surprise, in the sense of unexpectedness. Regarding the operations of the Kelly's ford column, and the occurrences in front of St. James' Church, there is no dispute; and it is only by implication that Major McClellan ascribes Buford's sudden withdrawal from our right to an actual repulse. On this point, following Major McClellan's example in other instances, I have thought it proper to speak from my personal knowledge. Military history could not expect an easier task than to reconcile our narratives; and it is only with a view to historic accuracy that I have denied the general terms of the official reports on his side that we were "driven across the river;" a statement which, being incorrect, may as well be corrected. The objects hoped to be gained by the reconnoissance were for once fully realized. The incidental fighting was very creditable to both sides, and it is simply a matter of fact, from which I argue nothing, that the nature of the fight was on our side more difficult than on Stuart's. The progress of the engagement brought him constantly into better position, enabling him to concentrate his troops within a very limited area around Fleetwood hill, while ours were operating from opposite points of the compass. If there was a sense of victory remaining with Stuart's men, it was natural on their seeing our men withdraw to the fords and recross the river; but there was not the

10

slightest sense of defeat on our side at nightfall, and the ultimate effects of the engagement were overwhelmingly in our favor.

The results of the battle of Beverly ford were manifold. It provided information which enabled General Hooker to move in good time to keep pace with Lee's army of invasion en route to Maryland and Pennsylvania; it chilled the ardor of Stuart's men, delaying his march, and, in fact, ruining his plans, which had soared high; it enabled General Pleasonton to anticipate him on the east flank of the Blue Ridge as he marched toward the Potomac, and to hold him in check by the well-fought battles of Aldie, Middleburg and Upperville, on the 17th, 19th and 21st of June, until Hooker's main army, followed by our cavalry, was north of the river, causing subsequent bewilderment and anxiety to General Lee throughout the campaign to the very eve of the battle of Gettysburg. In his official report General Lee declares that on the 27th of June, while his own army was at Chambersburg, "no report had been received that the Federal army had crossed the Potomac, and the absence of the cavalry rendered it impossible to obtain accurate information," though at this date the Army of the Potomac was already at Frederick City, Maryland. Again he says: "By the route Stuart pursued the Federal army was interposed between his command and our main body. The march toward Gettysburg was conducted more slowly than it would have been had the position of the Federal army been known." And, again, he mournfully reports: "It had not been intended to fight a general battle at such a distance from our base, unless attacked by the enemy; but, finding ourselves unexpectedly confronted by the Federal army, it became a matter of difficulty to withdraw through the mountains with our large trains." All this gain for our side and loss for General Lee sprang directly from the battle of Beverly ford and the consequent cavalry operations on the eastern flank of the Blue Ridge, south of the Potomac. It would be difficult to find in history the record of a cavalry battle or any battle of similar numbers on each side so fruitful of immediate, decisive results.

FLIGHT AND CAPTURE OF JEFFERSON DAVIS.

BY HON. JOHN H. REAGAN.

ON my return home, after an absence of a month, I find your letter of July 17th, inclosing a communication from General James H. Wilson to the Philadelphia WEEKLY TIMES, headed "Jefferson Davis' Flight from Richmond." You asked me to inform you how much truth there is in the statement of General Wilson, and say that you desire my answer for publication, and request me to make it full. My answer is at your disposal, and may be published or not, as you think best. I will answer this article as well as I can remember the facts at this date, and those which are material, so far as they come to my knowledge, were doubtless so impressed on my mind by the deep interest of the occasion that they will not be forgotten. I have in the outset to say that General Wilson must have written his statement from information derived from others, as he could not personally have known the facts about which he writes; and that he has either adopted the fanciful fiction of others, who know as little of the real facts as himself, or he has been egregiously imposed on. I have read the slip you send me twice carefully over; and if there is a single truth in it, outside of the great historical facts incidentally referred to, of the fall of Richmond and the surrender of General Lee, I have not discovered it. On the contrary, it is made up of statements which are utterly void of truth. I will call attention to some of them.

The statement has been made by General Wilson, as it has been made in many other newspaper articles, that "On the first Sunday in April, 1865, while seated in St. Paul's church, in Richmond,

Jefferson Davis received a telegram from Lee announcing the fall of Petersburg, the partial destruction of his army, and the immediate necessity of flight." On that point I make this statement : "On the Sunday referred to, I went by the War Department on my way to church. When at the department I was informed of two dispatches just received from General Lee, stating briefly the circumstances which made it necessary for him to withdraw his army from its position in front of Richmond and Petersburg at seven o'clock that evening, and that it would be necessary for the government archives and public property to be removed at once. On receiving this intelligence, not knowing that Mr. Davis had already received it, I walked toward his residence, which was a few hundred yards off, to confer with him about it, and on the way met him and Governor Lubbock, of his staff. We three then walked on to the Executive office. He then assembled his Cabinet, and sent for the Governor of Virginia and the Mayor of Richmond. Directions were then given to prepare the public archives for removal, and measures were considered and directions given to secure, as far as practicable, good order and safety to persons and property in the city until it should be surrendered. In this paper it is also said that, "Although he (Mr. Davis) could not have been entirely unprepared for this intelligence, it appears that he did not receive it with self-possession or dignity, but with tremulous and nervous haste ; like a weak man in the hour of misfortune, he left the house of worship and hurried home, where he and his more resolute wife spent the rest of the day in packing their personal baggage." And it is added that, "Those who are acquainted with the personal character of Mrs. Davis can readily imagine with what energy and determination she must have prepared her family for flight," etc. And that, "They may believe, too, that although heartsick and disgusted, there was nothing irresolute or vacillating in her actions."

I would express my surprise, if I could be surprised now by anything of this kind, that such a statement should come from any respectable source. Now, the truth is, Mr. Davis did not, "with tremulous and nervous haste, hurry home to his more resolute wife." From where I met him he went directly to the Executive office, where he remained nearly all day, and, if I remember right, a part of the night, looking after and giving directions in relation to public affairs, and seeming to take no notice of his private matters. He did not go to where his wife was, or act with her in preparing for flight; for neither she nor their children were in Richmond, or had been for three or four weeks before that time. And I am sure there is no man who saw Mr. Davis on that trying occasion but was impressed with his calm and manly dignity, his devotion to the public interest, and his courage. It is apparent that one object of this statement is to try to produce the impression that Mr. Davis, in the hour of extreme peril, had forgotten his great office and trust, and descended to the care of his personal baggage while the Confederate Government was dissolving; and that another of its objects was to show that, on this great occasion, he was irresolute, tremulous, nervous, and wanting in self-possession and dignity. Nothing could be further from the truth; and I venture the statement that there is no one who saw him then, or who knew his character, who would not unhesitatingly contradict such a statement; and I venture the further suggestion that neither of these charges will ever be sustained, nor will any attempt ever be made to sustain them by any legitimate or trustworthy evidence, and that no man will make such charges who has respect for truth and a just regard for his own reputation. It is just for me to say that early in the war Mr. Davis allowed all his property to be destroyed or carried away from where it was in Mississippi without making any effort to save it, and the fact was then noted as an evidence of his entire unselfishness. It is further said in this paper that, "At nightfall everything was in readiness. Even the gold still remaining in the Treasury, not exceeding in all $40,000, was packed away among the baggage," etc. If it is meant by this statement simply that the money in the Treasury, gold and all, was taken with the archives and public property away from Richmond by the proper department officers, the statement is correct; but if it is meant by this insidious form of a statement to be understood that this or any other public money was taken from Richmond in Mr. Davis' baggage, then the statement is wholly untrue.

It is also said in this paper, when speaking of the train which carried Mr. Davis and other officers from Richmond, that, "This train, it is said, was one which had carried provisions to Amelia Court-House for Lee's hard-pressed and hungry army, and having been ordered to Richmond, had taken these supplies to that place, where they were abandoned for a more ignoble freight." This whole paragraph is ridiculously absurd. No supplies were then being carried from the South toward Richmond—I mean after Lee's retreat began. And it was a train of passenger, and not of freight cars, which carried the persons referred to, and was provided for the express purpose of carrying them off. General Wilson also says: "It is stated, upon what appears good authority, that Davis had, many weeks before Lee's catastrophe, made the careful and exacting preparations for his escape, discussing the matter fully with his Cabinet in profound secrecy, and deciding that, in order to secure the escape of himself and his principal officers, the 'Shenandoah' should be ordered to cruise off the coast of Florida to take the fugitives aboard. These orders were sent to the rebel cruiser many days before Lee's lines were broken," etc. If the writer believed he had respectable authority for so important a statement, why did he not advise his readers what his authority was? No such question, nor any other question as to the means of escape, or as to instructions to the "Shenandoah" to facilitate such an escape, was ever considered by the Cabinet; nor, so far as I know or believe, was any such question considered or discussed with any member of the Cabinet. I do not believe that any such subject was considered or discussed by Mr. Davis or any member of his Cabinet at any time, before or after the surrender of General Lee. Nor do I believe that any man who regards his reputation for truth will allow himself to be given as authority for this statement.

In confirmation of this view, I may state that when Mr. Davis was informed that General Sherman would allow him to leave the United States on a United States vessel, with whoever or whatever he pleased to take with him, his reply was that he would do no act which would place him under obligations to the Federal Government, and that he would not leave Confederate soil while there was a Confederate regiment on it. I referred to this afterward in conversation with Mr. Davis, and he told me I would remember that he was one of the Senators who refused to vote the honors of the United States Senate to General Kossuth, and that his reason was that Kossuth abandoned Hungary, and left an army behind him. I may also mention that after this General Breckenridge and myself proposed that we should take what troops we had with us and go westward, crossing the Chattahoochie between Atlanta and Chattanooga, and get as many of them across the Mississippi as we could, and in the meantime keep up the impression that Mr. Davis was with us, and for him to go to the coast of Florida and cross to Cuba, and charter a vessel under the English flag and go to Brownsville, Texas, and thence return and meet us to the west of the Mississippi. He refused to assent to this plan, on the ground that he would not abandon Confederate soil. I ought to add that we were influenced to make this suggestion, because we thought him so exhausted and enfeebled that we did not think he could make the trip by land to where it was hoped to embody the troops west of the Mississippi.

I know, too, that it was Mr. Davis' purpose to try to get to the west of the Mississippi before our troops were disbanded, and to get together as many as we could, he hoped sixty or eighty thousand, and place them where they and their horses could be subsisted on the beef and grass of Texas, and where they could not be flanked by railroads and navigable rivers, and there to try and hold out for better terms than unconditional surrender.

From all this it will be seen how absurdly untrue the statement of General Wilson is. The following passage is found in his paper: "When Davis and his companions left Richmond, in pursuance of this plan, they believed that Lee could avoid surrender only a short time longer. A few days thereafter the news of this expected calamnity reached them, when they turned their faces again toward the south. Breckenridge, the Secretary of War, was sent to confer with Johnston, but found him only in time to assist in drawing up the terms of his celebrated capitulation to Sherman. The intelligence of this event caused the rebel chieftain to renew his flight, but while hurrying onward some fatuity induced him to change his plans, and to adopt the alternative of trying to push through to the southwest," etc. I have answered so much of this as refers to the supposed plan of escape. The writer seems to have been in the same predicament as many others have been, who have sought to force or to make facts to suit fanciful theories. Mr. Davis and his Cabinet were not, when they left Richmond, laboring under the belief that General Lee could avoid surrendering only a short time. It was still hoped at that time that Generals Lee and Johnston might be able to unite their armies at some point between the armies of Generals Grant and Sherman, and turn upon and defeat one of them, and take their chances for defeating the other by fighting them in detail. If I knew then where the "Shenandoah" was, I have now forgotten, and I certainly never heard the subject mentioned of an intended or desired escape from the country by her.

I think I am entirely safe in saying that neither Mr. Davis nor any member of his Cabinet contemplated leaving the country when we left Richmond, but two of them afterward determined to do so. And I do not believe that Mr. Davis or any other member of his Cabinet afterward desired to leave the country. Mr. Trenholm, prostrated by a long and dangerous illness, resigned his position as Secretary of the Treasury while we were on our way south, and went to his home. Mr. Mallory, Secretary of the Navy, and Mr. Davis, Attorney General, went to their homes, and all of them remained there until put under arrest by the authority of the

United States. Mr. Davis and myself were captured while endeavoring to make our way to the west of the Mississippi for the purpose of continuing the struggle there, if practicable, long enough to get better terms. General Breckenridge was not sent to confer with General Johnston as soon as Mr. Davis heard of the surrender of General Lee, if that is what the writer means to assert. Mr. Davis and his Cabinet remained at Danville, Virginia, for several days after being informed of the surrender of General Lee, and then went to Greensboro', North Carolina, where they remained a week or two. It was after we had left Greensboro' for Charlotte, North Carolina, and had gone as far as Lexington, in that State, that Mr. Davis received a dispatch from General Johnston, requesting him to send him assistance in his negotiations with General Sherman. General Breckenridge and myself were then sent back by him to join General Johnston at his headquarters, near Hillsboro', and to aid him in his negotiations. This was done at this time, and at the suggestion of General Johnston, and not as soon as Mr. Davis heard of the surrender of General Lee, as supposed by General Wilson. Much as Mr. Davis, no doubt, respected and esteemed General Breckenridge, it is not true that he confided his hopes to him, or to any other single person. What is said by General Wilson about the "last council of the Confederacy," is, no doubt, a fancy sketch, intended to round up handsomely this fiction, unrelieved by a single fact.

If the writer of this paper is Major General Wilson, who was in command at Macon, Georgia, when we were captured, I shall regret that he has allowed himself to be the author of such a paper, as I felt, and still feel, under obligations to him for a personal favor when I was passing that place. When we reached Macon, where we remained a few hours, we were informed that Mr. Davis and Mr. Clay, of Alabama, who were there, would be sent on to Washington City, and that I and the other prisoners were to remain there. At my own request, I saw General Wilson, and applied to him to have the order so modified as to allow me to go on with Mr. Davis. I based this request on the ground that Mr. Davis was worn down by his labors, and in feeble health; that I was the only member of his Cabinet with him, and I hoped to be of some service to him; and as we had been together through the conflict, I desired to share his fortunes whatever they might be. After some remarks by him about the danger I would invoke on myself, and my reply that I had fully considered all that, he said that he would see if the order could not be changed, and before we left there we were notified that we were all to go together. While I regretted that some others were sent on, I was grateful to him for the favor done me.

Since writing the foregoing the Philadelphia WEEKLY TIMES, of July 7th, has been put in my hands, which contains what I suppose to be the whole of General Wilson's letter. Much of it appears to be an account of military orders and of military operations with which he was connected, and about which I have no personal knowledge. What I wrote above had only reference to the portion of his letter which was then before me (the first two paragraphs of it), and has no reference to what he afterward says about military operations His paper is long and I have not leisure now to review it fully. I will say, however, that he is in error as to many of his statements of facts, and as to many of his conclusions in that part of his letter which was not before me when I wrote the foregoing pages. For instance: "He says that after he was advised by General Sherman of the armistice which was entered into between him and General Johnston, and that one of its provisions was, 'that neither party should make any change of troops during the continuance of the armistice,'" he proceeds with this further statement: "Having heard from citizens, however, that Davis, instead of observing the armistice, was making his way toward the south with an escort, I took possession of the railroads and sent scouts in all directions in order that I might receive timely notice of his movements." He then confesses to having violated the terms of the armistice, but excuses himself by saying that he had *heard from citizens* that Mr. Davis was violating it by going south with an escort. He says the first he heard of the armistice was from Generals Cobb and Smith, at Macon, Georgia, on the 20th day of April. That after that he was advised of its existence by General Sherman, and that it was "intended to apply to my [General Wilson's] command." He also says that in a short time he was informed by General Sherman, by telegram, of the termination of hostilities, and surrender of General Johnston, on the 27th of April. Now the armistice was agreed to on the 18th of April, and on the 24th of April General Sherman notified General Johnston it would terminate in forty-eight hours, leaving the parties bound by its terms until the 26th of April. Mr. Davis was at Charlotte when the treaty and armistice was agreed to. *He remained there under the terms of the armistice until the notice of its termination was given by General Sherman, and until the expiration of the forty-eight hours, when it was finally terminated, and did not leave there until he learned of the surrender of General Johnston, which took place on the 27th of April.*

General Wilson says: "The first direct information of Mr. Davis' movements reached me on the 23d of April, from a citizen, now a prominent lawyer and politician of Georgia, who had seen him at Charlotte, North Carolina, only three or four days before, and had learned that he was on his way, with a train and escort of cavalry, to the south." This citizen may have seen Mr. Davis at the time named at Charlotte. But if he did, he saw him halted there, awaiting the result of the negotiations with General Sherman, and afterward the termination of the armistice, until the 27th or 28th of April, with perfect good faith and honor, and not violating a solemn engagement, always binding on the true soldiers and honorable men, as General Wilson confesses he was, after he had been notified by General Sherman that the armistice was binding on him. And this violation of faith was aggravated by the fact that Mr. Davis was then struggling with defeat and disaster, environed on all sides by two overwhelming forces of a victorious army; while General Wilson, by his own statement, knew these facts, and had the game all in his own hands, and would have been in no danger of losing any of his advantages by acting in good faith. I leave him and his readers to determine whether he was justified in such a breach of faith by idle rumors, which he has since had ample time and opportunity to know were untrue, as the whole history of this affair has long since been within his reach. There is a statement in General Wilson's letter which is important only as showing how the most minute facts can be mis-stated, where the error can by any means cast discredit on Mr. Davis. He states, in substance, that the ferryman, where we crossed the Ocmulgee river, had told Colonel Harnden that we had crossed the river about one o'clock in the morning. This, it may have been supposed, would produce the belief that we were in precipitate flight. Now the truth is we reached that river just at dusk, and crossed it before it was fully dark, and that Mr. Davis had made his regular rides since leaving Washington, Georgia, in the day and rested at night, with the single exception of having rode across the country, north of the Ocmulgee river, a part of one night, to reach and protect his family, whom he had not seen for several weeks, against threatened evil. There is one other statement made by General Wilson which is so gross a perversion of the truth that I must quote it at length and state what did occur. He says: "Shortly after the recognition of Mr. Davis by his captors, Colonels Pritchard and Harnden rode up to where the group were standing. Davis, recognizing them as officers, asked which of them was in command. As these officers were lieutenant colonels of different regiments, belonging to different brigades of different divisions, and had, therefore, probably never before met, except casually, much less compared dates of commission, they were somewhat taken aback at the question, and hesitated what answer to make. Whereupon Mr. Davis upbraided them with ignorance, reproached them with unchivalrous conduct in hunting down women and children, and finally declared with the air and manners of a braveo, that they could not have caught him but for his desire to 'protect his women and children.' 'How would you have prevented it, Mr. Davis?' said Colonel Pritchard. 'Why, sir, I could have fought you or eluded you.' 'As for fighting us, we came prepared for that,' replied the Colonel; 'it would have saved us some trouble, and, doubtless, you a good deal; but as for eluding us, I don't think your garb is very well adapted to rapid locomotion.'"

In relation to this statement I wish to say, with whatever of emphasis I can give my words, that I was present at the time Mr. Davis and Colonel Pritchard recognized each other, as was also Governor Lubbock, and that there is *not one truth stated* in this *whole* paragraph. Colonel Pritchard did not come up for some time after Mr. Davis was made a prisoner. When he rode up there was a crowd, chiefly of Federal soldiers, around Mr. Davis. He was standing and dressed in the suit he habitually wore. He turned toward Colonel Pritchard and asked: "Who commands these troops?" Colonel Pritchard replied, without hesitation, that he did. Mr. Davis said to him: "You command a set of thieves and robbers. They rob women and children." Colonel Pritchard then said: "Mr. Davis, you should remember that you are a prisoner." And Mr. Davis replied: "I am fully conscious of that. It would be bad enough to be the prisoner of soldiers and gentlemen I am still lawful game, and would rather be dead than be your prisoner." I have often since thought and spoken of this scene and colloquy. I cannot have forgotten the substance of it. I think I repeat very nearly, or quite the words used. Not one word was said by Mr. Davis about fighting or eluding our pursuers. Not one word was said by Colonel Pritchard about saving any trouble. Not one word was said about Mr. Davis' garb, for there was nothing in his dress or appearance to call for such a remark. Not one word was said by Mr. Davis about "protecting his women and children." He only pointed to the fact that they were being robbed. I doubt if Colonel Harnden had then reached where we were; but of this I do not profess to know. I only know that a few moments before his men were fighting Colonel Pritchard's, on the north side of the creek, near which we had camped, and that few or none of the men from the other side of the creek had then reached us. And I do not think General Wilson can have had the authority of Colonel Pritchard for this statement, for he knows the facts as they are, and I cannot think would falsify them in this way.

Was this miserable falsehood about Colonel Pritchard saying to Mr. Davis, "I don't think your garb is very well adapted to rapid locomotion," intended to form another link in the chain of evidence to show that, when captured, Mr. Davis was disguised as a woman? Is it to be quoted by the next person who may write an article revamping this despicable slander, as additional and conclusive *evidence* that he was so disguised, and made conclusive by the fact that Colonel Pritchard so called attention to this disguise in the midst of the assemblage then around Mr. Davis? Outside of those who robbed the ladies and children, and those who rummaged among their wrappings, as this writer describes, I cannot believe there was one man in those two commands base enough to allow himself to be made the author of this false statement. I will not go through the disgusting details of falsehoods by which, in cold blood, twelve years after the war, when sensational statements and the bitterness of passion, and even the wish by falsehood to wrong an enemy, should have died away, General Wilson revamps and remodels the story of Mr. Davis' disguise. I will only make this statement as to what then occurred to show that if Mr. Davis had sought to disguise himself he could not have done so for want of time, and the facts show that it was impossible for him to have conceived and executed a plan of disguise. I was not immediately with him when we were attacked. Governor Lubbock, Colonel Johnston, Colonel Wood, and myself had slept under a tree, something like a hundred yards from where Mr. Davis and his family camped. We went into camp before nightfall the evening before, and had no fears of the presence of an enemy. We were misled as to our security for the time being by the following facts: We were getting well south in Georgia, with a view to turn Macon and Montgomery and pass through the piney wood country to the south of these cities, where the population was more sparse, and where the roads were not so much frequented. We were to cross the Ocmulgee river below, where it could be forded, and where there were not many ferries. On approaching that river we expected to encounter trouble, if the Federal authorities knew the course we were traveling. In this event we supposed the ferries would be guarded. When we crossed the river, about dusk, we found no opposition, and, at the same time, learned that there was a considerable cavalry force at Hawkinsville, twenty-three miles up the river from where we crossed it.

Learning that this force was so near, and seeing that the ferries were not guarded, we concluded our course was not known at that time, and traveled rather slowly the succeeding day, and went into camp, early in the evening before we were captured, with the understanding from Mr. Davis that he, Mr. Harrison, his staff officers and myself would probably go on after supper and leave his family, then supposed to be out of reach of danger, which caused us to leave our course and join them. I state all this to show our feeling of temporary security, and the reasons why we felt and acted as we did. The first warning we had of present danger was the firing just across the little creek we were camped on, which took place between the Wisconsin and Michigan cavalry, between day-dawn and full light. Colonel Pritchard, as I afterward learned from him, had some time before posted one part of his command across the road in front of us, and the other part across the road in the rear of us, and behind the little creek on which we were encamped. The firing was between these troops in rear of us and the Wisconsin troops, who were pursuing us on the road we had traveled. When this firing occurred, as Mr. and Mrs. Davis both told me afterward, Mr. Davis started out of his tent, saying to his wife, "those people have attacked us at last." (Meaning the men whom we had heard intended to rob Mr. Davis' train the night we quit our course, and went across the country to the north of the Ogeechee river.) "I will go and see if I can stop the firing; surely I will have some authority with Confederates yet." His staff officers and myself were camped about one hundred yards in the direction of the firing from him, and he supposed we were being fired on, as he told us afterward. As he stepped out of his tent, as he told me that day, he saw the troops which had been posted in front of us, and which were under the immediate command of Colonel Pritchard, in full gallop toward him, and within some sixty yards of his tent. He turned to his wife and said: "It is the Federal cavalry, and they are on us." As he turned to go out again, I understood his wife threw a waterproof cloak around his shoulders; he stepped out, and was immediately put under arrest. Directly afterward, Lubbock and myself went to him, where he was surrounded by the soldiers. He then had no cloak or other wrapping on him; was dressed in a suit of Confederate gray, with hat and boots on just as usual. Directly after this, and about the time the firing ceased between Colonel Pritchard's and Colonel Harnden's troops across the creek (I say Colonel Harnden because General Wilson says they were his, for I did not before know what officer commanded them), it was that the conversation above alluded to took place between Mr. Davis and Colonel Pritchard.

From these facts the impossibility of Mr. Davis' disguise, as charged, will be seen.   And it is out of these facts that the story of his disguise no doubt grew, with all the varied forms, more or less elaborate, it has been made to assume by sensational and reckless writers, who seem to have been willing to originate and circulate any story which they thought would gratify hate and bring ridicule on the leader of a brave people, who had risked all and lost all in a cause as dear to them as life; and under whom vast armies had been organized, many great battles had been fought, and a mighty struggle carried on for four years, which had shaken this continent, and arrested the attention of the civilized world; and which was then being supported by a million Federal soldiers, as was afterward shown by President Johnson; the leader of a cause sustained by a more united people, with clearer convictions of what was involved in the struggle, probably, than any people who ever engaged in revolution, if others may so call it, not simply to preserve slavery, but to secure the rights of local self-government, and friendly government, to a homogeneous and free people; and to secure protection against a government hostile to their interests and to an institution which had been planted in this country in early Colonial times by the Christian powers of Europe, in what they understood to be the humane policy of civilizing and Christianizing a people so barbarous then that they sacrificed, ate, enslaved, and sold each other; an institution which existed in nearly all the States of the Union when the Declaration of Independence was made, and when the Federal Constitution was adopted; an institution which was protected by the Constitution and laws of the United States, and of all the States in which it existed.   It was a struggle, whatever it may be fashionable to say about it now, of a comparatively weak people, with limited resources, against a people of more than twice their strength, and of vastly superior resources; of an unorganized people, without an army or navy or treasury, against a powerful government with all these at command; a struggle which cost more than half a million of lives, and caused the sacrifice of probably ten billions of dollars' worth of property, to gratify a fierce and aggressive fanaticism against the weaker section, and against the traditions, the Constitution and laws of the country.   But for this, history will write it down that there would have been no such war, no such sacrifice of life, and no such sacrifice of property, and the country might have gone on in its grand career the freest, the most prosperous and happy the world ever saw.

The time will some day come when the questions which led to

this war, and which have grown out of it, and the acts and motives of those who participated in it, will be discussed with candor and fairness, and with freedom from the passions and prejudices which still in some degree surround them. Then the real tiuth will be known, and those who come after us will, no doubt, do that justice to each side which neither can be expected to do to the other now, rapidly as we have advanced from the fierce passions of war toward a patriotic and fraternal restoration of good will.

WAR AS A POPULAR EDUCATOR.

BY JOHN A. WRIGHT.

WHEN the historian comes to write a truthful narrative of our civil war, the many able and varied accounts of different incidents connected therewith, that have been published in the WEEKLY TIMES, will be a source of profound satisfaction. No statement that will shed any light upon the causes, that will illustrate the condition of the people, or the progress of that dreadful contest, will be considered as useless. In the hope of contributing something toward a true history, it is here proposed to make a short statement of the general condition of the people other than of the Southern States, and more particularly of the State of Pennsylvania, when the insurrection in the South became an assured fact. The mutterings of discontent that for thirty years previous to 1861 had been heard from the South had made but little impression on the minds of the staid people of Pennsylvania. Their faith in the form of government, and the successful working for many years of the institutions engrafted into it, had given them a settled confidence in its efficiency to deal justly with all parts of the country. The people of Pennsylvania could not entertain the thought that the majority could inflict any wrong upon the minority that would be irreparable, or that would warrant any resort to rebellious measures. This conviction was no mere sentiment; it was based on an educated understanding of the principles which underlie the government itself. It is not claiming too much to argue that the marked agreement in the opinions of the people, on the questions which were raised at that time affecting the teachings of the

Constitution of the United States, was largely due to the education received by them in the public and private schools of the Commonwealth. This fact should be carefully noted by the school authorities, and the fullest provision be made in the future for the study of the history of our continent, of the government, and the principles on which the Constitution of the nation is founded.

To the general education of the people in 1861 is due the calmness of their conduct and the fixedness of their purpose. It was not the rush of youthful fire, which over-rode the wiser and more cautious thoughts of middle and old age, nor was it the yieldings of youth to the influence of older minds; but the expression of public opinion was a unit, the result of education. The only question that was deemed worthy of discussion, when the act of attempted dissolution was enacted, was not the right connected with it, but the humanitarian question of avoiding the horrors of a civil war. In connection with this educated thought of the people there was a moral training. The people of Pennsylvania were disposed to leave the solution of the slavery question to the disposition of the people of the South, and they fully understood that it was a difficult social question to manage. But when, through the great prosperity that the system of slavery had brought to the South, after many years of depression, they were convinced that its social character was to be fully merged into political efforts to secure its enlargement and continuance, then the moral sentiment was aroused in opposition to such extension of its borders and attempts at making it a permanent institution in this country, which was in opposition to their view of the true principles of the form of government. This condensed statement represents the condition of public opinion on these questions in 1860. The political sentiments and partisan relations of the people rapidly changed from the beginning of 1860. The exciting general election of that year brought out a full discussion of the prominent political questions, and as any party was supposed to sympathize with possible rebellion, so far was that party in the minority. Yet even then the probability of such a result as civil war was not accepted, nor could the people comprehend what it meant, for, with the exception of the Indian war, and the war with Mexico, their knowledge of war was as read of in books.

The financial condition of the country in the beginning of 1861 was unpromising. The difficulties of 1857 had not been forgotten; the traces and effects of the financial troubles of that year were still apparent. The country was but slowly recovering. Labor was still unemployed; wages were low; the prices of real estate had receded;

11

prices of the products of the soil and of manufactures were not remunerative, and a large amount of money laid idle for want of profitable employment. The difficulty of making collections in the Southern country increased the financial dilemma, and as the fact grew upon the people that war was inevitable, the certainty of immense losses to the merchants of the North caused further depression, and, with the announcement of war, there was an almost total collapse of credit and destruction of values. For a time the people were at sea without a compass or rudder. National growth or development always moves in lines; not like the tree that develops its branches and twigs equally, and makes, when grown, one of the most beautiful of God's creations; but nations develop as certain ideas take possession of its people, and such are run out until it is necessary to take up a new thought to preserve the results of the last. So there is always a want of completeness, of roundness, in national thought, practice and growth. When lines of thought in a nation become antagonistic, the result must be the destruction of both or the supremacy of one. To solve such questions, war comes in as the final arbiter. It is as yet a necessity. Wars between civilized people have been caused, in the past, more by diversity of opinion than by desire for conquest, and will be for years to come. War tests principles. When the successful thought assumes its position after war, it will be found to have elevated the people, advanced and enlarged their ideas, and given them a consciousness of power they did not have before they passed through this trying ordeal.

But the realities of war the people of Pennsylvania did not understand nor appreciate. The military spirit had almost died out from the impulse it received after the close of the Mexican war. Here and there, throughout this broad Commonwealth, could be occasionally heard the fife and drum, and the tramp, tramp of a few badly-drilled volunteers. Public opinion was not favorable to military organizations, and their efforts on parade were a subject of sport. It was much easier to pay a militia fine than to go through the expense and drudgery of a drill. The people thought the small national army was sufficient to man a few forts, keep up the pretense of a military organization, and take care of the Indians. They had no fear of a foreign war, and Mexico had been taught its lesson. The military school at West Point was considered by many people as a useless expense. For what good, they would ask, would be militia trainings or organized volunteer regiments, of what service an expensive army organization, when the country has no foes? The people of this country were in a position unlike those of any other nation. They did not feel directly the control of the General Government. They paid no government taxes; such as were raised were indirect. In no way was the hand of the General Government openly laid upon them or visible. So far, then, as their immediate interests were concerned, everything tended to give the people a sense of security, and the remotest thought was of a possible war. When, then, war was actually declared by the South, by firing on the flag of the country at Fort Sumter, on the 14th of April, 1861, the thrill that went through every nerve of the people of the North was a startling sensation. It wakened them up to a new fact—the struggle of ideas had commenced; war was inevitable. Whatever of secret hostility there might have been in certain quarters to the success of the North, was forbidden expression. The first gun fired at Sumter cemented the North. The thrill that awoke the people of this country to a realization of the fact of war, woke up with it their patriotism as founded upon education, religious teaching, moral principles, and the innate love of country. The education of the people enabled them to understand the issues made, with the propable consequences of any possible result, and as they thought, their minds grew and developed until they felt that the responsibility of the future of this great continent was upon them; that the great test of the democratic form of government was placed in their hands to determine. This sense of responsibility was shared by all classes, and the voice of the people of the North was so unanimous that to oppose it was at the risk of personal safety. There was then no hesitation as to what to do; but how to do it was the problem.

Here was war upon the people; war by land and by sea. There was entire unpreparedness as to organization in most of the loyal States, and in none less than in Pennsylvania. There were a few of the trained officers who served in the Mexican war available, and some of the ex-officers of the regular army, both those who had resigned after years of service, and graduates of West Point who had served in the army the legal time. Many of these were physically unfitted for duty. Yet when the call was made for 75,000 men— three months' men—the eagerness to be accepted showed the feeling of the people, and their confidence in their ability to master the new science. It required but a short experience for the people to learn that a good and reliable soldier is composed of neither hirelings nor vagabonds; but the best material to be found is necessary to constitute an army that will be obedient to orders, and submit to the severe discipline that is required. The old notion that to be a good soldier a man must lose his identity and become a machine, is an error. The experience of this country, and of Germany, in its recent war with France, proved that an intelligent soldiery is more reliable, and the degree of reliability is in proportion to the intelligent appreciation of the causes that produced the war, and what was to be done.

A very striking evidence of the want of preparation for war was exemplified in the absence of any government troops in the city of Baltimore on the 19th of April, 1861, when the Massachusetts regiment, a uniformed and well drilled body of men, was attacked on its passage through that city by a hastily gathered mob, and a large number of soldiers from the city of Philadelphia, under Colonel Small, were driven back because they were without arms and ammunition; and, further, that the General Government were deprived at that date of access northward by rail and by telegraph. It may surprise many, when they learn that for several days after the 19th of April, 1861, almost the entire correspondence between the Eastern, the Middle, and the Western States, and the government at Washington, was carried by private messengers, sent daily by various routes from Harrisburg to Washington, and *vice versa*, under the instructions of Governor A. G. Curtin. The necessities of the situation after the government's requisition for three months' men was filled, developed the importance of something more than a militia organization for the protection of the people and their property in the State of Pennsylvania. What the future might produce the wisest men at that time could not foresee. What effect a possible success on the part of the South might have been on the position of some of the leading men in the North, was unknown.

The Governor of Pennsylvania, A. G. Curtin, with great wisdom and foresight, recommended to the Legislature of that State the formation of fifteen full regiments—thirteen to be of infantry, one of light artillery, and one of cavalry—to be known as the "Reserve Volunteer Corps of Pennsylvania," to be used firstly in the defense of the State, and, secondly, to be transferred to the authority of the General Government if not required by the State—thereby covering any probable situation that the chances of war might produce. The eagerness to enter the army in defense of the life of the nation very rapidly filled these regiments. They were organized and officered under the authority of Governor Curtin, as well as clothed, equipped and provisioned at the expense of the State. The history of this organization, the only one of its kind in the States, has been often and well written, and as long as the State of Pennsylvania maintains a separate existence, or the records of history preserve the sad story of the civil war, so long will be preserved the record of the bravery and skill of the men and officers of the Reserve Corps of the State of Pennsylvania. After the inglorious defeat at Bull Run—a battle between undrilled men, where the chances of success or defeat were at best but equal—the terror and dismay which prevailed over the North was rapidly quieted when it was known that Governor Curtin had offered this Reserve Corps to the General Government for three years' service. It was a nucleus around which a new army might be formed, and one that could maintain its ground in defense of the capital after the discharge of the three months' men, and until rein-forced by the soldiers of other States. The best that could be done, in the haste to join the regiments for the three months' service, was to push the men forward to the front as rapidly as they were mustered into service; but here was a body of men, while their drill had not been completed, and to soldiers of older service would have been but raw recruits, yet they had the organization and accepted the idea of long and hard service, and very rapidly adapted themselves to the new situation.

The battle of Bull Run, the return of the three months' men, the attack and defense of Fort Sumter, the early efforts of the navy, very rapidly educated the people in what war was, and how it was to be met. With success, the public mind exhibited a constant tendency to go back to its state of quiet. Adversity aroused the people, and developed increased determination and energy. The change that the first year of the war produced in the condition of the people was marked. The government becoming the employer, there was a demand for labor, for all kinds of manufactured goods and articles, for the productions of the soil, for the building and armament of ships of war, and war material. The inventive powers of the people were taxed to produce deadlier weapons and more destructive guns, to increase certainty of result in attack, as well as safety in defense. Very many of the inventions thus worked out have been adopted and modified by the experienced engineers and artillerists of the Old World, and have given our makers of firearms a pre-eminence which secures them large orders from these governments. The "Monitor," the Gatling, the breech-loading guns, both great and small, and many others might be mentioned in this list of inventions thus used. The impetus to productions of all kinds, arising from the demands for government supplies, and the heavy tariffs that was placed on imported goods through the increased price of gold, gave the fullest employment to the people. Emigration rapidly increased, and as the country was losing its best men on the battle-fields and in the hospitals, their places were rapidly filled by the hardy emigrants. The abundance of money and apparent prosperity gave rise to an undue spirit of speculation. The people acted as though the money expended by the government, and the lives lost, was so much added to the value of property in place of properly considering it as a loss; and it did seem at one time as if the higher the prices of land, of labor, and material rose, the greater was the demand for all. These things gave the appearance of the highest state of prosperity, and did much to make many people look upon war as the legitimate road to success. Among the civilized nations of the earth the United States has, in proportion to the means of her people, occupied a high place in the line of humanitarian institutions. War means the wounding of men, the presence of diseases which come from exposure, hardships, irregularities of living and overtasking of powers of endurance. It means mental as well as physical agony; it makes widows and orphans, leaving them helpless and poor; it takes away from old age the support of the strong-armed son; the tendency of war on the morals of men in the army is bad, the excitement of the passions, the absence of home restraints and home comforts operate injuriously.

The presence of all these liabilities and evils to which the men were exposed who offered their lives in defense of their country excited in the people an earnest desire and a feeling of imperative duty to provide for them in the way best fitted to meet the varied demands. The medical department of the government developed great ability in the professional part of its work and great inventive power in planning hospitals, ambulances, couches, chairs, etc., many of which should be added to the list of improvements which foreign governments have adopted. In the French and German war the hospital accommodations were largely copies of the plans worked out by the officers in charge of the medical department of our army. Wherever permanent hospitals were built, every aid and attention that could be furnished by the voluntary contribution of the people, both male and female, were gladly offered—whether these contributions were in the form of flowers to enliven the sufferer, and of enticing cookery to tempt the appetite, of willingness to be eyes, arms or hands to write the letters of love to those at home, or whatever was needed that would comfort the invalid. The Sanitary Commission and the Christian Commission were as ready to afford all the comfort and aid they could on the field of battle or in the far off temporary hospital as in the permanent hospital. Aid was tendered the widow and the orphans, and the aged fathers and mothers were not neglected. Every care was taken that all moral influences should be placed around the men. Everything was done that would in any way contribute to the comfort and well-being of the men engaged in the service of the country; and, while no amount of attention will remove the sufferings and hardships that go with war, yet it was found to be possible to ameliorate some of their sufferings and to provide for the living. The State of Pennsylvania again, through the recommendation of Governor A. G. Curtin, who was as ready to recommend the care of all sufferers by the war as he was to urge by his eloquent voice the people to arms in defense of the nation, provided for the education and sustenance of the orphan children of dead soldiers. This noble institution has done a great work, and many will rise to call the State blessed.

From a quiet, peaceful people, but little interested in the world's progress, innocent of a knowledge of the arts of war, cultivating the soil, digging in the mines, melting the ore, handling goods—though these were done with little profit—quietly awaiting better times, with ill-will to no nation or section of our own country, with confidence in the perpetuity of the government, and faith in its power, though unseen, to protect them, if needed, with their school-houses and churches conveniently placed and well attended; from this state of almost pastoral quiet they had been awakened on one Sabbath morning in April, 1861, and in a year they are a restless, nervous people, thoroughly absorbed in a great civil war, accounts reaching them daily, and almost hourly, of a success here, or a defeat there, with the lives of their friends, their relatives—brothers, sons, husbands at peril; this people talk and think of war, its management, its strategies, its losses, and its honors, as though they had been students of war all their lives. Those at home are at work for those in the field or on the sea; the women prepare bandages, and nurse the sick and wounded in place of the lighter employments of a home-life. The people have learned what it is to support the government, and their means are poured out in its defense; for if their government fails, they see but little hope for the future. The children in the school-houses are taught about war; the playful drill of the boys, the play-gun and cannon, are instilling into them what may be the necessities of the future; the girls are as proud of their boy-soldiers as the maiden when the country places its laurel wreath of honor on her beloved. The churches are crowded with thoughtful worshipers, prayers are earnest; there is something to pray for. It is a test of the God they worship—the deliverance of the Israelites from bondage is in their minds, and when the cloud is darkest they see light through the darkness. The people are in deep earnest, every power is strained. What a change one year has produced. The real condition of the people before the war will be, perhaps, as well understood by the contrast with that of 1862 and succeeding years. That this war has produced like effects with all other wars of principle is unquestioned. The people of this country lived a century in the four years of war. The realities of life with its probabilities were taught them by a new teacher. They learned the value of a stable government, the necessity that in its Constitution there must exist all power to perpetuate and preserve its life; that this continent can only be developed under a strong government, and made a safe home for the millions that will till its fields, cultivate its fruits, clear its forests, mine its ores, teach its children, and give higher education to its people in all the arts and sciences that will add to their happiness. This war taught the people their strength and their ability to meet promptly and adequately every emergency, and developed the great truth that a republican form of government can withstand and overcome an internal revolution. This truth is the more strongly marked by the character, ability and perseverance of the people of the revolting States. The war was a hard, bloody struggle—but man's salvation is by the same emblem.

FIRE, SWORD, AND THE HALTER.

BY GENERAL J. D. IMBODEN.

THE years 1862 and 1864 were the most eventful of the war in the Shenandoah Valley. During the spring of the first, "Stonewall" Jackson made his famous twenty-eight days' campaign, with 13,000 men, against Generals Milroy, Banks, Fremont and Shields, driving them all out of the valley, with their aggregate forces of about 64,000 men. In 1864 the Federal operations were conducted successively by Generals Sigel, Hunter and Sheridan, when that splendid valley was desolated and scourged with fire and sword. It is proposed in this paper merely to give some account of General David Hunter's performances during his brief command in June and July, 1864, of the Federal forces in the Valley, and to lay before the people of this country, and especially of the Northern States, some facts that may explain why here and there are still found traces of bitter feeling in many a household in the South, not against the government of the United States, but against some of the agents and means employed by them in the name of the government, to crown their arms with success. As long as the present race inhabiting that famous and glorious Valley, and their descendants, retain the characteristics that inspired them with unbounded admiration for, and heroic devotion to, Lee and Jackson, as their ideals of Christian soldiers, the memory of General David Hunter will live and be handed down through the generations to come—it may be, in the long future, only by legend and tradition—in connection with deeds that illustrate how far the passions, fanaticism, and hate engendered by civil war can drag a man down, from the boasted civilization of our age and country, to the

(169)

barbarism and implacable personal animosities of that long period of cruel persecution, oppression, and outrage which, by the common consent of mankind, we denominate "The Dark Ages." These are strong expressions, but if the facts to be detailed do not justify them, then the people of the Shenandoah Valley, from whom General Hunter sprung, as an offshoot—transplanted to New Jersey—of one of the most honorable, numerous and distinguished family connections in Virginia, have lost the high sense of justice and love of right which even political opponents and belligerent enemies have freely accorded them in peace and war. What I write is history—every fact detailed is true, indisputably true, and sustained by evidence, both Confederate and Federal, that no man living can gainsay, and a denial is boldly challenged, with the assurance that I hold the proofs ready for production whenever, wherever, and however required. Perhaps no one now living was in a better position to know, at the time of their occurrence, all the details of these transactions than myself.

On the 21st of July, 1863, after General Lee had withdrawn his army from the battle-field of Gettysburg to Virginia, he, by special order, assigned me to the command of "The Valley District," in Virginia. The "district" embraced all that part of Virginia west of the Blue Ridge Mountain, and so far to the southwest as the James river, in Bottetourt county. It was created as a separate territorial command in 1861–2, for General Jackson, and continued as such after his death up to the close of the war. I held the command of the district up to December, 1864, except at short intervals, when the exigencies of the service required a larger body of troops than I had to be sent into the Valley, under officers of higher rank, who, of course, would assume command of me and the district till called away, when it would revert to me again. The position I thus held in my native valley and among my own people, not only made me cognizant of all that transpired when in command myself, but when officers in higher rank and their troops were sent to defend the Valley, they naturally looked to me for information about the enemy and his doings, and consulted freely with me; so that I knew everything that was going on on our side, and I had a hand in it.

Sigel's defeat at New Market, on the 15th of May, 1864, by a force less than one-half his own, proved in the end a great calamity to the people of the Valley, as it undoubtedly led to a change of Federal commanders; and the women and children of that country who experienced the mild military rule of the gentlemanly and

brave German, and of General Hunter successively, had cause to
regret that the former lost his command by a disastrous conflict
with their husbands, brothers and fathers at New Market, where
men fought men from "early morn till dewy eve," and a successor
was appointed, who soon enlarged the field of martial enterprise till
it embraced as fit objects of his valor and his vengeance the helpless,
unarmed and defenseless : decrepid age, gentle womanhood, and innocent childhood sharing alike the unpitying hostility of an army
commander whose prototype their Scotch-Irish ancestors had taught
them to abhor by the traditions they had brought over of the career
of Claverhouse on the Scottish border—a man whose deeds in the
end proved no small impediment to the union of England and Scot-
land, because of the bitter animosities their cruel nature had excited
to such a degree that even time had failed to obliterate them.

About the 1st of June, Hunter, having been reinforced to the
full extent of Sigel's losses in men and munitions, began his advance
upon Strasburg, up the Valley toward Staunton; Averill and Crook
moving simultaneously from the Kanawha region, in West Virginia,
so as to effect the junction of all their forces about the middle of the
month at Staunton, and thence move on Lynchburg.   When Hunter
took up his line of march, I had less than one thousand Confederate
soldiers in the Valley, General Breckenridge having not only withdrawn his own troops after the battle of New Market, but taking also
my largest regiment, the Sixty-second Virginia, to the aid of General
Lee, who was sorely pressed by General Grant with overwhelming
numbers on that memorable march from the Rappahannock to the
James.   Having full information of the combined movements of
Hunter, Crook, and Averill, and of their strength and purpose to
unite in the Valley, I communicated it to General Lee and the Confederate Secretary of War, announcing my utter inability to cope
with them successfully with only about one thousand veteran
soldiers.   General Lee informed me that he could not then send me
any assistance from the army near Richmond, but would direct
General William E. Jones, who was in Southwestern Virginia, to
come to my aid with every available man he could raise; and that I
might retard Hunter's advance as much as possible, he ordered me
to call out the "reserves" of Rockingham and Augusta counties.
These "reserves" were an improvised militia force composed of old
men over fifty years of age, and boys between sixteen and eighteen,
and were armed with shot-guns, hunting rifles and such odds and
ends of firearms as a state of war had scattered through the country.
To this order about seven hundred old men and boys responded,

chiefly mounted, and that generally on farm work-horses. My policy was to avoid a collision with any larger body of Hunter's troops than his advance guard, and to inform the people that we were falling back slowly in expectation of large reinforcements then on their way to my support. I knew that any such statement would be repeated to the enemy, and cause him to advance with great caution. On the afternoon of the 2d we had our first skirmish near Lacy Springs, a few miles north of Harrisonburg. The next day, I was pressed so hard that I had to fall back to the south bank of the North river, at Mount Crawford, seventeen miles from Staunton, losing a few men killed and wounded during the afternoon. Hunter camped at Harrisonburg. I made a rather ostentatious display of a purpose to dispute seriously the passage of the river next day, by throwing up some works on the hill tops overlooking the bridge and felling trees in the fords for several miles above and below.

During the night about two thousand men, sent forward by General Jones, joined me. To my dismay I found they were not generally organized in bodies larger than battalions, and in companies and fragments of companies hastily collected from Southwestern Virginia, between Lynchburg and Tennessee, and in large part indifferently armed. Indeed, many of the men were convalescents taken from the hospitals, and furloughed dismounted cavalrymen who had gone home for a remount, and were taken possession of by General Jones wherever he could find them, and hurried by rail through Lynchburg and Staunton to the front. I spent the entire night of the 3d in obtaining a list of all these small bodies of men, out of which by daybreak on the 4th I had composed, on paper, two brigades and assigned officers to their command. General Jones arrived at my headquarters a little after sunrise, and on reviewing my operations on paper, he adopted them, and at an early hour in the morning the various detachments were aggregated in their respective temporary brigades. During the day General Vaughan, of Tennessee, with from six hundred to eight hundred of his greatly reduced brigade, also joined us. We now had a force of something over four thousand men, including one regular and excellent six-gun battery, and one extemporized artillery company of "reserves," from Staunton, with five guns. Hunter, with eleven thousand superbly-appointed troops of all arms, was only eight miles distant in our front, and Crook and Averill, with seven thousand more, only two days' march in our rear; the two bodies rapidly approaching each other, and we between them in the condition I have just described, and with no hope of further assistance. Obviously our policy was to fight Hunter at the earliest moment, and possibly defeat him, and then turn upon Crook and Averill and do the best we could. Generals Jones, Vaughan and myself were all of the same grade brigadiers, Jones being the senior by a few months, and Vaughan ranking me also by a little older commission than mine. Jones, of course, assumed the command. He was an old army officer, brave as a lion, and had seen much service, and was known as a hard fighter. He was a man, however, of high temper, morose and fretful to such a degree that he was known by the soubriquet of "Grumble Jones." He held the fighting qualities of the enemy in great contempt, and never would admit the possibility of defeat where the odds against him were not much over two to one. So that when he took command of our little army, consisting of only a part of my brigade, not over one thousand men; Vaughan's Brigade, six hundred to eight hundred men; the two temporary conglomerate brigades under Colonels Brown and Jones, of about one thousand men each, and about seven hundred "reserves," a total of between four thousand and four thousand five hundred men, including the two batteries, he was entirely confident that he could whip Hunter. We fully expected an attack early on the morning of the 4th. The enemy not appearing, however, up to ten o'clock, I sent a regiment of cavalry—the Eighteenth Virginia, under Colonel George W. Imboden—to Hunter's side of the river to find out what he was doing. In a couple of hours it was ascertained that he had left the main road leading from Winchester to Staunton, and was marching to the southeastward to Port Republic, at the junction of the North and South rivers, which unite there near the foot of the Blue Ridge and form the Shenandoah. This flank movement disappointed and somewhat disconcerted General Jones. It imposed on him the necessity of a night march over roads he had never seen to get in position between Port Republic and Staunton.

As we were in my native county, Augusta, I knew every road, and almost every farm over which Hunter would pass. I did not, therefore, hesitate to urge on General Jones to let me select the point of conflict with Hunter. He consented to this, and I chose the crest of what is known as "Mowry's hill," an eminence overlooking the beautiful little vale of Long Meadow run, about eight miles northeast of Staunton. To this ground Jones decided to move on the night of the 4th, and in the morning throw up some works to cover our most vulnerable points. He ordered me to place my cavalry close in front of Hunter during the night, as we knew he would camp at Port Republic, and to avoid any risky engagement in the morning, to obstruct his advance as much as I could, so as to give our infantry time to strengthen their position as much as possible before the general battle, which we expected to come off about noon on the 5th. I took position during the night about two miles from Hunter's outposts. He began his march about daybreak, and by sunrise we came in collision with his cavalry so unexpectedly that I became more seriously engaged than I intended or my instructions warranted, and had great difficulty in extricating my command from what, for a little while, was a most perilous position. As it was, I lost one of my best companies, Captain F. M. Imboden's, of the Eighteenth Virginia Cavalry, which was cut off from all support, overpowered and captured.

Our next stand was made near Piedmont, where, to my amazement and against my solemn and angry protest, General Jones had decided to fight, instead of at Mowry's hill, three miles further back. We were formed in *echelon*, leaving a gap of nearly four hundred yards between our right and left wings. The two first assaults made on our left wing, where Jones commanded in person, were gallantly repulsed, but General Hunter discovering the fatal gap in our line between the right and left wings, rapidly formed a column of attack under cover of some woods, and, sweeping rapidly down on our exposed centre, pierced the line at this point, and striking the right flank of our left wing, doubled the line back on itself, resulting in the wildest confusion and great loss to us. The brave and gallant Jones was instantly killed when most heroically endeavoring to change his alignment to receive the blow he saw descending so portentously on his centre. A braver soldier never lived, and had he survived that day I doubt not he would have manfully admitted the error his over-confidence led him into. I never learned the reason for his change of plans, but infer that it was occasioned by a telegram he had received the night before from General Lee, and which the enemy found on his body, to the effect that no additional troops could be sent to the Valley for several days, and he must therefore fight Hunter as quickly as possible, and beat him back before Crook's and Averill's advent on the scene; and as Hunter had the day before flanked our position at Mount Crawford, making considerable detour by way of Port Republic, I think Jones concluded that his opponent sought to evade a conflict till the last possible moment, thus increasing the probabilities of a junction with Crook and Averill; and that if such was his purpose he would either not attack us at Mowry's hill, or would seek to flank it by another detour either to the right or left. Reasoning thus, and entirely confident that if he could engage Hunter anywhere that day he could beat him, he disregarded topographical considerations of advantage, and sought his enemy at the nearest point.

Our loss was over 1,500 in killed, wounded and captured, but if the pursuit had been more vigorous it would have been far worse for us. The cavalry did make a demonstration after the battle, but my cavalry brigade, and about seventy-five or eighty Tennessee rifle-men on foot, and McClanahan's six-gun battery, arrested their charge and drove them back, when we were permitted to move off without further molestation. The next day Hunter proceeded to Staunton, only eleven miles from the battle-field, and was there joined by Crook and Averill, increasing his force to some 18,000 men. We camped that night at Fisherville, seven miles east of Staunton, on the Chesapeake and Ohio Railroad, and next morning fell back to Waynesborough, at the western base of the Blue Ridge, where we supposed Hunter would attempt to cross Rockfish Gap on his way to Lynchburg. Up to his occupation of Staunton, where his army was so much strengthened by Crook and Averill as to relieve his mind of all apprehension of disaster, his conduct had been soldiery, striking his blows only at armed men. But at Staunton he com-menced burning private property, and, as will be seen further on, the passion for house-burning grew upon him, and a new system of war-fare was inaugurated that a few weeks afterward culminated in the retaliatory burning of Chambersburg. At Staunton his incendiary appetite was appeased by the burning of a large woolen mill that gave employment to many poor women and children, and a large steam flouring mill, and the railway buildings. He made inquiries, it was said, for my own residence; but as I had sold it, a few months before, to a man of "loyal" proclivities, it was spared.

Hunter remained two or three days at Staunton, and on the 9th of June moved toward Lexington, on his route to Lynchburg. On the 8th, General Breckenriage arrived at Rockfish Gap with a small force drawn from General Lee's army, and assumed command, and immediately began preparing for the defense of Lynchburg. General John McCausland, with his cavalry brigade, was ordered to keep in front of Hunter, and delay and harass him as much as possible, a task which he performed with signal ability, skill, and bravery. Hunter having sent General Duffie, with the brigade under his command, into the county of Nelson, east of the Blue Ridge and south of Rockfish Gap, I was ordered in pursuit and to protect Lynchburg, which was almost defenseless, from surprise by this cavalry detachment. The people of Nelson and Amherst counties, never having had the enemy before in their midst, were greatly excited and alarmed, and brought to me the wildest reports of the enemy's doings, and the most exaggerated accounts of his strength. Such information embarrassed me so much from its apparently authentic and yet often contradictory character that I decided to reach Lynchburg as soon as possible, and by a route that would enable me to save from destruction the bridges on the Orange and Alexandria Railroad, one of the lines of communication between Richmond and Lynchburg essential to the defense of the latter. I accomplished this object, but failed to encounter Duffie, who recrossed the mountains and joined Hunter at Lexington. On his march from Staunton to Lexington, when near Brownsburg, General Hunter ordered a thing to be done, so abhorrent to all our ideas of war between Christian and civilized powers, that a simple recital of the facts, without further comment, will answer all the purposes of history.

At the breaking out of the war, David S. Creigh, an old man of the highest social position, the father of eleven sons and daughters, beloved by all who knew them for their virtues and intelligence, resided on his estate, near Lewisburg, in Greenbrier county. His reputation was of the highest order. No man in the large county of Greenbrier was better known or more esteemed; few, if any, had more influence. Beside offices of high public trust in civil life, he was an elder in the Presbyterian church of Lewisburg, one of the largest and most respectable in the Synod of Virginia. In the early part of November, 1863, there being a Federal force near Lewisburg, Mr. Creigh, on entering his house one day, found a drunken and dissolute soldier there using the most insulting language to his wife and daughters, and at the same time breaking open trunks and drawers, and helping himself to their contents. At the moment Mr. Creigh entered, the ruffian was attempting to force the trunk of a young lady teacher in the family. Mr. Creigh asked him to desist, stating that it was the property of a lady under his protection. The villian, rising from the trunk, immediately drew a pistol, cocked it, pointed it at Mr. Creigh, and exclaimed: "Go out of this room. What are you doing here? Bring me the keys." Mr. Creigh attempted to defend himself and family, but a pistol he tried to use for the purpose snapped at the instant the robber fired at him, the ball grazing his face and burying itself in the wall. They then grappled, struggled into the passage, and tumbled down stairs, the robber on top. They rose, and Mr. Creigh attempted to wrest the pistol from the hands of his adversary, when it was accidentally discharged, and the latter wounded. They struggled into the portico, where the ruffian again shot at Mr. Creigh, when a negro woman, who saw it all, run up with an axe in her hand, and begged her master to use it. He took it from her and dispatched the robber. After consultation and advice with friends it was decided to bury the body, and say nothing about it.

The troops left the neighborhood, and did not return till June, 1864, when they were going through to join Hunter. A negro belonging to a neighbor, having heard of the matter, went to their camp and told it. Search was made, the remains found, and Mr. Creigh was arrested. He made a candid statement of the whole matter, and begged to be permitted to introduce witnesses to prove the facts, which was refused, and he was marched off with the army, to be turned over to General Hunter, at Staunton. On the 10th of June, Hunter camped near Brownsburg, on the farm of the Rev. James Morrison. About dark, a rather elderly man knocked at the door, announcing himself as the Rev. Mr. Osborn, of Uniontown, Pennsylvania, a chaplain in the army. He requested to see Mr. Morrison, stating that they had with the army a citizen of Greenbrier, whose name was Creigh, who was about to be executed; his doom had just been announced to him. He stated that Mr. Creigh claimed to be well acquainted with Mr. Morrison, and asked an interest in his prayers, as he was closely confined in a negro cabin, and no communication would be permitted with him. All efforts to visit him that night were in vain. He was first ordered to be executed that night, but was indulged to live till morning, that he might write to his family. The next morning, a little after daylight, he was brought out, put into a wagon, and conveyed up a little vale, about a quarter of a mile north of the house, and in full view of it, and was there hanged and left hanging till after the army had departed, when the wife of the venerable minister—he being too feeble—with such assistance as she could get, took down the body, wrapped it in a blanket, and buried it in a grave dug on the spot. Mr. Creigh had no trial, no witnesses, no counsel nor friends present, but was ordered to be hanged like a dog for an act of duty to his helpless wife and daughters.

From Brownsburg General Hunter proceeded to Lexington, encountering only such delay as McCausland could effect with a single brigade of cavalry. At Lexington he enlarged upon the burning operations begun at Staunton. On his way, and in the surrounding country, he burnt mills, furnaces, storehouses, granaries, and all farming utensils he could find, beside a great amount of

12

fencing, and a large quantity of grain. In the town he burnt the Virginia Military Institute, and all the professors' houses except the superintendent's (General Smith's), where he had his headquarters, and found a portion of the family too sick to be removed. He had the combustibles collected to burn Washington College, the recipient of the benefactions of the Father of his Country by his will; but, yielding to the appeals of the trustees and citizens, spared the building, but destroyed the philosophical and chemical apparatus, libraries and furniture. He burned the mills and some private stores in the lower part of the town. Captain Towns, an officer in General Hunter's army, took supper with the family of Governor John Letcher. Mrs. Letcher having heard threats that her house would be burned, spoke of it to Captain Towns, who said it could not be possible, and remarked that he would go at once to headquarters and let her know. He went, returned in a half hour, and told her that he was directed by General Hunter to assure her that the house would not be destroyed, and she might, therefore, rest easy. After this, she dismissed her fears, not believing it possible that a man occupying Hunter's position would be guilty of wilful and deliberate falsehood to a lady. It, however, turned out otherwise, for the next morning, at half-past eight o'clock, his assistant provost marshal, accompanied by a portion of his guard, rode up to the door, and Captain Berry dismounted, rang the door-bell, called for Mrs. Letcher, and informed her that General Hunter had ordered him to burn the house. She replied: "There must be some mistake," and requested to see the order. He said it was verbal. She asked if its execution could not be delayed till she could see Hunter? He replied: "The order is peremptory, and you have five minutes to leave the house." Mrs. Letcher then asked if she could be allowed to remove her mother's, her sister's, her own and her children's clothing. This request being refused, she left the house. In a very short time they poured camphene on the parlor floor and ignited it with a match. In the meantime Miss Lizzie Letcher was trying to remove some articles of clothing from the other end of the house, and Berry, finding these in her arms, set fire to them. The wardrobe and bureaus were then fired, and soon the house was enveloped in flames. Governor Letcher's mother, then seventy-eight years old, lived on the adjoining lot. They fired her stable, within forty feet of the dwelling, evidently to burn it, too; but, owing to the active exertions of Captain Towns, who made his men carry water, the house was saved. While Hunter was in Lexington, Captain Mathew X. White, residing near the town, was arrested, taken about two miles, and, without trial, was shot, on the allegation that he was a bushwhacker. During the first year of the war he commanded the Rockbridge Cavalry, and was a young gentleman of generous impulses and good character. The total destruction of private property in Rockbridge county, by Hunter, was estimated and published in the local papers at the time as over $2,000,000. The burning of the Institute was a public calamity, as it was an educational establishment of great value.

From Lexington he proceeded to Buchanan, in Bottetourt county, and camped on the magnificent estate of Colonel John T. Anderson, an elder brother of General Joseph R. Anderson, of the Tredegar Works, at Richmond. Colonel Anderson's estate, on the banks of the Upper James, and his mansion, were baronial in character. The house crowned a high, wooded hill, was very large, and furnished in a style to dispense that lavish hospitality which was the pride of so many of the old-time Virginians. It was the seat of luxury and refinement, and in all respects a place to make the owner contented with his lot in this world. Colonel Anderson was old— his head as white as snow—and his wife but a few years his junior. He was in no office, and too old to fight—hence was living on his fine estate strictly the life of a private gentleman. He had often, in years gone by, filled prominent representative positions from his county. There was no military or public object on God's earth to be gained by ruining such a man. Yet Hunter, after destroying all that could be destroyed on the plantation when he left it, ordered the grand old mansion, with all its contents, to be laid in ashes.

From Buchanan he proceeded toward Lynchburg, by way of the Peaks of Otter; but on arriving within four miles of the city, where a sharp skirmish occurred between General Crook's command and three brigades under my command, at a place called the Quaker Meeting-House, he ascertained that General Early was in town with Stonewall Jackson's old corps. This was enough for him. That night he began a rapid retreat toward Salem, leaving his cavalry to make demonstrations on Early's lines long enough to give him a good day's start. He thus made his escape with little loss—the heaviest of it consisting of some ten or twelve field-guns that fell into our hands near Salem. He escaped through the mountains into West Virginia, and reached the Ohio by way of the Kanawha Valley. If he had been attacked the evening of the affair at the Quaker Meeting-House, or had been vigorously pursued early next morning, I think the probabilities are that his entire army would have been captured. They were weary from long marching, and, from all accounts, greatly demoralized after the retreat began. Indeed, it was currently reported, and generally believed on our side, that Hunter was, himself, in so much alarm for his personal safety that it incapacitated him to direct the retreat, and that General Crook, in fact, saved their army. After Hunter's retreat, General Early moved down the Valley, and, in July, menaced Washington, before Hunter had time to get around to its defense. But I do not intend to detail Early's operations. After a few days on the north side of the Potomac, he came back to the Virginia side, whither Hunter followed.

I shall conclude this already long narrative by citing a few more instances of Hunter's incendiarism in the Lower Valley. It seems that, smarting under the miserable failure of his grand raid on Lynchburg, where, during a march of over two hundred miles, the largest force he encountered was under Jones at Piedmont, and he routed that, thus leaving the way open to reach Lynchburg within three days, destroy the stores there and go out through West Virginia unmolested, he had failed to do anything but inflict injury on private citizens, and he came back to the Potomac more implacable than when he left it a month before. His first victim was the Hon. Andrew Hunter, of Charlestown, Jefferson county, his own first cousin, and named after the General's father. Mr. Hunter is a lawyer of great eminence, and a man of deservedly large influence in his county and the State. His home, eight miles from Harper's Ferry, in the suburbs of Charlestown, was the most costly and elegant in the place, and his family as refined and cultivated as any in the State. His offense, in General Hunter's eyes, was that he had gone politically with his State, and was in full sympathy with the Confederate cause. The General sent a squadron of cavalry out from Harper's Ferry, took Mr. Hunter prisoner, and held him a month in the common guard-house of his soldiers, without alleging any offense against him not common to nearly all the people of Virginia, and finally discharged him without trial or explanation, after heaping these indignities on him. Mr. Hunter was an old man, and suffered severely from confinement and exposure. While he was thus a prisoner, General Hunter ordered his elegant mansion to be burned to the ground, with all its contents, not even permitting Mrs. Hunter and her daughter to save their clothes and family pictures from the flames; and, to add to the desolation, camped his cavalry within the inclosure of the beautiful grounds, of several acres, surrounding the residence, till the horses had destroyed them.

His next similar exploit was at Shepherdstown, in the same

county, where, on the 19th of July, 1864, he caused to be burned the residence of the Hon. A. R. Boteler, "Fountain Rock." Mrs. Boteler was also a cousin of General Hunter. This homestead was an old colonial house, endeared to the family by a thousand tender memories, and contained a splendid library, many pictures, and an invaluable collection of rare and precious manuscripts, illustrating the early history of that part of Virginia, that Colonel Boteler had collected by years of toil. The only members of the family who were there at the time were Colonel Boteler's eldest and widowed daughter, Mrs. Shepherd, who was an invalid, her three children, the eldest five years old and the youngest eighteen months, and Miss Helen Boteler. Colonel Boteler and his son were in the army, and Mrs. Boteler in Baltimore. The ladies and children were at dinner when informed by the servants that a body of cavalry had turned in at the gate, from the turnpike, and were coming up to the house.

It proved to be a small detachment of the First New York Cavalry, commanded by a Captain William F. Martindale, who, on being met at the door by Mrs. Shepherd, coolly told her that he had come to burn the house. She asked him by what authority. He told her by that of General Hunter, and showed her his written order. On reading it, she said: "The order, I see, sir, is for you to burn the houses of Colonel Alexander R. Boteler and Mr. Edmund I. Lee. Now this is not Colonel Boteler's house, but is the property of my mother, Mrs. Boteler, and therefore must not be destroyed, as you have no authority to burn her house." "It's Colonel Boteler's *home*, and that's enough for me," was Martindale's reply. She then said: "I have been obliged to remove all my personal effects here, and have several thousand dollars' worth of property stored in the house and outbuildings, which belongs to me and my children. Can I not be permitted to save it?" But Martindale curtly told her that he intended to "burn everything under roof upon the place." Meanwhile, some of the soldiers were plundering the house of silver spoons, forks, cups, and whatever they fancied, while others piled the parlor furniture on the floors, and others poured kerosene on the piles and floors, which they then set on fire. They had brought the kerosene with them, in canteens strapped to their saddles. Miss Boteler, being devoted to music, pleaded hard for her piano, as it belonged to her, having been a gift from her grandmother, but she was brutally forbidden to save it; whereupon, although the flames were roaring in the adjoining rooms, and the roof all on fire, she quietly went into the house, and seating herself for the last time before the instrument, sang her favorite hymn: "Thy will be done." Then shutting down the lid and locking it, she calmly went out upon the lawn, where her sick sister and the frightened little children were sitting under the trees, the only shelter then left for them.

Martindale's written order from Hunter also embraced another Virginia home. He burned it, too. The story is told by the gifted mistress of that household in the following letter, which was delivered to Hunter. I have been furnished a copy, with permission to publish it. This letter will live in history for its eloquence and sublime invective:

SHEPHERDSTOWN, VA., July 20th, 1864.

General Hunter:—

Yesterday, your underling, Captain Martindale, of the First New York Cavalry, executed your infamous order and burned my house. You have the satisfaction ere this of receiving from him the information that your orders were fulfilled to the letter; the dwelling and every outbuilding, seven in number, with their contents, being burned. I, therefore, a helpless woman whom you have cruelly wronged, address you, a Major General of the United States Army, and demand why this was done? What was my offense? My husband was absent— an exile. He never had been a politician or in any way engaged in the struggle now going on, his age preventing. This fact your chief-of-staff, David Strother, could have told you. The house was built by my father, a Revolutionary soldier, who served the whole seven years for your independence. There was I born; there the sacred dead repose. It was my house, and my home, and there has your niece (Miss Griffith), who has tarried among us all this horrid war up to the present moment, met with all kindness and hospitality at my hands. Was it for this that you turned me, my young daughter and little son out upon the world without a shelter? Or was it because my husband is the grandson of the Revolutionary patriot and "rebel," Richard Henry Lee, and the near kinsman of the noblest of Christian warriors, the greatest of generals, Robert E. Lee? Heaven's blessing be upon his head forever! You and your government have failed to conquer, subdue or match him; and, disappointed, rage and malice find vent on the helpless and inoffensive.

Hyena-like, you have torn my heart to pieces! for all hallowed memories clustered around that homestead; and, demon-like, you have done it without even the pretext of revenge, for I never saw or harmed you. Your office is not to lead, like a brave man and soldier, your men to fight in the ranks of war, but your work has been to separate yourself from all danger, and with your incendiary band steal unaware upon helpless women and children, to insult and destroy. Two fair homes did you yesterday ruthlessly lay in ashes, giving not a moment's warning to the startled inmates of your wicked purpose; turning mothers and children out of doors, your very name execrated by your own men for the cruel work you gave them to do.

In the case of Colonel A. R. Boteler, both father and mother were far away. Any heart but that of Captain Martindale (and yours) would have been touched by that little circle, comprising a widowed daughter just risen from her bed of illness, her three little fatherless babes—the oldest not five years old—and her heroic sister. I repeat, any *man* would have been touched at that sight. But, Captain Martindale! one might as well hope to find mercy and feeling in the heart of a wolf bent on his prey of young lambs, as to search for such qualities in his bosom. You have chosen well your agent for such deeds, and doubtless will promote him!

A colonel of the Federal army has stated that you deprived forty of your officers of their commands because they refused to carry out your malignant mischief. All honor to their names for this, at least! They are *men*—they have human hearts and blush for such a commander!

I ask who, that does not wish infamy and disgrace attached to him forever, would serve under you! *Your* name will stand on history's page as the Hunter of weak women and innocent children; the Hunter to destroy defenseless villages and refined and beautiful homes—to torture afresh the agonized hearts of the widows; the Hunter of Africa's poor sons and daughters, to lure them on to ruin and death of soul and body; the Hunter with the relentless heart of a wild beast, the face of a fiend, and the form of a man. Oh, Earth, behold the monster! Can I say, " God forgive you ? " No prayer can be offered for you! Were it possible for human lips to raise your name heavenward, angels would thrust the foul thing back again, and demons claim their own. The curses of thousands, the scorn of the manly and upright, and the hatred of the true and honorable, will follow you and yours through all time, and brand your name *infamy! infamy!*

Again, I demand why have you burned my house? Answer as you must answer before the Searcher of all hearts; why have you added this cruel, wicked deed to your many crimes ?

HENRIETTA E. LEE.

I have only recited the more prominent incidents of Hunter's brief career in the Valley of Virginia. The United States Government could not stand it, his army could not stand it, as many of his prominent officers yet living tell how keenly they felt the stigma such acts—beyond their control—brought on them. Shortly after the date of Mrs. Lee's letter he was removed, to the honor of the service, and General Sheridan was his successor—of his career, perhaps, anon! If the people of Chambersburg will carefully read this record of wanton destruction of private property, this "o'er true tale" of cruel wrong inflicted on the helpless, they will understand why, when goaded to madness, remuneration was demanded at their hands by General Early, and upon its refusal retaliation was inflicted on the nearest community that could be reached, and it was their misfortune to be that community. Contrast Lee in Pennsylvania, in 1863, and Hunter in Virginia, in 1864, and judge them both as history will.

UNION VIEW OF THE EXCHANGE OF PRISONERS.

BY GENERAL ROBERT S. NORTHCOTT.

I HAVE been a regular reader of the "Unwritten History of the Late War," as published in the WEEKLY TIMES. I read the history of the exchange of prisoners by Judge Ould, the Confederate Commissioner of Exchange, in which Secretary Stanton and other Federal officers are charged with violating the cartel, while the Confederate authorities are represented as acting in good faith. I believe that I will be able to show that all the obstructions to the exchange of prisoners during the late war were the result of bad faith in the President of the Southern Confederacy. On the 2d of July, 1862, a cartel was agreed upon by the belligerents, in which it was stipulated that all prisoners captured by either party should be paroled and delivered at certain points specified within ten days after their capture, or as soon thereafter as practicable. This was to be done in all cases except those in which commanding generals on the battle-field paroled their prisoners by agreement. No other paroles were valid. If a guerrilla chief captured a foraging party, and paroled those who composed it, it amounted to nothing, and if their officers ordered them into immediate service, it was no violation of the cartel.

In March, 1863, the gallant General A. D. Streight, then Colonel of the Fifty-first Indiana Infantry, by order of General Rosecrans, made a raid at the head of a picked brigade, setting out from Murfreesboro, Tennessee, and proceeding into the northern part of Alabama, and thence into Northern Georgia. When he had advanced as far as Rome, Georgia, he was intercepted by the Con-

(184)

federate General Forrest, with a largely superior force, and his retreat being cut off, he was compelled to make the best terms he could with his enemy. General Forrest gave him as liberal terms of surrender as he could expect. It was stipulated that Colonel Streight and his officers and men were to be paroled and passed into the Federal lines at as early a period as practicable. General Forrest furnished Colonel Streight with a copy of the terms of surrender, and him and each of his officers with a copy of his parole, and they were sent to Richmond to await a flag-of-truce boat to convey them into the Federal lines. When they arrived at Richmond, Colonel Streight and all his commissioned officers were confined in Libby prison, while the enlisted men belonging to his command were forwarded into the Federal lines; but Colonel Streight's copy of the terms of surrender, and the duplicate paroles of himself and officers, were taken from them, and they were informed that President Davis had decided that they should not be conveyed within the Federal lines, according to the terms of their surrrender, but that they would be returned to Alabama upon a requisition from Governor Shorter, to be tried by the courts of that State upon a charge of abducting slaves (a few negroes had been found as camp followers of Streight's army, at the time of his surrender). Here was a violation of the cartel by Jeff Davis himself. He ignored the action of one of his military commanders, who, in the exercise of his power, had committed himself to a line of conduct that Davis, as his superior, should have seen was executed in good faith.

Colonel Streight and his officers were, accordingly, retained in Libby to await the pleasure of the President of the Southern Confederacy to return them to the State of Alabama, there to be tried for negro stealing. This was the merest child's play; for, although negroes were found with Streight's army, President Davis and Governor Shorter both knew that it would be impossible to fasten the crime of negro stealing upon Colonel Streight, or any of his officers. They knew that Federal army officers were not bound to return runaway slaves; but the whole matter was trumped up for the purpose of punishing a gallant commander and his brave officers for having the courage to raid two hundred miles into the enemy's country. Here was a direct violation of the cartel. But he was guilty of other violations of it. In the winter of 1863, he issued an order forbidding the exchange of any officers belonging to the command of General Milroy, who then occupied Winchester, Virginia, with a considerable force. This he did without any just cause, for neither General Milroy, nor any of his officers, had violated the laws of civilized warfare.

But to return to Colonel Streight and his officers. They were retained in Libby, expecting every day to be sent to Alabama; but, in the meantime, Colonel Ludlow, the United States Commissioner of Exchange, arrived upon a flag-of-truce boat at City Point, near Richmond, with one hundred Confederate prisoners to exchange for Colonel Streight and his officers. Judge Ould, in compliance with instructions received from his President, informed Colonel Ludlow that Colonel Streight and his officers had been demanded by Governor Shorter, of Alabama, and that the Confederate Government had decided to comply with this demand, and, consequently, could not send them; but he would send all the other officers except Streight's command, and give him credit for the one hundred Confederate officers. There were not a dozen Federal officers in prison at that time beside Streight's command. He proposed sending the full equivalent for the hundred as soon as they should be captured. Of course, Colonel Ludlow refused to accede to this proposition, but answered Judge Ould that unless Streight and all his officers were delivered he would return with the Confederate prisoners. Judge Ould persistently refusing to send Streight and his officers, Colonel Ludlow, accordingly, returned with them.

Another violation of the cartel by the Confederate authorities came about in the following manner: Generals Morgan, Imboden, Ferguson, McNeil, and other guerrilla chiefs had captured a considerable number of Federal soldiers, made up of small foraging parties, stragglers, etc., and paroled them when and where captured, in order to avoid the trouble and expense of conveying them to any of the points designated in the cartel. These paroles not being valid, the men accepting them were ordered to duty immediately; but these paroles were all charged to the Government of the United States. After General Grant had captured Vicksburg, and paroled Pemberton's army, every member of that army was declared exchanged, as an offset to the irregularly paroled Federal prisoners, when the former amounted to three times as many as the latter. At this time the Federal Government had a large excess of prisoners; but, as the Confederate Government had violated the cartel whenever any advantage was to be gained by it, it was deemed expedient not to exchange. Shortly after the Vicksburg exchange, Judge Ould proposed to exchange man for man, according to rank, provided the party having the excess would parole them. This was an act of cool effrontery; for, had the Federal Government acceded to it, the Confederacy would have claimed the right to retain Streight and his men, all officers commanding negro soldiers, all negro prisoners, and all others against whom they could have trumped up charges. They had then gone so far that they refused to release chaplains and surgeons. They would have obtained 20,000 men above an equivalent for the Federal prisoners which they held. These 20,000 would have been thrown into the field, judging from the former course of the Confederate authorities.

The Confederate Government either did not understand the usages of civilized warfare, or else violated them wilfully Federal officers, who fell into their hands, were frequently condemned to close confinement in damp cells, upon frivolous charges. In the summer of 1863, General Neal Dow was captured near Port Hudson, Louisiana, and first sent to Richmond, and confined in Libby prison, but was shortly transferred to Pensacola, Florida, and placed in close confinement upon some frivolous charge. He was kept there a few months, and then returned to Libby, without being tried, or even knowing what the charges against him were. Captains Sawyer and Flinn were condemned by lottery to suffer death by hanging without any just cause. The gallant General Harry White was subjected to much annoyance, and his exchange refused and delayed, because he was a member of the State Senate of Pennsylvania, and had he been exchanged, he would probably have resumed his place in the Senate, which would have given his party one majority in that body. Notwithstanding the Federal Government frequently offered liberal terms of exchange for him, the Confederates persistently refused, and on the 25th of December, 1863, he was sent to Salisbury, North Carolina, and there placed in close confinement. He was kept there and in other Southern prisons until the following September, when he made his escape, and succeeded in reaching the Federal lines at Knoxville, Tennessee. Such treatment as General White received was violative of the rules of civilized warfare.

The treatment of General Goff, of West Virginia, by the Confederates, was more reprehensible, if possible, than that of General White. General Goff, at the time of his capture, was Major of the Fourth West Virginia Cavalry. He was confined in Libby prison with other Federal officers for a short time, when it was concluded to place him in close confinement, as a hostage for a Confederate Major, by the name of Armsey, who had been condemned to be executed by hanging, but whose sentence had been commuted to fifteen years' solitary confinement in Fort Delaware by President Lincoln. This Armsey, at the beginning of the war, was a citizen of Harrison county, West Virginia. At the beginning of the war he took part with the rebellion, and was commissioned major. Some time in the spring of 1863, Armsey returned to his home, which was then in the Federal lines, and commenced recruiting clandestinely for the Confederate service, and while engaged in this work was captured, and condemned to death by hanging. When the finding of the court-martial was presented to the President for approval, he commuted the sentence to solitary confinement, as above stated. Though the proceedings in Armsey's case were regular, and in strict accordance with the usages of war, the Confederate Government protested against his punishment, and when Major Goff was captured, resolved to put him into like confinement as Armsey, as a measure of retaliation, and Major Goff was accordingly taken from Libby to Salisbury, and placed in close confinement, and kept there for several months. Major Goff had been guilty of no infraction of the laws of war. He was then very young, and belonged to a wealthy and influential family, residing in the same county as Armsey, and he was punished as a hostage more to gratify the private malice of some Confederates, who suggested it, than for any principle involved. Officers in command of negro troops were treated with all kinds of indignity, when they were so unfortunate as to fall into rebel hands. On one occasion, two line officers, commanding negro troops, were captured with two negro soldiers. Upon their arrival at Libby prison a small apartment was extemporized, and all four confined together, and the officers compelled to mess with the negroes as a measure of degradation.

In December, 1863, General Benjamin F. Butler was made Federal Commissioner of Exchange, by an order from the War Department. The Confederate Government refused to communicate with him, because Jeff Davis had, at one time during Butler's military administration at New Orleans, issued a proclamation, solemnly and pompously declaring General Butler an outlaw. All communications from the Confederate Government, for a time, were addressed to Major Mulford, who was in command of the flag-of-truce steamer; but the Confederates soon saw their folly, and subsequently treated with General Butler in relation to the exchange of prisoners. But the refusal to treat with General Butler was another obstruction thrown in the way of the exchange of prisoners used by the Confederate Government.

A cartel binds both belligerent parties, and when one party violates it for the purpose of gaining some advantage, the other party is not bound to abide by the obligations of the contract. That the Confederate Government first violated the cartel, there can be no doubt. The forbidding of the exchange of General Milroy's officers, was a violation of it; the holding of, and refusing to exchange, Streight and his officers, was a violation; the sentence of Sawyer and Flinn to be hung, was a violation; the declaring of the Vicksburg prisoners exchanged, was a violation; the refusal to exchange officers commanding negroes, was a violation; the treatment of General White, and the treatment of General Goff, were direct infractions, as was the holding of surgeons and chaplains as prisoners of war.

It must be borne in mind that President Davis issued his orders declaring General Butler an outlaw, and had refused to exchange General Streight and his officers, before the United States Government refused to return Confederate prisoners; and even after the first infraction of the cartel, the government at Washington continued to send Confederate prisoners to Richmond, until the refusal to exchange Streight and his officers. The truth is, the Federal Government found it impossible to continue the general exchange of prisoners without giving the Confederate Government the power to deal unjustly with many of the Federal officers who fell into their hands. Had Jefferson Davis and his confederates been permitted to keep Streight and his officers, and turned them over to the Governor of Alabama, to have a mock trial in his State courts, on the false charge of negro stealing, and condemned to imprisonment at hard labor in the Alabama penitentiary; had they been permitted to hang Sawyer and Flinn, and commit indignities upon other Federal officers whom they desired to maltreat, they would, of course, have been glad to continue the exchange. But the demand of the Confederates just amounted to this: They must hang or keep in close confinement every Federal officer against whom they chose to prefer charges of a violation of the laws of war, and all officers commanding negro troops, while they required the Federal Government to return to them all prisoners captured. They acted all the time as if the Federal Government were bound to a strict obedience to the laws of war, while they were exempt from that obedience, because they were rebels. They hung spies, and denied the Federal Government that right. They assumed the right to declare that officers commanding negro troops, and negro troops themselves, were not entitled to the humanities of war. They assumed that the United States should not be governed by the accepted code of warfare, but by one specially manufactured for them by the Confederate Government. By this code, if a commander of the Union army hung a spy, the Confederate Government would hang a Federal

soldier or officer of equal rank, who was no spy, by way of retaliation.   By this code, the United States Government were required to
deliver all the Confederate prisoners captured, while the Confederate
Government should be permitted to retain any prisoners they chose,
and condemn them to execution, or otherwise maltreat them.

So far as the treatment of prisoners while confined in the Confederate military prisons is concerned, I have carefully refrained
from saying anything, and I have written this chapter only to vindicate the truth of history.

THE MORALE OF GENERAL LEE'S ARMY.

BY REV. J. WILLIAM JONES, D. D.

IN his testimony before the "Committee on the Conduct of the War," Major General Joseph Hooker says: "Our artillery had always been superior to that of the rebels, as was also our infantry, *except in discipline;* and *that,* for reasons not necessary to mention, never did equal Lee's army. With a rank and file *vastly inferior to our own, intellectually and physically,* that army had, *by discipline alone,* acquired a character for steadiness and efficiency unsurpassed, in my judgment, in ancient or modern times. We have not been able to rival it, nor has there been any near approximation to it in the other rebel armies." [Italics mine.]

I do not propose to enter upon any "odious" comparison between the Army of the Potomac and the Army of Northern Virginia, as to the character of the men who composed them; yet, I think I shall be able to show that General Hooker is entirely mistaken in attributing the confessed superiority of the Army of Northern Virginia to "*discipline alone,*" and that this army was composed of a body of men who, in all the qualities which go to make up what we call *morale,* were rarely, if ever, equaled, and never surpassed by any army that ever marched or fought "in all the tide of time."

The very circumstances which produced the organization of that army called into it the flower of the South. On the memorable 17th day of April, 1861, the day on which the Virginia Convention passed its Ordinance of Secession, I witnessed at the little village of Louisa Court-House, Virginia, a scene similar to those enacted all over the South, which none who saw it can ever forget. The "Louisa Blues," a volunteer company, composed of the very best young men of the county, were drilling at noon on the Court green, when a telegram from Richmond ordered them to be ready to take a train of cars at sundown that evening. Immediately all was bustle and activity; couriers were sent in every direction to notify absentees, and in every household busy fingers and anxious hearts were engaged in preparing these brave volunteers to meet promptly the call of their native Virginia. There was scarcely a laggard or a skulker in the whole company. Delicate boys, of scarcely sixteen, vied with gray-haired fathers in eagerness to march to the post of duty, and an hour before the appointed time that splendid company (numbering considerably more than its original roll strength) gathered at the depot, where an immense crowd had assembled to see them off. An aged minister of the Gospel spoke words of earnest counsel, and led the multitude in fervent prayer that the God of Jacob might go forth with these patriot soldiers, keep them in the way whither they went, and bring them back to their homes in safety and peace; but, above all, that he would shield them from the vices of the camp, and lead them into paths of righteousness.

The man of God is interrupted by the shrill whistle of the iron horse—the train dashes up to the depot, all are soon aboard, and, amid the waving of handkerchiefs, the cheers of the multitude, and the suppressed sobs of anxious mothers, wives, sisters, and daughters, those noble men go forth at the bidding of the sovereign power of their loved and honored State. At Gordonsville they are joined by companies from Staunton, Charlottesville, and the University of Virginia; and Orange, Culpepper, and other counties along the route swell their numbers as they hasten to the capture of Harper's Ferry, and the defense of the border. The call of Virginia now echoes through the land, and from seaboard to mountain valley the tramp of her sons is heard. Maryland, the Carolinas, Georgia, Florida, Alabama, Mississippi, Kentucky, Tennessee, Arkansas, Louisiana, Missouri, and distant Texas, catch the sound—her sons in every clime heed the call of their mother State; and these rush to our Northern border—the very flower of the intelligence, the wealth, the education, the social position, the culture, the refinement, the patriotism, and the religion of the South—to form the armies of the Shenandoah, and Manassas, and Norfolk, which those masters of the art of war, J. E. Johnston and Beauregard, moulded into what was afterward the famous Army of Northern Virginia, with which our peerless Lee won his series of splendid victories.

It was common for the Northern press to represent that "secession leaders" betrayed the people of the South, and led them unawares and unwilling into "the rebellion," and many of the so-called "histories" still insist that the "Union" men of the South were forced against their will into "the revolt." Never were a people more misrepresented. The simple truth is, that after Mr. Lincoln issued his proclamation, calling for troops to coerce sovereign States, there ceased to be any "Union" party in the South, and the people of every class and every section prepared for resistance to the bitter end, and *forced their leaders* to join the secession movement. A public sentiment was at once formed, which not only impelled our best men to enter the army, but branded, as a "skulker," the able-bodied young man who failed to do so. This spirit affected the character of all of the armies of the Confederacy, and none more than the Army of Northern Virginia.

The colleges of the South were deserted, and professors and students alike enlisted. The "learned professions" were suspended, and the office abandoned for the camp. The hum of the workshop ceased, the plough was left in the furrow, the ledger was left unposted, in many instances the pastor enlisted with the men of his flock, and the delicate sons of luxury vied with the hardy sons of toil in meeting patiently the hardships, privations, and sufferings of the camp, the march, the bivouac, or the battle-field. I remember that the first time I ever saw the "Rockbridge Artillery"—that famous battery which was attached to the "Stonewall Brigade" at the first battle of Manassas, with Rev. Dr. (afterward General) Pendleton as its captain—it had as private soldiers in its ranks no less than seven Masters of Arts of the University of Virginia (the highest evidence of real scholarship of any degree conferred by any institution in this country), a large number of graduates of other colleges, and a number of others of the very pick of the young men of the State, among them a son of General R. E. Lee, and a score or more of theological students. Two companies of students of the University of Virginia were mustered into service, and fully nine-tenths of the five hundred and fifty students, who were at the University that session, promptly entered the Confederate service—most of them the Army of Northern Virginia—as private soldiers.

When Rev. Dr. Junkin, of Pennsylvania, who was then president of Washington College, Lexington, Virginia, called a meeting of his faculty to devise means of punishing the students for raising a secession flag on the dome of the college, the day after Virginia seceded, he found the faculty in hearty sympathy with the students;

13

and while the doctor resigned his position, and went North, the students formed a volunteer company, and marched to the front under Professor White as their captain. Even Dr. Junkin's own sons threw themselves heartily into the Confederate struggle, while his son-in-law left his quiet professor's chair at Lexington to become the world-famous "Stonewall Jackson." The president of Hampden-Sidney College, Virginia (Rev. Dr. Atkinson), entered the service at the head of a company of his students. Major T. J. Jackson marched the corps of cadets of the Virginia Military Institute from the parade-ground at Lexington at precisely twelve o'clock on the day he received orders from the Governor of the Commonwealth, and all these young men entered active service. Indeed, every college in Virginia, and throughout the South, suspended its regular exercises, and the "midnight lamp" of the student was exchanged for the "camp-fires of the boys in gray."

There might have been seen in the ranks of one of the companies a young man who met every duty as a private soldier with enthusiasm, but who carried in his haversack copies of the Greek classics, which he read on the march or around the camp-fires, who has, since the war, borne off, at a German university, the highest honor ever won there by an American; who now fills the chair of Greek in one of the most important universities at the South, and who has already won a place in the very front rank of American scholars. I remember another (a Master of Arts of the University of Virginia), whom I found lying on an oilcloth during an interval in the battle of Cold Harbor, in 1864, oblivious of everything around him, and deeply absorbed in the study of Arabic, in which, as in other Oriental languages, he has perfected himself, since the war, at the University of Berlin, and by his own studies in connection with the professorship he fills, until he has now no superior, and scarcely an equal, in that department in this country. In winter quarters, it was very common to organize schools, in which accomplished teachers would guide enthusiastic students into the mysteries of Latin, Greek, modern languages, and the higher mathematics.

One single shot of the enemy, at first Fredericksburg, mortally wounded Colonel Lewis Minor Coleman (professor of Latin at the University of Virginia), who was widely known and loved as the accomplished scholar, the splendid soldier, the high-toned gentleman, and the humble Christian; Randolph Fairfax, one of the most accomplished young men and brightest Christians in the State; and Arthur Robinson, a grandson of William Wirt, and a worthy son of an illustrious sire.

I count it my proud privilege to have entered the service as "high private in the rear rank" of the famous old Thirteenth Virginia Infantry, and I do not hesitate to affirm that (while that regiment was not superior to others of our army in *morale*) it would be impossible to pick out of any community in the land a nobler body of men than they were. Our colonel was A. P. Hill, who, by gallantry and skill, and solid merit, rose to the rank of lieutenant general; achieved a reputation for the highest qualities of the soldier, and on that last sad day at Petersburg, with a sick furlough in his pocket, yielded up his noble life in an attempt to restore his broken lines. Our lieutenant colonel was James A. Walker, who won his wreath and stars by cool courage and notable skill; who was the last commander of the old "Stonewall Brigade;" who led Early's old division to Appomattox Court-House, and who has since occupied a prominent position; is now Lieutenant Governor, and exerts a potent influence in the affairs of the Commonwealth. Our major was J. E. B. Terrill, one of the very best drill-masters in the service, whose gallantry was conspicuous on every occasion, and whose well-merited appointment as brigadier general the Confederate Senate confirmed at the very hour at which he fell at Bethesda Church, in June, 1864, while leading the old Fourth Virginia Brigade in a heroic charge. Our company officers were, many of them, men fitted for the highest command, and among the rank and file were those competent, in every respect, to command a brigade, or even a division. There were not a few private soldiers in that army who were wealthy planters, merchant princes, leading citizens, men of rank and influence, at home.

It has been a subject of general remark that since the war our Governors, legislators, Congressmen, Senators, Judges, city and county officers, our leading business and professional men, the engineers on our railroads, the professors in our colleges, and even our preachers, have been, as a rule, selected from among those who "wore the gray." The Radical press has sneered at this, and held it up as a proof of the existence of a "rebellious spirit" still in the South. It is true that there is a feeling among our people that they owe something to the men who risked their lives for what they believed to be the cause of justice and right; but the real truth of the matter is that when we look for one of our *best* men to fill any position of honor, emolument or trust, we naturally turn to a Confederate soldier—for the native talent, education, and moral worth of the South were in our army.

But the *religious* element which entered that army, or was developed in it, has absolutely no parallel in all history. Our

noble old chief (General Lee) was a Christian, not merely in profession, but in reality, and did everything in his power to promote
the moral and spiritual welfare of his army.   The piety of
"Stonewall" Jackson is as historic as his splendid military achievements, and the influence which he exerted for the religious good of
his officers and men can never be fully known in this world.   These
noble leaders had at the first the co-operation of such Christian
soldiers as Generals D. H. Hill, T. R. Cobb, A. H. Colquitt, J. E. B.
Stuart, W. N. Pendleton, John B. Gordon, C. A. Evans, John
Pegram, and a large number of other general, field, staff, and subordinate officers; and, during the war, Generals Ewell, Longstreet,
Hood, Pender, R. H. Anderson, Rodes, Paxton, Baylor, and a
number of others made professions of religion.   Of the first four
companies from Georgia, which arrived in Virginia, three of the
captains were earnest Christians, and fifty of one of the companies
belonged to one church.   I remember one single regiment which
reported over four hundred church members, when it first came into
service, and another regiment which contained five ministers of the
Gospel—a chaplain, one captain, and three privates.

I have not space to give the details, but I have in my possession
the minutes of our Chaplains' Association, my diary carefully kept at
the time, files of our religious newspapers, a large number of letters
and memoranda from chaplains and army missionaries, and other data,
going to show that the world has rarely witnessed such revivals as we
had in Lee's army from the autumn of 1862 to the close of the war.   I
never expect to address such congregations, or to witness such results,
as we *daily* had in that army.   I frequently preached to several
thousand eager listeners, and I have seen over five hundred inquirers
after the way of life present themselves at one time, and have
witnessed hundreds of professions of conversion at one service.   I
preached one day in Davis' Mississippi Brigade to a large congregation who assembled in the open air, and sat through the service with
apparently the deepest interest, notwithstanding the fact that a
drenching rain was falling at the time.   Upon several occasions I
saw barefooted men stand in the snow at our service, and one of the
chaplains reported that in February, 1864, he preached in the open
air to a very large congregation, who stood in snow several inches
deep during the entire service, and that he counted in the number
fourteen barefooted men.   And this eagerness to hear the Gospel
was even more manifest during the most active campaigns.   On
those famous marches of the Valley campaign of 1862, which won
for our brave fellows the *soubriquet* of "Jackson's Foot Cavalry," I

never found the men too weary to assemble in large numbers at the evening prayer-meeting, and enter with hearty zest into the simple service. At half-past seven o'clock in the morning the day of the battle of Cross Keys, a large part of Elzey's Brigade promptly assembled on an intimation that there would be preaching; the chaplain of the Twenty-fifth Virginia Regiment (Rev. Dr. George B. Taylor, now a missionary to Italy) was interrupted at "thirdly," in his able and eloquent sermon, by the advance of the enemy, and soon the shock of battle succeeded the invitations of the Gospel.

The morning Early's Brigade was relieved from its perilous position at Warrenton White Sulphur Springs, on the second Manassas campaign, and recrossed to the south side of the Rappahannock, one of the largest congregations I ever saw, assembled for preaching. A fierce artillery duel was going on at the time, across the river, and a shell would occasionally burst nearer than was entirely comfortable; but the service went on, despite this strange church music, and the woods rang with hundreds of strong voices, swelling the strains of an old hymn, which recalled precious memories of home, and the dear old church of other days, as, at the same time, it lifted tender hearts up to the God whom they worshiped. Just as the last stanza of the last hymn, before the sermon, had been finished, and the preacher arose to announce his text, an immense rifle-shell fell in the very centre of the congregation, and buried itself in the ground, just between the gallant colonel of the Thirteenth Virginia and one of his captains. Fortunately, it failed to explode, and only threw dirt over all around. There was, of course, some commotion in that part of the congregation; but quiet was soon restored, and the chaplain announced his text, and was proceeding with his sermon, when Colonel Walker informed him that, if he would suspend the service, he would move the brigade back under shelter of the hill. Accordingly, the command was moved back (a member of an artillery company was wounded just as our rear left the ground), and I preached to one of the most solemnly attentive congregations it was ever my fortune to address. At "early dawn" of the next day, we moved on that splendid march which threw "the foot cavalry" on Pope's flank and rear, and compelled him (despite his general orders) to look to his "lines of retreat," and to realize the now prophetic words of that famous order: "Disaster and shame lurk in the rear." Alas! many of those gallant fellows heard that day, on the Rappahannock, their last message of salvation.

The night before the last day at the second Manassas, Colonel

W. H. S. Baylor was in command of the old Stonewall Brigade, of which he was made brigadier general the very day he was killed. Sending for his friend, Captain Hugh White, he said to him: "I know the men are very much wearied out by the battle of to-day, and that they need all of the rest they can get to fit them for the impending struggle of to-morrow; but I cannot consent that we shall seek our repose until we have had a brief season of worship, to thank God for the victory of to-day, and to beseech His continued protection and blessing during this terrible conflict." The men were quietly notified that there would be a short prayer-meeting, and nearly the whole of the brigade, and a number from other commands, assembled at the appointed place. The service was led by Rev. A. C. Hopkins, of the Second Virginia Infantry—one of those faithful chaplains who was always at the post of duty, even though it should be the post of danger. Captain Hugh White entered into the meeting with the intelligent zeal of the experienced Christian. Colonel Baylor joined in with the fervor of one who had but recently felt the preciousness of a new-born faith in Christ, and it was a solemn and impressive scene to all. In the great battle which followed, the next day, Colonel Baylor, with the flag of the "Stonewall" Brigade in his hands, and the shout of victory on his lips, fell, leading a splendid charge, and gave his noble life to the cause he loved so well. Hard by, and about the same moment, Captain White was shot down, while behaving with most conspicuous gallantry; and these two young men had exchanged the service of earth for golden harps, and fadeless crowns of victory.

I remember that on the comparatively quiet Sabbath with which we were blessed at Cold Harbor, in June, 1864, I preached four times to large and deeply solemn congregations. The service at sundown was especially impressive. Fully three thousand men gathered on the very ground over which had been made the grand Confederate charge which swept the field at Cold Harbor and Gaines' Mill, on the memorable 27th of June, 1862. It was a beautiful Sabbath eve, and all nature seemed to invite to peace and repose; but the long lines of stacked muskets gleaming in the rays of the setting sun, the tattered battle-flags rippling in the evening breeze, the scattering fire of the picket line in front, the occasional belching of the artillery on the flanks, and the very countenances of those powder-begrimed veterans of an hundred fights, all spoke of victories in the past, and terrible conflicts yet to come. The whole scene was inspiring, and as I gazed into those eager, upturned faces, and saw that

"Something on the soldier's cheek
Washed off the stain of powder,"

I tried, with an earnestness I have rarely, if ever, commanded, to tell them the story of the Cross—to hold up Christ as "the way, the truth, and the life"; and I remember that there were quite a number who, at the close of the service, signified their personal acceptance of the way of salvation.

All during that memorable campaign, as well as in the trenches at Petersburg, the revival spirit was unabated, and incidents of thrilling interest occurred. I have in my possession carefully collated statistics, to show that, during the four years of its existence, at least *fifteen thousand* soldiers of the Army of Northern Virginia professed faith in Christ, and that these professions were as genuine and as lasting as those of any of the churches at home.

These statistics are not given at random, but are very carefully compiled from the minutes of our Chaplains' Association, the reports of chaplains and army missionaries made at the time, and other sources of information, which fully satisfied me that *fifteen thousand* is a really low estimate of the number of converts. And as to the genuineness of these professions, I am prepared to prove that in their after lives in the army—their triumphant deaths—or the conduct of the survivors since the war, these army converts *as a rule* (of course there were some cases of sad backsliding, as there have been in every revival since the days of Judas Iscariot and Simon Magus) gave as conclusive evidence of the genuineness of their conversion, as is ever found in revivals at home. Among our chaplains there were some of the ablest and most devoted men in all of the evangelical denominations. We had some inefficient men, of course, and the hard jokes which irreligious officers sometimes perpetrated at the expense of their chaplains (such as telling one making for the rear, when the battle was growing hot, "You have been preaching about what a sweet place heaven is, and, now that you have a chance to go there in a few minutes, you are running away from it"), were, doubtless, well deserved. And yet an intimate acquaintance with the chaplains of the Army of Northern Virginia, enables me to say as I do, without reserve, that they were, as a class, as self-sacrificing, devoted a band of Christian workers as the world has seen since apostolic times. The public sentiment, among both officers and men, in that army, would speedily drive away a chaplain who was unfaithful to his trust.

Religion became among us such a real, living, vital *power* that even irreligious officers came to recognize and encourage it—many of them having preaching regularly at their headquarters, and

treating the chaplains and missionaries with the greatest courtesy
and respect. I can testify that, in constant intercourse with our
officers, from Generals Lee, Jackson, Ewell, Stuart, A. P. Hill, Early,
J. B. Gordon, J. A. Walker, and others of highest rank down to the
lowest rank, I was never treated otherwise than with marked
courtesy, kindness, and respect, and I usually found them ready to
give me their cordial co-operation in my work.

I have dwelt at such length on the *morale* of Lee's army,
because this was the key to its *discipline*. In the sense in which
the term is understood in the regular armies of Europe, or of the
United States, we *really had no discipline*. The degraded punish-
ments resorted to in those armies; the isolation of the officers from
the privates; the mere machine performance of duty, and the
carrying out of any routine, simply because discipline required it,
were almost unknown in our army. The private mingled in freest
social intercourse with his officers, and learned to obey them, because
he loved them, and loved the common cause for which they fought.
Right or wrong (and I do not propose to discuss that question here),
the soldiers of the Army of Northern Virginia enlisted from a
thorough conviction that they were defending the principles of
constitutional freedom—the humblest private in the ranks could
"give a reason for the faith that was in him"—indeed, could make
an argument in favor of the justice of his cause, which it would
puzzle the ablest lawyer on the other side to answer. And thus
they marched forth gayly to battle, and needed not the spur of
discipline to drive them on.

Personal devotion to their leaders was also an important element
in their discipline and *morale*. They ceased their loud murmurs
against retreating from Darksville without fighting Patterson,
because their honored chief ("old Joe Johnston") said it was best
not to do so, and they started with the utmost enthusiasm from
Winchester to Manassas, because he told them, in general orders,
that it was "a forced march to save the country." They would
march, many of them barefooted, thirty or forty miles a day, because
"Old Stonewall" said they must "press forward" to accomplish
important results, and because he would frequently gallop along the
column and give them a chance to cheer him. And they would
make the welkin ring with "General Lee to the rear," while they
counted it all joy to fight five times their numbers when the eyes of
their idolized chief were upon them. General Hooker was certainly
right in testifying that Lee's army had "acquired a character
for steadiness and efficiency unsurpassed in ancient or modern

times;" but it was not from "discipline alone," but because each individual was a hero, and the *morale* of the whole army such as the world has never seen.

I could fill a volume with incidents of individual heroism on the part of private soldiers in that army. I have space for only a few. At first Fredericksburg, just after Lawton's Georgia Brigade (under the command of Colonel Atkinson) had driven the enemy out of the woods on Early's front, and made their gallant dash across the plain (the men growling loudly at being ordered back, saying, "If it had been those Virginia fellows that made the charge, 'Old Jubal' would have let them drive the Yankees into the river"), a Georgia boy, who seemed to be not over sixteen, rushed up to me with his two middle fingers shattered, and exclaimed (mistaking me for a surgeon), "Doctor, I want you, please, to cut off these fingers and tie them up as soon as you can. The boys are going into another charge directly, and I want to be with them." I procured him a surgeon, the wound was dressed, and the brave boy hurried to the front again. At Cedar Creek, on the 19th of October, 1864, Sergeant Trainum, the color-bearer of the Thirteenth Virginia Infantry, was surrounded by a number of Sheridan's troopers, but—exclaiming, "You may kill me, but I will never give up my colors"—he fought until he fell insensible, and the flag was stripped from his body, around which he had wrapped it.

Looking through a port-hole in the trenches, below Petersburg, one day, a sudden gust of wind lifted my hat off, and landed it between the two lines. Private George Haner, of Company D, Thirteenth Virginia Regiment, at once stepped up, and offered to get my hat for me. I peremptorily forbade his doing so, as I knew the great risk he would run; but the fearless fellow soon disappeared, and before long returned with the hat. "How did you manage to get it?" I asked. "Oh! I crawled down the trench leading to our picket line, and fished it in with a pole." "Did not the Yankees see you?" "Oh, yes! they shot at me eight or ten times; but that made no difference, so they did not hit me." Poor fellow, he was afterward killed, bravely doing his duty. I frequently saw men in the trenches at Petersburg watching the shell from the enemy's mortars, as they came over, claiming some particular one as "my shell," and scarcely waiting for the smoke from the explosion to clear away, before eagerly rushing forward to gather up the scattered pieces, which were sold to the ordnance officer for a few cents (Confederate money) per pound. They called shells which went far to the rear, "quartermaster hunters;" and one day a gallant fellow (utterly reckless of personal danger in his eagerness for a joke) mounted the parapet, the target of many sharpshooters, and pointing to a shell that was flying over, exclaimed: "A little further to the right. Captain B—— (the name of a worthy quartermaster) is down yonder under the hill."

Upon another occasion, I saw a good-natured fellow frying some meat on the side of the trench, while the Minnie balls of the sharpshooters whistled all around him. At last, one struck in his fire, and threw ashes in his frying-pan, when he quietly moved to the other side of the fire, as if to avoid smoke, and went on with his culinary operations, coolly remarking: "Plague on those fellows; I expect they will spoil all my grease yet, before they quit their foolishness."

I have frequently seen men of that army display a fortitude under severe suffering, a calm resignation or ecstatic triumph in the hour of death, such as history rarely records. A noble fellow, who fell at Gaines' Mill, on the 27th of June, 1862, said to comrades who offered to bear him from the field: "No! I die. Tell my parents I die happy. On! on to victory! Jesus is with me, and can render all the help I need." Another, who fell mortally wounded at second Manassas, said to me, in reply to my question as to what message I should send home for him: "Tell father that it would be very hard to die here on the roadside without seeing him, or any of the loved ones at home; but I have fallen at the post of duty, and, as I have with me the 'friend that sticketh closer than a brother,' He maketh it all peace and joy." A Georgia soldier, who was shot through the mouth, during the battle of the Wilderness, and unable to speak, wrote in my note-book this sentence: "I am suffering very much; but I trust in Christ, and am perfectly resigned to His will. I am ready still to serve Him on earth, or to go up higher, just as He may see fit to direct." Another, who was mortally wounded in the "bloody angle" at Spottsylvania Court-House, said to me, with a radiant smile: "Well, my hours on earth are numbered. But what care I for that? Jesus says, 'Him that cometh unto me, I will in no wise cast out.' Now I have gone to Him, and I am happy in the assurance that He will not falsify His word, but will be true to His promise."

As the great cavalry chief, General J. E. B. Stuart, was quietly and calmly breathing out his noble life, he said to President Davis, who stood at his bedside: "I am ready and willing to die, if God and my country think that I have fulfilled my destiny and discharged my duty." Colonel Lewis Minor Coleman, of the University of

Virginia, who fell mortally wounded at first Fredericksburg, and lingered for some weeks in great agony, uttered many sentiments which would adorn the brightest pages of Christian experience, and, among other things, sent this message to his loved and honored chieftains : "Tell Generals Lee and Jackson that they know how a Christian soldier should *live ;* I only wish they were here to see a Christian soldier *die !* " Not many months afterward Jackson was called to "cross over the river, and rest under the shade of the trees," and left another bright illustration of how Christian soldiers of that army were wont to *die.* Colonel Willie Pegram, "the boy artillerist," as he was familiarly called, left the University of Virginia, at the breaking out of the war, as a private soldier, rose to the rank of colonel of artillery (he refused a tender of promotion to the command of an infantry brigade), upon more than one occasion elicited high praise from A. P. Hill, Jackson, and Lee, and, at the early age of twenty-two, fell on the ill-fated field of Five Forks, gallantly resisting the overwhelming odds against him. His last words were : *"I have done my duty, and now I turn to my Savior."*

And thus I might fill pages with the dying words of these noble men, which are, indeed, "apples of gold in pictures of silver," and show that they were taught by God's spirit how to live, and how to die. But I have already exceeded my allotted space, and must hasten to close. No! it was not *discipline alone* which made the Army of Northern Virginia what it was—which gave to it that heroic courage, that patience under hardships, that indomitable nerve under disaster, and that full confidence in its grand old chief, and in itself, that won, against fearful odds, a long series of splendid victories, and which, even in its defeat, wrung from Horace Greeley the tribute, "The rebellion had failed, and gone down, but the rebel army of Virginia and its commander had *not* failed ;" and from Swinton, in his "Army of the Potomac," the following graceful eulogy : " Nor can there fail to arise the image of that other army, that was the adversary of the Army of the Potomac, and which who can ever forget that once looked upon it ?—that array of tattered uniforms and bright muskets—that body of incomparable infantry, the Army of Northern Virginia, which, for four years, carried the revolt on its bayonets, opposing a constant front to the mighty concentration of power brought against it ; which, receiving terrible blows, did not fail to give the like ; and which, vital in all its parts, died only with its annihilation."

It was a noble band of intelligent, educated, patriotic soldiers, with a *morale* such as the world has rarely, if ever, witnessed—men who were devoted to their leaders, and to the cause for which they fought, who were very heroes in the fight, but who submitted with no bitter, or unmanly murmurings, when their idolized chieftain told them that he was "compelled to yield to overwhelming numbers and resources;" who have preserved unsullied their honor as they have observed to the letter the terms of their parole, and who will transmit to posterity, as a proud legacy, the story of their deeds as they marched, and fought, and suffered, and counted it all joy to be members of "Lee's army."

GENERAL MEADE AT GETTYSBURG.

BY COLONEL JAMES C. BIDDLE.

In order to understand fully the battle of Gettysburg, and to appreciate General Meade's services on that occasion, it will be necessary to refer briefly to some of the preceeding events. Two great battles had been recently fought between the contending forces in Virginia—at Fredericksburg and at Chancellorsville—both resulting in the defeat of the Army of the Potomac. At Fredericksburg, that army, under the command of General Burnside, assaulted the enemy in a position naturally strong and thoroughly fortified, and was repulsed with heavy loss. General Meade, in this action, won great distinction. Holding the left of our line with his noble division, the Pennsylvania Reserve Corps, he made an impetuous assault on the enemy's right, broke into his lines, and drove him from his works for over a half mile, capturing over two hundred prisoners, and several standards. In this advanced position, in which General Meade was left without support, he encountered heavy reinforcements of the enemy, who poured into his lines a destructive fire of infantry and artillery, not only in front but also on both flanks. Meade, unwilling to abandon the advantage he had gained, called repeatedly and earnestly for reinforcements, but in vain, and after a loss of nearly forty per cent. of his command, he was compelled to fall back, which he did without confusion. The history of the war does not contain the record of a more gallant assault, and by his brilliant conduct on this occasion, General Meade added to his already high reputation in the army. Soon after, in the latter part of December, 1862, he was promoted to the command of the Fifth Army Corps.

In the following May was fought the battle of Chancellorsville, the result of which caused the most universal gloom and depression. We cannot here enter, at any length, into the history of that battle. It will be sufficient to call to mind how the Army of the Potomac, reorganized and reinforced, in the best of spirits, and confident of victory, led by General Hooker, who enjoyed its confidence to a very high degree, went forth to meet its old antagonist, the Army of Northern Virginia. It was again doomed to disappointment, and after a short and unsuccessful campaign, it recrossed the Rappahannock, disheartened—not demoralized—for it is the crowning glory of the Army of the Potomac that it never faltered under misfortunes which would have been fatal to the efficiency of most armies. It has been well said: "Not the Army of the Potomac was beaten at Chancellorsville, but its commander;" for the truth is, that the army, as a whole, did not fight in that battle, but the different corps were attacked by Lee and beaten in detail. The Eleventh Corps, badly posted, was surprised by superior numbers, and routed. The Third Corps, which had been sent out to follow the enemy, who was supposed to be in retreat, was cut off from the rest of the army by the rout of the Eleventh Corps, and was compelled to sustain alone, and for several hours, the attack of Lee's whole force, until it fell back, gallantly fighting, upon the rest of the army—the First, Second, Fifth, and Twelfth Corps, only parts of some of these corps being engaged. Lee then turned upon Sedgwick, who was advancing from Fredericksburg, and drove him across the Rappahannock. This was on the 5th of May, and the same night the whole army recrossed the river, the Fifth Corps, under General Meade, covering the retreat. In this battle Lee had sixty thousand men, Longstreet's Corps having been sent to operate south of the James river; Hooker had not less than ninety thousand men.

Lee's successes at Fredericksburg and Chancellorsville, necessarily dispiriting to our troops, had a contrary effect upon the Army of Northern Virginia, whose *morale* was thereby raised to the highest pitch, and who became inspired with the belief that it could defeat the Army of the Potomac under any circumstances. Colonel Freemantle, of the British service, who was with General Lee at Gettysburg, in writing of that battle, says: "The staff officers spoke of the coming battle as a certainty, and the universal feeling was one of profound contempt for an enemy whom they have beaten so constantly, and under so many disadvantages." Lee himself was emboldened by these victories; and induced, as he says, by "important considerations," doubtless under the conviction, too, that the Army of the Potomac would be handled in Pennsylvania as at Chancellors-ville, he determined upon an offensive campaign, the object of which was the capture of Philadelphia, Baltimore, and Washington. The end he hoped to attain was the long coveted recognition by foreign powers of the Southern Confederacy, its consequent successful establishment, and the complete humiliation of the Union cause. Accordingly, on the 22d of June, after a series of bold movements in Virginia, he ordered the advance of his army, under Ewell, into Maryland; and on the 24th and 25th, his two remaining corps, under Longstreet and Hill, crossed the Potomac at Williamsport and Shepherdstown, and followed Ewell, who had already advanced into Pennsylvania as far as Chambersburg. The Army of the Potomac crossed on the 25th and 26th, at Edwards' Ferry, and was concentrated in the neighborhood of Frederick, Maryland.

It was under these circumstances that, at two A. M. of June 28th, General Meade, still in command of the Fifth Corps, received from General Hardie, of the War Department, the order of the President placing him in command of the Army of the Potomac. This order was a complete surprise to General Meade, and it is not too much to say that by it he was suddenly called to a position in which, for a time, the fate of the country was in his hands. One false step now, and the Union cause was lost; for if Lee had succeeded in his plans for this campaign, the capture of Vicksburg, and other victories in the West, would have been of little avail. General Meade was as modest as he was brave, and while he never sought promotion, he never shrank from the responsibility which it brought. We shall see that he bore himself so well in this grave crisis, that within six days after he assumed command, by his rare energy and skill, he accomplished a difficult march, and fought successfully, with an army inferior in numbers to that of his adversary, the greatest battle of the war.

Immediately after receiving the order placing him in command, General Meade sought an interview with General Hooker, and used every effort to obtain information concerning the strength and position of the different corps of our army, and the movements of the enemy. General Meade, in his evidence before the Committee on the Conduct of the War, says: "My predecessor, General Hooker, left the camp in a very few hours after I relieved him. I received from him no intimation of any plan, or any views that he may have had up to that moment, and I am not aware that he had any, but was waiting for the exigencies of the occasion to govern him, just as I had to do subsequently."

On assuming command, General Meade addressed his army in the following characteristic order:

By direction of the President of the United States, I hereby assume command of the Army of the Potomac. As a soldier, in obeying this order—an order totally unexpected and unsolicited—I have no promises or pledges to make. The country looks to this army to relieve it from the devastation and disgrace of a hostile invasion. Whatever fatigues and sacrifices we may be called upon to undergo, let us have in view constantly the magnitude of the interests involved, and let each man determine to do his duty, leaving to an all-controlling Providence the decision of the contest. It is with just diffidence that I relieve in the command of this army an eminent and accomplished soldier, whose name must ever appear conspicuous in the history of its achievements; but I rely upon the hearty support of my companions in arms to assist me in the discharge of the important trust which has been confided to me.

Our army at this time consisted of the First Corps, General Reynolds; Second, General Hancock; Third, General Sickles; Fifth, General Sykes (who succeeded General Meade); Sixth, General Sedgwick; Eleventh, General Howard, and Twelfth, General Slocum; the cavalry under General Pleasonton, and the artillery under General Hunt, the Chief of Artillery. Nothing was known of General Lee excepting that he was north of us threatening Harrisburg. It should be mentioned here that we had been reduced in material strength by the expiration of the term of service of many of the two years' and nine months' regiments, while the enemy had been reinforced by the return of Longstreet's Corps. Two corps of our army were on the north side of the Sharp Mountain, separated from the main column by the ridge. General Meade ordered these corps to recross the ridge, and on the morning of June 29th, put his whole force in motion, his right flank covering Baltimore, and his left opposing Lee's right. General Meade says of his own intentions in this movement: "My object being, at all hazards, to compel the enemy to loose his hold on the Susquehanna, and meet me in battle at some point. It was my firm determination, never for an instant deviated from, to give battle wherever and as soon as I could possibly find the enemy." On the night of June 29th, Lee learned that the Army of the Potomac, which he thought was still in Virginia, was advancing northward, threatening his communications. He therefore suspended the movement on Harrisburg, which he had ordered, and directed Longstreet, Hill, and Ewell to concentrate at Gettysburg. On the night of the 30th, after the Army of the Potomac had made two days' marches, General Meade heard that Lee was concentrating his army to meet him, and being entirely ignorant of the nature of the country in front of him, he at once instructed his engineers to select some ground having a general reference to the existing position of the army, which he might occupy by rapid movement of concentration, and thus give battle on his own terms, in case the enemy should advance across the South Mountain. The general line of Pipe Clay creek was selected, and a preliminary order of instructions issued to the corps commanders, informing them of this fact, and explaining how they might move their corps and concentrate in a good position along this line. This measure was made the ground of an accusation that General Meade had ordered a retreat. The mere statement of the nature of the order is of itself a sufficient refutation of the charge. General Humphreys, one of the ablest officers in our army, in speaking on this subject, says : "These instructions stated, 'Developments may cause the commanding general to assume the offensive from his present positions.' Not many hours after, new developments did cause him to change his plans, but these instructions evince that foresight which proves his (Meade's) ability to command an army. In similar circumstances, the agreement between Wellington and Blucher to concentrate their two armies—nearly double the number of Napoleon—far to the rear, in the vicinity of Waterloo, has been esteemed a proof of their great ability."

On June 30th, General Meade had sent General Reynolds, who commanded the left wing of our army, to Gettysburg, with orders to report to him concerning the character of the ground there, at the same time ordering General Humphreys to examine the ground in the vicinity of Emmetsburg. But while thus active in his endeavors to ascertain the nature of the several positions where he could fight Lee, he, at the same time, continued to press forward his army, and concentrate it so that he could with ease move it toward any point. On the morning of July 1st, our advance, consisting of the First and Eleventh Corps, under General Reynolds, arrived at Gettysburg, and there found Buford's Division of cavalry already engaged with the enemy. Reynolds, with that quickness of perception, which was one of his most marked characteristics, saw at a glance that here was the ground on which the great contest must be fought out. In the language of General Meade : "He immediately moved around the town of Gettysburg, and advanced on the Cashtown road, and, *without a moment's hesitation,* deployed his advanced division, and attacked the enemy, at the same time sending orders for the Eleventh Corps, General Howard, to advance as promptly as possible." Then it was that Reynolds fell, the greatest soldier the Army of the Potomac ever lost in battle. We have seen, with regret, a statement recently made that General Meade had failed to

14

do justice to his services and to his memory. This statement does injustice to General Meade, between whom and General Reynolds existed a strong personal friendship, and we feel sure that both these gallant soldiers, now in their graves, would disapprove of the publication of anything calculated to convey so wrong an impression. The above quotation from Meade's official report is proof that he appreciated General Reynolds' action on the first day at Gettysburg, and, subsequently, on the occasion of the presentation to him of a sword by the Pennsylvania Reserve Corps, he thus spoke, in words that express most eloquently the regret and admiration with which he cherished the memory of his fallen comrade and friend : "This reunion awakens in my heart a new sorrow for an officer whom it vividly recalls to my mind, for he commanded the division when I commanded one of the brigades. He was the noblest as well as the bravest gentleman in the army. I refer to John F. Reynolds. I cannot receive this sword without thinking of that officer. When he fell at Gettysburg, leading the advance, I lost not only a lieutenant of the utmost importance to me, but, I may say, that I lost a friend, aye, even a brother."

While the contest was going on between the enemy and our advance, General Meade was at Taneytown, about thirteen miles distant, in the centre of his army. Owing to the direction of the wind, the sound of Reynolds' guns did not reach his headquarters, and he did not hear until one P. M. of the same day that a portion of our troops had met the enemy, and that Reynolds had fallen. General Meade at once sent General Hancock to Gettysburg, with orders to assume command of all the troops, and to report to him concerning the practicability of fighting a battle there. General Meade has been criticised for sending General Hancock to command officers who were his superiors in rank, but that he was justified in doing so is made apparent by the following extract from a dispatch from General Buford, an able and distinguished officer, received by General Meade after Hancock had gone to the front :

HEADQUARTERS FIRST CAVALRY DIVISION,
July 1st, 1863—3.20 P. M.

* * * General Reynolds was killed early this morning. In my opinion there seems to be no directing person.   JOHN BUFORD.

Being satisfied, from the reports of officers returning from the field, that General Lee was about to concentrate his whole army there, General Meade, without waiting to hear from Hancock, issued orders to the Fifth and Twelfth Corps to proceed to the scene of action. At 6.30 P. M. he received the first report from General

Hancock, in which that officer said: "We can fight here, as the ground appears not unfavorable, with good troops." General Meade at once issued orders to all his corps commanders to move to Gettysburg, broke up his headquarters at Taneytown, and proceeded himself to the field, arriving there at one A. M. of the 2d. He was occupied during the night in directing the movements of the troops, and as soon as it was daylight, he proceeded to inspect the position occupied, and to make arrangements for posting the several corps as they should arrive. By seven A. M. the Second and Fifth Corps, with the rest of the Third, had reached the ground, and soon after the whole army was in position, with the exception of the Sixth Corps, which arrived at two P.M. after a long and fatiguing march. General Sedgwick says, in relation to this march: "I arrived at Gettysburg at about two o'clock in the afternoon of July 2d, having marched thirty-five miles from seven o'clock the evening previous. I received, on the way, frequent messages from General Meade to push forward my corps as rapidly as possible. I received no less than three messages, by his aides, urging me on."

As soon as the Sixth Corps had arrived, General Meade left his headquarters, and proceeded to the extreme left, to attend to the posting of the Fifth Corps, which he had ordered over from the right, and also to inspect the position of the Third Corps, about which he was in doubt. When he arrived on the ground, at about four P. M., he found that General Sickles, instead of connecting his right with the left of General Hancock, as he had been ordered to do, had thrown forward his line three-quarters of a mile in front of the Second Corps, leaving Little Round Top unprotected, and was, technically speaking, "in air"—without support on either flank. General Meade at once saw this mistake, and General Sickles promptly offered to withdraw to the line he had been intended to occupy, but General Meade replied: "You cannot do it. The enemy will not let you get away without a fight." Before he had finished the sentence, his prediction was fulfilled. The enemy opened with artillery from the woods on our left, and the action was begun. Soon large masses of infantry from Longstreet's Corps were thrown upon Sickles, the enemy at the same time sending a heavy force toward Little Round Top, the key to the whole position. General Warren, Meade's chief engineer, was holding this important point, with a few men whom he had collected together. General Meade sent several staff officers to urge forward the column under General Sykes, which was coming up with all possible speed, and which fortunately soon arrived. General Sykes at once threw a strong force upon Round Top, and succeeded in holding it against the enemy's assaults, after a fearful struggle.

In the meantime, the attack upon General Sickles was continued with great fury, and after a stubborn and gallant resistance, during which General Sickles was wounded, the Third Corps was compelled to fall back, shattered and broken, and to re-form behind the line originally intended to be held. Caldwell's Division of the Second Corps was sent by General Hancock to assist in checking the advance of the enemy, but after a severe struggle, in which Caldwell lost one-half of his command, the enemy enveloped his right and forced him back. The division of General Ayres was then struck on the right and rear, but with great courage it fought its way back through the enemy to its original line. General Humphreys, with his division, held the right of the line of the Third Corps. Although severely pressed by the enemy, he did not retire until ordered to do so, and then, judging that a rapid backward movement would demoralize his men, and make it difficult to rally them on the crest, he determined to withdraw slowly. He succeeded in this difficult movement, but with the loss of nearly one-half of his division. At length, when the enemy made a last furious charge on the crest, they were met by fresh troops, which had been sent by General Meade from other portions of the line, and were repulsed. General Meade, during this encounter, brought forward in person a brigade of the Twelfth Corps, and in the early part of the action his horse was shot under him. Finally, about sunset, a counter charge was made by our troops, in which the remnants of Humphrey's Division joined, and had the satisfaction of bringing back the guns they had previously lost. The division of Regulars, under General Ayres, led the assault on the right of the Fifth Corps, and pressed the enemy on the centre, but on the left they were outflanked and driven back. General Sykes at once ordered forward the Pennsylvania Reserves, who, led by General Crawford, made a gallant charge, and, after a sharp contest, the enemy retired. This ended the action on our left, but at eight P. M. it was suddenly renewed on our right by General Ewell, who made a powerful attack on our lines with the divisions of General Early and General Johnson, the former at Cemetery Hill and the latter at Culp's Hill. General Howard, who held the ground at Cemetery Hill, succeeded in repulsing the enemy, with the assistance of Carroll's Brigade of the Second Corps, which had been sent to his support by General Hancock. At Culp's Hill, the extreme right was held by only one brigade of the Twelfth Corps, the remainder of that corps not having yet returned from the left.

This brigade, commanded by General Greene, resisted the assault with great firmness, and, aided by Wadsworth's Division of the First Corps, finally succeeded in repulsing the enemy, who, however, advanced and occupied the breastworks on our furthest right, vacated by Geary's Division of the Twelfth Corps, which position they held during the night.

Thus ended, at ten P. M., the second day of the battle. Both armies had fought with a desperation which proved that they realized the tremendous issues which hung upon the conflict, but the result was indecisive. Lee had gained what he calls "partial successes," Longstreet having taken possession of our advanced position on the left, and Ewell had a foothold within our lines on the right. But our main line remained intact, and the army, although wearied by long marches and hard fighting, was ready and anxious to renew the contest. Both officers and men had acquired from this day's experience a firm confidence in their new commander. General Meade's prompt and rapid movement of troops from one part of the line to another, wherever the enemy pressed most heavily, had made them feel that they were under the lead of a general who had the ability to handle the army effectively. Fredericksburg and Chancellorsville had shown how little the valor of the troops could accomplish when incompetently led; at Gettysburg, under a skilful and able leader, their bravery and heroic endurance were rewarded with victory. A Latin proverb says: *"Formidabilior cervorum exercitus duce leone, quam leonum, cervo."*

The battle was renewed at daylight on the 3d, on our right. During the night, General Meade had returned the portion of the Twelfth Corps, that had been sent over to the left, to its former position, and a terrible struggle took place for the possession of the ground which had been occupied by General Ewell the night before. General Lee had hoped, by holding this ground, to turn our position, but General Geary, with his division, assisted by troops from the Sixth Corps, attacked the enemy, and, after a severe engagement, which lasted five hours, he drove them from our lines with heavy loss. This action terminated at ten A. M., and was followed by several hours of perfect quiet, when, suddenly, the enemy opened upon us a terrific artillery fire, with not less than one hundred and twenty-five guns. Our batteries, which had been posted by General Hunt, the efficient Chief of Artillery, replied with about seventy guns—the nature of the ground not admitting of the use of more. This artillery duel, which lasted an hour and a half, was the most severe experienced anywhere during the war. The air was filled with bursting shells and solid shot, and the very earth shook with the resounding cannon. General Meade well understood that the object of the enemy in this fire was to demoralize our men, preparatory to making a grand assault. He, therefore, directed our artillery to slacken their fire, and, finally, to cease altogether, with the view of making the enemy believe that they had silenced our guns, and thus bring on their assault the sooner. It resulted as he desired. Soon Lee's attacking column, composed of Pickett's Division, supported by Wilcox and Pettigrew, made a most gallant and well-sustained assault on our lines, advancing steadily, under a heavy artillery fire from the guns Lee thought he had silenced, to within musket range of our infantry. Here they were met by a terrible volley from Hays' and Gibbon's divisions, of the Second Corps. Pettigrew's command, composed of raw troops, gave way, and many of them were made prisoners; but Pickett's men, still undaunted, pressed on, and captured some of the intrenchments on our centre, crowding back the advanced portion of Webb's Brigade, which was soon rallied by the personal efforts of its commander. General Meade had ordered up Doubleday's Division and Stannard's Brigade of the First Corps, and, at this critical moment, General Hancock advanced, and Pickett's brave men were driven back with terrible loss. All their brigade commanders had fallen—one of them, General Armistead, being wounded and captured inside of our batteries. No one could have witnessed the conduct of the Southern troops, on this occasion, without a feeling of admiration, mingled with regret that such heroic courage and brave determination had not been displayed in a better cause. On our side the loss was very heavy, General Hancock and General Gibbon being among the wounded. When General Meade heard that Hancock, who had rendered conspicuous service throughout the battle, was wounded, he said to General Mitchell, of Hancock's staff, who had brought him the news: "Say to General Hancock that I thank him in my own name, and I thank him in the name of the country, for all he has done."

As soon as the assault was repulsed, General Meade went to the left of our lines and ordered Crawford's Division, the Pennsylvania Reserves, to advance. This division met a portion of Hood's command and attacked them, capturing many prisoners and seven thousand stand of arms. By this action Crawford regained possession of nearly all the ground lost by Sickles the day before, and rescued our wounded, who had lain for twenty-four hours entirely uncared for. While our artillery and infantry were thus engaged, our cavalry was doing good service on both flanks. General Farnsworth, on our left, with one brigade, made a gallant charge against the enemy's infantry; and, on our right, General Gregg successfully resisted an attempt of General Stuart to pass to our rear while Pickett attacked us in front.

Thus ended, in victory for the Union army, the battle of Gettysburg, one of the greatest battles on record—great in its results, as well as in the skill and valor with which it was fought. Of the private soldiers of the army, who names are unknown to fame, it must be said, that men did never show more courage, more patience, and firm endurance, than did the rank and file of the grand old Army of the Potomac in this battle, and during the trying marches which preceded it. In this imperfect account it has been impossible to do justice to, or even to mention, many who most distinguished themselves in the great contest. All did their duty zealously, some with more, some with less ability. But among the men who will ever be remembered in connection with that proud day in our history, General Meade will stand foremost as the "*facillime princeps*," the leader under whose command the glorious result was achieved.

The loss of the Army of the Potomac in this battle was twenty-three thousand—that of the enemy could not have been less than thirty thousand. At the close of the action, General Meade issued the following address to his troops:

> The Commanding General, in behalf of the country, thanks the Army of the Potomac for the glorious result of the recent operations.
>
> Our enemy, superior in numbers, and flushed with the pride of a successful invasion, attempted to overcome, or destroy this army. Utterly baffled and defeated, he has now withdrawn from the contest.
>
> The privations and fatigue the army has endured, and the heroic courage and gallantry it has displayed, will be matters of history to be ever remembered. Our task is not yet accomplished, and the Commanding General looks to the army for greater efforts to drive from our soil every vestige of the presence of the invader.
>
> It is right and proper that we should, on suitable occasions, return our grateful thanks to the Almighty Disposer of events, that, in the goodness of his Providence, He has thought fit to give voice to the cause of the just.

It had been General Meade's intention to order a general advance from our left, after the close of the action; but, owing to the lateness of the hour, and the wearied condition of the army, with a "wisdom that did guide his valor to act in safety," he abandoned the movement he had contemplated. For this he has been severely censured. General Howard, in an article in the *Atlantic Monthly*, of July last, says: "I have thought that the fearful exposure of General Meade's headquarters, where so much havoc was occasioned by the enemy's artillery, had so impressed him that he did not at first realize the victory he had won." The reverse of this is true. General Meade was not in the least "demoralized" by the enemy's fire, but realized fully the exact condition of affairs. Lee had been repulsed, not routed, and, if Meade had yielded to his own inclination to attack, he would have been repulsed himself, and would thus have thrown away the fruits of his great victory. That this view is correct, is proved beyond all doubt by the following passage, from Mr. William Swinton's "History of the Army of the Potomac." Mr. Swinton says:

> I have become convinced, from the testimony of General Longstreet himself, that attack would have resulted disastrously. "I had," said that officer to the writer, "Hood and McLaws, who had not been engaged; I had a heavy force of artillery; I should have liked nothing better than to have been attacked, and have no doubt that I should have given those who tried as bad a reception as Pickett received."

On July 4th, Lee, during a heavy storm, withdrew from our front, and on the 11th took up a position at Williamsport, on the Potomac. He was closely followed by Meade, who came up with him on the 12th, and who found him in a position naturally almost impregnable, and strongly fortified. Meade's impulse was to attack at once, but, after consultation with his corps commanders, he abstained from ordering an assault until he could more fully reconnoitre the enemy's position. On the morning of the 14th, a reconnoissance in force, supported by the whole army, was made at daylight; but, on the night of the 13th, Lee had recrossed the Potomac. There was a great deal of clamor at the time, because Meade did not destroy or capture Lee's army at Williamsport; but Meade, conscious that he had acted wisely, always felt that history would do him justice. Had he assaulted, he would certainly have been defeated, and the result would have been disastrous not only to the army, but to the country, for a defeat to our army there would have opened the road to Washington and the North, and all the fruits of Gettysburg would have been dissipated. A brief reference to the subsequent experience of the Army of the Potomac will confirm the truth of this assertion. In May, 1864, we began the campaign with one hundred and fifteen thousand men, and after Spottsylvania Court-House were constantly receiving heavy reinforcements. General Lee had about sixty thousand men. And yet, with this great preponderance of strength, we assaulted the enemy again and again, in positions not so strong as the one held at Williamsport, always without success and with terrible loss. From the crossing of the Rapidan, on May 5th, to the unsuccessful assault on the enemy's works at Petersburg, June 18th, a period of about six weeks, the Army of the Potomac lost not less than seventy thousand men. In the battles between the Army of the Potomac and the Army of Northern Virginia, in no case was a direct assault upon an intrenched position successful.

There is evidence that the enemy were anxious to be attacked at Williamsport. In the "History of the Pennsylvania Reserve Corps," by Mr. J. R. Sypher, a letter is quoted from the Rev. Dr. Falk, who was in the enemy's lines at that place. Dr. Falk says:

I was at the College of St. James, to which, on account of its commanding position, very many officers of the highest rank came to reconnoitre Meade's lines. From the conversation of these officers among themselves, and with us, it was evident that they most ardently desired to be attacked. "Now we have Meade where we want him." "If he attacks us here, we will pay him back for Gettysburg." "But the old fox is too cunning." These and similar expressions showed clearly that they believed their position strong enough to hold it against any attacking force.

The country has never realized how much it owes to General Meade's moral firmness in resisting his strong desire to attack the enemy here and at Gettysburg, and in view of the vital issues depending upon his action on these occasions, it may be said of him, as truly as it was said of Fabius:

Unus homo nobis cunctando restituit rem ;
Non ponebat enim rumores ante salutem.
(One man by delay restored to us the State, for he preferred the public safety to his own fame.)

Although General Meade needs no eulogy, his great deeds speaking for him more eloquently than any words, it may not be out of place to say something concerning his character as a soldier and as a man. As a soldier he was singularly modest and unassuming. He did his duty always in a quiet and undemonstrative way, and was entirely free from what may be called the tricks of popularity. He never claimed credit for services rendered by others, nor did he exaggerate those rendered by himself. On the night of July 3d, at Gettysburg, after the final repulse of the enemy, when every man in the army felt elated with the great victory, he prepared a dispatch to the General-in-chief so moderate in tone that one of his staff officers said to him: "You ought to boast a little more, General, for the country will not appreciate what you have done, unless you do so." General Meade replied: "I would rather understate our success than claim greater results than I have accomplished," and the dispatch was sent as he had written it. General Meade gave to the country his best energies from the beginning to the end of the war, and from July, 1863, until the final mustering out of our armies, as commander of the Army of the Potomac, he held a position not second in importance to that occupied by any other officer. Not only is there an entire absence of undue boasting in his dispatches and orders during all this period, but he was ready at all times to speak in words of praise of other generals, some of whom had received honors which his friends believed rightfully to belong to him.

As the commander of an army, General Meade was prompt to plan, and quick to execute; always ready for every possible movement of the enemy; fertile in expedients to meet unlooked-for emergencies; full of vigor, but not rash; firm, patient, and self-reliant. He showed these great qualities, not only in the campaign through which we have followed him, but in many others; and we may say here that, if the true history of the campaigns in Virginia, from the Wilderness to Appomattox Court-House, shall ever be written, the country will be surprised to hear how much was done by one whose name is hardly connected in the public mind with these achievements. The more General Meade's career is studied, the greater does his ability as a soldier appear; and lest we should seem to over-estimate him, we give the opinion of General Lee, the man of all others best qualified to judge of the skill of our generals. In an article written by Colonel J. Esten Cooke, who served in the Southern army, on the staff of General J. E. B. Stuart, that officer says:

General Lee esteemed the late General Meade very highly as a soldier, declaring that he was the *best officer in the Federal army*, and had "given him more trouble than any of them."

General Grant, too, has put on record his estimate of Meade's ability. Writing not long before the closing campaign of the war, he said:

General Meade is one of our truest men, and ablest officers. He has been constantly with the Army of the Potomac, confronting the strongest, best appointed, and most confident army of the South. He therefore has not had the opportunity of winning laurels so distinctly marked as have fallen to the lot of other generals. But I defy any man to name a commander who would do more than Meade has done, with the same chances. General Meade was appointed [Major General in the Regular army] at my solicitation, after a campaign of most protracted, and covering more severely-contested battles than any of which we have any account in history. I have been with General Meade through the whole campaign, and I not only made the recommendation upon a conviction that this recognition of his services was fully won, but that he was eminently qualified for the command such rank would entitle him to.*

General Meade was emphatically a Christian soldier, and never forgot his responsibility to a higher power. Caring more for the approval of his conscience than for the applause of his countrymen, no consideration could ever swerve him from the course he knew to be right; and on more than one occasion he deliberately chose to endanger his own reputation, rather than risk unnecessarily the lives of his men. For he was a man who "gained strength by prayer, and knew no guide but duty." In speaking of him in this respect, we cannot better conclude than by quoting the following extract from the address delivered at his funeral, by Bishop Whipple, of Minnesota:

If I asked any of you to describe our brother's character, you would tell me that he had a woman's gentleness, with the strength of a great-hearted man. I believe it was the lessons of Christian faith, inwrought into a soldier's life, which made him know no guide but duty, which made him so kind to the helpless, which placed him foremost in all public works, and made his name a household word in all your homes. During the dark days of our civil war, I happened to be in Washington. He telegraphed me to come and celebrate Easter in his camp, with the Holy Communion. It was a strange place for Easter flowers and Easter songs, and the story of the Resurrection, but I do not recall a sweeter service, nor one more redolent of the peace of heaven. Of the bronzed veterans who knelt beside the Lord's table, some, like Williams and Meade, are sleeping with the dead; others are scattered far, and busy in life's work. That day I knew that we had in our camp centurions who feared God and prayed always. The world loves to tell other stories of public men; and, perhaps, no eye but God's sees the record of the conflict of human souls in the battle of life. Death came suddenly, without the sound of a footfall; there were a few days when friends waited on medical skill, but his heart was in the country whither he was going. He looked to the Savior, the only one in heaven or earth who could help him. He asked for the Holy Communion, and by the Lord's table gathered manna for the journey; the words of penitence, and the look of faith, were blended with his dying prayers, and he fell asleep.

Our country had no greater soldier, no truer man, than George G. Meade, the skilful general, the incorruptible patriot, the pure, honorable, chivalrous, Christian gentleman. We need such men in the army and in the State, always and everywhere. Long may we cherish his memory, and honor his virtues.

---

* General Grant subsequently, when he became President of the United States, overslaughed General Meade by appointing to the vacant Lieutenant Generalship General Sheridan, Meade's junior in rank. This was unjust, not only to General Meade, but to the Army of the Potomac, which had displayed such wonderful fortitude and courage during the protracted and bloody campaign of which General Grant speaks, and which deserved that, by the promotion of its commander to this high rank, the government should recognize the paramount importance of its services in bringing the war to a successful end. It is far from our intention to say anything in disparagement of General Sheridan, who was a brave and able officer, but as General Grant "defies any man" to name an abler commander than Meade. and as Meade ranked Sheridan, the injustice is apparent.

MR. LINCOLN AND THE FORCE BILL.

BY HON. A. R. BOTELER.

A FEW days before the close of the Thirty-sixth Congress, which will be remembered as the eventful Congress that immediately preceded the war, I received a number of letters from conservative sources, similar in their import to the following from a well-known Union man, who was at that time a member of the Virginia Legislature:

RICHMOND, VA.,
February 25th, 1861.

My Dear Sir: Let me say to you, in all earnestness, that the passage, at this time, of Mr. Stanton's Force bill will do us, in Virginia, infinite harm. The disunionists, one and all, will clap their hands in very ecstacy, if the measure prevails. Already, some of the conservative friends in the convention have given way. Many, I fear, will follow. The States' rights sensibilities of our people are already wounded. If the bill passes, I verily believe that an ordinance of Secession will be passed in two days thereafter. For God's sake, for the country's sake, *do not let it pass!*   Yours, truly,

JOS. SEGAR.

HON. A. R. BOTELER, House of Representatives, Washington, D. C.

The bill referred to in the foregoing letter had been reported to the House, on the 18th of February, from the Committee on Military Affairs, by its chairman, the Hon. Benjamin Stanton, of Ohio. It extended the provisions of the Act of 1795, "for calling forth the militia," and those of the Act of 1807, "for the employment of the land and naval forces of the United States," so as not only to place the latter—the regular army and navy—at the disposal of the incoming President, but also to confer on him the plenary power to call out and control the militia, and to authorize him, beside, to accept the services of an unlimited number of volunteers,

(220)

who should be on the same footing as the regular forces of the United States, and whose officers should all be commissioned by himself.

On the day after the introduction of the bill, and before an opportunity was had to examine its provisions, an attempt was made to pass it without debate, under the operation of the previous question. This effort, however, was successfully resisted, and a limited discussion of it was allowed, which lasted, at intervals, until the 1st of March—the Friday before Mr. Lincoln's inauguration— when it was understood that the measure would then be put upon its passage, so that the Senate might have an opportunity to act upon it before the end of the session. Observing Mr. Stanton's anxiety that day to get the floor for the avowed purpose of having the bill disposed of without further delay, and, knowing that if he should call it up, it would be carried by a large majority, inasmuch as the secession of the cotton States, and the consequent withdrawal of their members of Congress, had left the conservatives of both Houses completely in the power of the extremists of the dominant party, I resolved to make a personal appeal to him, in the forlorn hope that, possibly, he might be persuaded to refrain from pressing his measure to a vote. Accordingly, I went over to his desk, and used every argument I could think of to induce him to forego his determination. But all in vain. He was utterly obdurate; and I finally said to him:

"Mr. Stanton, your bill is thwarting the efforts of the conservative men of Virginia, who are striving to prevent her secession, and to avert the calamity of civil war. If you persist in its passage, the effect will be to convince our people that the policy of coercion is a foregone conclusion. The secessionists of our State convention at Richmond, though now in a minority, will be enabled thereby to carry their point, and Virginia will be forced out of the Union against her will."

"Well!" said he, folding his arms, and leaning back in his chair, "Well, what if she does go? If that is to be her course, so be it. I have contemplated the possibility of such a contingency for some time past. Governor Winslow, over there, can tell you of a talk I had with him on the subject two years ago. I said then, as I say now, that in the event of a separation of the North and South on the basis of our respective systems of labor—slave and free—I suppose we'll have to submit to it; and I have made up my mind to do so, provided we can keep up our social and commercial intercourse unrestricted between the sections."

"Though I have never allowed myself," said I, "to look forward to such a contingency, and don't believe that there will be a permanent separation of the two sections on the basis of their labor systems, notwithstanding the untoward action and attitude of the cotton States, yet I consider it to be the bounden duty of us all in this crisis to do everything in our power to prevent the possibility of such a calamity. And as an ounce of prevention is worth a pound of cure, I, therefore, beg and entreat you not to press this bill of yours."

"'Tis useless," he replied, "to say anything further. I'm sorry that I cannot comply with your request; for the bill must pass, and pass the House this evening."

"Am I then to understand," I asked, "that this is a party measure, and one that Mr. Lincoln approves of?"

To which he replied by telling me that he himself had originated it; that no one else was responsible for its provisions, and that he had never spoken to Mr. Lincoln on the subject.

Whereupon I remarked, "I am very glad to hear that, and will myself speak to him about it without delay I don't know him personally, but this is no time to stand on ceremony; so I shall go to him at once and ascertain, if possible, his opinion of the policy of such a movement as yours at this particular juncture; and, perhaps," I added, as I turned to leave him, "Mr. Lincoln may not be so inflexible as you are in this matter, and can be induced to exert his influence to stop it in the Senate if too late to do so in the House."

"Yes, that's likely!" was his laconic rejoinder, qualified by an incredulous laugh.

On my way to the cloak-room, I stopped to speak to two of my colleagues, Messrs. Thomas S. Bocock and Muscoe R. H. Garnett, who were standing together in the area outside the bar of the House. Mentioning my purpose to see Mr. Lincoln, and the object of the visit, I requested them, if Stanton should call up the bill in my absence, to do me the favor to filibuster on it until I could get back to record my vote against it, which they promised to do; I, on my part, promising to report to them the particulars of my proposed interview. It was about four o'clock in the afternoon when I left the Capitol, and driving rapidly to Willard's, where the President-elect had a suite of rooms fronting the avenue, the first person I met on reaching the hotel was an old acquaintance from the county of Berkeley, Virginia, Colonel Ward H. Lamon, Mr. Lincoln's law partner and *compagnon de voyage* from Springfield to Washington, who, on learning my wishes, kindly undertook to ascertain if Mr.

Lincoln, whom he had just left alone, would see me. He soon came down with an invitation to walk up stairs, and as I did so, accompanied by the Colonel, I noticed that the corridors were strictly guarded by policemen—an unnecessary but natural precaution under the circumstances of apprehension and excitement that then prevailed in Washington.

On being introduced, Mr. Lincoln greeted me with great kindness and cordiality. "I'm glad to see you," said he; "always glad to see an Old Line Whig. Sit down."

Apologizing for disturbing him, I said: "I've no doubt that the unusual demands now made on your time and energies require you to have more rest than is likely to be allowed you here by the public; but my visit is not one of conventional formality or idle curiosity, as I come upon an important matter now pending in the House, and, therefore, trust that I am not trespassing too far on your courtesy in calling this evening."

"Not a bit of it," he replied; "not a bit. I'm really glad you have come, and wish that more of you Southern gentlemen would call and see me, as these are times when there should be a full, fair, and frank interchange of sentiment and suggestion among all who have the good of the country at heart. So draw up your chair, and tell me what's going on in the House to-day."

Thus encouraged, showing him a copy of Stanton's Force bill, I called his attention to some of its extraordinary features, and to the fact that it was "bristling all over with war." I spoke of the angry feeling it had excited in Congress, and of the painful anxieties it had caused throughout Virginia; how it had demoralized the members of her State convention, and was frustrating the patriotic efforts of her conservative citizens to keep her from seceding. I told him, also, how determined the friends of the measure were to force it through the House that evening, and how much reason there was to fear that its passage would do irreparable injury to the cause of the Union. "Consequently, Mr. Lincoln," said I, "I have ventured to come to you to tell you frankly what I think of the policy of this bill—to ask your opinion of it, and to invoke your influence in having it defeated."

While I was making these remarks, Mr. Lincoln listened to me with patient politeness, and when I paused for a reply, he said: "You must allow me the Yankee privilege of answering your questions by first asking a few myself. During the late Presidential canvass, were you not chairman of the National Executive Committee of the party that supported Bell and Everett?"

"Yes," said I, "of the Constitutional Union party."

"The campaign motto or platform of which," he continued, "was *'The Union, the Constitution, and enforcement of the laws'?*"

"It was," I replied; "and I think that it was not only the briefest, but about the best and most comprehensive platform that could have been adopted for that canvass."

"And you still stand by it, of course?" said he.

"I certainly do," was my reply.

"Then," he remarked, "there is no reason why we should not be of the same mind in this emergency, if I understand the meaning of your platform. How do you, yourself, interpret it?"

"It's meaning," I answered, "is obvious. It has nothing hidden in it—nothing more than meets the eye. We go for *'the Union'* as our fathers made it—to be a shield of protection over our heads, and not a sword of subjugation at our hearts; for *'the Constitution'* as they designed it, to be equally binding on both sections, North as well as South, in all its compromises, and in all its requirements; and for *'the enforcement of the laws'* by peaceable and constitutional means, not by bayonets—Federal bayonets, especially, Mr. Lincoln."

"Then your idea is," said he, "that Federal bayonets should not be used for the enforcement of laws within the limits of a State?"

"As a general rule, unquestionably not," I answered; "but, of course, there are exceptional cases, such as have already occurred—cases of invasion, insurrection, etc.—when the civil authorities of a State, finding themselves inadequate to the duty of protecting their people, or unable to enforce the laws within the limits of their jurisdiction, may rightfully require the Federal forces to assist them; in which event, it becomes the duty of the General Government, on application of the Legislature of the State, or of its Executive, when the Legislature cannot be convened, to furnish the required aid."

"And, now," said he, "to apply your platform to the present condition of affairs in those Southern States of the Union which are assuming to be no longer part of it. How about enforcing the laws in them, just now—the laws of the United States?"

"Inasmuch," I replied, "as the difficulties of doing so peaceably, under existing circumstances, are exceeded only by the dangers of attempting it forcibly, the practical question to be determined beforehand is whether the experiment is worth a civil war. Which consideration," I added, "brings us back to the object of my visit, and I therefore again take the liberty of asking if you approve of

Congress passing such a Force bill now as this of Stanton's, and whether you will not aid us in defeating it?"

"Of course," said he, "I am extremely anxious to see these sectional troubles settled peaceably and satisfactorily to all concerned. To accomplish that, I am willing to make almost any sacrifice, and to do anything in reason consistent with my sense of duty. There is one point, however, I can never surrender—that which was the main issue of the Presidential canvass and decided at the late election, concerning the extension of slavery in the Territories."

"As to that matter," I replied, "however important it may have heretofore seemed to some persons, we can well afford to remit it to the remote future, when there may be a practical necessity for its consideration, inasmuch as it has dwindled into utter insignificance before that portentous issue now so unexpectedly before us."

"Unexpectedly, indeed, and portentous enough in all conscience!" said he; "but I trust that matters are not as bad as they appear."

"Bad as they certainly are," I replied, "they will be infinitely worse before long if the utmost care be not taken to allay the present excitement, and to preserve the existing status between the sections until some such plan as that of Mr. Crittenden's, for a general convention, can be carried into effect, which, as the Peace Conference here has failed to secure a compromise, is the ultimate reliance left us for that object." I then went on to say: "Mr. Lincoln, it may seem presumptuous in me to express my opinion to you on these subjects so decidedly. But I speak frankly, because I feel deeply their vital importance to the whole country, and especially to the people of the district which I represent, which is a border district, stretching along the Potomac from the Alleghenies to tidewater, and which, in the event of a sectional civil war, will not only be the first to suffer from its effects, but will feel them first, last, and all the time, and in all their intensity. I speak to you as a Union man, from a Union county, of a Union district, of a Union State—a State which has done more to make and to maintain the Union than any of her sister States have had it in their power to do, and which now, from her known conservatism, her acknowledged prestige in national politics, and her geographical position, midway between the angry sections, can do more than any other State to preserve the peace and to bring about, by her mediatorial influence, a satisfactory adjustment of these fearful complications in spite of the opposition of those twin foes of the Union—the fanatical faction of Abolitionists in the North, and that of the no less fanatical secessionists *per se* in the South—provided only that a little more time be allowed her to continue her

15

patriotic efforts to these ends. You will, therefore, I trust, not impute my earnestness to presumption when I say to you, in all sincerity, that the passage of this Force bill will paralyze the Unionists of Virginia, and be the means of precipitating her into secession—a calamity which, at this juncture, will unquestionably involve the whole country in a civil war."

After a silence of some seconds, during which Mr. Lincoln seemed to be absorbed in thought, he presently looked up with a smile, and said: "Well, I'll see what can be done about the bill you speak of. I think it can be stopped, and that I may promise you it will be."

Thanking him most cordially and sincerely for his kindness in acceding to my request, I then inquired if I might announce from my place in the House that he did not approve of the measure.

"By no means," said he, "for that would make trouble. The question would at once be asked, what right I had to interfere with the legislation of this Congress. Whatever is to be done in the matter, must be done quietly."

"But, as I have promised two of my colleagues," said I, "to let them know the result of this interview, I hope you will at least allow me to acquaint them, confidentially, with the substance of your conversation?" To this he assented, and warmly thanking him again, I got up to take leave; but, on his insisting that I should resume my seat, I remained in conversation with him some fifteen minutes longer. As what subsequently passed between us had no special bearing on the object of my visit, it is needless now to make any further reference to it, except to say, that it served to deepen the impression already made upon me by the interview, that Mr. Lincoln was a kind-hearted man; that he was, at that time, willing to allow the moderate men of the South a fair opportunity to make further efforts for a settlement of our intestine and internecine difficulties, and that he was by no means disposed to interfere, directly or indirectly, with the institutions of slavery in any of the States, or to yield to the clamorous demand of those bloody-minded extremists, who were then so very keen to cry "havoc!" and "let slip the dogs of war;" and afterward so exceedingly careful, with the characteristic caution of their kind, to keep out of harm's way during the continuance of hostilities. Having concluded my visit, I was about to return to the Capitol, when, perceiving that the House flag was down (a recess having been ordered from five until seven o'clock the same evening), I went at once to my room (at Willard's, where I boarded that winter), and employed myself until dinner in making full notes of the foregoing conversation, while it was fresh in my memory.

On the re-assembling of the House that evening, naturally anxious to know what would be the fate of the Force bill, I closely watched the proceedings; some of which, upon a proposition to suspend the rules, to receive the report of the Peace Congress, were of an exciting character, and afforded a significant illustration of the truth of the proverb that "extremes meet;" for when the ayes and nays were called, Abolitionists and Secessionists *per se* were found voting together against the suspension. It was nearly ten o'clock before Mr. Stanton succeeded in getting the bill up for consideration, and immediately thereupon, a leading Republican member from Mr. Lincoln's own State (Mr. Washburne, our distinguished Minister to France), moved an adjournment; but a question of order having arisen, Mr. Washburne's motion was not entertained. Shortly afterward, Mr. Stanton moved the previous question on the engrossment of the bill, which was followed by another motion to adjourn, made by a prominent Republican from Pennsylvania (Mr. Hickman), which was not put to vote, because the floor had not been yielded to Mr. Hickman by Mr. John Cochrane, of New York, who was entitled to it, but who himself, before taking his seat, renewed the motion for an adjournment; and although it was well understood on both sides of the House that Cochrane's motion involved the fate of the bill, it was finally agreed to by a vote of seventy-seven to sixty. So the House adjourned that evening, and the Thirty-sixth Congress expired on the following Monday, without having given to Mr. Lincoln the power asked for—to call out the militia, and to accept the services of volunteers. Yet, alas! in little more than a month thereafter, he allowed himself to be persuaded to issue his proclamation for that purpose, the sad results of which are recorded on the bloodiest pages of our country's history.

THE FIRST ATTACK ON FORT FISHER.

BY BENSON J. LOSSING, LL.D.

THERE exists, I think, much misapprehension in the public mind concerning the first attack on Fort Fisher, at the mouth of the Cape Fear river, by National land and naval forces, late in December, 1864. I was an eye and ear witness of that event, and several months afterward I visited the ruined fort with a citizen of Wilmington, who was familiar with the facts on the Confederate side. Wilmington, on the Cape Fear river, almost thirty miles from the sea, was, for a long time, the chief goal of the British blockade-runners, which brought supplies for the Confederates. These were swift-moving steam-vessels, of medium size, with raking smoke-stacks, and painted a pale gray, or fog-color. They were almost invisible, even in a slight mist on the ocean, and they continually eluded the vigilance and the power of the active and watchful blockading squadron on the coast of North Carolina. To protect these supply-ships, and to prevent National vessels from entering the Cape Fear river, forts and batteries had been constructed by the Confederates on the borders of the sea, at the mouth of that stream. The chief of these defenses was Fort Fisher, a formidable earthwork of an irregular quadrilateral trace, with exterior sides, of an average of about two hundred and fifty yards. Its northeastern angle, which was nearest the sea, approached high-water mark within one hundred yards. From that salient to the water was a strong stockade, or wooden palisade. The land-face of the fort occupied the whole width of the cape, known as Federal Point. It mounted twenty-six guns, nineteen of which were in a position

(228)

to sweep the narrow, sandy cape, on which it stood. These being exposed to an enfilading fire from ships on the sea, were heavily traversed with sand; the tops of the traverses rising full six feet above the general line of the interior crests, and affording bomb-proof shelters for the garrison. At a distance, these traverses had the appearance of a series of mounds. The slopes of the parapet were well secured by blocks of thick marsh-sods. The quarters of the men were wooden shanties, just outside the works, and to the north of it. All along the land-front of the fort, and across the cape from the ocean to the river, was a stockade, and on the beach, along the sea-front, were the wrecks of several blockade-runners. Many torpedoes were planted near each front of the fort. Near the end of Federal Point was an artificial hill of sand, about fifty feet in height, called Mound Battery. On this two heavy columbiads were mounted. Between Fort Fisher and this lofty battery was a line of intrenchments, on which were mounted sixteen heavy guns. These intrenchments ran parallel with the beach. Back of these, and extending across to the Cape Fear river, was a line of rifle-pits; and on the shore of the stream, across from Mound Battery, was another artificial sand-hill, thirty feet in height, with four cannon upon it, and named Battery Buchanan. These constituted the defenses on Federal Point, and commanded the entrance to the Cape Fear river by New Inlet. About seven miles southwest from Fort Fisher, at Smithville, on the right of the old entrance to the Cape Fear, was Fort Johnson; and about a mile south of that was Fort Caswell. The latter and Fort Fisher were the principal guardians of the port of Wilmington. At Baldhead Point, on Smith's Island, was Battery Holmes.

These were the works which the government proposed to turn or assail after Farragut had effectually closed the port of Mobile, in August, 1864. Wilmington was then the only refuge for blockade-runners on the Atlantic and Gulf coasts. The National Government considered several plans for capturing and holding the city of Wilmington. One, submitted by Frederic Kidder, of Boston, seemed most promising of success. Mr. Kidder proposed to have a fleet of flat-bottomed steamers rendezvous at Beaufort, fifty or sixty miles up the coast, on which should be placed about twelve thousand soldiers under a competent commander. These were to be suddenly landed on the main at Masonboro' Inlet and marched directly upon Wilmington. At the same time a strong cavalry force should move rapidly from Newbern, tear up the railway between Wilmington and Goldsboro', and, if possible, destroy the bridge over the Cape

Fear river, ten miles above the first-named town. It was known that no formidable defenses near Wilmington would oppose a force coming over from the sea. This plan was submitted by Mr. Kidder, early in 1864, to General Burnside, who was then recruiting men in New York and New England to fill up his corps—the Ninth. That energetic officer was so pleased and interested in the plan that he submitted it to the government, and received from the War Department full permission to carry it out. For that purpose he collected a large force at Annapolis, and was almost ready to go forward in the execution of the plan, when the campaigns in Virginia and Georgia were arranged by General Grant, and Burnside and the Ninth Corps were called to the Army of the Potomac. The expedition against Wilmington was abandoned, and its capture was postponed for nearly a year.

In the summer of 1864, General Charles K. Graham submitted a plan for the seizure of Wilmington. It was suggested by Kidder's plan. It proposed to have a force of cavalry and infantry, a thousand strong, collectively, and a section of artillery, go out from Newbern (then held by the National forces) and strike the railway between Wilmington and Goldsboro' with destructive energy, while two picked squadrons of cavalry and two thousand infantry, with a good battery, should land at Snead's ferry, at the mouth of New river, forty-one miles from Wilmington. This force should then march on that city, while another, composed of twenty-five hundred infantry, with ten pieces of artillery, should land at Masonboro' Inlet and push on toward Wilmington. It was believed that the menaces of these several bodies of troops would so distract and divide the Confederates that the capture of Wilmington would be an easy task. Circumstances prevented an attempt to execute General Graham's plan.

Meanwhile, arrangements had been made by the government for an attack, by land and water, on the forts at the entrance to Mobile Bay, which were crowned with success. Similar arrangements were made to assail the forts at the entrance to the Cape Fear river. So early as August, 1864, armored and unarmored gunboats began to gather in Hampton Roads. Full fifty of these were there in October, under the command of Admiral David D. Porter, who had performed signal services on the Mississippi and other inland waters in the Southwest. Among them were several vessels of the "Monitor" class and the "New Ironsides," a powerful vessel, built at Philadelphia, having a wooden hull covered with iron plates four inches in thickness, and at her bow an immense wrought-iron beak, constituting her the most formidable "ram" in existence. She carried sixteen eleven-inch Dahlgren guns, two two hundred-pound Parrott guns, and four twenty-four-pound howitzers, making her aggregate weight of metal two hundred and eighty-four thousand eight hundred pounds. She was propelled by a screw moved by two horizontal engines, and was furnished with sails and completely bark-rigged. This was the most formidable vessel in Porter's fleet, and fought Fort Fisher gallantly without receiving a wound. After that she returned to the place of her nativity, where she was dismantled and allowed to repose at League Island, just below Philadelphia, until accidentally destroyed by fire on Sunday, about the middle of December, 1866.

While this naval armament was gathering in Hampton Roads, Governor Andrews, of Massachusetts, had laid Mr. Kidder's plan before the government, and it was again approved. The proponent was sent for, and he accompanied Admiral Porter from the National Capital to Hampton Roads. At Fortress Monroe, they had an interview with Lieutenant General Grant, who also approved the plan, and agreed to send the bulk of Sheridan's army, then in the Shenandoah Valley, to execute it. Again the supreme necessities of the service interfered. The movements of the Confederates in the Valley detained Sheridan there; and, as no competent force of cavalry could be had to make the co-operating movement from Newbern with forces at Masonboro' Inlet, the plan was again abandoned. Then measures for making a direct attack upon the Cape Fear defenses were pressed with energy.

In September, Generals Godfrey Weitzel and Charles K. Graham had made a reconnoissance of Fort Fisher by means of the blockading squadron. Rumors of this movement had reached the Confederates. On the fall of the Mobile forts, they perceived that their only hopes of receiving supplies from the sea rested on their ability to keep open the port of Wilmington to blockade-runners. The reconnoissance implied a meditated attempt to close it. Their suspicions were confirmed by the gathering of the formidable naval force in Hampton Roads. Then they hastened to strengthen Fort Fisher and its dependencies, by erecting new military works and increasing its garrison. The skilful engineer and judicious commander, General W. H. C. Whiting, was in charge of the Confederate forces in that region, in the absence of General Braxton Bragg, who had gone to Georgia with a greater portion of the Confederate troops at and around Wilmington, to oppose General Sherman's march from Atlanta to the sea. The fact that General Bragg had gone to Georgia, with most of the troops in Eastern North Carolina, was communicated to General Grant at the close of November, and he considered it important to strike the blow at Fort Fisher in the absence of that general. Grant had held a consultation with Admiral Porter in Hampton Roads, and it was agreed that the lieutenant general should provide 6,500 troops from the Army of the James, then under the command of General Benjamin F. Butler, to co-operate with the fleet. The immediate command of the troops was given to General Weitzel. Orders were issued for the soldiers and transports to be put in readiness at Bermuda Hundred (at the junction of the Appomattox and James rivers), to move as speedily as possible; and in the instructions given to General Butler (who accompanied the expedition), on the 6th of December, it was stated that the first object of the effort was to close the port of Wilmington, and the second was the capture of that city. He was instructed to debark the troops between the Cape Fear river and the sea, north of the north entrance (or New Inlet) to the river. Should the landing be effected while the Confederates still held Fort Fisher and the batteries guarding the entrance to the river, the troops were to intrench themselves, and, by co-operating with the navy, effect the reduction and capture of these places, when the navy could enter the river, and the port of Wilmington would be sealed. General Butler was further instructed that, "Should the troops under General Weitzel fail to effect a landing at or near Fort Fisher, they will be returned to the armies operating against Richmond, without delay."

A part of the plan of the operations against Fort Fisher was the explosion of a floating mine, containing between two and three hundred tons of gunpowder, so near the works that they might be destroyed, or the garrison be so paralyzed by the shock as to make the conquest an easy task. General Butler had proposed this expedient, having read of the destructive effects, at a considerable distance, of the explosion of a large quantity of gunpowder in England. He made the suggestion to the government, just as he was about to depart for the city of New York to preserve order during the Presidential election. It was submitted to experts. Among these was the late Richard Delafield, then Chief Engineer of the Army, who made an elaborate report, in which he showed that experience had taught the impossibility of very serious injury being done, in a lateral direction, by the explosion of unconfined gunpowder. He fortified his opinion by diagrams, showing the form of Fort Fisher and the other defenses, and concluded that the experiment would certainly result in failure. Captain Henry A. Wise, Chief of the

Ordnance Bureau, gave it as his opinion that no serious damage would be done beyond five hundred yards from the point of explosion. At a consultation of experts, at the house of Captain Wise, who had been summoned by Mr. Fox, the Assistant Secretary of the Navy, the subject was fully discussed, and it was concluded that it would be worth while to try the experiment, with a hope that the explosion might be effectual. When General Butler returned from New York, he found that the powder experiment was to be tried, and that preparations for it were being made. This matter caused some delay in the movements of the navy, and the expedition was not ready to sail before the 13th of December.

At this juncture I arrived at Hampton, accompanied by two Philadelphia friends (Ferdinand J. Dreer and Edward Greble), on my way to the headquarters of the army at City Point. While breakfasting at a restaurant I heard a person say, "The general is here." "What general?" I inquired. "General Butler," he answered. "He is at Fort Monroe." I had a private letter of introduction to General Butler, and letters from the Secretaries of War and Navy, and from President Lincoln, requesting officers of the United States service, who should read them, to give me every facility consistent with the rules of the service for obtaining historical materials. We went to the fort; I sent in my credentials to General Butler, and we were invited to his quarters, where we were introduced to his wife and daughter. Turning to me the General asked, "Did you ever see a naval fight?" I replied in the negative. "If you will go with me," he said, "I will show you one of the greatest naval contests on record." "Of course, I cannot ask *where* it will occur," I answered; "but I will inquire about how long we shall be gone?" "A week or ten days," the General replied. I guessed the destination to be Fort Fisher. "I will go," I said; but, recalling the words, remarked, "I cannot leave these gentlemen, who are traveling with me." "Invite them to go along," said the General. We consulted a few moments, and agreed to go. In the afternoon we accompanied General Butler on a visit to Admiral Porter, in his flag-ship, the "Malvern," lying in the Roads. On our return we were directed to be on board the Ben Deford, Butler's headquarters' ship, at eight o'clock the next morning. The vessel did not sail that day, and we visited the battle-field at Bethel, a few miles up the Virginia Peninsula, where the gallant son of Mr. Greble was slain at the beginning of the war.

The troops that composed the expedition against Fort Fisher were the divisions of Generals Ames and Paine, of the Army of the

James. Those of the latter were colored troops. They arrived at Hampton Roads in transports from Bermuda Hundred, on the morning of the 9th of December, when General Butler notified the Admiral that his troops were in readiness, and his transports were coaled and watered for only ten days. The Admiral said he would not leave before the 13th, and must go into Beaufort harbor, on the North Carolina coast, to obtain ammunition for his "monitors." The 13th being the day fixed for the departure of the fleet, at three o'clock in the morning of that day General Butler sent all the transports but his own ship up the Potomac some distance, where they remained all day. This was to mislead the Confederates, and divert their attention from his real designs. At night they returned and anchored under the lee of Cape Charles. On the following morning the Ben Deford left her moorings at Hampton, joined the fleet of transports, and all went out to sea. As we moved from the wharf a solitary cannon at Fortress Monroe fired a parting salute, and ladies on the ramparts, standing near the great Rodman gun that dwarfed them into dolls, waved an adieu with fluttering white handkerchiefs. The Ben Deford bore Generals Butler, Weitzel and Graham, and their respective staff officers, and Colonel Comstock of General Grant's staff, as his representative. The atmosphere was cloudless and serene; and all the afternoon the white beach and a continuous fringe of an almost unbroken pine forest along the North Carolina coast was visible. The transports dotted the sea at wide intervals; and when, at past midnight, we passed "Stormy Cape Hatteras," in the light of the waning moon, the heaving bosom of the ocean was as unruffled as a lake on a calm summer's day. On the evening of the 15th, we reached the appointed rendezvous, twenty-five miles at sea east of Fort Fisher, and out of reach of discovery by the Confederates on the shore. The rest of the transports soon gathered around us, and constituted a social community in the watery waste. There we waited three days for the arrival of the vessels of war, which had gone to sea the day before the departure of the transport-ships. The weather was delightful. There was a dreamy repose in the air like that of the delicious Indian summer, and the mercury rose to seventy-five degrees in the shade on the deck of the Ben Deford. This continued until the 18th. Meanwhile, all eyes had been turned anxiously northward to catch a glimpse of the expected war fleet, but disappointment came with each morning and evening.

Never was the sea more favorable for landing troops on the beach, and executing the details of the expedition, than during those three calm days. Delay caused the golden opportunity to be lost. On Sunday afternoon, the 18th, a chilling breeze came from the southeast, bringing with it a slight mist, the harbinger of an approaching storm. White-caps soon garnished the bosom of the ocean, and the wind constantly freshened. Toward sunset, the shadowy forms of vessels appeared on the hazy northern horizon. They were the heralds of Porter's magnificent fleet of warriors—the most formidable naval armament ever put afloat on the sea. There were fifty-eight strongly-armed vessels, fully manned, and four of them were "monitors." They gathered around us at twilight; and when the night set in, dark and lowering, their numerous lights on deck, and in the rigging, some white, and some colored, gave the pleasing impression of a floating city on the bosom of the great deep; and so it was. Very soon there was brisk signaling, with blazing torches, between the Ben Deford and the "Malvern;" and, at eight o'clock, General Butler departed for the latter in his gig to confer with Admiral Porter. On his return, he announced that it was intended to explode the floating mine, near Fort Fisher, at one o'clock in the morning, and to land the troops for attack, if possible, soon after the dawn of day.

The floating mine, or powder-ship, was a propeller of two hundred and ninety-five tons burden, named "Louisiana." She was disguised as a blockade-runner, in form and color, with two raking smoke-stacks—one real, the other a sham. A light deck above the water-line contained two hundred and fifteen tons (four hundred and thirty thousand pounds) of gunpowder, placed first in a row of barrels standing on their ends, the upper ones open, and the remainder in bags, each containing sixty pounds. The latter were stowed in tiers above the barrels. To communicate fire to the whole mass simultaneously, four separate threads of the Gomez fuse were woven through it, passing through each separate barrel and bag. At the stern, and under the powder-charged deck, was placed a heap of pine wood and other combustible materials, which were to be fired by the crew, when they were to escape in a swift little steamer employed for the purpose. Clock-work, by which a percussion-cap might be exploded, and ignite the fuse; short spermaceti candles, which would burn down, and fire the fuse, and a slow match, that would work in time with the candles, were all employed. The plan was to choose a favorable state of the weather for landing troops in launches on the beach, explode the powder-ship after midnight, and debark the troops at dawn, to take advantage of the effects of the explosion on the fort and garrison.

Warned that the explosion would take place in the "small hours" of the morning, we watched on deck until far past midnight, and were disappointed. The vessels had moved, in the darkness, to a point about twelve miles from Fort Fisher. Ignorant of what might be the effect of the explosion in the air at that distance, the engineers of the vessels caused the steam to be much lowered, to avoid a possible explosion of the boilers, in case of a sudden relief from atmospheric pressure. But the grand spectacle was not exhibited. It was evident that the water was too rough for troops to land, and the attack was postponed. The wind increased in violence the next day, and toward evening assumed the aspects of a gale. The low-decked "monitors" were frequently submerged, only their revolving turrets being visible. The transports had been coaled and watered, as we have observed, for only ten days, and that time had now been consumed in waiting for warriors and voyaging; and, by the advice of Admiral Porter, the unarmed fleet went to Beaufort, seventy miles up the coast, for a new supply. We were before the furious gale all night, and, with difficulty, threaded the sinuous channel into Beaufort harbor the next morning, just in time to escape the severest portion of the tempest, the heaviest, our pilot told us, that had been experienced on that coast in thirty years. There we remained until Saturday, the 24th. On Friday, when the ships were replenished, and the storm had passed by, General Butler sent one of his aides (Captain Clark), in an armed tug, to inform Porter that the transports, with the troops, would be at the rendezvous, off Fort Fisher, at six o'clock in the evening the next day. Clark returned at sunrise on Saturday, and reported that Porter had determined to explode the powder-ship at one o'clock that morning, and begin the attack without waiting for the troops. Butler could not believe the report to be correct, because the presence of the troops to co-operate in the attack would be essential to the success of the costly experiment of the powder-ship.

We departed for the rendezvous on Saturday morning. Between three and four o'clock in the afternoon, when we were off Masonboro' Inlet, and while standing on the bow of the Ben Deford with General Weitzel, I called his attention to small white flacculent clouds that appeared and disappeared at irregular intervals near the southern horizon. "Porter is at work," he said. "The 'clouds' are the smoke of exploding bombshells." Very soon we met an ammunition-box; then a dozen, and then an acre of them, floating in the sea. The testimony of these mute witnesses of a combat was soon confirmed by the sullen roar of artillery that fell upon the ear. We arrived at the scene of conflict just as it had ceased. A heavy pall of sulphurous smoke, made blood-red by the setting sun behind it, hung in the still air over Fort Fisher. Porter had, indeed, caused the "Louisiana," under the command of the intrepid Captain Rhind, to follow in the wake of a blockade-runner, at midnight, to within three hundred yards of the northeast salient of Fort Fisher. There she was anchored, and at two o'clock in the morning the powder was exploded without any sensible effect upon the fort or the garrison. The shock was felt like a slight earthquake at Newbern and Beaufort, but the garrison of Fort Fisher thought it was the effect of the bursting of the boiler of a blockade-runner. Probably not one-tenth of the powder was ignited. The fort seemed untouched by the explosion, for the edges of the parapet remained as sharply defined as ever.

Ten hours later Admiral Porter opened his heavy artillery on Fort Fisher and Mound Battery, and in the course of a few hours he hurled eight thousand shells upon them. The brief and feeble responses made by the guns of these defenses deceived the Admiral, and he believed he had disabled them all. At the middle of the afternoon he sent a dispatch to the Secretary of the Navy, in which he said that in half an hour after getting the ships in position he silenced Fort Fisher, but there *were no troops to take possession,* and he was "merely firing at it to keep up practice." "The forts," he said, "are nearly demolished, and as soon as troops come we can take possession." He added: "All that is wanted now is troops to land to go into them." How utterly deceived and mistaken the Admiral was appears from a statement of General Whiting, who said that no damage was done to Fort Fisher; that only one man was killed, and three were severely and nineteen were slightly wounded, and that only five gun-carriages were disabled and not a gun was bruised. The complaint of the absence of troops, by Admiral Porter, seems disingenious and ungracious under the circumstances, and was unjust to the army, which, as we have seen, had waited for the motions of the fleet already six days. And had the Admiral waited a few hours for the troops, which, he had been informed, would be there that day, he would have had them in full co-operation with him. As it was, he had defeated the intentions of both branches of the service concerning the powder-vessel, by causing it to be exploded when the army, in consequence of waiting for the navy, was, by the advice of the Admiral, seventy miles from the scene of action. Butler and Porter made arrangements to renew the attack the next morning at eight o'clock. Orders were given for us all to breakfast at six.

Preparations for the next day's serious work were completed at an early hour, and the young staff officers, who generally kept the deck merry with songs and jokes and conundrums until midnight, retired soberly at nine o'clock on that, to them, momentous Christmas eve.

The morning dawned brightly. It was the Christian Sabbath and the recurring birthday of the Prince of Peace. The fleet was not ready before ten o'clock, when the conflict was begun by light-draft gunboats shelling batteries on the shore, to clear the way for landing troops on the beach. Very soon the larger vessels began to hurl heavy missiles upon the main works. For several hours the bombardment continued without intermission. At a little past noon the transports were moved within eight hundred yards of the beach. A few shells sent from the land batteries exploded near us, and one passed directly through one of the smaller gunboats. Finally, these batteries were silenced by broadsides from the "Brooklyn," whose one hundred-pound guns were effective. Soon afterward the launches were prepared and filled with a part of Ames' Division (about one-third of all the troops present) and moved for the shore. General Curtis was the first to make the beach. We saw his tall, commanding figure bear forward the Stars and Stripes and plant them on a deserted battery. The act was greeted by loud cheers from the transports, and the bands struck up "Yankee Doodle." It was then about three o'clock. The "Malvern" passed near the Ben Deford, and Admiral Porter, standing on the wheel-house, called out to General Butler, saying: "There is not a rebel within five miles of the fort. You have nothing to do but march in and take it." This was another grave mistake, and led the Admiral to make most unkind reflections upon the military commander in his report two days afterward. At that moment, according to the testimony of General Whiting, there were two hundred and fifty more men in Fort Fisher than on the previous day, and behind its uninjured sand walls were *nine hundred effective men*, in good spirits, who, secure in their bomb-proofs, kept up a lazy response to the bombardment from the sea-front all day. The guns on the land-front were drawn back behind the traverses, and so excessively enfilading was the fire of the fleet, that not one of the nineteen cannons was seriously injured.

General Weitzel, the immediate commander of the National troops, accompanied by General Graham and Colonel Comstock, pushed a reconnoitering party to within five hundred yards of Fort Fisher, accepting the surrender, on the way, of the garrison of Flag Pond Hill Battery, consisting of sixty-two men, who were sent to the fleet. The skirmishers went within seventy-five yards of the fort, where nearly a dozen were wounded by the bursting of shells from the fleet. One soldier ran forward to the ditch and captured a flag, which the shells had cut from the parapet; and Lieutenant Walling, of the One Hundred and Forty-second New York Regiment, seeing a courier leave the sally-port, near the Cape Fear, rushed forward, shot the messenger, took his pistols from the holsters and a paper from his pocket, and, mounting the dead man's mule, rode back to the lines. The paper contained an order from Colonel Lamb, the immediate commander of the fort, for some powder to be sent in.

General Butler did not go on shore, but in the tug Chamberlain he moved to Fort Fisher, abreast the troops, and kept up communication with Weitzel by signals. Meanwhile, the remainder of Ames' Division had captured over two hundred North Carolinians, with ten commissioned officers, from whom Butler learned that Hoke's Division had been detached from the Confederate army at Petersburg for the defense of Wilmington; that two brigades were then within two miles of Fort Fisher, and that others were pressing on. The weather was now murky, and a heavy surf was beginning to roll in, making it impossible to land any more troops. Weitzel, who had thoroughly reconnoitred the fort, reported to Butler that in his judgment, and that of the officers with him, a successful assault upon it, with the troops at hand, would be impossible, for the moment the fleet should cease firing, the parapets would be fully manned and its nineteen heavy guns would sweep the land. It was also evident that the Confederate force outside of Fort Fisher, and near it, was much larger than that of the Nationals. Considering all of these things, Butler ordered the troops to withdraw and re-embark. While doing so, at twilight, the guns of the navy ceased work, when those of Fort Fisher sent a storm of grape and canister-shot after the retiring troops. It was impossible to get them on board that night, and it was thirty-six hours before they were rescued from their perilous position. On the following day the transports departed for Hampton Roads, leaving the fleet lying off Fort Fisher, with its ammunition nearly exhausted. The National loss, in this attack, was about fifty men killed and wounded, nearly all by the bursting of six heavy Parrott guns of the fleet. The Confederate loss was three killed, fifty-five wounded, and three hundred made prisoners.

The failure to capture Fort Fisher produced keen disappointment, and Admiral Porter's misleading report caused widespread indignation. Experts say, in the light of facts revealed, that the army officers acted wisely in not attacking. It seems to me that the chief cause of our failure may be found in the lack of co-operation with the land forces at the beginning. During the delay caused by the first day's waiting for the fleet at the rendezvous, and the succeeding gale, the Confederates were apprised of the expedition, and took sufficient measures to meet and frustrate it. Wilmington was denuded of troops, and the army was waiting for the fleet off Fort Fisher on the middle of December. At that time the garrison of the fort consisted of only six hundred and sixty-seven men. When Weitzel stood before it on Christmas day, it was nine hundred strong, and at least seven thousand men were within forty-eight hours' march of it.

MORGAN'S INDIANA AND OHIO RAID.

BY GENERAL BASIL W. DUKE.

THE expedition undertaken by General John H. Morgan, in the summer of 1863, and known as the "Indiana and Ohio Raid," serves more than any other effort of his active and adventurous career to illustrate his audacious strategy, and an account of it may be read with some interest as a contribution to the history of the *late civil war. I shall endeavor, therefore, as requested, to narrate its principal incidents; and, in order that a proper understanding of its purpose and importance as a military movement may be had, I must be allowed a brief description of the relative conditions and attitude of the two contending armies in Tennessee and Kentucky at that date. Indeed, if I hope to vindicate General Morgan's reputation from the charge of senseless audacity to which this raid gave rise, I should premise by saying that in this, as in all similar enterprises, he planned and conducted his operations with reference to those of the army to which he was attached, and with strict regard to the exigencies of the general campaign. While chiefly employed in what the French term *la petite guerre*, he directed his movements in accordance with the programme of the "great war."

The military situation in General Bragg's department was ominous of ill-fortune to the Confederates. Bragg's army, always inferior to the one opposing it, in numerical strength, had recently been greatly reduced by large detachments summoned by General Joseph E. Johnston, to aid in his projected movement to relieve Vicksburg. It was confronted at Tullahoma by the vastly superior forces of Rosecrans. General Simon Buckner was holding East

16   (241)

Tennessee with a force entirely inadequate to the defense of that important region. General Burnside was concentrating in Kentucky, for the invasion of East Tennessee, a force variously estimated at from twenty to more than thirty thousand men. It was estimated that on the Kentucky and Tennessee border there were, at least, ten or twelve thousand Federal troops, under the command of a General Judah, five thousand of which were excellent cavalry. This body was in a position to threaten the right flank of the Confederate army at Tullahoma if it should remain there, or greatly embarrass its movements if it retreated. General Bragg did not doubt that there would be an early advance of this formidable line—that Rosecrans would press on him, and Burnside simultaneously fall upon Buckner—and he knew that the Confederate positions could not be held. So soon as he fully realized the danger, he determined, as the only means of saving his attenuated army from utter annihilation by the enemy's masses, to promptly retreat to the south of the Tennessee river. But retreat to the army in front of Rosecrans was in no wise easy or free from hazard. To cross the Tennessee, with the Federal columns pushing close on its rear and flanks, threatened danger to that army almost as serious as a battle. Nor could battle be avoided, or long delayed, even if this retreat was successfully accomplished. The Confederate General knew that somewhere in the vicinity of Chattanooga he would have to turn upon his foes and fight. It was no longer possible to defend Middle Tennessee. A greater sacrifice, the evacuation of East Tennessee—the citadel of the Confederacy—was, perhaps, necessary. But retreat, continued too far, would degenerate into flight, and bring speedy ruin.

After the safe withdrawal of his army from Tullahoma to the new line south of the Tennessee, Bragg's chief object would be to delay Judah and Burnside—the latter especially—and to retard their advance and junction with Rosecrans until after reinforcements he was expecting from Virginia should arrive. He even hoped that circumstances might be so ordered as to prohibit a part of these forces, at least, from appearing in season for the decisive battle he intended to deliver. In this strategic emergency he saw no means of diverting the attention of the enemy, and of securing the much-needed time for the consummation of his plans, save by an energetic use of his cavalry. While vigorously pushing Rosecrans' outposts with the divisions of Martin and Wharton, in accordance with this policy, he designed for Morgan, in pursuance of the same plan, a far more important service. The latter was instructed to move rapidly with two thousand men of his division in the direction of Louisville, capture that city, if possible, and proceed thence into Middle and Eastern Kentucky, inviting pursuit by all the Federal forces who could thus be lured away from the vicinity of the anticipated conflict. By such a raid General Bragg believed that Judah could be so thoroughly employed as to leave him no leisure time to harass the withdrawal of the Confederates from Tullahoma; and he was confident that, if it should be more than usually active and prolonged, it might even engage the attention and arrest the march of Burnside.

Morgan had foreseen the necessity of such a diversion, and had long eagerly looked forward to a campaign in the Northern border States. Months before, he received intimation that he would be dispatched on this service, and believing the period to consummate his favorite hope was approaching, he had sent men to examine the fords of the upper Ohio. Ardently agreeing with General Bragg that a cavalry raid, judiciously managed, would do much to assist in extricating the army from its difficult and perilous situation, he yet differed with his superior in regard to one important feature of the proposed expedition. He argued that it should not be confined to Kentucky, and urged that he should be allowed to cross the Ohio. The people of Kentucky, he said, were grown accustomed to raids, and no longer prone to magnify the numbers of those who made them. The Federal Government, too, cared little to guard Kentucky against such incursions, and certainly would sacrifice no military advantage to do so. A dash into Kentucky would be decided too soon to effect any positive good, but a raid into Indiana and Ohio, he contended, would bring all the troops under Judah and Burnside in hot haste after him; would keep them engaged for weeks, and prevent their participation in Bragg's battle with Rosecrans—the object of greatest moment. Notwithstanding the sound military reasons why Rosecrans' plans should not be interrupted by the withdrawal of troops upon which he relied for their execution, the alarm and the clamor in those States would be so great that the administration would be forced to heed their outcry, and furnish soldiery for their protection.

His earnest representations, however, wrought no change in the views of his chief, and he was ordered to conduct the expedition in the manner which General Bragg, who was unwilling to risk the loss of so large a body of his cavalry, had first directed. But so positive were Morgan's convictions that, in order to be of any benefit in so grave a crisis, his raid should be extended to northern territory, he deliberately resolved to disobey the order restricting his operations to Kentucky; and, although he well knew that the chances of disaster were multiplied ten-fold by such a step, he made up his mind to take it. When he declared this determination, those with whom he advised made no effort to dissuade him from it, perfectly obvious as were the hazards to be encountered, and the serious breach of discipline involved in the infraction of the instructions given him. There was much in the idea of an enterprise so bold and exciting that found favor in the eyes of men trained to war under Morgan. In their judgment, informed by a long experience in just such service, his view of the situation was the correct one. And, at any rate, his resolve was fixed, and opposition would have been useless. It would have been easier to halt the stag-hound in full stretch after his quarry, than to have induced him to abandon this purpose. I do not remember to have ever seen General Morgan's remarkable military genius so vividly indicated as when he sketched his plan of that raid, and predicted its general events. Concealing from himself in no wise the dangers before him, and fairly calculating all the adverse chances, he explained, as he traced his proposed course upon the map, the expedient by which he expected to avoid every difficulty as it should arise. In these conferences he exhibited in a marked degree his extraordinary power of anticipating the effect of his own action upon his opponents, and of calculating what they would do; and more than once afterward, when Indiana and Ohio guides proved stubborn or recusant, and our devious march seemed about to end in abrupt disaster, I had occasion to recall his previous delineation of it, and wonder at his singular faculty of arriving at a correct idea of the nature and features of a country of which he was informed only by maps, and the most general description. While conceding that, from first to last, his progress would be attended with unusual difficulty and peril, he anticipated very serious danger at four points only, viz., at the crossing of the Cumberland river, the crossing of the Ohio, the march past Cincinnati, and, if compelled to attempt it, the recrossing of the Ohio. He hoped, however, to be relieved from the necessity of this latter risk by joining General Lee's army, if it should still be in Pennsylvania.

On the 2d of July, 1863, with two brigades of cavalry, aggregating an effective strength of twenty-four hundred and sixty men, and a battery of four field-pieces, he commenced the passage of the Cumberland, at Burksville. The heavy rains, of eight or ten days' duration, just previously, had immensely swollen the river. Its banks no longer confined the volume of its waters; its width was far greater than usual, and its current very strong and rapid. No large boats could be procured, and the only means of transportation for the men and artillery were small rafts, constructed by lashing canoes together, and making a flooring upon them of fence-rails. The horses were forced to swim, and, after laboring through the fierce stream and painfully climbing the crumbling, treacherous bank, they stood panting and trembling, in little groups, until comforted by the arrival of their masters. With such inadequate facilities, the passage of the river was necessarily tedious; but something worse than hard work, and loss of time, was to be apprehended. As has already been intimated, this, the initiatory step of the expedition, was one of the most perilous. Judah's cavalry was stationed only twelve miles distant from Burksville, where it had been concentrated immediately when Morgan appeared upon the border. It was more than double our entire strength, and if its commander had closely watched the river, and had attacked vigorously when our passage was partially effected, not only would the raid have been crushed in its inception, but we would have been cut to pieces. It is possible that his vigilance had been deceived by the apparent withdrawal of our regiments, after they had remained inactive for nearly a week upon the banks of the river; and he may have believed that, having recruited men and horses in the fertile and grassy valleys where they had been encamped, Morgan intended to seek safer proximity to Bragg. But, even if the Federal commander was beguiled into such a delusion by demonstrations made with no other view than to mislead him, his negligent watch was inexcusable. So far from himself trusting to chance, Morgan, finding the river unguarded, and not even observed by videttes, chose the very time that the difficulty of getting over was the greatest, for the reason that the attempt would then be least expected.

The result verified the accuracy of his calculations. Information of our movements was not transmitted to the enemy until late in the day, and it was not until nearly three in the afternoon that a column of about one thousand strong approached Burksville, so closely as to threaten the First Brigade, of which some eight hundred men were, by that hour, across. This force was promptly disposed to receive the advancing cavalry, and the ground about a mile back of the village being favorable, the greater part of it was placed in ambuscade. The Federals, unsuspectingly, trotted into the trap, and, recoiling before one stinging volley, delivered at short range, rushed back in confusion. General Morgan, at the head of a reserve of two hundred men, whom he had kept mounted, pressed the retreat so energetically that he dashed into Judah's camp along with the fleeing squadrons. For a few minutes there ensued a scene of indescribable turmoil, which promised to become a panic of the entire Federal command. Tents were overthrown, men were trampled down by their comrades rushing blindly about, riderless horses plunged in every direction, and the startled soldiers thronged and huddled together in fear and amazement, which paralyzed them while it lasted. But even while the Confederates were firing into their faces, and the confusion seemed irremediable, the discipline of these veterans reasserted itself, and their coolness began to return. Rallying in squads, without alignment or formation, for which there was no time, they poured a quick and continuous fire upon their assailants. Two or three pieces of artillery, wheeled rapidly into position, opened like a succession of thunder-claps, and raked the road along which the Confederate column was charging. To have continued the attack would have been madness, and Morgan, drawing off his riders as suddenly as he had brought them on, retired, leaving his adversaries so stupefied by the unexpected blow he had dealt them that they remained quietly in camp until next morning. But before that morning's sun had risen, Morgan had gotten everything across the angry flood, and was miles away upon the road to Northern Kentucky. Thus actually had he, from the nettle "danger," plucked the flower "safety."

It would be impossible, even were it desirable, to give, in the limits of an article like this, a detailed account of all the minor incidents which make up the history of an expedition of this character; and, of course, the numerous personal adventures of constant occurrence, when such a body of daring, reckless cavalrymen were threading or forcing their dubious way through the multitude of foes encompassing them, cannot well be told. The acts of individual prowess, the "hairbreadth escapes" which add such zest to the campaign, and afford the veteran "fighting his battles o'er again" exhaustless themes of interest or amusement, will scarcely be worth recital, unless the *raconteur*, forsaking all graver topics, devotes exclusive attention to them. The usual concomitants of a cavalry raid, the petty, but often sharp and desperately contested combats between small scouting parties, the fatal duels between videttes and pickets, which, trifling as they seem, yet fearfully swell the tale of blood and death, were uncommonly frequent in the six days during which we were traversing the breadth of Kentucky. Our line of march brought us in contact with the enemy far oftener than General Morgan wished, for he was anxious to economize his strength for the long, tough strain that he was yet to encounter. Nevertheless, as we had no choice but to pass through points strongly garrisoned, or avoid them by deflections from the direct route which would have greatly lengthened the march, and, perhaps, enabled the cavalry force we had eluded at the Cumberland, and now following, to overtake and attack us, we were forced to fight more than once when little inclined to do so. On the evening of the 3d, our advance guard and the Second Kentucky found a sharp skirmish with Woodford's regiment necessary to win the right of way through Columbia. On the 4th, one of the hottest collisions I ever witnessed occurred between five or six hundred men of the Third, Fifth, and Sixth Kentucky Regiments of ours, and a Michigan regiment four or five hundred strong, at the crossing of Green river. The officer commanding this Federal detachment had selected an exceedingly strong position, and had fortified it hastily, but skilfully. Summoned to surrender, he answered that the 4th of July was not " a good day for surrender." The assault was spirited and resolute, but was repulsed, and, after severe loss, we marched around the position without taking it. On the 5th, we attacked and captured Lebanon, occupied by a Kentucky infantry regiment. Two Michigan cavalry regiments advanced to relieve the garrison, but were driven off. The fighting lasted several hours, and the town was badly battered by our artillery. On the 6th, the column passed through Bardstown without meeting with resistance, although it was a point where we had anticipated serious opposition. On the same evening we crossed the Louisville and Nashville Railroad, at the Lebanon Junction, thirty miles from Louisville, and ascertained that a large and satisfactory panic was prevailing in that city.

We had now run the gauntlet of garrisoned towns, and passed the cordon of cavalry detachments stretched through Middle and Southern Kentucky. Judah's cavalry, under General Hobson, was following us, but was far in the rear. We had reason to believe the distance between us was hourly increasing. Our column marched the more rapidly and constantly, and uncertainty about our course would delay Hobson. Finding that we had not attacked Louisville, and had turned to the left, he would naturally suppose that we were seeking to escape through Western Kentucky. It was improbable that he would divine Morgan's intention to cross the Ohio.

On the 8th, before mid-day, we reached Brandenburg, and the Ohio river rolled before our eyes. Never before had it looked so mighty and majestic—and so hard to cross. A small detachment, under picked officers, had been sent in advance to capture steamboats, and had successfully accomplished its mission. We found two large boats awaiting us, and preparations to cross were instantly commenced. At this point the Ohio is about one thousand yards wide, and the Indiana shore, just opposite, favorable for the landing of the boats and disembarkation of men and horses. A dense mist which had overspread the surface of the river during the morning, suddenly lifted just before noon as one of the steamboats was about to push off with the Second Kentucky and Ninth Tennessee, which two regiments (leaving their horses for the nonce) were detailed as the first to cross. Almost simultaneously with the disappearance of the foggy curtain which had obstructed our view of the farther bank, and before the quickened eye well had time to take in the situation, our glances were attracted by the spouting flashes from, perhaps, a hundred rifles, aimed from the very spot where the boat must land, and quickly followed by the long, leaping flame and sullen roar of a field-piece. The range was too great for the small-arms to do danger, but several shell from the piece smashed into the groups scattered about the wharf, before it was silenced, and two or three men were wounded. General Morgan at once ordered the section of three-inch Parrotts, which made part of the battery, to be brought up. A few well-directed shots from these dispersed this party of hospitable Indianians, whose eager haste to welcome us anticipated our actual arrival in their State, and although they tried hard to save their artillery they were forced to abandon it. The boat immediately shoved across, and the two regiments which she carried sprang ashore, formed, and pressed forward, under fire from the party just before driven back by the steel guns, but which had retreated no further than a wooded ridge some five hundred yards from the river, where they either rejoined or were reinforced by another body of about the same strength.

Before more troops could be put over an interruption occurred, which threatened to stop all further proceedings. A river gunboat, small but vicious, put in an appearance, and opened fire alternately upon the men on the Indiana shore, the boats, and the troops in town. She carried three guns, and it was evident that, if well and boldly handled, it was possible for her to become mistress of the situation. So long as she remained within range, it would have been suicidal to have attempted to pass the river. A single well-aimed shot would have sent either boat to the bottom, and caused the loss of every man on board. But delay would be equally fatal. If the gunboat should do no more than stand guard over the ferry, and hold us inactive, we were ruined. Two of our strongest and best regiments were already dangerously compromised. Separated from the main body by the broad torrent, and, in that most awkward of all predicaments for cavalry, cut off from their horses, they might be attacked at any moment by overwhelming odds, while debarred retreat or assistance.

We were only thirty or forty miles from Louisville. So soon as a true comprehension of the situation was obtained there, a sufficient force might be sent thence to capture our comrades on the Indiana side, and successfully resist our passage, even if the gunboat should then release us from durance. Moreover, although Hobson might be mystified for a short period in regard to our movements, his doubt could not last long, and nothing could be more certain than, if we were detained twenty-four hours, he would be upon us, reinforced, perhaps, by every Federal cavalry detachment in Central Kentucky. We were not strong enough to cope with the half of such a force, for our original total of twenty-four hundred and sixty was now diminished by one hundred and fifty or sixty men, killed and wounded in the engagements sustained on the march, and some two hundred detached for necessary diversions. It was a sheer, absolute necessity that the gunboat should be sunk, or driven off, and the Parrotts were posted on a small hill, immediately overlooking the river, and set to work at her in dead earnest. Nothing loth, she instantly accepted the challenge, and, turning her broadside to the battery, gave back shot for shot.

Crowding upon the bluffs, the men watched this duel with intense interest. The hardiest veterans of the command, inured to a service in which every day brought its peculiar peril, every hour had its hazard, paled, and breathed thick and hard with keen excitement. For once, General Morgan's coolness and self-command forsook him, and he could not disguise the emotion he felt. No one realized so thoroughly as he the magnitude and imminence of the danger to which delay exposed him. No one knew so well the importance of promptly accomplishing this invasion, now that he had notified the people of Indiana that he was about to enter their territory. The news was speeding over the State. Everywhere resistance was being organized. He felt that he must cross that river at once; to be free to fight or flee, to elude the danger by celerity of movement, or quell it by audacious aggression. But the feeling with which every man in our ranks regarded that scene was quite different from that which conflict, grown familiar with custom, usually evoked. That wide, strong current, pouring steadily along, as if in contemptuous indifference of our struggles, divided us from a momentous future. Thrice our number of eager enemies were upon our track. The broad States of Kentucky and Tennessee separated us from the retreating Confederate armies. When we passed the great river, we would be confronted by the angry and hostile *North*—a vast and infuriated population, and a soldiery outnumbering us twenty to one. We were throwing down the gauntlet to the "nation." We could expect no such sympathy as in Kentucky often guided our movements, and rendered us valuable aid. But we knew that the whole people would rise in arms, and rush from all quarters against us. Our march would be incessantly harassed. The omnipresent telegraph would constantly tell of our course. Railroads would bring fresh assailants from every point of the compass, and we would have to undergo this ordeal—night and day, with no intermission, not an hour of safety—for nearly seven hundred miles.

After a contest of perhaps an hour, but which, to the impatient spectators, seemed interminable, the gunboat backed out and steamed up the river. Whether she had sustained injury from our guns or had exhausted her ammunition, we never knew. Without speculating about the cause of her withdrawal, we witnessed it with an exquisite sense of relief. Both boats were immediately crowded with men and horses to their fullest capacity, and the crossing was resumed and hastened with all possible dispatch. About five P. M. the gunboat returned, accompanied by a consort, causing us lively apprehension. They hovered in sight until dark, and once came so near as to elicit a few shots from the Parrotts, by way of protest, but made no further effort to interrupt the ferriage. Both brigades and the artillery were gotten over by midnight and encamped not far from the river. The panic of the people was excessive. Leaving their houses with doors unlocked and ajar, they fled into the woods, and concealed themselves so effectually that, thickly settled as was that portion of the State, we did not see the face of one citizen, man, woman, or child, until after noon of the next day. At Corydon, the first town through which our march conducted us, we encountered a spirited resistance from a considerable body of militia, who, selecting a position where the road ran between two rather abrupt hills, had erected a long barricade of timber, from which they opened a brisk fire upon the head of the column. The advance guard charged this work on horseback, and as it was too high for the horses to leap, and too strong to be broken down by their rush, some sixteen or eighteen men were unnecessarily lost. A demonstration upon the flank, however, quickly dislodged the party, and we entered the town without further molestation.

On the following day, before we reached Salem, we found parties of militia thick along the road, and at that place several hundred were collected, while squads were rapidly coming in from all directions. To attack instantly was the only policy proper with these fellows, for although they were raw and imperfectly armed, they would fight, and if we had hesitated in the least, might have become dangerous. The Second Regiment, dashing at full speed into the town, dispersed this body with trifling loss on either side.

I have seen the number of militia called out in the two States to resist this raid estimated at one hundred and fifty thousand. I know not how correct this may be, but I am confident that I quite often saw as many as ten thousand per diem, and it wasn't always a "good day" for militia. To men, accustomed as we were to the sparsely populated Southern States, drained by the demands of the war, the dense, able-bodied male population of Indiana and Ohio was as astonishing as it was disagreeable, and we never collided with an exceptionally stubborn gang without cursing the lack of patriotism which kept them at home and out of the army. Sending out detachments in every direction, General Morgan was enabled to prevent, in some measure, a concentration of the large bodies of militia. This method also caused his actual strength to be greatly magnified, and occasioned perplexity and doubt in regard to the course of his march, and the points at which he was really striking. Very nice calculation and careful management, however, was necessary to guard against their permanent separation from the main body.

At Vienna, where we tapped the telegraph lines, General Morgan obtained the first reliable information he had gotten, since crossing the river, of the movements of the regular troops under Burnside and Judah. I use the term "regular" in contradistinction to "militia." He learned that an immense force of infantry was being disposed to intercept him, and that points on the river were already being occupied by the soldiery. Threatening Madison, the most dangerous of these points, with one regiment, he turned due northward, toward Vernon, where heavy bodies of militia were concentrating. Amusing the officer in command here with a demand for his surrender, and apparent preparations for battle, he flanked the town without fighting, and urged his march rapidly in the direction of Cincinnati. He had learned the fact that Burnside was in that city, and inferred therefrom that a strenuous effort would be made to capture or rout him in that neighborhood. He expected to find the enemy in strong force along the line of the Hamilton and Dayton Railroad, and between Hamilton and Cincinnati. He believed that if he could elude this danger his ultimate success would be assured, unless the Ohio should be so high that boats could convey troops to the upper fords. It was important, therefore, to deceive General Burnside in regard to the point where he would cross this railroad. Accordingly, so soon as he reached Harrison, on the Indiana and Ohio line, and twenty-five miles from Cincinnati, he dispatched a strong detachment in the direction of Hamilton, and bivouacked the entire command on the road leading to that place, as if he meant to pursue it. But, that afternoon, when he thought time enough had elapsed for the news of this demonstration to have reached Burnside, he pressed directly for Cincinnati. In a few hours the detachment which had maneuvred toward Hamilton rejoined him by a flank march across the country. As he had expected, General Burnside, believing Hamilton to be his objective point, sent there the greater part of the troops posted at Cincinnati and in the vicinity. Hoping, although, of course, not knowing, that this could be done, and that Cincinnati would be left with a garrison no stronger than the absolute defense of the place might require, Morgan marched with unusual celerity, and penetrated into the suburbs of the city. This threat had the anticipated effect. The troops remaining there, about twenty-five hundred or three thousand in number, were withdrawn from the outskirts to the interior of the city, under the impression that it was about to be attacked, but uncertain where the blow would be delivered. Our advance videttes were instructed to cut the telegraph wires, so that no troops could be recalled, and also to chase in the pickets on every road; and thus feigning assault, while really bent on escape, the column cautiously wound its way through the populous environs of the big town.

So long as I live I shall never forget that night march around Cincinnati. We had now been almost constantly in motion for eleven days and nights, and gone nearly four hundred miles. It had been a period of almost total deprivation of rest and sleep; for, when not marching, we had been fighting, or hard at work. The column was incumbered with the men wounded in Indiana; and those still in the saddle, reduced in number to less than two thousand, were worn with the enormous fatigue consequent upon such exertions, of which no one, who has not had a similar experience, can form the slightest conception. The Second Brigade had comparatively little trouble, for it was in front, and General Morgan rode at its head with the guides. But the First Brigade was embarrassed beyond measure. If the regiment in the rear of the advance brigade had been kept "closed up," and held compactly together, the entire column would have been directed by the guides. But, although composed of the very best fighting material, this regiment had always been under lax discipline, and the effect was now observable. Its rear companies would straggle, halt, and delay all behind them. When forced to proceed, they would move at a gallop. A great gap would thus be opened between the two brigades, and we, who were in the rear, were obliged to grope our way without assistance. At the frequent junctions of roads, which occur in the suburbs of so large a city, we were compelled to consult all sorts of indications to ascertain the right path. The night was intensely dark, and it was necessary to light torches at all such points. The horses' tracks, on paved and dusty streets, so constantly traveled, afforded no clue to the route our comrades had taken; but we could trace it by noticing the manner in which the dust "settled" or floated. On a calm night, the dust occasioned by the passage of a large body of cavalry will remain in the air for minutes, and moves slowly in the direction followed by those who have disturbed it. We were, also, aided by remarking the slaver which had been dropped from the mouths of the horses.

At every halt men would fall asleep, and even drop from their saddles, and the officers were compelled to exercise constant vigilance to keep them in ranks. Daylight returned just as we reached the Little Miami Railroad, the last point at which we anticipated immediate danger, and, after the trials of the night, its appearance was gratefully hailed. Our progress was continued, however, save an hour's halt, in sight of Camp Dennison, to feed the horses, until we reached Williamsburg, where we rested, after a march of ninety-seven miles, and, for the first time during the raid, slept the sleep of the righteous who know not fear.

Our experience in Ohio was very similar to that in Indiana. Small fights with the militia were of hourly occurrence. They hung about the column, incessantly assaulting it; keeping up a continuous fusilade, the crack of their rifles sounded in our ears without intermission, and the list of killed and wounded was constantly swelling. We captured hundreds daily, but could only break their guns and turn them loose again. They finally resorted to one capital means of annoyance, by felling trees and barricading the roads. The advance guard was forced to carry axes to cut away these blockades.

While thus pleasantly occupied, we learned that Vicksburg had fallen, and General Lee, after Gettysburg, had retreated from Pennsylvania. The information did not conduce to improve our *morale*. General Morgan had managed, in both Indiana and Ohio, to successfully avoid any serious engagement, and as his progress through the latter State drew near its conclusion, he was more than ever anxious to shun battle. At Pomeroy, where we approached the river again, a large force of regular troops appeared; but, although our passage by the place was one sharp, continuous skirmish, we prevented them from gaining a position that would have forced us into a decisive combat.

On the night of the 18th, we encamped again on the banks of the Ohio, at the little village of Portland, not far from Buffington Island. This was the point where Morgan had planned to recross the river (when he first contemplated the raid), in the event he could not join General Lee in Pennsylvania; and here was the scene of the disaster which closed the expedition, and virtually terminated his own career of almost unparalleled success. An important element in his calculations, when he was planning this enterprise, was the fact that, after what is known as the "June rise" in the Ohio, the river generally runs down, and becomes fordable, at certain points, in the latter part of July. But this "rise," produced by the melting of the snow in the mountains, came, this year, not in June, but in July, so that the ford at Buffington, usually quite shallow and practicable in the latter month, was, in 1863, deep and difficult. We were unfortunate, also, in arriving at Portland after nightfall, and feared to attempt, in the solid gloom, and without guides, the passage of the stream. Men and horses were alike exhausted; a train of vehicles of every description, filled with wounded men, and the artillery, had to be crossed. If we missed the ford, as we might easily do in the darkness, many lives would be lost.

General Morgan knew that he would probably be attacked on the following day. He at once, and correctly, conjectured that the troops we had seen at Pomeroy were a portion of the infantry which had been sent from Kentucky to intercept us, and that they had been brought by the river from Cincinnati to Pomeroy. He knew that if the boats could pass that place, they could run up as far as Buffington's Island. The transports would certainly be accompanied by small gunboats. Against these, small-arms would be useless, and our artillery ammunition was nearly exhausted. Moreover, an attack from the forces under Hobson was to be apprehended, for our recent delays had enabled him to gain rapidly upon us.

It is needless to dwell upon the anxiety of the commander in such a situation, and impossible to describe the despondency which now assailed the subaltern officers and the men. The latter, demoralized by tremendous and constant toil, and forced and long-continued abstinence from sleep, for the first time doubting a successful issue of their efforts, lay down along the river shore in dogged despair.

They forgot their long experience of victory; they seemed, temporarily, to discard the confidence which they had hitherto unreservedly given their general; they could think only of the safety and repose which were just beyond the river, but separated from them by difficulties they saw no means of overcoming. At the first streak of dawn, five hundred men, detailed for that service, advanced to carry an earthwork thrown up at the entrance to the ford, and which on the previous night had been occupied by three hundred Federal infantry, and had mounted two heavy guns. They found the work abandoned, and the guns rolled over the bluff. But as this detachment moved on down the Pomeroy road, which it was instructed to guard while the main body was fording, a sharp rattle of musketry suddenly announced that it had encountered an enemy. This turned out to be Judah's advance guard, and sustained a smart loss in killed and wounded, beside a piece of artillery and some fifty men captured. One of Judah's staff was wounded, and his adjutant general made prisoner.

Our triumph, however, was short-lived. The Federal infantry, eight or ten thousand strong, instantly deployed and advanced, flanked by three regiments of cavalry. Two pieces of our battery were taken at the first onset. They were no great loss, inasmuch as but three cartridges remained to the guns, and the bores were so clogged with dust and dirt that they could scarcely be loaded. Our effective strength was now little more than eighteen hundred. The men were almost without ammunition; it had either been shot away in the frequent skirmishes, or worn out in the cartridge-boxes. Nevertheless, they formed with alacrity, and prepared for a resistance which should secure a safe retreat. And it would have been successfully done had not Hobson arrived just at this crisis with three thousand men and attacked our right flank.

If the reader will picture in his mind a long valley, which may be roughly described as in the shape of an enormous V, one side of which is a wooded, ridgy hill, and the other the river; if he will imagine this angle crowded with Confederates, while Judah pressed into the opening, Hobson aligned his command upon the ridge, and three gunboats steamed up the river and took position at short range on the left, he will have formed a tolerably accurate idea of the situation. The only means of egress from the valley left open to us was at the apex or northern end—the river runs here nearly due north and south. Upon the level and unsheltered surface of this river bottom we were exposed to a tremendous direct and cross-fire from twelve or thirteen thousand small-arms, and fifteen pieces of artillery. The screams of the shells drowned the hiss of the bullets; coming from three different directions, and bursting between the two lines formed at right angles—a disposition we were compelled to adopt in order to confront both assailants—the air seemed filled with metal, and the ground was torn and ploughed into furrows. Only some twenty-five men were killed, and about eighty wounded. The open, skirmish line formation, which our system of tactics prescribed, saved us from heavier loss.

The odds were too overwhelming and too apparent for the contest to have lasted long, even had the men been in better fighting condition. After sustaining the attack for little more than half an hour, we began to retreat, at first in good order. The upper end of the valley was filled with wagons and ambulances, whose wounded and terror-stricken occupants urged the scared horses to headlong flight. Often they became locked together, and were hurled over as if by an earthquake. Occasionally a solid shot, or unexploded shell would strike one, and dash it into splinters. As the retreating battalions neared the point of exit, and discovered that only two narrow roads afforded avenues of escape, they broke ranks and rushed for them. Both were instantly blocked. The remaining section of artillery was tumbled into a ravine, during this mad swirl, as if the guns had been as light as feathers. The gunboats raked the roads with grape, and the Seventh and Eighth Michigan Cavalry dashed into the mass of fugitives. In a moment the panic was complete, and the disaster irretrievable.

Between seven and eight hundred of the command were captured on this field. Some three hundred swam the river at a point twenty miles above. Several were drowned in the attempt to do so. General Morgan succeded in withdrawing about a thousand men from the fight, and effected their reorganization, although closely pursued and continually attacked by cavalry. This was a last effort, gallant but unavailing. Fresh thousands met him everywhere. He was baffled at every point, and, finally, about a week later, surrounded and obliged to surrender.

Thus ended a raid which, in boldness of conception and purpose, vigor and skill of execution, and importance of object, has no equal in the history of such enterprises. The soldier who carefully studies it will pronounce that its failure was not disgraceful, and that even success could have furnished no stronger proof, than did its conduct, of the genius and nerve of its author.

ON THE FIELD OF FREDERICKSBURG.

BY HON. D. WATSON ROWE.

EVERY one remembers the slaughter and the failure at Fredericksburg; the grief of it, the momentary pang of despair. Burnside was the man of the 13th of December; than he, no more gallant soldier in all the army, no more patriotic citizen in all the republic. But he attempted there the impossible, and, as repulse grew toward disaster, lost that equal mind, which is necessary in arduous affairs. Let us remember, however, and at once, that it is easy to be wise after the event. The Army of the Potomac felt, at the end of that calamitous day, that hope itself was killed—hope, whose presence was never before wanting to that array of the unconquerable will, and steadfast purpose, and courage to persevere; the secret of its final triumph. I have undertaken to describe certain night-scenes on that field famous for bloodshed. The battle is terrible; but the sequel of it is horrible. The battle, the charging column, is grand, sublime. The field after the action and the reaction is the spectacle which harrows up the soul.

Marye's Hill was the focus of the strife. It rises in the rear of Fredericksburg, a stone's throw beyond the canal, which runs along the western border of the city. The ascent is not very abrupt. A brick house stands on the hillside, whence you may overlook Fredericksburg, and all the circumjacent country. The Orange plank road ascends the hill on the right-hand side of the house, the telegraph road on the left. A sharp rise of ground, at the foot of the heights, afforded a cover for the formation of troops. Above Marye's Hill is an elevated plateau, which commands it. The hill is

17

part of a long, bold ridge, on which the declivity leans, stretching from Falmouth to Massoponax creek, six miles. Its summit was shaggy and rough with the earthworks of the Confederates, and was crowned with their artillery. The stone wall on Marye's Height was their "*coigne* of vantage," held by the brigades of Cobb and Kershaw, of McLaws' Division. On the semi-circular crest above, and stretching far on either hand, was Longstreet's Corps, forming the left of the Confederate line. His advance position was the stone wall and rifle-trenches along the telegraph road, above the house. The guns of the enemy commanded and swept the streets which led out to the heights. Sometimes you might see a regiment marching down those streets in single file, keeping close to the houses, one file on the right-hand side, another on the left. Between the canal and the foot of the ridge was a level plat of flat, even ground, a few hundred yards in width. This restricted space afforded what opportunity there was to form in order of battle. A division massed on this narrow plain was a target for Lee's artillery, which cut fearful swaths in the dense and compact ranks. Below, and to the right of the house, were fences, which impeded the advance of the charging lines. Whatever division was assigned the task of carrying Marye's Hill, *debouched* from the town, crossed the canal, traversed the narrow level, and formed under cover of the rise of ground below the house. At the word, suddenly ascending this bank, they pressed forward up the hill for the stone wall and the crest beyond.

From noon to dark Burnside continued to hurl one division after another against that volcano-like eminence, belching forth fire, and smoke, and iron hail. French's Division was the first to rush to the assault. When it emerged from cover, and burst out on the open, in full view of the enemy, it was greeted with a frightful, fiery reception from all his batteries on the circling summit. The ridge concentrated upon it the convergent fire of all its enginery of war. You might see at a mile the lanes made by the cannon balls in the ranks. You might see a bursting shell throw up into the air a cloud of earth and dust, mingled with the limbs of men. The batteries in front of the devoted division thundered against it. To the right, to the left, cannon were answering to each other in a tremendous deafening battle-chorus, the burden of which was—

Welcome to these madmen about to die.

The advancing column was the focus, the point of concentration, of an arc—almost a semi-circle—of destruction. It was a centre of attraction of all deadly missiles. At that moment that single division was going up alone in battle against the Southern Confederacy, and was being pounded to pieces. It continued to go up, nevertheless, toward the stone wall, toward the crest above. With lips more firmly pressed together, the men closed up their ranks and pushed forward. The storm of battle increased its fury upon them; the crash of musketry mingled with the roar of ordnance from the peaks. The stone wall and the rifle-pits added their terrible treble to the deep bass of the bellowing ridge. The rapid discharge of small-arms poured a continuous rain of bullets in their faces; they fell down by tens, by scores, by hundreds. When they had gained a large part of the distance, the storm developed into a hurricane of ruin. The division was blown back, as if by the breath of hell's door suddenly opened, shattered, disordered, pell-mell, down the declivity, amid the shouts and yells of the enemy, which made the horrid din demoniac. Until then the division seemed to be contending with the wrath of brute and material force bent on its annihilation. This shout recalled the human agency in all the turbulence and fury of the scene. The division of French fell back—that is to say, one-half of it. It suffered a loss of near half its numbers.

Hancock immediately charged with five thousand men, veteran regiments, led by tried commanders. They saw what had happened; they knew what would befall them. They advanced up the hill; the bravest were found dead within twenty-five paces of the stone wall; it was slaughter, havoc, carnage. In fifteen minutes they were thrown back with a loss of two thousand—unprecedented severity of loss. Hancock and French, repulsed from the stone wall, would not quit the hill altogether. Their divisions, lying down on the earth, literally clung to the ground they had won. These valiant men, who could not go forward, would not go back. All the while the batteries on the heights raged and stormed at them. Howard's Division came to their aid. Two divisions of the Ninth Corps, on their left, attacked repeatedly in their support.

It was then that Burnside rode down from the Phillips House, on the northern side of the Rappahannock, and standing on the bluff at the river, staring at those formidable heights, exclaimed, "That crest must be carried to-night." Hooker remonstrated, begged, obeyed. In the army to hear is to obey. He prepared to charge with Humphrey's Division; he brought up every available battery in the city. "I proceeded," he said, "against their barriers as I would against a fortification, and endeavored to breach a hole sufficiently large for a forlorn hope to enter." He continued the cannonading on the selected spot until sunset. He made no impression upon their works, " no more than you could make upon the side of a mountain of rock." Humphrey's Division formed under shelter of the rise, in column, for assault. They were directed to make the attack with empty muskets; there was no time there to load and fire. The officers were put in front, to lead. At the command they moved forward with great impetuosity; they charged at a run, hurrahing. The foremost of them advanced to within fifteen or twenty yards of the stone wall. Hooker afterward said : " No campaign in the world ever saw a more gallant advance than Humphrey's men made there. But they were put to do a work that no men could do." In a moment they were hurled back with enormous loss. It was now just dark; the attack was suspended. Three times from noon to dark the cannon on the crest, the musketry at the stone wall, had prostrated division after division on Marye's Hill.

And now the sun had set; twilight had stolen out of the west and spread her veil of dusk; the town, the flat, the hill, the ridge, lay under the " circling canopy of night's extended shade." Darkness and gloom had settled down upon the Phillips House, over on the Stafford Heights, where Burnside would after awhile hold his council of war.

The shattered regiments of Tyler's Brigade of Humphrey's Division were assembled under cover of the bank where they had formed for the charge. A colonel rode about through the crowd with the colors of his regiment in his hand, waving them, inciting the soldiers by his words to re-form for repelling a sortie. But there was really little need for that. Longstreet was content to lie behind his earthworks and stone walls, and with a few men, and the converging fire of numerous guns, was able to fling back with derision and scorn all the columns of assault that madness might throw against his impregnable position. The brick house on the hill was full of wounded men. In front of it lay the commander of a regiment, with shattered leg, white, still, with closed eyes. His riderless horse had already been mounted by the general of the division; about him, in rows, the wounded, the dying, a few of the dead, of his own and other commands. The fatal stone wall was in easy musket range; in a moment, with one rush, the enemy might surround the building. Beyond the house, and around it, and on all the slope below it, the ground was covered with corpses. A little distance below the house, a general officer sat on his horse—the horse of the wounded colonel lying above. It was the third steed he had mounted that evening. The other two lay dead. He was all alone; no staff, not even an orderly. His face was toward the house and the ridge. He pointed to the stone wall. "One minute more," he said, "and we should have been over it." He did not reflect that that would have been but the beginning of the work given him to do. He praised and blamed, besought and even swore; to be so near the goal, and not to reach it. When he saw a party of three or four descending the hill, he ordered them to stop, in order to renew the attack. After little they did what was right, quietly proceeded to the foot of the hill and joined their regiments. All the while stretcher-bearers were passing up and down. Descending, they bore pitiable burdens. A wounded man, upheld by one or two comrades, haltingly made his slow way to the hospital, followed by another and another. The colonel was conveyed by four men to the town, in agony, on a portion of a panel of fence torn down in the progress of the charge. The stretcher-bearers, not distinguishing between persons, had taken whatsoever one they first saw that needed their assistance; moreover, there was no time for selection. The next minute all the wounded on the hillside might be in the hands of the Confederates.

There was the darkness which belongs to night. The regiments had re-formed around their respective standards. They presented a short front compared with the long lines that had gone up the steep, hurrahing. The Southerners were quiet and close behind their works. It seemed that they would not sally forth. Then from each regiment a lieutenant, with a small party, went up the ascent, and sought in the darkness what fate had befallen the missing, and brought succor to the wounded. They went from man to man, as they lay on the ground. In the obscurity it was hard to distinguish the features of the slain. They felt for the letters and numbers on the caps. The letters indicated the company, the numbers denoted the regiment. Whatsoever man of their regiment they discovered, him they bore off, if wounded; if dead, they took the valuables and mementos found on his person, for his friends, and left him to lie on the earth where he had fallen, composing his limbs, turning his face to the sky. They found such all the way up; some not far from the stone wall, a greater number near the corners of the house, where the rain of bullets had been thickest.

At nine o'clock at night, the command was withdrawn from the front, and rested on their arms in the streets of the town. Some sat on the curbstones, meditating, looking gloomily at the ground; others lay on the pavement, trying to forget the events of the day in sleep. There was little said; deep dejection burdened the spirits of all. The incidents of the battle were not rehearsed, except now

and then. Always, when any one spoke, it was of a slain comrade—
of his virtues, or of the manner of his death; or of one missing,
with many conjectures respecting him. Some of them, it was said,
had premonitions, and went into the battle not expecting to survive
the day. Thus they lay or sat. The conversation was with bowed
head, and in a low murmur, ending in a sigh. The thoughts of all
were in the homes of the killed, seeing there the scenes and sorrow
which a day or two afterward occurred. Then they reverted to the
comrade of the morning, the tent-sharer, lying stark and dead up on
Marye's Hill, or at its base. A brave lieutenant lay on the plank
road, just where the brigade crossed for the purpose of forming for
the charge. A sharpshooter of the enemy had made that spot his
last bed. It was December, and cold. There was no camp-fire, and
there was neither blanket nor overcoat. They had been stored in a
warehouse preparatory to moving out to the attack. But no one
mentioned the cold; it was not noticed. Steadily the wounded were
carried by to the hospitals near the river. Some one, now and then,
brought word of the condition of a friend. The hospitals were a
harrowing sight; full, crowded, nevertheless patients were brought
in constantly. Down stairs, up stairs, every room full. Surgeons,
with their coats off and sleeves rolled up above the elbows, sawed
off limbs, administered anæsthetics. They took off a leg or an arm
in a twinkling, after a brief consultation. It seemed to be, in case
of doubt—off with his limb. A colonel lay in the middle of the
main room on the first floor, white, unconscious. When the surgeon
was asked what hope, he turned his hand down, then up, as much as
to say it may chance to fall either way. But the sights in a field
hospital, after a battle, are not to be minutely described. Nine
thousand was the tale of the wounded—nine thousand, and not all
told.

After midnight—perhaps it was two o'clock in the morning—
the brigade was again marched out of the town, and, filing in from
the road, took up a position a short distance below the brick house.
It was on the ground over which the successive charges had been
made. The fog, however, obscured everything; not a star twinkled
above them; nothing could be discerned a few feet away. The
brick house could not be seen, though they were close to it. Looking
back toward the town, lying on the river bank, over the narrow plain
which lay below, one could not persuade one's self it was not a sheet
of water unruffled in the dim landscape. Few lights, doubtless, were
burning at that hour in the town. None could be seen. You would
not have supposed that there was a town there. A profound stillness

prevailed, broken by no other sound than the cries of the wounded. On all the eminence above, where Longstreet's forces lay, there was the silence of death. With the night, which had brought conviction of failure, the brazen throats of Burnside's guns had ceased to roar. It was as if furious lions had gone, with the darkness, to their lairs. Now and then an ambulance crept along below, without seeming to make any noise. The stretcher-bearers walked silently toward whatever spot a cry or a groan of pain indicated an object of their search. It may not have been so quiet as it seemed. Perhaps it was contrast with the thunder of cannon, and shriek of shell, and rattle of musketry, and all the thousand voices of battle.

When, on the return to Marye's Heights, the command first filed in from the road, there appeared to be a thin line of soldiers sleeping on the ground to be occupied. They seemed to make a sort of row or rank. It was as if a line of skirmishers had halted and lain down; they were perfectly motionless; their sleep was profound. Not one of them awoke and got up. They were not relieved, either, when the others came. They seemed to have no commander—at least none awake. Had the fatigues of the day completely overpowered all of them, officers and privates alike? They were nearest the enemy, within call of him. They were the advance line of the Union army. Was it thus that they kept their watch, on which the safety of the whole army depended, pent up between the ridge and the river? The enemy might come within ten steps of them without being seen. The fog was a veil. No one knew what lay, or moved, or crept a little distance off. The regiments were allowed to lie down. In doing so, the men made a denser rank with those there before them. Still those others did not waken. If you looked closely at the face of one of them, in the mist and dimness, it was pallid, the eyes closed, the mouth open, the hair was disheveled; besides, the attitude was often painful. There were blood-marks, also. These men were all dead. Nevertheless, the new comers lay down among them, and rested. The pall of night concealed the foe now. The sombre uncertainty of fate enveloped the morrow. One was saved from the peril of the charge, but he found himself again on Marye's Hill, near the enemy, face to face with the dead, sharing their couch, almost in their embrace, in the mist and the December night. Why not accept them as bed-fellows? The bullet that laid low this one, if it had started diverging by ever so small an angle, would have found the heart's blood of that other who gazed upon him. It was chance or Providence, which to-morrow might be less kind. So they lay down with the dead, all in line, and were lulled asleep by the monotony of the cries of the wounded scattered everywhere.

At this time three officers rode out from the ranks, down the hill, toward the town. They sought to acquire a better knowledge of the locality. They were feeling about in the fog for the foot of the hill, and the roads. After they had gone a little distance, one of them was stationed as a guide-mark, while the two others went further, reconnoitering or exploring. He who was thus left alone found himself amid strange and melancholy surroundings. Meditation sat upon his brow, but to fall into complete revery was impossible. The hour and the scene would intrude themselves upon his thoughts of what had befallen. The dead would not remain unnoticed. The dying cried out into the darkness, and demanded succor of the world. Was there nothing in the universe to save? Tens of thousands within ear-shot, and no footstep of friend or foe drew near during all the hours. Sometimes they drew near and passed by, which was an aggravation of the agony. The subdued sound of wheels rolling slowly along, and ever and anon stopping, the murmur of voices and a cry of pain, told of the ambulance on its mission. It went off in another direction. The cries were borne through the haze to the officer as he sat solitary, waiting. Now a single lament, again voices intermingled and as if in chorus; from every direction, in front, behind, to right, to left, some near, some distant and faint. Some, doubtless, were faint that were not distant, the departing breath of one about to expire. They expressed every degree and shade of suffering, of pain, of agony; a sigh, a groan, a piteous appeal, a shriek, a succession of shrieks, a call of despair, a prayer to God, a demand for water, for the ambulance, a death-rattle, a horrid scream, a voice, as of the body when the soul tore itself away, and abandoned it to the enemy, to the night, and to dissolution. The voices were various. This, the tongue of a German; that wail in the Celtic brogue of a poor Irishman. The accent of New England was distinguishable in the thin cry of that boy. From a different quarter came utterances in the dialect of a far off Western State. The appeals of the Irish were the most pathetic. They put them into every form—denunciation, remonstrance, a pitiful prayer, a peremptory demand. The German was more patient, less demonstrative, withdrawing into himself. One man raised his body on his left arm, and extending his right hand upward, cried out to the heavens, and fell back. Most of them lay moaning, with the fitful movement of unrest and pain.

At this hour of the night, over at the Phillips' House, Burnside, overruling his council of war, had decided, in desperation, to hurl the Ninth Corps next day, himself at its head, against that self-same eminence. The officer sat on his horse, looking out into the spectre-making mist and darkness. Nothing stirred; not the sound of a gun was heard; a dread silence, which one momentarily expected to be broken by the rattle of fire-arms. All at once he looked down. He saw something white, not far off, that moved and seemed to be a man. It was, in fact, a thing in human form. In the obscurity one could not discern what the man was doing. The officer observed him attentively. He stooped and rose again; then stooped and handled an object on the ground. He moved away, and again bent down. Presently he returned, and began once more his manipulations of the former object. The chills crept over one. The darkness and the gloom, and the contrasted stillness from the loud and frightful uproar of the day, except for the intermittent cries of the wounded and dying, groans intermingled with fearful shrieks, and cries for water, and this thing, man or fiend, flitting about on the field, now up, now down, intent on his purpose, seeing nothing else, hearing nothing, seemingly fearing nothing, loving nothing; the hill all overstrewn with dead and the debris of artillery, and mutilated horses—it was a ghostly, weird, wicked scene, sending a shudder through the frame.

"Who goes there?" at the length the officer said, and rode forward.

"A private," the man replied, and gave his regiment and company.

"What are you doing here at this hour?" and so questioning he saw that the man was engaged in putting on the clothes of a dead soldier at his feet.

"I need clothes and shoes," he said, "and am taking them from this dead man; he won't need them any more."

"You, there! you are rifling the dead; robbing them of their watches and money. Begone!" And the man disappeared into the night like an evil bird that had flown away.

Where he had stood lay the dead man, who had fallen in the charge, stripped of his upper clothing; robbed of his life by the enemy, robbed of his garments by a comrade, alone on the hillside, in the darkness, waited for in some far off Northern home.

The three officers returned to their posts. Toward morning the general commanding the brigade came out, and, withdrawing his troops a little distance to the rear, took up a new position, less exposed than the former line. The captains were cautioned to leave none of their men unwarned of the movement. Nevertheless, a few of them were not distinguished from the dead, and were left where they lay. An orderly sergeant, waking from sound sleep, induced by the fatigues of the day, opened his eyes, and looked about him on all sides with surprise and wonder. His company and regiment were gone. The advance line, of which they had formed a part, had disappeared. He saw no living or moving thing. He started up and stood at gaze. What to do now? Which way to go? He concluded that the regiment had moved farther forward, and, going first to the left, and then up along a piece of fence, he saw the hostile line a short distance before him. Falling down, he crept on hands and knees, descending the hill again until he reached the road. An officer, anxious when the withdrawal was ordered that no one should remain behind for want of notice, waited until the regiments had moved away, then passed along the line just abandoned. He saw a man lying on his side, reposing on his elbow, his head supported on his hand, his left leg drawn up. You would have been certain he dozed, or meditated, so natural and restful his posture. Him he somewhat rudely touched, and thus accosted : "Get up and join your company. We have moved to the rear." The reclining figure moved not, made no response. The officer bent over him, and looked closely—he was a corpse.

At length the dawn appeared—the mist was dispelled. With the coming of morning, the command was again taken into the town.

A CAMPAIGN WITH SHARPSHOOTERS.

BY CAPTAIN JOHN D. YOUNG.

LONG before the close of the campaign of 1863, in the late war between the States, the Army of Northern Virginia, as well as its historic antagonist, the Army of the Potomac, had completely inaugurated the system of fighting from behind earthworks. So universal had become this method of defense that intrenching tools formed part of the soldier's regular equipment as much as he did his arms of offense, and the spade and mattock were ranked almost equal in importance with the sabre and rifle. The use of trenches by the Confederate army was dictated by a consideration higher than the mere effort of the individual to protect his own life. It was, on public grounds, a matter of dire necessity; its numbers, reduced by disease and death in hospital and field, were far from being recuperated by the conscription, sweeping as it was, of 1864. It was apparent to all that every life must be husbanded, and that every advantage of position must be taken, both as to nature and the addition of art, to render the weaker side able to cope with its adversaries. Thus it came to pass that whenever a line was formed or a position occupied where there was any likelihood of attack, trenches were dug at once and earthworks thrown up, which were elaborated and extended as the approach of the enemy increased the chances of an action. These preparations extended even to the picket-line. The remains of this vast system of defense are to be seen at this day, and will long be regarded as notable monuments of that long and desperate strife, whose other sequels, we hope and believe, are now being gradually effaced by the pitying touch of time and the wise counsels of later statesmanship. The chain of earthworks around Petersburg was fifty miles in extent; being an effort, which proved futile in its ultimate issue, to make the inanimate soil, however "sacred," supply the absence of flesh and blood. In the campaign of 1864 the necessity of still further utilizing the limited forces of the army loomed up as of prime consideration. It was also noticed that a great part of the fighting fell on the pickets; that these troops were time and again pushed in on the main body, and that, as a general thing, being unable to resist the slightest exhibition of force in their front, they roused the line when driven in, and caused the greatest trouble and annoyance.

Up to this time picket and outpost duty of all kinds was performed by details drawn haphazard from the various companies of the regiments constituting a brigade; a single regiment or even company being rarely sent as a body on this kind of service. These promiscuous details were usually placed under officers with whom they were as utterly unacquainted as each man was with his right and left file. As a natural consequence, the details failed to act in the presence of the enemy as a compact, confident body; for if there is any one thing more than any other that is well calculated to destroy the efficiency of a soldier, it is the suspicion that his comrades are going to give way. It is equally a confessed fact that, when satisfied of the courage and fidelity of one another, men who will fight at all will fight till overcome by hostile numbers. This was the state of things that presented itself to the leaders of the army in 1864. In the sharp economy of war, the use of works was a fixed fact and acknowledged advantage. Some improvement must now be made in the character of the troops who did the outpost duty. To remedy the inefficiency of the "details," and form a picket line that on sudden occasions might do the work of a line of battle; in short, by discipline and association, to render a small body of troops equal in strength and effectiveness to twice or even thrice their number—this was the problem, the solution of which was of no small labor to General Lee.

To accomplish such results no plan of organization presented itself in the formation of either army. The only thing known among military men that would in any degree approach the formation indicated, was the embodiment of a regiment for each division, after the manner of the Zouave regiments of the French service. There, as is known, to each division of the army is attached a corps, who act, as Kinglake aptly puts it, as "the spike-head of the division," being used either to push in, or else to ward off attack.

There was, however, a serious difficulty in the way of constantly employing a regiment on this kind of duty; for, while one regiment, taken as a whole, were always safe to be relied on for line fighting, it was well-nigh impossible to find such an organization in any division as combined all the qualities found necessary for single and determined picket fighting. Besides, at this time, it was considered a duty, not only extra dangerous, but otherwise specially onerous and distasteful; and regimental commanders were inclined to stand on their rights of only acting in their regular routine on the brigade roster. Therefore, it was decided, after long deliberation, to adhere to the old plan of details, but to introduce such improvements as would remedy the most obvious defects, especially that of having raw men and officers on every occasion that presented itself. To accomplish these ends an order was issued from division head-quarters for the formation of battalions, or corps of sharpshooters for each brigade. This order organized a body of troops that gained no little renown in the service. How often they stood before the fierce advance of the enemy, the unwritten history of the Army of Northern Virginia will attest; while their unmarked graves that fringe the lines from the Wilderness to Petersburg, and the thinned ranks they paraded on the last muster at Appomattox Court-House, will prove that in heroic devotion to duty they were second to none in an army that challenged the admiration of the world.

The organization and operation of the corps of sharpshooters of the Army of Northern Virginia will possess, if not for the general public, at least for the intelligent military student, the interest that naturally attaches to every movement new in the details of the service—a service the necessities of which developed many expedients before unknown in the annals and science of war. There were incidents connected with its manner of independent and advanced operations which cannot fail, from their unique and striking character, to possess a common interest for all. It was the fortune of the sharpshooters to experience all the romance and glamour of war; and to these was added enough of danger to make the service exciting and exhilarating. Placed between the lines of two great armies, they saw at least the beginnings of all movements, and had the first intimations of that pleasurable feeling—the *gaudia certaminis*—which battle ever brings to the heart of the true soldier. Their time was not spent in weary waiting for the order to advance; nor were they, except in rare instances, subjected to the trying ordeal of remaining quiet under fire, with no power to return the compliment. From the earliest opening of battle to its tragic close, the ears of the sharpshooters were made familiar with the peculiar music of the rifle, and their whole mind was exercised in the problem of affording as much annoyance as possible to the enemy. A battalion was composed of one commandant, eight commissioned officers, ten non-commissioned officers, one hundred and sixty privates, four scouts, and two buglers, specially selected, and drafted from each brigade. These were divided into four companies, equally officered. As it was a matter of the utmost importance that men should be chosen of tried courage and steadiness, who were good marksmen, and possessed of the requisite self-confidence, great care and caution were exercised in the drafts. Company commanders were ordered to present none for duty with the sharpshooters who did not come up to the standard; while the commandant of each battalion, assisted by his lieutenants, personally superintended the examination of all recruits offered for this branch of the service. The company officers in the corps were equally set apart for their military reputations with respect to zeal, intelligence, and personal gallantry. As soon as the requisite number of men was obtained, a separate camp was established, and in every respect the command was placed on an independent footing—reporting, as in case of a regiment, directly to brigade headquarters. Thus closely associated together, rank and file soon learned to know and to rely upon each other. Still further to increase this confidence, the companies were subdivided into groups of fours, something like the *comrades de battaille* of the French army. These groups messed and slept together, and were never separated in action, save by its casualties of disability and death. The further strengthening of this body of troops was hoped to be accomplished by thorough drill.

In order to assimilate the men and make them fully acquainted with the special character and details of the duties to which they were assigned, and above all to impart that sense of self-reliance so necessary for outpost fighting, a new system of drill and exercise was adopted. This scheme was presented in the form of a *brochure*, translated from the French by General C. M. Wilcox, and comprised the skirmish drill, the bayonet exercise, and practical instruction in estimating distances. In a short time men, eager to learn and easily handled, not only became proficient in their drill and excellent shots, but from frequent practice could correctly measure with a glance the distance intervening between themselves and the objects at which they aimed. The drill was conducted by signals on the bugle, as the line when deployed was too extended to be reached by the voice, or, when silence was requisite, by the wave of the sword of the officer in command. The sharpshooters were armed with the improved Enfield rifle; the scouts with rifles of Whitworth make, with telescopic sights. In order to preserve the *elan* of the corps, and to make the service sought after, it was ordered that this body should be exempt from all regimental or camp duty, and from all picket duty except in the face of the enemy. They were also assigned to the right of the column— the front in advance, the rear in retreat. This freedom from the irksome and distasteful duties of the camp, which were always especially detested by the average Confederate soldier—unaccustomed as he was to do any menial service for himself—made a place in the ranks of the sharpshooters an honor much to be desired. There was, in the very joyous nature of the service, something that had a great charm for the soldier, to which, to descend from sentiment to business, may be added the very general ambition at that time prevalent, and by no means confined to the line, to be among the first to handle the plunder of the enemy's camps. It was in this manner, as briefly above related, that the opening campaign of 1864 found every brigade of the Army of Northern Virginia provided with a body of picked troops to guard its front or clear the way for its advance. It was truly a "spike-head" of Toledo steel, which was not suffered to rust from disuse in the days that so quickly followed. It was kept bright and sharp by constant employment in the series of actions that lasted throughout that eventful year, beginning with the great battle of the Wilderness.

Though the sharpshooters were not employed in this engagement with any exclusive or even special reference to the method and distinctive purposes of their formation, it was the first action in which they fought as a separate organization, and as such deserves our notice; especially as some of its incidents, well worthy of record and remembrance, have never been honored by historic notice. Almost as soon as the leading divisions had engaged the enemy, the sharpshooters were detached and sent to the left of the plank road, to protect the flank of the troops ordered to Heth's support, and to fill a gap between Ewell and the troops on the right of the road. Moving forward, they passed long lines of artillery going into bivouac, well-knowing from the nature of the country that their services would not be needed; while riding about in a restless and eager manner, Colonel William Johnson Pegram was to be seen, asking through many a courier, dispatched one after another, if he could not get in a battery, or at least a section, and highly disquieted that his pieces should be silent at such a time. He forcibly recalled, in some respects, the figure of Lord Cardigan, at Balaklava, chewing his moustache, and cursing the luck of "Scarlett and the heavies." Colonel Pegram was invited to go in with us, and would probably have accepted—for battle had a powerful fascination for the calm, spectacled, studious, devout boy-colonel—but that he had been peremptorily ordered to remain with his guns and await developments. The sharpshooters moving in, found that the left of the road was clear; and Ewell, swinging laterally, soon filled up the gap which they had held, leaving them free to rejoin their command, which was actively engaged on the right-hand side of the road. The battalion moved less by sight than by faith in obeying this order; following the supposed line of the brigade's advance, and principally guided by the fire from the front, which grew in intensity and effect. Too much has been written in regard to the scenes of war, and too many living men actually witnessed these horrors and were part of the same, to render necessary any description of the advance through wounded men falling to the rear, through mounted men moving in haste and excitement, and through straggling parties who never failed to have urgent business somewhere in the rear, as soon as the business of these bloody days became critical. One little thing may be noted; the road was literally strewed with packs of playing-cards, thrown away by superstitious soldiers as they went into the fiery focus. It was a noticeable fact among the Confederate soldiers, that many who were regular gamblers, who would play "poker" or anything else all night if permitted, and who would carefully deposit the cards in their haversacks when the game was over, were very careful to throw them away as soon as firing began; after which they would load their guns and be ready to go in coolly. One figure that the command passed on its way forward will receive in time a more prominent and picturesque position than has yet been given it in the constellation of Confederate commanders—the calm, courteous, unselfish, gallant, patriotic A. P. Hill. Surrounded by his staff, this beloved general, whose custom it ever was to feel in person the pulse of battle, and who always stationed himself just behind his men in action, sat, a stately presence, anxiously awaiting the issue of events and sending up troops to support General Heth, who was sorely pressed.

"Face the fire and go in where it is hottest!" were the brief words in which the lieutenant general assigned the sharpshooters to their place in the battle. They were obeyed with a will; and the battalion soon found itself on the left of Lane's Brigade, where it fought on its own account till night put an end to the bloody contest.

Not till then did the battalion find its proper brigade, and resume its specific duties on the outpost petween the armies. A picket line in front was at once established, and the long watches of the night were spent in anxious conjecture of the issue of the enemy's fight, and the chances of its renewal on the morrow. No fires nor lights of any kind were allowed; and only the watery and feeble glimpses of the moon, then past her quarter, exposed the grim aspects of the bloody field, defining the outlines of silent and lifeless bodies, marking also the broken *debris* of battle and the patches of blood-soaked ground. Here the sharpshooters passed the first of many like nights —on the fringe of two mighty hosts, the deep stillness, unbroken except by the stray shots of pickets and the tramp of troops moving in their front. Several prisoners were picked up by the scouts, from whom the information was extracted that the enemy was in front, in strong force, and would advance at daylight. This intelligence was communicated to headquarters, while the sharpshooters, throwing up a temporary work of logs, camly awaited the appearance of morning, and with it, that of the enemy.

Nor were they disappointed; for at the first gray light there were movements in front which showed very clearly that something serious was on foot. In the direction of Ewell, to the right, the scattering fire of the night previous could be heard rapidly assuming the volume of a regular fusilade, which gathered force as it worked up to the left, increasing the activity of the enemy in the immediate front. Just as day fairly opened the memorable combat of May 5th began. Coming forward in loose order, the line of the enemy moved down upon us without the skirmishers either firing or cheering. The courage and discipline of the sharpshooters were never more severely tried than on this occasion; nor did they omit to respond to the high expectations of their superiors, receiving the enemy's charge with great steadiness, and continuing the unequal combat till both flanks were turned. The command, still unbroken, retired to the main line before the desperate odds it had engaged, having held the enemy in check over ten minutes, which proved a delay of most timely and providential interposition, as the following facts, which has never before transpired in connection with the battle, will attest; for the confident expectation with which the sharp-shooters withdrew—of re-forming on the main line and putting a stop there at once to the enemy's forward movement—was doomed to be a terrible disappointment, and a state of things was developed which might easily have led to the utmost disaster. By some unaccountable neglect the divisions of Generals Heth and Wilcox, which

18

had engaged the enemy on the evening before, still remained on the front line; some brigades having bivouacked where they found themselves when the fight was over, while others had gone into camp parked by regiments, and not even the pretense of a line of battle had been formed. One brigade rested with its naked flank perpendicular to the enemy's line. All this was done, or neglected, within a few hundred yards of the foe. No works had been thrown up, and when the Federal force broke the lines, there was no expectation of battle or danger. The men hastily aroused, thought of nothing but safety in flight, and "*sauve qui peut*" was the order of the day. The conditions were reversed, but the stampede exactly recalled the day when Jackson turned Hooker's right at Chancellorsville, and sent his Eleventh Corps with great speed to the rear. *This* time, however, we were not the pursuers, but the pursued. The enemy made good use of his opportunity, and as the panic-stricken Confederates fled in great confusion before his advance, it was apparent that all organized fighing by Heth and Wilcox was at an end for that time.

The day seemed irretrievably lost, and so it would have been except for the arrival of other troops. Moving rapidly through the entwining trees and matted undergrowth, in all haste to find the rear, we caught the gleam of bayonets in front of our disordered and plunging mass, and soon saw the dauntless mien and heard the steady tread of Longstreet's Corps, marching up to the relief, under the composed direction of "Old Pete" himself. Like Dessaix at Marengo, he arrived just in time "to win a victory." While some of the broken troops of Heth and Wilcox joined in the advance with Longstreet's column, others straggled back to the point at which they were first engaged the night before. The sharpshooters moved across the road, near by certain batteries of Poague's artillery, which had been planted on a slight plateau on the left of the road, and was at this time crowded with troops. General Hill and General Lee both occupied this position; the latter appearing intensely disgusted at the turn which affairs had taken. The ridiculous procedure of the ambulance corps, the teamsters, and the camp-followers generally, was singularly well calculated to aggravate this irritated feeling; for these people, supposing the day to have been lost, sought the rear with keen ardor, leaving the road so blockaded with sporadic plunder, and wagons turned upside-down, as to render difficult the movement of the supports. The "old man" was in no good humor, and had a business look about the eyes as he ordered the guns to be loaded with canister, and trained down the road. For five hundred yards in front of the plateau, the road ran perfectly smooth and straight, and was now filled with Federal troops, moving in column, but in no regular order; for all conformity had been sacrificed in the charge, and, beside, a great number of soldiers had converged into and advanced up the road, to escape the tangled undergrowth of the Wilderness. On the line came, firing and shouting, so closely following our own fugitives as to be mingled with them, and thus cause the cruel necessity of firing through the last of our own people to check the pursuit! A few rounds of canister did the work; and by this time fresh troops had come. Thus not only was a defeat, that seemed to be impending, averted, but a substantial victory was gained, though at a great sacrifice. For Longstreet, in himself a tower of strength, upon whose sturdy valor and fidelity General Lee leaned not less confidently, and not less worthily, than on Stonewall Jackson's, was taken from the field grievously wounded; while Jenkins, of South Carolina, and many other brave officers, had sealed in blood their devotion to the cause which their swords and their souls upheld. The Wilderness was a field well adapted, by the very nature of the country, to the operations of the sharpshooters; but so fierce had been the engagement that no opportunity was afforded them for the display either of maneuvres or marksmanship. The Wilderness battle has fitly been compared to the struggles of two giants, not unequally matched, who fruitlessly, yet frightfully, writhe and twist in each other's embrace until they are forcibly wrenched asunder.

The movement from the Wilderness to Spottsylvania Court-House was exceedingly arduous to the sharpshooters, who were compelled to march to the left flank of the column, deployed as if in regular line. At last the Court-House was reached; but it failed to afford the expected rest. Almost immediately the command was thrown forward, and began what appeared to be an endless picket fight. One day was the reflection of another, though the elements of exposure and excitement prevented their succession from becoming monotonous. At three o'clock, before light, the command would be moved out of the camp inside the main lines, and sent forward to relieve the regimental details who did guard duty at night. Arrived on the picket line, while darkness yet reigned, the men were placed in the rifle-pits, and, arranging themselves as comfortably as circumstances permitted, proceeded to make what their rations afforded in the way of breakfast. This was generally light, except when contributions had been levied from some contraband source, or the camp of the enemy had been put into requisition. Even during this daylight repast, the more adventurous would stop, at times, to take a shot at the gentlemen in front, while all had occasion to look about very sharply to keep their own brains from being knocked out. The rage after plunder was often fatal to some of our very best men. Some incidents of this passion are worth relating. A sergeant, named Warren, during the day killed a man a short distance in front of his pit, and at night, just before the command was relieved, moved quickly forward and possessed himself of the dead man's effects. It proved to be a rich haul, and next morning the men were wild for an attack, beholding in each hostile form the bearer of property, of which they burned to possess themselves. All day long they were taking what I may call pot-shots at the enemy's videttes, and in keeping away their friends, who might have otherwise removed the spoils. The impatience of the sportsmen was too great that night to wait till it was fully dark; they stole off in the gray dusk of the evening, and some of them—among whom was Sergeant Warren—returned no more. We passed, next morning, their bloated corpses, on the very spot where their operations had been so rashly begun. After this occurrence, stringent orders were issued against the practice of going outside of and beyond the lines. In this manner the command spent its days; sometimes on the outposts, sometimes in the rear; but always prepared to move at an instant's warning. It so happened that we were not on picket service on the 12th of May, a day long to be remembered as the bloodiest of all the horrible fights that raged along the lines, and only equaled in mortality, in proportion to the numbers engaged, by Cold Harbor, of the same year. The sharpshooters, however, saw and acted an important part of this stubborn engagement. Our position having been changed the night of the 11th to a road in rear of the works, we were startled the morning of the battle by the sudden apparition of a mounted officer, who dashed forward and shouted—without speaking to the general in command— "Right shoulder shift, arms! File left! Double quick, march!" "This way!" and away the sharpshooters went after him, not stopping to ask for his authority, or otherwise to "reason why." As the command hurried through the woods, the ears of the men were saluted with the familiar roll of musketry, and the occasional thunder of a big gun. As we *debouched* from the woods into the open, we came upon that fatal angle—the error, it is said, of General M. L. Smith, engineer-in-chief of the army—which gave so much trouble, and lost so many men, and which has passed into history as Johnson's salient. This angle had been early recognized as *the* weak point of our line, and was so much feared that the artillery which guarded it was withdrawn every night, and sent in early each morning before light.

The enemy in front of this salient was commanded by General Hancock, to whose skill and gallantry was intrusted an assault on our lines at that point. In the dusky light he came up with a rush; and just as our artillery, which was moving in battery at the same moment, galloped up, and unlimbered for action, it was captured. Only one piece or two was fired. The infantry of Johnson's Division were overpowered almost as speedily; but the supports came up promptly, and a hand-to-hand conflict ensued, during which the two forces were rarely as far apart as a dozen yards. At times, as if by mutual consent, there would be a cessation of the fire; but it would s⌐)n break out at some other point of the line, and, sweeping down, include the wasted antagonists in its folds. In the rear of each line were the supports, who were either to relieve the first line, or send in plenty of ammunition. There was no lack of ammunition that day.

The training of the sharpshooters in actual war was completed by these actions, and the efforts of their officers were conceded to be successful beyond the most sanguine expectations. These battalions had already established the best reputation among friend and foe for endurance and stubborn fighting. The knowledge that the sharpshooters held the picket lines enabled many a head to repose in peace of nights, undisturbed by visions of sudden attack, and the midnight call to arms. The battalion was now the very lightest of light troops in every particular of *impedimenta*. They carried absolutely nothing, save their arms and haversacks. The last were of but little use. The sharpshooters found it much less burdensome to make a raid for supplies on the line of the enemy than to carry knapsacks. When rations were ordered to be prepared for three days, they were generally cooked and eaten at the same time; not a difficult thing to do in the Confederate service, where the ration was scientifically calculated to the least that a man could live on. Sometimes blankets and fly-tents were carried, but only when there was to be a long march, and no immediate prospect of a fight. In the face of the enemy these daring corps usually threw away everything but their arms, and relied for provision on the chance of war. Their losses were heavy, but were easily filled by details of the best material of the line. The prestige of the sharpshooters were well kept up, and was the just subject of pride alike to their officers and at army headquarters. And so, when Grant changed his base, moving south, while Lee followed, describing the interior line, the sharpshooters brought up the rear of the latter, engaging in quite a number of unrecorded actions, gaining high credit for fighting, and occasionally rewarded by a good bit of plunder.

After General Grant's failure to break our front at Cold Harbor, he suddenly decamped, bag and baggage, for the south side of James river, masking his movement by covering his front with strong bodies of cavalry, supported by detached infantry. These covering troops were encountered at Riddle's shop, half way between Cold Harbor and the river, in such heavy force as to induce General Lee to suspend the movement then in progress of transferring Hill's Corps across the James. In leaving Cold Harbor, the sharpshooters were left on the picket line, and were not ordered to follow until ten A. M. Another delay resulted from the rifling of a bee-tree; and, before reaching Riddle's shop, the dropping fire notified the rear guard that the armies were at it again. At this point General Lee and his staff rode by rapidly to the front, hurrying as they did so the forward movement of the battalion. When we arrived on the ground we found that details from the brigade were already engaged with dismounted cavalry in front, with but poor success; while the advance of the whole corps was suspended till the force in front could be developed.

We were at once put in, and the three battalions detailed from Wilcox's Division were ordered to support us. As we had to move across an open field, the officer commanding the details flatly refused to go; and the commandant in charge, rightly judging that it was better to proceed alone than to depend on troops who would hang back, promptly decided to do without these supports, and ordered them back to the line, where they went with great cheerfulness. The word was then passed that both General Lee and General Hill would view the advance, and at the command "Forward!" a charge was made that swept the enemy from the field, disclosed his designs, and resulted in hurrying Hill's Corps forward to Petersburg, where its presence was greatly needed. When Petersburg was reached, the command was placed well on the right of the line, and the duties that developed upon the sharpshooters were, in consequence, very light. The men became fat and lazy on the accumulated captures of previous campaigns, and nothing more serious was attempted while the days dreamily glided by than an occasional "blockade" escapade into the city. This halcyon period was rudely disturbed by the combat of the 22d of June, on the line of the Petersburg and Weldon Railroad. This affair, brilliant in all respects to the Confederate cause, has been noticed so slightly heretofore that the details of the movement may well be given here, as its results in prisoners and guns, and, above all, in the fresh life imparted to the drooping spirits of the men, were of a magnitude not easy to be overstated. For a proper appreciation of the character of this action, some description is necessary of Major General William Mahone, the leader and moving spirit of the occasion. Mahone was a singular illustration of the fact that the Confederate service, while well calculated to develop the natural native aptitudes of its generals, did not afford all of them full scope for the exercise of the genius thus educed, but kept within narrow limits many high spirits which felt themselves capable of larger responsibilities, or wider fields than the cramped resources of the South admitted of their undertaking. He was a man of high personal courage and magnetic presence. A stern disciplinarian, he was greatly respected by his men, who, in the hour of battle, never fought so well as when under his immediate command. His frequent selection for the conduct of most delicate and difficult movements proved the high esteem in which he was held by General Lee. He was an officer in whom, it may be said, were blended the strategic qualities of Soult, and the ardent gallantry of Vandamme. Closely watching his front at all times, he never failed to strike the enemy whenever an opportunity offered, and his blows were always felt.

When General Grant, with the intention of more closely enveloping Petersburg, applied his old maneuvre of extending his left, he moved forward the Second and Sixth Army Corps for the purpose of seizing the Weldon Railroad. The movement was begun by the Second Corps, which marched to the Federal left and took position west of the Jerusalem plank road, their right connecting with the Fifth Corps. This movement at once drew out a strong force of Confederates to confront it, and a slight skirmish was the result. This happened on the 21st of June. That same night the Sixth (Federal) Corps moved up in rear of the Second Corps, and on a line parallel with it. It thus happened that when General Birney, commanding the Second Corps, swung forward his left more closely to envelop the Confederate works, a gap was created between the Second and Sixth, which widened as the turning movement progressed. General Mahone promptly noticed the bad formation of this part of the line, and himself suggested to General Lee the feasibility of attacking the left flank of Birney, then thrown well forward in the air. The march of Mahone's Division to the front was concealed from the enemy by the nature of the ground over which it passed to get into position. Nor, indeed, was his departure from the works observed; for, with great circumspection, even in details, he ordered the men to leave them one by one, dropping to the rear as if for any other purpose than that of going out to fight. The places of the absentees were gradually filled by an extension of the lines. In order to follow up the movement, the division of General Wilcox was dispatched to the right of Mahone, and was expected to render him support by moving to the front and connecting with his (Mahone's) right, and by afterward conforming with the latter's movements. The plan was a good one, and its results might have been very momentous. Mahone, moving cautiously to the front, holding his troops well in hand, furiously assaulted the left of Birney in flank and rear, carrying the line and capturing whole regiments and batteries. Penetrating further in the gap with one of his brigades, he struck the right of the Sixth Corps, and here rested, after vainly waiting for the expected support, which never came. After securing his guns and prisoners, Mahone returned to his works.

We will now follow the division of General Wilcox. These troops, moving well to the right, took position at some distance from the Weldon road. When the sharpshooters were sent forward they soon developed a strong skirmish line of the enemy, which was speedily broken; and an advance still further disclosed an open field with no enemy in front except a skirmish line and the ordinary reserve. Evidently the left of the Sixth Corps was near at hand. Two brigades of the division were moved into position, and the inevitable intrenchments soon began to appear; but beyond a sharp picket fire in front there was no fighting. All the evening we heard the firing to our left, and as it increased in volume an officer of the division staff was sent out to the picket line and informed the officer in charge that the division would withdraw at once from its position; that it must do its best to hold the line with both its flanks unprotected, and, if forced back, was to make a run for it. The sharpshooters kept up a steady fight, and were glad to perceive that there was no disposition on the part of the enemy to advance; on the contrary, they seemed rather nervous lest *we* should do so. At nightfall, however, unwonted signs of activity among them were to be observed. Fresh troops were moved into line; the rattle of accoutrements and canteens could be heard, and the officers' words of command all indicated preparations for an early advance. The word was passed down our line to give them one volley and then retire. When it was well dark, on the Federals came at a charge. Greatly to our relief we could hear the officers shouting out, "Hold your fire for the line of battle!" This was just the thing *we* wanted. We gave them one volley and broke for the rear like quarter-horses.

There was a line of cavalry pickets in our rear; but these were alarmed at the shouting of the enemy and at once decamped, nor did they draw rein until they reached their camp. The fact that the sharpshooters got away without losing a man in the race, proved that they, on occasion, could show a clean pair of heels. Late that night it was learned that Wilcox arrived on the ground in rear of Mahone too late to be of any service. The ground had been reached by a retrograde movement. This ended this brilliant affair, which, successful as it was, was greatly marred in execution by the manner in which General Mahone was supported. If the division of Wilcox had been moved to the front, the Confederates would have completely turned and enveloped the left flank of the Sixth Corps; and these troops caught between two fires must have suffered great losses. It is a significant fact, with regard to the various movements conducted by General Mahone, which reflected such lustre on himself and on the Confederate arms, that at no time was he placed under the command of any division commander. So great was the confidence reposed by General Lee in his skill and energy, that in all cases he reported to the corps commander or directly to the general-in-chief.

Almost immediately following the movement on Reams' Station, in which the sharpshooters bore their full part, and bore it well, was the battle of the Crater, an action fought entirely by Mahone, from which he gained enduring fame. Here, also, the sharpshooters covered themselves with glory, being always in the van and doing full service there. Their commandant, Captain Broadbent, a man of gigantic strength and stature, especially distinguished himself by his reckless daring. Like the brave Major Ridge, who led the stormers at Ciudad Rodrigo, Broadbent was the first in the works and fell at the foot of the Crater wall, pierced, it was said, with no less than eleven bayonet wounds. After Mahone drove the enemy from the captured mine and retook the pieces, when the line was re-established, a Napoleon gun belonging to Pegram's Battery (which being just over the mine was blown up by its explosion), was found to be outside of the line, at some distance in front of them. It was then almost death to show a head along the line, and the great question was how to get that gun in. Finally some adventurous spirits, being inspired by the promise of a furlough, crept at night to the front, fixed a strong rope around the muzzle, and so dragged it in in triumph. In this action the artillery was specially well served, officers encouraging the men, both by their presence and example. One battery to the south of the mine was handled with a degree of gallantry which challenged all honor. It was here that Lieutenant

Colonel Frank Huger, of South Carolina, a young officer of great promise and of high personal courage, with his own hands worked one of the guns throughout the fight. The sharpshooters in this battle sustained heavy losses, having not only skirmished with the enemy during the entire evening, but also participating in the attack with the main line. The extent of the enemy's losses is known; and the battle itself lives, alone of Confederate victories, on the canvas of John E. Elder, of Richmond, whose picture is notable for the absence from it of every recognizable figure of those who bore part in the heroic labors and perils of the bloody day. After this battle the army had a long rest, unbroken except by an occasional fusilade over some wretched deserter.

At this time desertions from the Confederate army had become matters of such common occurrence that it was determined to put a stop to the evil by a summary execution of the law. When men had been taken for this offense, there was held what was called a corps court-martial; when they were found guilty they were re-manded to their respective commands, that the sentence might be carried out. The sentence was executed with all the formalities suitable to such occasions, and the scene was well calculated to strike terror to the hearts of those who contemplated the commis-sion of this gravest of all military offenses. The brigade charged with the duty of executing the sentence was drawn up without arms, forming three sides of a hollow square. The condemned man, with the firing party, was marched around the inside of the square, the band in front playing a dirge—usually the " Dead March in Saul." These parades were the most disgusting and disagreeable duty en-countered during the whole war. One can never forget the looks of the poor fellows moving slowly around to their death. Some were erect and composed; others so nearly dead from terrror at the approach of death as to be reduced almost to a state of coma. After moving around the circle of the troops, the condemned man was fastened to a stake and shot, and the brigades, filing slowly by the corpse, were dismissed to their quarters. There were, I am glad to say, no deserters from the sharpshooters, as was natural; for they were the *elite* of the army.

When the heavy winter days were ended and spring found us prepared to continue the unequal contest, General Lee, weary of waiting, his depleted command being somewhat strengthened by its long rest, determined to assume the initiative. Accordingly, on the 25th of March, a movement was made on our left (Fort Stedman), which proved a failure. That very evening Grant delivered his *riposte* in the shape of a sharp thrust on our right at "Battery 45." Our pickets—only details were on duty—were driven in, and forced back almost under the works. The next day General Lee made a personal inspection of this portion of the lines, in company with Lieutenant General Hill and his division commanders. The picket line, as it remained, was undoubtedly faulty in the last degree, and General Lee, vexed with the burden of so many and such heavy responsibilities, seemed by no means disposed to tax his mind further with the assumption of details of this description. Turning sharply to General Hill, he exclaimed: "Here are your troops and yonder is the enemy. If you can't establish your picket line, I can't do it for you." And with these words he rode away. General Hill that night ordered the sharpshooters of Wilcox to carry the crest in their front, and the next day found us strongly intrenched on a line commanding all the country before it. In moving to our right to meet the continued advances of the enemy in that direction, each day saw our works stripped of men, and each day found us fighting. The sharpshooters were in greater demand than ever before. It was a common thing for a general officer to request their assistance in the establishment of his picket lines. One instance of the kind is worthy of record. Three days before the enemy broke through the lines around Petersburg, they pushed up their skirmish line almost to our works, in front of General Cook, near Hatcher's run, with the view of masking their larger movements. Friday evening, a battalion of sharpshooters of Wilcox's Division received orders to report to General Cook for duty. On reaching the quarters of that officer, they were informed that the command was told off for "nervous duty" in front of his line. We were placed in position with them by Captain Stephen W. Jones, a famous officer of sharpshooters in command of Cook's Corps. That night the battalion moved on the enemy, and with but slight loss captured their rifle-pits and re-established the picket line. The next day occurred the great break up and the death of A. P. Hill.

It was under most singular circumstances that Lieutenant General A. P. Hill, an officer whose name will ever be inseparably connected with the glory of the Army of Northern Virginia, met his death. When the Federal commander for the last time applied his favorite tactics, and extended his left flank to envelop our right, General Hill's Corps was massed at and beyond Hatcher's run, though a portion of his command held the works from "Battery 45" to the extreme right. His headquarters were still established near Petersburg. On Saturday evening he left the front at Hatcher's run, there being no indication at that point of a forward hostile movement. This the writer knows, as having obtained permission from General Hill himself to return to Petersburg, and having ridden up the lines in company with him and his staff. Next morning before dawn the enemy carried several points of his line by reason of its extension, and the attenuation of its defense. Moving across the country, the victorious Federals re-established their pickets in the direction of the river. General Hill, apprised of this state of things at his headquarters, at once dispatched such of his staff as were with him to report the facts to General Lee, and to see what could be done toward repairing the disaster. Accompanied by a few couriers, he rode immediately afterward toward Hatcher's run, with the view of rejoining the main body of his command. He was repeatedly urged not to attempt the undertaking; but his sole and laconic reply was, "I must get to my corps."

As the General and his party proceeded upon their way they found the country filled with detached bodies of Federal infantry, straggling and plundering. The first lot of these stragglers which was come across, uncertain of their strength, and perhaps awed by the appearance of a general officer—a sentiment natural to disciplined soldiery—quietly surrendered, and were sent to Petersburg in charge of three couriers. Accompanied only by Sergeant Tucker, General Hill continued on his way till, on reaching a point some four miles from Petersburg, on the plank road, they saw before them two Federal infantrymen. These men, seeing the mounted Confederates, took cover behind a tree. Hill, without hesitation, called to Tucker to ride them down; and, pushing forward in advance, received their fire with fatal effect. Thus perished, in the prime of life, a gallant officer, who had engaged in more pitched battles than he numbered years; who organized and fought with eminent success and daring the famous Light Division, and who handled the Third Corps of the army with the same vigilance, efficiency, and fidelity which distinguished him in lower commands, and which so singularly recalled his image to the dying eyes both of Lee and Jackson. In tone, in character, and in military force, he was strikingly like Bessieres; and his death may also be compared with that of the commander of the Old Guard, who lost his life in an insignificant skirmish on the eve of the great battle of Lutzen. His death was peculiarly unfortunate at this time; but even his magnetic presence—and no man's was more so—could hardly have redeemed the fortunes of the day. In fact, the army was so broken as almost to have lost its military attitude.

With the beginning of the retreat began also the most arduous labors of the sharpshooters. To this body was assigned the duty of protecting the rear of the wearied and worn battalions of Lee that now moved slowly up the line of the Southside Railroad, contesting the way inch by inch with the determined pursuer. At Farmville a decided stand was made, and here the rear guard was joined by Fitz Lee and his cavalry. The fighting on the retreat, except in rare instances, did not reach the dignity of pitched battles; but one action that took place near Farmville deserves the record it has so far received from no pen or tongue. When the army reached this point, the conduct of operations in the rear was intrusted to Major General Fitz Lee, of cavalry fame; an officer who, after the death of Stuart, ranked first in the army for energy, *elan*, and all other qualities that make the ideal *beau sabruer*. With a small column of infantry, and such of his own command as he was yet able to hold together, Fitz Lee stoutly guarded the rear of the retreating army. As the main column passed the bridge in rear of Farmville, Fitz Lee in person held the town, gradually diminishing his front, which was closely pressed by the enemy, till there remained with him but a handful of brave men. Seated on horseback, near the bridge, he calmly watched the preparations for firing it, and directed the movements of the last groups that filed across. There he sat, a grand figure, in his own person the last remnant of the Army of Northern Virginia; and, like Marshal Ney at the bridge Kowno, he fired the last shot, and was the last to cross. As the final man was seen to be over, and when the bridge itself was in flames, the soldiers supposing him to be a vidette, shouted to him to ride across. Lee turned slowly toward them, ordering them to hurry across, and, adding, "I am Fitz Lee," plunged into the river below the bridge. He gained the opposite bank in safety, but not without difficulty and danger, and the quick fire of the horse artillery from the other side soon gave assurance of his presence among the guns.

Hemmed in on all sides at Appomattox, General Robert E. Lee's only hope was to cut his way through, and, by the abandonment of his guns and baggage, to force his path to the mountains. Having formed this resolution, Gordon was promptly dispatched forward, while the left flank was protected by moving in the four battalions of Wilcox's sharpshooters. Two of these were engaged, and two more were moving into action. But a period to the fighting of the sharpshooters and of all the rest of that "incomparable infantry" was now close at hand. When Custer rode through the Confederate lines, an officer of General Lee's staff was at once sent to recall the sharpshooters, and the sound of their bugles to "Cease firing!" in a few minutes silenced forever the guns of the Army of Northern Virginia.

THE DRAFT RIOTS IN NEW YORK.

BY MAJOR T. P. M'ELRATH.

THE story of the New York draft riots of 1863 has been related with more or less completeness by every historian of the civil war. No thoroughly accurate account, however, has yet been published. The chroniclers appear to have confined their researches to surface events, and have been either ignorant of the true circumstances attending the suppression of the riots, or desirous of keeping those circumstances concealed. At that particular juncture a large portion of the city's militia force was absent at the seat of war, a fact which gave rise to the opinion that the riots had been previously planned instead of being, as it really was, a sudden and spontaneous insurrection. Through the same cause, also, the civil authorities were crippled, and the task of restoring order was thrown into the hands of the few Federal troops then stationed in the vicinity of New York. It is probable that the city was a gainer in the end by this state of things, which in the outset appeared so unfortunate. The interference which the regular troops encountered at the hands of the State officers—growing out of the jealousy of the local militia commander—doubled the period of the rioters' triumph, and coupled with his inefficiency throughout, suggests forcibly what might have been the consequence, had he been in absolute command.

Early in the summer it had been announced from Washington that a compulsory addition was to be made to the armies in the field by means of a general conscription. The quota of the city of New York was fixed at 12,500, and that of Brooklyn at 5,000. Colonel Robert Nugent, of the Sixty-ninth New York Volunteers—a captain in the Thirteenth United States Infantry—was detailed as assistant provost marshal general, and established his headquarters in Leonard street. The business of his department was conducted with quiet discretion, and the bugbear of a draft, which at first had created great consternation, in the course of time lost its terrors, as people became accustomed to its contemplation. Still there was a deep-seated hostility to the proposed conscription, which the political opponents of the war fostered as sedulously as they dared, with the hospitalities of Fort Lafayette and its sturdy commandant, Martin Burke, staring them in the face.

On Monday, June 29th, Governor Seymour, in Albany, received private information that a deep laid conspiracy was on foot in New York to resist the draft. Hastening to the city the details of the plot were communicated to him from the same source, to the effect that a large body of deserters, 1,800 strong, acting in concert with another large body of "Copperheads" were banded together to oppose the draft. Arms were to be obtained for the revolutionists by a simultaneous attack on the State arsenal in Seventh avenue, and on the Seventh Regiment armory, to be made during the night of July 3d, when it was believed that the noise and confusion attendant upon ushering in the national holiday would render the movements of the leaders in the daring project less liable to be observed. Governor Seymour held a council with Mayor Opdyke and General Sanford. Strong guards were posted at the places threatened with attack. The police authorities were privately notified, and Superintendent Kennedy detailed trusty officers to watch the armories, and to report the slightest circumstance of an unusual character that might occur in their neighborhood. Having made preparations for the assault General Sanford left the city on Friday morning, confiding the management of affairs to General Spicer. The night passed quietly, however. No attack was made, no conspirators exposed themselves to arrest, and the Governor and the small circle whom he had admitted to his confidence satisfied themselves that the whole affair was a hoax, gotten up with the mischievous intent of creating an alarm. The incident, however, revealed the existence of a dangerous under-current of sentiment in New York, at that time, hostile to the war policy of the government, and competent to impress itself with fatal distinctness upon the minds of the ignorant masses who make up so large a portion of that city's foreign population. The "Peace party," as the opposition styled itself, was carrying things with a high hand. At a meeting in the Twenty-second ward, held shortly after the 4th of July, the approaching conscription was denounced in bitter terms, and the President and his Cabinet were stigmatized as "murderers" and "despots." The train was, beyond a doubt, being carefully laid, when an unexpected spark brought about a premature explosion.

The 11th of July was the date appointed for the draft to begin. As that day fell on Saturday its selection was particularly ill-advised, the Sabbath holiday which followed affording the ignorant masses, as well as the disaffected element of the population, an opportunity for studying into the situation through the morning papers, and of discussing the prospect over their liquor—the probable result of which might have been easily foreseen. Some slight impediments had been placed in the way of the enrolling officers, but nothing had occurred to excite apprehensions of any outbreak, and the first day's work of conscription passed off in a quiet and orderly manner. The drafting took place in the deputy provost marshal's office, at the corner of Forty-sixth street and Third avenue, and 1,236 names were peacefully drawn that day out of the 1,500 called for from the Twenty-second ward. It was believed that the popular enthusiasm created by the routing of Lee's army had effectually silenced the anti-war party. Some hopeful ones expressed the belief that the contest was so near its close that even if the draft went on the conscripts would never be called for in the field. Then that fatal Sunday intervened. On the following morning the papers stated that the Irish laboring classes in the Twentieth ward, where the draft was to be held that day were in a state of intense excitement, and threatened to resist it to the utmost.

The threat was speedily put into execution. The Sunday deliberations had evidently led to a determination to break up the drafting depot in Third avenue. About nine o'clock in the morning fifty rough and rowdyish-looking fellows were observed, by persons doing business on the East river, in the region of Grand street, prowling along the wharves and picking up recruits. Gaining insolence by increase of numbers, they entered the foundries and warehouses, and by persuasion and threats induced the workmen to join them. Simultaneously with this movement a similar one was progressing on the west side. About ten o'clock a large body of laboring men and ill-favored ruffians, armed mostly with clubs and bludgeons, after holding a brief parley in a vacant lot near Central Park, marched down Forty-seventh street to Third avenue. The deputy marshal's office was immediately entered, Captain Jenkins and his assistants retreating precipitately through a rear door. The wheel containing the names was carried away safely, but all the books and papers that could be found were destroyed, and the building itself was set on fire. Police Superintendent Kennedy, who was driving across the town on a tour of inspection, observed the flames, and leaving his wagon at the corner of Forty-sixth and Lexington avenue, proceeded unsuspiciously and unarmed on foot to the scene of the disturbance. Although not in uniform he was recognized. In an instant he was set upon and beaten so brutally that when, after a race for life of several blocks, he was happily rescued from his pursuers and carried in a market wagon to the police headquarters in Mulberry street, his colleagues failed to recognize him. He was the first person assaulted in the riot. Police Commissioner Acton immediately realized the situation. He assumed command, and dispatching what police were available (forty-four in number) to the scene of the riot, telegraphed to each of the thirty-two precincts covered by the Metropolitan police for the whole reserve force to be concentrated at the headquarters. This wise step was taken just in time, for soon afterward the rioters had cut down the telegraph poles and destroyed all communication between the headquarters and the upper precincts of the city.

A futile effort had meanwhile been made to subdue the rioters in Third avenue by a force of between forty and fifty invalid soldiers, who were ordered to the aid of the deputy provost marshal from the Park barracks. These soldiers held the key of the situation in their hands. The mob up to this period was entirely without definite organization, and destitute of leaders, and was wholly incapable of maintaining its ground against a resolute attack of disciplined troops. But either through a mistaken sense of their own superiority, or a misguided disposition to leniency, the soldiers contented themselves with firing a harmless volley over the heads of the rioters. The latter, who a moment before were wavering, saw their opportunity immediately. They rushed upon the soldiers, wrested from them their yet unloaded weapons, and drove them in wild confusion down the avenue. Two of the soldiers were beaten down, and left for dead on the pavement. Others would doubtless have suffered a similar fate, had they not fortunately encountered in their flight the police force sent by Commissioner Acton. The mob, having tasted blood after receiving its baptism of fire, was by this time worked up into a state of uncontrollable frenzy. Brandishing clubs and muskets above their heads, and yelling, and shouting, they rushed down the avenue like a torrent. Sergeant McCredie, who commanded the police, expecting speedy reinforcements, deployed his men in line across the street, and, as the head of the disorderly column approached, he ordered a charge. Despite

19

their overwhelming numbers, the mob could not withstand this onset of a disciplined force. Step by step, they were driven back three blocks. By the time Forty-sixth street was reached, however, Sergeant McCredie's little band was thoroughly exhausted. The expected reinforcements did not arrive. A large body of rioters, who had slipped out of the way into Forty-fifth street, seeing the paltry number of police before whom they were retreating, emerged again into the avenue, in rear of the latter, thus hemming them in on every side. Fighting was no longer in the question. The brave little force broke and fled, every man seeking his own safety, and all eventually escaped, though nearly every one of the party was severely beaten and wounded. This first triumph of the mob was achieved about noon. The excitement had spread rapidly through the city, and at that hour Third avenue, from the Cooper Institute to Forty-sixth street, was black with human beings—the sidewalks, housetops and windows being all crowded with rioters, or spectators. It was estimated that fifty thousand persons were thus congregated within the stretch of thirty blocks along the avenue.

The attention of the mob having been drawn away in the manner related from the building they had set on fire, the firemen succeeded in subduing the flames, after four houses had been burned to the ground. It is deserving of notice that, while these terrible scenes were being enacted in the Ninth district, the draft in the Eighth district, at 1190 Broadway, under Captain Manierre, was going on without molestation. It was adjourned at noon, and the policemen in attendance hastened to the aid of their comrades on the east side. In the meantime the work of destruction progressed, but in an irregular and desultory manner, clearly indicating the absence of previous arrangement. The news of the uprising, as it spread through those portions of the city where the low Irish dwelt, stirred up the dregs of the population, and they came thronging forth in great numbers, so that at almost every turn a mob was discernible. Splitting up into several sections, as different objects attracted them, they would rejoin and separate without apparently any concert of action. A shout and a cry in one direction would call off a throng, while a similar shout in another direction would attract a portion thither. The armory, at the corner of Second avenue and Twenty-first street, was captured from the police detailed to hold it, and the rioters, after arming themselves, destroyed all the material they could not carry away. Several of the attacking party were killed in this encounter. One detachment started for Captain Manierre's drafting office, at the corner of Broadway and Twenty-ninth street, which they burned down. The rich goods in the stores on the block of Broadway, between Twenty-eighth and Twenty-ninth streets, turned the attention of the mob to plunder. It was estimated that the active rioters in this crowd were not over one hundred in number, but they were attended by an enormous horde, including women and children, who displayed a skilled expertness in appropriating property. Watches, bracelets, jewelry, and valuable goods of all kinds disappeared from the stores, as if by magic, and in an hour's time the whole block had been devastated and set on fire. It was completely destroyed. Simultaneously with these two outrages, a third and larger squad of rioters broke away in the direction of the Colored Orphan Asylum, on Fifth avenue and Forty-third and Forty-fourth streets.

The old antipathy of the Irish to the negroes had already been given full vent, and since noon had manifested itself in various parts of the city—even those remote from the scenes of worst outrage—by a sort of desultory persecution of black people wherever they were met. The station-houses were filled with the hounded creatures seeking protection; and about the time of the attack on the orphan asylum, a colored cartman had been murdered, mutilated, hanged, and burned, in Clarkson street, under circumstances of atrocity unparalleled in civilized communities. On their way, the mob stopped to sack and burn two valuable dwellings, on Lexington avenue, after which the orphan asylum was subjected to a pillage, which lasted nearly two hours; and the edifice was then, despite the earnest efforts of the firemen, burned to the ground. The inmates had been removed before the mob's arrival. Soon after this, the crowd, flushed with success and maddened with liquor, made a demonstration on the police headquarters. They were met, in Broadway, near Amity street, by Inspector Daniel Carpenter, who, after a brief struggle, drove them back with terrible punishment. No more spirited fight took place during the entire riots than this one, in which a desperate mob, armed with every description of weapon, and numbering several thousand, was totally routed by two hundred policemen, armed solely with their clubs. A similar scene was enacted at about seven o'clock in the evening, when an attack was made on the *Tribune* building. Here, again, the crowd was enormously in excess of the police; and here, again, the latter swept the ruffianly assailants before them like chaff before an autumn breeze. This ended the heavy fighting of the day, though minor disturbances occurred at various points during the evening, including the burning of Postmaster Wakeman's house, in Eighty-sixth street. The custom-house and sub-treasury, in Wall street, were under guard; and General Sanford, commanding the city military, had collected some men for the protection of the State arsenal, in Seventh avenue. But, throughout the deadly occurrences of the day, he had not dispatched a single body of soldiers to assist the police in quelling the mob.

At the beginning of July, the military post of the city and harbor of New York was commanded by Brevet Brigadier General Harvey Brown, Colonel of the Fifth United States Artillery. The headquarters of the Department of the East, under General Wool, were in New York city. The "post" headquarters were at Fort Hamilton, where, as Adjutant of the Fifth Artillery, I performed the additional duty of Acting Assistant Adjutant General. The "post" comprised all the forts and military commands, excepting Governor's Island, in the vicinity of New York, together with the hospital and convalescent depots at Hart's and Riker's Islands and Willett's Point. The garrison of this rather comprehensive post, exclusive of the volunteers who passed through it in a continuous stream, on their way from Northern hospitals, to rejoin their commands in the field, was constituted as follows: At Fort Hamilton, the headquarters, and two mounted batteries (Dupont's and Piper's) of the Fifth Artillery; headquarters Second Battalion Twelfth United States Infantry, Major Bruen, commanding, and the Eleventh Regiment New York Volunteer Heavy Artillery, Colonel W. B. Barnes. Fort Ethan Allen (Sandy Hook), Company F, Twelfth Infantry, Captain H. R. Putnam, commanding. Fort Richmond, Company H, Twelfth Infantry, Captain Walter S. Franklin, commanding. Fort Lafayette, one company of the Ninth United States Infantry, under Lieutenant Wood; Lieutenant Colonel Martin Burke, Third United States Artillery, commanding. Fort Schuyler, Twentieth and Twenty-eighth New York Batteries, First Lieutenant B. F. Ryer, Twentieth Battery, New York Volunteer Artillery, commanding. New York city, a volunteer guard at the Park barracks, designated the Invalid Corps.

Beside the above-named commands, there was a company of infantry at Fort Hamilton known as the "Permanent Guard," which had been organized by myself a few weeks previous in compliance with instructions from department headquarters. The garrison of that post—being composed of light artillery—had special duties to perform incident to the mounted service which, in addition to their not being armed with muskets, precluded their being detailed for the general garrison guard and fatigue duty. The "Permanent

Guard" was in its way a "crack" organization. My orders authorized me to take from all the volunteer troops, convalescents and furlough men in the harbor, whatever private soldiers I might select, not to exceed one hundred and eighty in number, and by dint of careful selection and occasional changes—substituting good material for poor—the company became eventually a type of the cream of the volunteer army. No two men in it belonged necessarily to the same regiment; all had seen hard service in the field, and all were willing to pass a portion of their terms of enlistment in protecting Fort Hamilton from invasion. The severest punishment I could inflict was to ship an undesirable soldier to his regiment. The name I adopted in mild imitation of the celebrated "Permanent Party" of Governor's Island. Their association with the regulars excited in them a wholesome spirit of emulation. I succeeded in having them equipped in every respect the same as the Twelfth Infantry; had their clothing made over by a company tailor to fit them; fed them well with the accumulations of the company fund; held them down to strict discipline, and in a short time I found myself in charge of as orderly, self-possessed, and "natty" a company as any officer need desire to command. The gallant service they performed in the July riots, and the eagerness displayed by the regular infantry officers in New York during that period to lead them, showed the sterling metal of which they were composed, and justify me in claiming for the "Permanent Guard of Fort Hamilton" the place it is entitled to in the history of that deadly outbreak. On July 4th telegraphic orders were received from Washington to dispatch the two batteries from Fort Hamilton to the Army of the Potomac at Chambersburg, and the "Permanent Guard" thus became the only effective garrison of the post. The aggregate strength of General Brown's command at that time was less than 500.

About two o'clock on the afternoon of Monday, July 13th, having occasion to visit the telegraph office just outside the military inclosure of Fort Hamilton, I was informed by the operator that communication with the city had been in some way cut off. No word of any disturbance had reached us at the Narrows. Shortly afterward a mounted orderly from General Wool's headquarters made his appearance, bearing an order to send immediately to New York a portion of the troops from Fort Lafayette, and half the company then garrisoning Fort Richmond. While I was proceeding to carry this order into execution General Brown arrived from the city and expressed great surprise at the small number of men—about eighty—specified in General Wool's order. As the tug was then in sight which was to carry the detachment to New York, General Brown ordered me, without delay, to get all the troops at Forts Hamilton, Lafayette, Richmond, and at Sandy Hook, in readiness to move at a moment's notice, while he proceeded to the city to provide transportation for them. This first detail of troops sent to New York consisted of one platoon of Company H, Twelfth United States Infantry, from Fort Richmond, and Lieutenant Wood, Ninth United States Infantry, with his company (fifty-four strong), from Fort Lafayette—the whole under the command of Captain Walter S. Franklin. These troops were ordered by General Brown, upon landing, to report to Colonel Nugent at the corner of Broadway and Leonard street; and as that officer was found to be at the Seventh avenue arsenal, they were dispatched without delay to that point. Captain Franklin, on arriving at the arsenal, found everything already in the state of confusion that prevailed there during the whole period of the disturbances. Nobody seemed to know who was in command—militia staff officers were displaying great activity in a purposeless way; and excepting a single sentry at the front entrance, there was literally no guard established over the building. A detachment of marines arriving from the Brooklyn Navy Yard, Captain Franklin used them to clear away the noisy crowd that had congregated in the avenue and established a line of sentries along the four streets by which that post was approached.

In the meanwhile, after ordering the remainder of the regular troops in the harbor to be in readiness, and making provision to replace them with volunteers, I occupied myself at Fort Hamilton in an effort to improvise for the occasion a section of light artillery, which I knew would be valuable in street fighting. The two batteries, on their departure a few days previous, had carried with them every trained horse and driver, and all the equipments at the post. There remained, however, two guns, brass six-pounders, which had belonged to Bragg's celebrated battery in the Mexican war, and which, having been condemned, had for several years past performed ornamental service on Governor's Island, and, more lately, had been utilized for drill instruction by the batteries of the Fifth Artillery. A couple of hours' effort enabled me to rig together a harness for the post quartermaster's horses, a wheel and a lead team to each piece. The quartermaster's teamsters supplied the drivers, and a sufficient number of volunteers were detailed to serve as cannoneers. This motley battery was completed by my assigning the drum major of the Fifth Artillery as chief of one of the pieces, and the commissary sergeant as the chief of the other, and placing a volunteer officer of heavy artillery in command of the whole, with orders to make every effort to report to General Brown, at the St. Nicholas Hotel. As the horses were unused to that kind of pulling, I was in great doubt about the guns ever reaching New York; but my concern on that score was greatly modified by the reflection that none of the men accompanying them knew anything respecting their use. My doubts as to the horses turned out to be groundless, though those respecting the men were fully realized.

About eight in the evening two steamboats reported to me at Fort Hamilton. On one of these I placed a company of volunteer artillery to replace at Sandy Hook Captain Putnam's company of the Twelfth Infantry, which latter I ordered to return on the same boat to New York. On the other boat I proceeded myself with the "Permanent Guard," and the remainder of the troops already referred to from Forts Lafayette and Richmond, numbering in all about one hundred and forty soldiers. Landing at the foot of Spring street I marched, in a heavy shower, up to the St. Nicholas Hotel, where I was ushered into General Wool's office, in one of the parlors. The apartment was crowded with officers and civilians. Among the latter I recognized several of the most prominent merchants of New York engaged in earnest discussion with General Brown. Approaching Major Christensen, General Wool's adjutant general, I inquired what had been going on in the city that day, for as yet I was ignorant of the details. Major Christensen's reply was characteristic. "Good God! McElrath, this is the one spot in New York where the least is known of what is taking place!" The course of events showed that the refreshing ignorance admitted by Major Christensen prevailed at General Wool's headquarters without interruption through the riots, despite the intelligent staff with which he was surrounded. Reporting my arrival to General Brown, I was informed that having declined to serve under General Sanford when ordered to do so by General Wool, he had, at his own request, been relieved from duty. I replied that I should like then to be relieved also, but he requested me to report to General Wool, which I did. A more arbitrary piece of absurdity has seldom been recorded in military annals than this attempt to place, at a critical juncture, a veteran of nearly fifty years' service in the regular army in a position subordinate to an unpracticed militia officer, simply because the latter held higher rank by State commission. General Wool, however, was firm in spite of the earnest remonstrances of the gentlemen present, and General Brown was equally determined. Happily for the welfare of New York city, the matter was compromised during the night by the interposition of Mayor Opdyke and others, and General Brown the next morning assumed command of all the government troops in the city, and took up his quarters at the police headquarters in Mulberry street, where he and Commissioner Acton concerted measures which speedily reduced the rioters to submission. No effective steps were taken to accomplish this purpose until these two gentlemen formed their alliance, and no steps other than those which they carried out tended in any degree whatever to that end.

In the meanwhile, I had reported to General Wool, who nervously ordered me to take my command to the arsenal, and to carefully avoid any encounter with a mob on my way thither, as it was imperative to reinforce General Sanford promptly. No obstacle was offered, however, to our progress, and we reached the arsenal about eleven o'clock. General Sanford was there in command, but did not wear any vestige of uniform, either then, or at any time during the riots. About midnight, word was received that a mob was preparing to assault the arsenal. A few minutes later General Sanford put on his hat, and, bidding us good-night, with the assurance that he should look in again in the morning, he departed for his private residence. This resembled his behavior on the 3d of the month, as above related. Two staff officers remained and entertained us for the rest of the night with a dispute as to which was in command. About two A. M., Lieutenant Wood arrived at the arsenal with the section of artillery from Fort Hamilton, which had succeeded in reaching the St. Nicholas Hotel, and he and I made a transfer of commands, he taking my infantry and I assuming charge of the artillery. The staff officers desired me to bring the guns inside the building, but as that was preposterous, I persuaded them to allow me to put them in battery at the corners of Thirty-fifth and Thirty-sixth streets, pointing up and down Seventh avenue. Rumors reached us, from time to time, of disorderly gatherings moving about the city; but, as I have already stated, no further violence was attempted by the mob until Tuesday morning.

The 14th of July dawned clear and lovely. In the lower part of the city some attempt was made in the morning to resume business, but in the upper districts stores and residences remained closed. Second and Third avenues were the rallying points, but the rioters, being without leaders, hesitated as to their course of action. Early in the morning Inspector Carpenter, with two hundred and fifty police, started on a reconnoissance from the Mulberry street headquarters. About the same time one of the staff officers at the arsenal ordered the officer whom I had placed in command of the section, while I went to breakfast at a restaurant, in the next block, to accompany a detachment under Colonel O'Brien, Eleventh New York Volunteers, to Yorkville, where fighting was reported to be in progress. The lieutenant was refused permission to notify me, and when I returned to the arsenal I was thunder-struck to find that my guns, and men, and horses had disappeared, nobody seemed to know whither! Seeking out the staff officer who had performed the brilliant *coup*, I gave him my opinion of his conduct in the language it merited, and had the satisfaction of being informed, in return, that "the regular army officers were always trying to ride over the militia!" My occupation in that quarter being gone, I returned to General Brown, for assignment to whatever other duty might offer itself.

It was no easy matter to accomplish this. No street cars were running, and it would have been sheer fool-hardiness to undertake to make the trip on foot, alone. Two livery stables were near by, but in neither could I induce a driver to undertake the risky job. Finally, the proprietor of one of the stables declared that he would drive me down himself. A coach was driven out, and cautioning me to keep the curtains down and to have my revolver ready for use, he started briskly across the town. It seemed like passing through a deserted city! Up Thirty-sixth street to Fifth avenue, and down that thoroughfare to Fourteenth street, every house we passed was closed, with curtains down and blinds tight shut. Neither cars nor stages were running, and, excepting occasional glimpses of people grouped together at distant points down the side streets, we did not see a living creature until, after turning into Broadway, we approached Amity street. From that point Broadway was crowded as far, almost, as the eye could reach, with citizens eager to hear what was occurring in the disaffected districts. I found General Brown at the St. Nicholas Hotel, and was instructed to serve on his personal staff, Lieutenant Colonel Frothingham, aide-de-camp, having been detailed as his adjutant general. In the meanwhile, the section with Colonel O'Brien's command had encountered a mob at Second avenue and Thirty-fourth street. Carpenter's policemen had just before inflicted a severe punishment upon this gang, and threatening demonstrations were made toward O'Brien, who attempted to awe the crowd by a discharge of blank cartridges. This cleared the streets and Colonel O'Brien, who appears to have been operating thus far on his own responsibility, marched down town and reported to General Brown for orders. As he was in too excited a condition to be fit to intrust with a command, his services were declined, and his company melted away as mysteriously as it had sprung into existence. The unfortunate colonel undertook to return to his residence. As he was passing through Thirty-second street, he was attacked by the very ruffians whose lives he had so unwisely spared, and after being subjected to horrible brutalities, was dragged almost naked into his own back yard, where he died in agony, surrounded by a howling crowd of ferocious men and women.

This tragedy was a type of the acts that were being perpetrated in twenty different parts of the city. The mob had asserted itself, and the spirit of pandemonium was set loose. It is impracticable to give a detailed account of all the riotous and murderous transactions. Detachments of police and military were incessantly setting out from the Mulberry street headquarters, returning for a brief rest, and then sallying forth again. Wherever a mob was encountered, it was charged upon relentlessly, with utter disregard to the relative strength of the two forces; and in every case the rioters were repulsed with heavy loss. Finally, they ceased showing fight on the open streets, and, at the first appearance of their determined pursuers, broke and fled, to assemble again at some distant point, and resume their work of havoc. In all the proceedings, from Tuesday morning on, no co-operation was received from General Sanford by General Brown or Commissioner Acton. Members of volunteer regiments, who chanced to be in the city, tendered their services; and nearly four hundred citizens were sworn in at police headquarters, as specials, receiving clubs and badges. Business was closed down town, and the merchants and bankers resolved to volunteer, in companies of one hundred each, to serve under the military. William E. Dodge was made captain of one of these companies. The armory, at White and Elm streets, was guarded by a mixed command of the Eighty-fourth New York Militia and some Zouaves. The sub-treasury and custom-house were similarly defended. In front of the government stores, in Worth and White streets, the Invalid Corps and a squad of marines patrolled, while howitzers, loaded with grape and canister, stood ready for action. All this time the fight was going on in every direction, while the constant ringing of fire-bells contributed to increase the constantly-spreading terror of the citizens. The negro population were hunted down mercilessly, and the ferryboats were crowded through the day by the poor wretches, fleeing for their lives.

Scenes of violence and carnage, such as I have described, prevailed in the streets of New York from Monday noon until Thursday night. The political sentiment, which displayed itself in the original assault on the draft office, in Third avenue, disappeared after that demonstration, and thenceforward the mob was actuated solely by an instinct of rapine and plunder. The limits of this sketch will not admit a recital of every encounter between the rioters and the city's defenders. Outbreaks would occur simultaneously in widely-separated sections of the city, compelling the police and military to split up into small detachments. These latter would combine, as they happened to meet in the streets, so that it would be impossible to give a connected narrative of the services of any individual portion of the command. I will, accordingly, briefly summarize the principal occurrences of the riots not yet described:

THURSDAY, July 14.—Lieutenant Wood, Ninth Infantry, commanding the mixed detachment from the Narrows, being assaulted, about ten A. M., in Pitt street, fired on the mob, killing fourteen and wounding seventeen. He dispersed, at the point of the bayonet, another mob in Division street. The "Permanent Guard" received special mention for its gallantry in both the above actions. Captain Dilks, with two hundred policemen, had a desperate fight, on Second avenue, near Thirtieth street, with over one thousand rioters, whom he routed with severe loss. Later in the day, the mob returned, in increased numbers, and overpowered the police, but were again repulsed, by Captain Franklin (Twelfth Infantry), after a spirited fight, in which a number of rioters were killed. Mayor Opdyke's house was partially sacked by a mob of boys. An attack was made on some houses at Forty-sixth street and Fifth avenue, which was suppressed by Captain Putnam (Twelfth Infantry), with a loss to the rioters of forty men. The residence of James Gibbon, a relative of Horace Greeley, in Twenty-ninth street, between Seventh and Eighth avenues, was emptied of its contents. Brooks Brothers' clothing store, in Catharine street, was ransacked, until Captain Franklin came to the rescue. Four barricades were erected in Ninth avenue, near Thirty-fifth street, which Captain Wilkins, with the Governor's Island troops, captured and destroyed after a lively fight. My section, of which I had resumed command after it was rescued from Colonel O'Brien, was attacked at Thirty-sixth street and Seventh avenue. I went into battery, but my raw gun detachments worked clumsily, and the mob vanished like smoke into the side streets. As the excitement was intense in that neighborhood, and General Sanford was apprehensive for the safety of the arsenal, I bivouacked where I was, having the "Permanent Guard," under Lieutenant Porter, First United States Artillery, as my support.

WEDNESDAY, July 15.—Several thousand rioters, who were

sacking houses and hanging negroes to lamp-posts at Thirty-second
street and Eighth avenue, were driven off by Colonel Mott, with a
squadron of cavalry, and a battery of the Eighth New York
Volunteer Artillery. All through that day, from points in the city
five miles apart, came the news of riots and calls for help. One of
the latter was from General Sanford, asking to be relieved of some
of the negroes who had taken refuge in the arsenal, so that he could
make room for more soldiers. Several colored men were hung to
lamp-posts near Twenty-seventh street and Seventh avenue, and a
force of one hundred and fifty infantry was sent in the afternoon by
General Sanford to disperse the mob. The soldiers returned, however, without attempting to clear the streets, and almost while they
were still in sight the rioters had recommenced their occupation of
plunder and murder. Late in the day, a fight took place in First
avenue, between Eighteenth and Nineteenth streets, between a
desperate mob and a force of militia and enrolled citizens. Colonel
Jardine, of the Ninth New York Volunteers, was shot, and crippled
for life, and the troops were repulsed until Captain Putnam, with
his company, and the "Permanent Guard," under Captain Shelley,
acting aide-de-camp, were sent by General Brown to the rescue.

THURSDAY, July 16.—At an early hour in the morning the
Seventh Regiment New York Militia, which had been summoned
home by telegraph, arrived, and the other militia regiments followed
during the day. By this time the riot was regarded as practically
over. Mayor Opdyke had the day previous issued a proclamation,
calling on the citizens to resume their avocations. It was also
announced from Washington that the draft had been suspended, and
the Common Council appropriated $2,500,000 toward paying $300
exemption money per man to the poor who might be drafted.
General Brown, however, and Commissioner Acton remained
steadily at their posts. The riotous spirit, which for three days and
nights had held the metropolis by the throat, though crushed, was
not yet wholly extinguished. The "Permanent Guard" had
encounters during the day with rioters on Fourth avenue, near
Grammercy Park, and in Fifty-second street, near Eleventh avenue.
A heavy fight took place about one P. M. at Jackson's foundry, at
First avenue and Twenty-eighth street. The mob, driven to final
desperation, rallied repeatedly after being dispersed by the soldiers,
and renewed their attack. The troops were so divided, engaged in
patroling the city, that it was night before a sufficient force could be
concentrated by General Brown to finish the work of subjugation.
Captain Putnam, with several companies under his command, earned

this crowning honor, and, about ten P. M., in a heavy thunder-storm, finished successfully the last fight of the New York riots.

While these military operations were in progress, other influences were being exerted for the restoration of peace and order, none of which, however, had any perceptible effect. Governor Seymour arrived in New York on Tuesday, and issued a proclamation, notifying the insurgents that the only opposition to the conscription that could be allowed was an appeal to the courts, the right of every citizen to make which would be maintained, and urging all to stand firmly by the authorities in sustaining law and order in the city. It was soon urged upon the Governor, however, that more rigorous measures were demanded, and, becoming convinced that such was the case, he issued a second proclamation, declaring the city in a state of insurrection. It was too late, however. Opposition to the conscription had, hours before, faded from the minds of the frenzied rioters, and the glare of the incendiaries' torch blinded them to the inevitable consequences of their misdoing. Later on that same day, Governor Seymour was induced to speak from the steps of the City Hall to an immense gathering of the people, among whom, it is probable, there were many who had participated in the outrages which had been committed. The Governor made a few remarks, intended to allay the popular excitement, and earnestly counseled obedience to the laws and the constituted authorities. He also read a letter, containing a statement that the conscription had been postponed by the authorities in Washington. This speech of Governor Seymour, owing to his well-known affiliation with the opposition, was severely criticised by his political opponents, chiefly on account of his opening it with the words, "My friends." While he was speaking, however, his previous proclamation showed that he was exerting his influence for suppressing the insurrection, and he could hardly be expected to address a peaceable audience with the invective applicable to red-handed rioters and incendiaries. In his remarks he expressed his belief that the conscription act was illegal, and announced his determination to have it tested in the courts. In dwelling upon these points he may have violated good taste, but it must be borne in mind that his purpose was to soothe an unusual popular excitement, and that he was justified in using whatever reasonable arguments were available for that purpose. In his official acts and proclamations during the riots, Governor Seymour expressed himself in very different phrases. There was better ground for censure in the attitude assumed by Archbishop Hughes toward the rioters. Although that

prelate had yielded on Wednesday, July 15th, to the pressure
exerted upon him by issuing a brief address to the Irish, urging
them to abstain from violence, he caused to be published at the
same time a long letter to Horace Greeley, expressing his sympathy
with the opponents of the war, and his belief that the Irish were
the victims of oppression. On Thursday Archbishop Hughes issued
a call for a meeting at his residence, at Madison avenue and Thirty-
sixth street, on the following day, of "the men of New York who
are now called in many of the papers rioters." At the time
appointed between three thousand and five thousand persons assembled there, and listened to a sensible exhortation to good conduct, at
the conclusion of which they returned to their homes as peaceably
as they had come together. Such an effort, if made four days
earlier, would have prevented incalculable suffering and loss.

The riots were brought to an end on the evening of Thursday,
July 16th, and the city immediately resumed its customary aspect,
while the authorities proceeded to calculate the amount of damage
that had been sustained. The exact number of rioters killed was
never ascertained. It was reported, how truly I cannot say, that the
remains of many of them were secretly carried into the country for
burial. Governor Seymour, in his next annual message, stated that
"the number of killed and wounded is estimated by the police to be
at least one thousand." The mortality statistics for the riot week at
the City Inspector's office showed an increase of four hundred and
fifty over the average weekly mortality, including ninety deaths from
gun-shot wounds. The increase for the month was twelve hundred.
A large number of wounded persons probably died during the following week. Only three policemen were killed. The damage to
property was more precisely estimated. A committee was appointed
by the county supervisors to audit claims for damages, for all of
which the county was responsible under law. Claims were presented
to the amount of $2,500,000, of which $1,500,000 were allowed, and
were paid as expeditiously as possible.

On July 17th, an unexpected order was received from the War
Deparment relieving General Brown from the command of the city
and harbor of New York, General Canby being sent from Washington to assume the position. On the following day, General Wool
was superseded by Major General John A. Dix. Old age and consequent infirmity rendered the removal of General Wool from so
responsible a command a matter of perfect propriety, but the citizens
of New York, conscious of the debt of gratitude they owed to General Brown, were very reluctant to see him so peremptorily supplanted

at the very moment of his and their triumph. The orders in both cases were dated the 15th, and, doubtless, had their origin in a supposition at the War Office that so extensive an outbreak must, in some degree, be attributed to the inefficiency of the commanding officers. To a certain extent such an impression was correct. The strong contrast presented throughout the riots by the conduct of the three generals between whom the command was nominally divided enabled observers, even during the height of the excitement, to recognize the difference between capacity and titled incompetency. General Wool, in his temporary office at the St. Nicholas Hotel, unconscious of the real condition of things, and issuing orders contrary to reason and to military precedent, and General Sanford, in citizens' dress, jealously locking himself up for three days in the arsenal, collecting about him eagerly every soldier he could lay his hands upon, and in no single instance initiating a movement against the rioters of sufficient consequence to receive mention in the daily journals, were types of prejudiced inefficiency; while General Brown, on duty without intermission through four days and nights, covering the entire city of New York with a military force whose aggregate number was far smaller than the bodies of rioters with which any one of its detachments came into collision, co-operating generously with the sturdy Police Commissioners, and bending his whole energies to the single task of carrying out their plans for saving the city, was emphatically the man for the occasion. I have before me, as I write, General Brown's order-book, in which are transcribed the orders he issued during these four eventful July days. They cover nearly all the movements I have referred to above, beside many that I have not alluded to—such as sending troops to protect the down town wharves, to the aid of Brooklyn, of Harlem, and of Jersey City, to guard private residences, providing ordnance material and subsistence supplies, and the innumerable incidents of a campaign. Yet General Wool, in a letter written July 20th to Governor Seymour, asserted to himself the credit of all these precautions, and made a special boast of having, at the first outbreak, ordered to New York all the troops in the harbor, "leaving only small guards to protect the forts." I have already shown how General Brown was compelled to exert himself in order to accomplish this very thing which General Wool's order practically forbade.

A similar spirit was displayed by General Sanford in his report of July 25th to the Governor, in which he claims to have sent detachments "to all parts of the city, and the rioters were everywhere beaten and dispersed on Monday afternoon, Monday night, and Tuesday morning, and the peace of the city would have been entirely restored in a few hours but for the interference of Brevet Brigadier General Brown, who, in disobedience of the orders of General Wool, withdrew the detachments belonging to the General Government." Both of the letters referred to abound in mis-statements; but a further analysis of their prejudiced features is unnecessary in this place. The Police Commissioners of New York, and the merchants whose interests being at stake rendered them keen observers, were unanimous in attributing to General Brown the saving of the city from further inestimable damage. A number of representative citizens united on July 25th in presenting him with an elegant service of silver as a testimonial of their gratitude and esteem. The letter accompanying the present concluded with these words of sympathy: "Your memory will always remain with us safe from all detraction, and beyond all forgetfulnes." General Brown's command was now limited to the affairs of his regiment, the Fifth Artillery. I reported to him each morning at his residence for the day's instructions. Early in August, a few weeks after the riots, I presented myself, as usual, and was surprised and grieved to hear him remark: "I shall never give you orders again!" In response to my look of surprise, General Brown silently pointed to a paragraph among the telegraphic dispatches in that morning's issue of the New York *Times*, which he was reading on my arrival. It announced that Colonel and Brevet Brigadier General Harvey Brown had been retired from active service, to date from August 1st, by order of the President! This was the first notification he had received of his impending fate. In this abrupt manner was a faithful army service of forty-five years brought harshly to an end. Such is the reward which our republic sometimes bestows upon her honest servants who have patiently passed their lives in upholding her honor.

The foregoing condensed narrative is written from a purely military standpoint, with a view to placing in their true light the services performed in the New York riots by the United States troops under General Brown. All that I have written is substantiated by official documents on file at the department headquarters, copies of which are in my hands. My purpose being so restricted, much of equal interest to many minds has been necessarily omitted. That portion of the subject, however, I leave the politicians to relate, being satisfied to contribute, as my meed to history, this true chapter concerning the New York draft riots of 1863.

THE CAMPAIGN IN PENNSYLVANIA.

BY COLONEL W. H. TAYLOR.

FROM the very necessity of the case, the general theory upon which the war was conducted, on the part of the South, was one of defense. The great superiority of the North in men and material made it indispensable for the South to husband its resources as much as possible, inasmuch as the hope of ultimate success which the latter entertained, rested rather upon the dissatisfaction and pecuniary distress which a prolonged war would entail upon the former—making the people weary of the struggle—than upon any expectation of conquering a peace by actually subduing so powerful an adversary. Nevertheless, in the judgment of General Lee, it was a part of a true defensive policy to take the aggressive when good opportunity offered; and by delivering an effective blow to the enemy, not only to inflict upon him serious loss, but, at the same time, to thwart his designs of invasion, derange the plan of campaign contemplated by him, and thus prolong the conflict. The Federal army, under General Hooker, had re-occupied the heights opposite Fredericksburg, where it could not be attacked except at a disadvantage. Instead of quietly awaiting the pleasure of the Federal commander, in designing and putting into execution some new plan of campaign, General Lee determined to maneuvre to draw him from his impregnable position, and, if possible, to remove the scene of hostilities beyond the Potomac. His design was to free the State of Virginia, for a time, at least, from the presence of the enemy, to transfer the theatre of war to Northern soil, and, by selecting a favorable time and place in which to receive the attack which his

20

adversary would be compelled to make on him, to take the reasonable chances of defeating him in a pitched battle; knowing full well that to obtain such an advantage there, would place him in position to attain far more decisive results than could be hoped for from a like advantage gained in Virginia. But even if unable to attain the valuable results which might be expected to follow a decided advantage gained over the enemy in Maryland or Pennsylvania, it was thought that the movement would at least so far disturb the Federal plan for the summer campaign as to prevent its execution during the season for active operations.

In pursuance of this design, early in the month of June, General Lee moved his army northward by way of Culpepper, and thence to and down the Valley of Virginia to Winchester. The army had been reorganized into three army corps, designated the First, Second, and Third Corps, and commanded respectively by Lieutenant Generals Longstreet, Ewell, and A. P. Hill. The Second Corps was in advance, and crossed the branches of the Shenandoah, near Front Royal, on the 12th of June. Brushing aside the force of the enemy under General Milroy, that occupied the lower valley—most of which was captured, and the remnant of which sought refuge in the fortifications at Harper's Ferry—General Ewell crossed the Potomac river with his three divisions in the latter part of June; and, in pursuance of the orders of General Lee, traversed Maryland and advanced into Pennsylvania. General A. P. Hill, whose corps was the last to leave the line of the Rappahannock, followed, with his three divisions, in Ewell's rear. General Longstreet covered these movements with his corps; then moved by Ashby's and Snicker's Gaps into the Valley, and likewise crossed the Potomac river, leaving to General Stuart the task of holding the gaps of the Blue Ridge Mountains with his corps of cavalry. The Federal commander had meanwhile moved his army so as to cover Washington City; and, as soon as he was thoroughly informed, by Ewell's rapid advance, of the real intention of his adversary, he, too, crossed into Maryland. On the 27th of June, General Lee was near Chambersburg with the First and Third Corps, the Second being still in advance, but within supporting distance. With the exception of the cavalry, the army was well in hand. The absence of that indispensable arm of the service was most seriously felt by General Lee. He had directed General Stuart to use his discretion as to where and when to cross the river—that is, he was to cross east of the mountains, or retire through the mountain passes into the Valley and cross in the immediate rear of the infantry, as the movements of the enemy and his own judgment should determine; but he was expected to maintain communication with the main column, and especially directed to keep the commanding general informed of the movements of the Federal army.

The army continued to advance. On the 1st of July, General Lee reached Cashtown, and stopped to confer with General A. P. Hill, whose corps was concentrating at that point, and who reported that the advance of Heth's Division had encountered the cavalry of the enemy near Gettysburg. Instructions had been sent to General Heth to ascertain what force was at Gettysburg, and, if he found infantry opposed to him, to report the fact immediately, without forcing an engagement. No tidings whatever had been received from, or of our cavalry under General Stuart, since crossing the river; and General Lee was consequently without accurate information of the movements, or position of the main Federal army. An army without cavalry in a strange and hostile country is as a man deprived of his eyesight and beset by enemies; he may be ever so brave and strong, but he cannot intelligently administer a single effective blow. The sound of artillery was soon heard in the direction of Gettysburg. General Hill hastened to the front. General Lee followed. On arriving at the scene of battle, General Lee ascertained that the enemy's infantry and artillery were present in considerable force. Heth's Division was already hotly engaged, and it was soon evident that a serious engagement could not be avoided. Orders had previously been sent to General Ewell to recall his advanced divisions, and to concentrate about Cashtown. While *en route* for that point, on the morning of the 1st of July, General Ewell learned that Hill's Corps was moving toward Gettysburg, and, on arriving at Middletown, he turned the head of his column in that direction. When within a few miles of the town, General Rodes, whose division was in advance, was made aware, by the sharp cannonading, of the presence of the enemy in force at Gettysburg, and caused immediate preparations for battle to be made.

On reaching the scene of conflict, General Rodes made his disposition to assail the force with which Hill's troops were engaged, but no sooner were his lines formed than he perceived fresh troops of the enemy extending their right flank, and deploying in his immediate front. With this force he was soon actively engaged. The contest now became sharp and earnest. Neither side sought or expected a general engagement; and yet, brought thus unexpectedly in the presence of each other, found a conflict unavoidable. The

battle continued, with varying success, until perhaps three P. M.,
when General Early, of Ewell's Corps, reached the field with his
division, moved in on Rodes' left, and attacked the enemy with his
accustomed vigor and impetuosity. This decided the contest. The
enemy's right gave way under Early's assault. Pender's Division,
of Hill's Corps, had meanwhile been advanced to relieve that of
Heth; and Rodes, observing the effect of Early's attack, ordered his
line forward. There resulted a general and irresistible advance
of our entire line; the enemy gave way at all points, and were
driven in disorder through and beyond the town of Gettysburg,
leaving over five thousand prisoners in our hands. In this action
the force engaged on the Confederate side, as already stated, consisted
of the divisions of Heth and Pender, of Hill's Corps, and those of
Early and Rodes, of Ewell's Corps. On the side of the Federals
there was the First Corps, embracing the divisions of Wadsworth,
Doubleday, and Robinson; the Eleventh Corps, embracing the
divisions of Schurz, Barlow, and Steinwehr, and the cavalry force
under General Buford. The infantry force on each side was about
the same, and the preponderance in numbers was with the Federals—
to the extent of General Buford's cavalry command.

General Lee witnessed the flight of the Federals through
Gettysburg, and up the hills beyond. He then directed me to go
to General Ewell, and to say to him that, from the position which
he occupied, he could see the enemy retreating over those hills,
without organization, and in great confusion; that it was only
necessary to press "those people" in order to secure possession of
the heights; and that, if possible, he wished him to do this. In
obedience to these instructions, I proceeded immediately to General
Ewell, and delivered the order of General Lee; and, after receiving
from him some message for the commanding general in regard to
the prisoners captured, returned to the latter, and reported that his
order had been delivered. General Ewell did not express any
objection, or indicate the existence of any impediment, to the
execution of the order conveyed to him, but left the impression on
my mind that it would be executed. In the exercise of that
discretion, however, which General Lee was accustomed to accord to
his lieutenants, and probably because of an undue regard for his
admonition, given early in the day, not to precipitate a general
engagement, General Ewell deemed it unwise to make the pursuit.
The troops were not moved forward, and the enemy proceeded to
occupy and fortify the position which it was designed that General
Ewell should seize. Major General Edward Johnson, whose division

reached the field after the engagement, and formed on the left of Early, in a conversation had with me, since the war, about this circumstance, in which I sought an explanation of our inaction at that time, assured me that there was no hindrance to his moving forward; but that, after getting his command in line of battle, and before it became seriously engaged, or had advanced any great distance, for some unexplained reason, he had received orders to halt. This was after General Lee's message was delivered to General Ewell.

Such was the condition of affairs when darkness veiled the scene on the evening of the first day. The prevailing idea with General Lee was, to press forward without delay; to follow up promptly and vigorously the advantage already gained. Having failed to reap the full fruit of the victory before night, his mind was evidently occupied with the idea of renewing the assault upon the enemy's right with the dawn of day on the second. The divisions of Major Generals Early and Rodes, of Ewell's Corps, had been actively engaged, and had sustained some loss, but were still in excellent condition, and in the full enjoyment of the prestige of success and a consequent elation of spirit, in having so gallantly swept the enemy from their front, through the town of Gettysburg, and compelled him to seek refuge behind the heights beyond. The division of Major General Edward Johnson, of the same corps, was perfectly fresh, not having been engaged. Anderson's Division, of Hill's Corps, was also now up. With this force General Lee thought that the enemy's position could be assailed with every prospect of success; but, after a conference with the corps and division commanders on our left, who represented that, in their judgment, it would be hazardous to attempt to storm the strong position occupied by the enemy, with troops somewhat fagged by the marching and fighting of the first day; that the ground in their immediate front furnished greater obstacles to a successful assault than existed at other points of the line, and that it could be reasonably concluded, since they had so severely handled the enemy in their front, that he would concentrate and fortify with special reference to resisting a further advance just there, he determined to make the main attack well on the enemy's left, indulging the hope that Longstreet's Corps would be up in time to begin the movement at an early hour on the second. He instructed General Ewell to be prepared to co-operate by a simultaneous advance by his corps. General Longstreet was unexpectedly detained, however, as will best appear from the following extract from his report of the Gettysburg campaign. In speaking of his movements on the first day of July, he says:

Our march on this day was greatly delayed by Johnson's Division, of the Second Corps, which came into the road from Shippensburg, and the long wagon-trains that followed him. McLaws' Division, however, reached Marsh creek, four miles from Gettysburg, a little after dark, and Hood's Division got within nearly the same distance of the town about twelve o'clock at night. Law's Brigade was ordered forward to its division during the day, and joined about noon on the 2d. Previous to his joining I received instructions from the commanding general to move, with the portion of my command that was up, around to gain the Emmetts-burg road on the enemy's left. The enemy, having been driven back by the corps of Lieutenant Generals Ewell and A. P. Hill, the day previous, had taken a strong position extending from the hill at the cemetery along the Emmettsburg road. Fearing that my force was too weak to venture to make an attack, I delayed until General Law's Brigade joined its division. As soon after his arrival as we could make our preparations, the movement was begun. Engineers, sent out by the commanding general and myself, guided us by a road which would have completely disclosed the move. Some delay ensued in seeking a more concealed route. McLaws' Division got into position, opposite the enemy's left, about 4 P. M. Hood's Division was moved on farther to our right, and got into position, partially enveloping the enemy's left.

General Longstreet here explains the cause of the delay in bringing up his troops on the *first day ;* but, notwithstanding this, the divisions of Hood and McLaws (with the exception of Law's Brigade) encamped within four miles of Gettysburg at midnight of the 1st of July. He then received instructions to move *with the portion of his command that was then up*, to gain the Emmettsburg road on the enemy's left ; but fearing that his force was too weak to venture to make an attack, he delayed until Law's Brigade joined its division, about noon on the 2d. In this, General Longstreet clearly admits that he assumed the responsibility of postponing the execution of the orders of the commanding general. Owing to the causes assigned, the troops were not in position to attack until 4 P. M. One can imagine what was going on in the Federal lines meanwhile. Round Top, the key to their position, which was not occupied in the morning, they now held in force, and another corps (Sedgwick's) had reached the field. Late as it was, the original plan was adhered to. The two divisions of Longstreet's Corps gallantly advanced, forced the enemy back a considerable distance, and captured some trophies and prisoners. Ewell's Divisons were ordered forward, and likewise gained additional ground and trophies. On Cemetery Hill the attack by Early's leading brigades was made with vigor. They drove the enemy back into the works on the crest, into which they forced their way, and seized several pieces of artillery ; but they were compelled to relinquish what they had gained, from want of expected support on their right, and retired to their original position, bringing with them some prisoners and four stands of colors. In explanation of this lack of expected support, General Rodes, who was on General Early's right, states in his report, that after he had conferred with General Early on his left, and General Lane on his right, and arranged to attack in concert, he proceeded at once to make the necessary preparations; but as he had to draw his troops out of the town by the flank, change the direction of the line of battle, and then traverse a distance of twelve or fourteen hundred yards, while General Early had to move only half that distance, without change of front, it resulted that, before he drove in the enemy's skirmishers, General Early had attacked, and been compelled to withdraw.

The whole affair was disjointed. There was an utter absence of accord in the movements of the several commands, and no decisive results attended the operations of the second day. It is generally conceded that General Longstreet, on this occasion, was fairly chargeable with tardiness, and I have always thought that his conduct, in this particular, was due to a lack of appreciation, on his part, of the circumstances which created an urgent and peculiar need for the presence of his troops at the front. As soon as the necessity for the concentration of the army was precipitated by the unexpected encounter, on the 1st of July, with a large force of the enemy, near Gettysburg, General Longstreet was urged to hasten his march; and this, perhaps, should have sufficed to cause him to push his divisions on toward Gettysburg, from which point he was distant but four miles, early on the 2d. But I cannot say that he was notified, on the night of the 1st, of the attack proposed to be made on the morning of the 2d, and the part his corps was to take therein. Neither do I think it just to charge that he was alone responsible for the delay in attacking that ensued *after* his arrival on the field. I well remember how General Lee was chafed by the non-appearance of the troops, until he finally became restless, and rode back to meet General Longstreet, and urge him forward; but, then, there was considerable delay in putting the troops to work after they reached the field; and much time was spent in discussing what was to be done, which, perhaps, could not be avoided. At any rate, it would be unreasonable to hold General Longstreet alone accountable for this. Indeed, great injustice has been done him in the charge that he had orders from the commanding general to attack the enemy at sunrise on the 2d of July, and that he disobeyed these orders. This would imply that he was in position to attack, whereas General Lee but anticipated his early arrival on the 2d, and based his calculations upon it. I have shown how he was disappointed, and I need hardly add that the delay was fatal.

General Lee determined to renew the attack upon the enemy's position on the 3d of July. In his report of the campaign, in speaking of the operations of the second day, he says:

The result of this day's operations induced the belief that, with proper concert of action, and with the increased support that the positions gained on the right would enable the artillery to render the assaulting columns, we should ultimately succeed; and it was accordingly determined to continue the attack. The general plan was unchanged. Longstreet, reinforced by Pickett's three brigades, which arrived near the battle-field during the afternoon of the 2d, was ordered to attack the next morning; and General Ewell was directed to assail the enemy's right at the same time.

General Longstreet's dispositions were not completed as early as was expected. It appears that he was delayed by apprehensions that his troops would be taken in reverse as they advanced. General Ewell, who had orders to co-operate with General Longstreet, and who was, of course, not aware of any impediment to the main attack arranged to be made on the enemy's left, having reinforced General Johnson, whose division was upon our extreme left, during the night of the 2d, ordered him forward early the next morning. In obedience to these instructions, General Johnson became hotly engaged before General Ewell could be informed of the halt which had been called on our right. After a gallant and prolonged struggle, in which the enemy was forced to abandon part of his intrenchments, General Johnson found himself unable to carry the strongly-fortified crest of the hill. The projected attack on the enemy's left not having been made, he was enabled to hold his right with a force largely superior to that of General Johnson, and, finally, to threaten his flank and rear, rendering it necessary for him to retire to his original position about one P. M. General Lee then had a conference with General Longstreet, and the mode of attack, and the troops to make it, were thoroughly debated. I was present, and understood the arrangement to be that General Longstreet should endeavor to force the enemy's lines in his front. That front was held by the divisions of Hood and McLaws. To strengthen him for the undertaking, it was decided to reinforce him by such troops as could be drawn from the centre.

Pickett's Division, of Longstreet's Corps, was then up, fresh and available. Heth's Division, of Hill's Corps, was also mentioned as available, having been, in great measure, recuperated since its active engagement of the first day; so, also, were the brigades of Lane and Scales, of Pender's Division, Hill's Corps; and as our extreme right was comparatively safe, being well posted, and not at all threatened, one of the divisions of Hood and McLaws, and the greater portion of the other, could be removed out of the lines and be made to take part in the attack. Indeed, it was designed, originally, that the two divisions last named, reinforced by Pickett, should make the attack; and it was only because of the apprehensions of General Longstreet that his corps was not strong enough for the movement, that General Hill was called on to reinforce him. Orders were sent to General Hill to place Heth's Division and two brigades of Pender's at General Longstreet's disposal, and to be prepared to give him further assistance if requested. The assault was to have been made with a column of not less than two divisions, and the remaining divisions were to have been moved forward in support of those in advance. This was the result of the conference alluded to, as understood by me. Lieutenant General A. P. Hill appears to have had the same impression, for he says, in his report of the operations of his corps at this time:

> I was directed to hold my line with Anderson's Division and the half of Pender's, now commanded by General Lane, and to order Heth's Division, commanded by Pettigrew, and Lane's and Scales' Brigades, of Pender's Division, to report to Lieutenant General Longstreet, *as a support to his corps*, in the assault on the enemy's lines.

General Longstreet proceeded at once to make the dispositions for attack, and General Lee rode along the portion of the line held by A. P. Hill's Corps, and finally took position about the Confederate centre, on an elevated point, from which he could survey the field and watch the result of the movement. After a heavy artillery fire along the entire line, and at a given signal, the movement began, but the plan agreed on was not carried out. The only troops that participated in the attack were the divisions of Pickett (First Corps) and Heth (Third Corps)—the latter, since the wounding of General Heth, commanded by General Pettigrew—and the brigades of Lane, Scales, and Wilcox. The two divisions were formed in advance, the three brigades as their support. The divisions of Hood and McLaws (First Corps) were passive spectators of the movement. To one who observed the charge, it appeared that Pettigrew's line was not a continuation of that of Pickett, but that it advanced in *echelon*. It would seem that there was some confusion in forming the troops, for Captain Louis G. Young, of General Pettigrew's staff, says:

> On the morning of the 3d of July, General Pettigrew, commanding Heth's Division, was instructed to report to General Longstreet, who directed him to form *in the rear* of Pickett's Division, and support his advance upon Cemetery Hill, which would be commenced as soon as the fire from our artillery should have driven the

enemy from his guns, and prepared the way for the attack. And I presume that it was in consequence of this having been the first plan settled on, that the erroneous report was circulated that Heth's Division was assigned the duty of supporting that of Pickett. But the order referred to was countermanded almost as soon as given, and General Pettigrew was instructed to advance *upon the same line* with Pickett, a portion of Pender's Division acting as supports.

Wilcox's Brigade was ordered to support Pickett's right flank, and the brigades of Lane and Scales acted as supports to Heth's Division. General Lane, in his report, says:

> General Longstreet ordered me to form in rear of the *right* of Heth's Division, commanded by General Pettigrew. Soon after I had executed this order, putting Lowrance on the right, I was relieved of the command of the division by Major General Trimble, who acted under the same orders that I had received. Heth's Division was much longer than Lowrance's Brigade and my own, which constituted its only support, and there was, consequently, *no second line in the rear of its left.*

The assaulting column really consisted of Pickett's Division— two brigades in front, and one in the second line as a support—with the brigade of Wilcox in the rear of the right, to protect that flank; while Heth's Division moved forward on Pickett's left in *echelon*, or with the alignment so imperfect and so drooping on the left as to appear in *echelon*, with Lane's and Scales' Brigades in rear of its right, and its left without reserve or support, and entirely exposed. Thus the column moved forward. It is needless to say a word here of the heroic conduct of Pickett's Division; that charge has already passed into history as "one of the world's great deeds of arms." While, doubtless, many brave men of other commands reached the crest of the height, this was the only organized body that entered the works of the enemy. Much can be said in excuse for the failure of the other commands to fulfil the task assigned them. As a general rule, the peculiarly rough and wooded character of the country in which our army was accustomed to operate, and which, in some respects, was unfavorable for the maneuvres of large armies, was of decided advantage to us; for, in moving upon the enemy, through bodies of woods, or in a broken, rolling country, not only was the enemy at a loss how to estimate our strength, but our own men were not impressed with that sense of insecurity, which must have resulted from a thorough knowledge of their own weakness.*

---

* "The enemy's batteries soon opened upon our lines with canister, and the left seemed to stagger under to, but the advance was resumed, and with some degree of steadiness. Pickett's troops did not appear to be checked by the batteries, and only halted to deliver a fire when close under musket range. Major General Anderson's Division was ordered forward to support and assist the wavering columns of Pettigrew and Trimble. Pickett's troops, after delivering fire, advanced to the charge,

It was different here. The charge was made down a gentle slope, and then up to the enemy's lines, a distance of over half a mile, denuded of forests, and in full sight of the enemy, and perfect range of their artillery. These combined causes produced their natural effect upon Pettigrew's Division, and the brigade supporting it, caused them to falter, and finally retire. Then Pickett's Division, continuing the charge without supports, and in the sight of the enemy, was not half so formidable or effective as it would have been had trees or hills prevented the enemy from so correctly estimating the strength of the attacking column, and our own troops from experiencing that sense of weakness which the known absence of support necessarily produced. In spite of all this, it steadily and gallantly advanced to its allotted task. As the three brigades under Garnett, Armistead, and Kemper, approach the enemy's lines, a most terrific fire of artillery and small-arms is concentrated upon them; but they swerve not—there is no faltering; steadily moving forward, they rapidly reduce the intervening space, and close with their adversaries; leaping the breastworks, they drive back the enemy, and plant their standard on the captured guns, amid shouts of victory—dearly won and short-lived victory.

No more could be exacted, or expected, of those men of brave hearts and nerves of steel; but where are the supports to reap the benefit of their heroic efforts, and gather the fruits of a victory so nobly won? Was that but a forlorn hope, on whose success, not only in penetrating the enemy's lines, but in maintaining its hold against their combined and united efforts to dislodge it, an entire army was to wait in quiet observation? Was it designed to throw these few brigades—originally, at the most, but two divisions—upon the fortified stronghold of the enemy, while, full half a mile away, seven-ninths of the army, in breathless suspense, in ardent admiration and fearful anxiety, watched, but moved not? I maintain that such was not the design of the commanding general. Had the veteran divisions of Hood and McLaws been moved forward, as was

---

and entered the enemy's lines, capturing some of his batteries, and gained his works. About the same moment the troops that had before hesitated broke their ranks and fell back in great disorder, many more falling under the enemy's fire in retreating than while they were attacking. This gave the enemy time to throw his entire force upon Pickett, with a strong prospect of being able to break up his lines, or destroy him before Anderson's Division could reach him, which would, in its turn, have greatly exposed Anderson. He was, therefore, ordered to halt. In a few moments the enemy, marching against both flanks, and the front of Pickett's Division, overpowered it and drove it back, capturing about half of those of it who were not killed or wounded."—*Extract from the Official Report of General Longstreet.*

planned, in support of those of Pickett and Pettigrew, not only would the latter division, in all probability, have gained the enemy's works, as did that of Pickett, but these two would have been enabled, with the aid of Hood and McLaws, to resist all efforts of the enemy to dislodge them. The enemy closing in on Pickett's Brigades, concentrating upon that small band of heroes the fire of every gun that could be brought to bear upon them, soon disintegrated and overpowered them. Such as were not killed, disabled, and made captive, fell back to our lines.

It appears that General Longstreet deemed it necessary to defend his right flank and rear with the divisions of McLaws and Hood. These divisions, as before stated, constituted all of the Confederate line held by Longstreet's troops, and it is not apparent how they were necessary to defend his flank and rear. The nearest infantry force of the enemy, to our right, occupied the hills—Round Top and Little Round Top—and the only force that could be said to have threatened our flank and rear consisted of a few brigades of cavalry, so posted as to protect the enemy's left. It is not my purpose here to undertake to establish the wisdom of an attack on the enemy's position on the third day, which General Longstreet contends was opposed by his judgment, and of which he says he would have stayed the execution, had he felt that he had the privilege so to do; nor do I propose to discuss the necessities of his position, which he represents to have been such as to forbid the employment of McLaws' and Hood's Divisions in the attack; neither do I seek any other than a just explanation of the causes of our failure at that time; but well recalling my surprise and disappointment when it was ascertained that only Pickett's Division, and the troops from Hill's Corps had taken part in the movement, and with positively distinct impressions as to the occurrences just related, I deem it proper to record them for confirmation or refutation as the undisputed facts of the case, and the testimony of others, may determine.

After the assault on the enemy's works, on the 3d of July, there was no serious fighting at Gettysburg. The 4th passed in comparative quiet. Neither army evinced any disposition to assail the other. Notwithstanding the brilliant achievements of Ewell and Hill on the first day, and the decided advantage gained by Longstreet on the second, the failure of the operations of the third day, involving, as they did, but two divisions of the army, deprived us of the prestige of our previous successes, and gave a shadow of right to our adversary's claim of having gained a victory. Their exultation, however, should be tempered with moderation, when we consider that, after one day of absolute quiet, the Confederates withdrew from their front without serious molestation, and with bridges swept away, and an impassable river in rear, stood in an attitude of defiance until their line of retreat could be rendered practicable, after which they safely recrossed into Virginia. Then, again, so serious was the loss visited upon the Federals in the engagements of the first and second days, and so near success was the effort to storm their position on the third day, that they were themselves undecided as to whether they should stand or retreat. In discussing several councils, or conferences, held by General Meade with his corps commanders, General Sickles testified, before the Committee on the Conduct of the War, that the reason the Confederates were not followed up was on account of differences of opinion whether or not the Federals should themselves retreat, as "it was by no means clear, in the judgment of the corps commanders, or of the general in command, whether they had won or not."

It appears, from the official returns on file in the War Department, that on the 31st of May, 1863, the Army of Northern Virginia numbered: infantry, fifty-nine thousand four hundred and fifty-seven; cavalry, ten thousand two hundred and ninety-two; and artillery, four thousand seven hundred and two; of all arms, seventy-four thousand four hundred and fifty-one effectives. This was immediately before the invasion of Pennsylvania, and may be regarded as representing the maximum of General Lee's army in the Gettysburg campaign. On the 20th of July, 1863, after the return of General Lee to Virginia, his army numbered forty-one thousand three hundred and eighty-eight effectives, exclusive of the cavalry corps, of which no report is made in the return of the date last mentioned; allowing "eight thousand one hundred and twelve," a fair estimate for the cavalry, the effective total of the army on the 20th of July was forty-nine thousand five hundred. It appears, therefore, that General Lee's loss in the Pennsylvania campaign was nearly twenty-five thousand.

Concerning the strength of the Federal army, General Meade testified as follows, before the Committee on the Conduct of the War (second series, vol. i., p. 337): "Including all arms of the service, my strength was a little under one hundred thousand men—about ninety-five thousand. I think General Lee had about ninety thousand infantry, four thousand to five thousand artillery, and about ten thousand cavalry." Again, he testifies: "I think the returns showed me, when I took command of the army, amounted to about one hundred and five thousand men; included in those were the eleven thousand of General French." In this latter matter thee vidence is against General Meade. General Hooker, on the 27th of June, 1863, telegraphed to General Halleck, from Poolesville: "My whole force of *enlisted men* for duty will not exceed one hundred and five thousand (105,000)." This would make his total effective force (officers and men) full one hundred and twelve thousand. This dispatch was received by General Halleck at nine A. M. On reaching Sandy Hook, subsequently, on the same day, General Hooker telegraphed as follows, concerning the garrison at Harper's Ferry, under General French: "I find ten thousand men here in condition to take the field. Here they are of no earthly account. They cannot defend a ford of the river; and, as far as Harper's Ferry is concerned, there is nothing of it. As for the fortifications, the work of the troops, they remain when the troops are withdrawn. No enemy will ever take possession of them for them. This is my opinion. All the public property could have been secured to-night, and the troops marched to where they could have been of some service." This dispatch was received by General Halleck at 2.55 P. M. It is evident that the garrison at Harper's Ferry was not embraced in the returns alluded to by General Hooker in his first dispatch. Although General Halleck refused these troops to General Hooker, they were immediately awarded to General Meade, on his assuming command when General Hooker was relieved.

With t more accurate returns of the two armies at Gettysburg, we are left to form our conclusions as to their strength from the data given above. I put the Army of the Potomac at one hundred and five thousand, and the Army of Northern Virginia at sixty-seven thousand of all arms—fifty-three thousand five hundred infantry, nine thousand cavalry, and four thousand five hundred artillery—and believe these figures very nearly correct. In this estimate, I adopt the strength of the Federal army as given by its commander on the 27th of June, but four days before the first encounter at Gettysburg, excluding all consideration of the troops at Harper's Ferry, although General Meade, on assuming command, at once ordered General French to move to Frederick with seven thousand men, to protect his communications, and thus made available a like number of men of the Army of the Potomac, who would otherwise have been detached for this service.

On the side of the Confederates, the entire cavalry corps is included. That portion which General Stuart accompanied made a complete circuit of the Federal army, and only joined General Lee on the evening of the second day; and the brigades under Generals Jones and Robertson, which had been left to guard the passes of the Blue Ridge, did not rejoin the army until the 3d of July.

THE FIRST SHOT AGAINST THE FLAG.

BY MAJOR GENERAL S. WYLIE CRAWFORD.

THE passage of the Ordinance of Secession of the State of South Carolina found the General Government in possession of certain pieces of property ceded to the United States, in accordance with law, and mainly used for military purposes. An arsenal had been built within the corporate limits of the city of Charleston; it was a depot of supplies, and contained valuable stores. Within the same city were the custom-house and post-office. Of the three forts in the harbor, Fort Moultrie alone was garrisoned, and this by two companies of artillery, numbering about eighty men. Castle Pinckney, an old and crumbling work, close to the city, was the station of an ordnance sergeant only, whose principal duty consisted in the care of an harbor light that shone nightly from its parapet. Four miles down the bay, and commanding the channel entrance, stood Fort Sumter, in process of construction, and wholly defenseless. A large number of workmen, principally inhabitants of Charleston, were employed on its completion, which was conducted by the Engineer Department, under authority of an act of Congress. The importance of its position was early recognized by all, and the determination to possess it was, beyond all other considerations, the direct cause of hostilities. It was claimed that the State could not be said to have resumed her sovereignty until she exercised undisputed control over all the dependencies of her territory.

This question entered into every speech that was made, to keep up the spirit that was carrying the State onward, and in every document drawn up defining her position and marking her course. It was presented in official argument in every demand for the surrender of Fort Sumter, and in its solution the State was brought face to face with the General Government, and at a point from which neither felt that it could retire. In order to open negotiations, it was desired by the authorities of South Carolina that the existing status in the harbor should not be disturbed, and, early in November, the Congressional delegation of South Carolina waited upon the President to secure his consent to such an arrangement. It was asserted by them that such consent was obtained, and, although the existence of any obligation limiting his freedom of action was distinctly denied by Mr. Buchanan, in his letter to the commissioners, it was, nevertheless, relied upon by the authorities of South Carolina as affording time and opportunity for the discussion, and, perhaps, peaceable solution of the difficulties. Far ahead of the people, the leaders of the movement saw the necessity for vigorous action. They knew that, to maintain the Union, there would be war; but they, nevertheless, held out to the people that there would be no collision; and, in this, they were partially justified by the reiterated assertions of the partisan press in the North, and the opinions of men high in public position. Immediately upon the passage of the Ordinance of Secession by the State of South Carolina, a commission, consisting of three gentlemen of character, standing, and well-known public service—Messrs. Adams, Barnwell, and Orr— were sent to Washington to open communications with the government for a settlement of the important questions which immediately arose upon the assumption, by the State, of her new position. They were in actual communication with the President, when an event occurred which, while it awoke the country to a realization of the actual condition of things in the State of South Carolina, served equally to remove every scruple in the minds of doubting men, and to bind the whole State together firmly in a determined purpose of resistance.

Major Anderson, the commandant of the garrison of Fort Moultrie, fearing that he would be attacked, on the night of the 26th of December, after partially dismantling the fort, moved his entire command to Fort Sumter. Without awaiting explanation or the action of their commissioners in Washington, the authorities of the State proceeded to seize and occupy the forts in the harbor and the government property in the State. Fort Moultrie was garrisoned and the flag of South Carolina raised over it. The seizure of Castle Pinckney followed; the arsenal was seized and its contents appropriated. The engineers' office in Charleston was occupied and its valuable maps and records appropriated, and among them the entire details of the construction of Fort Sumter. The chief clerk was made an officer in the service of the State, and a messenger was sent to Major Anderson, by the Governor of the State, requiring him to return to Fort Moultrie. It was declined, and both sides commenced preparations for hostilities, that seemed now to be unavoidable. Whatever hopes might have been entertained by the authorities of a peaceful solution of the difficulties, were rudely shaken, if not abandoned, when it was known that the General Government acquiesced in the movement of Major Anderson, and refused to remand him to Fort Moultrie. At first the President was inclined to order Anderson to return to Fort Moultrie, and he authorized the transmission of a telegram to South Carolina that Anderson's movement was not only without, but against his orders; but he would go no further. The action of South Carolina in seizing the government property, and that specific instructions had been given by his Secretary of War authorizing just such a movement, restrained the President and rendered the restoration of the former status impossible. In vain was a "breach of faith" alleged, and the "personal honor" of the President said to be involved. In vain the commission in Washington urged their understanding of the pledge made to them. The President stood firm. "Should I return Major Anderson to Fort Moultrie," said he, "I might go back to Wheatland by the light of my burning effigies."

It is not the purpose of this paper to inquire how far the President had pledged himself to maintain the status in Charleston harbor. His great desire, as well as his intention, was, no doubt, to preserve that status until the close of his administration. This had become impossible. The South Carolina commissioners could accept nothing less, and they left Washington, after having transmitted to the President a communication, so offensive in its tone, and so personal in its character, that he declined to receive it. This decision was reached in a Cabinet council. When it was announced, the President turned to the Secretary of War, and said: "Reinforcements must now be sent." The Secretary of War, Mr. Floyd, whose resignation had been invited by the President, was virtually out of the government. Although he had given the very instructions which justified the movement of Major Anderson, he made the refusal of the President to restore the status in Charleston harbor the pretext for his action, and vacated his office. The movement of Major Anderson, however justified in a military point of view, led directly to such measures on

21

the part of the State authorities and of its people as to greatly increase the probabilities of a collision. But while the friends of peace did not cease their exertions, work on the batteries went steadily on in the harbor of Charleston. The policy of the President had changed. Major Anderson was not only to be maintained in his position; he was to be supplied, and reinforced, if possible. A large transport, the Star of the West, left New York on the 5th of January, and arrived off Charleston on the 9th. She was unarmed and without convoy, and as she attempted to enter the harbor she was fired upon from a hastily constructed battery near the entrance. She had passed this fire when Fort Moultrie opened upon her at long range, when, lowering her flag, she proceeded northward. From the fact that there were no guns of sufficient calibre in position at that time, as well as the absence of any instructions to meet such a contingency, Fort Sumter was silent. The gauntlet was thus distinctly thrown down; South Carolina boldly avowed the hostile step she had taken and asserted her determination to defend it. And yet the efforts of those who earnestly desired peace did not slacken.

Agents from the fort, and from the State, were sent to Washington to represent to the government the exact condition of things, and to ask its interference. Increased activity was immediately visible in the harbor of Charleston; skilful engineers selected the most eligible points for batteries, and field-works were rapidly erected. Emboldened by the result of the firing on the Star of the West, a formal demand for the immediate surrender of Fort Sumter was made by the Governor of South Carolina. On the 20th of January, a boat, bearing a white flag—the only means of communication between the fort and the State—appeared off Sumter. She brought two officials, "the Secretary of State and the Secretary of War of South Carolina," with a message from the Governor containing a demand for the immediate delivery of the work to the authorities of the State. The interview was characterized by every courtesy, and the demand sustained by earnest verbal representations. It was as firmly declined, and the matter referred to Washington. Long and elaborate discussions between the Secretary of War, Mr. Holt, and the envoy of the Governor, Colonel Hayne, followed. Lieutenant Hall, on behalf of Major Anderson, represented him as secure in his position. The envoy bore a demand for the surrender of the fort. Before this could be presented, nine of the Senators from the cotton States induced Colonel Hayne to postpone the delivery of the communication until they could ascertain whether the President would refrain from reinforcing the fort, provided the

Governor of South Carolina would also refrain from an attack upon it; but upon this being transmitted to the President, he at once authorized his secretary to state that Major Anderson had made no request for reinforcements, but should his safety require them, every effort would be made to supply them. On the 30th, Colonel Hayne presented his demand; but, as in the case of the commissioners originally sent by the State, the negotiations were not satisfactory, and an able and conclusive reply from the Secretary of War, Mr. Holt, was transmitted to the envoy of the Governor, which placed the whole subject beyond discussion.

It was now clear that the government at Washington intended to relieve Fort Sumter at its option. For the State, but one course, consistent with the attitude assumed by her, was to be pursued, and that was to close the harbor to all relief to the fort. Increased activity prevailed everywhere, and the scene that was daily presented from the parapet of Fort Sumter was well calculated to discourage all hope of peace. Troops and munitions of war moved to various points, and the garrison earnestly watched the daily progress of works intended for their destruction. The buoys had been taken up; the lights were extinguished, and pilots forbidden to bring ships bearing the United States flag into the harbor. Within Fort Sumter, as far as their limited means would allow, a similar activity was manifested by the garrison. Guns of heavy calibre were raised to the parapet, and placed in position; others were mounted in the casements below, and every resource was made use of to strengthen and arm the work, and to make effective the scanty material in their possession. Meantime, a provisional government had been organized by the States which had passed the Ordinances of Secession. Jurisdiction over the public property in the harbor of Charleston was assumed by it, and Brigadier General P. G. T. Beauregard, an officer of engineers, who had resigned his commission in the Army of the United States, was commissioned by the Confederate Government, and sent to Charleston to take command of the military operations. Daily reports were sent to Washington, by Major Anderson, of the condition of Fort Sumter and its garrison, and the government was fully informed of their pressing wants. On the 1st of February, 1861, in anticipation of the future, the women and children belonging to the garrison were sent northward. And thus, openly, without disguise of any sort, warlike preparations went on, from day to day, until the fort was surrounded by batteries, all bearing upon it and upon the channel by which any relief could reach it, and ready to open at any moment.

The month of March had come, and with it the close of the administration of President Buchanan. Congress had adjourned without an effort to avert the dangers threatening the nation. Whatever may be thought of the vacillating policy of President Buchanan, it is nevertheless true that he never at any time contemplated the surrender of the forts in Charleston harbor, however anxious he was to avoid a collision that would alarm the Border States, and precipitate war. His administration closed with the issues still unsettled, and the country steadily drifting to war. Up to the last moment the Confederate authorities had hoped that Sumter would be voluntarily evacuated, and they had at one time reason for the belief. An accredited agent from President Lincoln had visited the fort for the purpose of arranging for the removal of the garrison. An intermediary between the Secretary of State and the Confederate authorities, Associate Justice John A. Campbell, of the Supreme Court of the United States, had telegraphed on the 15th of March that he felt perfect confidence in the belief that Fort Sumter would be evacuated in five days; that no measure changing the existing status was contemplated; that the demand for the surrender should not be pressed; and again on the 21st and 22d of March he telegraphed that his "confidence" in the decision was unabated. In the meantime, however, other agencies were at work, of which he was probably ignorant, and which largely contributed to an immediate precipitation of hostilities. Soon after the occupancy of Fort Sumter, and up to the earlier days of President Lincoln's administration, Major Anderson had reported to his government that he was not in need of reinforcements, that he was secure in his position, that he could not be relieved without a struggle, and, in a later report, that in his opinion twenty thousand men would be necessary to take the batteries, and relieve him But as time passed, while reporting daily to his government, he brought finally the facts of his position so plainly to their notice, in a communication of the 1st of April, that action upon their part was imperative. He reported that his provisions were nearly exhausted, that his command would be without food in a few days, and that his condition was such that some measures for his relief must be taken. His communication engaged the immediate attention of the President and his Cabinet.

Yielding to the argument of a "military necessity," the written opinions of every member of the Cabinet, except the Postmaster General, Mr. Montgomery Blair, was in favor of the withdrawal of the garrison from the harbor of Charleston, when, suddenly, the whole purpose was changed, and an expedition to reinforce the fort was ordered. A dispatch of the following purport was forwarded to Major Anderson : He was told that his report had caused great anxiety to the President. It was hoped from his previous communication, and the report of the special messenger, Captain Fox, that he could hold out until the 15th of April, when an expedition was to have gone to his relief. He was directed, if possible, to hold out until the 12th of April, when the expedition would go forward, and, finding his "flag still flying," an effort would be made to provision him, and to reinforce him if resisted. As soon as this dispatch was sent to Major Anderson, it was followed by a messenger, Mr. Chew, the chief clerk of the State Department, to the authorities of South Carolina, informing them that an attempt to provision and relieve the fort would now be made. The messenger accomplished his mission, and barely escaped from the city of Charleston without molestation. Upon receipt of the message from the State Department, not a moment was lost by the officer in command of the Confederate forces in the harbor of Charleston. A telegram was at once sent to the Confederate Government, at Montgomery, with the information brought by the messenger, and instructions asked for. The reply betrayed no appreciation of the long and terrible war it inaugurated : "If you have no doubt of the authorized character of the agent," was the reply, "you will at once demand the evacuation of the fort, and, if this is refused, proceed in such manner as you may determine to reduce it."

On the morning of the 11th of April, the dawn of day disclosed an activity at once unusual and significant over the entire harbor. The waters were covered with vessels hastily putting to sea. An iron-clad floating-battery of four guns, the construction of which in Charleston had been watched by the garrison for months, was towed down the bay to a point at the western end of Sullivan's Island, where its guns bore directly upon Fort Sumter. A wooden dwelling on the beach, near the end of the island, was pulled down and unmasked a land work, mounting four guns, hitherto unknown to the garrison. Its fire would enfilade the most important battery of Fort Sumter, which was upon the parapet of the right flank of the work, and whose guns were mainly relied upon to control the fire from the heavy guns on Cumming's Point, that would take the fort in reverse. Bodies of troops were landed, and the batteries on shore fully manned, and every preparation completed, when, at four o'clock P. M., a boat under a white flag approached the fort. Two officials, aides-de-camp of the general commanding the Confederate forces in

the harbor, Colonel Chesnut and Captain S. D. Lee, were admitted
to the guard-room just inside the main entrance to the work.   They
bore a communication from the military commandant at Charleston,
and to the following effect: It stated that the Government of the
Confederate States had hitherto forborne from any hostile demonstration against Fort Sumter, in the hope that the General Government would voluntarily evacuate it in order to avert war, and that
there was reason to believe that such would have been the course
pursued, but that the Confederate Government could no longer
delay "assuming actual possession" of a fortification so important to
it.   The evacuation of Fort Sumter was demanded in the name of
the Government of the Confederate States.   All proper facilites were
tendered to Major Anderson for the removal of himself and his
command.   He was to take with him his company and private property, and to salute his flag upon taking it down.

Calling the officers of the garrison into his private room, he laid
the communication before them, and then, for the first time, made
known to them the confidential dispatch from the government,
received a few days previously, in which their determination to
relieve the fort was expressed, and instructions in regard to it conveyed.   In this communication authority was given him to capitulate
when the necessity of the case required it.   The conference of the
officers was long and earnest.   There was no thought for a moment
of acceding to the demand for the evacuation of the fort, and the
following reply was returned by Major Anderson: "That the demand
for the evacuation of the fort was one with which he regretted that
his sense of honor and his obligations to his government prevented
his compliance."   On receiving this communication the Confederate
officers left the fort.   The entire interview was characterized by
every courtesy, though more distant and formal than in previous
conferences.   They were followed to the main gate of the work by
Major Anderson, and the writer of this article.   As they were about
to embark, Major Anderson remarked in their hearing that he would
be starved out any way in a few days, if their guns did not batter
him to pieces, and this was repeated more specifically to the Confederate officers in reply to their inquiries on the subject.   As the boat
returned, the batteries around were covered with spectators all
anxiously watching the result of the mission.

Renewed activity prevailed.   Inside the fort powder was taken
from the magazines, which were now closed, ammunition was served
to the batteries and the details of the men made to serve them.
Careful instructions were given to use the utmost economy in regard

to what food was left, and the officers in command of the batteries were directed not to unnecessarily expose their men. Outside the fort, steamers, large and small, were plying in every direction. The buoy which marked the turn in the harbor from the main channel, and, which alone had been suffered to remain, was taken up at about five o'clock in the afternoon. Its place was supplied by three hulks loaded with combustible material, the evident object of which was to light the channel should the fleet, whose arrival was now hourly anticipated, attempt to enter by night. They were anchored directly under the guns of Fort Moultrie. In this state of preparation the night of the 11th of April closed upon the harbor. Toward midnight the officers of the garrison were aroused by the report of the officer of the day, that a boat under a white flag had arrived, and that two messengers from the Confederate authorities had again come to the work. It was now one and a half o'clock in the morning, when the aides of the military commandant of the Confederate forces, accompanied by Colonel Chisholm and Mr. Roger A. Pryor, of Virginia, entered the work. They bore a letter from Brigadier General Beauregard, commanding Provisional Army Confederate States of America, to Major Anderson, to the effect, that in consequence of the verbal observation made to his aides in relation to the condition of his supplies, and that he would soon be starved out, he had communicated the same to his government. The proposition was then made to him, that if he would state the time at which he would evacuate the fort, and that meanwhile he would agree not to use his guns against the Confederate forces unless theirs should be employed against Fort Sumter, General Beauregard would abstain from opening fire upon him, and that his aides were authorized to enter into such an arrangement.

Again the officers of the garrison were assembled in consultation, and a long deliberation followed. The question which engaged the most serious consideration was in regard to the provisions in the fort, and how far the men, who were now without sufficient or proper food, could be relied upon for resistance. The bread supplies of the garrison were exhausted; nothing remained but short rations of pork and coffee. Still it was earnestly desired that the utmost expectations of the government should be realized, and it was determined to hold out to the period desired by them, the 15th instant. It was agreed that the terms proposed, which would tie the hands of the garrison and neutralize its fire, could not be acceded to, and a reply to the following effect was made by Major Anderson: "That if provided with proper means he would evacuate the fort at noon on the

15th instant, provided he should not receive controlling instructions or additional supplies from his government; that he would not open the fire of his batteries unless compelled to do so by some hostile act or demonstration by the Confederate forces against his fort or the flag it bore." No sooner had Colonel Chesnut, the officer to whom it was handed, read the reply of Major Anderson than he pronounced it unsatisfactory, and made the following reply in writing:

FORT SUMTER, S. C., April 12, 1861—3.20 A. M.

SIR: By authority of Brigadier General Beauregard, commanding the Provisional forces of the Confederate States, we have the honor to notify you that he will open the fire of his batteries upon Fort Sumter in one hour from this time.

We have the honor to be, very respectfully, your obedient servants,

JAMES CHESNUT, JR.,
Aide-de-camp.

STEPHEN D. LEE,
Captain C. S. and A. D. C.

To MAJOR ROBERT ANDERSON, U. S. A., commanding Fort Sumter.

Positive instructions from the Confederate Government had been sent to their agent in Charleston harbor that if this last proposition to Major Anderson was refused by him, he should reduce the fort as his judgment decided to be most practicable. But little conversation followed the delivery, to the aides, of the reply of Major Anderson. An inquiry as to the exact time in the morning was made, which was found to be 3.30 A. M.

The Confederate officers left the fort without any formal leave-taking, and their boat soon disappeared in the darkness. Upon their arrival in Charleston, and the delivery of Major Anderson's response, a telegram was sent to Montgomery, informing the authorities that Major Anderson "would not consent." Inside the work, the men were informed of what had happened, and directed to await the summons to the guns. No fire was to be returned until daylight. The night was calm and clear, and the sea was still. Fires were lighted in all the Confederate works, when, at 4.30 A. M., the silence was broken by the discharge of a mortar from a battery near Fort Johnson, within easy range of the work; a shell rose high in the air, and burst directly over Fort Sumter; its echo died away, and all was still again; when, suddenly, fire was opened from every battery of the enemy. At daylight, all the guns of Fort Sumter opened, and the fire steadily continued all day. During the night of the 12th, the accurate range of the mortars lodged a shell in the parade, or about the work, at intervals of fifteen minutes. It was estimated that over twenty-five hundred shot and shell struck the fort during the first twenty-four hours. By morning, the fleet sent to our assistance appeared off the bar, but did not enter. At 8.30 on the 13th, the quarters took fire, from the effect of hot shot, and could not be extinguished, and soon the entire barracks were in a blaze. The barrels containing powder were thrown into the sea. At 1.20 on the 13th, the flagstaff, having been struck four times, was shot away, and the flag replaced upon the parapet. The firing upon the work was severe and continued; the return from the fort slow and feeble, sounding like signals of distress to the nation, and, finally, ceased altogether. Seeing the condition of things, a Colonel Wigfall pushed out in an open boat from Cumming's Point—unauthorized it is true—and, learning from Major Anderson that he would evacuate the fort upon the terms originally proposed to him, returned and communicated with General Beauregard, who immediately sent a commission authorized to arrange terms for the evacuation, which were soon agreed upon. The garrison was transferred to the large transport lying off the bar, and was soon on its way to the North. Many an eye turned toward the disappearing fort, and as it sunk at last upon the horizon the smoke-cloud still hung heavily over its parapet.

THE DALTON–ATLANTA OPERATIONS.

BY GENERAL JOSEPH E. JOHNSTON.

IT is stated on page 24 of General Sherman's "Memoirs" volume ii, that on the 1st of May, 1864, the strength of the three armies—of the Cumberland, of the Tennessee, and of the Ohio—with which General Sherman was about to invade Georgia, was ninety-eight thousand, seven hundred and ninety-seven men of all arms present for duty, with two hundred and fifty-four field-pieces. As the forces of the three departments furnishing these troops amounted at the time to two hundred and twenty-nine thousand, five hundred and twenty-four men present for duty (see Secretary of War's report, 1865, page 5), the strength of the invading army could have been doubled without leaving its communications insufficiently guarded. Therefore, General Sherman must have regarded the forces he assembled as ample for his object. That object was (see General Grant's letter, on page 26) "to move against Johnston's army, to break it up, and to get into the interior of the enemy's country as far as he could, inflicting all the damage he could against their war resources." That army was in front of Dalton, of forty-two thousand, eight hundred men, of all arms, present for duty, with one hundred and fifty field-guns. Its position had not been selected, but was occupied by accident. General Bragg took it for the encampment of a night in his retreat from Missionary Ridge; but the troops remained there because it was ascertained that the pursuit had ceased. During the previous winter General Gilmer, Chief Engineer of the Confederacy, had wisely provided a strong base for this army, by the intrenchment of Atlanta, and the engineers of the

(330)

army constructed some field-works at Resaca for the protection of the bridges there, and three very rough country roads from Dalton to Resaca were converted into good ones. In the spring the works there were considerably enlarged.

On the 5th of May, the Federal army was in order of battle three or four miles in front of Tunnel Hill. On the 6th, it approached Tunnel Hill; on the 7th, drove our advanced guard from that place, and placed itself, in the afternoon, near and parallel to Rocky Face, its right some distance below Mill Creek gap. On pages 32, 33, 34, and 35, General Sherman describes the operations of the 8th, 9th, and 10th, except the very sharp fighting. In his report, that of the 9th is characterized as almost a battle (see page 14). In these engagements the Confederates, who were completely sheltered by intrenchments, had almost no loss; but the Federal troops, standing on open ground and in great numbers, suffered very severely. On page 34, General Sherman claims to have surprised Johnston, by McPherson's arrival before Resaca on the 9th; forgetting, apparently, that his approach was discovered on the 8th (see his report, page 14), and that the place was found well prepared for defense, being held not by "one small brigade," as he supposed, but by a division—so intrenched as to be able to maintain itself a full day, at least. So if McPherson had attacked on the 9th, according to General Sherman's plan, Resaca could easily have been held against him until next morning, when the army, having left Dalton the night before, without the enemy's knowledge, would be ready to fall upon him from the rear, while holding his line of retreat. With twice his number on one side, and Resaca on the other, he could not have escaped. If the other course, suggested for McPherson by General Sherman, had been taken—that of "placing his whole force astride the railroad above Resaca"—Johnston must have marched against and assailed him in the same manner, with the same advantages. Either course suggested, taken by McPherson, would have compelled Johnston to attack him, and with such advantages of numbers and position as to secure his destruction. We never found it difficult to leave the presence of the Federal army at night without its knowledge. The retreat to the east, which General Sherman supposed that the Confederates would have attempted, was impossible. But even if it had been easy, they could not have hesitated to attack the Army of the Tennessee, in either of the cases supposed—opportunities for armies to fight detachments of half their strength are rarely offered in war.

General Sherman is mistaken in the opinion, appearing both in his report and memoirs, that the Confederate army at Dalton was brought to the verge of ruin by his movement through Snake Creek gap. This operation had been provided against by making Resaca strong enough to hold out at least a day against twenty thousand or thirty thousand men, and by the making of roads by which the Southern troops at Dalton could reach Resaca before their antagonists. Resaca was held, instead of Snake Creek gap, because it was nearer than the latter to the main Confederate position, and much farther from the Federal main body, and could be held by a smaller body of troops. This operation could have produced no better result than that gained—the abandonment of Dalton by the Southern army. Rocky Face, instead of covering Dalton, completely covered the Federal flank march to Snake Creek gap, and, therefore, was advantageous to him (General Sherman), and not to his adversary.

On page 32, General Sherman gives the impression that the position in front of Dalton was very strong, and he says in his report (page 73): "To strike Dalton in front was impracticable, as it was covered by an inaccessible ridge." This ridge covered the left flank, not the front, and terminated but two miles north of the position, which was east of the mountain, in ground as fit for the maneuvres of a large army as a tactician can expect to find in the interior of the Southern country. On page 35, the General writes that the bulk of the Southern army was "found (on the 13th) inside of Resaca. * * * A complete line of intrenchments was found covering the place." The two armies were formed in front of Resaca nearly at the same time; so that the Federal army could give battle on equal terms, except as to numbers, by attacking promptly— the difference being about ten to four. The two armies intrenched that day. There was very brisk fighting all day of the 14th— greatly to our advantage, for we were assailed in our intrenchments. General Sherman was misinformed as to the taking of an important ridge by the advance of McPherson's whole line, and bloody repulses of Confederate attempts to retake it—this on the 15th; there were no such occurrences. But on the 14th, about dusk, the left of our line of skirmishers—forty or fifty men—was driven from a slight elevation in front of our left; but no attempt was made to retake it.

The first paragraph on page 36 is inaccurate. The fighting on the 15th was to our advantage (none of it at night), for we were on the defensive—behind breastworks. As to capturing a four-gun intrenched battery with its men and guns: On the morning of the 15th, General Hood advanced one, eighty or one hundred yards. Soon after its fire opened the men and horses were driven off by an infantry fire from a ravine near. The Federal soldiers, who attempted to carry them off, were in like manner driven back by our musketry. So the unintrenched guns, without men, were left between the two lines until the Southern troops abandoned the position. What is said on page 36 might create the impression that the Southern army crossed the Oostenaula in consequence of the fighting described. It was because two bridges and a large body of Federal troops were discovered the afternoon of the 14th at Lay's ferry, some miles below, strongly threatening our communications by the indication of another flanking operation—covered by the river as the first had been by the ridge. To avoid this danger the Southern army crossed the Oostenaula about midnight, and moved along the railroad about seven miles. The 17th, it marched eight miles to Adairsville by eight o'clock A. M.; remained there till next morning (18th), and marched nine miles to Cassville before eleven o'clock; passed that day and the 19th there, and at one or two o'clock A. M. of the 20th marched to the Etowah, and crossed it early in the afternoon near the railroad.

On page 36 the difficulties overcome by the Federal army seem somewhat magnified, and its advantage of greatly superior numbers depreciated. The operations in question can scarcely be termed "rapid successes." Indeed, it is not easy to see the progress made in "breaking up Johnston's army" by the advance of the Federal army sixteen miles, at the expense of five days of sharp fighting, all to the advantage of its enemy.

The circumstances referred to on pages 40 and 41 are these (related in "Johnston's Narrative," pages 321 to 324): In the morning of May 19th, the Federal army was approaching Cassville, in two bodies, one following the railroad, the other the direct wagon road. Hardee's Corps was near the former, Polk's and Hood's at Cassville. Johnston determined to attack the column on the direct road with Polk's and Hood's Corps when the other was at Kingston, three hours' march to the west. Polk was to meet and attack the head of the column; Hood, marching a little in advance of him on a road on his right, was to join in the action as the enemy deployed. When the latter had marched some miles in the proper direction, he turned his corps and marched back and formed it facing to the east, about a mile east of Cassville, upon a wild report brought him, he said, by one of his aide-de-camps. Neither this information nor his action upon it was reported. As the plan depended on the distance between the two Federal columns for success, it was defeated by the loss of time produced by this erratic movement. The army was then drawn up in the best position it ever occupied, in which it skirmished during the afternoon. But at night General Hood's persistent declaration that he and General Polk would not be able to hold their ground an hour, caused the withdrawal of the army.

Page 43: The broken ground south of the Etowah can nowhere be called a "ridge of mountains." The route through it chosen by General Sherman was the least unfavorable. Page 44: The action at New Hope Church was the attack on Stewart's Division by Hooker's Corps. It began an hour and a half before sunset, and continued until dark, Stewart holding his ground. As the corps had a front equal only to that of the division, and was exposed to the musketry of five thousand infantry, and the canister of sixteen guns at short range, great execution must have been done in its ranks. Page 45: The "bloody battle" mentioned was an absurd attack on the Federal right, made without orders, by two Confederate brigades. It was quickly ended by the division commander, who drew back the troops as soon as he heard the firing, after they had lost three hundred men. But a real battle, which occurred the day before, is unnoticed—a carefully prepared attack upon our right by the Fourth Corps, supported by a division of the Fourteenth. The battle began about five o'clock P. M., and continued two hours. After the repulse of the assailants we counted about seven hundred dead within thirty yards of our line. The description of daily fighting on the same page is correct as to spirit and frequency; but as the Confederates were not permitted to leave their breastworks, the sallies and repulses were all Federal. Page 46: The Confederate army abandoned the line of New Hope Church on the 4th of June, because it was discovered that day that the Federal troops were moving by their left rear toward Allatoona, under cover of their line of intrenchments. On the same page, General Sherman claims that substantially during May he had fought over one hundred miles of most difficult country—from Chattanooga to Big Shanty. The fighting commenced at Tunnel Hill, thirty miles from Chattanooga, and he reached Big Shanty only on the 10th of June.

Page 49: "I always estimated my force at about double his; * * * but I also reckoned that in the natural strength of the country, in the abundance of mountains, streams and forests, he had a fair offset to our numerical superiority." Such being General Sherman's opinion, it is not easy to understand why he did not make his army one hundred and fifty thousand or two hundred thousand men. He knew the strength of the country, and it has been seen that, on the 5th of May, he had one hundred and thirty thousand men under his control, beside those assembled around him. Page

51: It is stated that the Seventeenth Corps, lately arrived, with new regiments, and returned furloughed men, "equaled the Federal losses by battle, sickness, and by detachments," so that the three armies still aggregated about one hundred thousand effective men. According to the table on page 136, they aggregated one hundred and twelve thousand eight hundred men. On the same page, below, it is said that the Confederates had signal stations and fresh lines of parapets on Kenesaw, Lost Mountain and Pine Mount. Kenesaw was not occupied by our (Southern) troops until the 19th, and Lost Mountain was abandoned on the 8th. Our only signal stations were on Kenesaw, as an observatory, and at headquarters. Page 53: The circumstances of General Polk's death were these: He had accompanied General Hardee and me to Pine Mount to reconnoitre. We placed ourselves in a battery near the summit, on the enemy's side. After seeing everything that interested us, we turned to leave the place. As we did so a cannon shot from a battery opposite, probably fired at a crowd of soldiers on the summit behind us, passed over us. A second came after about a minute, and a minute later, while we were walking slowly toward our horses, General Polk being on the very top of the hill, a third shot passed through the middle of his chest, from left to right. He was lifeless when I reached him in a few seconds, for we were but twenty or thirty feet apart. A brisk fire of artillery (shell) commenced soon after; there had been no volleys, and there was no signal station there.

Page 54: "We captured a good many prisoners, among them a whole infantry regiment, the Fourteenth Alabama, three hundred and twenty strong." The occurrences of the day made this highly improbable, if not impossible—it was the 15th. On the 16th, a company of skirmishers was forgotten in a change of position, and captured. Page 55: "The Confederate intrenchment was much smaller than that described—a ditch about two feet deep, the earth thrown up on the outside, making a parapet two feet and a half high, surmounted with a head log." We had no intrenching tools, a disadvantage for which all the mountain streams and forests of Georgia would not have compensated. Page 56: "These successive contractions of the enemy's line encouraged us and discouraged him, but were doubtless justified by strong reasons. On the 20th, Johnston's position was unusually strong;" by which his troops were greatly encouraged—indeed, made confident. Pages 59 and 60: The reports upon which General Sherman's telegram of the 23d was based, were extremely inaccurate. Johnston had not half so many miles of connected or other trenches as he. The Federal army had gained no

ground by fighting, unless the driving in of a few skirmishers can
be called so. The Southern army was never, during this part of the
campaign, driven from a position by fighting, or the fear of it; only
by danger to its communications, by the extension of the strongly
intrenched lines, which the enemy's greatly superior numbers enabled
him to make and man. The positions gained on the 21st, near the
south end of Kenesaw, and on a hill near, were outside of our position
—not occupied by our line, and if at all, only by pickets, and General
Sherman was deceived by reports of efforts to retake them and night
attacks, which were *never* made by our troops. If the Confederate
troops were so incessantly beaten, it is unaccountable that they were
permitted to remain before Marietta four weeks, and then shifted
their ground only to avoid losing their communications. The attack
on Hooker and Schofield on the 22d, was made against orders by
General Hood with Stevenson's Division, supported by Hindman's.
It was defeated by intrenched artillery. But the troops held the
ground they gained long enough to remove their dead and wounded.
On the 25th, an attack like this was made on Stevenson's Division
by the troops that had repulsed it on the 22d, and they were repelled
with as heavy a loss as they had inflicted then. But this affair
escapes General Sherman's notice.

Pages 60 and 61: The description of the attack on the Confederate army on the 27th of June, prepared from the 24th, and the
statement of the Federal loss, contrast strangely: "About 9 A. M. of
the day appointed the troops moved to the assault, and all along our
lines for ten miles a furious fire of artillery and musketry was kept
up. At all points the enemy met us with determined courage, and
in great force. * * * By half-past eleven the assault was over,
and had failed." The statement of loss was twenty-five hundred
killed and wounded. According to this, an army of Americans,
inured to war, was defeated by a loss of but two and a half per cent.
It is incredible. General Sherman's subordinates must have imposed
upon him. It is equally incredible that another army of American
veterans, as completely protected as men using arms can be, could
strike but two and a half per cent. of men exposed to their muskets
and cannon, in *seven lines* at least, in two hours and a half. The
writer has seen American soldiers, *not* inured to war, *win* a field with
a loss ten times greater proportionally.

Page 70: The Confederates are accused of burning their pontoon bridges after crossing the Chattahoochee. They did not
commit that folly.

On the 17th, it was reported that the Federal army was on the southeast bank of the Chattahoochee, from Roswell to Powers' ferry. That night General Hood was placed in command of the Southern army by telegraph. On the 18th, at his urgent request, Johnston forced the troops on the high ground, overlooking the valley of Peachtree creek from the south, to meet the advance of the Federal forces reported that morning by General Wheeler.

General Sherman's returns, on pages 24 and 136, shows ninety-eight thousand seven hundred and ninety-seven men present for duty May 1st; one hundred and twelve thousand eight hundred and nineteen June 1st, and one hundred and six thousand and seventy July 1st. Those of the Southern army show forty-two thousand eight hundred present for duty May 1st; fifty-eight thousand five hundred and sixty-two June 6th, and fifty-three thousand two hundred and seventy five July 1st. Fourteen thousandt wo hundred infantry and artillery and seven thousand cavalry were received in six detachments, coming at different times—all in May. General Sherman points out these additions to our forces, but says nothing of the reinforcements he received —except the arrival of the Seventeenth Corps (nine thousand men) June 8th. His reported losses in May, corrected by General Thomas (on page 5, report of Committee on Conduct of the War, supplementary part i), and the difference between the May and June returns above, show that he received above twenty-five thousand men in May alone. According to the table on page 133, before July 18th the Federal army lost in killed and wounded about twenty-one thousand men, of whom about twenty-five hundred were killed. The Southern army lost in the same time nine thousand nine hundred and seventy-two killed and wounded, of whom one thousand two hundred and eighty-eight were killed. The Southern officers believed that the Federal losses compared with theirs about as five to one. And circumstances justify that belief.

Except on three occasions, the Southern troops fought in their intrenchments, exposing scarcely a thirtieth of their persons, while their adversaries were fully exposed on open ground. Therefore, with equal marksmanship, they would have given thirty hits for one received. According to the reports of General Sherman's subordinates, they gave but two; or, on equal ground, would have made one effective shot to the enemy's fifteen—which is incredible. The more so, because a fire so utterly ineffective could not have repulsed or checked, in seventy days of such close and continued fighting as General Sherman describes, veteran American soldiers such as his. We had, too, direct proofs of the inaccuracy of these reports. After the action of June 27th (pages 60, 61), we counted one thousand

22

dead of the Army of the Cumberland lying before two of Hardee's divisions, very near, some against, our breastworks. The calculated proportion of wounded to killed is five to one; this would indicate a loss of six thousand *there*. But the officers of that army reported fifteen hundred and eighty killed, wounded, and *missing* (see page 223, above report)—less than two per cent. of the sixty thousand men of that army. The dead belonged to the first and second lines; and we could see seven exposed to our muskets and cannon, so that many others must have been killed. In like manner, on the 27th of May, we repelled an assault by four divisions, and counted seven hundred dead within thirty paces of our line. As five or six lines immediately behind these dead were exposed to our shot, there must have been considerable additional loss. Yet Federal officers reported but fourteen hundred as the entire loss, when it could not have been so little as four thousand. General Sherman does not allude to this action. In the engagement two days before (referred to on page 44), we had a much greater force engaged longer, and, therefore, must have inflicted a much greater loss. In the three actions, at least twenty-five hundred Federal soldiers must have been killed— as many as, according to Federal officers, were killed in all the fighting in ten weeks described by General Sherman, of which that in these three actions was not a fourth part.

The reports made to General Sherman charge his troops, indirectly, with being checked, repulsed, intimidated, by such losses as ordinary troops would have disregarded. This is incredible to those who, like the writer, have often witnessed the vigorous and persistent courage of American soldiers, the best of whom were not superior to General Sherman's. But the testimony of the ten thousand and thirty-six graves in the Union Cemetery at Marietta, of soldiers killed south of the Etowah, is conclusive. Less than two thousand of them fell in the actions about Atlanta. But at least three thousand were killed north of the Etowah, and buried at Chattanooga. As the towns and villages in the route of the Federal army were burned, there could have been no hospitals, and, therefore, few deaths by sickness south of Dalton. These proofs show that the estimate on page 357, "Johnston's Narrative," which General Sherman pronounces erroneous, is not much so, to say the least. On page 48, General Sherman claims to have taken three thousand two hundred and forty-five prisoners in May, because he had captured twelve thousand nine hundred and eighty-three in the four and a half months ending September 15th. We had no loss by capture in May, and only a little more than two hundred up to July 18th. The marches and the results of the fighting in that time did not enable the enemy to make prisoners. His successes and prisoners were subsequent. On page 49, General Sherman claims that the strength of the country, by mountains, streams, and forests, gave his enemy a fair offset to his numerical superiority. Between Dalton aud Atlanta, one sees but two *semblances* of mountains—Rocky Face, which covered the march by which he "flanked" Dalton and Kenesaw, less than two miles long. The country was no more unfavorable for the offensive than the Wilderness, or that on which Lee and McClellan fought near Richmond, or that between Amelia and Appomattox Court-Houses.

General Sherman certainly executed his plan of operations with great perseverance, skill, and resolution. But it is a question if that plan was the best. The results obtained, compared with those attainable, indicate that it was not. At Dalton, only the southern left flank was covered by Rocky Face, not its front; and an attack in front would have been on ground as favorable to the Federal army as its general could have hoped to find. With odds of near ten to four, he might well have thought the "breaking up of Johnston's army" attainable there. If defeated, Atlanta, its place of refuge, was one hundred miles off, with three rivers intervening; while the Federal army, if unsuccessful, had a secure refuge in Chattanooga, which was easily reached. At Resaca, the Federal general had a still better opportunity, for the two armies met there without intrenchments between them—the Federals having a line of retreat from their centre directly to the rear; while the Southern troops, formed near and parallel to the road to Atlanta, would have been driven from that road by defeat, and, consequently, destroyed. Battle at either place, whatever the result, would not have cost a fourth of the number of men actually lost. And success would have ended the campaign, and decided the war.

On page 39, General Sherman says: " Of course it was to my interest to bring him to battle as soon as possible." His overwhelming numbers ought to have made it possible at any time. The flanking operations forced the Southern army back to Atlanta, but could do no more. There it was safe in intrenchments much stronger than any it had previously occupied, and too extensive to be invested. And three railroads met there, either one capable of supplying the army. So it could have maintained itself there indefinitely, and so won the campaign with little more loss. This is no afterthought, but was expressed to General Hood when he took command. The Federal march to Jonesboro' caused, but did not compel, the abandonment of Atlanta. For if the Southern troops had remained in the place, the enemy would, in a few days, have been forced to return to his railroad. And, besides, Atlanta could have been sufficiently supplied from Macon, through Augusta; but at Jonesboro' the Federal troops could not be fed. This mode of gaining Atlanta made the acquisition of no great value. For the campaign continued, and General Sherman was occupied by General Hood until late in October, when he commenced the disastrous expedition into Tennessee, which left the former without an antagonist.

Bentonville—pages 303–4–5–6: Johnston attempted to unite the three little bodies of his troops near Bentonville, on the 18th of March, to attack the head of General Sherman's left column next morning, on the Goldsboro' road. Less than two-thirds had arrived at eight A. M. of the 19th, when the Federal column appeared and deployed, intrenching lightly at the same time. The fighting that day was a vigorous attack on our left, defeated in half an hour; then a similar one on our right, repulsed in like manner. About three o'clock, all the troops being in line, the Federal army was attacked, driven from its position, and pursued a mile and a half, into an extensive thicket, which compelled the Southern troops to halt when otherwise they were not opposed. Two hours after we were slightly attacked—by a reconnoitering party, probably; it was so easily repelled. We made *no other attack,* but held our ground till after nightfall, to carry off our wounded. Our army remained in line nearly parallel to the Goldsboro' road, to remove the wounded to Smithfield. Its flanks were somewhat thrown back—the left only of cavalry skirmishers. Butler's cavalry was observing the right Federal column; Wheeler's arrived from Averysboro' the evening of the 19th. Mower's movement (see page 304) was made after three o'clock; for he had proceeded but a mile and a half when attacked and driven back, about half-past four o'clock, being then in rear of our centre where orders could not reach him. So the skirmishing mentioned on page 304 must have been very brief. Our men, being intrenched, easily drove off the enemy. In reference to "wide discrepancies," General O. O. Howard's (right) wing fought only in this skirmish. Yet it is claimed (page 305) that its loss was but four hundred and eight, while it inflicted one of near two thousand, including wounded, on the Confederates—four times as great as that they suffered June 27th, by the assault of the whole Federal army (see page 61). It is claimed, also, on page 305, that the Southern army, which was successful in all the fighting and intrenched in most of it, lost fifty per cent. more than the Federals. These "discrepancies" cannot be charged to the Southern officers.

Meetings of Sherman and Johnston, April 17th and 18th: By a not unusual error of memory, General Sherman probably attributes to Johnston language that he heard in Raleigh the following evening (see pages 349 and 351). It could not have entered the mind of the latter that any of the class to which General Sherman belongs could entertain a suspicion that Mr. Davis was accessory to assassination. The object of our meeting, expressed in a letter in his report, page 137, was to make a general armistice—"to enable the civil authorities to enter into the needful arrangements to terminate the existing war." He said that this was impracticable, and offered such terms of surrender as were granted to the army of Northern Virginia. Johnston declined to capitulate, because the military condition in North Carolina was unlike that in Virginia, and proposed that they should agree upon preliminaries of peace, citing authorities. General Sherman assented, and in less than two hours the terms, drawn up and adopted next day, were agreed upon, except that General Sherman refused to include Mr. Davis and his Cabinet in the article (sixth) granting amnesty. This question was discussed till sunset, when they agreed to resume the subject next morning. General Breckenridge accompanied Johnston to the meeting, and Mr. Reagan put on paper the terms discussed the day before, which Johnston had given, and sent the paper after him. As soon as received, without any discussion aside, these terms were proposed to General Sherman, with the reminder that they had been almost accepted the day before. With this paper before him, General Sherman wrote rapidly that which was adopted and signed, which expressed in his language the terms discussed the day before. The terms of this convention show that there was no question of surrender, but of peace; nor of Johnston's power over other Confederate armies, for in the last paragraph both acknowledge that they had not the power, but pledge themselves to obtain it.

SOME RECOLLECTIONS OF GRANT.

BY S. H. M. BYERS.

LOOKING over my diary to-day, kept when a corporal in Company B, I find this half-faded entry: "This day our corps, the Seventeenth, McPherson commanding, marched from the Mississippi river up to Fort Gibson." While I was standing by the pontoon bridge watching the boys cross the bayou, I heard somebody cheering, and, looking round, saw an officer on horseback in a major general's uniform. He dismounted and came over to the very spot where I was standing. I did not know his face, but something told me it was Grant—Ulysses Grant, at that moment the hero of the Western army. Solid he stood—erect; about five feet eight, with square features, thin closed lips, brown hair, brown beard, both cut short and neat. "He must weigh one hundred and fifty pounds; looks just like the soldier he is. I think he is larger than Napoleon, but not much—he is not so dumpy; looks like a man in good earnest, and the rebels think he is." And this was the first time I saw Grant. I think I still possess some of the feeling that overcame me at that moment as I stood so near to one who held our lives and, possibly, our country's in his hands. I heard him speak: "Men, push right along; close up fast, and hurry over." Two or three men mounted on mules attempted to wedge past the soldiers on the bridge. Grant noticed it, and quietly said, "Lieutenant, send those men to the rear." Every soldier passing turned to gaze on him, but there was no further recognition. There was no McClellan, begging the boys to allow him to light his cigar by theirs, or inquiring to what regiment that exceedingly fine-marching company belonged to. There was no

Pope, bullying the men for not marching faster, or officers for some trivial detail remembered only by martinets. There was no Bonaparte, posturing for effect; no pointing to the Pyramids, no calling the centuries to witness. There was no nonsense, no sentiment; only a plain business man of the republic, there for the one single purpose of getting that command across the river in the shortest time possible. On a horse near by, and among the still mounted staff, sat the general's son, a bright-looking lad of about eleven years. Fastened to his little waist, by the broad yellow belt, was his father's sword—that sword on whose clear steel was soon to be engraved Vicksburg, Spottsylvania, the Wilderness, and Richmond. The boy talked and jested with the bronzed soldiers near him, who laughingly inquired where we should camp; to which the young field marshal replied: "Over the river!" Over the river! Ah! that night we slept with our guns in our hands; and another night, and another, saw more than one of our division camped beyond and over the river—in that last tenting-ground where the reveille was heard no more forever.

I next saw Grant on May 18th, 1863, and this time at the battle of "Champion Hills," in rear of Vicksburg. We had crossed the Mississippi river at Grand Gulf, and swung off east and north; had fought the battles of Port Gibson, Raymond, and Jackson, and were overtaking Pemberton's army hastening to the walls of Vicksburg. It was a very hot day, and we had marched hard, slept little, and rested none. Among the magnolias on Champion hills, the enemy, forty to fifty thousand strong, turned on us. Sherman's Corps was already engaged far on the right as we approached the field in that overpowering Mississippi sun. Our brigade was soon in line, on the edge of a meadow, or open field sloping toward the woods, where the enemy were concealed, and steadily firing upon us. We were in that most trying position of soldiers, for regulars even—being fired on without permission to return the shots. We were standing two files deep, bearing as patiently as we could not a heavy, but a steady fire from infantry, while an occasional cannon-ball tore up the turf in front or behind us. A good many men were falling, and the wounded were being borne to the rear of the brigade, close to an old well, whose wooden curb seemed to offer the only protection from bullets on the exposed line. "Colonel, move your men a little by the left flank," said a quiet, though commanding voice. On looking round, I saw immediately behind us Grant, the commander-in-chief, mounted on a beautiful bay mare, and followed by perhaps half a dozen of his staff. For some reason he dismounted, and most of his officers were sent off, bearing orders, probably, to other quarters of the field. It was Grant under fire. The rattling musketry increased on our front, and grew louder, too, on the left flank. Grant had led his horse to the left, and thus kept near the company to which I belonged. He now stood leaning complacently against his favorite steed, smoking—as seemed habitual with him— the stump of a cigar. His was the only horse near the line, and must, naturally, have attracted some of the enemy's fire. What if he should be killed, I thought to myself, and the army be left without its commander? In front of us was an enemy; behind us, and about us, and liable to overcome and crush us, were his rein- forcements. For days we had been away from our base of supplies, and marching inside the enemy's lines. What if Grant should be killed, and we be defeated here—in such a place, and at such a time? I am sure every one who recognized him wished him away; but there he stood—clear, calm, and immovable. I was close enough to see his features. Earnest they were; but sign of inward movement, there was none. It was the same cool, calculating face I had seen before at the bridge; the same careful, half-cynical face I afterward saw busied with affairs of State.

Whatever there may have been in his feelings there was no effort to conceal; there was no pretence, no trick; whatever that face was, it was natural. A man close by me had the bones of his leg shattered by a ball, and was being helped to the rear. His cries of pain attracted the attention of Grant, and I noticed the half-curious, though sympathizing shades, that crossed his quiet face as the bleeding soldier seemed to look toward him for help. Men have often asked if Grant were personally brave in battle. Bravery, like many other human qualities, is comparative. That Grant was fearless in battle would be hard to say. If he possessed true bravery, he also possessed fear. Brave men are not fearless men. The fools, the excited, and the drunken, are they who, fearless and unasked, run on to death. Where duty was, imposed or assumed, Grant feared not to stand, and his *sang froid* was as marked, and not more necessary, in the presence of bullets, as it afterward was in the presence of popular clamor and senseless political reproach. He was eminently and above all things a cool man, and that, I take it, was, in the exciting times in which he lived, the first great key to his success. He was not made hilarious by victory, nor was he depressed by defeat. His services had not been forced upon the country, nor was he oblivious to his country's claims. He recognized simple duty, and his worst enemies envied the ardor with which that duty was performed. He was called a born soldier, but was, in fact, nothing of the kind. He was simply a man of correct methods and a fixed will. The same methods and the same will would have led men to call him a born railway director, or a born anything to which he had once in good earnest turned his hand. As a young soldier he had lacked opportunity. He lived in a land where neither soldiers nor poets were wanted. There were no wars, no romances, and little history. If he had tried business a little as a farmer, a tanner, a surveyor, or what not, it was not in good earnest. It was a makeshift for the occasion. The war was Grant's opportunity, and he was at the age and had the disposition to seize it. But his military renown was not of luck alone. It was earned blow by blow.

We had not waited many minutes at the meadow when an orderly dashed up to Grant, and handed him a communication. Then followed an order to move rapidly to the left, and into the road. The fire grew heavier, and the air seemed too hot to be borne. "Forward!" came a second order, all along the line—"Forward! double quick!" Everybody shouted "double quick," as the noise was becoming terrific. We had forgotten to fix bayonets! what forgetfulness! and again the screaming was, "Fix bayonets! fix bayonets!" I had been selected by the colonel, just as we entered the road, to act as sergeant major, and I now ran behind and along the line, shouting at the top of my voice, "Fix bayonets!" The orders were not heard, and we were charging the enemy's position with bare muskets. A moment more and we were at the top of the ascent, and among thinner wood and larger trees. The enemy had fallen back a few rods, forming a solid line parallel with our own; and now commenced, in good earnest, the fighting of the day. For half an hour we poured the hot lead into each others' faces. We had forty rounds each in our cartridge-boxes, and, probably, nine-tenths of them were fired in that half hour. For me it was the first real "stand up and fight," as the boys called it, of my life. Of skirmishes, I had seen many, and had been under fire; but this was a real battle, and what Grant himself might have called "business." I tried to keep cool, and determined to fire no shot without taking aim; but a slight wound in the hand ended my coolness, and the smoke of the battle soon made aim-taking mere guessing. One rebel officer I noticed, through the smoke, directly in front of me on horseback. That was my mark, and I must have fired twenty times at him before his form disappeared. I remember how, in the midst of it all, a young lad—he could not have been more than sixteen—came running up to me, and weeping, cried: "My regiment—my regiment is gone—has run! What shall I do?" "Here's the place," I said, "pitch in!" and pitch in he did. He was of metal, that boy, and kept his place with the bravest veteran in the line. Hotter and hotter grew the fight, and soon this same boy cried: "Look—look behind us," and, sure enough, the regiment to our left had disappeared, and we were flanked.

"Stop! halt! surrender!" cried a hundred rebels, whose voices seem to ring in my ears to this very day. But there was no stopping, and no surrender. We ran, and ran manfully. It was terribly hot, a hot afternoon under a Mississippi sun, and an enemy on flank and rear, shouting and firing. The grass, the stones, the bushes, seemed melting under the shower of bullets that was following us to the rear. We tried to halt, and tried to form. It was no use. Again we ran, and harder, and farther, and faster. We passed over the very spot where, half an hour before, we left Grant leaning on his bay mare and smoking his cigar. Thank God! he was gone. The dead were still there, and the wounded called pitiably to us to halt and help them as we ran headlong to the rear. Like ten thousand starving and howling wolves the enemy pursued, closer and closer, and we scarcely dared look back to face the fate that seemed certain. Grant had seen it all, and in less time than I can tell it a line of cannon had been thrown across our path, which, as soon as we had passed, belched grape-shot and canister into the faces of our pursuers. They stopped, they turned, and they, too, ran, and left their dead side by side with our own. Our lines, protected by the batteries, rallied and followed, and Champion hills was won, and with it was won the door to Vicksburg. Three army corps had taken part in the fight—Sherman's, McClernand's, and McPherson's. One division of the enemy passed us and got to our rear, thus escaping being captured with the thirty thousand who surrendered on that birthday of the nation in 1863.

Grant passed along the lines, after the fight, as we stood in the narrow roads, waiting to pursue the enemy to their works at Vicksburg. Every hat was in the air, and the men cheered till they were hoarse; but, speechless, and almost without a bow, he pushed on past, like an embarrassed man hurrying to get away from some defeat. Once he stopped, near the colors, and, without addressing himself to any one in particular, said: "Well done!" It was midnight before we halted for the night; and then, before lying down, we called the roll, and found how many comrades were left coldly sleeping under the magnolias of Champion hills. My best friend was killed, and our mess had three that night instead of the six who had shared our rations in the morning at reveille. In a few weeks

Vicksburg was added to the victor's crown. The siege, though not especially long, had been severe. On the 22d of May, Grant, under the impression that the enemy had been demoralized by their defeat at Champion hills, gave ear to the general cry of soldiers and officers to "storm the works." On the 19th, we had assaulted and failed. For days the batteries had been receiving enormous additions of ammunition, and, all the morning of the day designated for the attack, Vicksburg trembled under the most terrific cannonade from every gun on the line. Men were detailed to spring before the advancing line, with ladders and planks to aid us in getting over ditches. It was a forlorn hope—this little party of brave men, advancing with their ladders to certain death. At the given signal, the storming lines uncovered, and, advancing, were met by the most terrible crashing of musketry. The ditches were deep and wide, and the earthworks, bristling with red-mouthed cannon, were very high. At places, too, the enemy were outside of the breastworks, hidden behind bags of sand, from which they, with safety to themselves, delivered a galling fire. Others, again, during the night, had dug holes more than breast-deep, in which they stood, as the line advanced, and picked off, at ease, our men with ladders.

Still, in face of all this, and in the heat of a broiling sun, our troops advanced to the very ditches, only to be driven back by a fire that no body of soldiers could withstand. It was of no use; we were attempting the impossible. Many lives were being sacrificed, and nothing gained. Some of the breastworks we could not have entered from the front, even had there not been an enemy within. On the afternoon of the same day, we attempted the charge again, with the same result. Afterward, when Vicksburg was ours, I walked, time and again, over the very ground where we had so desperately fought, and looked at the forts which we had sought to storm, reflecting on the extreme madness of the undertaking. The result of the attack, however mortifying it must have been to Grant himself, did not lessen his cool and fixed determination to possess Vicksburg before a step in any other direction should be taken. Silently, this one feeling was communicated to every soldier of his army. There were no loud proclamations, orders, or manifestos as to what would next come. There were no promises of victory to the North, no threats of humiliation to the South; but every soldier knew that, as we had intrenched before Vicksburg, we would stay there until the city had surrendered. There was no doubt, no fears. We knew that our commander was a man of business, with certain regular, fixed methods and determinations, and that, just then, it was his particular business to take that particular town. So, we said, as we lay in the rifle-pits: "Let us make ourselves comfortable; for here we stay till the last enemy in our front has become our prisoner."

But Grant was not the only commander at Vicksburg with cool pluck, brave heart, and fixed determination. Logan, the fearless; the accomplished McPherson, the Bayard of the West, were there; and Sherman, the brilliancy of whose deeds were soon to eclipse even those of his great commander. What restless energy was there—what pluck among both officers and men. How many the incidents of daring—of risk, sacrifice, and of camp humor, even on the "ragged edge" of danger. Sometimes a flag-of-truce came out—often on business intent, to collect the wounded, or bury the dead; but an occasional one as a "feeler," to learn incidentally, or perhaps directly, if there was still hope. It was told of Sherman how one of these flag-of-truce officers one day asked the grim general, in a haughty tone, "How long he calculated it would take the Yankees to reduce the heroic city?" The prompt reply was: "You don't know me, perhaps. My name is Sherman. My enemies in the North sometimes call me 'Crazy Sherman;' but, in my sane moments, I have said this war may last seventeen years yet; and I know of no place where I should so soon spend seven of them as right here, before Vicksburg." The rebel said "Good day," and returned to the forts, where it was soon whispered round that, with such a man besieging them, the city was doomed.

Our army occupied the anomalous position of being besiegers and besieged at the same time. Pemberton's army was in front of us in the works, while the army of his confederate, Johnston, almost surrounded us from behind, and was vigilant in seeking either an opportunity to break through and join the forces in Vicksburg or lend them a helping hand in getting out. Many were the adventures, grim sports and escapes we had as we lay for weeks between these two lines of the enemy. The noise of the bombardment was constant, the click of the rifles on the line of pickets never ceased day or night, and many were the deceptions practiced by the pickets of both armies as they stood within speaking distance of each other to induce a show of "heads" above the long lines of rude rifle-pits. I remember how, one day, I and two of my companions fired for an hour at a rebel who kept for ever hopping up and down behind the sand bags and calling constantly, "Try again, will you, Mr. Yankee?" Finally the figure mounted up in full view, when we discovered we were cheaply sold, as the daring rebel was a stuffed suit of old clothes on a pole, while the mockery came from the real rebel, safe behind the sand bags. Another one, more reckless, however, placed himself in the open embrasure of a low earthwork for a moment, and shouted "Fire!" In an instant he lay stretched dead in the embrasure. An effort was made by his comrades to pull away his body, but shots were constantly fired into the opening at every one daring to show himself for an instant. They tried to pull the body away with poles, but in vain; the firing increased almost to the dignity of an action, and finally a battery joined in the conflict over the poor corpse which, darkness hiding the combatants, they were at last able to secure. I have thought since then, owing to the risks run on his behalf, that the poor man was possibly not dead after all, but sadly wounded, and lying there under the hot sun dying—with help so near and yet so powerless to save.

But incidents though as dangerous, touching the ludicrous, also occurred. I recall how a young Federal sergeant foolishly insisted on exposing himself to the fire of the enemy by creeping over the earthwork and surveying the lines with an opera-glass, borrowed during his raids from some planter's house. The captain had repeatedly and vainly warned him against his recklessness, till one sunny morning, while engaged in his usual observations with glass to eye, a bullet fired from an unlooked-for quarter smashed the glass in his hand. Our boys, seeing he was not killed, but rejoicing at the warning, gave cheers for the rebel who fired the shot. It was a close shave, but our sergeant was cured of reckless curiosity. Another incident, not less ludicrous, occurred the morning on which we assaulted the works of Vicksburg. I had been detailed to bring cartridges to my regiment, which had advanced out of the hollow in which it lay and over the brow of the hill under a heavy fire. The firing was still going on, but the regiment lay down unharmed, when cartridges were called for. I went back, but found the boxes of a 1,000 "58s" too heavy to carry, and so strapped two of them over the back of a strong mule, and started to the front. I walked and led the mule, while a companion followed, administering a wagon-whip from behind. On emerging from the breastworks it was necessary to hurry over a little rise in full·view of the enemy. It was but a dozen rods to a spot of safety in the hollow. We took a good start at a run, and emerged into full view of the forts, not a hundred rods away, when the beast, true to his instincts, took it into his head at this particular crisis to stop stock-still. Persuasion, pulling, whooping, separate or combined, helped nothing. There he stood, fixed as the general of the army himself, and apparently ten times as cool. What could be done? Bullets were whizzing about our heads and ears, two had skinned up the boxes on the mule's back, and the next moment some sharpshooter might, and certainly would, pick us off forever. We couldn't run; the ammunition was pressingly needed. It was too hot to remain there, and go we could not. Again my comrade whipped, both shouted, and I pulled and tugged till, suddenly, halter and bridle both slipped over the mule's head. Free from restraint, he was disposed to run, and run he did—but fortunately in the right direction. We, too, ran faster, possibly, than did the mule. He was caught in the right place, unloaded and tied to a bush, where, in a few hours, when the line fell back, he was left standing as an outpost, being probably seized upon and eaten by the hungry soldiers of Pemberton's army. I have often wondered since then how that mule was accounted for at Washington. Was he reported stolen, captured, or simply

" Died on the field of honor?"

During the long weeks of the siege, the common soldiers saw Grant daily; not exhibiting himself for the sake of being cheered and cheaply glorified, but patiently examining the little details necessary to the safety and comfort of the army. Near my regiment was an Ohio battery of brass six-pounders, and it was not uncommon to see the commander walk over and aim the guns himself or watch with intense interest the effect of some particular shot. His own tents, though not as exposed, were as close to the lines of the enemy as were the huts of the soldiers on duty. He was commanding his troops from the front, not from the rear. He lived in his army, and was himself not only its director, but a part of it. He was a private soldier in command, a corporal in the uniform of a general. Enormous quantities of ammunition had been furnished the batteries, and Grant proposed celebrating the anniversary of the nation by pouring hot lead into Vicksburg. Pemberton certainly expected as much, and offered to surrender in time. What days those were to us, the common soldiers of the army, as we lay in the trenches of Vicksburg! It was here that I got my first commission, and, in a very few days, the first order I had the honor of reading to a regiment of bronzed soldiers in line contained the words :

Vicksburg has capitulated. At ten to-morrow morning, July 4th, 1863, the garrison, thirty thousand in number, will march outside the works and surrender their arms.

U. S. GRANT.

There was a shout, a throwing up of hats; then came a silence. "Not true, not true; too good, too good!" cried many. But the colonel said, "Praised be God! it is true; Grant never jests;" and again the woods rang with grateful shouts. Some danced wildly about, all shouting and shaking hands, and a few even rolled on the grass in deliriums of joy, that our nation's birthday should be welcomed in a way like that. As for me, I saw again the boys in blue marching down the court-house steps of my native village, off over the lawn, and away to death and glory. Some of them were then beside me, and joining in the maddening shouts of victory. I could not shout; my heart was too full, my joy too great. That night I wrote in my diary: "This day has rewarded me a thousand times for all the sacrifices, hardships, dangers, and vicissitudes of two years as a private soldier." I went to my little tent, made of bushes, and writing my mother a letter, told how gloriously Vicksburg was won, and how her boy had helped to take it. I inclosed to her, too, a copy of my commission in one of the fighting regiments, and closed by asking if she were not glad her boy was not too young to be a soldier? Her answer brought me her blessing and her prayer, and I was doubly rewarded.

We at once turned and pursued the enemy in our rear, under Johnston. The Vicksburg prisoners were to go back to a camp of parole, and for days we marched along the country road side by side— lines of the "blue" and lines of the "gray." It was a strange sight— those two armies that only a few hours before had been hurling destruction and death at each other, now walking in silence, side by side; they to prison, we in pursuit of their retreating comrades; we glowing in victory, they saddened in defeat. There were no jeers as we marched along; no reproaching, no boasting, and no insults. On the contrary, we recognized an honorable foe, crippled but not dead; and many were the little kindnesses received on that strange and silent march, by Pemberton's men, from the boys of Grant's army. Many a ration was divided, many a canteen filled, and many were the mutual, sympathizing wishes that the cruel war might soon be over. I recall how a soldier, observing one of the prisoners footsore, weary with the march, and almost fainting, relieved him by taking from him his heavy burden, and fastening it on top of his own, carrying it for miles. The prisoners, seeing the incident, cheered, and I think more than one honest, kindly man of that stranger train was touched to tears. Pemberton rode at the head of his prisoner column, silent and sad. He as well as all the officers of of his army, were in the full gray uniform of the South, and though prisoners, their swords still hung in the scabbards at their sides. Many of them were mounted on the thin steeds that had survived the hunger of the siege. When Grant passed us, and the boys cheered, the curiosity of the rebels was extreme; and I was told that at one point they even joined in the shouts that welcomed him.

In September, I was allowed a short leave of absence to visit my home in the far West. As I went down to the docks, the boat on which I was to have had passage blew up, killing many soldiers and negroes. Later, I got on another steamer, which on our way up the river stuck on a sand-bar for days. My leave was for but a month, and in this vexing way was the time so precious to me being lost. At last I got home, saw my friends, and after eight days there, the only time spent at home during the whole four years' war, I hurried back to join my corps, which was then on its march to Chattanooga. There I saw Grant, the last time for many months, preparing for the great battles of Missionary Ridge and Lookout Mountain. I was under Sherman now, and joining in the charge made by a part of Smith's Division, on the right wing of Bragg's army, was surrounded and captured. It was the last battle of my life. I saw my sword, and pistols, and purse divided among a corporal and two privates, who came near shooting each other on account of the trophies captured from the young Yankee. I also saw, however, from the top of Mission Ridge, the flying enemy, and the grand advance of Thomas' and Sherman's armies. I was a prisoner!

What I experienced during more than fifteen months in the prisons of Libby, Columbia, Charleston, and elsewhere, will not be related here. In September, 1864, the Libby prisoners, seven hundred in number, and all officers, were transferred from Charleston to a camp in the woods, on the Congaree river, near Columbia, South Carolina. There seemed but one outlook ahead for us, and that was a lingering death, unless hastened by some attempt to escape. I had got away twice, for a few days at a time, but was recaptured, and my position made even worse than before. In December, Sherman had made that brilliant march to the sea, and in February was engaged in that still more arduous campaign through the Carolinas to Richmond. I learned that his army was approaching Columbia, and for the third time attempted to get away. I escaped the guards, and, aided by an old slave, secreted myself in Columbia, and witnessed the evacuation by the rebels, and the grand entry of Sherman's army. Sherman, with his characteristic kindness, sought out myself and others who had been prisoners, and who had escaped, and cared for the wants of all. I was given, for the time, a place on his staff. What a change it was, from the degradation, the starving, the suffering of a mistrusted prisoner to the headquarters of the most brilliant general of modern times. Sherman was marching northward with an army of ninety thousand men in four columns, on as many different roads, all bearing on some designated point. One day he would ride with this column, the next day with that; but whenever he appeared among the soldiers it was one loud and continued cheer for "Billy Sherman." Here was the general whom everybody knew, and whom everybody loved. If Grant had been the creator of the Western army, Sherman was its idol. He was, indeed, looked upon as a sort of common property, in which every man in the army had a special and particular interest. I speak knowingly, as one who was a private soldier, and who associated with private soldiers under him. In the tent, in the bivouac, in the rifle-pits, the men's faith in his consummate generalship never faltered. On the march his name was more than respected—it was loved ; and whenever he appeared, the knapsacks of the boys grew lighter, the step brisk, and the face bright. It was in this march through the Carolinas I again saw so much of the influence of that presence on the soldiery. It rained nearly all the time ; the roads were horrid, and had to be corduroyed with poles and rails half the way ; the wagons and the artillery stuck in the mire hourly, and the soldiers had to drag them out with their own hands. Every stream had to be bridged, every quagmire filled, and every mile skirmished with the enemy.

There was not a tent in the army. Even the general slept in the woods, under "plys," in deserted houses, or lone churches along the way. On right and left, before and behind, was an enemy; quagmires were under foot, and continued rain overhead; yet through all this the boys tugged and fought, and amidst their tugging sang and cheered. It was the magnetism of one really great man. It was "Billy Sherman." His approach to the line of march was the signal for shoutings that I have heard taken up and repeated for miles ahead. Riding alongside the regiments struggling through the mud or the underbrush at the roadside, he would often speak to the nearest soldiers with some kind and encouraging word. Nor was it unusual to hear private soldiers call out to him, knowing his kind heart would give them no rebuff. At headquarters there was little pretense, and no show. When evening came a convenient spot in the woods was usually sought out, a few tent plys were stretched, and a rail fire built in front. The mess-chest was opened, and a hasty but substantial meal was enjoyed, amid conversation on almost every topic but the war. On this he was oftenest silent, preferring

23

to keep his own judgment, hopes and fears to himself. He wrote most, probably all, of his own dispatches, leaving his staff little or nothing to do. After supper he studied his maps in the fire-light, or heard the reports from the other columns for the day. He was last in bed at night, and first in the saddle in the morning. Dinner consisted of a light lunch at twelve; all dismounted at the roadside, and an hour's rest brought us again to the saddle. So the days passed, and the enemy was continually pushed or beaten back from each and every chosen position.

At Fayetteville a tugboat met us in answer to a message sent by one of Sherman's scouts to Wilmington. The general seized the opportunity to report his progress to the Secretary of War, at Washington, and to General Grant, then with his army before Richmond. At the breakfast-table that Sunday morning he announced his intentions, and I was to be the lucky one to go. That night a few of us ran down the Cape Fear river to the sea, and a ship bore me around Cape Hatteras, across to Fortress Monroe, and up the James to Grant. I found him in a little board cabin of two rooms. He stood talking with a delegation of Northern citizens, who had come down ostensibly to encourage the army, but in reality to interfere with the plans of its commander by insisting on giving some pet advice. In those days everybody thought himself fit to command an army, and the newspapers seemed to be all edited by major generals, so full were they of warning instructions, "We told you so's," etc. I was announced to Grant as a bearer of dispatches from Sherman, whose army I soon learned had not been heard from since cutting loose from its base at Savannah, the greatest anxiety being felt for its safety the country over. Grant took my hand and conducted me into the little back room, closing the door behind us. The dispatches, which I had sewed up in my clothes, were turned over and carefully read, and I saw with what a glow his face lighted up as he read of the continued successes of his friend and co-commander. He hurried them through again, rose to his feet, and for a moment paced the little room; then suddenly opening the door he called General Ord, who was in the adjoining room, to come in and hear the good news from Sherman. Bad news of some misfortune to Sherman's army had been telegraphed to Richmond by Wade Hampton, of the enemy's army, the day before. The reports had come through the lines to Grant in most exaggerated form. "Glorious!" cried Ord, "glorious! I was beginning to have my fears, but——" "Not a bit! not a bit!" replied Grant. "I knew him. I knew my man. I expected him to do just this, and he has done it." I was then questioned as to many a detail of Sherman's last movements. "We have been in perfect ignorance," said Grant, "of all these things; you have brought me the first authentic news. How about Kilpatrick?" And I told him how, a few nights before, this officer had been surprised in bed, and his staff all captured; how he fled to the swamp, rallied his men, and, returning, chased Wade Hampton completely from the road. Grant and Ord both laughed heartily. "And this, then, was the disaster to Sherman's army, of which the rebels had been boasting so loudly. I expected just exactly as much," said Grant.

Kilpatrick had, in fact, a most laughable adventure with a narrow escape, however, for life. He was at Sherman's headquarters the day after the surprise, and I heard him telling how he was chased, and his staff captured and put up stairs in a house, where they remained while he rallied his men in the swamp, and surprised Hampton in return, and to more purpose, too, than he himself had been surprised. He lost a couple of hundred of prisoners, however, and some horses. But Kilpatrick kept his ground and lived to lead his dashing cavalry on many another field. "How do the men seem off for shoes and for coats?" asked Grant. I replied, if suffering, there was no complaint. At that moment a fierce and sudden cannonade commenced at some point on the enemy's line. An officer was called and ordered off to see what it meant. "It is one of the usual make-believes that we are having daily," said Grant. I asked if an engagement was expected. He replied it was quite possible at any hour; but his own opinion was that Lee at that very moment might be getting ready to try and escape from Richmond, and that this thundering cannonade was one of his preparatory ruses to attract attention. The correctness of his opinion was proven in a few days, when Lee and his whole army fell back from Richmond, only to be captured at Appomattox Court-House. Grant mentioned that the Secretary of War, Mr. Stanton, was there from Washington, and would visit him that evening, and suggested that he should take charge of my other papers and turn them over to him. He was then kind enough to ask about my own personal experiences, especially my life in prison, and if I, too, confirmed the horrible tales of suffering that had met his ears daily. I gave him a list of what we had to eat for months, told him that the prisoners were in rags, that not a single garment had ever been given to them since their capture, and some of them had been in the enemy's hands for eighteen months. He expressed his sorrow; surprise he had none; and added that their sufferings would soon be over, as he believed the war would very soon terminate. "You would like to go home at once, wouldn't you?" he said, again going to the door and asking Rawlins, his chief-of-staff, to have leave of absence and pass made out for me. He signed the papers, and thanked me for my promptness.

It was the last time I ever saw Grant in uniform. I went to my home in the far West. I was, as a soldier, almost alone; yet in a few days I saw the little fragment of the company, of which I had been a member, returning from the war. They were veterans then. I, too, was a veteran. I heard the drums beating, and again I went down to the village, and there saw the "boys" paraded for the last time on the green grass of the court-house yard; on the very spot, indeed, where, four years before, we had been mustered in. There was not so much room required now, as then. Twenty-seven bronzed faces were all that were left of a hundred stout youths who had stood on that same spot but four short years before. There was no cheering now, as then; the silence was painful, almost. Many of the wives, and mothers, and sisters who were there before, were not there again—they could not be. In their desolate homes they sat, and, like Rachel, wept and would not be comforted. Their soldiers had been left behind; had been mustered out on the red battle-field many a day before. I have left my native village since then—I could not stay there. The recollections that always crowded upon my mind when passing the green court yard made it impossible.

CHARACTERISTICS OF THE ARMIES

BY H. V. REDFIELD.

FOR the first three years of the war my home in Tennessee was surrounded by the armed hosts of one army, and then the other (and sometimes both at once, or so near it as to be uncomfortable), and my opportunities for observation were good. When the war broke out, the people of our portion of lower East Tennessee calculated upon exemption from its ravages. I remember vividly how the old citizens, in whom I had implicit confidence, shook their heads with prophetic earnestness, saying that we would see no soldiers of either army, "as they couldn't get their cannons over these mountains." The leading merchant, the leading minister, and the leading physician were of this opinion, and the solemn judgment of three such distinguished men was, in my mind, all but conclusive. Yet, alas! the village knowledge of war proved as illusive as that of Betsey Ward, when her old man, the immortal A. Ward, was prancing up and down the room, musket in hand, "drilling." The cellar-door being open, a sudden right-about wheel threw him in, nearly breaking his neck. "Are you hurt, deary?" exclaimed Mrs. A. W., running to the hole, and putting her question in the direction of the groans below. "Go away!" shouted Ward; "what do you know about war?" Well, when the war was over our little circle of prophets, or those of them who lived through it, knew more about it than they did when it commenced. They found that mountains were no barrier to cannon, and that "terrible armies with banners" swept past them back and forth with the apparent ease that a pendulum swings in its course.

From near the beginning the Southern soldiers were with us—
squads, companies, and regiments. They were almost always well
behaved. Of course they "scouted," and arrested ultra Union men,
and carried them away from their families, and did many hard and
cruel things; but they did not pillage, or wantonly destroy property,
and they paid for forage and animals in Confederate currency,
which was at first very good money. Looking back at it impartially—
and I pledge myself to try and write the truth—I am constrained to
say that the Southern soldiers, as a mass, at the beginning of the war,
were gentlemen. Even our chickens roosted securely near their
camps. Indeed, for the first year of the war, I do not recall an
instance of theft in our neighborhood by the Southern soldiers. At
first the greater portion of them seemed to have little conception of
the magnitude of the job they had undertaken. They thought the
war would soon be over; that the Yankees would not fight very
much, and all hands could go home before the end of the year.
They conceived it to be more of a frolic than a real war. Indeed,
the Southern troops were ultra sanguine at the beginning, counting
upon a united South and a divided North, and a timid enemy
without taste for war and gunpowder. Occasionally, one wiser than
the rest would shake his head ominously, and say that Southern
independence could only be established after a most desperate and
bloody contest; but such were regarded as men made melancholy
by a cross in love, or an absent sweetheart, far, far away, or the
dyspepsia, or constitutional melancholy. In fine, such gloomy
persons were laughed at.

All the talk about the ability of one Southern man to make
away with five of the enemy, and all the prophecies about the war
as "only a frolic," was ended, in the part of the country where I
was, by the crushing Confederate defeat at Mill Spring, Kentucky,
January 19th, 1862. Here the idol of the Tennesseeans, General
Felix K. Zollicoffer, was killed, and his command put to utter rout.
I was living fully one hundred and fifty miles south of this battle-
field; yet it is a fact that some of the panic-stricken soldiers
stampeded that distance before they got over their fright! I saw
some of them on horses without saddles, both men and animals
having a wild look in the eyes, as if awakened from a terrible dream.
At Knoxville, the fugitives had to be "herded" and guarded.
Some went to that city, some to Chattanooga, and, indeed, they
spread out over the face of the country like frightened cattle.
Perhaps this panic was not equaled in the whole course of the war.
It certainly served the purpose of awakening the Southern soldiers,

in this part of the country, from the dream that "the Yankees" would be easily discouraged and overcome. The whole affair was extremely humiliating to the Confederates. Not only was their army defeated, but utterly routed and broken up, and its com- mander killed. Zollicoffer's death was tragic. At first, the action seemed favorable to the Southern troops, and Zollicoffer advanced at the head of his men. He was in advance, and came upon a Kentucky (Federal) regiment in a piece of woods. The commander of this regiment, Colonel Fry, shot Zollicoffer dead, and his body fell into their hands. This victory was the first considerable Union victory of the war. After that, the magnitude of the conflict dawned upon the people of the western portion of the Confederacy. It was "an eye-opener," and dispelled the delusions they had been cherishing.

A month after, Fort Donelson and Nashville fell, and the Con- federate plans of campaign in the West were all broken up. General John B. Floyd (Secretary of War under Buchanan), who had escaped from Donelson, came through our neighborhood in retreat. The soldiers were much dispirited, and Floyd himself was rather melan- choly. He camped near us two or three days, resting his men on their long retreat. Hearing that there were many Union men in the neighborhood, he sent word for them to come in; that his soldiers should not molest them. Nor did they. The General made a speech to the citizens, explaining how it was that he escaped from Donelson. "I shall never be captured in this war," said he, "for I have a long account to settle with the Yankees, and they can settle it in hell!" The General did not lose heart in the success of the Confederacy; but it was plain, from his remarks, which I heard, that the magnitude of the conflict had dawned upon him at Donelson as it never had before. Some of the Union men would not hear his speech out, but left the room. Floyd was very unpopular among this class of citizens, owing to the wide belief that he had been active in precipitating the Southern States into secession.

It was about the 1st of March that Floyd came through on his way to Chattanooga. In two months—May 1st, 1862—the first "Yankees" appeared in our neighborhood. It was a company of the Tenth Ohio Infantry. A few of them had impressed horses, and came into town as though shot out of a gun. The others fol- lowed on foot, in close order. The more ultra of the Southern people ran away. The Union people were delighted. But their delight was brief, for the soldiers set about indiscriminate robbery. One Union citizen was knocked down in his own house, in the presence of his family, and robbed of four thousand dollars. By the aid of General O. M. Mitchell, he subsequently recovered the most of this money; but the conduct of the soldiers, on this occasion, was a stunning blow to the Union people. It happened that the company were foreigners, and, however valuable they might be as fighters, they had an eye to pillage. They stole more in a few hours than the Southern soldiers, in the same immediate neighborhood, had stolen in the whole course of the war up to that time. This company returned in the direction of Huntsville, Alabama, the same day, and we saw no more Federals for about five weeks. Meantime, the Southern soldiers came in, and from that time until the close of the war the citizens were first treated to one side and then the other. Near the close of 1863, I left that part of the country, and went North; but, having been within both lines and both camps, my opportunities for observing the characteristics of the two armies were excellent. Beside, I had kinsmen and friends in each army operating in that region, and through them I had many inside views of camp life, and opportunities to contrast the traits of each army.

The Union army was altogether the best fed. Early in 1862 the Confederates ceased to have coffee. Indeed, they had not from the first anything like a regular supply. Soon after meat and flour began to grow scarce. But the abundance of coffee which the Federals had was worth several regiments of men to that side. I personally knew of an amusing instance of coffee alone drawing three soldiers into the Federal army. Not far from us lived a family whom I will call Blank—father and two sons. The father was among the first to volunteer in the Southern army and fight for his "rights," although he was utterly impecunious, having no negroes or much of anything else. He was captured, paroled and came home until exchanged. The Federal army came near, and his two sons, then at man's estate, went down to the Union "camp" to see how things looked. They met friends there and were bountifully fed upon crackers and coffee. This last was a luxury which they had long been deprived. They actually enlisted to get plenty of coffee and "grub." When the old man heard of this performance he started for the camp to get his sons out of the "scrape." He got in, got some of that good coffee, and enlisted for the war and fought it through with his two sons! Thus coffee captured recruits. The reader may doubt this story, but I can vouch for its truth. The parties are all yet living, and not long ago I saw the old man, and, indeed, have known him for many years. Through the whole war the superior food of the Union army was a powerful lever upon that side. After the first year the Confederates had little coffee, and their food became very indifferent. In the spring of 1863, I spent two days in the camp of a Confederate cavalry brigade, and their food was simply flour and beef, nothing else. They had not an ounce of salt, and it was not to be got for love or money. They mixed the flour with water, baked it, and roasted the beef on the end of a stick. I could but contrast their style of living with that of the well fed and splendidly equipped Federal army, with their full rations of coffee pork, beef, salt, bread, and beans, and convenient cooking vessels.

In clothing, there was no comparison. The Southern uniform was supposed to be gray, but the soldiers wore homespun of all colors. Of overcoats they had no regular supply Blankets were very scarce. Ditto woolen shirts and socks. The splendid double-thick overcoat which every Federal soldier had was usually warmer than every article of clothing that the Southern soldier had combined. I do not think that the Confederate Government attempted to issue overcoats to their men. At least I never saw any among them that bore resemblance to uniformity. But it was in cavalry equipment that the Federal soldier stood out pre-eminently superior. And over all, he had an oil-cloth blanket which fitted around the neck, keeping the whole person dry, as well as protecting arms and ammunition. Much of the Southern cavalry was ridiculously equipped. In one regiment I have seen four or five different kinds of rifles and shot-guns, all sorts of saddles, some with rope stirrups, many of the saddles without blankets; all sorts of bridles, and in fact a conglomerate get-up fairly laughable. The horses were usually fed on raw corn on the cob. Baled hay, sacked corn, and oats, such as the Union army had, was rather a rarity on the other side. I speak of what fell under my own observation. The stock of the Southern army, horses and mules, never looked as well as that of the Union army. The animals of the two armies could be distinguished even if no men were about. Animals in the Union army were not only better fed, but better attended, better groomed, and cared for. Another point of difference was the superior brightness and cleanliness of the Northern arms. The muskets and bayonets, and brass ornaments upon the ammunition boxes always looked bright and cleanly. In the Southern army there was never this care to keep the guns bright and free from dirt and rust.

The first time I visited a large camp of the Union army, I was struck with the convenience of everything as compared with Southern camps. This was afterward repeatedly verified. The Northern soldiers, although they might be in camp but a few days, would busy themselves constructing beds up off the ground, usually by driving forked sticks, and laying rails and bits of plank across. If in the woods, they utilized small boughs and leaves in preparing beds, and the larger limbs in building shelters from the sun and rain to cook in, etc. Indeed, whenever they went into camp they were as busy as bees arranging for health and comfort. On the other side, the Southerners rarely troubled themselves to provide these little comforts. In camp they were usually idle. The scenes of busy industry, which we always saw in the Northern camp, were never duplicated in the other. And as to filth, the Union camps were almost incomparably cleaner. The difference was amazing, and one could but wonder why there should be this great contrast. In the Southern camp you could hardly go twenty steps without getting into filth of some sort, while in the camp of the other side all deposits of filth were carefully removed out of the way. Much of the sickness which scourged the Southern army, particularly in the early stages of the war, is attributable, no doubt, to the filthy condition of their camps.

The little comforts and conveniences, which the Northern soldiers arranged for themselves in their temporary habitations, was perhaps but a reflex of their home life. One soldier knew how to make himself comfortable in his temporary quarters, and preferred this duty to idleness, while the other preferred to take it easy. There was always a scene of bustling activity about the Federal encampments, very noticeable when compared to the laxity and idleness of the other side.

In the wagon trains of the respective armies there was a great difference. Right here it is proper to say that I speak exclusively of the Western armies, knowing nothing whatever from observation of the Eastern armies. The wagons of the Federals were uniform in size and make, and much stronger and heavier than the wagons of the Confederates; beside, there were more of them. That is, ordinarily, a brigade of Union troops on the march would have about twice as many wagons as a detachment of Confederates of equal size. Confederate army wagons were not uniform in size and build. They usually had the appearance of having been picked up about the country, as well as made to order after several different patterns. The Federal wagons when on the move were covered with canvas, and this was generally kept white and clean, and upon it, in plain black lettering, was the brigade, division, and corps to which the wagon belonged. In a camp of a hundred wagons, a man could pick out the one he wanted, without asking a question, as each was distinctly marked upon both sides of the canvas. Not so with the Confederate wagons. There was among them a lack of uniformity in build, style, and size, and no general attempt was made to designate them by lettering. Also, Federal harness and "gearing," in strength, uniformity, and adaptability was greatly superior to the hastily improvised, and often weak and faulty harness and "gearing," employed with the Confederate teams. Indeed, through the whole transportation department of the Union service there was much more system, order, and business stability than in the same department of the Confederates. From the very shoes upon the mules' feet to the hat on the driver's head, the wagon transportation system of the Federals was superior. There was a strength, uniformity, system, and durability about it that was conspicuous when compared with the rather slip-shod wagon transportation of the Confederates.

One of the most marked differences in the *personnel* of the two armies was the far greater propensity of the Federals to pillage. When the Union troops were around we all had to look out for our money, jewels, watches, vegetables, pigs, cows, and chickens. All the men, of course, would not pillage, but there were always some in each regiment who laid hold of everything they could steal, whether of much use to them or not. And much of that which was of no earthly use they sometimes wantonly destroyed. I had in my charge a small building filled with articles usually kept in a country store. This they repeatedly broke into, carrying off what they chose and destroying what they did not want. They kindled a fire in the fireplace, and burned up several pairs of hames worth two dollars and a half a pair —using them for firewood. A hundred or two bibles, belonging to the American Bible Society, they tore up and scattered about the floor, or made fires of them. Such utter and wicked waste I had not thought human beings could be guilty of. No unoccupied building was exempt from their ravages, and few that were occupied. No amount of fastenings could protect a building from the insatiate ravages of the pillagers. Nothing was too sacred to be stolen or destroyed, and it was almost impossible to secrete anything from their search. Money buried was dug up and appropriated; valuables hidden in the most unheard-of places were searched out. A neighbor put a ham of meat in a writing-desk, but it was found. Another secreted a sum of gold under his house, but the "fresh dirt" betrayed it, and they took it. We had some money and jewelry which we thought would be safest in a cupboard in the sitting-room. It happened that all the family went into another room for about three minutes, and hearing footsteps came hastily back, but the cupboard was broken open and the valuables gone. Some of General Turchin's men committed this robbery, and I made every effort to recover; but it was no use. Seldom was a valuable recovered when once the pillagers got hold of it. Not all the soldiers would do this; perhaps not one in fifty were robbers, but there were robbers in every regiment. When the Federal army first came among us we had about sixty chickens, and every night we would hear the "squak! squak!" of the fowls as they were hurried away to the soldiers' mess-kettles. An old rooster that had been with us for four years we imagined would be rather tough eating, and I remember that I rather enjoyed hearing his "squak! squak!" which grew fainter and fainter, as the soldiers ran away with him. I knew that they had a tough dose, and that unless the rebellion held out pretty well it would be over before they could get him cooked to a point that his tough ligaments and muscles could be masticated. At last all of our chickens were gone but one. An old hen, solitary and alone, occupied the roost. We thought we would save her for a "nest egg," as it were, until the cruel war was over. We put her in the cellar. A kitchen stood over this cellar. That night was dark and stormy. Two soldiers came, saying that they were separated from their regiment, could not find it in the darkness, and begged that they might sleep on the floor in the kitchen, anywhere, to be out of the storm. We gave them permission. Early in the morning they were gone, taking with them our last old hen.

The remarkable difference in the pillaging propensities of the two armies may be accounted for on the ground, first, that the Federal army was in an enemy's country, and all things were considered legitimate game, and little inquiry made whether or not the owners were Union people. Second, the foreign element in the Federal army was very large, and with them was the riff-raff from the large cities, who entered the army more from motives of pillage than patriotism. Regiments raised in cities were always more troublesome as pillagers than those from the rural districts. In the Southern army these conditions did not exist. There were no enlistments in that army prompted by motives of invasion and pillage. And there were few large cities to send out "wharf rats," roughs, and pickpockets into the army. Beside, the foreign element in the Southern army was very small. And for this reason, I doubt if the whole Southern army had been poured into the North, that the robbery and pillage would have been as great as that which marked the course of the Federal army in the South. The *personnel* of the two armies differed widely in the points above-mentioned. The pillagers and robbers in the Federal army did not spare the Union people. The first who came to our neighborhood committed several outrageous robberies, and it happened that the victims in every instance were Union men. This had an unhappy effect, one of the victims, at least, thereafter transferring his sympathies from the Union side to the Confederate, on account of his ill-treatment. The outrages, robberies, and pillaging which took place wherever the Union army moved, is traceable to a small minority of the soldiers, and almost invariably to the foreign element among them, enlisted in the large cities. The officers used to say in explanation that every flock had black sheep, and that a thousand men, picked up promiscuously, would always contain a few desperate characters, who went from motives of plunder. This is no doubt true, but the bummer element in the Union army was certainly larger than in the other. I have known regiments of Southern troops to encamp around premises for weeks, and not even rob a hen-roost; but when the other side came, then chickens and all other movable property, animate and inanimate, had to be under the eye of its owner, and often this did not protect it.

The Confederates usually paid for what they took for the use of the army in Confederate money. Indeed, payment was the rule seldom violated. The Federals, when upon organized foraging ex-peditions, usually gave receipts for what they took, which were payable upon proof of loyalty, on the part of the claimant. But it was from the foraging of irresponsible soldiers, without an officer, that the people mostly suffered. Often in our neighborhood would they kill a fine cow, for instance, take a quarter, or what they could conveniently carry, and leave the rest to waste. In fact, every living animal fit for food was in constant danger from irresponsible Federal foragers and stragglers. When men are hungry, they must eat, and eat they would, when they could get anything, whether Union or Secession; but the Union soldiers were by far the most inveterate, wasteful and reckless foragers. The farmers and country people, who traded in the camps of both armies, had to skin their eyes when in the camp of the "Yankees," as they called them. A farmer of my acquaintance took a barrel of cider into a Union camp near by. The barrel held forty gallons. He had sold about twenty quarts, at twenty cents a quart, when, to his intense amazement, the barrel was empty! Come to investigate, he found that the soldiers had bored up through the wagon-bed, and into the barrel, and slyly but rapidly drawn the contents into their canteens! Another farmer had a very large sack of peaches upon a mule, which he led. By a sly, quick motion a soldier cut the string, and away went the peaches over the ground and the soldiers after them. The farmer came home without a cent, saying that "them Yankees" were the d—dest sharpest folks in a trade he ever heard of! Another farmer lost nearly all of a wagon-load of apples by a very simple process. Two soldiers engaged him in violent "argument" upon theology, while a whole regiment swarmed around the rear of the wagon, and stole the most of the apples before the hard-shell Baptist, who was attempting to peddle them, knew what was going on—or rather off. He came home offering to bet that the Yankees could steal the shortening out of a gingercake without breaking the crust. Another dealer had a barrel of brandy, which he put into the depot over night, with other military stores which were guarded. Surely, he thought, that brandy is safe. In the morning he found the barrel just where he had left it, but it was wonderfully light! In the night, the soldiers had crawled under the floor, bored up through and into the barrel, and drained the last drop into their canteens. The owner joined the apple pedler in the opinion that the irrepressible Yankees could take the shortening out of a gingercake without breaking the crust.

Both armies had a weakness for vegetables. The regulation diet not embracing them to any great extent, this mania for vegetables, and particularly for potatoes, is accounted for. But the Southern soldiers very rarely entered gardens, and took without permission. The others did, or many did. And in this I noticed that the pillagers in the Union army were the few, and not the many. We had quite a lot of Irish potatoes in the garden, and where one Federal soldier slipped over the fence and stole them, ten would come to the front door and ask for them, or offer to buy. Yet the one in ten, or even one in twenty, gave the whole army a bad name. The Union soldiers did a thriving business with the country people, swapping off coffee and salt for potatoes and vegetables. They had an abundance of coffee, while within the Confederate lines there was scarcely any. Even the pickets of the two armies used to exchange papers and coffee for tobacco. The Confederates had an abundance of tobacco, but no coffee, while the Union troops had coffee, but tobacco was scarce. For some time the Tennessee river, near us, was the line. It was nothing unusual for the soldiers to swim across to each other and make exchanges of coffee, tobacco, and papers. And in all these transactions I never knew an instance of bad faith on either side.

The discipline in the Union army, in many respects, appeared to be best. That is, there was less insubordination and more respect for officers. There was stronger individuality about the Southern soldier, and he was far more apt to "talk back" to his superior than were the Federals. Frequently have I seen Southern soldiers splitting the mud with their feet and the air with oaths, as they pranced up and down the streets, promising to "get even" with such and such an officer when the war was over and all were on an equality again. "Just wait until this thing is over, and I can give him a fair fight," was about the way the case was put. But I have not heard of the settlement of any of these momentous difficulties since the surrender. Among Southern officers of lower rank there always seemed to me to be more ill-feeling for certain of their superiors, and lack of confidence, than I ever had an opportunity of noticing on the other side. But jealousies and bickerings are common to all humanity, only it did seem to me there were more of it in the Southern army than the other; and, too, more disposition to saddle the responsibility of disaster upon the shoulders of their commanders. I may have mentioned that it used to seem to me that the Southern troops were more liable to "panics" and stampedes than the others. This may be because I happened to have personal knowledge of three "panics" among Southern soldiers, and never chanced to witness anything of the sort on the other side. The Federals always appeared to me to be more self-possessed and cooler in the hour of danger, and I have seen them in some trying situations. The "panics" among the Southern troops that I happened to know of, from seeing some of the fugitives, was the famous Fishing creek panic, the Battle creek panic, and the Bridgeport panic. The Battle creek affair was very ridiculous. Two cavalry regiments were camped near us. Hearing there were some "Yankees" near the head of Battle creek they sallied forth in the early morning to scoop them up. They went out in fine style, and in the best of spirits. The commander, I believe, was Colonel Adams. Late in the afternoon a few cavalry came dashing through the town, bareheaded and covered with mud "Get out of the way!" they cried; "the Yankees are right behind us! We are all cut to pieces!" And on they went. Soon more came, and then the whole command, riding rapidly, some bareheaded, and all in a hurry, and apparently badly scared. Before dark they were all through, and left us in momentary expectation of seeing the victorious Federals. They did not get along, however, until noon next day. Come to get at the truth of the matter, the advance of the cavalry had been fired into and "seen" more Yankees than they expected, whereupon a "panic" seized the whole command and they fled most ingloriously and ridiculously. Yet they were good soldiers. They simply "took a panic." Only one man was killed, and he from the fall of his horse. The Bridgeport panic was equally ridiculous, some of Ledbetter's men on that occasion actually crowding one another off the bridge into the river in their fright. Had the Federal commander ran his cannon around to the hill on the upper side of the bridge, and which fully commanded it, he could have bagged the whole lot. The nearest approach to a panic I ever saw among the Union troops was in October, 1863, when Wheeler's cavalry got in behind the lines and burned a train of five hundred loaded wagons at Anderson's, in Seynatchie valley. Yet the panic was among the teamsters, and this was perhaps justifiable. The squads of Federal cavalry from all directions started right out after the enemy instead of away from them.

The Federal cavalry made the best appearance, owing to their uniform, better equipment, and better fed horses; but at first, certainly the Southerners were altogether the best riders. I have seen some of the Texas cavalry perform feats almost incredible, such as riding at full gallop, leaning over toward the ground, picking up a stone and throwing it, and dropping hats on the ground and coming back at full gallop and picking them up without the least abatement in speed. Inspired by such as this, and the consciousness of perfect horsemanship, the Southerners at first underrated the Northern cavalry, but soon after learned to respect this branch of the service. I remember reading in a Southern paper a ridiculous account of what was to be expected from "Yankee tailors and shoemakers on horse." The sequel was not quite so cheerful." At the beginning the Southern cavalry was no doubt superior; but toward the close it is a question if the superiority did not shift to the other side, mainly owing to the excellent equipments of this branch of the Union service. The superiority of Federal cavalry equipment has been more fully mentioned in another place. Gradually their skill in horsemanship equaled their equipment, and then the Union cavalry became of extraordinary efficiency.

For about a year and a half, one end of the Nashville and Chattanooga road was in possession of one army, and the other end held by the other. They "see-sawed" up and down its line, raided upon it, and fought over every inch of it. So far as each side could hold possession, they erected "stockades" at the important stations and bridges to protect them from raids. These stockades were usually made of oak logs, set endwise in the ground, covered with like heavy timber, and with loop-holes for defense. Without artillery, they could hardly be reduced. The superiority of the stockades built by the Union troops, over those built by the Confederates on the same line of road, was striking. The Union troops bestowed an immense amount of labor on theirs, making them of square timber, massive, and enduring, and perfect in every particular, while those put up by the Confederates were feeble and ridiculous imitations, showing not one-tenth of the labor and skill that the Federals bestowed upon theirs. These little stockades were, to my mind, significant illustrations of the characteristics of the two armies. What the Northern troops built was of an enduring and substantial character, and constructed with the highest skill, while Southern works of the same character were loosely thrown together, with little skill and less labor, negroes usually being put to such service. In the construction of hospitals and warehouses the same difference was noticeable. Confederate buildings, no matter for what purpose to be employed, were slovenly built, showing little skill and great economy of labor, and little display of the "knack" of making them convenient. The "public works" of the Confederates were about as short-lived as the Confederacy itself.

War horrors predominated in our neighborhood; but the humorous side was not altogether lacking. A brigade, one day, camped around the premises of a neighbor of ours. He was sitting on the fence (for the purpose, as he said, of saving one rail at least), contemplating the destruction going on all around. One soldier was killing a calf, another was after the pigs, another was milking the cows, hundreds were burning rails, others were taking off the well bucket and rope, some were digging for "hidden treasures," and, altogether, the scene was rather lively. Our neighbor looked for some time, saying nothing, doubtless from inability to do the subject justice, when he broke out: "Gentlemen, if I live through this war, I shall never fear hell!" When Bragg retreated from Tullahoma, a large part of his army passed through our neighborhood. The soldiers were much discouraged. Within a few months, they had retreated all the way from before Nashville—about one hundred and thirty miles—and, in all that time, they declared they had not been whipped. "It's bad enough to run when we are whipped," said one of the soldiers; "d—n this way of beating the Yankees and then running away from them!" I asked one of the officers, an acquaintance, to what point they were retreating. "To Cuba," he replied, sharply, "if old Bragg can get a bridge built across from Florida!" On the same retreat, a couple of soldiers stopped at a house near us,

24

and proposed to swap horses, as theirs were worn out. Our neighbor trotted out two, and offered them a bargain. One of his horses, however, had a very white head and face. "That one won't do," said one of the soldiers; "the enemy could see that face a mile." "No," said the other soldier, quickly, "that's no objection; for the other end of Bragg's cavalry is always toward the Yankees!" So they took the white-faced horse and went on, satisfied that the rear only would point toward the enemy during the remainder of the war. This happened just as I have related it, and shows something of the spirit of Bragg's army on the famous retreat from Tullahoma.

When General John B. Floyd retreated from Fort Donelson to Chattanooga, he passed near us, and made a speech to the people of the neighborhood, as I have before related, in which he said that he would "never be taken alive by the Yankees, that he had a long settlement to make with them, which they might settle in h——l." I was telling a Federal soldier of this, an Irishman, when he broke out: "That's all right—we'll be ripresented thar, too!" A lady living near us, hearing that the Federal army was coming, took some corn to the side of the mountain, buried it, and covered the spot with leaves. A few days after a blue coat appeared at the door. "Madam," said he, "I found some corn on the side of the mountain, which I am told is yours. I came to tell you that you should hide it better, as our boys will get it!" Another neighbor, having lost all his bacon but one large "middling," hid that in his writing-desk. A squad of cavalry officers swooped down upon him, searched his house, and found the bacon. Said one soldier to another: "Ain't it a pity we're in such a hurry, we can't stop to cook and eat this bacon?" They thought it very sad, indeed, that they should find such a treasure, and not be able to make immediate use of it. Another neighbor had two wagon loads of bacon when the Federal advance was near. He hustled one load across the Tennessee river in a hurry, and came back for the other. When he returned to the south side of the river again, he found that the Southern troops had eaten the last morsel of his first load, and were lying in wait for the second. He broke down completely. "It's just no use," he said, "to try to save anything in this war." One day a squad of Federal cavalry were searching the house of a neighbor for plunder. They threw the beds on the floor, emptied the contents of the trunks out, climbed up into the garret, and upset things generally in their mad chase for hidden treasures. While one of the soldiers was up to his elbows in the sacred contents of a trunk, he said to the owner, who stood near, pale and trembling, "What sort of a man is Dr. B. ?" referring to a physician of the neighbor-hood. "Why, sir, he is a gentleman," was the reply. "Oh, *that* don't signify anything," said the pillager. "*I'm* a gentleman; I meant what is his politics?" Our neighbor, although badly fright-ened, could not help laughing at the pillager's opinion of what constituted a gentleman.

The Confederates were fierce in their pursuit of conscripts. All able-bodied men, between the ages of eighteen and forty-five, were held to military service, and those who did not enter volun-tarily were caught, if possible, and put in. To prevent this the Union men, who had not left the country, used to hide out in the woods and mountains. A gentleman of my acquaintance, hearing that the conscript officers were to make a raid in his neighborhood on a certain night, went into the woods. It was pitch dark, and he wandered about until he came to a tree top. He crawled into that, and went to sleep. In the morning he found that the tree top was in the centre of the road by which the conscript officers would approach! The position was about the most dangerous he could have selected in the whole neighborhood. Two other men went far up the side of the mountain, built a fire, and went to sleep. The fire could be plainly seen from town, and the conscript officers went to it and bagged their men. Two others hid in a cave, and built a fire, feeling great security. The heat from the fire loosened the rocks above, which fell down, breaking a leg for each of the men. They crawled out, and gave themselves up, saying that they might as well go to war at once as to have their legs snapped off in that style.

I could write much of the humors of the war, but these few anecdotes will show to the reader that, horrible as war is, it has its comical and ridiculous features.

THE UNION CAVALRY AT GETTYSBURG.

BY MAJOR GENERAL D. M'M. GREGG.

IN considering the importance of the part taken by the cavalry of the Army of the Potomac, in the Gettysburg campaign, it will not be amiss to refer briefly to the circumstances under which the volunteer cavalry was organized, and the difficulties and hindrances which were met, and had to be overcome, in bringing it to the high state of efficiency that characterized it at the opening of that campaign. During the fall of 1861, and the winter following, there had been established in camps about Washington, regiments of men with horses, intended for the volunteer cavalry service. These regiments had been formed hastily by uniting companies of men from different parts of the same State, and after this the organization was completed by the appointment of the field officers by the Governor of the State. Naturally enough, very many improper appointments were made, and the result was the failure of many of the regiments to make any progress in preparing themselves for the duties of cavalry in the field. The absence or laxity of discipline, inattention to police and sanitary regulations, ignorance of their duties on the part of officers, and dissensions producing discontent and insubordination (growing out of the claims of rival candidates for appointments), unfortunately obstructed too many of the regiments. In some instances, the colonels were aged men of local influence, whose patriotic zeal, associated with an imagined dash of character, led them to enter an arm of service, the fatigues and hardships of which compelled an early return to their homes; in others, they were men who had been selected for any other reason than even their supposed fitness to command, and these, by their incapacity or unwillingness to learn their duties, fell under the contempt of their commanders. The enlisted men were the very best material, and these furnished non-commissioned officers of intelligence and peculiar fitness for their offices. Of the company officers, many had been wisely chosen, and were willing to both learn and practice their duties.

The condition of the horses in many of the camps was as bad as possible. Of these, many when received were totally unfit for cavalry service, having been taken without inspection by competent examiners, from dishonest contractors, or from government corrals, superintended by dishonest examiners. With some exceptions, whatever care was given the horses, was at such times as best suited the convenience of the individual trooper, and as the horses generally stood in mud to their knees, unless their masters were prompted by exceptionally humane feelings, the intervals between feedings and waterings were distressingly long. In many of the regiments, when their condition was the worst possible, the well-intentioned subordinate officers and enlisted men asked the War Department or their State authorities to detail young, but experienced, officers of the regular cavalry, or the appointment of civilians who had served in European armies, to command their regiments. This was done; and the officers so selected, on taking command, were from the first encouraged by the hearty spirit in which officers and enlisted men entered into the work of reform and improvement. Schools for instruction in tactics and in the rules and articles of war were established; officers, as well as enlisted men, were drilled in the school of the squad and upward, the camps were changed, better police and sanitary regulations enforced, strict discipline maintained, inefficient officers were discharged by the examining board, and their vacancies given deserving non-commissioned officers.

When the Army of the Potomac moved, in the spring of 1862, to the Peninsula, it was accompanied by a cavalry force, the volunteer regiments of which were in a surprising state of serviceability, considering the short time and the unfavorable circumstances under which their real organization had been effected. The regular regiments were in their habitual state of efficiency. During this campaign the cavalry won for itself no particular distinction. The volunteer regiments were distributed among the different corps of the army; the country was very generally heavily wooded, or covered the with dense undergrowth; the armies were in close proximity, and ordinarily intrenched; the space between the lines obstructed by felled timber, and the roads barricaded, and, for the greater part of the time, impassable, because of the almost unfathomable mud. There was no proper field for cavalry operations, and if there had been, nothing could have been done; for, while it was the fashion to sneer at the cavalry, there was a remarkable fondness displayed at corps, division, and brigade headquarters of infantry for the presence of numerous and well-mounted orderlies; details for this ornamental and often menial duty, and those for the most grossly absurd picket and escort duty, absorbed pretty much the entire cavalry.

Returning from the Peninsula, the cavalry disembarked at Alexandria, in condition very unfitted for the hard service that was expected of it in the Maryland campaign of the fall of 1862. But little improvement was made, and, with some noted exceptions, nothing strikingly brilliant was accomplished by it until General Hooker took command of the Army of the Potomac. Then it was at last thought that the cavalry, properly organized and taken care of, and employed in legitimate duty, might become an important element of that grand army. The rebel cavalry under Stuart, and his lieutenants, the younger Lees, had from the onset been very efficient. It was composed of the best blood of the South—officers and enlisted men had been accustomed all their lives to the use of fire-arms, and were well practiced in horsemanship. Its strength had not been frittered away in petty details, but preserved for the heavy blows which it, from time to time, inflicted on our lines of communication, and means of transportation.

General Hooker organized his cavalry into a corps, commanded by General Stoneman, the division commanders being Generals Pleasonton, Buford, Averill, and D. McM. Gregg. Soon after this organization was made, the cavalry, save a part detained to take part in the battle of Chancellorsville (where it did distinguished service), left the lines of the army on what is known as the Stoneman raid. Without considering at all the material results of that raid, which, if not so great as expected, were lessened by the adverse issue of the battle in which our army engaged at Chancellorsville, its moral result was to convince the cavalry engaged in it of its ability to do whatever might thereafter be required when employed in its proper sphere. General Pleasonton now succeeded to the command of the corps, and the work of preparation for future campaigns went forward with the greatest enthusiasm and zeal. To this time, for the reasons heretofore given, the prestige of success had steadily remained with the rebel cavalry in its greater and more important undertakings, but the time was now at hand for its transfer to our side, there to remain to the close of the war, not, however, without our enemy making, at all times and places, the most desperate and gallant efforts to win it back.

In the early part of June, 1863, the rebel cavalry corps was assembled about Brandy Station, and in front of that point on the Rappahannock river. There had been reviews and inspections preparatory to making some great movement; this was suspected to be northward, and not directly against the forces confronting on the river. The strength of Stuart's command at this time was subsequently ascertained to have been about twelve thousand horsemen, divided into five brigades, with sixteen pieces of light artillery. Had this force gotten off undiscovered, and reached Pennsylvania without having fought the battle of Brandy Station, and subsequently been defeated at Aldie, Middleburg, and Upperville, the fertile valleys, busy towns, and wealthy cities of our beloved State would have been devastated to an extent beyond ordinary estimate. But this was not to be. On Saturday and Sunday, June 6th and 7th, General Pleasonton assembled his corps about Warrenton Junction and Catlett's Station, rations, forage, and ammunition were issued, and every trooper was put in the best possible condition for a ceremonious visit to our neighbors opposite. On Monday evening, General John Buford, with his two brigades and light batteries, and a small supporting column of infantry, moved to the vicinity of Beverly Ford, and General Gregg, with his own and Colonel Duffie's divisions, and light batteries, moved to Kelly's Ford, six miles below, and here was found another small column of infantry. The strength of these two commands was about nine thousand cavalry.

At daylight, on Tuesday, June 9th, General Buford, with his regular and volunteer brigades crossed the Rappahannock at Beverly Ford and surprised the enemy's pickets, driving them back upon their camps and intrenchments, and maintained for hours a most obstinate fight with a force largely superior to his own. His advance was through a rough, wooded country, which afforded the enemy every defensive advantage, but his regiments, led by such soldiers as Colonel Davis, of the Eighth New York (killed in the action), Major Morris, of the Sixth Pennsylvania, and Captain Merritt, of the Second Regulars, and others of like character, were not to be stopped by ordinary resistance; and by their repeated mounted charges, and advances as dismounted skirmishers, the enemy was driven back to a line strongly held by a large number of field-pieces supported by troops.

General Gregg, with his own and Colonel Dufie's command,

crossed at the same time at Kelly's Ford. Agreeably to orders from the corps commander, Colonel Dufie proceeded at once to Stevensburg to take position, while Gregg marched directly upon Brandy Station, which, owing to the number of miles to be marched and obstructions met in the roads, he did not reach until some hours after Buford's attack had been made. Upon an open plain, his brigades, led by Colonels Kilpatrick and Wyndham, fell upon the enemy so furiously that General Stuart's headquarters were captured. There were no reserves, but at once the entire command charged the enemy, and here, at last, were two forces of cavalry, on favorable ground, all mounted, struggling for victory with sabre and pistol. Brigade met brigade, and the blue and the gray met in hand-to-hand strife, and many gallant horsemen went down that day on a field whose glories have not often been surpassed. Moving on a short interior line, the mass of the rebel mounted force was speedily concentrated at the point of danger, so as to give it largely the preponderance in numbers. Dufie's command, at Stevensburg, having encountered there some of the enemy, could not be gotten on the field in time to take part in the engagement; still the contest was maintained until the arrival of rebel infantry from Culpepper; after this a junction was made by the two divisions, and toward evening, leisurely and unmolested, all recrossed the Rappahannock.

The object of the reconnoissance had been fully accomplished —the numbers, position, and intentions of the enemy fully discovered. On the morrow this cavalry giant was to have marched for Pennsylvania. No further objection was offered to his departure, as we felt sure his stature was somewhat shortened, and his gait would show a limp. Our total loss in killed, wounded, and a small number of prisoners, was about five hundred; the enemy's, from reports published in the Richmond papers, greater. The result of this engagement created the greatest enthusiasm in our regiments; the virtues of those who fell were fondly told by their surviving comrades, and acts of conspicuous gallantry and daring were applauded and remembered for imitation on other fields. Even now, when there is a meeting of any of those who fought at Brandy Station, and the talk falls upon the fight, the pulse quickens and the eye brightens as the story is repeated.

Our cavalry was again reorganized in two divisions, commanded respectively by Generals John Buford and D. McM. Gregg, and to each division were attached two light batteries. Everything necessary was done in preparation for an active campaign. The division formerly commanded by General Averill (who had been transferred to another field) was consolidated with Gregg's, and the new division was named the second; an additional brigade was formed in it, commanded by Colonel I. Irvin Gregg, the other two being commanded respectively by General Kilpatrick and Colonel McIntosh. The two divisions were soon put in motion toward the Potomac, but did not take exactly the same route, and the Army of the Potomac followed their lead. The major part of the rebel army, having moved in advance, entered the Shenandoah Valley by the passes of the Blue Ridge, either for the purpose of masking the movements of the rebel infantry, or else to discover the whereabouts of and to impede the march of our army. The advance of Stuart's command had reached Aldie, and here, on June 17th, began a series of skirmishes, or engagements, between the two cavalry forces, all of which were decided successes for us, and terminated in driving Stuart's cavalry through the gap at Paris.

On June 17th, Kilpatrick's Brigade, moving in the advance of the Second Division, fell upon the enemy at Aldie, and there ensued an engagement of the most obstinate character, in which several brilliant mounted charges were made, terminating in the retreat of the enemy. On June 19th, the division advanced to Middleburg, where a part of Stuart's force was posted, and was attacked by Colonel Irvin Gregg's Brigade. Here, as at Aldie, the fight was very obstinate. The enemy had carefully selected a most defensible position, from which he had to be driven step by step, and this work had to be done by dismounted skirmishers, owing to the unfavorable character of the country for mounted service. On the 19th, Gregg's Division moved on the turnpike from Middleburg in the direction of Upperville, and soon encountered the enemy's cavalry in great force. The attack was promptly made, the enemy offering the most stubborn resistance. The long lines of stone fences which are so common in that region, were so many lines of defense to a force in retreat; these could be held until our advancing skirmishers were almost upon them, but then there would be no escape for those behind—it was either to surrender as prisoners or to attempt to escape across the open fields beyond, to fall before the deadly fire of the carbines of the pursuers. Later in the day, General Buford's Division came in on the right and took the enemy in flank; then our entire force, under General Pleasonton, and supported by a column of infantry, moved forward and dealt the finishing blow. Through Upperville the pursuit was continued at a run, the enemy flying in the greatest confusion; nor were they permitted to re-form, until night put a stop to further pursuit at the mouth of the gap.

Our losses in the fighting of these three days amounted to five hundred in killed, wounded, and missing; of the latter, there were but few. The enemy's loss was much greater, particularly in prisoners. Our captures also included light guns, flags, and small-arms.

The Army of the Potomac, moving in pursuit of Lee, was required to protect itself on one side from any possible attack of the enemy, and to extend its protection, on the other side, to Washington. These successful engagements of our cavalry left our infantry free to march, without the loss of an hour, to the field of Gettysburg, where the Army of the Potomac was destined to deliver the blow which, more than any other, was to determine the issue of the rebellion.

The limits of this article will forbid following our divisions of cavalry on their marches to Gettysburg. It must be mentioned that at Frederick, Maryland, the addition of the cavalry formerly commanded by General Stahl, made it necessary to organize a third division, the command of which was given to General Kilpatrick. General Buford, with his division, in advance of our army, on July 1st, first encountered the enemy in the vicinity of Gettysburg. How well his brigades of regulars and volunteers resisted the advance of that invading host, yielding only foot by foot, and so slowly as to give ample time for our infantry to go to his support, is well known to every one familiar with the history of the great battle. General Kilpatrick's division marched from Frederick well to the right, at Hanover engaged the enemy's cavalry in a sharp skirmish, and reached Gettysburg on the 1st, and on the left of our line, on the 3d, one of his brigades, led by General Farnsworth, gallantly charged the enemy's infantry, even to his line of defenses, and protected that flank from any attack, with the assistance of General Merritt's regular brigade. General Gregg's Division, having crossed the Potomac at Edwards' Ferry, in rear of our army, passed through Frederick, and, on the afternoon of July 1st, was at Hanover Junction, and reached Gettysburg on the morning of the 2d, taking position on the right of our line. On the 3d, during that terrific fire of artillery, which preceded the gallant but unsuccessful assault of Pickett's Division on our line, it was discovered that Stuart's cavalry was moving to our right, with the evident intention of passing to the rear, to make a simultaneous attack there. What the consequence of the success of this movement would have been, the merest tyro in the art of war will understand. When opposite our right, Stuart was met by General Gregg, with two of his brigades (Colonels McIntosh and Irvin Gregg), and Custer's Brigade of the Third

Division, and, on a fair field, there was another trial between two cavalry forces, in which most of the fighting was done in the saddle, and with the trooper's favorite weapon—the sabre. Without entering into the details of the fight, it need only be added, that Stuart advanced not a pace beyond where he was met; but after a severe struggle, which was only terminated by the darkness of night, he withdrew, and on the morrow, with the defeated army of Lee, was in retreat to the Potomac.

Thus has been outlined the services of the cavalry of the Army of the Potomac, during the Gettysburg campaign. No period of its history is more glorious, nor more fondly dwelt upon by those who were for a long time identified with the cavalry arm. Whatever credit its services deserve, must be fully shared by the light batteries of the regular service, and Martin's New York Volunteer Battery, which were attached to the divisions, and rendered such service as could only result from perfect discipline and the highest professional skill and training.

A RUSE OF WAR.

BY CAPTAIN JOHN SCOTT.

WHEN General Butler landed at City Point and Bermuda Hundreds, in the spring of 1864, with an army of thirty thousand men, and accompanied and guarded by gunboats and iron-clads, why he did not at once occupy Petersburg, to obtain which afterward cost so much blood to the Federal army, is a question, the answer to which is not very obvious. Petersburg, on the line of the railway leading south from Richmond, the heart of the Southern Confederacy was distant twenty miles from City Point, with which it was connected by a railway, a navigable river, and a broad highway in good condition, and passing through a level country not occupied by the military forces of the enemy. I propose to furnish what I thought then, and think now, to be an answer to this question. It will be a modicum of information, which may prove useful to the historian, when he comes to gather up all the facts for an impartial history of the four years' war, which has left scars even on the Constitution. It will, moreover, be doing justice to the memory of Major General George E. Pickett, a distinguished officer of the Southern army, whose reputation is dear to us all of the South.

To render my brief narrative intelligible to the reader not particularly informed of the military facts to which it has reference, it will be necessary first to state the situation in the Department of North Carolina with which Petersburg was embraced, or so much of it as affected that point. General Pickett was still in command at Petersburg, though he had been relieved, when General Butler, with

(380)

his large army, suddenly occupied City Point. His troops were engaged in an expedition to North Carolina, with the exception of a single regiment of infantry belonging to Clingman's Brigade, not more than five or six hundred strong; nor had the troops of General Beauregard, who had succeeded to the command of the department, yet arrived. The strong defenses of the town were unoccupied. It was only necessary for the Federal commander to send up a detachment of his army to occupy them, and cut the communications of Richmond with the South, the seat of its principal resources. Why so vital a point as Petersburg at that time was, should have been left unguarded, and its defenses sent off in search of objects of secondary importance, I do not know. The biographer of General Pickett, Colonel Walter Harrison, states, in his interesting volume, that General Pickett, as early as the preceding November, had penetrated the enemy's design to make an expedition up James river against Petersburg, and, in a personal interview with the Confederate authorities, had represented this contingency and the unprotected state of that town. He had even carried his representations to General Lee, who had referred him to General Beauregard, with whom, in consequence, he had had an interview at Weldon. "But," says Colonel Harrison, "the expedition to Plymouth was at this time put on foot; much valuable time was wasted, and the troops which should have been ordered at once to Petersburg were kept in North Carolina doing little or nothing, while Pickett was left in Petersburg with merely a handful of men." Colonel Harrison continues: "General Beauregard was in no way responsible for this. He had no control over these troops, and I have understood strongly urged their being hastened to Petersburg to support Pickett." But the danger to Petersburg, from the direction of the lower James, was apparent to others beside General Pickett. A gentleman of Petersburg had, but a short time before the arrival of General Butler, pointed out to me on one of the military maps of the day that Bermuda Hundreds would probably be the point which the enemy would next strike. The eyes, which should have seen everything, appear to have been alone blinded to this vulnerable point.

Not long before the occurrences of these events I had been ordered to report for duty to General Pickett, whom I found in Petersburg. As the town was vacant of soldiers, I employed the leisure in examining its fortifications, and in other ways that pleased me. I was in my quarters early in the day, when I was suddenly summoned to report to General Pickett. I found everything astir, and he informed me of the occupation of City Point by the forces commanded by General Butler. He told me I was the only cavalry officer on the ground, and that he wished me to take a party of cavalry to reconnoitre Butler's position, to remain in the vicinity of his outposts, and, if possible, induce the belief that I commanded but an advance body of troops, and that he might soon expect an attack. But that, in truth, he had no troops with which to defend Petersburg, and that the place would be captured unless General Butler could be amused with this false opinion, until Beauregard could arrive from the South. I inquired where I should find my cavalry command. He told me that he had none, but that he would exert himself to get together a body of mounted citizens, and that with these I must perform that duty. With characteristic energy he set about to improvise such a command as he had described, and in that chivalrous community it was not long before I found myself at the head of a body of thirty mounted citizens, armed with such weapons as each man could obtain. My most serious difficulty was in procuring a horse for my own use. But I succeeded in buying a very fine one, for which I had to pay a price large even in the depreciated currency of the war. One cavalryman who had been at home on a furlough, was the only enlisted soldier who joined me, and the only one who was killed on this tour of duty. As we passed beyond the limits of Petersburg, on the City Point road, we saw encamped on our right the regiment of North Carolina infantry, as if thrown forward to engage General Butler, and what guns we had were mounted on the fortifications on that side. It was evident that our brave commander was not dismayed, and that he was ready to use every available force at his disposal.

Toward the close of the day we came in view of the enemy's outposts, and at once began the work of observation, taking care to make as great display of our force as possible, but when night closed in we retired to the rear. These tactics were repeated the next day, and the next. There was a barn which stood outside the Federal lines, equi-distant between us, which contained a supply of forage. The Federals would occupy it by day, but would be withdrawn at night, when my men would visit it to procure food for their animals. When we first came in sight of the enemy's pickets, General Roger A. Pryor, now a brilliant advocate of the New York bar, who was at that time in Petersburg, and had joined us as a volunteer, was very solicitous that we should engage them. But I would not allow it to be done. I did not explain to him General Pickett's orders, and he retired from what appeared to be so purposely and inglorious a service. A collision with my loose array I knew might spoil the

A RUSE OF WAR.

plan, and disclose the sham we were attempting to impose on the enemy. Thus things continued till the third or fourth day, when a reconnoissance in force, preceded by a line of skirmishers, issued from the Federal lines, and advanced on the Petersburg road. I was informed at that time by a gentleman, a resident of the neighborhood, that some colored troops had visited in the vicinity of their camp, and had been told by the negroes of the insignificant nature of my force, and the true condition of affairs, and this reconnoissance had been sent to find out the truth. My men had been broken into several small parties, and scattered along the enemy's front. With one of them I fell back before the skirmishers until we reached the point at which the railway and the highway crossed. There I halted my party and allowed the skirmishers to approach near, the consequence of which was that my horse was fatally wounded in the head. But I was soon mounted on another and resumed the retreat. While we were passing through a body of woods, or rather as we were emerging from it, it was discovered that a detachment of cavalry had been thrown in advance of the skirmishers, and were making a dash at us. A hot chase ensued, but we passed safely into the Southern lines, which had been established at no great distance ahead of us. A round of our musketry emptied several saddles, and compelled a disorderly retreat. My little command never reassembled, but the object had been achieved. When I went to report to General Pickett he received me cordially, and was well pleased with his game of bluff with General Butler. But for this bold conception of Pickett's, Petersburg would have been occupied, Richmond isolated, the catastrophe accelerated, and General Butler would have been the hero of the war. It was his object to cut the railroad, as was proved by his attack at Port Walthall Junction, where he was repulsed by the gallant Haygood, as well as by the unsuccessful attempt of Cantz's Cavalry Division to the south of the town. Had General Butler been informed of the condition of things, a richer prize was within his grasp, and fair Petersburg, like another Helen, would have yielded herself his captive. This was my only contact with Pickett's men during the bloody war. Soon after I was ordered to take command of the troops stationed for the defense of the High Bridge.

RECOLLECTIONS OF GENERAL REYNOLDS.

BY GENERAL T. F. M'COY.

AFTER the battle of Antietam, the army, being exhausted from the extraordinary fatigues, exposures, and losses of the protracted campaigns of the past summer, took position for rest and reoccupation on the late battle-field, and in the region of country adjacent, north of the Potomac, the enemy occupying the country south of the river —the river being the general dividing line between the two armies. Reynolds' Corps occupied the long picket line on the river. Rickett's Division, of which our brigade was a part, was in this corps. The brigade commander was rather of a dashing character, an officer of experience and gallantry, and had a keen eye for a comfortable position for his headquarters, and would run risks of capture rather than deprive himself of a good and choice spot for this purpose. In pursuance of this he fixed his headquarters in the little village of Mercersville, in the most desirable house, and right on the picket line, on the bank of the river, and in a dangerous position, as the river at this point was both narrow and shallow. The camp of the brigade was a half mile in rear of this line, and in a comparatively safe place. Ordinarily, for an officer of rank to have his headquarters on or very near the picket line, with the enemy's line in rather close proximity, would not be regarded as safe, or in accordance with strict military rule. In this case, the river intervening, of course modified it materially in the judgment of the officers. Yet an enterprising party of the enemy, familiar with the ground as they might have been, could have almost any night dashed into Mercersville, and carried off the general and his staff, and the reserve picket would likely have gotten upon the ground in time to have seen them vanish beyond the river.

Only a week or two elapsed when our brigade commander obtained a leave of absence, and an order was issued by the division commander assigning another officer to the command. This necessitated a removal to the village, and a more familiar acquaintance with the surroundings. The few weeks of command here looms up as a most unpleasant period in that officer's military experience. There was nothing at that time interesting in or about the village; indeed, everything almost seemed to be the reverse. The citizens, however, so far as could be ascertained, claimed to be loyal to the old flag. Most of the persons visible were very hard-looking cases, and most of them lounged about, or were attracted about, one or two very unattractive taverns, where it was quite certain bad whisky was freely issued, and perhaps more freely used, and that, too, to the detriment of morals, health, and discipline, notwithstanding a "boy in blue" kept watch, day and night, musket in hand, not very far from the spigot. A few of them, as well as many others from different quarters, had passes from General McClellan, which was about the only thing that gave them any fair degree of grace, and on this ground were allowed to pass the river, and enter the enemy's lines.

The next most interesting and attractive object to the citizens of the vicinity, was one of the old-fashioned fish-baskets in the middle of the stream, just opposite the village. Persons could approach this basket along the wing walls that formed the dam from either side of the river; for this reason, it was regarded as affording convenience for any small party of the enemy to enter our lines without the use of a boat, and thus required at our hands special attention. The commanding officer was greatly annoyed by persons requesting passes to visit the fish-basket, and was frequently troubled to reconcile the giving of a pass for this purpose with the general order from army headquarters—not to allow any one to cross the river unless he could show a pass signed by the general-in-chief. The thing was as wisely managed as could be under the peculiar circumstances, having in view the important fact of preserving the fish from getting into the hands of the enemy. To have allowed this, would have been distressing to the flesh. The pleasant recollection remains of the fact of the fish always reaching the north bank of the river, and contributing aid and comfort to loyal and patriotic appetites. This incident is mentioned as being the only thing in the character of a fish-basket that became an object of

25

solicitude during the war, so far as the writer has any recollection.
Interesting periods, however, can be recalled after this when such an
object would have excited the greatest care and attention, for fresh
river fish would ever be a welcome and happy change for the tough,
changeless army ration of fresh beef, so productive of uneasy sleep,
and so worrying upon the soldiers' digestion. The mention of fresh
rations brings to my recollection a communication received about
this time from General Reynolds, who was at this early period of the
war as rigid in protecting the beef and mutton of the rebel citizens as
McClellan himself; indeed, in this he was but carrying out the standing orders of the commander-in-chief. The communication was
dated Headquarters First Army Corps, October 21st, 1862, and in
the general's own handwriting, and for this reason is preserved as a
precious memento of our lamented corps commander. It was in
these words: "It is represented that some of your men have crossed
the river and have been killing sheep belonging to Mr. Shepherd.
You will take such measures as to prevent this at once." This letter
was signed, "John F. Reynolds, Brigadier General, Commanding,"
and did not come through the regular military channel, the General
not seeming to be a stickler in the observance of red tape.

No copy of the reply to this communication was retained, but a
suitable one was promptly made, and, of course, the general commanding the corps was respectfully informed that he had been misinformed as to any of the soldiers of the brigade referred to engaging
in any such recreation, as they had not, so early in the war, attained
that degree of discipline as to secure subsistence in that way. It
might be supposed that in less than a year from this period, when
the army had undergone a little necessary demoralization in this
direction and secured a little more patriotic wisdom on this interesting point, that these soldiers would have accepted a little subsistence
of this kind; and doubtless the general would have thought it of so
contraband a character as to have saved himself the writing, and his
orderly the time of conveying, dispatches on the subject.

For weeks the army had been resting, and at the same time
preparing for a movement against the enemy, and almost daily
orders were issued of a preliminary character. For the week previous
to the movement, we were kept in hourly, yea, constant, expectancy for
the final marching orders. While in this excited condition, an orderly
dashed up with the following communication from General Reynolds,
dated at his headquarters, October 25th, 1862:

The general commanding desires you will question Mrs. ——, wife of ——,
who will cross to your headquarters to-day, as to the position and movements of the

enemy, and forward to these headquarters all the information you may gather from her.

The names of these persons are omitted, lest they might suffer even at this late day for their loyalty. Mrs. —— encountered no difficulty in crosssng the river, and presented herself about ten o'clock in the forenoon. The result of the interview with her will appear in the following reply to the foregoing letter, which was promptly forwarded to the general's headquarters :

I have the honor to report, for the information of Major General Reynolds, commanding the corps, that Mrs. ——, named in your communication of this date, has called at these headquarters, and has given me the following information: "I live about four miles and a half from Martinsburg, on the road to Shepherdstown, in the lines of the rebel army. The rebel infantry all left that neighborhood on Thursday night of this week. I think the whole rebel army was there. When they left they moved toward Winchester. Stuart's cavalry have been left. The number I do not know. They have torn up the railroad and everything belonging to the road at Martinsburg, and down toward Kearneyville. They took up the cross-ties and burnt them, putting the rails on the fire. They are treating the Union citizens badly, and using and destroying their property." This is all of any importance that Mrs. —— seemed to know in reference to the movements and conduct of the enemy.

The next day, the whole army was in motion for the designated points on the river, to cross in pursuit of the enemy. It was reported, at or about the time, that for the reason that McClellan was tardy in making this movement he was removed, a few days after crossing into Virginia, from the command of the army, and was succeeded by General Burnside. This may or may not have been the reason. It is only our purpose to speak of it as an interesting fact that made a deep impression at the time, and one that may be referred to, after a lapse of fourteen years, as an important and interesting crisis in the history of that army, that did the greatest amount of fighting, was the best disciplined, and the greatest army of the rebellion.

It is a well known fact that the removal of McClellan caused an extraordinary sensation in the army. There can be no gainsaying the fact that at this time he was the idol chieftain of the Army of the Potomac. His taking leave, a final leave, of that great and noted army, a few days after, at Warrenton, was an extraordinary spectacle, and one long to be remembered by those who witnessed it. In any army with less intelligence and less patriotism, demoralization and disintegration might have resulted. This interesting occasion was an illustration of the oft-asserted fact that American bayonets *think*, and that it is not man-worship, but patriotism; not the hero-chieftain, but the noble good cause, the flag of the country and what that flag represented, that governed the rank and file, and prompted to years of toil and suffering, and to deeds of noble daring.

With the cannon's roar that celebrated this deeply interesting scene, and memorable military pageant of tears and cheers, of floating banners, and proudly marching columns, the period of "hero worship" in the Army of the Potomac passed away forever. Heroes, it is true, rose and fell after this in quick succession; but stern war, determined, uncompromising war, now more than ever became the moving power, thought and cry of the thinking masses of the loyal people of the land. The popular irresistible public sentiment was impelling the mighty columns of that great army to close up to the now historic bloody lines of the Rappahannock and the Rapidan, and there, and on many bloody battle-fields far beyond, almost regardless of whose hand wielded the sceptre of command, thousands upon thousands gallantly fought, bled, and died to vindicate the flag of the nation, and to preserve the existence and unity of the great and good government transmitted to us by the fathers of the Revolution. The great cause of the Union loomed up more and more prominently as the mighty struggle progressed, and at length Appomattox witnessed its triumph, and to-day more than forty millions of freemen are enjoying its blessed fruits.

As before remarked, our brigade commander had no personal acquaintance with General Reynolds, not even to the extent of knowing him by sight, if he rode along the lines. It may, therefore, be worth while to notice the manner his acquaintance was formed, as it may illustrate a pleasant trait in his character. The army was on the move. Our corps, and perhaps one or two others, by different roads, concentrated at the little village of Berlin, two or three miles southeast of Harper's Ferry, after having greatly suffered from a snow-storm in making a march over South Mountain. The Potomac was crossed here on pontoons, and from thence the line of march was continued down the Loudon valley, running parallel with the Valley of the Shenandoah, in which the rebel army was moving at the time. While on this movement, in the heart of this beautiful valley, General Ricketts, commanding our division, being himself a mile or two in the advance, communicated, by a staff officer, an order that when the brigade arrived at a certain angle in the road, upon which it was then moving, that it should leave the road and march in another direction, a diagonal way across the fields. Before the head of the column reached this point, it was met by a modest looking officer, entirely alone, exhibiting no special insignia of rank, and supposed at the time to be an ordinary staff officer. He addressed the brigade commander in a mild, pleasant way, at the same time joining him and riding in the same direction. He seemed to have a knowledge that the column had been ordered to leave the road, and said it was a wrong or mistaken order, but did not assume that he had any authority to order otherwise, and kept riding along until the two officers were one or two hundred yards in advance of the troops. The strange officer's manner was observed to be somewhat peculiar, as he kept watching the head of the column; and it being near the turning off point, and being satisfied that the brigade commander was not going counter to the order of his division commander at his mere suggestion, or request, and being satisfied, doubtless, that he was not regarded as of much account, decided it would be necessary for him to indicate higher rank and authority. Turning his head again, and finding that in another minute the head of the brigade would change direction, and leave the road, unless otherwise ordered, he says to the brigade commander: "Direct your orderly to return to the column, and have it continue its advance on the road." The quiet, dignified manner in which these words were uttered made an impression that he might be more than what he seemed to be. His full character was not yet understood, and hesitation to comply was manifested. The orderly having overheard the words, and knowing the officer, had turned his horse and was ready, and anxious, to bear the order to the officer commanding the leading regiment. As the crisis in this little episode had now come, the modest stranger found it necessary to assert more fully his position and authority. In a calm and moderate tone, peculiar to him, he said: "General Reynolds orders that the column shall continue its march in this direction." These words opened the eyes of the officer in command. No sooner said than done. The orderly was off at full speed, and the order communicated just in proper time. The officer was not slow in recognizing his superior. Finding himself in the presence, and in company with his corps commander, he was no little alarmed and embarrassed, and being about to take respectful leave and retire to his proper place, the General requested him to ride along in company with him, which the officer was pleased to do for some considerable distance, and now looks back upon it as one of the pleasant reminiscences of his early experience in the war, and as his first introduction to an officer who was then eminent, and who afterward became so distinguished.

Two or three days after this pleasant incident, when our brigade was leading the advance, the day being warm, dry, and dusty, we observed some distance forward a party of officers, dismounted, in a field skirting the road, very busily engaged in efforts to extinguish an extensive fire, raging in the dry grass and fences. On approaching nearer we found the party to consist of General Reynolds and his staff. It was now ascertained that they had, in their desire to prevent unnecessary devastation, voluntarily undertaken to stem the advance of an enemy who, not despising their rank, yet seemed to entertain supreme contempt for their numbers. It, therefore, became necessary to call in reinforcements. The brigade promptly furnished them, the fiery enemy was routed, and the march resumed. In this incident we may infer the kindness of heart and the respect for strict observance of military law by which the general was governed; this being in the infantile period of the war, and when it was conducted under the system of the old regulations, which were soon found not to be well adapted in certain particulars to this peculiar and cruel war. The close of this year seemed to have ended such fastidiousness. Fences, crops, barns, and houses, railroads, and even towns were afterward swept away by the surging and resistless tide of war, when in the way of an advancing army, or when used as a shield for the enemy, or when necessary to the subsistence and comfort of the army.

In a few weeks, after the occurrence of the incident just mentioned, the bloody battle of Fredericksburg took place, in which Reynolds' Corps was a prominent actor, and was the only corps in our whole army that met with any considerable degree of success in that great battle. That corps, in withdrawing from that sanguinary field, felt like a victor, as it was, indeed, for it charged upon and broke the enemy's lines on their right, and, if prompt support had been rendered, the right flank of Lee's army would have been turned, his position made untenable, and a great victory for the Army of the Potomac, rather than a bloody repulse, would have been the result.

Twice during the winter, in the way of official duty, we met General Reynolds in his tent at corps headquarters. Our duty was to report to him for orders and instructions, and on these occasions the interviews were brief and the words few. He impressed us as being mild and gentlemanly in manner, and an officer of not a very numerous class of old army officers who knew how to treat volunteers in such a way as to secure their respect and confidence. The next we saw of Reynolds was at the great review of his corps in April, 1863, at Belle Plain, by President Lincoln. This was his last review, and but a short time before the battle of Chancellorsville. In this movement, for the first three days, his corps was making demonstrations against Fredericksburg. Here we saw the general cross the Rappahannock, on the pontoon bridge, in gallant style, under a heavy fire of shell. Three days after this he visited our division, then on the right of the army at Chancellorsville, his corps having arrived upon this battle-ground the evening before, in time to take the place of the Eleventh Corps, then just swept from its position by Stonewall Jackson's famous flank attack, in which Jackson himself found a soldier's death, and the Confederacy lost one of its greatest heroes. Once again we remember seeing General Reynolds. It was when on the march to the world-renowned battle-field of Gettysburg. He was standing on a little eminence near his headquarters, looking, doubtless, with a just pride at his splendid corps, as it filed past him into camp for the night. This was the last time our eyes rested upon that noble officer and patriot. That vision often looms up in the memories of the great rebellion. A few days thereafter he fell. A distinguished officer of his staff says:

On the night before the battle, General Reynolds retired to his room about midnight, and rose early, as was his usual practice. On the march from our head-quarters, at the Red Tavern, he was very reticent and uncommunicative to all around him, as was his wont. He was, in this respect, an entirely different man from any other general officer with whom I served during the war, having very little, if anything, to say to any one, other than to communicate to them such orders as he desired executed. He would, while upon the march, ride miles without having any conversation with any one. Our ride to Gettysburg formed no exception to this rule. From this you can see that no conclusion could be arrived at as to what his feelings and presentiments were upon that day. I consider him one of the finest and most thorough soldiers which the civil war brought before the country.

The whole army was shocked at the death of General Reynolds. His corps deeply felt his loss. This great Commonwealth, of whom he was a native, mourned over his death. In him the national cause lost a powerful supporter and leader. The officers of his corps testified their appreciation of his services, and their high regard for him as their commander and comrade, by the erection of a monument to his memory. With the historian's record of the great battle of Gettysburg, Major General John F. Reynolds' bright name and fame will pass down to posterity.

Were a star quenched on high,
For ages would its light,
Still traveling downward from the sky,
Shine on our mortal sight.

So, when a great man dies,
For years beyond our ken,
The light he leaves behind him
Upon the paths of men.

THE BATTLE OF FLEETWOOD.

BY MAJOR H. B. M'CLELLAN.

THE services rendered by the cavalry of the armies contending upon the soil of Virginia, have not been fully appreciated by those who have as yet attempted the story of the war. During the last two years of the war no branch of the Army of the Potomac contributed so much to the overthrow of Lee's army as the cavalry, both that which operated in the Valley of Virginia and that which remained at Petersburg. But for the efficiency of this force, it is safe to say, that the war would have been indefinitely prolonged. From the time that the cavalry was concentrated into a corps under General Pleasonton, until the close of the war, a steady progress was made in discipline, *esprit du corps*, and numbers. Nothing was spared to render this arm complete. Breech-loading carbines of the most approved patterns were provided; horses and accoutrements were never wanting, and during the last year of the war Sheridan commanded as fine a body of troops as ever drew sabre.

On the other hand, two causes contributed steadily to diminish the numbers and efficiency of the Confederate cavalry. The government committed the fatal error of allowing the men to own their own horses, paying them a *per diem* for their use, and the muster valuation in cases where they were killed in action; but giving no compensation for horses lost by any of the other casualties of a campaign. If a man's horse were killed, disabled, or worn out in the service, he must return to his home to procure another; and the strength of the command was constantly reduced below its reported "effective total" by the large number of men absent upon "horse details," as they were called.   Toward the close of the war many were unable to remount themselves, and hundreds of such dismounted men were collected in a useless crowd, which was dubbed "Company Q."   The second cause was the failure or inability of the government to supply good arms and accoutrements.   Our breech-loading guns were nearly all captured from the enemy, and the same may be said of the best of our saddles and bridles.   From these causes, which it was beyond the power of any cavalry commander to remedy, there was a steady decline in the numbers of the Confederate cavalry, and, as compared with the Federal cavalry, a decline in efficiency. But the men remained the same in courage and devotion, and to the very end the best blood in the land rode after Stuart, Hampton, and the Lees.   But while the superior efficiency of the Federal horse is certainly to be acknowledged, a Confederate cavalryman may be pardoned in dissenting from some of the statements made by General D. McM. Gregg, in his able article on "The Union Cavalry in the Gettysburg Campaign."   In the first place, when stating the force of the cavalry under Stuart's command in June, 1863, General Gregg falls into the very common error of largely over-estimating his adversary.   He states that the Confederate cavalry numbered "about twelve thousand horsemen, divided into five brigades, with sixteen pieces of artillery."   The brigade organization is stated correctly; our artillery consisted of five batteries of four guns each—in all twenty guns; but in estimating Stuart's horsemen at the battle of Brandy Station, June 9th, 1863, at twelve thousand, General Gregg nearly doubles our effective strength.

As Assistant Adjutant General of the Cavalry, it was within my province to know its strength.   Three grand reviews were held in Culpepper—on the 22d of May, and on the 5th and 8th of June, 1863. At the first of these reviews there were present only the three brigades of Hampton, and the two Lees.   Private memoranda, now in my possession, show about four thousand men, exclusive of pickets, in the saddle upon that day.   Before the second review Stuart was joined by Robertson's North Carolina Brigade, and by W. E. Jones' Virginia Brigade, and on the 31st of May, 1863, the "total effective" of the cavalry division was reported as nine thousand five hundred and thirty-six.   To rightly estimate the force with which Stuart fought the battle of the 9th of June, 1863, there must be deducted from this number the men absent on special duty—"horse details"—the entire brigade of Robertson, the Fourth Virginia Cavalry, and the Second South Carolina Cavalry.   It must also be stated that of Fitz

Lee's Brigade only four squadrons of sharpshooters were engaged, and these at the very close of the battle. When these deductions are made, it will appear that Stuart's available force did not much exceed, if at all, six thousand men. Again, in speaking of the time when General Pleasonton assumed command, General Gregg states: "To this time, for the reasons heretofore given, the prestige of success had steadily remained with the rebel cavalry in its greatest and more important undertakings; but the time was now at hand for its transfer to our side, there 'to remain to the close of the war.' * * *"

I propose to show that the battle of the 9th of June, as a passage-at-arms, was a victory for the Southern cavalry. I could also show that Stuart was not, as General Gregg states, subsequently defeated at Aldie, Middleburg, and Upperville; but that he successfully performed his task of guarding the flank of Lee's army while passing into Maryland, although falling back from Aldie to Upperville, before a superior force of cavalry, supported by at least seven regiments of infantry. I would remind General Gregg that the last charge in the cavalry battle at Gettysburg was made by the Southern cavalry; that by this charge his division was swept behind the protection of his artillery, and that the field remained in the undisputed possession of Stuart, save that from the opposite hills a fierce artillery duel was maintained until night. I would remind him how the Federal cavalry was handled after Gettysburg, on the road between Hagerstown and Williamsport, when this "limping cavalry giant" raised the siege of our wagon trains which were huddled together on the bank of the Potomac. I would remind him of "The Buckland Races," on the 19th of October, 1863, when Kilpatrick's Division was chased, with horses at full gallop, from within three miles of Warrenton to Buckland Mills, and only by this rapid flight escaped being crushed between Hampton's and Fitz Lee's Brigades. Nor must the battle near Trevillian's Station, in June, 1864, be forgotten, where the entire strength of the cavalry of both armies was concentrated. Had Sheridan been able to carry out his plans, the speedy evacuation of Richmond must have followed; but he was met and successfully opposed by Hampton, and in a two days' battle was so severely crippled that he was compelled to abandon his designs, and retire during the night to a place of safety. Nor can Hampton's famous "Cattle Raid" be passed over, where two thousand five hundred fat beeves were snatched from the guardianship of this same Federal cavalry, and safely conveyed within the Confederate lines at Petersburg, despite very vigorous efforts on the part of General

Gregg himself, if I mistake not, for their recovery. No! No! *"The prestige of success" did* rest finally and forever with the Federal horsemen, but there were many bright days between times, when the Confederate troopers could exult in conscious victory; and on the last day, glory, as of the setting sun, crowned the arms of the remnant of Fitz Lee's old brigade, when, under the gallant Munford, they made, at the High Bridge, near Farmville, a successful charge —the last charge of the war. No more accomplished commander, no harder fighter than General Gregg was to be found in the Federal army, and no one can afford better than he gracefully to acknowledge the achievements of the Southern Horse.

"The Fight at Brandy Station," or "The Battle of Fleetwood," as Stuart called it, was one of the most splendid passages-at-arms which the war furnished. General R. E. Lee was commencing the movement of his army which resulted in the Gettysburg campaign, and had already moved Ewell's Corps to the vicinity of Culpepper Court-House. On the 7th of June, he notified General Stuart that he would review his cavalry on the next day. This review was held on the 8th of June, on the broad open fields which lie between Brandy Station and Culpepper Court-House. On the evening of the same day the brigades were moved down toward the Rappahannock, preparatory to the crossing, which it was contemplated to make the next day. Fitz Lee's Brigade, commanded by Colonel Thomas T. Munford, having charge of the pickets on the upper Rappahannock, was, with the exception of the Fourth Virginia Cavalry, moved across the Hazel river. W. H. F. Lee's Brigade was stationed on the road to Welford's ford; Jones' Brigade on the road to Beverly's ford, and Robertson's Brigade on the farm of John Minor Botts, picketing the lower fords. Hampton's Brigade was held in reserve. One battery of horse artillery was sent with Fitz Lee's Brigade across the Hazel river; the remaining four batteries accompanied Jones' Brigade. The object of the movement contemplated for the next morning was not to make an extensive cavalry raid, but to place the command in such position as best to protect the flank of our army while marching northward. Orders were issued to march at an early hour on the 9th, and, ignorant of any concentration of the enemy's cavalry on the opposite side, the battalion of horse artillery bivouacked close to Beverly's ford, in advance of Jones' Brigade. The position was an exposed one, and nearly resulted in serious loss.

With everything in readiness for an early start, Stuart himself bivouacked on the night of the 8th, on Fleetwood Hill, so-called from the name of the residence there situated. The hill is between

Brandy Station and the river, about half a mile from the station, and commands the open plain around it in every direction. At the very first dawn of day the firing of the pickets at Beverly's ford notified us that an attack had been made; and soon reports came in from Jones and from Robertson that the enemy had effected a crossing at both Beverly's and Kelley's fords. The condition of the horse artillery was, for a time, exceedingly critical. The advance of the enemy was pressed with vigor, and there was nothing between the guns and danger, save the squadron on picket. Guns and wagons were harnessed in haste, and retired in much confusion, until the arrival of Jones' grand guard, the Seventh Virginia, checked the enemy. No serious loss occurred save that Major Beckham's desk, in which he had placed the order of march received by him the previous night, was jostled out of his wagon in its hasty retreat, and fell into the enemy's hands, thus revealing to him authoritatively part of the information which he had come to obtain. Retiring to the vicinity of St. James' Church, the artillery was placed in position for action, and the whole of Jones' Brigade having now been brought forward, the advance of the enemy was still further checked until Hampton, with four of his regiments, took position upon Jones' right, and a junction was effected with W. H. F. Lee's Brigade upon the left. At the earliest report of the enemy's advance, Robertson moved to the support of his pickets, and encountered a party of the enemy near Brown's house, about two miles from Kelley's ford. This brigade was not, however, engaged during any part of the day. With matters in this position the fight continued for more than two hours, with no decisive result on either side, save that the Confederate cavalry held their position against every attack. It is the concurrent opinion of Generals Hampton and Jones, and of Major Beckham, as expressed in their official reports, that they could not have been dislodged by the force which had developed itself in their front. The enemy's infantry had been freely used, both as a support, and as an attacking force, but the effort to dislodge our troops from the first position they assumed near the church had entirely failed.

But, meanwhile, the situation was becoming serious in another direction, and that, too, while we were ignorant of the danger. Before sending Hampton into action, Stuart had ordered that one of his regiments be detached to guard our rear at Brandy Station; but learning from Robertson that a column of the enemy was moving upon Stevensburg, this regiment, the Second South Carolina, Colonel M. C. Butler, was ordered to that point, which is about five miles from Brandy Station. The Fourth Virginia, Colonel Wickham, was shortly after sent in the same direction. Relying upon these regiments and upon Robertson's Brigade to protect his rear from an attack by way of the lower fords, Stuart proceeded to the front at St. James' Church to urge on the battle; and as the field was geographically so extensive, he stationed his adjutant (the writer) upon Fleetwood Hill, directions having been given to the brigades and detached regiments to communicate with that point as headquarters. Every scrap of the camp was removed toward Culpepper Court-House, and there remained nothing upon the hill but the adjutant and his couriers. A six-pound howitzer from Chew's Battery, under charge of Lieutenant Carter, which had been retired from the fight near the river because its ammunition was nearly exhausted, was halted at the bottom of the hill; a circumstance which afterward proved to be our salvation. Perhaps nearly two hours had elapsed since Stuart had mounted for the front, when an individual scout reported to me that the enemy was advancing from Kelley's ford in force and unopposed upon Brandy Station, and that he was now directly in our rear. Not having personal acquaintance with the man, and deeming it impossible that such a movement could be made without opposition from Robertson's Brigade, I ordered the scout to return and satisfy himself by a closer inspection that he had not mistaken some of our troops for the enemy. In less than five minutes the man came back with the report that I could now satisfy myself, as the enemy was in plain view. And so it was! Within cannon-shot of the hill, a long column of the enemy filled the road which here skirted the woods, and were pressing steadily upon the railroad station, which must in a few moments be in their possession. How could they be prevented from also occupying the Fleetwood Hill, the key to the whole position? Matters looked serious! But it is wonderful what results can sometimes be accomplished with the smallest means. Lieutenant Carter's howitzer was brought up and boldly pushed beyond the crest of the hill; a few imperfect shells and some round shot were found in the limber chest; a slow fire was at once opened upon the marching column; and courier after courier was dispatched to General Stuart to inform him of the peril. It was all important to gain time; for should the enemy once plant his artillery upon this hill it would cost many valuable lives to retake the position, even if that could at all be accomplished. We must retain this position or suffer disastrous defeat, inclosed between the divisions of Buford and Gregg. But the enemy was deceived by appearances. There was not one man left upon the hill beside those belonging to the howitzer section and myself; for I had sent away even my last courier with an urgent appeal for speedy help. Instead of moving a small force forward to an immediate attack, which would, of course, have been successful, three rifled-guns were unlimbered, and a fierce cannonade was commenced, and continued while troops were preparing for the assault. My first courier found General Stuart as incredulous concerning the presence of the enemy in his rear as I had been; but simultaneous with my second message came the sound of the cannonading, and there was no longer room for doubt. The nearest point from which a regiment could be sent was Jones' position, not less than two miles distant from Fleetwood. Two of his regiments, the Twelfth Virginia, Colonel Harman, and White's Thirty-fifth Virginia Battalion, were immediately withdrawn from his line and ordered at a gallop to meet this new danger. But minutes expanded seemingly into hours to those anxious watchers on the hill, who feared, lest, after all, help *could* not arrive in time. But it *did* come. The emergency was so pressing that Colonel Harman had no time to form his regiment in squadrons, or even platoons.

He reached the top of the hill as Lieutenant Carter was retiring his gun after having fired his very last cartridge. Not fifty yards below Sir Percy Wyndham was advancing a strong regiment in magnificent order, in column of squadrons, with flags and guidons flying, directly upon the hill, and to meet this attack the Twelfth Virginia was compelled to move forward instantly, though disordered by a hard gallop, and in column of fours. The result was a recoil, which extended for a time to White's Battalion, which was following close after. Stuart reached the hill a few moments later, and, satisfied that he had here to encounter a large force of the enemy, he ordered both Jones and Hampton to withdraw with the artillery from the Beverly's ford road and concentrate upon Fleetwood Hill. And now the first serious contest was for the possession of this hill, and so stubbornly was this fought on either side, and for so long a time, that all of Jones' regiments, and all of Hampton's, participated successively in the charges and counter-charges which swept across its face. At one time Gregg would have possession, at another Stuart; but at no time did Gregg retain possession sufficiently long to bring up his guns to the crest. He did, indeed, advance three guns to the foot of the hill; but there they were destined to remain. On the other hand, Stuart did gain position little by little. How fierce this struggle was, and with what determined gallantry fought by both sides, may, perhaps, best be shown by an extract from Major Beckham's report. He says:

The pieces first placed on Fleetwood Hill were under the command of Lieutenant Carter, of Chew's Battery, and had been repeatedly charged by the enemy and retaken by our cavalry; and at the time that the two guns of McGregor's were brought toward the crest of the hill, it was very doubtful which party had possession of it. The two guns were, however, moved up rapidly, and scarcely had they reached the top (and before they could be put in position), when a small party of the enemy charged them. The charge was met by the cannoneers of the pieces. Lieutenant Ford killed one of the enemy with his pistol; Lieutenant Hoxton killed one, and private Sully, of McGregor's Battery, knocked one off his horse with a sponge-staff. Several of the party were taken prisoners by the men at the guns.

Aid was close at hand for these gallant cannoneers. Cobb's Georgia Legion, under Colonel P. M. B. Young, cleared the hill of the enemy, and concerted charges, made by other regiments of Hampton's and Jones' Brigades, placed it securely in our possession. And now covetous eyes were cast toward the foot of the hill, where stood those three rifled guns, and around them the battle raged fiercely. Three times were they over-ridden by the Confederate Horse, and twice were they retaken by their friends.* But Colonel Lomax, with the Eleventh Virginia, made the last charge, and the guns remained with us. One was disabled, the other two serviceable. These two points decided the struggle in our favor, and Brandy Station was soon cleared of its unwelcome visitors, who were hurried back along the road upon which they had advanced. The pursuit was continued by Lomax and Hampton, until checked by *the fire of our own artillery,†* for the dust and smoke of the conflict was so great that from the position of the artillery, friends could not be distinguished from foes.

But the question of further pursuit of Gregg's Division was soon decided for us by General Buford, who made a heavy attack upon W. H. F. Lee's Brigade, upon our left, beyond the Barbour House, at the same time advancing with infantry and cavalry through the open fields from the direction of St. James' Church, threatening another attack upon the Fleetwood Hill, and forming, subsequently,

---

* This statement has been courteously questioned by Colonel Thomas, of the First Pennsylvania Cavalry. My authority is this: "Stuart states, in his report, that the Thirty-fifth Virginia Battalion penetrated to the enemy's artillery, but were driven back." Major Flournoy, commanding the Sixth Virginia Cavalry, states: "We charged and took the battery, but were unable to hold it." Colonel Lomax, Eleventh Virginia Cavalry, says: "I charged the enemy on the right of the Culpepper Court-House road, capturing a battery of three guns and many prisoners."—*See Official Report of Battles, Richmond,* 1864. These circumstances might easily have escaped Colonel Thomas' notice, on a field so confused and dusty.

† See Reports of Stuart, Hampton, and Lomax.

a junction with Gregg's Division. The fight upon the left was obstinate and bloody, and our troops maintained their ground with difficulty, until the opportune arrival of Colonel Munford with Fitz Lee's Brigade, who attacked the enemy in flank at Green's house and Welford's, with sharpshooters and artillery, causing them to fall back toward the river, upon which our pickets were established at nightfall. Knowing that a force of infantry was present with both of the columns which had attacked him, and believing that the enemy's cavalry alone outnumbered ours, General Stuart had applied to General Lee for an infantry support, which arrived about four o'clock in the afternoon. This force, a portion of Ewell's Corps, was stationed to protect the Fleetwood Hill, and to support the brigades of the two Lees on our left. But the battle was virtually over before their arrival, and they did not fire a gun. Their presence, however, revealed to General Pleasonton another item of information which he had set out to obtain.

While these events were transpiring near Brandy Station, affairs wore a far different complexion near Stevensburg, to which point Colonel M. C. Butler's Second South Carolina, and Colonel W. C. Wickham's Fourth Virginia Cavalry had been sent to oppose the advance of Duffie's Division. On his arrival near Willis Madden's house, Colonel Wickham found Butler already engaged with the enemy. Before dispositions could be made, either to receive or make an attack, a charge of the enemy produced some confusion in a portion of the line of the Second South Carolina, which extended to the Fourth Virginia. The whole regiment became demoralized, and ran from the enemy's charge without firing a gun. They were pursued through the town of Stevensburg, and for some distance beyond, nor could the men be rallied until satisfied that the enemy's pursuit had ceased. In his report, Stuart says: "This regiment usually fights well, and its stampede on this occasion is unaccountable." In fact, the Fourth Virginia was one of our largest and best regiments. The men were deeply humiliated by this disgraceful conduct. Through their colonel they presented to General Stuart an humble confession of their fault, and a promise that they would wipe out their disgrace upon the next field of battle—a promise which the future history of the regiment fully redeemed. This affair cost us some valuable lives. The bursting of one shell killed Lieutenant Colonel Frank Hampton, brother of General Wade Hampton, and Captain Farley, volunteer aide-de-camp to General Stuart, and carried away the foot of Colonel M. C. Butler, necessitating amputation of the leg, and depriving his regiment of his valuable services for many months.

In summing up the results of this battle it must be remembered that Robertson's Brigade, which numbered more than a thousand men, did not, at any time in the day, participate in the fighting.*

---

*Inasmuch as General Robertson has, in the Memphis *Appeal*, complained of injustice done him by the references which I have made to his operations, I append his own reports of this day's work, as follows:

HEADQUARTERS CAVALRY BRIGADE,
June 12th, 1863.

MAJOR H. B. McCLELLAN,
Assistant Adjutant General, etc.:

Major :—On 9th instant, according to orders, my brigade proceeded to within two miles of Kelley's ford to check the enemy's advance upon the railroad, near which our forces were engaged. I dismounted a portion to oppose the enemy's infantry in the woods. The enemy's cannon had just opened, when several orders were received to fall back rapidly to Brandy Station, the Yankees being in my rear. I had reported their advance upon Stevensburg and Brandy, and was ordered, through Lieutenant Johnston, to hold the ground in my front. One regiment of my brigade was then ordered to move rapidly to the General's headquarters, the other was instructed to cover the right and rear of Hampton's Brigade. Both regiments were, subsequently, drawn up in line of battle to repel the advance of the enemy's columns, which finally moved to the left. One of my regiments was then ordered in that direction. I accompanied it, and, in accordance with instructions, deployed it as skirmishers, to hold that wing until reinforcements should arrive. The other regiment remained with Hampton.

My command, although opposed to the enemy during the entire day, was not at any time actively engaged. Will make a detailed report.

Very respectfully,
(Signed)   B. H. ROBERTSON,
Brigadier General, Commanding Cavalry.

Deeming this report unsatisfactory, General Stuart required another from General Robertson, which was furnished, as follows:

HEADQUARTERS CAVALRY BRIGADE,
June 13th, 1863.

MAJOR H. B. McCLELLAN,
Assistant Adjutant General, Headquarters Cavalry Division:

Major :—In answer to yours just received, have the honor to make the following statement:

About two miles this side of Kelley's ford, at Brown's house, I think, I met Captain White falling back from his picket line. He reported that five regiments of infantry and a large amount of cavalry had crossed the river, and were slowly advancing toward the railroad. Just then the enemy's line of skirmishers emerged from the woods, and I at once dismounted a large portion of my command, and made such disposition of my entire force as seemed best calculated to retard their progress. I immediately sent scouting parties to my right, and went forward myself to ascertain what was transpiring there. I soon learned that the enemy was advancing upon the Brandy Station road, and dispatched Captain Worthington with the information. Soon afterward the enemy was reported moving upon Stevensburg, in large force. I ordered Lieutenant Holcombe to report the fact to the Major

26

He allowed himself to be occupied in an almost useless observation
of the enemy, who had thrown a small force into his front, after
crossing at Kelley's ford. Nor did Colonel Munford, with Fitz Lee's
Brigade, reach the field until after noonday, and only participated,
with his sharpshooters, in repelling the last attack of Buford upon
our left. The brunt of the battle was borne by the three brigades
of Jones, W. H. F. Lee, and Hampton, and from the last one regiment

---

General commanding, who informed me that a force had been sent to Stevensburg,
and that troops were at Brandy Station. Before receiving this message, I had contemplated making an attack in rear, should it meet the General's approval. I, therefore, sent Lieutenant James Johnston to report to General Stuart, who sent me
orders to hold my front. A division of my force was impossible, as I needed them
all. I consider it extremely fortunate that my command was not withdrawn from
the position it occupied (which was a very strong one), as the enemy's force, consisting of infantry, artillery, and cavalry, was marching directly upon the right
flank of our troops, engaged in front of Rappahannock Station. I had not force
sufficient to hold in check (and it was vitally important to do so) this body, and, at
the same time, follow the flanking party. All the facts may be summed up, as follows: Before my arrival the enemy's cavalry had turned off to the points upon
which they intended to march. They had posted artillery, cavalry, and infantry so
as to cover this movement, or, if unopposed, march upon the railroad. Had I pursued the flanking party, the road I was ordered to defend would have been left
utterly exposed. I acted according to orders, and the dictates of judgment. I came
to this army resolved that my official conduct should meet the approbation of my
military superiors, and whenever, in their opinion, I deserve censure, I shall most
cheerfully submit to official investigation.

Very respectfully, Major, your obedient servant,
(Signed)   B. H. ROBERTSON,
Brigadier General, Commanding Cavalry.

[*Indorsement.*]

HEADQUARTERS CAVALRY DIVISION,
June 13th, 1863.

Respectfully forwarded. It is very clear that General Robertson intended to
do what was right. At the time Lieutenant Johnston reported to me, it was too
late for any movement to have been made from General Robertson's front, and it
would have been extremely hazardous for him to have interposed his command
between the enemy's artillery, and the column of cavalry that had passed on his
right flank. *At the time he arrived on the spot, it is presumed he could have made the
detachment to get to the front of the flanking column, and delay its progress.*

(Signed)   J. E. B. STUART,
Major General.

See *Reports of Battles, Richmond,* 1864.

As to what force occupied General Robertson's attention, near Brown's house,
I quote the following from letters recently received from General D. McM. Gregg,
commanding Federal cavalry:

"In reply to your question as to what force I left near Kelley's ford, when I
advanced on Brandy Station, on June 9th, 1863, from my recollection. I would say,

was detached. Taking, therefore, General Gregg's statement, that the Union cavalry in this engagement numbered about nine thousand men, and that both his and Buford's Divisions were supported by infantry, it cannot be denied that General Stuart was opposed by a force which largely outnumbered his own. As trophies of the battle Stuart could number three pieces of artillery (a loss of which General Gregg makes no mention), three regimental and three company flags, three hundred and sixty-three prisoners captured, beside horses, pistols, sabres, and carbines. Our total loss, making an extreme estimate of that in White's Battalion, from which no report was received, was four hundred and eighty-five.† In regard to the loss in Pleasonton's command, it may be stated that one of the Northern newspapers, of about that date, contained a list of one hundred and ninety-two wounded, who were received into *one* hospital in Alexandria from this battle. Doubtless many were placed in other hospitals. But add to this number the prisoners sent to Richmond, and we find a loss of five hundred and fifty-five, without counting those killed on the field. The total number of casualties probably exceeded seven hundred men. The laurel crown remains with General Gregg, and he can well afford to acknowledge that, though his men fought long and well, they met more than equals at Brandy Station on the 9th of June, 1863.

---

none at all. I know of no reason why I should have done so, for after I crossed, General Russel followed with about fifteen hundred infantry, and directed his march upon General Buford's flank."

And again: "In my official report there is no mention of my having sent any cavalry with the infantry; if I sent any at all, it must have been a mere detachment. You will observe that General Pleasonton makes no mention of artillery having accompanied the infantry."

These quotations abundantly justify my remarks. General Robertson was expected to observe the road upon which General Gregg advanced; but Gregg attained our rear, and nearly effected a disastrous surprise.

† See Stuart's report.

THE UNION MEN OF MARYLAND.

BY HON. W. H. PURNELL, LL.D.

"YET truth, which only doth judge itself, teacheth that the inquiry of truth, which is the love-making or wooing of it, the knowledge of truth, which is the enjoying of it, is the sovereign good of human nature."— *Francis Bacon.*

In our late terrible and bloody civil war, Maryland was claimed by both sides. In each of the contending armies her sons were to be found fighting bravely, and it is well known that her people were much divided in sentiment. The late Henry Winter Davis always indignantly denied that a majority of the people of Maryland were ever, at any time, on the side of secession; and he was deeply hurt by the suspicion and coldness that were sometimes shown by the National authorities in their treatment of his State. He resented, with all the ardor of his nature, the wholesale denunciation that not a few of the Northern papers heaped upon her. He was grieved that the President-elect, Mr. Lincoln, should have deemed it prudent to pass through her great city clandestinely on his way to Washington to be inaugurated. This event did, indeed, manifest a want of confidence in the city of Baltimore, at least, if not in the State of Maryland. President-elect Lincoln had intended, after his reception by the Pennsylvania Legislature, at Harrisburg, on the afternoon of February 22d, 1861, to go to Baltimore, on the 23d, by the Northern Central Railway; but was, with difficulty, induced by the advice of friends, and against the indignant protest of his military companion, the brave Colonel Sumner, to change his mind, return to Philadelphia, take a sleeping-car on the Philadelphia, Wilmington and Baltimore Railroad, and thus, unrecognized, to complete the remain-

(404)

der of his journey to the National capital. His family went on the
Northern Central Railway, by the special train intended for him.

It was charged that there existed, in Baltimore, a conspiracy to
assassinate the President; but I am not aware that any reliable evidence
has ever been produced to sustain the charge. The Albany
Evening Journal, of that time, says: "The friends of Mr. Lincoln
do not question the loyalty and hospitality of the people of Maryland;
but they were aware that a few disaffected citizens, who sympathized
warmly with the secessionists, were determined to frustrate,
at all hazards, the inauguration of the President-elect, even at the
cost of his life." The Baltimore *Clipper*, a strong Union newspaper,
most positively asserted that there was no conspiracy. The
Baltimore *American*, another Union journal, said: "Ample precautions
were taken to guard against any violation of the public peace.
A large police force was detailed for duty at the depot, * * *
and these measures of Marshal Kane, even if they had failed to
restrain any expression of disapprobation, would certainly have
secured Mr. Lincoln from any insult, had such been intended." The
whole article in the *American* clearly shows that that paper never
thought of the existence of any assassination plot, but attributed the
excitement partly to the natural curiosity of the people, and partly
to the unpopularity of certain injudicious and ostentatious friends
of the President, who wished to welcome him with a public demonstration.
When the train, in which the President was expected,
arrived at the Northern Central depot, there was a large, noisy, and
disorderly crowd there, but the police prevented any injury to the
unpopular persons alluded to. There was no appearance of organization,
and there were no persons of prominence in the tumultuous
crowd. If, then, there was a well-organized plot to take the life of
the President-elect, its leaders could not have been present on that
occasion, nor were they ever discovered. Most likely the report
arose from mere idle talk and empty bluster. It did, however,
seriously discredit the State of Maryland throughout the North.

This prejudice against the State was deepened by a subsequent
occurrence. On the 19th of April, 1861, two regiments, going to
Washington in response to the President's call, were assaulted in
the streets of Baltimore by a mob, and three soldiers killed and
several severely wounded. The Massachusetts regiment, by the help
of their own muskets, and under the protection of the Mayor and
police, did succeed, after a trying ordeal, in getting through to the
Washington depot. The other, a Pennsylvania regiment, under the
command of Colonel Small, was pressed upon by the mob, and

ordered by one of Governor Hicks' militia generals to turn back, and, being unarmed, were compelled to obey. The soldiers of the Massachusetts regiment, after exercising great forbearance, at length fired upon the crowd, killing several persons, some of them, as it was alleged, innocent spectators. The excitement throughout the city was intense; exaggerated reports were circulated; the number of citizens killed was magnified from ten to two hundred; youths from sixteen to twenty years of age, armed to the teeth, were seen running wildly about the streets. The thoroughfares were filled with people telling and hearing but one side of the story, and firing one another with the spirit of vengeance. An impromptu mass meeting assembled in Monument Square; the Mayor was called out; the Governor, who had been in the city for several days, was sent for, and appeared; a Maryland flag was hoisted over his head, and his views clamorously demanded. He responded, by declaring that he would suffer his right arm to be torn from his body before he would raise it to strike a sister State. That night, so it is charged, the Governor agreed to an order for the destruction of the bridges on the Philadelphia, Wilmington and Baltimore, and the Northern Central Railroads, in order to prevent the passage of any more troops through Maryland to Washington. It is but justice to Governor Hicks to state, that he always denied that he had authorized any such proceeding. However, the bridges were destroyed.

On Thursday, the 18th day of April, I went from Annapolis to Baltimore. I had expected to find some excitement among the Baltimore people in consequence of the assault upon Fort Sumter and its surrender, which last event had occurred on the Sunday previous, the 14th; but, to my regret, I found the excitement at fever-heat. The Southern sympathizers were open and fierce in the expression of their views; the Union men were more moderate, but firm. The first congregated to hear fiery speeches from their leaders, and loudly applauded the condemnation of Mr. Lincoln's proclamation for troops. Governor Hicks, who had gone to Baltimore on the 17th, and had ascertained the state of feeling, issued his proclamation on the 18th, counseling peace and neutrality on the part of the people of Maryland. It had little or no effect. It was not bold enough to suit the the temper of the times. It was something of a wet blanket to the Union men, and the secessionists despised it and took courage. Thus matters stood on the morning of the 19th. No speaker had directly counseled an attack upon the troops that might pass through, but the incitements were all in that direction, and there were idle, restless, and reckless spirits at hand—few it may be;

but enough to make the onslaught, and there was an abundance of fuel when once the flame was kindled. When the troops came it seemed to be a surprise to all, police as well as citizens; but a mob soon collected and began to hoot and jeer, and finally to throw stones and bricks. Some Union men came forward and endeavored to restrain the crowd and to protect the troops, but they were overborne, and the mob worked its will with the results above given. Mayor Brown, in a letter, dated April 20th, replying to Governor Andrews, who had requested him to have the Massachusetts dead taken care of and forwarded to Boston, says: "No one deplores the sad events of yesterday in this city more deeply than myself; but they were inevitable. Our people viewed the passage of armed troops to another State through the streets as an invasion of our soil, and could not be restrained."

On the day of the riot, I dined at Barnum's Hotel, where I had been stopping since the day before. Marshal Kane came in, and taking a seat at the table near Mr. Robert Fowler, afterward State Treasurer, they began to talk of the attack upon the troops, Mr. Fowler severely blaming the police department for not preventing the perpetration of such an outrage. The Marshal answered, in substance, as follows: "The administration at Washington was to blame for not giving the city authorities timely notice of the coming of the troops. He could and would," he said, "have arranged to pass the troops safely." He added, that he was afraid the affair would be misunderstood in the North, and the people in that section, becoming infuriated, would cry out for vengeance on Baltimore. I withdrew before the conversation was concluded. In the evening, during the progress of a secession meeting, held in front of Barnum's, I saw Marshal Kane eject from the hotel three men who came to the clerk's desk demanding the whereabouts of Senator Sumner. Upon inquiry, I learned that Mr. Sumner had been at the hotel in the forepart of the day, but, by the advice of friends, had withdrawn to a private house. Colonel Kane appeared to be very active and successful in his endeavors to keep the peace. In the morning, I read with astonishment his famous dispatch to Bradley Johnson:

BALTIMORE, April 19th, 1861.

Thank you for your offer. Bring your men in by the first train, and we will arrange with the railroad afterward. *Streets red with Maryland blood.* Send express over the mountains and valleys of Maryland and Virginia for the riflemen to come without delay. Fresh hordes will be down on us to-morrow (20th). We will fight them or die.

GEORGE P. KANE.

Colonel Kane may have been influenced, however, by the desire to shield Baltimore from the indiscriminate violence anticipated by him and others from an aroused and indignant North.

The unexpected turn things had taken, greatly discouraged the Union men, and some sought their homes in despair; but I saw a large number, in the course of the day and night, that were as firm and determined as ever. The Hon. Alexander H. Evans volunteered as an aide to the Governor, and exerted himself as far as possible to rescue him from the secession influences by which he was surrounded on that unfortunate day.

On the morning of the 20th, I was sent for by the Hon. Henry Winter Davis, and requested to accompany him to Washington. I understood that a mob had visited his house twice; he was not at home, as he had just returned that morning. I found him much agitated, but hopeful and resolute. We started for Washington in the afternoon, driving out to the Relay, and taking the train there. When we reached the Annapolis Junction, Mr. Davis said, upon reflection, he thought I could do more good by returning to Annapolis and "stiffening up the Governor." On arriving at Annapolis, I saw an unusually large number of persons at the depot, and was prepared to witness some demonstrations of secession sympathy; but all were as polite and courteous to me as ever, and there was a general expression of regret at the occurrences in Baltimore. In the evening, I called to see the Governor. He was much prostrated and very desponding; complained of loss of sleep; said he had been put in a false position by the administration; that he was a true Union man still, but they were taking the ground from beneath him by rash and hasty measures; that he supposed all of us would be regarded as traitors, and Maryland treated as if she had attempted to secede. I endeavored to reassure him, and expressed my earnest sympathy with him in his trying position. After conferring with him about some provision for the safety of his family, in case the mob from Baltimore should seek him in Annapolis, of which, however, I had not the slightest apprehension, we discussed the question of convening the Legislature. I begged him to adhere to his former and often-repeated resolution not to call it, but he was manifestly inclined to think the time had come to share his great responsibility with that body. On Sunday night he made up his mind, and on Tuesday he issued his proclamation, fixing the 26th as the day of meeting.

On Monday, the 22d, the Governor came up State House Hill, looking composed and seeming to be quite cheerful. I inquired his conclusion about the Legislature; he replied he should call it, and would prepare his proclamation immediately. The wish was then expressed that the State might as speedily as possible be filled with Federal bayonets. There were several gentlemen standing around, and the Governor, putting his hand on my shoulder, whispered: "That is exactly what I wish." Yet, the day before, he would not grant General Butler, who was in Annapolis harbor, permission to land his troops. He afterward protested against the seizure of the Annapolis and Elk Ridge Railroad, and fixed upon Frederick City for the meeting of the General Assembly, in order to free that body from the presence of Federal troops. He asked the President to send no more soldiers into Maryland. He proposed to the administration to submit the questions between the North and the South to Lord Lyons, the British Minister, for arbitration. He very tardily responded to the President's call for troops, and when he did so, he required an assurance from the Secretary of War that all the forces raised in Maryland should be kept within her own borders.

From things like these Mr. Greeley was led to sneer at him as the "model Union Governor," forgetting that he, himself, had said: "Let the wayward sisters go." There was, indeed, throughout the North a prevalent suspicion of Maryland Unionism. Even Mr. Lincoln, with all his acuteness and all his means of knowledge, and with a Maryland representative in his Cabinet, harbored doubts, though he was very cautious in expressing them. The Hon. Alexander H. Evans, before mentioned, relates a ludicrous incident, which serves to show the lurking suspicion in the President's mind. After the 19th of April riot Mr. Evans made application to the President on behalf of the Union men of Cecil county for a thousand stand of arms. "You shall have them," said Mr. Lincoln; and then, with that well-known, but indescribable expression playing around his mouth, he added, after a pause, "but are you quite certain which way they will point them?" It must be admitted that appearances gave room for doubt; and yet I firmly believe that Winter Davis was right in claiming for a majority of the Maryland people a fealty to the Union. There were many secessionists—not a few, able, earnest, and fearless; but the real, true sentiment of the mass of the people was on the other side. Governor Hicks, too, notwithstanding some mistakes, and despite the overawing of him on the 19th of April, was a Union man to the core. I knew him well, and for more than three years had been in almost daily intercourse with him.

In dealing with the Union question he had endeavored to practice in the State the same Fabian tactics that President Lincoln so successfully carried out in his management of National affairs. This policy on the part of the Governor was a wise one—at least it was so up to the 18th of April, 1861. He paid respect to the opinions and humored the prejudices of the great body of his people, being himself, in fact, one of them. He possessed great personal popularity. His appearance told much in his favor. He had a downright honest look—a very John Bull he was—softened with a most benevolent expression of countenance. Of medium stature, thick set, rather corpulent, with broad head and face, strong features, prominent chin, mouth shutting firmly down upon molar teeth in front, easy in address, and of dignified carriage, he gave assurance of a man that could do the State some service. He had not the learning of the schools, for he had come up from the ranks, where, in his youthful days, one could scarcely find even that little learning which Pope calls "a dangerous thing."

But he had used his natural gifts to some purpose. He was a close observer, and had studied men until he knew well how to capture them. Beside, he was really kind-hearted, and delighted to do favors. For years he had been the leading Whig in his native county of Dorchester, on the Eastern Shore, and when that old and honored party suddenly declined and died, he joined the Know-Nothing or American organization, "to beat the Democrats." He was elected Governor, in 1857, and had given himself earnestly and faithfully to the discharge of his important duties. At the breaking out of the civil war, he was about sixty years of age, and in appearance was strong and robust, but, in fact, his health was seriously impaired; and he had recently suffered severe family bereavement which greatly unnerved him. In the late Presidential election, Maryland had cast her electoral vote for Breckenridge, who had received not quite a thousand more of the popular vote than Bell, and who, if the nearly six thousand votes cast for Douglas, and the little more than two thousand cast for Lincoln be counted, was in an actual minority. A large majority of the secessionists were found among the voters for Breckenridge; but by no means were all who supported him for secession, for such able and influential men as the Hon. Reverdy Johnson, the Hon. John W. Crisfield, and the Hon. Henry H. Goldsborough, may be taken to represent thousands of others that stood boldly for the integrity of the Union. There were, of course, a number of the Bell men who took the other side; and there were a great many men that sympathized with the South, and yet loved the Union. There were many strong ties between the people of Maryland and the people of the more Southern States. Beside the common property interest in slavery, there was constant intercourse between the people, and the commercial interests of the city of Baltimore were largely dependent upon the South. When the appeal was made that Maryland must go with Virginia, the Union men found it most difficult to answer in the negative with satisfaction to the people; in truth, while Virginia seemed to hesitate, Governor Hicks deemed it prudent to assent to the proposition, feeling hopeful that the "Mother of States" would preserve her allegiance. The complications in which our people were involved may be imagined; and a full appreciation of them would bring a favorable judgment both to the State and its Governor. Robert Burns aptly says:

> "What's done we partly may compute,
> But know not what's resisted."

Governor Hicks received a communication from prominent citizens, shortly after the election, in 1860, requesting him to call an extra session of the Legislature, in order to consider the condition of the country, and to determine what course Maryland should take. The members of the Legislature had been elected in the fall of 1859, mainly on State issues, and were not authorized to represent the people on the momentous questions pending in 1861. The Governor promptly refused to make the call. He was solicited again and again, privately and publicly, by individuals and by county meetings, but he most decidedly declined to do so. He resisted all blandishments, threats, and importunities. A commissioner from Mississippi, a native of Maryland, came to him and invited the co-operation of Maryland, but the Governor declined to accept the invitation. He pursued the same course with the Alabama commissioner, speaking bold, firm words for the Union. He was talking and writing constantly, and encouraging and receiving encouragement in the interest of the Union. Many public gatherings throughout the State passed resolutions commending his course. Such eminent men as the Hon. Reverdy Johnson, Hon. A. W. Bradford, and William H. Collins, Esq., sustained him by eloquent and powerful arguments, made through the press and directly to the people.

The Hon. Henry Winter Davis, not a politic man like the Governor, and, therefore, distrusted by the latter as imprudent and rash, declared himself an unconditional Union man, and by his untiring energy, unequaled eloquence, and matchless ability, did much to mould public opinion, and, eventually, succeeded in bringing a strong party to his own advanced position. He never followed the people; he led them—nor did he care to see how near

they were to him. He marched straight on, taking no step backward, and looking neither to the right nor the left. Governor
Hicks admired him greatly, but shunned him. The Hon. Montgomery Blair, who was the only prominent man in Maryland that
had supported Mr. Lincoln in 1860, by his non-partisan course after
his accession to the Cabinet, making everything subordinate to the
preservation of the Union, obtained great influence with the
Governor, and was regarded as a safe counselor. Both Judge Blair
and Mr. Davis contended strongly that the people of Maryland were
on the side of the Union, and they were right, for notwithstanding
all the mistakes of the National administration, all temptations,
associations, adverse influences, and provocations, no considerable
portion of them ever declared for secession. Indeed, as far as I can
recollect, such a declaration was confined to an out-of-the-way
meeting, composed of a mere handful of men. Even after the 19th
of April riot, when things had a very bad look in Baltimore, an
election for delegates to the Legislature resulted in a withering
rebuke of secession. There was but one set of candidates, and they
were men of ability and integrity of character, not open and avowed
secessionists, but opposed to coercion; and yet, in the midst of all
the prevailing excitement, they received, out of a voting population
of more than thirty thousand, only nine thousand votes.

In May, 1861, at the special election for the extra session of
Congress, all the Union candidates were elected except one, and he
was beaten by a "Union and Peace" candidate. In November,
1861, the Governor and all the other members of the Union State
ticket were elected, with a large majority of both branches of the
Legislature. General Butler, in May, 1861, replying to Governor
Andrews, who found fault with him for offering to suppress an
apprehended slave insurrection at or in the neighborhood of
Annapolis, declares that he had found, by intercourse with the
people there, that they were not rebels, but a large majority of
them strongly for the Union. He also expresses confidence in the
Governor.

But, after all, the critical time was between the election of
Lincoln and his inauguration. There had been a fierce partisan
conflict, and the party in power had lost and expected to be removed
from the places they held so long. The expiring Buchanan administration was supine and inert. Maryland was at the very door of
the capital—her great city overshadowing it. Let us suppose that
she had been disloyal, and that in all those months she had bent her
energies to the plotting of treason; that her Governor had come to

an understanding with the Governors of the other Southern States, and perfected arrangements for resistance accordingly, would Mr. Lincoln have been inaugurated and installed in power at Washington? Would not the Confederate authorities have held the National capital, and, consequently, have had their independence acknowledged by the leading power of Europe?

Is it too much, then, to claim for Maryland that her fidelity to her obligations in the early days of secession perserved the National capital for the installation of the lawfully-elected President; materially shortened the internecine strife, and, under God, determined possibly the ultimate issue of the mighty contest? When other States are honored, let her not be despised. When others are mentioned with affection and gratitude, let her name not be left out.

LEE IN PENNSYLVANIA.

BY GENERAL JAMES LONGSTREET.

It has been my purpose for some years to give to the public a detailed history of the campaign of Gettysburg from its inception to its disastrous close. The execution of this task has been delayed by reason of a press of personal business, and by reason of a genuine reluctance that I have felt against anything that might, even by implication, impugn the wisdom of my late comrades in arms. My sincere feeling upon this subject is best expressed in the following letter, which was written shortly after the battle of Gettysburg, when there was a sly undercurrent of misrepresentation of my course, and in response to an appeal from a respected relative, that I would make some reply to my accusers:

CAMP, CULPEPPER COURT-HOUSE,
July 24th, 1863.

My Dear Uncle:—Your letters of the 13th and 14th were received on yesterday. As to our late battle I cannot say much. I have no right to say anything, in fact, but will venture a little for you, alone. If it goes to aunt and cousins it must be under promise that it will go no further. The battle was not made as I would have made it. My idea was to throw ourselves between the enemy and Washington, select a strong position, and force the enemy to attack us. So far as is given to man the ability to judge, we may say, with confidence, that we should have destroyed the Federal army, marched into Washington and dictated our terms, or, at least, held Washington, and marched over as much of Pennsylvania as we cared to, had we drawn the enemy into attack upon our carefully-chosen position in its rear. General Lee chose the plans adopted; and he is the person appointed to choose and to order. I consider it a part of my duty to express my views to the commanding general. If he approves and adopts them, it is well; if he does not, it is my duty to adopt his views, and to execute his orders as faithfully as if they were my own. I cannot help but think that great results would have been obtained had my views

(414)

been thought better of; yet I am much inclined to accept the present condition as for the best. I hope and trust that it is so. Your programme would all be well enough, had it been practicable, and was duly thought of, too. I fancy that no good ideas upon that campaign will be mentioned at any time, that did not receive their share of consideration by General Lee. The few things that he might have overlooked himself were, I believe, suggested by myself. As we failed, I must take my share of the responsibility. In fact, I would prefer that all the blame should rest upon me. As General Lee is our commander, he should have the support and influence we can give him. If the blame, if there is any, can be shifted from him to me, I shall help him and our cause by taking it. I desire, therefore, that all the responsibility that can be put upon me shall go there, and shall remain there. The truth will be known in time, and I leave that to show how much of the responsibility of Gettysburg rests on my shoulders.   *   *   *

Most affectionately yours,

J. LONGSTREET.

To A. B. LONGSTREET, LL.D., Columbus, Ga.

I sincerely regret that I cannot still rest upon that letter. But I have been so repeatedly and so rancorously assailed by those whose intimacy with the commanding general in that battle gave an apparent importance to their assaults, that I feel impelled by a sense of duty to give to the public a full and comprehensive narration of the campaign from its beginning to its end; especially when I reflect that the publication of the truth cannot now, as it might have done then, injure the cause for which we fought the battle. The request that I furnish this history to the WEEKLY TIMES comes opportunely, for the appeal just made through the press by a distinguished foreigner for all the information that will develop the causes of the failure of that campaign, has provoked anew its partisan and desultory discussion, and renders a plain and logical recital of the facts both timely and important.

After the defeat of Burnside at Fredericksburg, in December, it was believed that active operations were over for the winter, and I was sent with two divisions of my corps to the eastern shore of Virginia, where I could find food for my men during the winter, and send supplies to the Army of Northern Virginia. I spent several months in this department, keeping the enemy close within his fortifications, and foraging with little trouble and great success. On May 1st, I received orders to report to General Lee at Fredericksburg. General Hooker had begun to throw his army across the Rappahannock, and the active campaign was opening. I left Suffolk as soon as possible, and hurried my troops forward. Passing through Richmond, I called to pay my respects to Mr. Seddon, the Secretary of War. Mr. Seddon was, at the time of my visit, deeply considering the critical condition of Pemberton's army at Vicksburg, around which General Grant was then decisively drawing his lines. He informed me that he had in contemplation a plan for concentrating a succoring army at Jackson, Mississippi, under the command of General Johnston, with a view of driving Grant from before Vicksburg by a direct issue-at-arms. He suggested that possibly my corps might be needed to make the army strong enough to handle Grant, and asked me my views. I replied that there was a better plan, in my judgment, for relieving Vicksburg than by a direct assault upon Grant. I proposed that the army then concentrating at Jackson, Mississippi, be moved swiftly to Tullahoma, where General Bragg was then located with a fine army, confronting an army of about equal strength under General Rosecrans, and that at the same time the two divisions of my corps be hurried forward to the same point. The simultaneous arrival of these reinforcements would give us a grand army at Tullahoma. With this army General Johnston might speedily crush Rosecrans, and that he should then turn his force toward the north, and with his splendid army march through Tennessee and Kentucky, and threaten the invasion of Ohio. My idea was that, in the march through those States, the army would meet no organized obstruction; would be supplied with provisions and even reinforcements by those friendly to our cause, and would inevitably result in drawing Grant's army from Vicksburg to look after and protect his own territory. Mr. Seddon adhered to his original views; not so much, I think, from his great confidence in them, as from the difficulty of withdrawing the force suggested from General Lee's army. I was very thoroughly impressed with the practicability of the plan, however, and when I reached General Lee I laid it before him with the freedom justified by our close personal and official relations. The idea seemed to be a new one to him, but he was evidently seriously impressed with it. We discussed it over and over, and I discovered that his main objection to it was that it would, if adopted, force him to divide his army. He left no room to doubt, however, that he believed the idea of an offensive campaign was not only important, but necessary.

At length, while we were discussing the idea of a western forward movement, he asked me if I did not think an invasion of Maryland and Pennsylvania by his own army would accomplish the same result, and I replied that I did not see that it would, because this movement would be too hazardous, and the campaign in thoroughly Union States would require more time and greater preparation than one through Tennessee and Kentucky. I soon discovered that he had determined that he would make some forward movement, and I finally assented that the Pennsylvania campaign might be brought to a successful issue if he could make it offensive in strategy, but defensive in tactics. This point was urged with great persistency. I suggested that, after piercing Pennsylvania and menacing Washington, we should choose a strong position, and force the Federals to attack us, observing that the popular clamor throughout the North would speedily force the Federal general to attempt to drive us out. I recalled to him the battle of Fredericksburg as an instance of a defensive battle, when, with a few thousand men, we hurled the whole Federal army back, crippling and demoralizing it, with trifling loss to our own troops; and Chancellorsville as an instance of an offensive battle, where we dislodged the Federals, it is true, but at such a terrible sacrifice that half a dozen such victories would have ruined us. It will be remembered that Stonewall Jackson once said that " we sometimes fail to drive the enemy from a position. They always fail to drive us." I reminded him, too, of Napoleon's advice to Marmont, to whom he said, when putting him at the head of an invading army, " Select your ground, and make your enemy attack you." I recall these points, simply because I desire to have it distinctly understood that, while I first suggested to General Lee the idea of an offensive campaign, I was never persuaded to yield my argument against the Gettysburg campaign, except with the understanding that we were not to deliver an offensive battle, but to so maneuvre that the enemy should be forced to attack us—or, to repeat, that our campaign should be one of offensive strategy, but defensive tactics. Upon this understanding my assent was given, and General Lee, who had been kind enough to discuss the matter with me patiently, gave the order of march.

The movement was begun on the 3d of June. McLaws' Division of my corps moved out of Fredericksburg, for Culpepper Court-House, followed by Ewell's Corps, on the 4th and 5th of June. Hood's Division and Stuart's cavalry moved at the same time. On the 8th, we found two full corps (for Pickett's Division had joined me then), and Stuart's cavalry, concentrated at Culpepper Court-House. In the meantime a large force of the Federals, cavalry and infantry, had been thrown across the Rappahannock, and sent to attack General Stuart. They were encountered at Brandy Station, on the morning of the 9th, and repulsed. General Lee says of this engagement: "On the 9th, a large force of Federal cavalry, strongly supported by infantry, crossed the Rappahannock at Beverly's ford, and attacked General Stuart. A severe engagement ensued, continuing from early in the morning until late in the afternoon, when

27

the enemy was forced to recross the river with heavy loss, leaving four hundred prisoners, three pieces of artillery, and several colors in our hands." The failure of General Lee to follow up his advantage by pouring the heavy force concentrated at Culpepper Court-House upon this detachment of the Federals, confirmed my convictions that he had determined to make a defensive battle, and would not allow any casual advantage to precipitate a general engagement. If he had had any idea of abandoning the original plan of a tactical defensive, then, in my judgment, was the time to have done so. While at Culpepper, I sent a trusty scout (who had been sent to me by Secretary Seddon, while I was at Suffolk), with instructions to go into the Federal lines, discover his policy, and bring me all the information he could possibly pick up. When this scout asked me very significantly where he should report, I replied: "Find me, wherever I am, when you have the desired information." I did this because I feared to trust him with a knowledge of our future movements. I supplied him with all the gold he needed, and instructed him to spare neither pains nor money to obtain full and accurate information. The information gathered by this scout led to the most tremendous results, as will soon be seen.

General A. P. Hill, having left Fredericksburg as soon as the enemy had retired from his front, was sent to follow Ewell, who had marched up the Valley and cleared it of the Federals. My corps left Culpepper on the 15th, and with a view of covering the march of Hill and Ewell through the Valley, moved along the east side of the Blue Ridge, and occupied Snicker's and Ashby's gaps, and the line of the Blue Ridge. General Stuart was in my front and on my flank, reconnoitering the movements of the Federals. When it was found that Hooker did not intend to attack, I withdrew to the west side, and marched to the Potomac. As I was leaving the Blue Ridge, I instructed General Stuart to follow me, and to cross the Potomac at Shepherdstown, while I crossed at Williamsport, ten miles above. In reply to these instructions, General Stuart informed me that he had discretionary powers from General Lee; whereupon I withdrew. General Stuart held the gap for a while, and then hurried around beyond Hooker's army, and we saw nothing more of him until the evening of the 2d of July, when he came down from York and joined us, having made a complete circuit of the Federal army. The absence of Stuart's cavalry from the main body of the army, during the march, is claimed to have been a fatal error, as General Lee says: "No report had been received (on the 27th) that the enemy had crossed the Potomac, and the absence of the cavalry rendered it impossible to obtain accurate information." The army, therefore, moved forward, as a man might walk over strange ground with his eyes shut. General Lee says of his orders to Stuart: "General Stuart was left to guard the passes of the mountains and to observe the movements of the enemy, who he was instructed to harass and impede as much as possible, should he attempt to cross the Potomac. In that event, General Stuart was directed to move into Maryland, crossing the Potomac on the east or west of the Blue Ridge, as in his judgment should be best, and take position on the right of our column as it advanced."

My corps crossed the Potomac at Williamsport, and General A. P. Hill crossed at Shepherdstown. Our columns were joined together at Hagerstown, and we marched thence into Pennsylvania, reaching Chambersburg on the evening of the 27th. At this point, on the night of the 29th, information was received by which the whole plan of the campaign was changed. We had not heard from the enemy for several days, and General Lee was in doubt as to where he was; indeed, we did not know that he had yet left Virginia. At about ten o'clock that night, Colonel Sorrell, my chief-of-staff, was waked by an orderly, who reported that a suspicious person had just been arrested by the provost marshal. Upon investigation, Sorrell discovered that the suspicious person was the scout Harrison that I had sent out at Culpepper. He was dirt-stained, travel-worn, and very much broken down. After questioning him sufficiently to find that he brought very important information, Colonel Sorrell brought him to my headquarters and awoke me. He gave the information that the enemy had crossed the Potomac, marched northwest, and that the head of his column was at Frederick City, on our right. I felt that this information was exceedingly important, and might involve a change in the direction of our march. General Lee had already issued orders that we were to advance toward Harrisburg. I at once sent the scout to General Lee's headquarters, and followed him myself early in the morning. I found General Lee up, and asked him if the information brought by the scout might not involve a change of direction of the head of our column to the right. He immediately acquiesced in the suggestion, possibly saying that he had already given orders to that effect. The movement toward the enemy was begun at once. Hill marched toward Gettysburg, and my corps followed, with the exception of Pickett's Division, which was left at Chambersburg by General Lee's orders. Ewell was recalled from above—he having advanced as far as Carlisle. I was with General Lee most of that day (the

30th). At about noon, the road in front of my corps was blocked
by Hill's Corps and Ewell's wagon train, which had cut into the
road from above. The orders were to allow these trains to precede
us, and that we should go into camp at Greenwood, about ten miles
from Chambersburg. My infantry was forced to remain in Greenwood until late in the afternoon of the 1st; my artillery did not get
the road until two o'clock on the morning of the 2d.

General Lee spent the night with us, establishing his headquarters, as he frequently did, a short distance from mine. General
Lee says of the movements of this day : " Preparation had been made
to advance upon Harrisburg; but, on the night of the 29th, information was received from a scout that the enemy had crossed the Potomac,
was advancing northward, and that the head of his column had already
reached South Mountain. As our communication with the Potomac
were thus menaced, it was resolved to prevent its further progress in
that direction by concentrating our army on the east side of the
mountains." On the morning of the 1st, General Lee and myself
left his headquarters together, and had ridden three or four miles,
when we heard heavy firing along Hill's front. The firing became
so heavy that General Lee left me and hurried forward to see what
it meant. After attending to some details of my march, I followed.
The firing proceeded from the engagement between our advance and
Reynolds' Corps, in which the Federals were repulsed. This rencontre was totally unexpected on both sides. As an evidence of the
doubt in which General Lee was enveloped, and the anxiety that
weighed him down during the afternoon, I quote from General R.
H. Anderson the report of a conversation had with him during the
engagement. General Anderson was resting with his division at
Cashtown, awaiting orders. About ten o'clock in the morning he
received a message notifying him that General Lee desired to see
him. He found General Lee intently listening to the fire of the
guns, and very much disturbed and depressed. At length he said,
more to himself than to General Anderson : " I cannot think what
has become of Stuart; I ought to have heard from him long before
now. He may have met with disaster, but I hope not. In the
absence of reports from him, I am in ignorance as to what we have
in front of us here. It may be the whole Federal army, or it may
be only a detachment. If it is the whole Federal force we must
fight a battle here; if we do not gain a victory, those defiles and
gorges through which we passed this morning will shelter us from
disaster."

When I overtook General Lee, at five o'clock that afternoon, he said, to my surprise, that he thought of attacking General Meade upon the heights the next day. I suggested that this course seemed to be at variance with the plan of the campaign that had been agreed upon before leaving Fredericksburg. He said: "If the enemy is there to-morrow, we must attack him." I replied: "If he is there, it will be because he is anxious that we should attack him—a good reason, in my judgment, for not doing so." I urged that we should move around by our right to the left of Meade, and put our army between him and Washington, threatening his left and rear, and thus force him to attack us in such position as we might select. I said that it seemed to me that if, during our council at Fredericksburg, we had described the position in which we desired to get the two armies, we could not have expected to get the enemy in a better position for us than that he then occupied; that he was in strong position and would be awaiting us, which was evidence that he desired that we should attack him. I said, further, that his weak point seemed to be his left; hence, I thought that we should move around to his left, that we might threaten it if we intended to maneuvre, or attack it if we determined upon a battle. I called his attention to the fact that the country was admirably adapted for a defensive battle, and that we should surely repulse Meade with crushing loss if we would take position so as to force him to attack us, and suggested that, even if we carried the heights in front of us, and drove Meade out, we should be so badly crippled that we could not reap the fruits of victory; and that the heights of Gettysburg were, in themselves, of no more importance to us than the ground we then occupied, and that the mere possession of the ground was not worth a hundred men to us. That Meade's army, not its position, was our objective. General Lee was impressed with the idea that, by attacking the Federals, he could whip them in detail. I reminded him that if the Federals were there in the morning, it would be proof that they had their forces well in hand, and that with Pickett in Chambersburg, and Stuart out of reach, we should be somewhat in detail. He, however, did not seem to abandon the idea of attack on the next day. He seemed under a subdued excitement, which occasionally took possession of him when "the hunt was up," and threatened his superb equipoise. The sharp battle fought by Hill and Ewell on that day had given him a taste of victory. Upon this point I quote General Fitzhugh Lee, who says, speaking of the attack on the 3d: "He told the father of the writer [his brother] that he was controlled too far by the great confidence he felt in the fighting qualities of his people, who begged simply to be 'turned loose,' and by the assurances of most of his higher officers." I left General Lee quite late on the night of the 1st. Speaking of the battle on the 2d, General Lee says, in his official report: "It had not been intended to fight a general battle at such a distance from our base, unless attacked by the enemy; but, finding ourselves unexpectedly confronted by the Federal army, it became a matter of difficulty to withdraw through the mountains with our large trains."

When I left General Lee on the night of the 1st, I believed that he had made up his mind to attack, but was confident that he had not not yet determined as to when the attack should be made. The assertion first made by General Pendleton, and echoed by his confederates, that I was ordered to open the attack at sunrise, is totally false. Documentary testimony upon this point will be presented in the course of this article. Suffice it to say, at present, that General Lee never, in his life, gave me orders to open an attack at a specific hour. He was perfectly satisfied that, when I had my troops in position, and was ordered to attack, no time was ever lost. On the night of the 1st I left him without any orders at all. On the morning of the 2d, I went to General Lee's headquarters at daylight, and renewed my views against making an attack. He seemed resolved, however, and we discussed the probable results. We observed the position of the Federals, and got a general idea of the nature of the ground. About sunrise General Lee sent Colonel Venable, of his staff, to General Ewell's headquarters, ordering him to make a reconnoissance of the ground in his front, with a view of making the main attack on his left. A short time afterward he followed Colonel Venable in person. He returned at about nine o'clock, and informed me that it would not do to have Ewell open the attack. He, finally, determined that I should make the main attack on the extreme right. It was fully eleven o'clock when General Lee arrived at this conclusion and ordered the movement. In the meantime, by General Lee's authority, Law's Brigade, which had been put upon picket duty, was ordered to rejoin my command, and, upon my suggestion that it would be better to await its arrival, General Lee assented. We waited about forty minutes for these troops, and then moved forward. A delay of several hours occurred in the march of the troops. The cause of this delay was that we had been ordered by General Lee to proceed cautiously upon the forward movement, so as to avoid being seen by the enemy. General Lee ordered Colonel Johnston, of his engineer corps, to lead and conduct the head of the column. My troops, therefore, moved forward under guidance of a special officer of General Lee, and with instructions to follow his directions.

I left General Lee only after the line had stretched out on the march, and rode along with Hood's Division, which was in the rear. The march was necessarily slow, the conductor frequently encountering points that exposed the troops to the view of the signal station on Round Top. At length the column halted. After waiting some time, supposing that it would soon move forward, I sent to the front to inquire the occasion of the delay. It was reported that the column was awaiting the movements of Colonel Johnston, who was trying to lead it by some route by which it could pursue its march without falling under view of the Federal signal station. Looking up toward Round Top I saw that the signal station was in full view, and, as we could plainly see this station, it was apparent that our heavy columns was seen from their position, and that further efforts to conceal ourselves would be a waste of time.

I became very impatient at this delay, and determined to take upon myself the responsibility of hurrying the troops forward. I did not order General McLaws forward, because, as the head of the column, he had direct orders from General Lee to follow the conduct of Colonel Johnston. Therefore, I sent orders to Hood, who was in the rear and not encumbered by these instructions, to push his division forward by the most direct route, so as to take position on my right. He did so, and thus broke up the delay. The troops were rapidly thrown into position, and preparations were made for the attack. It may be proper just here to consider the relative strength and position of the two armies. Our army was fifty-two thousand infantry; Meade's was ninety-five thousand. These are our highest figures, and the enemy's lowest. We had learned on the night of the 1st, from some prisoners captured near Seminary Ridge, that the First, Eleventh, and Third Corps had arrived by the Emmetsburg road, and had taken position on the heights in front of us, and that reinforcements had been seen coming by the Baltimore road, just after the fight of the 1st. From an intercepted dispatch, we learned that another corps was in camp, about four miles from the field. We had every reason, therefore, to believe that the Federals were prepared to renew the battle. Our army was stretched in an elliptical curve, reaching from the front of Round Top around Seminary Ridge, and enveloping Cemetery Heights on the left; thus covering a space of four or five miles. The enemy occupied the high ground in front of us, being massed within a curve of about two miles, nearly concentric with the curve described by our forces. His line was about one thousand four hundred yards from ours. Any one will see that the proposition for this inferior force to assault and drive out the masses of troops upon the heights, was a very problematical one. My orders from General Lee were "to envelop the enemy's left, and begin the attack there, following up, as near as possible, the direction of the Emmetsburg road."

My corps occupied our right, with Hood on the extreme right, and McLaws next. Hill's Corps was next to mine, in front of the Federal centre, and Ewell was on our extreme left. My corps, with Pickett's Division absent, numbered hardly thirteen thousand men. I realized that the fight was to be a fearful one; but being assured that my flank would be protected by the brigades of Wilcox, Perry, Wright, Posey, and Mahone, moving *en echelon*, and that Ewell was to co-operate by a direct attack on the enemy's right, and Hill to threaten his centre, and attack if opportunity offered, and thus prevent reinforcements from being launched either against myself or Ewell, it seemed possible that we might possibly dislodge the great army in front of us. At half-past three o'clock the order was given General Hood to advance upon the enemy, and, hurrying to the head of McLaws' Division, I moved with his line. Then was fairly commenced what I do not hesitate to pronounce the best three hours' fighting ever done by any troops on any battle-field. Directly in front of us, occupying the peach orchard, on a piece of elevated ground that General Lee desired me to take and hold for his artillery, was the Third Corps of the Federals, commanded by General Sickles. My men charged with great spirit and dislodged the Federals from the peach orchard with but little delay, though they fought stubbornly. We were then on the crest of Seminary Ridge. The artillery was brought forward and put into position at the peach orchard. The infantry swept down the slope and soon reached the marshy ground that lay between Seminary and Cemetery Ridges, fighting their way over every foot of ground and against overwhelming odds. At every step we found that reinforcements were pouring into the Federals from every side. Nothing could stop my men, however, and they commenced their heroic charge up the side of Cemetery Ridge. Our attack was to progress in the general direction of the Emmetsburg road, but the Federal troops, as they were forced from point to point, availing themselves of the stone fences and boulders near the mountain as rallying points, so annoyed our right flank that General Hood's Division was obliged to make a partial change of front so as to relieve itself of this galling flank fire. This drew General McLaws a little further to the right than General Lee had anticipated, so that the defensive advantages of the ground enabled the Federals to delay our purposes until they could occupy Little Round Top, which they just then discovered was the key to their position. The force thrown upon this point was so strong as to seize our right, as it were, in a vice.

Still the battle on our main line continued to progress. The situation was a critical one. My corps had been fighting over an hour, having encountered and driven back line after line of the enemy. In front of them was a high and rugged ridge, on its crest the bulk of the Army of the Potomac, numbering six to one, and securely resting behind strong positions. My brave fellows never hesitated, however. Their duty was in front of them and they met it. They charged up the hill in splendid style, sweeping everything before them, dislodging the enemy in the face of a withering fire. When they had fairly started up the second ridge, I discovered that they were suffering terribly from a fire that swept over their right and left flanks. I also found that my left flank was not protected by the brigades that were to move *en echelon* with it. McLaws' line was consequently spread out to the left to protect its flank, and Hood's line was extended to the right to protect its flank from the sweeping fire of the large bodies of troops that were posted on Round Top.* These two movements of extension so drew my forces out, that I found myself attacking Cemetery Hill with a single line of battle against no less than fifty thousand troops.

My two divisions at that time were cut down to eight or nine thousand men, four thousand having been killed or wounded. We felt at every step the heavy stroke of fresh troops—the sturdy regular blow that tells a soldier instantly that he has encountered reserves or reinforcements. We received no support at all, and there was no evidence of co-operation on any side. To urge my men forward under these circumstances would have been madness, and I withdrew them in good order to the peach orchard that we had taken from the Federals early in the afternoon. It may be mentioned here, as illustrative of the dauntless spirit of these men, that

---

* The importance of Round Top, as a *point d' appui*, was not appreciated until after my attack. General Meade seems to have alluded to it as a point to be occupied, " if practicable," but in such slighting manner as to show that he did not deem it of great importance. So it was occupied by an inadequate force. As our battle progressed, pushing the Federals back from point to point, subordinate officers and soldiers, seeking shelter, as birds fly to cover in a tempest, found behind the large boulders of its rock-bound sides, not only protection but rallying points. These reinforcements to the troops already there, checked our advance on the right, and some superior officer, arriving just then, divined from effect the cause, and threw a force into Round Top that transformed it, as if by magic, into a Gibraltar.

when General Humphreys (of Mississippi) was ordered to withdraw his troops from the charge, he thought there was some mistake, and retired to a captured battery, near the swale between the two ridges, where he halted, and, when ordered to retire to the new line a second time, he did so under protest.* Our men had no thought of retreat. They broke every line they encountered   When the order to withdraw was given, a courier was sent to General Lee, informing him of the result of the day's work.

Before pursuing this narrative further, I shall say a word or two concerning this assault. I am satisfied that my force, numbering hardly thirteen thousand men, encountered during that three and a half hours of bloody work not less than sixty-five thousand of the Federals, and yet their charge was not checked nor their line broken until we ordered them to withdraw. Mr. Whitelaw Reid, writing a most excellent account of this charge to the Cincinnati *Gazette*, says: "It was believed, from the terrific attack, that the whole rebel army, Ewell's Corps included, was massed on our centre and left, and so a single brigade was left to hold the rifle-pits on the right, and the rest hurried across the little neck of land to strengthen our weakening lines." He describes, too, the haste with which corps after corps was hurried forward to the left to check the advance of my two-thirds of one corps. General Meade himself testifies (see his official report) that the Third, the Second, the Fifth, the Sixth, and the Eleventh Corps, all of the Twelfth, except one brigade, and part of the First Corps, engaged my handful of heroes during that glorious but disastrous afternoon. I found that night that four thousand five hundred and twenty-nine of my men, more than one-third of their total number, had been left on the field. History records no parallel to the fight made by these two divisions on the 2d of July at Gettysburg. I cannot refrain from inserting just here an account of the battle of the 2d, taken from a graphic account in the New York *World*. It will be seen that the correspondent treats the charge of my thirteen thousand men, as if it were the charge of the whole army. The account is as follows:

He then began a heavy fire on Cemetery Hill. It must not be thought that this wrathful fire was unanswered. Our artillery began to play within a few moments, and hurled back defiance and like destruction upon the rebel lines. Until six

---

* The troops engaged with me in the fight of the 2d were mostly Georgians, as follows: The four Georgia brigades of Generals Benning, Anderson, Wofford, and Semmes, General Kershaw's South Carolina Brigade, General Law's Alabama Brigade, General Barksdale's (afterward General Humphrey's) Mississippi Brigade, and General Robertson's Texas Brigade.

o'clock the roar of cannon, the rush of missiles, and the bursting of bombs filled all the air. The clangor alone of this awful combat might well have confused and awed a less cool and watchful commander than General Meade. It did not confuse him. With the calculation of a tactician, and the eye of an experienced judge, he watched from his headquarters, on the hill, whatever movement under the murky cloud which enveloped the rebel lines might first disclose the intention which it was evident this artillery firing covered. About six o'clock P. M. silence, deep, awfully impressive, but momentary, was permitted, as if by magic, to dwell upon the field. Only the groans—unheard before—of the wounded and dying, only a murmur, a warning memory of the breeze through the foliage; only the low rattle of preparation of what was to come embroidered this blank stillness. Then, as the smoke beyond the village was lightly borne to the eastward, the woods on the left were seen filled with dark masses of infantry, three columns deep, who advanced at a quick step. Magnificent! Such a charge by such a force—full forty-five thousand men, under Hill and Longstreet—even though it threatened to pierce and annihilate the Third Corps, against which it was directed, drew forth cries of admiration from all who beheld it. General Sickles and his splendid command withstood the shock with a determination that checked but could not fully restrain it. Back, inch by inch, fighting, falling, dying, cheering, the men retired. The rebels came on more furiously, halting at intervals, pouring volleys that struck our troops down in scores. General Sickles, fighting desperately, was struck in the leg and fell. The Second Corps came to the aid of his decimated column. The battle then grew fearful. Standing firmly up against the storm, our troops, though still outnumbered, gave back shot for shot, volley for volley, almost death for death. Still the enemy was not restrained. Down he came upon our left with a momentum that nothing could check. The rifled guns that lay before our infantry on a knoll were in danger of capture. General Hancock was wounded in the thigh, General Gibbon in the shoulder The Fifth Corps, as the First and Second wavered anew, went into the breach with such shouts and such volleys as made the rebel column tremble at last. Up from the valley behind, another battery came rolling to the heights, and flung its contents in an instant down in the midst of the enemy's ranks. Crash! crash! with discharges deafening, terrible, the musketry firing went on. The enemy, re-forming after each discharge with wondrous celerity and firmness, still pressed up the declivity. What hideous courage filled the minutes between the appearance of the Fifth Corps and the advance to the support of the rebel columns of still another column from the right, I cannot bear to tell. Men fell, as the leaves fall in autumn, before those horrible discharges. Faltering for an instant, the rebel columns seemed about to recede before the tempest. But their officers, who could be seen through the smoke of the conflict galloping, and swinging their swords along the lines, rallied them anew, and the next instant the whole line sprang forward, as if to break through our own by mere weight of numbers. A division from the Twelfth Corps, on the extreme right, reached the scene at this instant, and at the same time Sedgwick came up with the Sixth Corps, having finished a march of nearly thirty-six consecutive hours. To what rescue they came their officers saw and told them. Weary as they were, barefooted, hungry, fit to drop for slumber, as they were, the wish for victory was so blended with the thought of exhaustion that they cast themselves, in turn, *en masse* into line of battle, and went down on the enemy with death in their weapons and cheers on their lips. The rebel's camel's back was broken by this "feather." His line staggered, reeled, and drifted slowly back, while the shouts of our soldiers, lifted up amid the roar of musketry over the bodies of the dead and wounded, proclaimed the completeness of their victory.

It may be imagined that I was astonished at the fact, that we received no support after we had driven the Federals from the peach orchard and one thousand yards beyond. If General Ewell had engaged the army in his front at that time (say four o'clock) he would have prevented their massing their whole army in my front, and while he and I kept their two wings engaged, Hill would have found their centre weak, and should have threatened it while I broke through their left and dislodged them. Having failed to move at four o'clock, while the enemy was in his front, it was still more surprising that he did not advance at five o'clock with vigor and promptness, when the trenches in front of him were vacated, or rather held by one single brigade (as General Meade's testimony before the Committee on the Conduct of the War states). Had he taken these trenches and scattered the brigade that held them, he would have found himself in the Federals' flank and rear. His attack in the rear must have dislodged the Federals, as it would have been totally unexpected—it being believed that he was in front with me. Hill, charging upon the centre at the same time, would have increased their disorder and we should have won the field. But Ewell did not advance until I had withdrawn my troops, and the First Corps, after winning position after position, was forced to withdraw from the field with two corps of their comrades within sight and resting upon their arms. Ewell did not move until about dusk (according to his own report). He then occupied the trenches that the enemy had vacated (see General Meade's report). The real cause of Ewell's non-compliance with General Lee's orders was that he had broken his line of battle by sending two brigades off on some duty up the York road. General Early says that my failure to attack at sunrise was the cause of Ewell's line being broken at the time I did attack. This is not only absurd, but impossible. After sunrise that morning, Colonel Venable and General Lee were at Ewell's headquarters discussing the policy of opening the attack with Ewell's Corps. They left Ewell with this definite order: that he was to hold himself in readiness to support my attack when it was made. It is silly to say that he was ready at sunrise, when he was not ready at four o'clock when the attack was really made. His orders were to hold himself in readiness to co-operate with my attack when it was made. In breaking his line of battle he rendered himself unable to support me when he would have been potential. Touching the failure of the supporting brigades of Anderson's Division to cover McLaws' flank by *echelon* movements, as directed, there is little to be said. Those brigades acted gallantly, but went astray early in the fight. General Anderson, in his report, says: "A strong fire was poured upon our right flank, which had become detached from McLaws' left." General Lee, alluding to the action of these two brigades, says: "But having become separated from McLaws, Wilcox's and Wright's Brigades advanced with great gallantry, breaking successive lines of the enemy's infantry, and compelling him to abandon much of his artillery. Wilcox reached the foot and Wright gained the crest of the ridge itself, driving the enemy down the opposite side; but having become separated from McLaws, and gone beyond the other two brigades of the division they were to attack in front and on both flanks, and compelled to retire, being unable to bring off any of the captured artillery, McLaws' left also fell back, and it being now nearly dark, General Longstreet determined to await the arrival of Pickett." So much for the action of the first day.

I did not see General Lee that night. On the next morning he came to see me, and, fearing that he was still in his disposition to attack, I tried to anticipate him, by saying: "General, I have had my scouts out all night, and I find that you still have an excellent opportunity to move around to the right of Meade's army, and maneuvre him into attacking us." He replied, pointing with his fist at Cemetery Hill: "The enemy is there, and I am going to strike him." I felt then that it was my duty to express my convictions; I said: "General, I have been a soldier all my life. I have been with soldiers engaged in fights by couples, by squads, companies, regiments, divisions, and armies, and should know, as well as any one, what soldiers can do. It is my opinion that no fifteen thousand men ever arrayed for battle can take that position," pointing to Cemetery Hill. General Lee, in reply to this, ordered me to prepare Pickett's Division for the attack. I should not have been so urgent had I not foreseen the hopelessness of the proposed assault. I felt that I must say a word against the sacrifice of my men; and then I felt that my record was such that General Lee would or could not misconstrue my motives. I said no more, however, but turned away. The most of the morning was consumed in waiting for Pickett's men, and getting into position. The plan of assault was as follows: Our artillery was to be massed in a wood from which Pickett was to charge, and it was to pour a continuous fire upon the cemetery. Under cover of this fire, and supported by it, Pickett was to charge.

Our artillery was in charge of General E. P. Alexander, a brave and gifted officer. Colonel Walton was my chief of artillery; but Alexander, being at the head of the column, and being first in position, and being, beside, an officer of unusual promptness, sagacity, and intelligence, was given charge of the artillery. The arrangements were completed about one o'clock. General Alexander had arranged that a battery of seven eleven-pound howitzers, with fresh horses and full caissons, were to charge with Pickett, at the head of his line, but General Pendleton, from whom the guns had been borrowed, recalled them just before the charge was made, and thus deranged this wise plan. Never was I so depressed as upon that day. I felt that my men were to be sacrificed, and that I should have to order them to make a hopeless charge. I had instructed General Alexander, being unwilling to trust myself with the entire responsibility, to carefully observe the effect of the fire upon the enemy, and when it began to tell to notify Pickett to begin the assault. I was so much impressed with the hopelessness of the charge, that I wrote the following note to General Alexander: "If the artillery fire does not have the effect to drive off the enemy or greatly demoralize him, so as to make our efforts pretty certain, I would prefer that you should not advise General Pickett to make the charge. I shall rely a great deal on your judgment to determine the matter, and shall expect you to let Pickett know when the moment offers."

To my note the General replied as follows: "I will only be able to judge the effect of our fire upon the enemy by his return fire, for his infantry is but little exposed to view, and the smoke will obscure the whole field. If, as I infer from your note, there is an alternative to this attack, it should be carefully considered before opening our fire, for it will take all of the artillery ammunition we have left to test this one thoroughly; and, if the result is unfavorable, we will have none left for another effort; and, even if this is entirely successful, it can only be so at a very bloody cost." I still desired to save my men, and felt that if the artillery did not produce the desired effect, I would be justified in holding Pickett off. I wrote this note to Colonel Walton at exactly 1.30 P. M.: "Let the batteries open. Order great precision in firing. If the batteries at the peach orchard cannot be used against the point we intend attacking, let them open on the enemy at Rocky Hill." The cannonading which opened along both lines was grand. In a few moments a courier brought a note to General Pickett (who was standing near me) from Alexander, which, after reading, he handed to me. It was as follows: "If you are coming at all, you must come at once, or I cannot give you proper support; but the enemy's fire has not slackened at all; at least eighteen guns are still firing from the cemetery itself." After I had read the note, Pickett said to me: "General, shall I advance?" My feelings had so overcome me that

I would not speak, for fear of betraying my want of confidence to him. I bowed affirmation, and turned to mount my horse. Pickett immediately said: "I shall lead my division forward, sir." I spurred my horse to the wood where Alexander was stationed with artillery. When I reached him, he told me of the disappearance of the seven guns which were to have led the charge with Pickett, and that his ammunition was so low that he could not properly support the charge. I at once ordered him to stop Pickett until the ammunition had been replenished. He informed me that he had no ammunition with which to replenish. I then saw that there was no help for it, and that Pickett must advance under his orders. He swept past our artillery in splendid style, and the men marched steadily and compactly down the slope. As they started up the ridge, over one hundred cannon from the breastworks of the Federals hurled a rain of canister, grape, and shell down upon them; still they pressed on until half way up the slope, when the crest of the hill was lit with a solid sheet of flame as the masses of infantry rose and fired. When the smoke cleared away, Pickett's Division was gone. Nearly two-thirds of his men lay dead on the field, and the survivors were sullenly retreating down the hill. Mortal man could not have stood that fire. In half an hour the contested field was cleared and the battle of Gettysburg was over.

When this charge had failed, I expected that, of course, the enemy would throw himself against our shattered ranks and try to crush us. I sent my staff officers to the rear to assist in rallying the troops, and hurried to our line of batteries, as the only support that I could give them, knowing that my presence would impress upon every one of them the necessity of holding the ground to the last extremity. I knew if the army was to be saved, those batteries must check the enemy. As I rode along the line of artillery, I observed my old friend Captain Miller, Washington Artillery, of Sharpsburg record, walking between his guns and smoking his pipe as quietly and contentedly as he could at his camp-fire. The enemy's skirmishers were then advancing and threatening assault. For unaccountable reasons, the enemy did not pursue his advantage. Our army was soon in compact shape, and its face turned once more toward Virginia. I may mention here that it has been absurdly said that General Lee ordered me to put Hood's and McLaws' Divisions in support of Pickett's assault. General Lee never ordered any such thing.* After our troops were all arranged for assault, General Lee

* Colonel Taylor says that General Lee, in his presence, gave me orders to put Hood's and McLaws' Divisions in this column of attack. This I deny, and do not

rode with me twice over the lines to see that everything was arranged according to his wishes. He was told that we had been more particular in giving the orders than ever before; that the commanders had been sent for, and the point of attack had been carefully designated, and that the commanders had been directed to communicate to their subordinates, and through them to every soldier in the command, the work that was before them, so that they should nerve themselves for the attack, and fully understand it. After leaving me, he again rode over the field once, if not twice, so that there was really no room for misconstruction or misunderstanding of his wishes. He could not have thought of giving any such an order. Hood and McLaws were confronted by a largely superior force of the enemy on the right of Pickett's attack. To have moved them to Pickett's support, would have disengaged treble their number of Federals, who would have swooped down from their rocky fastnesses against the flank of our attacking column, and swept our army from the field. A reference to any of the maps of Gettysburg will show from the position of the troops that this would have been the inevitable result. General Lee and myself never had any deliberate conversation about Gettysburg. The subject was never broached by either of us to the other. On one occasion it came up casually, and he said to me (alluding to the charge of Pickett, on the 3d), "General, why didn't you stop all that thing that day?" I replied that I could not, under the circumstances, assume such a responsibility, as no discretion had been left me.

Before discussing the weak points of the campaign of Gettys-

---

suppose he will claim that any one else heard the order. If the reader will examine any of the maps of Gettysburg, he will see that the withdrawal of these two divisions from their line of battle would have left half of General Lee's line of battle open, and by the shortest route to his line of supplies and retreat. Fully one-half of his army would have been in the column of assault, and half of Meade's army would have been free to sally out on the flank of our column, and we should have been destroyed on that field of battle, beyond a doubt. Of course, if we assume that Meade would place his army in line of battle, and allow us to select our point of attack, we could have massed against it, and rushed through. But this assumption would be absurd. The only way for those divisions to have been moved, was to have attacked the heights in front. But this attack had been tried, and failed the day before. If Pickett had shown signs of getting a lodgment, I should, of course, have pushed the other divisions forward to support the attack. But I saw that he was going to pieces at once. When Colonel Freemantle (Her Majesty's service) approached me (see his account), and congratulated me on Pickett's apparent success, I told him that his line would break in a moment—that he was not strong enough to make a serious impression. My assertion was correct. To have rushed forward my two divisions, then carrying bloody noses from their terrible conflict the day before, would have been madness.

burg, it is proper that I should say that I do so with the greatest affection for General Lee, and the greatest reverence for his memory. The relations existing between us were affectionate, confidential, and even tender, from first to last. There was never a harsh word between us. It is, then, with a reluctant spirit that I write a calm and critical review of the Gettysburg campaign, because that review will show that our commanding general was unfortunate at several points. There is no doubt that General Lee, during the crisis of that campaign, lost the matchless equipoise that usually characterized him, and that whatever mistakes were made were not so much matters of deliberate judgment as the impulses of a great mind disturbed by unparalleled conditions. General Lee was thrown from his balance (as is shown by the statement of General Fitzhugh Lee) by too great confidence in the prowess of his troops and (as is shown by General Anderson's statement) by the deplorable absence of General Stuart and the perplexity occasioned thereby. With this preface I proceed to say that the Gettysburg campaign was weak in these points— adhering, however, to my opinion that a combined movement against Rosecrans, in Tennessee, and a march toward Cincinnati would have given better results than could possibly have been secured by the invasion of Pennsylvania: First, the offensive strategical, but defensive tactical, plan of the campaign, as agreed upon, should never have been abandoned after we entered the enemy's country. Second, if there ever was a time when the abandonment of that plan could have promised decisive results, it was at Brandy Station, where, after Stuart had repulsed the force thrown across the river, we might have fallen on that force and crushed it, and then put ourselves in position, threatening the enemy's right and rear, which would have dislodged him from his position at Fredericksburg, and given us the opportunity for an effective blow. Third, General Stuart should not have been permitted to leave the general line of march, thus forcing us to march blindfolded into the enemy's country; to this may be attributed, in my opinion, the change of the policy of the campaign. Fourth, the success obtained by the accidental rencontre on the 1st, should have been vigorously prosecuted, and the enemy should have been given no time to fortify or concentrate. Fifth, on the night of the 1st, the army should have been carried around to Meade's right and rear, and posted between him and his capital, and we could have maneuvred him into an attack. Sixth, when the attack was made on the enemy's left, on the 2d, by my corps, Ewell should have been required to co-operate by a vigorous movement against his right, and Hill should have moved against his centre. Had this

28

been done, his army would have been dislodged, beyond question. Seventh, on the morning of the 3d it was not yet too late to move to the right and manœuvre the Federals into attacking us. Eighth, Pickett's Division should not have been ordered to assault Cemetery Ridge on the 3d, as we had already tested the strength of that position sufficiently to admonish us that we could not dislodge him. While the co-operation of Generals Ewell and Hill, on the 2d, by vigorous assault at the moment my battle was in progress, would, in all probability, have dislodged the Federals from their position, it does not seem that such success would have yielded the fruits anticipated at the inception of the campaign. The battle, as it was fought, would, in any result, have so crippled us that the Federals would have been able to make good their retreat, and we should soon have been obliged to retire to Virginia with nothing but victory to cover our waning cause.

The morals of the victory might have dispirited the North, and aroused the South to new exertions, but it would have been nothing in the game being played by the two armies at Gettysburg. As to the abandonment of the tactical defensive policy that we had agreed upon, there can be no doubt that General Lee deeply deplored it as a mistake. His remark, made just after the battle, " It is all my fault," meant just what it said. It adds to the nobility and magnanimity of that remark, when we reflect that it was the utterance of a deep-felt truth, rather than a mere sentiment. In a letter written to me by General Lee, in January, 1864, he says: " Had I taken your advice at Gettysburg, instead of pursuing the course I did, how different all might have been." Captain T. J. Gorie, of Houston, Texas, a gentleman of high position and undoubted integrity, writes to me upon this same point as follows: "Another important circumstance which I distinctly remember was in the winter of 1864, when you sent me from East Tennessee to Orange Court-House with dispatches for General Lee. Upon my arrival there, General Lee asked me in his tent, where he was alone with two or three Northern papers on his table. He remarked that he had just been reading the Northern official report of the battle of Gettysburg; that he had become satisfied, from reading those reports that, if he had permitted you to carry out your plans on the third day, instead of making the attack on Cemetery Hill, we would have been successful." I cannot see, as has been claimed, why the absence of General Lee's cavalry should have justified his attack on the enemy. On the contrary, while they may have perplexed him, I hold that it was additional reason for his not hazarding an attack. At the time the attack was ordered, we were fearful that our cavalry had been destroyed. In case of a disaster, and a forced retreat, we should have had nothing to cover our retreat. When so much was at stake as at Gettysburg, the absence of the cavalry should have prevented the taking of any chances.

As to the failure of Stuart to move with the army to the west side of the Blue Ridge, I can only call attention to the fact that General Lee gave him discretionary orders. He doubtless did as he thought best. Had no discretion been given him, he would have known and fallen into his natural position—my right flank. But authority thus given a subordinate general, implies an opinion on the part of the commander that something better than the drudgery of a march along our flank might be open to him, and one of General Stuart's activity and gallantry should not be expected to fail to seek it. As to Ewell's failure to prosecute the advantage won on the 1st, there is little to be said, as the commanding general was on the field. I merely quote from his (General Ewell's) official report. He says: "The enemy had fallen back to a commanding position that was known to us as Cemetery Hill, south of Gettysburg, and quickly showed a formidable front there. On entering the town, I received a message from the commanding general to attack the hill, if I could do so to advantage. I could not bring artillery to bear on it; all the troops with me were jaded by twelve hours' marching and fighting, and I was notified that General Johnson was close to the town with his division, the only one of my corps that had not been engaged, Anderson's Division, of the Third Corps, having been halted to let them pass. Cemetery Hill was not assailable from the town, and I determined, with Johnson's Division, to take possession of a wooded hill to my left, on a line with and commanding Cemetery Hill. Before Johnson got up the Federals were reported moving to our left flank—our extreme left—and I could see what seemed to be his skirmishers in that direction. Before this report could be investigated by Lieutenant T. T. Turner, of my staff, and Lieutenant Robert Early, sent to investigate it, and Johnson placed in position, the night was far advanced." General Lee explains his failure to send positive orders to Ewell to follow up the flying enemy as follows: "The attack was not pressed that afternoon, the enemy's force being unknown, and it being considered advisable to await the arrival of the rest of our troops. Orders were sent back to hasten their march, and, in the meantime, every effort was made to ascertain the numbers and positions of the enemy, and find the most favorable point to attack."

Pursuit "pell-mell" is sometimes justified in a mere retreat. It is the accepted principle of action in a rout. General Early, in his report of this day's work, says "the enemy had been routed." He should, therefore, have been followed by everything that could have been thrown upon his heels, not so much to gain the heights, which were recognized as the rallying point, but to prevent his rallying at all in time to form lines for another battle. If the enemy had been routed, this could and should have been done. In the "Military Annals of Louisiana" (Napier Bartlett, Esq.), in the account of this rout, he says: "Hays had received orders, through Early, from General Ewell (though Lee's general instructions were subsequently the reverse) to halt at Gettysburg, and advance no further in case he should succeed in capturing that place. But Hays now saw that the enemy were coming around by what is known as the Baltimore road, and were making for the heights—the Cemetery Ridge. This ridge meant life or death, and for the possession of it the battles of the 2d and 3d were fought. * * * Owing to the long detour the enemy was compelled to make, it was obvious that he could not get his artillery in position on the heights for one or two hours. The immediate occupation of the heights by the Confederates, who were in position to get them at the time referred to, was a matter of vital importance. Hays recognized it as such, and presently sent for Early. The latter thought as Hays, but declined to disobey orders. At the urgent request of General Hays, however, he sent for General Ewell. When the latter arrived, many precious moments had been lost. But the enemy, who did not see its value until the arrival of Hancock, had not yet appeared in force." General Hays told me, ten years after the battle, that he "could have seized the heights without the loss of ten men." Here we see General Early adhering to orders when his own conviction told him he should not do so, and refusing to allow General Hays to seize a point recognized by him as of vast importance, because of technical authority, at a moment when he admitted and knew that disregard of the order would only have made more secure the point at issue when the order was given.

Before closing this article, I desire to settle finally and fully one point, concerning which there has been much discussion, viz.: The alleged delay in the attack upon the 2d. I am moved to this task, not so much by an ambition to dissolve the cloud of personal misrepresentation that has settled about my head, as by a sense of duty which leads me to determine a point that will be of value to the historian. It was asserted by General Pendleton, with whom the carefulness of statement or deliberateness of judgment has never been a characteristic, but who has been distinguished for the unreliability of his memory, that General Lee ordered me to attack the enemy at sunrise on the 2d. General J. A. Early has, in positive terms, indorsed this charge, which I now proceed to disprove. I have said that I left General Lee late in the night of the 1st, and that he had not then determined when the attack should be made; that I went to his headquarters early the next morning, and was with him for some time; that he left me early after sunrise and went to Ewell's headquarters, with the express view of seeing whether or not the main attack should be made then, and that he returned about nine o'clock; and that after discussing the ground for some time, he determined that I should make the main attack, and at eleven o'clock gave me the order to prepare for it. I now present documents that sustain these assertions.

The first letter that I offer is from Colonel W. H. Taylor, of General Lee's staff. It is as follows:

NORFOLK, VA., April 28th, 1875.

Dear General—I have received your letter of the 20th instant. I have not read the article of which you speak, nor have I ever seen any copy of General Pendleton's address; indeed, I have read little or nothing of what has been written since the war. In the first place, because I could not spare the time, and in the second, of those of whose writings I have heard, I deem but very few entitled to any attention whatever. I can only say, that I never before heard of the "sunrise attack" you were to have made, as charged by General Pendleton. If such an order was given you I never knew of it, or it has strangely escaped my memory. I think it more than probable that if General Lee had had your troops available the evening previous to the day of which you speak, he would have ordered an early attack; but this does not touch the point at issue. I regard it as a great mistake on the part of those who, perhaps because of political differences, now undertake to criticise and attack your war record. Such conduct is most ungenerous, and I am sure meets the disapprobation of all good Confederates with whom I have had the pleasure of associating in the daily walks of life. Yours, very respectfully,

W. H. TAYLOR.

To GENERAL LONGSTREET.

The next letter is from Colonel Charles Marshall, of General Lee's staff, who has charge of all the papers left by General Lee. It is as follows:

BALTIMORE, MD., May 7th, 1875.

Dear General—Your letter of the 20th ultimo was received, and should have had an earlier reply, but for my engagements preventing me from looking at my papers to find what I could on the subject. I have no personal recollection of the order to which you refer. It certainly was not conveyed by me, nor is there anything in General Lee's official report to show the attack on the 2d was expected by him to begin earlier, except that he notices that there was not proper concert of action on that day. * * * * Respectfully,

CHARLES MARSHALL.

To GENERAL LONGSTREET, New Orleans.

Then a letter from General A. S. Long, who was General Lee's Military Secretary:

BIG ISLAND, BEDFORD, VA., May 31st, 1875.

Dear General—Your letter of the 20th ultimo, referring to an assertion of General Pendleton's, made in a lecture delivered several years ago, which was recently published in the *Southern Historical Society Magazine* substantially as follows: "That General Lee ordered General Longstreet to attack General Meade at sunrise on the morning of the 2d of July," has been received. I do not recollect of hearing of an order to attack at sunrise, or at any other designated hour, pending the operations at Gettysburg during the first three days of July, 1863. * * *

Yours, truly,   A. S. LONG.

To GENERAL LONGSTREET.

I add the letter of Colonel Venable, of General Lee's staff, which should of itself be conclusive. I merely premise it with the statement that it was fully nine o'clock before General Lee returned from his reconnoissance of Ewell's lines:

UNIVERSITY OF VIRGINIA, May 11th, 1875.

GENERAL JAMES LONGSTREET:

Dear General—Your letter of the 25th ultimo, with regard to General Lee's battle order on the 1st and 2d of July at Gettysburg, was duly received. I did not know of any order for an attack on the enemy at sunrise on the 2d, nor can I believe any such order was issued by General Lee. About sunrise on the 2d of July I was sent by General Lee to General Ewell to ask him what he thought of the advantages of an attack on the enemy from his position. (Colonel Marshall had been sent with a similar order on the night of the 1st.) General Ewell made me ride with him from point to point of his lines, so as to see with him the exact position of things. Before he got through the examination of the enemy's position, General Lee came himself to General Ewell's lines. In sending the message to General Ewell, General Lee was explicit in saying that the question was whether he should move all the troops around on the right, and attack on that side. I do not think that the errand on which I was sent by the commanding general is consistent with the idea of an attack at sunrise by any portion of the army. Yours, very truly,

CHAS. S. VENABLE.

I add upon this point the letter of Dr. Cullen, Medical Director of the First Corps:

RICHMOND, VA., May 18th, 1875.

GENERAL JAMES LONGSTREET:

Dear General—Yours of the 16th ult. should have received my immediate attention, but before answering it, I was desirous of refreshing my memory of the scenes and incidents of the Gettysburg campaign by conversation with others who were with us, and who served in different corps of the command. It was an astounding announcement to the survivors of the First Army Corps that the disaster and failure at Gettysburg was alone and solely due to its commander, and that had he obeyed the orders of the commander-in-chief that Meade's army would have been beaten before its entire force had assembled, and its final discomfiture thereby made certain. It is a little strange that these charges were not made while General Lee was alive to substantiate or disprove them, and that seven years or more were permitted to pass by in silence regarding them. You are fortunate in being able to call upon the Adjutant General and the two confidential officers of General Lee's staff for their testimony in the case, and I do not think that you will have any reason to fear their evidence. They knew every order that was issued for that battle, when and where attacks were to be made, who were slow in attacking, and who did not make attacks that were expected to be made. I hope, for the sake of history and for your brave military record, that a quietus will at once be put on this subject. I distinctly remember the appearance in our headquarter camp of the scout who brought from Frederick the first account that General Lee had of the definite whereabouts of the enemy; of the excitement at General Lee's headquarters among couriers, quartermasters, commissaries, etc., all betokening some early movement of the commands dependent upon the news brought by the scout. That afternoon General Lee was walking with some of us in the road in front of his headquarters, and said: "To-morrow, gentlemen, we will not move to Harrisburg as we expected, but will go over to Gettysburg and see what General Meade is after." Orders had then been issued to the corps to move at sunrise on the morning of the next day, and promptly at that time the corps was put on the road. The troops moved slowly a short distance, when they were stopped by Ewell's wagon trains and Johnson's Division turning into the road in front of them, making their way from some point north to Cashtown or Gettysburg. How many hours we were detained I am unable to say, but it must have been many, for I remember eating a lunch or dinner before moving again. Being anxious to see you I rode rapidly by the troops (who, as soon as they could get into the road, pushed hurriedly by us, also), and overtook you about dark at the hill this side of Gettysburg, about half a mile from the town. You had been at the front with General Lee, and were returning to your camp, a mile or two back. I spoke very exultingly of the victory we were thought to have obtained that day, but was surprised to find that you did not take the same cheerful view of it that I did ; and presently you remarked, that it would have been better had we not fought than to have left undone what we did. You said that the enemy were left occupying a position that it would take the whole army to drive them from, and then at a great sacrifice. We soon reached the camp, three miles, perhaps, from Gettysburg, and found the column near by. Orders were issued to be ready to march at "daybreak," or some earlier hour, next morning. About three o'clock in the morning, while the stars were shining, you left your headquarters and rode to General Lee's, where I found you sitting with him *after sunrise* looking at the enemy on Cemetery Hill. I rode then into Gettysburg, and was gone some two hours, and when I returned found you still with General Lee. At two or three o'clock in the day I rode with you toward the right, when you were about to attack, and was with you in front of the peach orchard when Hood began to move toward Round Top. General Hood was soon wounded, and I removed him from the field to a house near by. * * *   I am yours, very truly,

J. S. D. CULLEN.

I submit next an extract from the official report of General R. H. Anderson:

Upon approaching Gettysburg, I was directed to occupy the position in line of battle which had first been vacated by Pender's Division, and to place one brigade and battery of artillery a mile or more on the right. Wilcox's Brigade and Captain Ross' battery, of Lane's battalion, were posted in the detached position, while the other brigades occupied the ground from which Pender's Division had first been moved. We continued in position until the morning of the 2d, when I received orders to take up a new line of battle, on the right of Pender's Division, about a mile and a half further forward. In taking the new position, the Tenth Alabama Regiment, Wilcox's Brigade, had a sharp skirmish with the body of the enemy who had occupied a wooded hill on the extreme right of my line. * * * Shortly after the line had been formed, I received notice that Lieutenant General Longstreet would occupy the ground on my right, and that his line would be in a direction nearly at right angles with mine, and that he would assault the extreme left of the enemy and drive him toward Gettysburg.

From a narrative of General McLaws, published in 1873, I copy the following:

On the 30th of June, I had been directed to have my division in readiness to follow General Ewell's Corps. Marching toward Gettysburg, which it was intimated we would have passed by ten o'clock the next day (the 1st of July), my division was accordingly marched from its camp and lined along the road in the order of march by eight o'clock the 1st of July. When the troops of Ewell's Corps (it was Johnson's Division in charge of Ewell's wagon trains, which were coming from Carlisle by the road west of the mountains) had passed the head of my column, I asked General Longstreet's staff officer, Major Fairfax, if my division should follow. He went off to inquire, and returned with orders for me to wait until Ewell's wagon train had passed, which did not happen until after four o'clock P. M. The train was calculated to be fourteen miles long, when I took up the line of march and continued marching until I arrived within three miles of Gettysburg, where my command camped along a creek. This was far into the night. My division was leading Longstreet's Corps, and, of course, the other divisions come up later. I saw Hood's Division the next morning, and understood that Pickett had been detached to guard the rear. While on the march, about ten o'clock at night, I met General Longstreet and some of his staff coming from the direction of Gettysburg, and had a few moments conversation with him. He said nothing of having received an order to attack at daylight the next morning. Here, I will state, that until General Pendleton mentioned it about two years ago, when he was on a lecturing tour, after the death of General Lee, I never heard it intimated even that any such order had ever been given.

I close the testimony on this point by an extract from a letter from General Hood. He writes:

I arrived with my staff in front of the heights of Gettysburg shortly after daybreak, as I have already stated, on the morning of the 2d of July. My division soon commenced filing into an open field near me, when the troops were allowed to stack arms and rest until further orders. A short distance in advance of this point, and during the early part of the same morning, we were both engaged in company with Generals A. P. Hill and Lee in observing the position of the Federals. General Lee, with coat buttoned to the throat, sabre belt around his waist, and field-glasses pendant at his side, walked up and down in the shade of large trees near us, halting, now and then, to observe the enemy. He seemed full of hope, yet at times buried in deep thought. Colonel Freemantle, of England, was ensconced in the forks of a tree not far off, with glasses in constant use, examining the lofty position of the Federal army. General Lee was seemingly anxious that you should attack that morning. He remarked to me: "The enemy is here, and if we do not whip him, he will whip us." You thought it better to await the arrival of Pickett's Division, at that time still in the rear, in order to make the attack, and you said to me, subsequently, while we were seated together near the trunk of a tree : "General Lee is a little nervous this morning. He wishes me to attack. I do not wish to do so without Pickett. I never like to go into a battle with one boot off."

`Having thus disproved the assertions of Messrs. Pendleton and Early in regard to this rumored order for a sunrise attack, it appears that they are worthy of no further recognition; but it is difficult to pass beyond them without noting the manner in which, by their ignorance, they marred the plans of their chief on the field of battle. Mr. Pendleton robbed Pickett's Division of its most important adjunct, fresh field artillery, at the moment of its severest trial, and thus frustrated the wise and brilliant programme of assault planned by General Alexander, and without the knowlekge of that officer. (See narrative of General Alexander in the *Southern Historical Monthly* for September, 1877.) General Early broke up General Lee's line of battle on the 2d of July by detaching part of his division on some uncalled-for service, in violation of General Lee's orders, and thus prevented the co-operative attack of Ewell, ordered by General Lee.

It is proper to discuss briefly, at this point, the movements of the third day. The charge of that day, as made by General Pickett, was emphatically a forlorn hope. The point designated by General Lee as the point of attack, seemed to be about one mile from where he and I stood when he gave his orders. I asked him if the distance that we had to overcome under a terrific fire was not more than a mile. He replied: "No, it is not more than fourteen hundred yards." So that our troops, when they arose above the crest, had to advance this distance under the fire of about half of the Federal army before they could fire a shot. Anything less than thirty thousand fresh veterans would have been vainly sacrificed in this attempt. The force given me for this work was Pickett's Division (or rather a part of it), about five thousand five hundred men, fresh and ready to undertake anything. My supporting force of probably eight thousand men, had bloody noses and bruised heads from the fight of the previous day, and were not in physical condition to undertake such desperate work. When fresh they were the equals of any troops on earth; but every soldier knows that there is a great difference between fresh soldiers and those who have just come out of a heavy battle. It has been charged that the delay of the attack on the 3d was the cause of the failure of Ewell to co-operate with Pickett's attack. Colonel Taylor says that Ewell was ordered to attack at the same time with me, mine being the main attack. He says : "General Longstreet's dispositions were not completed as soon as was expected. * * * General Ewell, who had orders to co-operate with General Longstreet, and who was, of course, not aware of any impediment to the main attack, having reinforced General Johnson, during the night of the 2d, ordered him forward early the next morning. In obedience to these instructions, General Johnson became hotly engaged before General Ewell could be informed of the halt that had been called upon our right."

Let us look at the facts of this. Instead of "making this attack at daylight," General Ewell says: "Just before the time fixed for General Johnson's advance, the enemy attacked him to regain the works captured by Stuart the evening before." General Meade, in his official report, says: "On the morning of the 3d, General Geary, having returned during the night, attacked, at early dawn, the enemy, and succeeded in driving him back, and reoccupying his former position. A spirited contest was maintained along this portion of the line all the morning, and General Geary, reinforced by Wharton's Brigade, of the Sixth Corps, maintained his position, and inflicted very severe loss on the enemy." Now to return to my end of the line. At about sunrise General Lee came to me and informed me that General Pickett would soon report to me, and then ordered that his troops were to be used as a column of assault, designating the point of assault, and that portions of the Third Corps were to be used in support. About seven o'clock General Pickett rode forward and stated that his troops would soon be upon the field, and asked to be assigned his position. Colonel W. W. Wood, of Pickett's Division, in his account of the day, says: "If I remember correctly, Pickett's Division and the artillery were all in position by eleven A. M." Hence, we see that General Geary attacked General Ewell at least one hour before I had received my orders for the day; that at the very moment of my receiving these instructions General Ewell was engaged in a "spirited contest;" that this contest had continued several hours before General Pickett's troops came upon the field, and that the contest was virtually over before General Pickett and the artillery were prepared for the battle. When these arrangements were completed, and the batteries ordered to open, General Ewell had been driven from his position, and not a footstep was made from any other part of the army in my support. That there may have been confusion of orders on the field during the second and third days, I am not prepared to deny; but there was nothing of the kind about the headquarters of the First Corps.

I have not seen the criticism of the Comte de Paris upon the campaign, but I gather from quotations that he adduced as one of the objections to the invasion of Pennsylvania, that the Federals would do superior fighting upon their own soil. The Confederates, whom I have read after, deny that this is true. Although not technically correct, the Comte is right in the material point. The actual fighting on the field of Gettysburg, by the Army of the Potomac, was not marked by any unusual gallantry, but the positions that it occupied were held with much more than the usual tenacity of purpose.

There is little to say of the retreat of General Lee's army to the Potomac. When we reached South Mountain, on our retreat, we learned that the Federal cavalry was in strong force, threatening the destruction of our trains then collecting at Williamsport, and that it was also intercepting our trains on the road, and burning some of our wagons. Upon the receipt of this intelligence General Lee ordered me to march as rapidly as possible to the relief of our trains. By a forced march we succeeded in clearing the road, and reached Williamsport in time to save our supply trains. We then took position covering the crossing there and at Falling Water, a short distance below. As the other corps arrived they were assigned positions, and we went to work as rapidly as possible to strengthen our line with field works. On the 13th, General Lee informed me that the river had fallen sufficiently at Williamsport to allow us to ford, and that the bridge at Falling Water had been repaired, and that he would, that night, recross the river with his entire army. I suggested, as a matter of convenience, and to avoid confusion, that it might be better to pass the trains over that night, with everything not essential to battle, and let his troops remain in position until the night of the 14th; that, if the rest of his line was as strong as mine, we could easily repulse any attack that might be made, and thus recover some of the prestige lost by the discomfiture at Gettysburg. After we crossed the Potomac we soon found that the Federals were pushing along the west side of the Blue Ridge, with the purpose of cutting off our retreat to Richmond. General Lee again sent my corps forward to prevent this effort on the part of General Meade, and we succeeded in clearing the way and holding it open for the Third Corps, that followed us. General Ewell, however, was cut off, and was obliged to pass the mountains further south. The First Corps reached Culpepper Court-House on the 24th.

In the month of August, 1863, while lying along the Rapidan, I called General Lee's attention to the condition of our affairs in the West, and the progress that was being made by the army under General Rosecrans in cutting a new line through the State of Georgia, and suggesting that a successful march, such as he had started on, would again bisect the Southern country, and that when that was done the war would be virtually over. I suggested that he should adhere to his defensive tactics upon the Rapidan, and reinforce from his army the army lying in front of Rosecrans—so that it could crush that army, and then push on to the West. He seemed struck with these views, but was as much opposed to dividing his army as he was in the spring when I first suggested it. He went down to Richmond to arrange for another offensive campaign during the fall. While there several letters passed between us, only two of which I have preserved in connected form. The result of this correspondence was, however, that I was sent with two divisions—Hood's and McLaws'—to reinforce our army then in Georgia. The result of this movement was the defeat of Rosecrans, at Chickamauga, when the last hope of the Confederacy expired with the failure of our army to prosecute the advantage gained by this defeat. The letters are appended herewith:

(Confidential.)   [*Copy.*]

RICHMOND, August 31st, 1863.

LIEUTENANT GENERAL J. LONGSTREET,
   Headquarters Army of West Virginia:

General—I have wished for several days past to return to the army, but have been detained by the President. He will not listen to my proposition to leave to-morrow.

I hope you will use every exertion to prepare the army for offensive operations, and improve the condition of men and animals. I can see nothing better to be done than to endeavor to bring General Meade out and use our efforts to crush his army while in the present condition.

The Quartermaster's Department promise to send up three thousand bushels of corn per day, provided the cars can be unloaded and returned without delay. I hope you will be able to arrange it so that the cars will not be detained. With this supply of corn, if it can be maintained, the condition of our animals should improve.

Very respectfully and truly yours,

[Signed]   R. E. LEE,
                                                    General.

[*Copy.*]

HEADQUARTERS, September 2d, 1863.

General—Your letter of the 31st is received. I have expressed to Generals Ewell and Hill your wishes, and am doing all that can be done to be well prepared with my own command. Our greatest difficulty will be in preparing our animals.

I don't know that we can reasonably hope to accomplish much *here*, by offensive operations, unless we are strong enough to cross the Potomac. If we advance to meet the enemy on this side, he will, in all probability, go into one of his many fortified positions. These we cannot afford to attack.

I know but little of the condition of our affairs in the West, but am inclined to the opinion that our best opportunity for great results is in Tennessee. If we could hold the defensive here with two corps, and send the other to operate in

Tennessee, with that army, I think that we could accomplish more than by an advance from here.

The enemy seems to have settled down upon the plan of holding certain points by fortifying and defending, while he concentrates upon others. It seems to me that this must succeed, unless we concentrate ourselves, and at the same time make occasional show of active operations at all points.

I know of no other means of acting upon that principle at present, except to depend upon our fortifications in Virginia, and concentrate with one corps of this army, and such as may be drawn from others, in Tennessee, and destroy Rosecrans' army.

I feel assured that this is practicable, and that greater advantages will be gained than by any operations from here.

I remain, general, very respectfully, your obedient servant,

[Signed]   JAMES LONGSTREET,
                                    Lieut. General.

GENERAL R. E. LEE, Commanding, etc.

It will be noticed by those who have watched the desultory controversy maintained upon this subject, that after I had proved the fallacy of General Pendleton's and General Early's idea of a sunrise attack, they fall back upon the charge that I delayed bringing my troops into action, waiving all question of an order from General Lee. I have shown that I did not receive orders from General Lee to attack until about eleven o'clock on the 2d; that I immediately began my dispositions for attack; that I waited about forty minutes for Law's Brigade, by General Lee's assenting authority; that by especial orders from General Lee, my corps marched into position by a circuitous route, under the direction and conduct of Colonel Johnson, of his staff of engineers; that Colonel Johnson's orders were to keep the march of the troops concealed, and that I hurried Hood's Division forward in the face of those orders, throwing them into line by a direct march, and breaking up the delay occasioned by the orders of General Lee. I need only add that every movement or halt of the troops on that day was made in the immediate presence of General Lee, or in his sight—certainly within the reach of his easy and prompt correction. I quote, in this connection, the order that I issued to the heads of departments in my corps on the 1st. I present the order as issued to Colonel Walton, of the artillery, similar orders having been issued to the division commanders:

[*Order.*]

HEADQUARTERS FIRST ARMY CORPS,
NEAR GETTYSBURG, July 18—5.30 P. M.

Colonel—The commanding general desires you to come on to-night as fast as you can, without distressing your men or animals. Hill and Ewell have sharply engaged the enemy, and you will be needed for to-morrow's battle. Let us know where you will stop to-night. * * * Respectfully,

G. M. SORRELL,
A. A. General.

To COLONEL J. B. WALTON, Chief of Artillery.

I offer, also, a report made by General Hood touching this march. He says:

> While lying in camp near Chambersburg, information was received that Hill and Ewell were about to come into contact with the enemy near Gettysburg. My troops, together with McLaws' Division, were at once put in motion, upon the most direct road to that point, which we reached, after a hard march, at or before sunrise on July the 2d. So imperative had been our orders to hasten forward with all possible speed, that on the march my troops were allowed to halt and rest only about two hours during the night from the 1st to the 2d of July.

It appears to me that the gentlemen who made the above-mentioned charges against me have chosen the wrong point of attack. With their motives I have nothing to do; but I cannot help suggesting that if they had charged me with having precipitated the battle, instead of having delayed it, the records might have sustained them in that my attack was made about four hours before General Ewell's. I am reminded, in this connection, of what a Federal officer, who was engaged in that battle, said to me when we were talking over the battle, and the comments it had provoked. He said: "I cannot imagine how they can charge you with being late in your attack, as you were the only one that got in at all. I do not think their charge can be credited."

In conclusion, I may say that it is unfortunate that the discussion of all mooted points concerning the battle was not opened before the death of General Lee. A word or two from him would have settled all points at issue. As it is, I have written an impartial narrative of the facts as they are, with such comments as the nature of the case seemed to demand.

THE CAMPAIGN OF GETTYSBURG.

BY MAJOR GENERAL ALFRED PLEASONTON.

THE history of the Army of the Potomac in the Gettysburg campaign has never been written. That army was unfortunate in having two commanders, General Hooker having been relieved at Frederick City, Maryland, about a week before the battle of Gettysburg, by General Meade. General Meade's report of the campaign embraces only the time he was in command, and, as a consequence, the operations of the army up to Frederick City are not recorded, except in subordinate reports. As the commander of the Cavalry Corps of the Army of the Potomac, I occupied the same personal relations to the commanders of that army—Generals Hooker and Meade—that General Longstreet held with General Lee. I, therefore, feel constrained to review the campaign of Gettysburg, as presented by General Longstreet, to enable the public to arrive at a proper understanding of the relative merits of the armies of the North and South in that campaign. General Longstreet states that on the 3d of June, 1863, the movement of General Lee's army from Fredericksburg commenced, and that on the 8th two full corps and Stuart's cavalry were concentrated at Culpepper Court-House. He further says: "That on the 9th of June, a large force of Federals, cavalry and infantry, had been thrown across the Rappahannock, and sent to attack Stuart. They were encountered at Brandy Station, on the morning of the 9th, and repulsed." General Longstreet also expresses the opinion that if there was an occasion which justified General Lee in departing from his plan of campaign, viz., offensive strategy and defensive tactics, it was at this battle of Beverly ford,

(447)

and that Lee should have fallen upon this command with his whole force and crushed it.

Now for the facts on our side. General Hooker, having received reports from different sources early in June, 1863, that General Lee was quietly withdrawing his army from Fredericksburg toward Culpepper Court-House, wanted positive information on the subject; so he directed me to make a reconnoissance in force toward Culpepper, to attack the enemy, if necessary, and force him to display his infantry; but not to return without positive information of Lee's whereabouts. My command consisted at this time of two divisions of cavalry and six batteries of horse artillery, and I suggested to General Hooker, in view of what he required, that I should be reinforced with some infantry. The General told me to take what infantry I wanted, but not to fail, as he considered the information to be obtained of the utmost importance to the coming campaign. I selected three thousand infantry, under Generals Ames and D. A. Russell. On the 8th of June, I directed General Gregg to cross the Rappahannock at Kelly's ford, at daylight on the morning of the 9th, with the Second Division of cavalry and Russell's infantry, while I would cross with Buford's Division of cavalry and Ames' infantry, and join him at Brandy Station. The two fords were about eight miles apart, Brandy Station being nearly in the apex of the triangle, three miles south of the river, and a good position from which to operate on Culpepper, in case it became necessary to move in that direction. The movement was a reconnoissance in force to gain information. It was my duty not to seek a fight and not to avoid one—to distribute my force in such manner as to give the best opportunities for obtaining the information desired; at the same time to be within supporting distance in case of an action, and to withdraw and report to General Hooker as soon as my task was accomplished. The evening of the 8th of June a heavy rain laid the dust and enabled me to place the command near Beverly ford without attracting the notice of the enemy. To my surprise, General Lee had no pickets on the north side of the Rappahannock. I ordered my command to bivouac without fires, and be ready at four o'clock in the morning. The next morning, with Colonel Davis, of the Eighth New York Cavalry, who was to lead the advance, I reconnoitred the ford, and found the circumstances favorable for a surprise of the enemy on the opposite side, in case he was there in force.

The north bank of the river commanded the southern, and, with the exception of a few cavalry pickets, scattered up and down the river, nothing was to be seen. The roaring of the water over the dam just above the ford would prevent the sound of cavalry from being heard in making the passage of the river, while a dense fog on the river, extending some distance on the other side to the position occupied by the enemy's mounted pickets, would screen from observation any body of troops while crossing. It was decided, therefore, to attack immediately, and, if possible, capture the enemy's-pickets and supports before the main body could be notified of the movement. Accordingly, at five o'clock, Colonel Davis gallantly led the Eighth New York Cavalry through the ford, and, charging the reserve of the pickets, took them by surprise, and, after a short resistance, they were overpowered. Most unfortunately, at that moment the captain of the picket rode up to Colonel Davis and shot him through the head, but was immediately killed by Davis' adjutant. The death of Colonel Davis caused a temporary delay; but, hearing of it, I crossed the river, and was soon to the front. By this time at least three regiments were over—a sufficient force to hold the position until the entire command should cross. On the north side I had placed three batteries in a position which commanded our flanks, and the crossing was completed. It was at this time a trooper fired a blank cartridge from a battery in their rear, and this roused the sleeping soldiers of Stuart's cavalry. Stuart's headquarters were not more than a quarter of a mile from the ford, and we pushed our advance with such vigor that we captured it, with a copy of his orders and other important papers indicating the campaign Lee intended to make. In obedience to his orders, Stuart was to have crossed Beverly ford that morning to destroy the railroad to Alexandria, for the purpose of delaying the Army of the Potomac in its movement north; while that Lee intended to cross the Potomac in the neighborhood of Poolesville and the Monocacy, from the other communications captured, was evident.

Stuart, stung at being surprised, soon had his command in action, and did some splendid fighting that day to recover his position. The whole of my line was engaged at once, and for a time it was charge and counter-charge. Nothing could have been finer than the gallantry displayed by the troops on both sides; but my command knew they had gained an advantage, and they were determined to keep it. The desperate attacks of Stuart could not move them. I had sufficient information, after the capture of Stuart's headquarters, to have authorized the withdrawal of my command to the north side of the river, but hearing General Gregg's guns in the direction of Brandy Station, and knowing he would expect me to connect with him in that vicinity, I directed General Buford to advance his right, while

29

the left was extended in the direction of Brandy Station. The enemy's cavalry, well supplied with artillery, fought with great stubbornness, and it was one o'clock in the day before I made any communication with Gregg. He informed me that he had been actively engaged all day; that the enemy were running trains full of infantry from Culpepper to Brandy Station, and massing them in the woods near the residence of John Minor Botts. Gregg was then directed to withdraw and recross the river at the railroad bridge, which he did without difficulty. I held my position, covering Beverly ford, until Gregg's crossing was assured, and then withdrew. The last gun was fired at seven in the evening.

Such was the action of Beverly ford, which General Longstreet calls Brandy Station. It was a reconnoissance in force, in which some of the hardest fighting of the war had to be done. It accomplished more than was expected, by not only establishing the fact that Lee was at Culpepper in force, but it apprised General Hooker of General Lee's intention to invade the North. In reporting to General Hooker the result of my reconnoissance, I stated I was of the opinion that Stuart was not now likely to cross the river. The General, however, thought it best for my command to remain in the vicinity of Warrenton Junction until the 16th of June, and Stuart never made any attempt to cross the river during that time. Such, then, was one result of the attack on the 9th. A second result was to change the direction of Lee's army toward the Shenandoah, instead of attempting to cross the Potomac near Washington, forcing that army to operate on an exterior line. The third result was to give the Army of the Potomac the initiative, based on the knowledge of General Lee's intentions. Did General Lee know that Stuart's papers had been lost? Did he or Stuart suppose they were in my possession? At all events, General Longstreet's experienced military sagacity impressed him with the necessity of changing the plan of campaign, and with their whole force make a determined effort to crush me. No ordinary attack, which had been repulsed, would have been considered by Longstreet as worthy of any such distinguished attention. I claim, therefore, that the services of the nine thousand splendid soldiers of my command could not have been more brilliant or more important to the army and the country in their results.

On the evening of the 16th of June, the cavalry corps encamped near Manassas, the Army of the Potomac occupying positions between that point and Fairfax Court-House. After consultation with General Hooker it was decided that I should proceed by the way of Aldie, through the Bull Run mountains, into Loudon Valley, to ascertain if Lee's army or any portion of it were in that vicinity. I started early on the 17th, made a long march of twenty-five miles, and about five o'clock in the afternoon, shortly after we had entered the pass, met the enemy's cavalry coming through. After a hard fight for several hours, we drove them back to the west side of the mountains. On the 18th and 19th, we were again engaged, and forced them beyond Middleburg, about nine miles from Aldie, and on the 21st, advancing with Buford on the road to Union, and Gregg on the Upperville road, we swept the Loudon Valley to the base of the Blue Ridge, fighting our way the whole distance. Near Upperville the fighting was severe, several brigades, on each side, being engaged in charging each other; but such was the dash and spirit of our cavalry that the enemy could not withstand it, and retreated through Ashby's gap badly worsted. General Buford, on the right, sent some parties to the top of the Blue Ridge, and they reported large masses of infantry and camps in the Shenandoah Valley toward Winchester. There being no infantry in the Loudon Valley, it was evident General Lee did not intend to cross the Potomac lower down than Shepherdstown. These facts were reported to General Hooker on the night of the 21st of June, and he shortly after set the army in motion for the vicinity of Frederick City, Maryland, Buford's Division of cavalry taking up a position at Middletown, to the west of Frederick City.

I desire, here, to call attention to General Longstreet's statement, in which he ignores all the operations of Stuart's cavalry from the 17th to the 21st of June. General Longstreet states that he was occupying Ashby's and Snicker's gaps at that time with his corps, and communicated with General Stuart. He knew, therefore, that General Stuart had been most actively engaged from the 17th of June, attempting to push through the Bull Run mountains, in order to ascertain the whereabouts of General Hooker's army. Stuart had been doing his best to execute General Lee's orders, which were "to harass the enemy, and to impede him as much as possible should he attempt to cross the Potomac." Such were General Lee's orders to Stuart, and to execute them it was his first duty to find out where the Army of the Potomac was located. This he was doing when he attempted to pass the Bull Run mountains; but, unfortunately for Stuart, the enemy harassed him so much, and drove him back into Ashby's gap in such condition that he was unable to reach the Potomac in time to see the enemy cross. General Stuart, at Ashby's gap on the 21st of June, was as ignorant of the position of Hooker's army as were Generals Lee and Longstreet, on the 27th of June, at Chambersburg. That Lee and Longstreet should have hurried on to Chambersburg under such conditions, is best explained by the ancient adage : "Whom the gods wish to destroy they first make mad." Generals Lee and Longstreet lay great stress on the absence of Stuart's cavalry as one of the principal causes of failure of the campaign on their side. I have shown that the two divisions of the cavalry corps of the Army of the Potomac had effectually prevented Lee's cavalry from obtaining any information in Virginia with reference to the movements of that army. Now, on arriving at Frederick City, Maryland, my corps was reinforced by a third division, commanded by Kilpatrick, Custer, and Farnsworth, and it is assuming nothing to assert that what had been done by my two divisions in Virginia could be accomplished by three divisions with more ease and certainty in Maryland.

Two days after I arrived at Frederick City, General Meade relieved General Hooker of the command of the Army of the Potomac. On assuming the command, General Meade sent for me, and in strong terms deprecated the change in commanders with a battle so near at hand, acknowledged his ignorance with regard to the army in general, and said he would be obliged to depend a great deal upon me to assist him. Our relations were of the most cordial and friendly character, and I soon gave him to understand my views, for we then knew that Lee's army was moving toward Chambersburg. I told him that Lee would make for Gettysburg, and that if he seized that position before we could reach it we should have hard work to get him out, and that to prevent his doing so would depend more on the cavalry than anything else. I called his attention to a division of cavalry near Frederick City, which he might place under my command, and I would like to have officers I would name specially assigned to it, as I expected to have some desperate work to do. The General assented to my request, and upon my naming the officers, he immediately telegraphed to have them appointed brigadier generals. This was his first dispatch to Washington, and in the afternoon he received the reply making the appointments, and directing the officers to be assigned at once. They were Custer, Merritt, and Farnsworth; all three young captains, and two of them, Custer and Farnsworth, my aides-de-camp. While the General and myself were in conversation in reference to the campaign a second dispatch was brought him, stating that Stuart, with his cavalry, were making a raid near Washington City, and had cut the wires, so that we had no telegraphic communication. I laughed at this news, and said Stuart has served us better than he is aware of; we shall now have no instructions from the aulic council until we have a battle. General Meade, however, took the matter very seriously; thought I should take all the cavalry and capture Stuart; that the government would expect him to do so. I assured him that Lee was of more importance to us than Stuart; the latter was in a false position and useless to Lee, and that it was a maxim in war never to interfere with the enemy when he was making a false move. That Stuart could only join Lee by recrossing the Potomac, which would occupy so much time as to prevent his being in the next battle; or he must pass round to the north of our army, in which event I should have the cavalry so placed that he would not be able to escape us. General Meade then decided to leave the affair with me, and, as I expected, three or four days after, near a place called Hanover, Kilpatrick's Division met Stuart's command loaded down with plunder, which was recaptured, and, after a severe fight, Stuart was compelled to make such a detour that he only joined Lee at Gettysburg on the second day of the battle, July 2d.

The Army of the Potomac was in motion by the 28th of June, moving north from Frederick City. In arranging the line of march of the different corps, I was impressed with the idea that General Meade considered that General Lee would move toward Harrisburg and cross the river in that vicinity. He spoke of it to me more than once. I could not believe it, although General Longstreet states that, at one time, General Lee did entertain that idea. The general line of march of the army was too much to the east for a rapid concentration on Gettysburg, and believing that General Lee understood the advantages of that position as well as I did, I was determined to occupy it first. I, therefore, ordered Buford, with the first division of cavalry, to move from Middletown by the way of Emmettsburg to Gettysburg, and to hold that position at all hazards until the army could support him. In obedience to these orders, Buford arrived at Gettysburg on the afternoon of June 30th, and obtaining information that Lee was in force on the Cashtown road, he moved out on that road some four miles beyond Gettysburg, and encamped for the night. Early next morning General A. P. Hill attacked him in force, but the nature of the ground was such that Buford, with his splendid fighting, restrained the superior force against him until Reynolds and Howard and others came up, and saved the position to the Army of the Potomac. General Longstreet states that this rencontre " was totally unexpected on both sides." The above statement shows that the General is mistaken in supposing the rencontre was unexpected on our side. Buford's judgment in believing he would be attacked in heavy force on the morning of the 1st of July, and going out four miles to meet it the night before, was what saved to us the position. Had he waited an attack at Gettysburg, he would have been driven from the place before any support could have arrived.

General Meade had his headquarters on the 1st of July at a place called Taneytown, about eighteen miles to the east of Gettysburg. It was about noon of that day I received a dispatch from General Buford, stating the enemy had attacked him in force early that morning four miles from Gettysburg; that he had fought them desperately for several hours to retard their progress; that Howard, with the Eleventh Corps, and Reynolds, with the First Corps, had arrived on the field; that Reynolds had been killed while bringing his corps into action; there appeared to be no directing head, and if General Meade expected to secure that position, the sooner he marched the army there the better. I immediately showed this dispatch to General Meade, when he decided to move on Gettysburg, and sending for General Hancock, whose corps was nearest to Gettysburg, he ordered him to proceed at once to that point, directing his corps to follow him, and to take command of the forces engaged. At the same time orders were sent to the different corps of the army to march on Gettysburg without delay. The time occupied in making these arrangements detained General Meade until after dark, when we proceeded to Gettysburg, and arrived at General Howard's headquarters on Cemetery Hill after midnight.

At daylight on the morning of the 2d of July, General Meade requested me to ride over the position with him, and we were engaged in that duty until ten o'clock, by which time the disposition of the different corps, as they should arrive, had been decided. In examining the position, General Meade was strongly impressed that our right was our weakest place, and on both the 2d and 3d of July he gave it his attention. On the 3d, during the artillery combat on our left, he took a position on a high mound between the right and left flanks, watching our right, and expecting a heavy attack in that direction. I had six batteries of horse artillery in reserve, and in case our right had given way, these batteries were to be sent to its support. But finding our right could not hold its own, and our batteries on the left had suffered, these splendid batteries were placed in position on the left in time to meet General Pickett's charge. I am not, therefore, surprised when General Longstreet states, "That when the smoke cleared away Pickett's Division was gone," and "that mortal man could not have stood that fire." I do not propose to follow General Longstreet through the details of the battle of Gettysburg. The charges of the Southern soldiers on the 2d and 3d of July were magnificent, and did them the highest honor. But this was not war. Napoleon I. laid down the maxim that a general who disregards the principles of war at the commencement of a campaign, finds himself overwhelmed by the consequences when the crisis of battle arrives. The campaign of Gettysburg is a good illustration of the truth of this maxim. General Lee violated the principles of strategy, and the results forced him to disregard those of tactics, and when after the repulse of his troops on the third day, he said, "it was all my fault," he nobly declared the true verdict in the case.

The battle of Gettysburg was over, and in speaking of the subsequent events of the campaign, I do so with reluctance. I was in the position to form a correct opinion of the failure of the army to follow General Lee, having been the constant companion of General Meade from the time he assumed the command at Frederick City. In justice to the General, I can state he did not desire the command, and considered it hazardous to change commanders at that time, and his position was far more difficult than it would have been had he been assigned the command at the commencement of the campaign. Personally very brave, an excellent corps commander, General Meade had not that grasp of mind, when thrown into a new and responsible position, to quickly comprehend and decide upon important events as they occurred. He required time to come to a decision, and this indulgence an active campaign never allows to a commanding general. From the time he assumed command of the army until after the battle of Gettysburg, the most important events were occuring with such rapidity, and with such resistless force, that his decisions were the consequences of these events rather than the operations of his individual intelligence.

From the suddenness of the repulse of the last charge on July 3d, it became necessary for General Meade to decide at once what to do. I rode up to him, and, after congratulating him on the splendid conduct of the army, I said: "General, I will give you half an hour to show yourself a great general. Order the army to advance, while I will take the cavalry, get in Lee's rear, and we will finish the campaign in a week." He replied: "How do you know Lee will not attack me again; we have done well enough." I replied that Lee had exhausted all his available men; that the cannonade of the two last days had exhausted his ammunition; he was far from his base of supplies; and, by compelling him to keep his army together, they must soon surrender, for he was living on the country. To this the General did not reply, but asked me to ride up to the Round Top with him; and as we rode along the ridge for nearly a mile, the troops cheered him in a manner that plainly showed they expected the advance. When we reached the Round Top everything was still in Lee's position with the exception of a single battery which was firing upon some of our skirmishers to prevent their advancing. I was so impressed with the idea that Lee was retreating that I again earnestly urged General Meade to advance the army; but instead of doing so, he ordered me to send some cavalry to ascertain the fact. Gregg's Division of cavalry started soon after, and at eight o'clock the next morning I received his report, stating that he was twenty-two miles on the Cashtown road, and that the enemy was not only retreating, but it was a rout, the road being encumbered with wounded and wagons in the greatest confusion.

On this report the two other divisions of cavalry were sent to intercept and harass Lee in crossing the Potomac; but the Army of the Potomac did not leave Gettysburg for four or five days after, and then passed by the way of South Mountain to the Antietam creek. In consequence of heavy rains the Potomac river was so much swollen that Lee could not cross, and the two armies were again brought face to face for two days. General Meade declined to attack, and Lee's army escaped. The cavalry rendered important service after the battle of Gettysburg, in pursuit. They captured large trains of wagons, many prisoners, and were in such position that, had General Meade followed Lee on the 4th of July, the surrender of Lee would have been unavoidable.

The two great objective points of the war were Washington and Richmond. Had Lee's army captured Washington and held it, the South would have been recognized by the nations of Europe, and the war would have been continued by the North under the greatest disadvantages. When the army of the Potomac entered Richmond, the Southern cause was considered lost in Europe, and the South surrendered. The recognition of the South by foreign governments entered largely into the political and military operations of the government at Richmond; and the invasion of Pennsylvania by General Lee, in 1863, cannot properly be explained by military reasons alone. The attempt to do this is the weak point of General Longstreet's defense of that campaign. The chances of that campaign from a military point of view were so much against General Lee, and the General himself was so conscious of them, that his effort to prosecute it can only clearly be understood when it is assumed the necessities of the South were so great as to compel the government at Richmond to direct the movement in order, if possible, to hasten their recognition by France and England. In the first place, Lee's army was not in a condition to make that campaign a success. A month before, at Chancellorsville, he had lost his ablest lieutenant, Stonewall Jackson, and the flower of his army. His army never recovered from that blow. It caused General Longstreet to say, "Such was the terrible sacrifice, that half a dozen such victories would have ruined us." The battle of Chancellorsville was properly the beginning of the Gettysburg campaign, and should be so considered in reviewing the military operations of the two armies. The Army of the Potomac never was in finer order than in June, when it moved from Fredericksburg, and it was ably handled throughout the campaign, and until after the battle of Gettysburg.

The army had three roads to concentrate on Gettysburg, viz.: the Emmettsburg road, the Taneytown road, and the Baltimore pike, and could naturally arrive there before Lee's army, coming from Chambersburg, on a single road through Cashtown. On the night of the 1st of July, we had more troops in position than Lee, and from that time victory was assured to us. Had Lee attacked on the morning of the 2d, he would have been repulsed, as he was when he did attack. The failure of Lee to make any impression on our right, which General Meade expected on both days, the 2d and 3d of July, showed that General Lee was either too weak, or did not have his army well in hand. As to General Lee maneuvring to our left, the supposition shows the ignorance existing of our position and the nature of the country. I had two divisions of cavalry, one in rear of our position, and one on Lee's right flank. This cavalry would have held Lee in check in any such movement, while the Army of the Potomac from Cemetery Hill would have swept down and turned Gettysburg into an Austrelitz. It would have been far better for General Lee and his army if they could have realized that the Army of the Potomac possessed generals fully equal to their own; that the mobility of the army for marching and maneuvring was equal, if not superior, to theirs, and that, in point of equipment, endurance, and tenacity, they were their superiors. It is one of the wisest maxims of war, "Never to hold an enemy in contempt." The South suffered for the violation of this rule the most bitter mortification and suffering, and none more so than the gallant men who strove to wring victory from despair at Gettysburg.

Three serious blunders deprived the Army of the Potomac of

the best fruits of their labors. The first of these was the change of commanders a few days before the battle. This delayed the movements of the army, and was near losing us the position at Gettysburg. It was singular that a government that claimed "never to swap horses while crossing a stream" should have done so in the most important crisis of the war. The second blunder was the neglect of the government to send fifty thousand of the seventy thousand men around Washington, by the way of the Baltimore and Ohio Railroad, to the south of the Potomac, to oppose the crossing of Lee. With the Army of the Potomac in his rear, and fifty thousand men to oppose his crossing, the war in Virginia would have ended in 1863, instead of 1865. The third blunder was the refusal of General Meade to follow the enemy after the repulse on the 3d of July. This lost the army all the advantages for which they had toiled and struggled for many long and weary days; but it could not detract from the glorious distinction and honor of the gallant soldiers who had humbled the best and proudest army the South ever put into the field.

The campaign of Gettysburg was the best campaign of the war on the Northern side. It was conducted on the truest principles of war, as established by the greatest masters, viz.: to separate the enemy from his base while securing your own base of operations. That the results of the campaign did not include the surrender of Lee's army, was due to the action and inaction of the government at Washington, and is another illustration of the matchless equipoise of great minds disturbed by unparalleled conditions, so graphically described by General Longstreet in his instance of General Lee at Gettysburg. While our Southern friends are discussing their campaign of Gettysburg, I would call their attention to a notable circumstance, viz.: that in the campaign of General Grant, from Culpepper to Richmond, General Lee pursued the same strategy and same tactics adopted by the Army of the Potomac in the campaign of Gettysburg. While General Grant is open to the severest criticism, in a military point of view, for operating on an exterior line, and leaving his adversary secure in his communications and bases of supplies (precisely the blunder committed by Lee in his Gettysburg campaign), Lee's reputation as a general rests on the splendid defense of Richmond, which he conducted in the years 1864 and 1865. The immense loss of life in General Grant's campaign against Richmond was due to his violation of the principles of war. The two campaigns are good illustrations that neither governments or generals can disregard the fundamental principles of war, without suffering immense sacrifices and with uncertain results of success.

To close as I began, that justice had not been done to the cavalry in the campaign of Gettysburg, the above review, in my opinion, clearly shows it. I can say they had greater opportunities for distinction than their companions in arms, and they so fully availed themselves of these advantages that, without their services, the record of the campaign would be like the play of "Hamlet" with the part of *Hamlet* left out. Further, the renown for all that is great and glorious in cavalry warfare they established for themselves in that campaign, made them the peers of the famous troopers of the Great Frederick, and the splendid horsemen who swept over the plains of Europe led by the white plume of the dashing Murat.

VAN DORN, THE HERO OF MISSISSIPPI.

BY MAJOR GENERAL DABNEY H. MAURY.

GENERAL EARL VAN DORN was, in the opinion of the writer, the most remarkable man the State of Mississippi has ever known. My acquaintance with him began in Monterey, in the fall of 1846. He was aide-de-camp then to General Persifor F. Smith, and was one of the most attractive young fellows in the army. He used to ride a beautiful bay Andalusian horse, and as he came galloping along the lines, with his yellow hair waving in the wind, and his bright face lighted with kindliness and courage, we all loved to see him. His figure was lithe and graceful, his stature did not exceed five feet six inches, but his clear blue eyes, his firm set mouth, with white strong teeth, his well cut nose with expanding nostrils, gave assurance of a man whom men could trust and follow. No young officer came out of the Mexican war with a reputation more enviable than his. After the close of that war he resumed his duties and position in the infantry regiment of which he was a lieutenant. In 1854 the Second Cavalry was organized, and Van Dorn was promoted to be major of the regiment. He conducted several of the most important and successful expeditions against the Comanches we have ever made, and in one of them was shot through the body, the point of the arrow just protruding through the skin. No surgeon was at hand. Van Dorn, reflecting that to withdraw the arrow would leave the barbed head in his body, thrust it on through, and left the surgeon little to do. When the States resumed their State sovereignty, he took a bold and efficient part in securing to Texas, where he was serving, all of the war material within her borders. Early in the war he was ordered to join the army under General Joe Johnston at Manassas; whence soon after, in February, 1861, he was ordered to take command of the Trans-Mississippi Department.

I was associated with him in this command as chief of his staff, and saw him daily for many months. He had conceived the bold project of capturing St. Louis and transferring the war into Illinois, and was actively engaged in preparing for this enterprise when he was summoned by General Price to Boston Mountain, where the forces of Price and McCulloch lay in great need of a common superior—for these two generals could not co-operate because of questions of rank. Therefore, Van Dorn promptly responded to Price's summons, and in a few hours was in the saddle and on his way to Van Buren. I went with him, and one aide-de-camp, an orderly, and my servant man Jem made up our party. Van Dorn rode a fine thoroughbred black mare he had brought from Virginia. I was mounted on a sorrel I had bought in Pocahontas a few hours before we set out. Except my sorrel mare, Van Dorn's black mare was the hardest trotter in the world, and as we trotted fifty-five miles every day for five or six days, we had a very unusual opportunity of learning all that a hard trotter can do to a man in a long day's march. Had it not been that we slept every night in a feather bed, that soothed our sore bones and served as a poultice to our galled saddle pieces, we would have been permanently disabled for cavalry service forever. My boy Jem alone enjoyed that trip. He rode in the ambulance all day and slept *ad libitum* day and night; and except when he got a ducking by the upsetting of a canoe in Black river, he was as happy as ever he had been since the last herring season on the Potomac. The battle of Elk Horn disturbed Jem's equilibrium even more than the upsetting of the canoe. The excitement of imminent danger, which was never a pleasing emotion to Jem, was kept up at Elk Horn much longer than in Black river, and I could not find him for three days—not, indeed, until we accidentally met on the route of our retreat, when, I must say, he showed great delight at "meeting up" with me again, and took to himself no little credit for the skill with which he had conducted the movements of that ambulance for the past three days. It had contained all of our clothing, and blankets, and camp supplies, of no little value to hungry and wearied warriors. The blankets and clothing were all right, but we found nothing whatever for the inner man. Jem was cheerful, and cordial, and comfortable, but we never could ascertain where he had the ambulance from the time the first shot was fired until the moment we encountered him in full retreat, and with the last sound of the battle died out in the distance behind him.

Van Dorn had planned the battle of Elk Horn well; he had moved so rapidly from Boston Mountain, with the forces of Price and McCulloch combined, that he caught the enemy unprepared, and with his divisions so far separated that, but for the inevitable indiscipline of troops so hastily thrown together, he would have destroyed the whole Federal army. By the loss of thirty minutes in reaching Bentonville, we lost the cutting off of Sigel with seven thousand men, who were hurrying to join the main body on Sugar creek. But we pushed him hard all that day; and after he had closed upon the main body, Van Dorn, leaving a small force to occupy the attention in front, threw his army, by a night march, quite around the Federal army, and across their only road by which retreat to Missouri could be effected. He handled his forces well— always attacking, always pressing the enemy back. When he heard of the death, in quick succession, of the three principal commanders of his right wing—McCulloch, McIntosh, and Hebert—and the consequent withdrawal from the attack of that whole wing, he only set his lips a little firmer; his blue eyes blazed brighter, and his nostrils looked wider, as he said, "Then we must press them the harder!" And he did, too; and he had everything moving finely by sundown, and all the enemy's line before us in full retreat at a run, and falling back into their wagon trains; when, by misapprehension on the part of the commander with our advanced troops, the pursuit was arrested, our forces withdrawn from the attack to go into bivouac, and the enemy was permitted to quietly reorganize his army and prepare for a combined attack upon us in the morning. During the night, we found that most of our batteries and regiments had exhausted their ammunition, and the ordnance train, with all the reserve ammunition, had been sent away, fifteen miles back, on the road along which we had come, and the enemy lay between. There was nothing left for Van Dorn but to get his train on the road to Van Buren, and his army off by the same route, and to fight enough to secure them. This he did, and marched away unmolested.

Arrived at Van Buren, Van Dorn addressed himself to the completion of the reorganization of his army, thenceforth known as the Army of the West; and it was there he gave an illustration of true magnanimity—very rarely known in ambitious men—by the offer he made to move with all his forces to reinforce General Sidney Johnston at Corinth. By this he surrendered the great independent command of the Trans-Mississippi Department, and all the plans he had formed, for the sake of his views of the best interests of their common country, and became a subordinate commander of an army corps instead of the commander-in-chief of an army. He hoped to reach Johnston in time for the battle of Shiloh, and had he done so, would have given a very different result to that critical battle. But Shiloh had been fought, and our army, under Beauregard, was occupying the works of Corinth when Van Dorn, with the Army of the West, sixteen thousand effectives, reached that point. We lay near Corinth more than six weeks, and three times offered battle to Halleck, who, with one hundred thousand men, was cautiously advancing as if to attack us. Three times our army, forty thousand strong, marched out of its intrenchments and advanced to meet Halleck and give him battle, but every time he drew back and declined it. In every council Van Dorn's voice was for war. May 30th, 1862, Beauregard evacuated his works in a masterly manner, and marched south, unmolested, to Tupelo, when he halted the army and held it ready for battle. In June, Van Dorn was ordered to go to Vicksburg, which was threatened with attack, and was in poor condition for defense. He evinced here great energy and ability. He repulsed the enemy's fleet, put the place in a good condition of defense, occupied Port Hudson, and there erected such works as enabled us for a year longer to control the Mississippi river and its tributaries, so as to keep open free intercourse with the trans-Mississippi, whence large supplies for the armies on this side were drawn. He organized an expedition against Baton Rouge during this time, which, but for the cholera, which swept off half of the force, and the untimely breaking down of the ram "Arkansas'" engine, when almost within range of the town, would have been a brilliant and complete success.

After this, Van Dorn urged General Price, who had been left at Tupelo with the Army of the West, when Bragg moved to Chattanooga, to unite all their available forces in Mississippi, carry Corinth by assault, and sweep the enemy out of West Tennessee. This, unfortunately, Price, under his instructions, could not then do. Our combined forces would then have exceeded twenty-five thousand effectives, and there is no doubt as to the results of the movement. Later, after Breckenridge had been detached with six thousand men, and Price had lost about four thousand on the Iuka expedition (mainly stragglers), the attempt on Corinth was made. Its works had been greatly strengthened, and its garrison greatly increased. Van Dorn attacked with his usual vigor and dash. His left and centre stormed the town, captured all the guns in their front, and broke Rosecrans' centre. The division comprising our right wing remained inactive, so that the enemy, believing our right was merely making a feint, detached Stanley, with six thousand fresh men, from his left and drove us out of the town.

Never was a general more disappointed than Van Dorn; but no man in all our army was so little shaken in his courage by the result as he was. I think his was the highest courage I have ever known. It rose above every disaster, and he never looked more gallant than when his broken army, in utter disorder, was streaming through the open woods which then environed Corinth and its formidable defenses. However much depression all of us showed and felt, he, alone, remained unconquered; and if he could have gotten his forces together, would have tried it again. But seeing that was impossible, he brought Lovell's Division, which, not having assaulted, was unbroken, to cover the rear and moved back to Chewalla, seven miles west of Corinth, encouraging officers and men to re-form their broken organizations as we marched along. No sooner did he halt at Chewalla than he gave orders to move in the morning to attack the enemy at Rienzi. But the condition of two of his three divisions was such that the generals advised against attempting any new aggressive movement until we could re-form and re-fit our commands. My division had marched from Chewalla to attack Corinth with four thousand eight hundred muskets the day but one before. We left in the approaches, and the very central defenses of Corinth, two thousand officers and men, killed or wounded; among them were many of my ablest field and company officers. The Missourians had lost almost as heavily; Lovell's Division alone, not having attacked the works at all, came off with but a trifling loss. It was, therefore, decided to move down to Ripley by the route we had so lately come over in such brave array, and with such high hopes. But before dawn the next morning, Van Dorn had moved the cavalry and pioneers on the road to Rienzi, still resolved to capture that place, and march around immediately and attack Corinth from the opposite direction.

The plan was worthy of Charles XII., and might have been successful; and Van Dorn only abandoned it when convinced that he would inevitably lose his wagon train, and that the army would feel he was rash. A friend said to him finally: "Van Dorn, you are the only man I ever saw who loves danger for its own sake. When any daring enterprise is before you, you cannot adequately estimate the obstacle in your way." He replied: "While I do not admit the correctness of your criticism, I feel how wrong I shall be to imperil this army through my personal peculiarities, after what such a friend as you have told me they are, and I will countermand the orders and move at once on the road to Ripley." Few commanders have ever been so beset as Van Dorn was in the forks of the Hatchie, and very few would have extricated a beaten army as he did then. One with a force stated at ten thousand men, headed him at the Hatchie bridge, while Rosecrans, with twenty thousand men, was attacking his rear at the Tuscumbia bridge, only five miles off. The whole road between was occupied by a train of near four hundred wagons, and a defeated army of about eleven thousand muskets. But Van Dorn was never, for a moment, dismayed. He repulsed Ord, and punished him severely; while he checked Rosecrans at the Tuscumbia until he could turn his train and army short to the left, and cross the Hatchie by the Boneyard road, without the loss of a wagon.

By ten P. M. his whole army and train were safely over the Hatchie, and with a full moon to light us on our way we briskly marched for Ripley, where we drew up in line of battle and awaited the enemy; but he not advancing, we marched to Holly Springs. When, in November, Van Dorn checked Grant's advance, he then occupied the works on the Tallahatchie, which he held for a month —Grant's force was sixty thousand, Van Dorn's was sixteen thousand. He then retired behind the Yallabusha to Grenada, and awaited Grant's advance until Christmas eve, 1862, when, leaving the army at Grenada, under Loring's command, he moved with two thousand horse around Grant's army, swooped down upon Holly Springs, captured the garrison, destroyed three months' stores for sixty thousand men, and defeated Grant's whole campaign and compelled him to abandon Mississippi. From that time Van Dorn resumed his proper *role* as a general of cavalry, in which he had no superior in either army. His extrication of his cavalry division from the bend of Duck river, equaled his conduct in the forks of the Hatchie.

In the spring of 1863, he was the chief commander of the cavalry of Bragg's army, then at Tullahoma; he had as brigade commanders Armstrong, Jackson, Cosby, and Martin, and, with about eight thousand men, was preparing to move across the Ohio. His command was bivouacked in the fertile region of Middle Tennessee. His headquarters were at Spring Hill, and almost daily he would engage the enemy with one of his brigades while the other three were carefully drilled. His horses were in fine order and his men in better drill, discipline and spirit than our cavalry had ever been. He was assassinated just as he was about to move on the most important enterprise of his life. I believe that in him we lost

30

the greatest cavalry soldier of his time. His knowledge of roads and country was wonderful. He knew how to care for his men and horses. His own wants were few; his habits simple; he was energetic and enduring; he deferred everything to his military duty; he craved glory beyond everything—high glory; there was no stain of vain glory about anything he ever did or said. As the bravest are ever the greatest, so was he simple and kind, and gentle as a child. I remember one evening on our ride across Arkansas, we stopped at the hospitable house of an old gentlemen (Dr. Williams) about one day's march this side of Van Buren. We were sitting on the portico —Van Dorn and I—when a little child came out to us; he called her to him, and soon had her confidence, and as she told him, in her child-like way, that she was an orphan, and spoke of her mother, lately dead, his eyes filled with tears, and I noticed that he slipped into her hand the only piece of gold he owned, and asked her to get with it something to remember him by.

The pre-eminent quality of his military nature was that he was unconquerable. Whether defeated or victorious, he always controlled his resources. As Napoleon said of De Soix, he was all for war and glory; and he had a just idea of glory. There was no self-seeking in him, and he would die for duty at any moment. His personal traits were very charming. His person was very handsome; his manners frank and simple; with his friends he was genial, and sometimes convivial; but never did I know him to postpone his duty for pleasure, or to pursue conviviality to a degree unbecoming a gentleman. Take him for all in all, he was the most gallant soldier I have ever known.

THE RIGHT FLANK AT GETTYSBURG.

BY COLONEL WILLIAM BROOKE-RAWLE.

It is but natural that the battle which proved to be the turning point of the Rebellion should attract more attention, and be more thoroughly studied, than any other. To some, it may seem late in the day to discuss a new phase of that fearful struggle; but to those still living who there "assisted," the whole subject is one of interest.

The "History of the Civil War in America," by the Comte de Paris, has been written to the end of the year 1862, with a degree of ability which is remarkable. In his search for the truth concerning the campaign of Gettysburg, for his forthcoming volume, that author has loosened an avalanche of newspaper and manuscript communications, especially from "our friends on the other side," and he may well hesitate before attempting to reconcile the many disputed questions which have arisen. So peculiar do the views of some writers appear to us, that we begin to distrust the memory of those days, and almost to question the general belief that the battle of Gettysburg was a victory for the Union arms. Some might be led to suppose that the dissensions among the Confederate leaders, rather than the ability with which General Meade handled his noble army, brought about the results of the battle. Indeed, it is almost becoming doubtful to the minds of many of the participants in the battle whether they were even present—so different from their recollections of the events do recent representations appear.

It has been insinuated by a gallant Confederate officer (Major H. B. McClellan, Assistant Adjutant General on the staff of General

J. E. B. Stuart), who, if indeed he were present, might be presumed
to have been in a position to judge correctly, that the cavalry
operations on the right flank of the Union army at Gettysburg
resulted victoriously for his cause. That this was not the case, will
be shown conclusively.

But little has been written of the operations of the cavalry
during the battle of Gettysburg. So fierce was the main engagement, of which the infantry bore the brunt, that the "affairs" of the
cavalry have almost passed unnoticed, yet on the right flank there
occurred one of the most beautiful cavalry fights of the war, and one
most important in its results. It may be confidently asserted that,
had it not been for General D. McM. Gregg and the three brigades
under his command on the Bonaughtown road, on July 3d, 1863,
that day would have resulted differently, and, instead of a glorious
victory, the name of " Gettysburg" would suggest a state of affairs
which it is not agreeable to contemplate. The neglect with which
this portion of the battle has been treated is due, in a great degree,
to the want of that self-assertion which was not uncommon among
the officers of our Cavalry Corps. The skilful leader, gallant officer,
and accomplished gentleman who was in command on the right
flank, has allowed his modesty and retiring disposition to stand in
the way of his claiming for himself and his division the laurels to
which they are entitled. The Second Cavalry Division, moreover,
was not a favorite among the newspaper correspondents. None of
them were attached nominally to its staff, nor allowed in its camps,
or among its men—for its commander saw the mischief which they
worked. He was appreciated the more for his rule, but there are
instances of others thereby gathering, in the ephemeral records of
the times, the glory which he had rightly earned, well knowing that
no public denial would come from him. It is but tardy justice
which is now being done to him and his command, and the importance of the operations on the right flank was never brought before
the public until the recent appearance of Major Carpenter's able
article, containing extracts from the official report of the Confederate General Stuart, which is of infinite importance to the true
history of the battle, but which the War Department, for some
reason, has hitherto refused to the public.*

* There has existed a wide-spread supposition that Stuart and his cavalry
were not even present at the battle of Gettysburg. This is partly owing to the fact
that, after the battles of Aldie and Upperville, Stuart became separated from Lee's
army, and was prevented from joining it, or from being of any assistance to its

General Meade, in his official report of the battle, merely refers to the fact that, on the 3d of July, "General Gregg was engaged with the enemy on our extreme right, having passed across the Baltimore pike and Bonaughtown road and boldly attacked the enemy's left and rear," and in his dispatches of that date he telegraphed in the evening to Washington: "My cavalry have been engaged all day on both flanks of the enemy, harassing and vigorously attacking him with great success, notwithstanding they encountered superior numbers, both cavalry and infantry." Swinton, in his "Campaigns of the Army of the Potomac," states that "during the action (July 3d) the cavalry had been operating on the flanks—Kilpatrick's Division on the left, and Gregg's Division on the right," and, in a note, "the scope of this work does not permit the recital of the details of the numerous cavalry affairs." And Bates, in his "History of the Battle of Gettysburg," which contains some good material, gives a few lines to an account of the operations on the right flank, correct in the main, but he erroneously locates Stuart with his cavalry on the right of the Confederate line.

In the official maps of the battle-field, recently published by the War Department, the responsible duty of designating thereon the positions of the different portions of the contending armies, has been assigned to Mr. John B. Bachelder. He also has paid but little attention in his studies of the battle to the operations of the cavalry, but in a memorandum, apparently accounting for the absence from other places of the Confederate cavalry command of General Stuart, he makes a half-hidden mention of "Gregg's Cavalry" on the maps, both of the 2d and 3d of July, as being engaged on those days outside their limits. He has fallen into error even in designating the roads on which those forces met. This may, in some degree, be owing to the fact, that the official surveys, from which the maps were prepared, have not been extended sufficiently far to the east to cover the field of the operations, though an equivalent quantity of

---

commander during its movements preceding the battle, by the interposition of Gregg's and Kilpatrick's Cavalry. Stuart was thereby compelled to make a wide detour, only reaching Lee on the 2d of July; and, owing to this separation, and the loss of the "eyes and ears" of his army, Lee had, to a great extent, to move in the dark. To the fact of Stuart's absence from Lee's army, many recent Confederate writers have attributed the resulst of the campaign, while others maintain that the two brigades, under Generals Robertson, and Jones, which did not accompany Stuart upon his independent movement, were amply sufficient for the purposes of observation.

country to the west, upon which no events of consequence occurred, has been included.*

Even among cavalry officers a want of appreciation has been shown. General Pleasonton, who, though nominally commanding the Cavalry Corps at the time, was not with any of his divisions, but, according to his own account, near General Meade in the rear of the infantry line of battle, instructing his distinguished chief "how, in half an hour, to show himself a great general," has recently written an article giving an outline of the valuable services of the cavalry of the Army of the Potomac preceding the battle of Gettysburg. He omits entirely to mention the important part it took in the battle itself. Though concluding in a general way with a glowing tribute to its services, it is difficult to ascertain from what he writes whether any portion of the corps of which he was the commander was actually engaged.

And finally, General Custer, who was temporarily serving under General Gregg with his brigade, forwarded independently an official report of the movements of his command, which, in some of its statements, is not entirely ingenuous. In the account referred to, he has taken to himself and his Michigan Brigade alone, the credit which, to say the least, others were entitled to share.

---

* Since this article was first published, the following letter has been received which, in justice to Mr. Bachelder, is now given in full:

OFFICE OF THE CHIEF OF ENGINEERS,
WASHINGTON, D. C., December 10th, 1878.

COLONEL WILLIAM BROOKE-RAWLE,

Sir—Your letter of 13th ultimo, transmitting an account of the operations of the cavalry command of General David McM. Gregg during the battle of Gettysburg, was referred to Mr. John B. Bachelder, who was employed by the War Department to plot the positions of the troops on the maps of Gettysburg battlefield, and has been returned endorsed as follows:

"In answer to the letter of Mr. William Brooke-Rawle, I have the honor to say that it is to be regretted that from the removed position of the field of operations of Gregg's Cavalry, it was found impracticable to embrace it in the general survey of the field without reducing the scale to an extent which would have defeated the object of the map, and this is the more to be regretted, as this affair was one of the most brilliant features of the battle, and, it is not improbable, saved the army from disaster. It was spoken of at the time, and I have always understood that a separate survey of Gregg's field would be made whenever an appropriation was granted for that purpose, which I heartily recommend.

"I am, sir, yours with respect,

"JNO. B. BACHELDER."

Very respectfully your obedient servant,

A. A. HUMPHREYS,

Brigadier General, Chief of Engineers.

The story of Gregg's fight has never been told. The task of telling it now has devolved upon the writer, who would have preferred that some other and abler hand had undertaken it. As it is, the following has at least the merit of being written by one who witnessed and participated in the events which he attempts to describe, and whose comrades are ready to sustain him in that which he relates.

In the movements of the Army of the Potomac after crossing that river in pursuit of the Army of Northern Virginia, the Cavalry Corps of the former, with its three divisions, operated in front and on the flanks. General Buford, with the First Division, took the left flank, General Kilpatrick, with the Third Division, the centre, and General Gregg, with the Second Division, which was the last of the army to leave Virginia, the right flank. This disposition was maintained as well as could be, but when the column of Stuart was struck, Kilpatrick was followed up by Gregg. In the concentration upon Gettysburg, Gregg, with the First and Third Brigades of his division, left Hanover at daybreak on the 2d of July, and about noon took position on the Bonaughtown (or Hanover) road, near its intersection with the Salem Church (or Low Dutch) road, and about three miles from the town. The First Brigade, commanded by Colonel John B. McIntosh, of the Third Pennsylvania Cavalry, consisted of his own regiment and the First New Jersey and First Maryland Cavalry regiments, and Captain A. M. Randol's Light Battery E of the First (regular) Artillery, four guns. It was temporarily depleted of one-half its strength by the loss of the First Pennsylvania and First Massachusetts Cavalry regiments, which had been detached for service with the Reserve Artillery and the Sixth Corps respectively. The Third Brigade, commanded by Colonel J. Irvin Gregg, of the Sixteenth Pennsylvania Cavalry, consisted of his own regiment and the Fourth Pennsylvania, First Maine, and Tenth New York Cavalry regiments. In addition to Randol's Battery, a section of the volunteer battery belonging to the Purnell Legion was with the division until the night of the 2d of July. This section, in the hurrying movements of concentration, had become separated from its proper command, and had been found, some days before, wandering around the country entirely on its own account. General Gregg took it along with him, and showed it some marching which astonished its fat and sleek horses and well-conditioned men. The Second Brigade of the division, under Colonel Pennock Huey, of the Eighth Pennsylvania Cavalry, had, on the 1st of July, been sent to Westminster, Maryland, to guard the army trains.

Since crossing the Potomac on the 27th of June, the column had marched steadily day and night. Previously, it had been on incessant duty since the opening of the campaign on the 9th of June at Brandy Station, and now, having been for many days without food or forage, the division arrived with wearied men and jaded horses upon the field of Gettysburg. Its numerical strength had, moreover, been considerably reduced, for many horses and men had dropped from exhaustion along the road. So much so was this the case that, in some regiments, it became necessary to consolidate the companies, reducing the number of squadrons in each to three or four.

Upon reaching the Bonaughtown road, pickets were thrown out, connecting with the infantry on the left, and extending well to the right of the road. The remainder of the command sought a little rest and shelter from the scorching heat, while from the ridges of hills could be seen the conflict between the infantry and artillery of the opposing armies. About seven o'clock in the evening a line of Confederate infantry skirmishers moved along our front, covering their main column, which proved to be a portion of Johnson's Division of Ewell's Corps, advancing to the attack of Culp's Hill. Screened by Brinkerhoff's Ridge from the position occupied by the cavalry, the enemy were not, at first, observed by the pickets, but a party of Confederate officers, making a reconnoissance to the summit of the ridge where it crosses the Bonaughtown road, disclosed their approach. The section of the Purnell Battery, in position on the road near the Howard house, planted two shells in their midst. At the same moment, those portions of McIntosh's Brigade which were not unsaddled, and which were drawn up near the Little house, mounted and moved forward. Several squadrons of the Third Pennsylvania and First New Jersey plunged down the hill and across Cress' Run, then dismounted and deployed at the double quick. Coming to the summit of Brinkerhoff's Ridge, the enemy's line of infantry was observed approaching also at a run. Along the summit there was a stone wall, which each party at once saw would command possession of the field, and each redoubled its efforts to secure it. The cavalry-men, however, reached it first—the enemy being but some ten yards off—and poured in a volley from their carbines which checked the advance of their adversaries. The enemy, after some ineffectual attempts to take the wall, retired to a more sheltered position, about two hundred yards off, and heavy firing was kept up until after nightfall. In the meantime, some of the artillery with the division was employed upon the columns of the enemy's infantry, which could be seen moving towards Culp's Hill in support of the bloody struggle for its possession. About ten o'clock in the evening, in accordance with orders from headquarters, General Gregg withdrew the skirmish line, substituting a picket line from the First New Jersey, and moved his command over to the Baltimore pike, where it took position on the south side of White Run, in the rear of the Reserve Artillery, and remained there during the night.*

On the morning of July 3d, General Gregg was directed to resume his position on the right of the infantry line, and make a demonstration against the enemy. Finding General Custer's Brigade of the Third Cavalry Division occupying his position of the previous day on the Bonaughtown road, Gregg placed his two brigades to the left of Custer's line, covering the right of the Twelfth Corps. A regiment was dismounted and deployed for some distance into the woods without finding anything in front. Scarcely had this been done, however, when, about noon, a dispatch from the commander of the Eleventh Corps, to General Meade, was placed in General Gregg's hands, notifying him that a large body of the enemy's cavalry had been observed, from Cemetery Hill, moving towards the right of our line. At the same time an order from General Pleasonton, commanding the Cavalry Corps, was received, directing that Custer's Brigade should at once join its division (Kilpatrick's) on the left. Accordingly, McIntosh's Brigade was ordered to relieve Custer's, and to occupy his position on the right of the Bonaughtown road, west of the Salem Church road.

In order to appreciate the positions of the opposing forces, it becomes necessary to examine the official report of General J. E. B. Stuart, now in the possession of the War Department, but which has never been published in full. After mentioning that his advance (Hampton's Brigade) had arrived in the vicinity of Gettysburg, on July 2d, just in time to repulse an attempt by some of our cavalry (under Kilpatrick) to reach the rear of the Confederate line, by way of Hunterstown, Stuart proceeds to state that he took position on the York and Heidlersburg roads. On the morning of the 3d, he moved forward to a new position to the left of General Ewell's left, and in advance of it, where, from the elevated ground, there was a view of the country for many miles. He was thus enabled to render Ewell's left secure, and at the same time to command a view of the routes leading to the rear of our lines. His purpose, as he himself states, was to effect a surprise on the rear of our main line of battle, and it is

---

* This position is within the limits of the official maps, but no mention is made of the two brigades thereon.

obvious that he intended to accomplish this by way of the Baltimore pike, and the roads hereafter described, simultaneously with Pickett's attack in front. In the concentration of his forces for this object, however, Hampton's and Fitzhugh Lee's Brigades, as he further states, unfortunately debouched into open ground, disclosing the movement, and causing the corresponding movement of a large force of our cavalry, and to this Stuart attributes his want of success. Although checked in his original design, nevertheless, he adds: "Had the enemy's main body been dislodged, as was confidently hoped and expected" (by Pickett's charge) "I was in precisely the right position to discover it and improve the opportunity. I watched keenly and anxiously the indications in his rear for that purpose, while in the attack which I intended (which was forestalled by our troops being exposed to view), his cavalry would have separated from the main body, and gave promise of solid results and advantages."

Stuart acknowledges that the position which he held was very strong, and he is fully justified in his description of it. A country cross-road branches off from the York turnpike about two and a half miles from Gettysburg, and runs in a southeasterly direction towards the Salem Church road, which connects the York and Baltimore turnpikes. About half the distance to the Salem Church road, and a mile from it, the road crosses Cress' Run, and then rises to the ridge mentioned by Stuart, and known as Cress' Ridge. A moderately thick piece of woods on the right, (as Stuart's line faced) ends at the crest of the ridge, affording protection and cover to the supports of the battery which was subsequently placed there. Screened by the piece of woods, and on the opposite side of the cross-road, is a large open space on the Stallsmith farm, where the Confederate leader was enabled to mass and maneuvre his cavalry without its being observed from our position.

Gregg's position was as inferior to Stuart's as the general line occupied by the main body of the Army of Northern Virginia was to that occupied by the Army of the Potomac. As Stuart says, the whole country for miles lay at his feet. The Salem Church road crosses the Bonaughtown road nearly at right angles, about three and a half miles southeast of Gettysburg, at the Reever house, and continues on about two miles further until it reaches the Baltimore pike about one and three-fourths miles southeast of its crossing over Rock creek and the rear of centre of our main line of battle.*

---

*A country road, parallel with the Salem Church road, and from a half mile to a mile nearer Gettysburg, runs from the Bonaughtown road, at the Howard

About three-fourths of a mile northeast from the intersection of the Salem Church and Bonaughtown roads, the cross-road above mentioned branches off to the northwest, towards Stuart's position and the York pike. A piece of woods, which, since the battle, has been reduced in extent, covered the intersection of the Salem Church road and the cross-road on the side towards the enemy's position, extending about equi-distant on each road from a lane leading down to John Rummel's house and farm buildings on the north, to the Lott house on the south, a total distance of about a half mile or more. One side of this woods faced the northwest and the enemy's position. Between the ridge on which the Reever house stands, and along which the Salem Church road runs, and the higher ridge occupied by Stuart, but nearer the latter, is a small creek known as Little's run, starting from the spring-house at Rummel's. The open ground between the two ridges, which was comparatively level, and which extended about a-half mile in width, by a mile in length, afforded an excellent opportunity for the maneuvring of cavalry. The Rummel farm buildings, eventually, became the key point of the field, which lies about three miles east of Gettysburg.

The force under Gregg numbered about five thousand men, though not more than three thousand were actually engaged in the fight which occurred on the ground described. It consisted of the three regiments of McIntosh's Brigade, Irvin Gregg's Brigade, and Custer's Brigade, which, as will appear, remained on the field. This last, known as the "Michigan Brigade," was composed of the First, Fifth, Sixth, and Seventh Michigan Cavalry regiments, commanded by Colonels Town, Alger, Gray, and Mann, respectively, and Light Battery M, of the Second (regular) Artillery, commanded by Lieutenant A. C. M. Pennington. On the other hand, Stuart had with him, as he states in his report, Hampton's, Fitzhugh Lee's, and W. H. F. Lee's Brigades of cavalry, to which was added, for the proposed movements of the day, Jenkins' Brigade of cavalry armed as mounted infantry with Enfield muskets. This entire force has been

---

house, along the valley of Cress' Run, and strikes the Baltimore pike by the bridge over White Run, less than a mile southeast of the bridge over Rock Creek, near which latter, by Powers' Hill, were the Reserve Artillery, and the ammunition trains. This, being a more direct one than the Salem Church road, was used by our troops for operating between the Baltimore pike and the Bonaughtown road, and, consequently, the rear of our main line of battle was even more accessible by this than by the road above described.

estimated by reliable Confederate authority at between six thousand
and seven thousand men.*

When McIntosh, with his command, came upon the ground,
shortly before one o'clock, for the purpose of relieving Custer, he
found the latter in position, facing Gettysburg, near the junction of the Bonaughtown and Salem Church roads, and covering
them. In his official report of the battle, Custer mistakes the names
of the roads on which he held position. He erroneously calls the
Hanover or Bonaughtown road the *York* pike, and the Salem Church
road the *Oxford* road. He states, however:

At an early hour on the morning of the 3d, I received an order, through a
staff officer of the brigadier general commanding the division, to move, at once, my
command, and follow the First Brigade on the road leading from Two Taverns to
Gettysburg. Agreeably to the above instructions, my column was formed and
moved out on the road designated, when a staff officer of Brigadier General Gregg,
commanding Second Division, ordered me to take my command and place it in
position on the pike leading from *York* to Gettysburg, which position formed the
extreme right of our battle on that day. Upon arriving at the point designated, I immediately placed my command in position, facing toward Gettysburg. At the same
time I caused reconnoissances to be made on my front, right and rear, but failed to
discover any considerable force of the enemy. Everything remained quiet till ten
A. M., when the enemy appeared on my right flank, and opened upon me with a
battery of six guns. Leaving two guns and a regiment to hold my first position,
and cover the road leading to Gettysburg, I shifted the remaining portion of my
command, forming a new line of battle at right angles to my former line. The
enemy had obtained correct range of my new position, and were pouring solid shot
and shell into my command with great accuracy. Placing two sections of Battery
M, Second (regular) Artillery, in position, I ordered them to silence the enemy's battery, which order, notwithstanding the superiority of the enemy's position, was successfully accomplished in a very short space of time. My line, as it then existed, was
shaped like the letter **L**, the shorter branch, formed of the section of Battery M, supported by four squadrons of the Sixth Michigan Cavalry, faced towards Gettysburg,
covering the Gettysburg pike; the long branch, composed of the remaining two
sections of Battery M, Second Artillery, supported by a portion of the Sixth Michigan Cavalry, on the right, while the Seventh Michigan Cavalry, still further to the
right and in advance, was held in readiness to repel any attack the enemy might
make coming on the *Oxford* road. The Fifth Michigan Cavalry was dismounted,
and ordered to take position in front of my centre and left. The First Michigan
Cavalry was held in columns of squadrons to observe the movements of the enemy.

---

* It seems, however, that a disinterested, and, therefore, more reliable authority
—the Comte de Paris—has estimated the numbers of the Confederate cavalry at from
one-third to one-half greater than those given above. It has been well said by a
recent writer, referring to the statement made by Stuart in his report that the
two brigades, which did not accompany him into Pennsylvania, were strong in
point of numbers: "As a rule, the forces on the Southern side are made out to be
so nearly non-existent, that one thinks of them as a shadowy army, like the ghostly
troops which pass before the Emperor in the French picture of the *Revue des Morts.*"

I ordered fifty men to be sent one mile and a half on the *Oxford* road, while a detachment of equal size was sent one mile and a half on the road leading from Gettysburg to *York*, both detachments being under the command of the gallant Major Webber, who, from time to time, kept me so well informed of the movements of the enemy that I was enabled to make my dispositions with complete success.

At twelve o'clock, an order was transmitted to me from the brigadier general commanding the division, by one of his aides, directing me, upon being relieved by a brigade from the Second Division, to move with my command and form a junction with the First Brigade, on the extreme left. On the arrival of the brigade of the Second Division, commanded by Colonel McIntosh, I prepared to execute the order.

The remaining portions of his account require re-statement for reasons already mentioned.

Upon notifying Custer of the orders to relieve him, McIntosh inquired as to his picket line and the position and force of the enemy. Nothing was said as to any previous firing, and everything was quiet at the time. Custer reported, however, that the enemy were all around, and that an attack might be expected at any moment from the right and rear. The First New Jersey, under Major Beaumont, was at once ordered out, mounted, to relieve Custer's lines, and took position in the woods on the Salem Church road, facing to the northwest. The Third Pennsylvania, under Lieutenant Colonel Jones, and First Maryland, under Lieutenant Colonel Deems, were drawn up in close columns of squadrons in a clover field west of the Lott house, awaiting developments. While in this position, and a few minutes after one o'clock, the tremendous artillery firing which preceded Pickett's attack began. Not being in the line of fire, however, the officers and men of the brigade, while allowing their horses to graze, looked with amazement upon the magnificent spectacle.

As soon as the Michigan Brigade had withdrawn from the field for the purpose of joining Kilpatrick near Round Top, McIntosh, who had looked well over the ground, determined to ascertain what force was in his front without waiting to be attacked. Accordingly, about two o'clock, he ordered Major Beaumont to deploy a strong skirmish line of the First New Jersey, and move it forward, under Major Janeway, towards the wooded crest, about half a mile in front of him, and a short distance beyond Rummel's, expecting there to find the enemy. This movement was a signal for the deployment of a skirmish line from Rummel's barn, where a strong picket force had been concealed, and which at once occupied a line of fences a short distance to the south. The First New Jersey, which had reached a stone and rail fence parallel with that occupied by the enemy, was dismounted and reinforced from the woods, and immediately became hotly engaged. Two squadrons of the Third Pennsylvania, under Captains Treichel and Rogers, were deployed, dismounted, to the left in the open fields, and another squadron of the same regiment, under Captain Miller, deployed, mounted, to the extreme right of the whole line, along the edge of the woods covering the cross-road, above mentioned, which ran towards the enemy's position.* One squadron of the First New Jersey, under Captain Hart, remained drawn up, mounted, in the woods, in support of the line. To meet this movement, the Confederate skirmish line was strongly reinforced from the woods in the rear by dismounted men, and a battery was placed in position on the wooded crest back of the Rummel house, and to the left of the cross-road.

The Confederate battery now opened fire, and McIntosh sent back for Randol and his guns, at the same time informing General Gregg of the state of affairs, that he was engaged with a greatly superior force, and requesting that Colonel Irvin Gregg's Brigade be sent up at the trot to support him. That brigade was yet some distance off, and Gregg, meeting Custer on the march in the opposite direction, ordered him to return and reinforce McIntosh, and to remain on the ground until the Third Brigade could be brought up. Custer, ever ready for a fight, was not loth to do so. Wheeling his column about, he moved up at once to McIntosh's support, and General Gregg, coming upon the field, took command of the forces. In the meantime, the enemy attempted to force our lines on the right, but their charge was gallantly repulsed by Miller's squadron of the Third Pennsylvania, and Hart's squadron of the First New Jersey, in the woods.

The enemy having filled the large barn at Rummel's with sharpshooters, who, while picking off our men, were completely protected from our fire, Captain Randol, upon coming on the ground, placed a section of his battery of three-inch light ordnance guns, under Lieutenant Chester, in position, well to the front, on the edge of an orchard, some distance to the left and beyond the Reever house, and opened upon it. Shell after shell struck the building, soon compelling the enemy to abandon it, and as they did so, the centre of our line advanced and occupied the enemy's line of fences and some of the outbuildings. Having thus pierced their line, a force was sent out to take the enemy in flank, while the left centre moved up to the line of fences, driving back the portions of Jenkins' Brigade which had occupied it. This movement caused the left of the enemy's line, held by portions of Hampton's and Fitzhugh Lee's

---

* Captain Walsh's squadron of the Third Pennsylvania had been sent out on picket duty still farther to the right, but was not actively engaged in the fight.

brigades, dismounted, to give way also, and their position was at once taken. The left, the centre, and the right centre of our line was thus advanced, while the right still rested on the woods on the cross-road, and the Sixth Michigan went into position along Little's Run, on the left rear of Treichel's and Rogers' squadrons, occupying the space thus opened, at the same extending to the left so as to cover the Bonaughtown road. Pennington's Battery of six guns, upon arriving on the ground, went into position on the side of the Bonaughtown road, a short distance west of the Spangler house, and about two hundred and fifty yards to the left and rear of Chester's section. Between the two Randol placed his second section, under Lieutenant Kinney, of the First Connecticut Heavy Artillery, an officer of the Reserve Artillery staff, who had volunteered to serve with the battery. By the accuracy of their firing and superior range, Randol's guns soon silenced the enemy's battery on the crest beyond Rummel's, near the cross-road, and Pennington's, some guns in position more to our left.

When the ammunition of the First New Jersey and Third Pennsylvania was becoming exhausted, the Fifth Michigan, armed with Spencer repeating carbines, was ordered to relieve them, and moved up, dismounted, to the front, along a fence which intersected the field lengthwise running at right angles to the skirmish line. The left came up the line occupied by Treichel's and Rodgers' squadrons of the Third Pennsylvania, behind a fence which was slightly retired from that occupied by the First New Jersey; but before the right could reach the more advanced fence occupied by the First New Jersey, a dismounted regiment from W. H. F. Lee's Brigade advanced in line to the support of the enemy's skirmishers, who were about to be cut off by the detachment sent out from Rummel's, and made a terrific onslaught along the line. Treichel's and Rogers' squadrons of the Third Pennsylvania, and that portion of the Fifth Michigan which had reached their line, held the ground stubbornly. After a while, when the fire had slackened, Treichel and Rogers, who had been ordered to retire when the Fifth Michigan came up, endeavored to withdraw their men. The enemy, believing it a symptom of retreat, advanced. The Third Pennsylvanians came back upon the line, and again and again this was repeated.

The First New Jersey remained at the line of fences until the last cartridge was used and the last pistol emptied, and then fell back upon the supports in the woods. This movement was taken advantage of by the enemy, and the First Virginia was at once ordered forward for a mounted charge upon our right centre. As it was seen to start, McIntosh rode over quickly to the Lott house, where he had left the First Maryland prepared for such an emergency. Gregg, however, upon coming on the field, had moved the regiment over to the right of the Salem Church road, to guard more effectually that important quarter. The Seventh Michigan, which was to take its place, was just then coming on the field from the direction of the Reever house in column of fours. Custer, who was near, also saw the emergency, ordered close column of squadrons to be formed at the gallop, and advanced with it to meet the attack.

As the First New Jersey fell back, the right of the two Third Pennsylvania squadrons, and that portion of the Fifth Michigan which had reached them, swung back behind the fence which ran parallel with the line of the charging column and intersecting the field lengthwise.

The Seventh Michigan, a new regiment, advanced boldly to meet the First Virginia, but on coming up to the stone and rail fence, instead of pushing across it, began firing with their repeating carbines. The First Virginia came on in spite of the heavy fire until it reached the fence from the other side. Both regiments fought face to face across the fence with their carbines and revolvers, while a scorching fire was centred upon the First Virginia from either flank. The enemy's dismounted line also came up, and assisted the First Virginia to pass the fence, whereupon the Seventh Michigan gave way in disorder, the enemy following in close pursuit.

The First Virginia, becoming strung out by this movement, was exposed to a terrific fire from the two batteries in front, and from the heavy skirmish lines on the flanks, while some of the Fifth Michigan, who had succeeded in mounting, advanced to assist the Seventh. It was more than even their gallantry could stand, and the First Virginia fell back on the supports which were fast advancing to its assistance. This was about three o'clock.

Just then there appeared in the distance, turning the point of woods on the cross-road by the Stallsmith farm, a brigade of cavalry.* It was manifest to every one that, unless this, the grandest attack of all was checked, the day would go hard with the Army of the Potomac. It was Stuart's last reserve and his last resource, for, if the Baltimore pike was to be reached, and havoc created in our rear, the critical moment had arrived, as Pickett was even then moving up to the assault of Cemetery Ridge.

---

* Stuart, in his official report, states that this force consisted of the First North Carolina Cavalry, and Jeff Davis Legion, but that gradually *the greater portion of his command* became involved in the hand-to-hand fighting.

In close columns of squadrons, advancing as if in review, with sabres drawn and glistening like silver in the bright sunlight, the spectacle called forth a murmur of admiration. It was, indeed, a memorable one. Chester, being nearest, opened at once with his section, at the distance of three-fourths of a mile. Pennington and Kinney soon did the same. Canister and percussion shell were put into the steadily approaching columns as fast as the guns could fire. The dismounted men fell back to the right and left, and such as could got to their horses. The mounted skirmishers rallied and fell into line. Then Gregg rode over to the First Michigan, which, as it had come upon the field some time before, had formed close column of squadrons between and supporting the batteries, and ordered it to charge. As Town ordered sabres to be drawn and the column to advance, Custer dashed up with similar orders, and placed himself at its head. The two columns drew nearer and nearer, the Confederates outnumbering their opponents as three or four to one. The gait increased—first the trot, then the gallop. Hampton's battle-flag floated in the van of the brigade. The orders of the Confederate officers could be heard by those in the woods on their left: "Keep to your sabres, men, keep to your sabres!" for the lessons they had learned at Brandy Station and at Aldie had been severe. There the cry had been: "Put up your sabres! Draw your pistols and fight like gentlemen!" But the sabre was never a favorite weapon with the Confederate cavalry, and now, in spite of the lessons of the past, the warnings of the present were not heeded by all.

As the charge was ordered the speed increased, every horse on the jump, every man yelling like a demon. The columns of the Confederates blended, but the perfect alignment was maintained. Chester put charge after charge of canister into their midst, his men bringing it up to the guns by the armful. The execution was fearful, but the long rents closed up at once. As the opposing columns drew nearer and nearer, each with perfect alignment, every man gathered his horse well under him, and gripped his weapon the tighter. Though ordered to retire his guns, towards which the head of the assaulting column was directed, Chester kept on until the enemy were within fifty yards, and the head of the First Michigan had come into the line of his fire. Staggered by the fearful execution from the two batteries, the men in the front line of the Confederate column drew in their horses and wavered. Some turned, and the column fanned out to the right and left, but those behind came pressing on. Custer, seeing the front men hesitate, waved his sabre

31

and shouted, "Come on, you Wolverines!" and with a fearful yell
the First Michigan rushed on, Custer four lengths ahead.

McIntosh, as he saw the Confederate column advancing, sent
his Adjutant General, Captain Walter S. Newhall, to the left, with
orders to Treichel and Rogers to rally their men for a charge on the
flank as it passed. But sixteen men could get their horses, and with
five officers they made for the battle-flag. Newhall, back once
more with the men of his own regiment, who, as he knew well,
would go anywhere, and sharing the excitement of the moment,
rushed in, by the side of Treichel and Rogers, at the head of the
little band. Miller, whose squadron of the Third Pennsylvania was
already mounted, and had rallied, fired a volley from the woods on
the right, as the Confederate column passed parallel with his line,
but one hundred yards off, and then, with sabres drawn, charged
down into the overwhelming masses of the enemy.

The small detachment of the Third Pennsylvania, under Treichel
and Rogers, struck the enemy first, all making for the color-guard.
Newhall was about seizing the flag when a sabre blow, directed at
his head, compelled him to parry it. At the same moment the
color-bearer lowered his spear and struck Newhall full in the face,
tearing open his mouth and knocking him senseless to the ground.
Every officer and nearly every man in the little band was killed or
wounded, although some succeeded in cutting their way clear through.
Almost at the same moment Miller, with his squadron of the Third
Pennsylvania, struck the left flank about two-thirds of the way down
the column. Going through and through, he cut off the rear portion
and drove it back past Rummel's, almost up to the Confederate
battery, and nothing but the heavy losses which he had suffered and
the scattering of his men prevented his going further, wounded
though he was.

In the meantime, the two columns had come together with a crash
—the one led by Hampton and Fitz Lee (for he, too, was there), and the
other by Custer—and were fighting hand-to-hand. McIntosh, with his
staff and orderlies, and such scattered men from the Michigan and other
regiments as he could get together, charged in with their sabres.
For minutes, which seemed like hours, amid the clashing of the
sabres, the rattle of the small-arms, the frenzied imprecations, the
demands to surrender, the undaunted replies, and the appeals for
mercy, the Confederate column stood its ground. Captain Thomas
of the staff, seeing that a little more was needed to turn the tide,
cut his way over to the woods on the right, where he knew he could
find Hart, with his fresh squadron of the First New Jersey. In the

melee, near the colors, was an officer of high rank, and the two headed the squadron for that part of the fight. They came within reach of him with their sabres, and then it was that Wade Hampton was wounded.

By this time the edges of the Confederate column had begun to fray away, and the outside men to draw back. As Hart's squadron, and the other small parties who had rallied and mounted, charged down from all sides, the enemy turned. Then followed a pell-mell rush, our men in close pursuit. Many prisoners were captured, and many of our men, through their impetuosity, were carried away by the overpowering current of the retreat.*

The pursuit was kept up past Rummel's, and the enemy were driven back into the woods beyond. The line of fences and the farm buildings which constituted the key-point of the field, and which, in the beginning of the fight, had been in the possession of the enemy, remained in ours until the end. All serious fighting for the day was over, for Pickett's simultaneous assault had also been repulsed, and the victory along the line was complete. Skirmishing, and some desultory artillery firing, was kept up at intervals by both forces until after nightfall, these disturbances being caused by the enemy's endeavors to recover their killed and wounded, who were lying thickly strewn over the field in our possession. At dark Stuart withdrew to the York pike, preparatory to covering the retreat of Lee's army towards the Potomac. In the evening, Custer's Brigade was ordered to join its division. Gregg remained all night in possession of the field, and in the morning started in pursuit of the retreating enemy.

The losses of the Confederate cavalry were unmistakably heavy, but have not been ascertained. General Gregg reported the losses in his division to be one officer and thirty-three enlisted men killed, seventeen officers and forty enlisted men wounded, and one officer and one hundred and three enlisted men missing—total, one hundred and ninety-five. These losses were suffered principally by the Third Pennsylvania and First New Jersey Cavalry regiments, which had borne the brunt of the fighting of the division. By the time the Third Brigade had come up, the Michigan Brigade had gotten so

---

* The successful result of this magnificent cavalry charge was attributed by the victors to the steadiness and efficiency with which they used the sabre, *en masse*, against greatly superior numbers of the enemy, many of whom had exchanged that weapon for the revolver. It should be a strong point, in the present discussions, in favor of the retention of the sabre as a cavalryman's weapon.

deeply into the fight that it could not be withdrawn. The Third Brigade had, consequently, been held in reserve close at hand during the fight, drawn up in position south of the Bonaughtown road, on either side of the Salem Church road.

Custer, in his official report, stated his losses to be nine officers and sixty-nine enlisted men killed, twenty-five officers and two hundred and seven enlisted men wounded, and seven officers and two hundred and twenty-five enlisted men missing—total, five hundred and forty-two.

It has been claimed that Gregg's fight at Gettysburg was the finest cavalry fight of the war. To borrow the language of Custer in his report of it: "I challenge the annals of warfare to produce a more brilliant or successful charge of cavalry than the one just recounted."

LEE AND GRANT IN THE WILDERNESS.

BY GENERAL C. M. WILCOX.

OF the many officers of distinction in the Union army, to whom independent and separate commands were intrusted, in popular opinion North, General Grant was regarded as the most successful, and in abilities the ablest; and for services rendered rewarded, both by Congress and the President, in a manner leaving no doubt as to the high appreciation in which they were held. He was promoted to the grade of lieutenant general, and assigned, on the 10th of March, 1864, by President Lincoln, to the command of the armies of the United States. This order placed, subject to his will, more armed men than any general of modern times ever commanded. The object to be accomplished by this law of Congress, and order of the President, concentrating the whole military power of the North in one officer, was the speedy overthrow of the Southern Confederacy, and the subjugation of its people. To effect this, Richmond must be taken; but preliminary to this, the Army of Northern Virginia must be either destroyed or captured. The annihilation of this army, the main support of the Confederacy, was esteemed by General Grant as his especial privilege, as it was his duty; and to facilitate this, he established his headquarters with the Army of the Potomac; so that, while giving a general supervision to other armies, he could personally control and direct the movements of this particular one, charged, in his opinion, with the highest mission.

The reputation of General Grant, before serving in Virginia, was due mostly to the capture of Fort Donelson and Vicksburg; and while, in a strictly military point of view, neither can be considered as very remarkable, yet each was followed by very decided, solid gains to the North. The first led to the evacuation of Nashville, Tennessee, and transferring the Union forces to the west of the Tennessee river; the last, followed speedily by the surrender of Port Hudson, virtually closed the Mississippi to the Confederacy and cut it in twain. Credit is due to General Grant for knowing where to direct his blows. Battles in which the greatest numbers are engaged, and most brilliant victories won, are not always followed by the best results to the fortunate side. When General Grant was assigned to duty as above stated, the Army of the Potomac, commanded by General Meade, lay in Culpepper county, Virginia, and, confronting it, across the Rapidan, was the Army of Northern Virginia. These armies had, with two exceptions, held the above positions since early in August following the battle of Gettysburg. The first was in October, when General Lee, although much reduced by detaching Longstreet South, crossed the Rapidan and advanced on Meade. The latter retired rapidly, not halting until he had crossed Bull Run. During this retreat of Meade a collision occurred at Bristoe Station between three of Hill's Brigades and the Fifth Corps, in which the former were worsted. General Lee returned to the Rapidan, and Meade to his old camp in Culpepper. The latter part of November (the second exception), Meade crossed the Rapidan below the Confederate right. General Lee changed front immediately, and moved rapidly to meet him. A slight skirmish occurred late in the afternoon. Next morning the Army of Northern Virginia took position in the rear of Mine run. The Union forces confronted it a week, retired at night, hurried back to the Rapidan, and recrossed into Culpepper without a battle but losing prisoners.

During the winter, while on the Rapidan, General Lee's troops —A. P. Hill's Corps—extended up the river as far as Liberty mills, six miles above Orange Court-House; Ewell's Corps on the right, below Clarke's Mountain, which was eight miles from Orange; Longstreet, after his return from East Tennessee, remained near Gordonsville, eight miles in rear. In general, while on the Rapidan, the troops were not regularly and well supplied with good and sufficient rations, nor was their clothing of the best; their *morale* was, nevertheless, excellent, and when spring came the camp was enlivened by the resuming of military exercises, drills, etc. In April, without any orders being given, there was a sending to the rear, by officers, of extra baggage, and a general but quiet preparation for the coming campaign, soon to be inaugurated early in May. There was at length a little stir among ordnance officers, a more than usual activity among those of the medical department; and finally, May 3d, an order was issued to have, in the language of the camp, "three days' cooked rations," thus putting an end to all supense. The Rapidan flows within a mile of Orange Court-House, runs little south of east, and empties into the Rappahannock eight miles above Fredericksburg. Two roads, the old pike and plank, connect Orange Court-House and Fredericksburg; they diverge at the Court-House, the first runs between the latter and the Rapidan, somewhat parallel, but at times two and a half miles or more apart; come together near Chancellorsville, soon separate again, but unite within six or seven miles at Tabernacle Church, and from that to Fredericksburg there being but one, the plank road. It would not be uninteresting to know the strength and organization of the two armies on the eve of entering upon this, their final, longest, most active, and laborious campaign. The Army of Northern Virginia numbered, of all arms, fifty thousand; forty-two thousand of this aggregate was infantry, divided into three corps of three divisions each—the three corps commanders and seven of the nine division commanders being West Point graduates. The cavalry commander, the chief engineer, chief of artillery, quartermaster and commissary, were all graduates; the medical director had been a surgeon in the United States Army.

The Army of the Potomac was reported by the Secretary of War to be one hundred and forty-one thousand one hundred and sixty-six, composed of three corps, Second, Fifth, and Sixth, to which the Ninth had recently been joined. It is probable that the strength of this army actually present may differ from that given in the Secretary's report—may have been less. Without knowing the strength of the cavalry and artillery, they may be estimated approximatively; and these two arms, together with the overestimate of the War Department, may be stated at twenty thousand, leaving one hundred and twenty-one thousand one hundred and sixty-six for the infantry. The Second and Fifth Corps had each four divisions; the other two, three each. The corps commanders and chiefs-of-staff of this army were graduates of the Academy; most of the division commanders are believed to have been graduates. In addition to superiority of numbers, the Federals were better fed, clothed, armed, and equipped, and had the means of providing for the sick and wounded in a manner the Confederates could not. In all these essentials with them were no deficiencies; their transportation was better, the condition of artillery and cavalry horses was better, as well as the more abundant means of keeping them in that state. General Grant is credited with the following words, and it is believed they expressed his design : " To hammer continuously against the armed force of the enemy and his resources, until by mere attrition, if nothing else," etc. These words make the impression that General Grant believed he had a serious undertaking on hand, and if his plan did not propose to make a sixty or ninety days' affair of it, it certainly did clearly indicate that his armies were to fight as long as there was a man left, or an armed enemy to oppose. General Grant, after deliberating whether he should cross the Rapidan above General Lee's left or below his right flank, decided upon the latter, which he is reported to have said, would " force him back toward Richmond, somewhere to the north of which he hoped to have a battle." It will be seen that he had mistaken his adversary. The Army of the Potomac, now directed by General Grant, began to move, twelve A. M., on the 4th of May, for the lower fords of the Rapidan. The Second Corps (Hancock's) being nearest the river, marched to Ely's ford, while Sedgwick's and Warren's (Sixth and Fifth Corps) moved to Germanna ford, six miles above, the last two corps preceded by Wilson's cavalry ; and by one P. M. of the 4th, Warren's (Fifth) Corps had crossed on a pontoon bridge, and, continuing his march, halted near the intersection of the old pike and Germanna ford road, and went into bivouac. Sedgwick's (Sixth) Corps crossed later in the afternoon, and camped near the ford. Wilson's cavalry advanced up the old pike to watch any move of the Confederates from that quarter. Hancock, preceded by Gregg's cavalry, crossed at Ely's ford, and by nine A. M. on the 4th, was at Chancellorsville ; there went into bivouac, having thrown the cavalry forward toward Todd's Tavern and Fredericksburg.

It is well to observe how accurately posted General Lee was as to the designs of the enemy, whose movement began at twelve A. M., while his own followed in a few hours—commencing at sunup in some cases, and earlier in others. General Lee's troops moved by the right flank ; two divisions of Hill's Corps (Heth's and Wilcox's) down the plank road toward Fredericksburg, and bivouacked near dark at Vidierville. Wilcox had made a long march, having been six miles above the Court-House. Ewell's Corps moved on the old pike, and halted for the night near Locust Grove. Anderson's Division, of Hill's Corps, remained behind to guard certain fords on the Rapidan. Longstreet's two divisions moved from Gordonsville, to follow, after reaching the plank road, in the rear of Hill. The army, that had been much separated, for convenience of passing the winter, was now being concentrated as it converged upon the enemy; and all in good spirits, notwithstanding the heavy odds known to be against them. Early in the morning of the 5th, Gregg's cavalry was ordered toward Hamilton's crossing, and the Second Corps moved toward Shady Grove, its right reaching out in the direction of the Fifth Corps, under orders for Parker's store, on the plank road. Warren's (Fifth) Corps moved toward this store, extending his right out in the direction of Sedgwick, at or near the old Wilderness tavern, to which place he was to move as soon as the road was free of other troops. With such orders, it was clear that no immediate encounter with the Confederates was anticipated; their flank being turned, it was probably believed, as before stated, that they would fall back toward Richmond. The different columns of the Union army began to move as ordered. Warren was nearest the Confederates, but he was ignorant of their close proximity; for the cavalry, that had been ordered forward on the old pike the preceding afternoon to observe the approach of the enemy in that direction, had, late in the evening, been recalled, and sent on a scout up the plank road as far as Parker's store. This store was near ten miles from Vidierville. The Confederates were on the march quite as early the morning of the 5th—Ewell on the old pike, Hill continuing on the plank road, Johnson's Division leading the advance, with Ewell and Heth's Division leading with Hill. Hill's troops had advanced beyond Mine run some miles, when several shots were heard far to the right, and soon after others directly in front. This firing was repeated, and at times in vivacity almost equal to an active infantry skirmish. That on the right was believed to be between the cavalry of the two armies on or near the Catharpin road, while that in front was between Kirkland's Brigade, of Heth's Division, and the enemy's cavalry, mostly dismounted. The fire in front occasioned but little delay. A few of the enemy's dead and wounded were seen on the roadside as the troops moved on. Near Parker's store, the flank of the column was struck by a small body of cavalry. They disappeared at once in a dense thicket; but a regiment (Thirty-eighth North Carolina, Colonel Ashford) of Scales' Brigade, Wilcox's Division, remained at this point until the wagons had passed.

Warren, to guard Sedgwick's right flank, and at the same time for his own protection as he moved from Germanna ford, ordered Griffin's Division forward on the old pike, while the remainder of the corps, with Crawford's Division leading, moved on a neighborhood road toward Parker's store. It was not long before Griffin met the Confederates; and as Crawford approached the plank road, he met the cavalry coming to the rear, reporting them advancing on that road also. Reports of General Lee's troops being on each of these two roads having been made, Crawford was ordered to halt, and informed that Griffin and Wadsworth would attack on the old pike. Getty's Division, of the Sixth Corps, took position on the plank road. The historian Swinton states this to have been at 8.20 A. M. Hill's two divisions were at least eight or nine miles from Parker's store at this hour. Ewell's Corps bivouacked the night of the 4th nearer the enemy than Hill had, and, resuming the march early the morning of the 5th, were first to engage the Federals. He had marched eight or nine miles. When the head of his column passed a short distance beyond a road that left the old pike and lead to Germanna ford, the enemy was discovered to be in front. Johnson's Division was formed in line to the left of the old pike, across the road running to Germanna ford, and was the first to receive the attack, made with such force and spirit that Johnson's right brigade (General John M. Jones) was forced back, and General Jones and his aide, Lieutenant Early, in endeavoring to restore order, were both killed. Battle's Brigade, of Rodes' Division, on the right of Jones' Brigade, shared a like fate. Jones' Brigade was believed by its division commander to have been forced back in consequence of the artillery having been changed in position or withdrawn without his knowledge. The other brigades of Johnson's Division held their ground. Early's Division was ordered up, and Gordon's Brigade of this, with Doles', Daniels', and Ramseur's brigades of Rodes' Division—Gordon on the right—advanced and drove the enemy back some distance. Johnson, in the meantime, was fighting heavily and successfully. Quite a number of prisoners and two pieces of artillery were captured.

After the Federals had been driven back there was a pause in the fighting, when Hays' Brigade of Early's Division moved around to the extreme left of Johnson's Division, in order to take part in the general forward movement; the brigade advanced, but, from oversight, was not supported, and was withdrawn. Later, Pegram's Brigade was ordered to the left of Hays, and was assailed with vigor, but repulsed the enemy, inflicting heavy losses. In Ewell's Corps, Brigadier Generals John M. Jones and Leroy A. Stafford were killed, and Brigadier General John Pegram wounded. The Federals had engaged Griffin's and Wadsworth's Divisions, supported by Robinson's Division and McCandless' Brigade, of Crawford's Division—all of Fifth Corps. When Warren's advance up the old pike was arrested, and the reported movement of the Confederates down the plank road had caused Crawford to halt before it was reached, Generals Grant and Meade had (according to Mr. Swinton) just reached the old Wilderness tavern, and each of these generals believed Warren had but a small force in his front, for General Lee's flank having been turned, he could not, in their opinion, have the boldness to assume the offensive. It was under such impressions that Warren received a peremptory order "to brush away the small force in his front"—and thus the battle began. The same historian states that at about nine A. M. General Meade, addressing some officers near him, said: "They have left a division to fool us here, while they concentrate and prepare a position toward the North Anna; and what I want is to prevent those fellows from getting back to Mine run." If General Meade was correctly quoted, it is evident that Mine run called up disagreeable reminiscences; he had been much criticised in the Northern press—and many think justly—for not attacking the Confederates while in position on that stream the December preceding. But had Generals Grant and Meade so willed, by being a little more active, they could have had the Second, Fifth, and Sixth Corps, probably ninety thousand infantry, all on Mine run, where it crossed the plank road, by or before sundown on the fourth, and would have been within a short distance of Hill's two divisions and in rear of Ewell's right.

General Warren failed "to brush away the small force in his front," and it was only this failure that corrected the errors into which Generals Grant and Meade had fallen in supposing General Lee would retire toward Richmond without a battle; and after this failure on the part of Warren to carry out his orders, Hancock, who had moved to Shady Grove, was recalled, and ordered to rejoin the other corps, and Sedgwick to take position on the right of Warren. Hancock arrived at three P. M., and formed in double line in front of the Brock road, and *began to intrench at once ;* but before completing the work was ordered to attack the enemy on the plank road, and drive him back to Parker's store. It will be seen that Hancock, like Warren, failed in carrying out his orders. There was some interval, near two and a half hours, between the fighting on the old pike and that on the plank road. Artillery and musketry had been heard on the former and ceased, leaving the result not satisfactorily known; but as the firing had receded in Ewell's front, the inference was that he had the better of Warren. There was no communication between Hill's two divisions on the plank road and Ewell's Corps on the old pike, and the intervening distance was uncertain. The head of Hill's column had been brought to a halt a little before three P. M. The Federals were known to be in great strength in the immediate vicinity. General Lee felt some uneasiness at the separation of these two corps. Heth's Division took position in line of battle across the plank road, and Wilcox was ordered to go with his division through the woods in the direction of the old pike and open communication with Ewell. Ten or fifteen minutes before this order to Wilcox was given, a line of the enemy's skirmishers came out into an open space of several acres, within less than two hundred yards of Generals Lee, Hill, and Heth. Seeing these officers and the soldiers near by, they retired at once into the wood without firing. These skirmishers had come from the direction in which Wilcox had to move.

Wilcox's move through the dense woods was slow for the first half mile; then came a field of that width, and about a house, several hundred yards distant in front, in this field, a party of the enemy was seen. One of his (Wilcox's) regiments was ordered forward at a run, and captured twenty or thirty, several officers being of the number. Two of Wilcox's Brigades (McGowan's and Scales') were left in the woods, near the the fence of the field, and reported by him to General Lee. From the house there was a good view of the old Wilderness tavern; the Federals could be seen about it. This was also reported, and Wilcox passed on with his brigades in quest of Ewell's right; crossed, a short distance beyond the house, Wilderness run; rose up in a field beyond, and into woods to the front and left, five or six hundred yards, his two brigades were ordered; but in a second field, and to the right of these woods, Gordon's Brigade, the right of Ewell's Corps, was found. Wilcox had hardly spoken to General Gordon when volleys of musketry were heard in the woods. He rode rapidly to rejoin his brigades, but near the woods met a courier from General Lee, bringing orders for him to return with all possible speed to the plank road, as Heth was attacked—the enemy known to be in heavy force. The two brigades were recalled at once, and returned with a little over three hundred prisoners. The musketry was heard in considerable volume on the plank road, and as Wilcox recrossed the open field, the enemy could be seen moving toward this road; his two brigades left near the field had been recalled, and when he arrived on the field of battle one of them (McGowan's) had already been ordered in, and the other (Scales') soon followed—the former across the road at right angles, the latter to the right of it, where the firing then seemed heaviest. The troops engaged could not be seen, the rattle of musketry alone indicating where the struggle was severest, and the points to which the reinforcing brigades should be sent. A third brigade (Thomas', of Wilcox's Division) was ordered on the left of the road to take position on the left of Heth, and fought in line nearly parallel to the road. The enemy were in the rear of the left of Heth. Thomas did not get into position on his left. The fourth and last brigade of Wilcox's (Lane's) went in on the right of the road and extreme right of the line, the musketry now raging furiously on the entire front. Wilcox rode forward down the road, found that McGowan's Brigade had swept like a gale through the woods, driving back all before it, and was much in advance of our lines, both on the right and left. It was deemed prudent to recall it to the main line. The firing, and of the severest kind, continued till after dark, and then slackened till eight, and soon after died out. The two divisions had held their ground, and captured a few prisoners. No artillery was used on this road by the Confederates; two pieces, believed to have been used by the Federals, were passed over in the road by McGowan's Brigade.

On the plank road Heth's and Wilcox's divisions, eight brigades, about thirteen thousand muskets, fought. Of these eight brigades, four were from North Carolina, one from South Carolina, one from Georgia and Mississippi each, one made up of Virginia and Tennessee troops. Contending against these on the Union side were, first, Getty's Division, Sixth Corps, soon reinforced by Birney's and Mott's Divisions, of the Second Corps; next, and before five P. M., Carroll's and Owen's Brigades, of Gibbon's Division, Second Corps; following these were two brigades of Barlow's Division, Second Corps; late in the afternoon Wadsworth's Division and Baxter's Brigade, of Robinson's Division, Fifth Corps. The statement made as to Federal troops engaged on the two roads, and throughout the two days' collision, is taken mostly from Swinton's "History of the Army of the Potomac." General Lee's infantry was composed of nine divisions; one (Pickett's) was absent below Richmond, and not included in the estimate of forty-two thousand for the infantry. This would give an average, therefore, of five thousand two hundred and fifty to each one of the eight divisions with General Lee. Wilcox's and Heth's were in excess of this average, the division of the former having seven thousand two hundred muskets present. In Ewell's Corps were two of the weakest divisions, Early's and Johnson's. Rodes' Division of this corps was the strongest in the army; but one brigade of this, Johnson's, was absent in North Carolina. Hoke's Brigade, of Early's Division, was also absent at Hanover Junction. Three of the eight divisions of infantry were absent on the 5th—Anderson's, of Hill's Corps, and two of Longstreet's.

There was less than twenty-six thousand Confederate infantry present at the first day's battle. If our estimate of the infantry of the Army of the Potomac be correct, ninety thousand of these were present on this day. Ewell had about eleven thousand muskets; opposed to these were Griffin's and Wadsworth's Divisions, Fifth Corps, supported by Robinson's Division and McCandless' Brigade, of Crawford's Division, of the same corps. It has been seen that Heth's Division alone received, on the plank road, the first attack, and bore the brunt of it till the arrival of Wilcox's brigades (McGowan's and Scales'), to be soon followed by Thomas' and Lane's Brigades, and that these reinforcing brigades were sent in on such points as were believed to be most sorely pressed, or where they could be best used. When the battle closed Wilcox was in front, and his line much disjointed—one brigade had fought nearly parallel to the road.

The historian Swinton, referring to this contest on the plank road, after it had been going on an hour or two, says: "The heavy firing borne to the ears of Generals Grant and Meade, at the old Wilderness tavern, attested the severity of the conflict that was going on at this important junction of roads (old pike and Brock roads). It was judged that the pressure on Hancock might be relieved by sending a force from Warren's Corps to strike through the forest southward, and fall upon the flank and rear of Hill." As there was about one and a half miles between Ewell and Hill, and fully a half mile of this an open field, in full view of the old field, and bald hill near the old Wilderness tavern, and as there was not a skirmish line, nor a piece of artillery, or even a vidette in this space, this move, or one on Ewell's right flank, might have been made at any time during the battle; and the chances were that it could have been made successfully if directed with ordinary skill and courage; in fact, with the supposed preponderance of numbers present on the Union side, both Ewell and Hill could have been attacked in flank and rear at the same time. About nine o'clock General Wilcox, from a partial examination made under difficulties— thick woods and darkness of the night—but mainly from reports of his officers, learned that his line was very irregular and much broken and required to be re-arranged. He repaired to General Lee's tent, intending to report the condition of his front, and to suggest that a skirmish line be left where the front then was, the troops be retired a short distance, and the line rectified. General Lee, at the time, was not over two hundred yards from the point General Wilcox had fixed for his own headquarters during the night, and was not over four hundred yards from where the battle had been fought. As General Wilcox entered the tent, General Lee remarked that he had made a complimentary report of the conduct of the two divisions on the plank road, and that he had received a note (holding it in his hand) from General Anderson, stating that he would bivouac at Vidierville for the night; but, he continued, "he has been instructed to move forward; he and Longstreet will be up, and the two divisions that have been so actively engaged will be relieved before day." General Wilcox, hearing this, made no suggestions about the line, as he was to be relieved before day. The failure to rearrange his line and the delay in the arrival of the three rear divisions, was near proving fatal to the Confederates.

By ten P. M. all was quiet; occasionally a man that had been sent to the rear on some errand, would be seen returning to the front. It seemed almost impossible to realize that so fierce a battle had been fought and terminating only two hours before, or that so many armed men were lying almost within reach,* ready to spring forward at early dawn to renew the bloody work. The night was clear and cloudless, but with the tall forest trees and thick underwood nothing could be seen save the road along which the wounded were now no longer borne. A line had been determined in the early hours of the night on which it would be suggested the newly arrived troops should form; but twelve, two, three o'clock came, and half-past three, and no reinforcements. An order was then sent to the rear for the pioneers to come to the front with axes, spades, etc., to fell trees and construct works. It was daylight before they came, and the enemy was found to be too close to permit their use. Clear daylight had come, but no reinforcing divisions. The struggle was renewed early in the morning of the 6th by Ewell striking the enemy on his extreme right flank (Seymour's Brigade), and involving the whole of the right two divisions, Wright's and Rickett's, of the Sixth Corps. This attack was followed soon by Hancock advancing a heavy force on the plank road. On this the Confederates were in no condition either to advance or resist an attack. Wilcox, in front, was in an irregular and broken line; Heth's men had slept close in rear, without regard to order. The corps commander had informed General Heth that the two divisions would be relieved before day,

---

* At an early hour of the night, after the battle was over, Colonel Baldwin, of the First Massachusetts Regiment, stepped a short distance to the front to get a drink of water from a stream quite near, and found himself in the midst of Confederates, and was made a prisoner. Colonel Davidson, Seventh North Carolina Regiment, became a prisoner to the Union forces in the same manner, and near the same place.

and hence this unfortunate condition of affairs at this critical moment. The tree-tops were already tinged with the early rays of the rising sun, but the enemy lay quiet; at length the sun itself was seen between the boughs and foliage of the heavy forest, and on the plank road the Confederates, eager to catch at straws in their unprepared state, began to have hopes that the Federals would not advance; but these were soon dispelled. A few shots were heard on Wilcox's right, and the firing extended rapidly along to the left, to the road and across this, and around to his extreme left, which was considerably in rear of his line on the right of the road. The musketry increased rapidly in volume, and was soon of the heaviest kind. Heth's men hurried to the rear, preparatory to re-forming line; the badly formed line of Wilcox received, unaided, this powerful column, which soon enveloped its flank. The fighting was severe as long as it lasted. Swinton says of it, "an hour's severe fighting."

While the firing was severe on the flank, a dense mass of Federals poured into the road from the thickets on either side, and the Confederates began to yield. Wilcox rode back rapidly to General Lee, found him where he had been the night before, and reported the condition of his command. His response was, "Longstreet must be here; go bring him up." Galloping to the road, the head of his corps, Kershaw's Division was met, and ordered to file at once to the right and get into line as quickly as possible, for fear his division would be forced back on it while forming. Less than a brigade had left the road when Longstreet in person arrived. He was informed where General Lee would be found—within one hundred and fifty yards. In the open space—old field—where General Lee's tent was at 9 P. M., and where he reappeared so early in the morning, was artillery—one or two batteries—on a gentle swell of the surface, in front descending and open for several hundred yards; the enemy were not within one hundred and fifty or two hundred yards of these guns. When Wilcox's men had fallen to the rear sufficiently to enable the guns to be used, they were directed into the woods, obliquely across the plank road; the enemy on the road could not see the guns. Wilcox's men, while Kershaw was uncovering the plank road, and before Fields' Division formed on the left of it, filed off the plank road and took position a half mile to the left, between Ewell's right and the troops on the plank road, filling up in part this long intervening unoccupied space. Later, Heth's Division took position on his right.

An extract will be made from Swinton, as he is often quoted, and, as far as my information goes, is in general quite accurate; in the extract will be found errors, but it would appear that he is hardly responsible for them.   Page 430 he says: "General Lee began the action by striking Grant's right flank, and some little while before the time ordered by Grant for renewal of the battle;" and again he says: "But as the left was the point at which, by common consent, the fiercest dispute took place, I shall, first of all, set forth the sequence of events on that flank.   When, at 5 A. M., Hancock opened his attack by an advance of his two right divisions under Birney, together with Getty's command (Owen's and Carroll's Brigades, Gibbon's Division, supporting), and pushed forward on the right and left of the Orange plank road, the onset was made with such vigor, and Lee was yet so weak on that flank, owing to the non-arrival of Longstreet, that for a time it seemed as though a great victory would be snatched.   At the same time Hancock opened a direct attack, Wadsworth's Division (Fifth Corps) assailed his flank, took up the action and fought its way across that part of the Second Corps posted on the right of the plank road.   The combined attack overpowered the Confederates, and after an hour's severe contest the whole hostile front was carried, and Hill's Divisions under Wilcox and Heth were driven for a mile and a half through the woods, under heavy loss, and back to the trains, and artillery, and Confederate headquarters."   This author, in a note at the bottom of page 431, says: "I use no stronger language than that employed by General Longstreet in a description he gave the writer of the situation of affairs at the moment of his arrival."   This combined attack of great strength was met by Wilcox's Division alone; it was followed by the enemy less than three hundred yards, filed out of the road to the left before it had reached the point where Kershaw's Division was then getting into line on the right, and moved over to the left as before explained.   Had it been forced back one and a half miles it would have run over Longstreet's command marching by the flank. It was not possible for General Longstreet, reaching the field at the time he did, to have known from what point and how far Wilcox's troops had been forced back.   The telegram of General Lee explaining this affair, he never saw, and may never have even heard of it at the time.   It was as follows: "Heth's and Wilcox's Divisions, in the act of being relieved, were attacked by the enemy and thrown into some confusion."

After Wilcox was forced back, the enemy did not press forward, as it was believed he would, but made a halt, probably to rectify alignments, no doubt much broken.   At all events, this was the supposition; but, whatever the cause—whether real or imaginary—

32

it afforded ample time for Anderson to arrive, and for Longstreet to form, and when Hancock renewed the advance, he was repulsed. It was about nine A. M. when the advance was resumed, according to Mr. Swinton, "to meet a bitter opposition, and, although furious fighting took place, he gained nothing." After this checking of Hancock, there was a lull in the contest for an hour or more; when, a little after twelve M., Longstreet moved forward, attacked Hancock's left, and drove it back (Mott's Division and a brigade of another division) in the wildest confusion. The whole line, as far as the plank road, was forced back, and re-formed on the line from which it had advanced in the morning. In this fight General Wadsworth was mortally wounded. He lived two or three days. On the right of the road, the Confederate left, General Longstreet was severely wounded, and Brigadier General Jenkins killed—these two by our own fire on the right of the road. There was now a suspension of hostilities till four P. M., when the Confederates advanced again—this time against Hancock in his first position of the morning. His left was driven back, and his intrenchments carried, the troops forced from them retiring in great disorder toward Chancellorsville. The Confederates were much disintegrated and too weak to hold what had been gained, and were driven out. The contest now ended on the plank road, the two lines being (on the plank road) where each was when the battle began. Nothing had been gained by the enemy; his losses had far exceeded those of the Confederates   The battle of the 6th closed with Ewell making a second attack on the right flank and rear of the Union army. This was made by Gordon's Brigade, of Early's Division, and Johnson's Brigade, of Rodes' Division. These brigades, Gordon's leading, struck the Federals (Rickett's Division) on its right flank, doubling it up and causing great confusion. At the same time, Pegram's Brigade, of Early's Division, advanced and attacked in front. A large number of prisoners were captured; among these were two general officers, Seymour and Shaler. This ended the struggle of the day. On this flank it had commenced, as has been seen, early in the morning; but the main battle on the 5th was on the plank road. With the Confederates, there were more troops engaged on the plank road (Kershaw's, Fields', and Anderson's divisions) on the 6th, and less on the old pike. It was the same with the Federals. On the Union side, early in the morning, on the plank road, there was the same force as on the previous evening; but after Wilcox was forced back, Getty's Division was held in the rear, and Stephenson's Division, of the Ninth Corps, thrown forward. Leasure's Brigade, of the

Ninth Corps, was also engaged. On the pike, early in the morning of the 6th, were Rickett's and Wright's Divisions, Sixth Corps; in the afternoon, Rickett's and the greater part of the Sixth Corps; Burnside's Corps (Ninth), with the exception of Stephenson's Division and Leasure's Brigade, not engaged. A body of troops, on the 6th, appeared in front of Wilcox's Division, then between Ewell and the Confederates, on the plank road; a few shots from a battery was all that was used against them. They were supposed to be of the Ninth Corps.

Such was the battle of the Wilderness. The impression has been made that the Federals attacked the Confederates in a position carefully selected. The latter had no advantage of position, as it has been seen that the two armies fought where they met. On the plank road, the Confederates had no cover, save that of the woods, until the 7th; the battle ceased on the 6th. And this was common to the two armies. It was different on this road with the Federals. On the old pike, the Federals were covered by works; the Confederates, if at all, slightly so. It would have shown but little enterprise on the part of the former, with their superiority of numbers, to have allowed the latter to intrench in their immediate presence. It has been seen that the Confederates acted on the offensive in the battle as often as the Federals. If the latter attacked on the old pike and the plank road on the 5th, and renewed the attack on the morning of the 6th on the latter, the Confederates began the battle of the 6th by attacking the enemy's right; and on the plank road, Longstreet made a vigorous attack, and in the midst of success was wounded seriously. Later in the day, the attack was renewed on the plank road, and intrenchments carried; and yet later, the Federal right attacked. The battle of the Wilderness was a Confederate victory. General Grant had crossed the Rapidan below the right flank of General Lee, and purposed to pass through the Wilderness toward Gordonsville, and down the railroad to Richmond. He hoped to have a battle to the north of Richmond, after having made his way through the Wilderness. General Meade was fearful the North Anna would be reached by the Confederates and fortified, and was also anxious lest they would get back to Mine run, ten miles in rear of where the Wilderness battle was fought. Having fought two days, General Grant left General Lee's front in the night of the 7th, and moved off by his left flank, and not in the direction proposed.

About nine A. M. on the 5th of May, Generals Grant and Meade rode up to the old Wilderness tavern; this was the first appearance of the former in what is called the Wilderness by citizens of Orange and Spottsylvania counties, Virginia. He was, personally, wholly ignorant of this section of Virginia, with its peculiar features. That he was not familiar with its topography, the following extract from his official report of this battle will show: "Early on the 5th, the advance, the Fifth Corps, Major General G. K. Warren commanding, met the enemy outside his intrenchments near Mine run." And after giving details of the battle, says: "On the morning of the 7th, reconnoissances showed that the enemy had fallen behind his intrenched line, with pickets to the front, covering a part of the battle-field." Mine run, at the date of the battle of the Wilderness, was well known North as the place where Generals Lee and Meade confronted each other for a week the winter previous, and it is also well known that the latter retired without a battle, and upon the grounds that the Mine run line was one of strength. General Grant's statement that the enemy were met outside his intrenchments near Mine run carries with it the inference that it was in the immediate vicinity of this intrenched position that General Lee was met; and the further statement, "reconnoissances made on the morning of the 7th showed they had fallen behind their intrenched line, with pickets covering a part of the battle-field," makes the impression that General Lee had sought the protection of the Mine run line. General Meade and the Army of the Potomac knew Mine run was ten or twelve miles in rear of the Wilderness battle-field; he and his army had passed an entire week near this run, made generally known to the country by his army retiring from it without fighting. The country about and near it was as well known to his army as to that commanded by General Lee; the Ninth Corps only were strangers in this section of Virginia.

Again, General Grant in his report, says: "From this" (General Lee having fallen behind his intrenched line, and Mine run being supposed to be the line) "it was evident to my mind that the two days' fighting had satisfied him of his inability to further maintain the contest in the open field, notwithstanding his advantage in position, and he would await an attack behind his works." And the inference legitimately drawn is, that it was an indisposition on his part to attack General Lee in this (Mine run) position, which had been regarded by General Meade as too formidable to assail, that made him hesitate and finally abandon General Lee's front, leaving scores of his dead unburied, and move off, not in the direction of Richmond, with the view, no doubt, of drawing General Lee out of this strong Mine run line. Of the casualties of the two armies, those of the Confederates are not known to the writer with sufficient accuracy to venture a statement; but those of the Army of the Potomac can be ascertained by referring to the report of the Surgeon General of the army; they are there given in detail, and it will be seen, upon examination, that the losses on the 5th and 6th of May—killed, wounded, and missing—when added, amount to thirty-seven thousand seven hundred and thirty-seven; and if to this prisoners be added, the entire loss to the Union side was over forty thousand. With losses so appalling in his first two days' collision with the Army of Northern Virginia, and believing his adversary to be under cover of the impregnable Mine run lines, General Grant abandoned the Wilderness and uncovered General Lee's front by moving off by his left flank, commencing the march soon after nightfall of the 7th.

THE "OLD CAPITOL" PRISON.

BY COLONEL N. T. COLBY.

THAT which is commonly known as the Old Capitol Prison, and which figured so conspicuously in the history of the late war, consisted, really, of two separate and distinct edifices, locally known by the names of the Old Capitol and the Carroll buildings, and were situated, the first, on the corner of Pennsylvania avenue and East First street, and the other on the corner of Maryland avenue and East First—a block apart, and both facing the Capitol building and East Capitol Park. The "Old Capitol" was so named from having been the temporary meeting-place of both Houses, I believe, after the destruction of the Capitol buildings by the English under Ross, in the war of 1812, and the other from its having been the property of the Carroll family, descendants of him of Carrollton— *vide* the signatures to the Declaration of Independence. Of course the use to which they were devoted in the late war was far enough from that for which they were originally constructed, and, in fact, in their earlier and better days, they earned, historically, a higher reputation than many more pretentious Washington edifices. The Old Capitol, especially, after its abandonment by Congress, was occupied as a fashionable boarding-house, and was largely patronized by the "*creme de la creme*" of the Southern dwellers in Washington. The great original nullifier, Calhoun, boarded here, and from out its doors went the gallant, but ill-fated, Commodore Decatur, the morning he met his enemy, Barron, at Bladensburg, in the duel that cost him his life. No brick walls, old or new, in the capital, have shut in stranger episodes and vicissitudes of life than these, and, I doubt not, each of

(502)

its four stories could many a tale unfold worthy special record of life at our National Capital in those comparatively primitive days. At the breaking out of our civil war they were not occupied, having, for lack of care, fallen into that neglected, down at the heel, slipshod condition of many buildings in Washington *then*, and there existed in their appearance little evidence either of their past greatness or future notoriety. Both buildings were of a size to indicate that they were built either for very large families, with many servants (which is probable, inasmuch as they were erected in the days when slavery made servants plentiful), or for boarding-houses, and contained in all forty or fifty rooms each—many of them quite large. Their tenantless condition, added to their roominess and location, doubtless, recommended them to a government suddenly and unexpectedly called upon to provide a place of confinement for many prisoners, and little outlay was needed to fit them for the purpose, as they always depended more upon the vigilance and care of the guards for the safe keeping of prisoners than upon bolts and bars. To be sure, there were iron bars at some of the windows; but as they were only inserted in the soft wood of the window frames it will be seen that they were only an apparent, and not real addition to security. Locks were attached to each door, and, with some addition to the cooking apparatus, the hotel was ready for its guests. A guard of about sixty men, under the command of a captain or lieutenant, was daily detailed from a neighboring infantry regiment, to each prison, doing regular guard duty, two hours on and four off, day and night.

The character of the prisoners was a matter of wide variation, differing in this particular from any other place of confinement. Especially is this true of the Old Capitol, where were held the prisoners of State particularly, such as parties charged with active disloyalty at the North, bounty frauds, counterfeiters of United States notes and other issues, contractors who had swindled the government, and, I doubt not, men who were arrested by detectives upon trumped-up charges simply to blackmail them, and who were wholly innocent. In fact, it would be quite unfair to assume that because one had been a prisoner here, that he was, therefore, a criminal, for I met *many* gentlemen there, *as prisoners, too*, whose claims to regard as gentlemen and men of refinement and social standing is *to-day* widely honored. *Per contra*, there were a few, and but a few, who gravitated naturally to a prison. In saying this I refer strictly to the civil prisoners, as among the prisoners of war there was the usual variety of humanity—generally of the better class—as very few privates of the Southern army found their way here, except they were special cases, either awaiting trial by court-martial or under sentence, and temporarily held there for the convenience of the government. Thus it was the pleasure of the authorities to regard those captured from Mosby's following ("guerrillas") as special cases, and I had some twenty of them—rough, dirty, ill-looking customers they were—in a large room on the fourth floor of the Old Capitol, fronting on the street. They were a turbulent and unruly set, and often amused themselves by throwing bricks (taken from an old fireplace in their room) at the sentinels on the pavement underneath their window, and, in one or two cases, barely escaped killing them. All other means failing, and provoked at last, I notified them that I had given orders to the guard to fire on any one showing himself at the window, and that they were responsible for it, and for the result. I am happy to say no one was injured, although they tested both the obedience and correct aim of the sentinel by putting one of their old hats on a stick and pushing it up to the window and getting a ball through it—but the brick throwing was ended.

It is proper to say, in this connection, that there was no means of punishing a refractory prisoner—as there were no "dungeons" in either prison—nor did I ever see a prisoner ironed beyond being handcuffed, and that only in very few cases and for a temporary purpose, and not once as a punishment. The food served was a soldier's full ration, cooked, and many purchased at neighboring restaurants (by written order) anything they wished, even wine and cigars; the privilege of so buying, however, being mostly confined to civilians, who often had plenty of money, which officers or soldiers rarely had. Of course, the money and valuables of each prisoner was taken from him on his entrance to the prison, and a receipt given him by the superintendent, but he was at liberty to draw it for legitimate uses as pleased him. Knives were also taken from the prisoners, and upon assuming the command of the prisons I receipted for, to my predecessor, among other valuables, something like a hundred thousand dollars in money and United States bonds and a *full bushel* of pocket-knives! I speak thus accurately of the *measure* as they were contained in two half-bushel measures, fairly level full, being those belonging to prisoners *then* in confinement, as well as to many hundreds who had been released or sent elsewhere and forgotten to ask for them. A noted English hotel thief, who was held by the authorities as a witness, gave up on his admission to the prison about five thousand dollars' worth of jewelry, mostly diamonds, and naively answered my query as to where he got them by saying concisely, "prigged 'em," *i. e.*, stole them. He was a gentlemanly-looking fellow, and seemed actually to believe his profession as matter of fact as any other, and frankly admitted it. A Jew was arrested and brought to prison charged with having come through the army lines from Dixie, and upon being searched, previous to assignment to quarters, was found to be wrapped in a long piece of muslin in which several hundred dollars in gold pieces were carefully sewed, and his misery in seeing them ripped ruthlessly from their hiding place was extreme, equaled only by the scorn which he regarded my receipt for the much-loved hoard. After a trial which restored him to freedom, however, he presented his scorned acknowledgment, and thought better of it when it returned to his possession his treasure. The war had made money plenty, and it often fell temporarily into strange and unaccustomed hands, and from prisoners charged with bounty frauds I received as high as twenty or thirty thousand dollars in notes and bonds—the results, doubtless, of their rascality. The jealousy of the authorities regarding the safe-keeping of this large amount of money is illustrated by the following incident: Standing in the prison yard upon one occasion while a detachment of prisoners were taking their daily airing, I was approached by one who begged a few minutes' conversation, the substance of which, after a slight preface, was the offer of five hundred dollars (which he held my receipt for, having given it up on his admission) if I would allow him to write a letter and forward it to its destination *unread*. Telling him I would communicate with him in regard to the matter later, he went to his room, from which I summoned him within an hour by the corporal of the guard and confined him alone in a small room on the ground floor, without windows, save in the door, and kept him there a week on strict bread and water diet, and a few days after he was released from prison upon an order from the War Department. Nor did I learn till long after that he was a Secret Service Agent and imprisoned specially to make me the offer he did, and that his report of his success was received with roars of laughter from his superior officers.

The fidelity with which the prisons were guarded is attested by the few escapes that occurred, only two that were successful taking place during my command of over a year. One from Carroll Prison of a Virginia colonel, who lowered himself from a third-story window with a rope made from his blanket; which rope, by the way, proved too short, and came near proving fatal to both life and escape. The night selected for the attempt was dark and rainy, and he carefully descended hand over hand till he felt the end of the rope; to reascend was impossible, and there was nothing for it but to drop, which he did, coming down on the pavement with a crash within six feet of the sentinel with his loaded musket. Probably no sweeter sound ever fell on the ear of that colonel than the dull, unmeaning click of the gun, which (doubtless owing to the rain) missed fire when leveled at his breast, the muzzle scarce a yard away ; and ere aid could come, he bounded off into the darkness and disappeared. The attempt was gallant enough to have proved a permanent success, but he was returned to me by General Lew Wallace, within a month, having been retaken in Baltimore.

Attempted escapes were more numerous, however, some of them of such a nature as, I think, to much interest the reader. One, especially, borders on the marvelous, and yet I vouch for its entire accuracy, and can substantiate it fully from documents now in my possession. It is as follows : A citizen of Maryland, whom, for the purpose of this narrative we will name Brown, was arrested and sent to the Old Capitol, charged with having killed a Union soldier in an affray during a drinking spree; and, as he was well known to be an ardent sympathizer with the Southern cause, it was inferred that he was influenced by that motive in the killing—but with this our story has nothing to do. He was an uneducated, ignorant, superstitious man—probably a sample of " poor white trash " of the South—and, as the result shows, easily imposed upon. He was assigned to a room on the fourth floor, in which there was already an occupant, who seemed ill-pleased to share his bed and board with a new comer, whose appearance he evidently did not admire. However, *nolens volens*, Brown was and must be his room-mate, as the crowded condition of the building made other disposition impossible, and thus was developed a plan to be rid of him, purely devilish, as follows : For a few days he manifested a friendly disposition toward Brown until he succeeded in winning his confidence. Then, one day, upon returning to the room after a visit to the prison yard, he informed Brown that he had overheard the colonel commanding the prisons giving orders preparatory to his (Brown's) execution by shooting, to take place the next morning. Believing this absurd tale, the effect on Brown was terrible, and so thoroughly was he frightened that he dashed about the room with wild cries of anguish and despair, and it was with much difficulty his companion could quiet him sufficiently to reveal a plan which he pretended he had safely arranged for his escape from the impending doom. Escape! it was heaven, and Brown listened with an eager ear to anything that promised half a chance, and with credulity marvelous, as the doom to him was frightful. Brown was then told that his room-mate had long followed the profession of an acrobat in a circus, and, consequently, could explain how it was possible to jump from any place, however far the distance, without injury, and it consisted, simply, in always starting from a spring board. All that was necessary was to get the board, jump into the yard beneath, scale the fence surrounding it, and he was free. And the half-crazed Brown agreed. Taking up one of the floor-planks, about two o'clock that morning, they ran it noiselessly out of the window, securing one end firmly to the window-sill. The night was dark, but the gas-lights in the yard below flickered on the paved surface of the ground, which echoed to the measured tread of the sentinels as they paced their midnight rounds. Bidding his mate "good-bye," Brown slowly emerged from the window on his hands and knees, crawling toward the extreme end of the narrow plank—bending more and more with his weight over the dizzy height. Reaching, at length, the end, he carefully arose into a standing position, and, following his instructor's orders, he began to spring the board more and more rapidly, finally bounding upward as high as the impetus thus acquired would carry him, and then down, down through the yielding air to the stones beneath. With terrible swiftness, just missing the point of a sentinel's bayonet as he passed, he struck the pavement. The guard, amazed and frightened, fled the length of the yard, and Brown, unhurt, sprang to his feet and dashed in headlong flight toward a pair of steps leading to the top of a shed, upon which, however, was located another sentinel, who successfully stopped his further efforts. Not a bone was broken, and he sustained no visible injury worthy of mention. Yet the leap could not have been less than forty or fifty feet, and the landing place a stone paved yard. His brain, however, was affected by the shock, and not long after he was shot and killed by one of the guards while attempting another escape—an attempt like the one above narrated, which no sane person would have dared, and the poor fellow met the very fate he so madly strove to escape.

Of the secret agents or spies in the service of the rebel government, there were some who achieved notoriety at least, and they were well represented at the Old Capitol, both male and female. Among the latter was Belle Boyd, who left the impression with those with whom she came in contact of a woman governed more by romance and love of notoriety than actual regard for the Southern cause. Undeniably good-looking, with a fine figure, and merry disposition, she could have been dangerous had she possessed equal good sense and good judgment. I believe the extent of the damage she inflicted on the Northern cause was in tempting from his loyalty a subordinate officer of the navy, whom it was affirmed she married. He also found his way to the prison, from which he dictated a challenge to the editor of the Washington *Star*, for some rather scornful allusions to himself and wife. They were both "light weights" in the profession.

Mrs. Baxley was a woman of far different character—educated, remarkably intelligent and cultivated, and with a steady courage any man might envy. She was a shrewd plotter of mischief to the North, and utterly fearless in its execution. Her intense hatred of a Yankee, with her whole-souled devotion to the Southern cause, often impelled her beyond the line of propriety and discretion, even to the verge of the ridiculous—never, however, to the peril of the cause she loved. The first time my attention was called to her case was by a note handed me by one of the guards, directed to the colonel commanding the prisoners, asking me to bring her an armful of wood! Of course, it meant defiance and insult, but provoked only a smile; and the next "break out" of her irrepressible hatred to Yankeedom had a tinge of tragedy rather than comedy. It was thus: Going once to the window of her room (which was located on the second-story of the building), she began a scathing and contemptuous criticism of the sentinel underneath, until, goaded by her tongue, he threatened to fire at her if she did not desist and leave the window. "Fire, then, you Yankee scoundrel! You were hired to murder women, and here is an opportunity to exercise your trade," was the reply. Stung by the words, and thinking to frighten her, he raised his piece, but aimed above her head, and fired, the ball crashing through the window over her. Not a muscle stirred as she still coolly faced the window as before, saying, contemptuously: "A shot worthy a Yankee; load and try another." She was arrested while within our army lines searching for her son, who had been wounded and captured in one of the great battles. He was sent to the prison where his mother was, and she had the privilege of seeing him often and of standing by his bedside when he died. He was buried from the prison and lies in the Congressional Cemetery, his mother being allowed to accompany his remains to their last resting place. She was accompanied to the cemetery in the same carriage by Mrs. Surratt (who was afterward hanged for complicity with President Lincoln's assassination), and a couple of guards detailed for the purpose. Mrs. Surratt was a large fleshy woman, and when first sent to the prison was not supposed to be guilty of anything very serious, or that could involve a risk to her life. Her daughter was her frequent visitor, and always was permitted to see her. At her trial she was removed from the Old Capitol, to which she never returned, having been tried, condemned, and executed at the Old Armory.

The murder of the President brought many unexpected guests to the prison, among whom I remember Junius Brutus Booth, a brother of Wilkes Booth; John S. Clarke, the renowned comedian; Mr. Ford, of Baltimore, owner of Ford's Theatre, in Washington, where Lincoln was shot; Dr. Mudd, who set the broken limb of the flying assassin, and who repented therefor in the Dry Tortugas; Spangler, the stage carpenter, who held a ready saddled horse at the back door of the theatre for Booth's escape, and many others supposed to have possible connection with, or knowledge of, the assassination. I gave to Junius Brutus Booth the knowledge of the death of his brother Wilkes, and the circumstances attending it, to which he sadly and sorrowfully answered, "Poor, misguided boy."

On the night of the murder of Lincoln there were eight hundred rebel officers in Carroll Prison, and I need hardly say it was crowded to its utmost capacity. Every grade of rank, from a second lieutenant to a major general, had its representative, and, as a rule, they were an intelligent, gentlemanly set of men, and, as I thought, worthy a better cause. I announced to them myself the news that fell so like a thunderbolt on the country of the cowardly murder of the President; and to their honor, I record it, that with two exceptions they united in condemning the act, and regretting its occurrence most heartily.

While Carroll Prison was thus crowded, it was attacked by a mob, and came near furnishing a bloody sequel to the death of Lincoln. It was when daily expectation of the announcement of the capture of his murderer was awaited with intense interest, that a sergeant and two privates were sent in charge of two prisoners, civilians, from the headquarters of the Provost Marshal, Colonel Ingraham, to deliver them at Carroll Prison, and it was surmised and believed that the prisoners were Booth and an accomplice. Instantly, they were followed by a crowd that rapidly increased in numbers and fierceness, till it seemed that the death of the entire party was inevitable. A mounted orderly, by another street, brought notice of their coming, and a warning to be prepared. But thirty men were to be spared, and they were at once drawn up before the entrance, and the orderly dispatched for more troops. Presently, the mob came in sight—a dense mass, numbering thousands—while just before them, driven like chaff before a gale, was the sergeant and his men, running, but bravely keeping their trust, always surrounding and defending the prisoners—now struck down by some missile, but instantly up again, making straight to the shelter of the prison, which at last they reached, bloody and bruised — all of them, especially the prisoners, half dead with blows and fright. Then the mob, cheated of its prey, crowded the street with fierce yells, and began hurling stones at the windows, and, finally, at the little force still guarding the front doors, till the ominous clicking of the gun-locks began to intimate that, with or without the orders of their officers, they would fire in self-defense. Anxiously they looked for the coming of assistance; but, compelled at last to either give up their trust or to attack, they suddenly deployed as skirmishers, and, with leveled bayonets, sprang forward at the word of command upon the rioters, who, dismayed and surprised, fled down the streets and alleys—not one being killed, and but few wounded with the bayonet. The prisoners, I need not add, were not Booth, or connected in any way with his crime, but they barely escaped with life.

The number of prisoners in " Carroll," as I said before, at this time, was the most serious test of its capacity, and was the result of some difficulty in obtaining speedy transportation for them to the prison depots further North and West. Many friends of the Southern officers confined here came to see them, and, in all cases, so far as my knowledge goes, were permitted to see them, and provide them with much-needed comforts; and, more than that, I allowed, in one case at least, a young major, who met here for the first time in four years his lady love and intended wife, to accompany her home to tea, only asking his word of honor that he would return at a given hour, which he punctually did. His name has escaped my memory; but if the few hours of pleasure he enjoyed upon that occasion be not yet gratefully remembered, then is he an ungrateful man. I recall, also, with pleasure now, that I, in testifying before a House committee, appointed to consider the propriety of retaliating the treatment our poor fellows received at Andersonville and other Southern prisons, condemned it as unworthy the name of any Christian people. When at last the order came to send away nearly all the eight hundred, I stood near the door as they marched out, and, with hardly one exception, they shook me by the hand, in saying their " good-bye," and expressed their sense of the kind treatment they had received.

Governor Vance, of North Corolina, Governor Letcher, of Virginia, and Governor Brown, of Georgia, were, for a few months, recipients of the hospitalities of the Old Capitol, and endured the tedium of prison life with the patient courage of true-hearted men. Before the breaking out of the war, and while the propriety of secession was being discussed in North Carolina, Governor Vance came out strong against it, stumping nearly the whole State in favor of "the Union as it was." Finding it in vain, and called upon to decide between "the devil and the deep sea," or in other words, whether he would be politically and socially ostracized by his friends, who had always stood staunchly by him in the State where he was born, reared, and educated, or go in with them in an undertaking which he foresaw would fail, like many another good man in the South he chose to live or fall among friends. Who could blame him? He saw the failure and scorned to evade the result by changing to a Unionist, as many far less worthy did, feeling that he had deliberately incurred the risk, and willing, deliberately, to expiate it. Possessing a keen perception of the humorous, cheerful, ready witted, with a vigorous intellect, a story-teller *par excellence*—surpassing even Senator Nye—and, really, the best extempore speaker for any and all occasions, with or without notice, carrying always his audience like a whirlwind—such was Governor Zebulon B. Vance, the pet and pride of the old North State.

I cannot refrain from an anecdote of himself, illustrative of the commencement of his political life and his popularity with all classes in his native State, as he himself related it. It was after his first election to a seat in the House of Representatives in Washington, and at about the age of thirty-eight years. He had attended the full session, and on his journey home had arrived at the end of railway travel, and was obliged to finish the journey by staging across the country. Full of the pride of being a member of Congress, and to see and be seen, he mounted a seat outside the coach with the driver of the vehicle, and away they rolled behind four sorry-looking steeds. The Jehu was evidently of the earth earthy, of the stable odorous, a ragged, seedy specimen of his order, and in strong contrast to our friend, the Governor, who sat by his side, dressed in the more decorous results of a fashionable Washington tailor—and no doubt happy in so being. Pride, however, was destined to the usual fall, the author of which humiliation being close at hand. A tall, cadaverous, lank, pale specimen of the race known as "clay banks," was sleepily leaning against a fence as they passed. He was shirtless and ragged, and his remnant of broad-brimmed hat sank ungracefully over and about his long hair, the only laudable use for which was to cover his dirty neck and face. Gravely he saluted the driver, with "Good-morning, Mr. Jobson," and then lifting lazily his eyes on Vance, he became suddenly galvanized with an unexpected recognition, to which he gave vent with a "Hell's blazes, Zeb Vance, is that yeow?" The Governor avers he did the rest of that journey as an inside passenger.

Governor Letcher was a fine specimen of a Virginian, frank, dignified, courteous, and generous, firm and unchangeable in his deliberate and matured purpose, and of inflexible integrity and honor.

General Edward Johnson occupied the same room with the above-mentioned Governors, and also a gentleman from Savannah named Lamar, and they exhausted thoroughly every means in their power to avert the tedium of confinement. Governor Vance, once looking from his window into the East Capitol Park, said, with a sigh, "How I would like to stretch my limbs with a brisk walk over there." I replied, by saying, "Put on your hat, then," and suiting the action to the word, he did so, and I led him down stairs and past the guard, and away he went and enjoyed his stroll hugely, returning in a few hours safe to his hotel.

One evening there arrived from the War Department an order to prepare for the reception of (as near as I can recollect) one hundred and fifty prisoners, who were coming from Baltimore, nearly all of whom were to be placed in solitary confinement and not allowed to communicate with each other. Now, every room in both prisons was occupied, and to carry out the command was simply impossible, and I did not attempt it. Their arrival was a fresh surprise, for the prisoners were some of the principal business men of Baltimore, with their employees—such gentlemen as Messrs. Johnson, Sutton & Co., Hamilton Easter & Co., Weesenfelt & Co., Charles E. Waters & Co., and many more. They were arrested by a leading detective for alleged selling of goods to be run through the blockade. I believe there was not a guilty man in the number, and that it was a put up job by the astute detectives, who knew that, being gentlemen of wealth, they could extort money from them by sufficient squeezing. Their coming brought a good influence in many ways, and many a poor devil then confined, with neither friends or money, could testify to their liberality and generosity, and benefited by the ill wind that blew these gentlemen into durance vile.

TORPEDO SERVICE IN CHARLESTON HARBOR.

BY GENERAL G. T. BEAUREGARD.

On my return to Charleston, in September, 1862, to assume command of the Department of South Carolina and Georgia, I found the defenses of those two States in a bad and incomplete condition, including defective location and arrangement of works, even at Charleston and Savannah. Several points—such as the mouths of the Stono and Edisto rivers, and the head-waters of Broad river at Port Royal—I found unprotected; though, soon after the fall of Fort Sumter, in 1861, as I was about to be detached, I had designated them to be properly fortified. A recommendation had even been made by my immediate predecessor that the outer defenses of Charleston harbor should be given up, as untenable against the iron-clads and monitors then known to be under construction at the North, and that the water line of the immediate city of Charleston should be made the sole line of defense. This course, however, not having been authorized by the Richmond authorities, it was not attempted, except that the fortifications of Cole's Island—the key to the defense of the Stono river—was abandoned, and the harbor in the mouth of the Stono left open to the enemy, who made it their base of operations. Immediately on my arrival I inspected the defenses of Charleston and Savannah, and made a requisition on the War Department for additional troops and heavy guns deemed necessary; but neither could be furnished, owing, it was stated, to the pressing wants of the Confederacy at other points. Shortly afterward, Florida was added to my command, but without any increase of troops or guns, except the few already in that State; and,

33   (513)

later, several brigades were withdrawn from me, notwithstanding my protest, to reinforce the armies of Virginia and Tennessee.

As I have already said, I found at Charleston an exceedingly bad defensive condition against a determined attack. Excepting Fort Moultrie, on Sullivan's Island, the works and batteries covering Charleston harbor, including Fort Sumter, were insufficiently armed, and their barbette guns without the protection of heavy traverses. In all the harbor works, there were only three ten-inch and a few eight-inch columbiads, which had been left in Forts Sumter and Moultrie by Major Anderson, and about a dozen rifle guns— unbanded thirty-two-pounders, made by the Confederates—which burst after a few discharges. There were, however, a number of good forty-two-pounders of the old pattern, which I afterward had rifled and banded. I found a continuous floating boom of large timbers, bound together and interlinked, stretching across from Fort Sumter to Fort Moultrie. But this was a fragile and unreliable barrier, as it offered too great a resistance to the strong current of the ebb and flood tide at full moon, especially after southeasterly gales, which backed up the waters in the bay, and in the Ashley and Cooper rivers. It was exposed, therefore, at such periods, to be broken, particularly as the channel bottom was hard and smooth, and the light anchors which held the boom in position were constantly dragging—a fact which made the breaking of the boom an easy matter under the strain of hostile steamers coming against it under full headway. For this reason, the engineers had proposed the substitution of a rope obstruction, which would be free from tidal strain, but little had been done toward its preparation. I, therefore, soon after assuming command, ordered its immediate completion, and, to give it protection and greater efficiency, directed that two lines of torpedoes be planted a few hundred yards in advance of it. But before the order could be carried out, a strong southerly storm broke the timber boom in several places, leaving the channel unprotected, except by the guns of Forts Sumter and Moultrie. Fortunately, however, the Federal fleet made no effort to enter the harbor, as it might have done if it had made the attempt at night. A few days later the rope obstruction and torpedoes were in position, and so remained, without serious injury, till the end of the war.

The rope obstruction was made of two heavy cables, about five or six feet apart, the one below the other, and connected together by a network of smaller ropes. The anchors were made fast to the lower cable, and the buoys or floats to the upper one. The upper cable carried a fringe of smaller ropes, about three-fourths of an inch in diameter by fifty feet long, which floated as so many "streamers" on the surface, destined to foul the screw propeller of any steamer which might attempt to pass over the obstruction. Shortly after these cables were in position, a blockade-runner, in attempting at night to pass through the gap purposely left open near the Sullivan Island shore, under the guns of Fort Moultrie, and of the outside batteries, accidentally crossed the end of the rope obstruction, when one of the streamers got entangled around the shaft, checking its revolutions. The vessel was at once compelled to drop anchor to avoid drifting on the torpedoes or ashore, and afterward had to be docked for the removal of the streamer before she could again use her propeller. The torpedoes, as anchored, floated a few feet below the surface of the water at low tide, and were loaded with one hundred pounds of powder, arranged to explode by concussion—the automatic fuse employed being the invention of Captain Francis D. Lee, an intelligent young engineer officer of my general staff, and now a prominent architect in St. Louis. The fuse or firing apparatus consisted of a cylindrical lead tube with a hemispherical head, the metal in the head being thinner than at the sides. The tube was open at the lower extremity, where it was surrounded by a flange; and, when in place, it was protected against leakage by means of brass couplings and rubber washers. It was charged as follows: In its centre was a glass tube filled with sulphuric acid, and hermetically sealed. This was guarded by another glass tube, sealed in like manner, and both were retained in position by means of a peculiar pin at the open end of the leaden tube; the space between the latter and the glass tube was then filled with a composition of chlorate of potassa and powdered loaf sugar, with a quantity of rifle powder. The lower part of the tube was then closed with a piece of oiled paper. Great care had to be taken to ascertain that the leaden tube was perfectly water-tight under considerable pressure. The torpedo also had to undergo the most careful test. The firing of the tube was produced by bringing the thin head in contact with a hard object, as the side of a vessel; the indentation of the lead broke the glass tubes, which discharged the acid on the composition, firing it, and thereby igniting the charge in the torpedo. The charges used varied from sixty to one hundred pounds rifle powder, though other explosives might have been more advantageously used if they had been available to us. Generally, four of the fuses were attached to the head of each torpedo, so as to secure the discharge at any angle of attack. These firing tubes or fuses were afterward modified to avoid the great risk consequent upon screwing them in place, and of having them permanently attached to the charged torpedo. The shell of the latter was thinned at the point where the tube was attached, so that, under water pressure, the explosion of the tube would certainly break it and discharge the torpedo; though, when unsubmerged, the explosion of the tube would vent itself in the open air without breaking the shell. In this arrangement, the tube was of brass, with a leaden head, and made water-tight by means of a screw plug at its base. Both the shell and the tube being made independently water-tight, the screw connection between the two was made loose, so that the tube could be attached or detached readily with the fingers. The mode adopted for testing against leakage was by placing them in a vessel of alcohol, under the glass exhaust of an air-pump. When no air bubbles appeared the tubes could be relied on. Captain Lee had also an electric torpedo, which exploded by concussion against a hard object; the electric current, being thus established, insured the discharge at the right moment.

Captain Lee is the inventor also of the "spar-torpedo" as an attachment to vessels, now in general use in the Federal navy. It originated as follows: He reported to me that he thought he could blow up successfully any vessel by means of a torpedo carried some five or six feet under water at the end of a pole ten or twelve feet long, which should be attached to the bow of a skiff or row-boat. I authorized an experiment upon the hulk of an unfinished and condemned gunboat anchored in the harbor, and loaded for the purpose with all kinds of rubbish taken from the "burnt district" of the city. It was a complete success; a large hole was made in the side of the hulk, the rubbish being blown high in the air, and the vessel sank in less than a minute.* I then determined to employ this important invention, not only in the defense of Charleston, but to disperse or destroy the Federal blockading fleet, by means of one or more small, swift steamers, with low decks, and armed only with "spar-torpedoes" as designed by Captain Lee. I sent him at once to Richmond, to urge the matter on the attention of the Confederate Government. He reported his mission as follows:

---

* Since writing the above, I have been informed by Captain F. Barrett, United States Navy, that he had invented the same "spar-torpedo" in the first year of the war, but it had not been applied by the Federals. In the spring of 1862, I had also recommended its use to General Lovell, for the defense of New Orleans, by arming river boats with it, to make night attacks on the enemy's fleet—but it was proposed to use it above water.

In compliance with your orders, I submitted the drawing of my torpedo and a vessel with which I propose to operate them, to the Secretary of War. While he heartily approved, he stated his inability to act in the matter, as it was a subject that appertained to the navy. He, however, introduced me and urged it to the Secretary of the Navy. The Secretary of War could do nothing, and the Secretary of the Navy would not, for the reason that I was not a naval officer, under his command. So I returned to Charleston without accomplishing anything. After a lapse of some months, I was again sent to Richmond to represent the matter to the government, and I carried with me the indorsement of the best officers of the navy. The result was the transfer of an unfinished hull, on the stocks at Charleston, which was designed for a gunboat—or rather floating battery, as she was not arranged for any motive power, but was intended to be anchored in position. This hull was completed by me, and a second-hand and much worn engine was obtained in Savannah, and placed in her. Notwithstanding her tub-like model and the inefficiency of her engine, Captain Carlin, commanding a blockade-runner, took charge of her in an attack against the "New Ironsides." She was furnished with a spar designed to carry three torpedoes of one hundred pounds each. The lateral spars suggested by you, Captain Carlin declined to use, as they would interfere very seriously with the movements of the vessel, which, even without them, could with the utmost difficulty stem the current. The boat was almost entirely submerged, and painted gray like the blockade-runners, and, like them, made no smoke, by burning anthracite coal. The night selected for the attack was very dark, and the "New Ironsides" was not seen until quite near. Captain Carlin immediately made for her; but her side being oblique to the direction of his approach, he ordered his steersman, who was below deck, to change the course. This order was misunderstood, and, in place of going the "bow on," as was proposed, she ran alongside of the "New Ironsides" and entangled her spar in the anchor-chain of that vessel. In attempting to back, the engine hung on the centre, and some delay occurred before it was pried off. During this critical period, Captain Carlin, in answer to threats and inquiries, declared his boat to be the Live Yankee, from Port Royal, with dispatches for the admiral. This deception was not discovered until after Carlin had backed out and his vessel was lost in the darkness.

Shortly after this bold attempt of Captain Carlin, in the summer of 1863, to blow up the "New Ironsides," Mr. Theodore Stoney, Dr. Ravenel, and other gentlemen of Charleston, had built a small cigar-shaped boat, which they called the "David." It had been specially planned and constructed to attack this much-dreaded naval Goliath, the "New Ironsides." It was about twenty feet long, with a diameter of five feet at its middle, and was propelled by a small screw worked by a diminutive engine. As soon as ready for service, I caused it to be fitted with a "Lee spar-torpedo," charged with seventy-five pounds of powder. Commander W. T. Glassel, a brave and enterprising officer of the Confederate States Navy, took charge of it, and about eight o'clock one hazy night, on the ebb tide, with a crew of one engineer, J. H. Tomb; one fireman, James Sullivan; and a pilot, J. W. Cannon, he fearlessly set forth from Charleston on his perilous mission—the destruction of the "New Ironsides." I may note that this iron-clad steamer threw a great deal more metal, at each broadside, than all the monitors together of the fleet; her fire was delivered with more rapidity and accuracy, and she was the most effective vessel employed in the reduction of Battery Wagner.

The "David" reached the "New Ironsides" about ten o'clock P. M., striking her with a torpedo about six feet under water, but fortunately for that steamer, she received the shock against one of her inner bulkheads, which saved her from destruction. The water, however, being thrown up in large volume, half-filled her little assailant and extinguished its fires. It then drifted out to sea with the current, under a heavy grape and musketry fire from the much-alarmed crew of the "New Ironsides." Supposing the "David" disabled, Glassel and his men jumped into the sea to swim ashore; but after remaining in the water about one hour he was picked up by the boat of a Federal transport schooner, whence he was transferred to the guardship "Ottawa," lying outside of the rest of the fleet. He was ordered at first, by Admiral Dahlgren, to be ironed, and in case of resistance, to be double ironed; but through the intercession of his friend, Captain W. D. Whiting, commanding the "Ottawa," he was released on giving his parole not to attempt to escape from the ship. The fireman, Sullivan, had taken refuge on the rudder of the "New Ironsides," where he was discovered, put in irons and kept in a dark cell until sent with Glassel to New York, to be tried and hung, as reported by Northern newspapers, for using an engine of war not recognized by civilized nations. But the government of the United States has now a torpedo corps, intended specially to study and develop that important branch of the military service. After a captivity of many months in Forts Lafayette and Warren, Glassel and Sullivan were finally exchanged for the captain and a sailor of the Federal steamer "Isaac Smith," a heavily-armed gunboat which was captured in the Stono river, with its entire crew of one hundred and thirty officers and men, by a surprise I had prepared, with field artillery only, placed in ambuscade along the river bank, and under whose fire the Federal gunners were unable to man and use their powerful guns. Captain Glassel's other two companions, Engineer Tomb and Pilot Cannon, after swimming about for a while, espied the "David" still afloat, drifting with the current; they betook themselves to it, re-lit the fires from its bull's-eye lantern, got up steam and started back for the city; they had to repass through the fleet and they received the fire of several of its monitors and guard-boats, fortunately without injury. With the assistance of the flood tide they returned to their point of departure, at the Atlantic wharf, about midnight, after having performed one of the most daring feats of the war. The "New Ironsides" never fired another shot after this attack upon her. She remained some time at her anchorage off Morris Island, evidently undergoing repairs; she was then towed to Port Royal, probably to fit her for her voyage to Philadelphia, where she remained until destroyed by fire after the war.

Nearly about the time of the attack upon the "New Ironsides" by the "David," Mr. Horace L. Hunley, formerly of New Orleans, but then living in Mobile, offered me another torpedo-boat of a different description, which had been built with his private means. It was shaped like a fish, made of galvanized iron, was twenty feet long, and at the middle three and a half feet wide by five deep. From its shape it came to be known as the "fish torpedo-boat." Propelled by a screw worked from the inside by seven or eight men, it was so contrived that it could be submerged and worked under water for several hours, and to this end was provided with a fin on each side, worked also from the interior. By depressing the points of these fins the boat, when in motion, was made to descend, and by elevating them it was made to rise. Light was afforded through the means of bull's-eyes placed in the man-holes. Lieutenant Payne, Confederate States Navy, having volunteered with a crew from the Confederate Navy, to man. the fish-boat for another attack upon the "New Ironsides," it was given into their hands for that purpose. While tied to the wharf at Fort Johnston, whence it was to start under cover of night to make the attack, a steamer passing close by capsized and sunk it. Lieutenant Payne, who, at the time, was standing in one of the man-holes, jumped out into the water, which, rushing into the two openings, drowned two men then within the body of the boat. After the recovery of the sunken boat Mr. Hunley came from Mobile, bringing with him Lieutenant Dixon, of the Alabama volunteers, who had successfully experimented with the boat in the harbor of Mobile, and under him another naval crew volunteered to work it. As originally designed, the torpedo was to be dragged astern upon the surface of the water; the boat, approaching the broadside of the vessel to be attacked, was to dive beneath it, and rising to the surface beyond, continue its course, thus bringing the floating torpedo against the vessel's side, when it would be discharged by a trigger contrived to go off by the contact. Lieutenant Dixon made repeated descents in the harbor of Charleston, diving under the naval receiving ship which lay at anchor there. But one day when he was absent from the city Mr. Hunley, unfortunately, wishing to handle the boat himself, made the attempt. It was readily submerged, but did not rise again to the surface, and all on board perished from asphyxiation. When the boat was discovered, raised and opened, the spectacle was indescribably ghastly; the unfortunate men were contorted into all kinds of horrible attitudes; some clutching candles, evidently endeavoring to force open the man-holes; others lying in the bottom tightly grappled together, and the blackened faces of all presented the expression of their despair and agony. After this tragedy I refused to permit the boat to be used again; but Lieutenant Dixon, a brave and determined man, having returned to Charleston, applied to me for authority to use it against the Federal steam sloop-of-war " Housatonic," a powerful new vessel, carrying eleven guns of the largest calibre, which lay at the time in the north channel opposite Beach Inlet, materially obstructing the passage of our blockade-runners in and out. At the suggestion of my chief-of-staff, General Jordan, I consented to its use for this purpose, not as a submarine machine, but in the same manner as the " David." As the " Housatonic" was easily approached through interior channels from behind Sullivan's Island, and Lieutenant Dixon readily procured a volunteer crew, his little vessel was fitted with a Lee spar torpedo, and the expedition was undertaken. Lieutenant Dixon, acting with characteristic coolness and resolution, struck and sunk the " Housatonic" on the night of February 17th, 1864; but unhappily, from some unknown cause, the torpedo boat was also sunk, and all with it lost. Several years since a " diver," examining the wreck of the " Housatonic," discovered the fish-boat lying alongside of its victim.

From the commencement of the siege of Charleston I had been decidedly of the opinion that the most effective as well as least costly method of defense against the powerful iron-clad steamers and monitors originated during the late war, was to use against them small but swift steamers of light draught, very low decks, and hulls iron-claded down several feet below the water line; these boats to be armed with a spar-torpedo (on Captain Lee's plan), to thrust out from the bow at the moment of collision, being inclined to strike below the enemy's armor, and so arranged that the torpedo could be immediately renewed from within for another attack; all such boats to be painted gray like the blockade-runners, and, when employed, to burn anthracite coal, so as to make no smoke. But, unfortunately, I had not the means to put the system into execution. Soon after the first torpedo attack, made as related, by the " David" upon the " New Ironsides," I caused a number of boats and barges to be armed with spar-torpedoes for the purpose of attacking in detail the enemy's gunboats resorting to the sounds and harbors along the South Carolina coast. But the Federals, having become very watchful, surrounded their steamers at night with nettings and floating booms, to prevent the torpedo boats from coming near enough to do them any injury. Even in the outer harbor of Charleston, where the blockaders and their consorts were at anchor, the same precaution was observed in calm weather.

The anchoring of the large torpedoes in position was attended with considerable danger. While planting them at the mouth of the Cooper and Ashley rivers (which form the peninsula of the city of Charleston), the steamer engaged in that duty being swung around by the returning tide, struck and exploded one of the torpedoes just anchored. The steamer sank immediately, but, fortunately, the tide being low and the depth of the water not great, no lives were lost. In 1863–4, Jacksonville, Florida, having been evacuated by the Confederates, then too weak to hold it longer, the Federal gunboats frequently ran up the St. John's river many miles, committing depredations along its banks. To stop these proceedings, I sent a party from Charleston under a staff officer, Captain Pliny Bryan, to plant torpedoes in the channels of that stream. The result was the destruction of several large steamers, and a cessation of all annoyance on the part of others. In the bay of Charleston, and adjacent streams, I had planted about one hundred and twenty-five torpedoes, and some fifty more in other parts of my department. The first torpedoes used in the late war were placed in the James river, below Richmond, by General G. R. Raines, who became afterward chief of the Torpedo Bureau. Mr. Barbarin, of New Orleans, placed, also, successfully, a large number of torpedoes in Mobile Bay and its vicinity.

To show the important results obtained by the use of torpedoes by the Confederates, and the importance attached now at the North to that mode of warfare, I will quote here the following remarks from an able article in the last September number of the *Galaxy*, entitled, "Has the Day of Great Navies Past?" The author says: "The real application of submarine warfare dates from the efforts of the Confederates during the late war. In October, 1862, a 'torpedo bureau' was established at Richmond, which made rapid progress in the construction and operations of these weapons until the close of the war in 1865. Seven Union iron-clads, eleven wooden war vessels, and six army transports were destroyed by Southern torpedoes, and many more were seriously damaged. This destruction occurred, for

the most part, during the last two years of the war, and it is suggestive to think what might have been the influence on the Union
cause if the Confederate practice of submarine warfare had been
nearly as efficient at the commencement as it was at the close of the
war.   It is not too much to say, respecting the blockade of the
Southern ports, that if not altogether broken up, it would have been
rendered so inefficient as to have commanded no respect from
European powers, while the command of rivers, all important to the
Union forces as bases of operations, would have been next to
impossible.

     *   *   *   *   *   *   *

"Think of the destruction this infernal machine effected, and
bear in mind its use came to be fairly understood, and some system
introduced into its arrangement only during the last part of the war.
During a period when scarcely any vessels were lost, and very few
severely damaged by the most powerful guns then employed in
actual war, we find this long list of disasters from the use of this new
and, in the beginning, much despised comer into the arena of naval
warfare.   But it required just such a record as this to arouse naval
officers to ask themselves the question, 'Is not the days of great
navies gone forever?'   If such comparatively rude and improvised
torpedoes made use of by the Confederates caused such damage, and
spread such terror among the Union fleet, what will be the consequence when skilful engineers, encouraged by governments, as they
have never been before, diligently apply themselves to the perfecting
of this terrible weapon?   The sucesses of the Confederates have
made the torpedo, which before was looked on with loathing—a
name not to be spoken except contemptuously—a recognized factor
in modern and naval warfare.   On all sides we see the greatest
activity in improving it."

I shall now refer briefly to the use in Charleston harbor of rifle
cannon and iron-clad floating and land batteries.   In the attack on
Fort Sumter, in 1861, these war appliances were first used in the
United States.   When I arrived at Charleston, in March of that year,
to assume command of the forces there assembling, and direct the
attack on Fort Sumter, I found under construction a rough floating
battery, made of palmetto logs, under the direction of Captain Hamilton, an ex-United States naval officer.   He intended to plate it
with several sheets of rolled-iron, each about three-quarters of an
inch thick, and to arm it with four thirty-two-pounder carronades.
He and his battery were so much ridiculed, however, that he could,
with difficulty, obtain any further assistance from the State govern-

ment. He came to me in great discouragement, and expressed, in vivid terms, his certainty of success, and of revolutionizing future naval warfare, as well as the construction of war vessels. I approved of Captain Hamilton's design, and, having secured the necessary means, instructed him to finish his battery at the earliest moment practicable. This being accomplished before the attack on Fort Sumter opened, early in April I placed the floating battery in position at the western extremity of Sullivan's Island to enfilade certain barbette guns of the fort which could not be reached effectively by our land batteries. It, therefore, played an important part in that brief drama of thirty-three hours, receiving many shots without any serious injury. About one year later, in Hampton roads, the "Merrimac," plated and roofed with two layers of railroad iron, met the "Monitor" in a momentous encounter, which first attracted the attention of the civilized world to the important change that iron-plating or "armors" would thenceforth create in naval architecture and armaments. The one and a half to two inch plating used on Captain Hamilton's floating battery has already grown to about twelve inches thickness of steel plates of the best quality, put together with the utmost care, in the effort to resist the heaviest rifle-shots now used. About the same time that Captain Hamilton was constructing his floating battery, Mr. C. H. Steven, of Charleston (who, afterward, died a brigadier general at the battle of Chickamauga), commenced building an iron-clad land battery at Cumming's Point, the northern extremity of Morris Island, and the point nearest to Fort Sumter—that is, about thirteen hundred yards distant. This battery was to be built of heavy timbers covered with one layer of railroad iron, the rails well fitted into each other, presenting an inclined, smooth surface of about thirty-five degrees to the fire of Sumter; the surface was to be well greased, and the guns were to fire through small embrasures supplied with strong iron shutters. I approved also of the plan, making such suggestions as my experience as an engineer warranted. This battery took an active part in the attack, and was struck several times; but, excepting the jamming and disabling one of the shutters, the battery remained uninjured to the end of the fight.

From Cumming's Point also, and in the same attack, was used the first rifled cannon fired in America. The day before I received orders from the Confederate Government, at Montgomery, to demand the evacuation or surrender of Fort Sumter, a vessel from England arriving in the outer harbor, signaled that she had something important for the Governor of the State. I sent out a harbor boat, which returned with a small Blakely rifled-gun, of two and a half inches diameter, with only fifty rounds of ammunition. I placed it at once behind a sand-bag parapet next to the Steven battery, where it did opportune service with its ten-pound shell while the ammunition lasted. The penetration of the projectiles into the brick masonry of the fort was not great at that distance, but the piece had great accuracy, and several of the shells entered the embrasures facing Morris Island. One of the officers of the garrison remarked after the surrender, that when they first heard the singular whizzing, screeching sound of the projectile, they did not understand its cause until one of the unexploded shells being found in the fort the mystery was solved. As a proof of the rapid strides taken by the artillery arm of the service, I shall mention that two years later the Federals fired against Fort Sumter, from nearly the same spot, rifle projectiles weighing three hundred pounds. Meantime I had received from England two other Blakely rifled cannon of thirteen and a quarter inches calibre. These magnificent specimens of heavy ordnance were, apart from their immense size, different in construction from anything I had ever seen. They had been bored through from muzzle to breech; the breech was then plugged with a brass block, extending into the bore at least two feet, and into which had been reamed a chamber about eighteen inches in length and six in diameter, while the vent entered the bore immediately in advance of this chamber. The projectiles provided were shells weighing, when loaded, about three hundred and fifty pounds, and solid cylindrical shots weighing seven hundred and thirty pounds; the charge for the latter was sixty pounds of powder. The first of these guns received was mounted in a battery specially constructed for it at "The Battery," at the immediate mouth of Cooper river, to command the inner harbor. As no instructions for their service accompanied the guns, and the metal between the exterior surface of the breech and the rear of the inner chamber did not exceed six to eight inches, against all experience in ordnance, apprehensions were excited that the gun would burst in firing with so large a charge and such weight of projectile. Under the circumstances it was determined to charge it with an empty shell and the minimum of powder necessary to move it; the charge was divided in two cartridges, one to fit the small rear chamber, and the other the main bore. The gun was fired by means of a long lanyard from the bomb-proof attached to the battery; and, as apprehended, it burst at the first fire, even with the relatively small charge used; the brass plug was found started back at least the sixteenth of an inch, splitting the breech with three or four distinct cracks, and rendering it useless.

With such a result I did not attempt, of course, to mount and use the other, but assembled a board of officers to study the principle that might be involved in the peculiar construction, and to make experiments generally with ordnance. The happy results of the extensive experiments made by this board with many guns of different calibre, including muskets, and last of all with the other Blakely, was that if the cartridge were not pressed down to the bottom of the bore of a gun, and a space were thus left in rear of the charge, as great a velocity could be imparted to the projectile with a much smaller charge, and the gun was subject to less abrupt strain from the explosion, because this air-chamber, affording certain room for the expansion of the gases, gave time for the inertia of the heavy mass of the projectile to be overcome before the full explosion of the charge, and opportunity was also given for the ignition of the entire charge, so that no powder was wasted as in ordinary gunnery. When this was discovered the remaining Blakely was tried from a skid, without any cartridge in the rear chamber. It fired both projectiles, shell and solid shot, with complete success, notwithstanding the small amount of metal at the extremity of the breech. I at once utilized this discovery. We had a number of eight-inch columbiads (remaining in Charleston after the capture of Sumter in 1861), which contained a powder-chamber of smaller diameter than the calibre of the gun. The vent in rear of this powder-chamber was plugged, and a new vent opened in advance of the powder-chamber, leaving the latter to serve as an air-chamber, as in our use of the Blakely gun. They were then rifled and banded, and thus turned into admirable guns, which were effectively employed against the Federal iron-clads. I am surprised that the new principle adapted to these guns has not been used for the heavy ordnance of the present day, as it would secure great economy in weight and cost. The injured Blakely gun was subsequently thoroughly repaired, and made as efficient as when first received.

In the year 1854, while in charge as engineer of the fortifications of Louisiana, I attended a target practice with heavy guns by the garrison of Fort Jackson, on the Mississippi river, the object fired at being a hogshead floating with the current at the rate of about four and a half miles an hour. I was struck with the difficulties of trailing or traversing the guns—forty-two pounders and eight-inch columbiads—and with the consequent inaccuracy of the firing. Reflecting upon the matter, I devised soon afterward a simple method of overcoming the difficulty by the application of a "rack and lever" to the wheels of the chassis of the guns; and I sent drawings of the improvement to the Chief of Engineers, General Totten, who referred them, with his approval, to the Chief of Ordnance. In the course of a few weeks the latter informed me that his department had not yet noticed any great obstacle in traversing guns on moving objects, and therefore declined to adopt my invention. When charged, in 1861, with the Confederate attack on Fort Sumter, I described this device to several of my engineer and artillery officers; but before I could have it applied I was ordered to Virginia to assume command of the Confederate force then assembling at Manassas. Afterward, on my return to Charleston, in 1862, one of my artillery officers, Lieutenant Colonel Yates, an intelligent and zealous soldier, applied this principle (modified, however) to one of the heavy guns in the harbor with such satisfactory results that I gave him orders to apply it as rapidly as possible to all guns of that class which we then had mounted. By April 6th, 1863, when Admiral Dupont made his attack on Fort Sumter with seven monitors, the "New Ironsides," several gunboats and mortar boats, our heaviest pieces had this traversing apparatus adapted to their chassis, and the result realized fully our expectations. However slow or fast the Federal vessels moved in their evolutions, they received a steady and unerring fire, which at first disconcerted them, and at last gave us a brilliant victory—disabling five of the monitors, one of which, the "Keokuk," sunk at her anchors that night. It is pertinent for me, professionally, to remark, that had this Federal naval attack on Fort Sumter of the 6th of April, 1863, been made at night, while the fleet could have easily approached near enough to see the fort—a large, lofty object, covering several acres—the monitors, which were relatively so small and low on the water, could not have been seen from the fort. It would have been impossible, therefore, for the latter to have returned with any accuracy the fire of the fleet, and this plan of attack could have been repeated every night until the walls of the fort should have crumbled under the enormous missiles, which made holes two and a half feet deep in the walls, and shattered the latter in an alarming manner. I could not then have repaired during the day the damages of the night, and I am confident now, as I was then, that Fort Sumter, if thus attacked, must have been disabled and silenced in a few days. Such a result at that time would have been necessarily followed by the evacuation of Morris and Sullivan's Islands, and, soon after, of Charleston itself, for I had not yet had time to complete and arm the system of works, including James Island and the inner harbor, which enabled us six months later to bid defiance to Admiral Dahlgren's powerful fleet and Gilmore's strong land forces.

GREGG'S CAVALRY AT GETTYSBURG

BY MAJOR J. EDWARD CARPENTER.

LITTLE has been written o.' the stubborn fight which took place on the 3d of July, 1863, on the right of the Union line at Gettysburg, between the cavalry command of General David McM. Gregg, and that of the Confederate Chief of Cavalry, General J. E. B. Stuart. In an article published in the WEEKLY TIMES of March 31st, 1877, entitled, "The Union Cavalry in the Gettysburg Campaign," by General Gregg, it is stated:

On the 3d, during that terrific fire of artillery which preceded the gallant but unsuccessful assault of Pickett's Division on our line, it was discovered that Stuart's cavalry was moving to our right with the evident intention of passing to the rear to make a simultaneous attack there. What the consequence of the success of this movement would have been, the merest tyro in the art of war will understand. When opposite our right, Stuart was met by General Gregg with two of his brigades (Colonels McIntosh and Irvin Gregg) and Custer's Brigade of the Third Division; and, on a fair field, there was another trial between two cavalry forces, in which most of the fighting was done in the saddle, and with the trooper's favorite weapon—the sabre. Without entering into the details of the fight, it need only be added that Stuart advanced not a pace beyond where he was met; but, after a severe struggle, which was only terminated by the darkness of the night, he withdrew, and on the morrow, with the defeated army of Lee, was in retreat to the Potomac.

In reply to this, Major H. B. McClellan, who was Assistant Adjutant General on the staff of General Stuart, writes in the same paper, October 20th, 1877:

I would remind General G.egg that the last charge in the cavalry battle at Gettysburg was made by the Southern cavalry; that by this charge his division was swept behind the protection of his artillery, and that the field remained in the

(527)

undisputed possession of Stuart, save that from the opposite hills a fierce artillery duel was maintained until night.*

Let us examine by the light of the official reports of the commanding officers of the contending forces these conflicting statements, and discover where the victory really remained, or who was defeated—Gregg or Stuart.

General Gregg, in his official report, dated July 25th, 1863, to Lieutenant Colonel A. J. Alexander, Assistant Adjutant General Cavalry Corps, says:

At twelve M. I received a copy of a dispatch from the commander of the Eleventh Corps to the Major General commanding the Army of the Potomac, that large columns of the enemy's cavalry were moving towards the right of our line. At the same time I received an order from Major General Pleasonton, through an aide-de-camp, to send the First Brigade of the Third Division to join General Kilpatrick on the left. The First Brigade of my division was sent to relieve the brigade of the Third Division. This change having been made, a strong line of skirmishers displayed by the enemy was evidence that the enemy's cavalry had gained our right, and were about to attack with the view of gaining the rear of our line of battle. The importance of stubbornly resisting an attack at this point, which, if successful, would have been productive of the most serious consequences, determined me to retain the brigade of the Third Division until the enemy were driven back. General Custer, commanding the brigade, satisfied of the intended attack, was well pleased to remain with his brigade.

Then follows a description of the disposition of his troops and the arrangement of his line of battle. The report then proceeds:

At this time the skirmishing became very brisk on both sides, and an artillery fire was begun by the enemy and ourselves. During the skirmish of the dismounted men the enemy brought upon the field a column for a charge. The charge of this column was met by the (Seventh) Michigan cavalry of the First Brigade, Third Division, but not successfully. The advantage gained in this charge was soon wrested from the enemy by the gallant charge of the First Michigan, of the same brigade. This regiment drove the enemy back to his starting point.

---

* It is remarkable that, among the numerous accounts from Confederate sources, of the operations of General Stuart's cavalry in the Gettysburg campaign, published among these "Annals of the War," until the appearance of this statement by Major McClellan, mention has not been made of the part taken by Stuart in the actual battle. Knowledge of this is certainly essential to a correct understanding of the great struggle. One might imagine that Major McClellan's assertion had been thrust forward as a feeler, to ascertain whether there was any one to take up the gauntlet for General Gregg and his command, who, for many years, have rested content with their achievements without boasting, and, if there were none ready to do so, to claim unequivocally a victory.

The very able paper of Colonel Brooke-Rawle, on "The Right Flank at Gettysburg," which appears in this series, furnishes the reader a careful, reliable, and truthful account of the engagement between Gregg and Stuart.

Other charges were made by the columns of the enemy, but in every instance were they driven back. Defeated at every point, the enemy withdrew to his left, and in passing the wood in which the First New Jersey Cavalry was posted, that regiment gallantly and successfully charged the flank of his column. Heavy skirmishing was still maintained by the Third Pennsylvania Cavalry with the enemy, and was continued until nightfall. During the engagement, a portion of this regiment made a very handsome and successful charge upon one of the enemy's regiments. The enemy retired his columns behind his artillery, and at dark withdrew from his former position. At this time I was at liberty to relieve the First Brigade, Third Division, which was directed to join its division. Our own and the enemy's loss, during this engagement, was severe. Ours, one officer killed, seventeen officers wounded, and one officer missing; enlisted men killed, thirty-three; wounded, forty; missing, one hundred and three.

On the morning of the 4th, I advanced to the enemy's position, but found him gone. Following toward Hunterstown, I found many of his wounded abandoned. From these we learned that the enemy had been severely punished and his loss heavy. One general officer of the enemy was seriously wounded. * * * * *

It will be seen that General Gregg fought a defensive fight. That "the importance of *stubbornly resisting* an attack at this point, which, if successful, would have been productive of the most serious consequences," determined him "to retain the brigade of the Third Division until the enemy were driven back." This, then, was all that he strove to accomplish—to drive the enemy back in case he should attack. Again, Gregg's report says: "Other charges were made by the columns of the enemy, but in every instance were they *driven back*. Defeated at every point the enemy withdrew to his left," etc. If, then, Gregg succeeded in resisting the attack made upon him by Stuart, it is evident that the victory belongs to and was properly claimed by him.

Let us now turn to the official report of General Stuart, which is dated August 20th, 1863, and is addressed to Colonel R. H. Chilton, Chief-of-Staff, Army of Northern Virginia. The report, after detailing the movements of Stuart's forces prior to his arrival in the vicinity of Gettysburg, gives the following account of his operations during the battle :*

---

* The portion of General Stuart's report referring to the operations of his command *during* the battle of Gettysburg is now for the first time printed. The original report, in the possession of the War Department, is one connected paper, giving a history of the part taken by his troopers from the very beginning to the close of the campaign. That portion of the report which refers only to Stuart's operations *after* Gettysburg, commencing with the paragraph next to the last of the extract here quoted, "during the night of the 3d," etc., was published by the Southern Historical Society (Vol. II., Southern Historical Society Papers, page 65) as an entire report, and is entitled "General J. E. B. Stuart's Report of Operations after Gettysburg." It may be unjust to the editors of that magazine to

34

My advance reached Gettysburg July 2d, just in time to thwart a move of the enemy's cavalry* upon our rear by way of Hunterstown, after a fierce engagement, in which Hampton's Brigade performed gallant service, a series of charges compelling the enemy to leave the field and abandon his purpose. I took my position that day on the York and Heidelburg roads, on the left wing of the Army of Northern Virginia.

On the morning of the 3d of July, pursuant to instructions from the commanding general (the ground along our line of battle being totally impracticable for cavalry operations), I moved forward to a position to the left of General Ewell's left, and in advance of it, where a commanding ridge completely controlled a wide plain of cultivated fields stretching toward Hanover on the left, and reaching to the base of the mountain spurs, among which the enemy held position. My command was increased by the addition of Jenkins' Brigade, who, here, in the presence of the enemy, allowed themselves to be supplied with but ten rounds of ammunition, although armed with the most approved Enfield muskets.

I moved this command and W. H. F. Lee's secretly through the woods to a position, and hoped to effect a surprise upon the enemy's rear. But Hampton's and Fitz Lee's brigades, which had been ordered to follow me, unfortunately *debouched* into open ground, disclosing the movement, and causing a corresponding movement of a large force of the enemy's cavalry. Having been informed that Generals Hampton and Lee were up, I sent for them to come forward, so that I could show them, at a glance, from the elevated ground I held, the situation, and arrange for further operations. My message was so long in finding General Hampton that he never reached me, and General Lee remained, as it was deemed inadvisable, at the time the message was delivered, for both to leave their commands.

Before General Hampton had reached where I was, the enemy had deployed a heavy line of sharpshooters, and were advancing towards our position, which was very strong. Our artillery had, however, left the crest, which it was essential for it to occupy, on account of being too short range to compete with the longer-range guns of the enemy; but I sent orders for its return. Jenkins' Brigade was chiefly employed dismounted, and fought with decided effect until the ten rounds were expended, and then retreated, under circumstances of difficulty and exposure, which entailed the loss of valuable men. The left, where Hampton's and Lee's brigades were, by this time became heavily engaged as dismounted skirmishers.

My plan was to employ the enemy in front with sharpshooters, and move a command of cavalry upon their left flank from the position lately held by me, but the falling back of Jenkins' men (that officer was wounded the day previous, before reporting to me, and his brigade was commanded by Colonel Ferguson, Sixteenth Virginia Cavalry) caused a like movement of those on the left, and the enemy, sending forward a squadron or two, were about to cut off and capture a portion of our dismounted sharpshooters.

To prevent this, I ordered forward the nearest cavalry regiment (one of W. H. F. Lee's) quickly to charge this force of cavalry. It was gallantly done, and about the same time a portion of General Fitz Lee's command charged on the left, the First Virginia Cavalry being most conspicuous. In these charges the impet-

---

suggest that the cause of truth is not advanced by the publication of the tail-end of General Stuart's report, which chronicles the events of his successful flight into Virginia, and by consigning to oblivion that portion which narrates the defeat of his forces in the greatest effort made by him during the campaign—the battle itself.

* Under Kilpatrick.

uosity of these gallant fellows, after two weeks of hard marching and hard fighting on short rations, was not only extraordinary, but irresistible. The enemy's masses vanished before them like grain before the scythe, and that regiment elicited the admiration of every beholder, and eclipsed the many laurels already won by its gallant veterans. Their impetuosity carried them too far, and the charge being very much prolonged, their horses, already jaded by hard marching, failed under it. Their movement was too rapid to be stopped by couriers, and the enemy perceiving it, were turning upon them with fresh horses. The First North Carolina Cavalry and Jeff Davis Legion were sent to their support, and gradually this hand-to-hand fighting involved the greater portion of the command, till the enemy was driven from the field, which was now raked by their artillery, posted about three-quarters of a mile off, our officers and men behaving with the greatest heroism throughout.

Our own artillery commanding the same ground, no more hand-to-hand fighting occurred, but the wounded were removed and the prisoners (a large number) taken to the rear. The enemy's loss was unmistakably heavy—numbers not known. Many of his killed and wounded fell into our hands. That brave and distinguished officer, Brigadier General Hampton, was seriously wounded twice in this engagement. Among the killed was Major Connor, a gallant and efficient officer of the Jeff Davis Legion. Several officers and many valuable men were killed and wounded, whose names it is not now in my power to furnish, but which, it is hoped, will be ultimately furnished in the reports of regimental and brigade commanders.

Notwithstanding the favorable results obtained, I would have preferred a different method of attack, as already indicated, but I soon saw that entanglement, by the force of circumstances narrated, was unavoidable, and determined to make the best fight possible. General Fitz Lee was always in the right place, and contributed his usual conspicuous share to the success of the day. Both he and the gallant First Virginia begged me, after the hot encounter, to allow them to take the enemy's battery, but I doubted the practicability of the ground for such a purpose.

During this day's operations I held such a position as not only to render Ewell's left entirely secure, where the firing of my command, mistaken for that of the enemy, caused some apprehension, but commanded a view of the routes leading to the enemy's rear. Had the enemy's main body been dislodged, as was confidently hoped and expected, I was in precisely the right position to discover it, and improve the opportunity. I watched keenly and anxiously the indications in his rear for that purpose; while in the attack which I intended, (which was forestalled by our troops being exposed to view,) his cavalry would have separated from the main body, and gave promise of solid results and advantages. After dark I directed a withdrawal to the York road, as our position was so far advanced as to make it hazardous at night, on account of the proximity of the enemy's infantry.

During the night of the 3d of July, the commanding general withdrew the main body to the ridges west of Gettysburg, and sent word to me to that effect, but his messenger missed me. I repaired to his headquarters during the latter part of the night, and received instructions as to the new line, and sent, in compliance therewith, a brigade (Fitz Lee's) to Cashtown to protect our trains congregated there. My cavalry and artillery were somewhat jeopardized before I got back to my command by the enemy's having occupied our late ground before my command could be notified of the change. None, however, were either lost or captured.

During the 4th, which was quite rainy, written instructions were received from the commanding general as to the order of march back to the Potomac.

It appears, then, according to his own narrative, that General Stuart moved his command and W. H. F. Lee's secretely through the woods to a position, "*and hoped to effect a surprise upon the enemy's rear.*" Did he accomplish his object? Stuart further says: "My plan was to employ the enemy in front with sharpshooters, and move a command of cavalry upon their left flank from a position lately held by me." But in the next sentence, he proceeds to state the reasons why this plan was not successful, and further on in the report he squarely acknowledges his failure:

Notwithstanding the favorable results obtained, I would have preferred a different mode of attack, as already indicated, but I soon saw that entanglement by the force of circumstances narrated, was unavoidable, and determined to make the best fight possible. * * * Had the enemy's main body been dislodged, as was confidently hoped and expected, I was in precisely the right position to discover it and improve the opportunity. I watched keenly and anxiously the indications in his rear for that purpose; while in the attack which I intended, which was forestalled by our troops being exposed to view, his cavalry would have separated from the main body, and gave promise of solid results and advantages. After dark I directed a withdrawal * * * My cavalry and artillery were somewhat jeopardized before I got back to my command by the enemy's having occupied our late ground.

A nice discrimination is not required to detect throughout Stuart's report a desire to explain why his attack upon Gregg was unsuccessful. First, his column *debouched* into the open ground, and gave notice of his intended attack to his enemy; next, the rout of Jenkins' Brigade caused a like movement to those on the left; then the impetuosity of the First Virginia carried them too far, and their horses failed under it, and finally, a withdrawal to the York road was directed by Stuart, because his advanced position was hazardous on account of the proximity of the enemy's infantry. The two reports are harmonious in that one (Gregg's) claims to have successfully resisted an attack, and the other (Stuart's) admits that he was not successful in his operations against the right and rear of the Union line. The reports seem to conflict somewhat in their statements regarding the result of the charges made by certain contending regiments, but an analysis of the statements made by each, will go far toward harmonizing them, and the truth may easily be eliminated. It should be borne in mind that it is a weakness of human nature to cover up our failures, as far as possible, and to set forth our successes prominently. Especially is this true when we feel and know that everything has been done to insure success that a more than ordinary prudence, ability, and bravery could dictate.

There can be but one opinion of the fighting qualities of General Stuart's command at Gettysburg. Those who opposed his attempt to reach the rear of the Union lines, have every reason to remember the valor and intrepidity of his troopers. But in Gregg, he had "a Roland for his Oliver," and in a fair fight, in an open field, with no surprise on the one side or the other, he was, in plain language, simply defeated in all that he undertook to accomplish—and the more one seeks for the truth on this subject the more certainly must he come to this conclusion. I was not aware, until I had read Major McClellan's article, before alluded to, that there had been a claim to a victory over Gregg, at Gettysburg, made by Stuart. The results of the battle were so overwhelmingly on the side of Gregg, it would seem, that the blindest prejudice alone could construe the victory to his opponent.

Stuart describes the charge of one of W. H. F. Lee's regiments and a portion of Fitz Lee's command, including the First Virginia Cavalry, as very successful—"the enemy's masses vanished before them like grain before the scythe;" but he adds, "their impetuosity carried them too far," "their horses, already jaded," "failed under it." "The First North Carolina Cavalry and Jeff Davis Legion were sent to their support, and gradually this hand-to-hand fighting involved the greater portion of the command," etc. Here is a half hidden acknowledgment that after the first charge, which Gregg admits was not successfully met by the Seventh Michigan Regiment, the attacking column was obliged to retire before the charge of the First Michigan Regiment. The difference between the reports of the two commanders here being that Stuart mentions the repulse in the mildest language, while Gregg writes of it in glowing terms: "The advantage gained in this charge was soon wrested from the enemy by the gallant charge of the First Michigan Cavalry of the same brigade. This regiment drove the enemy back to his starting point."

There remains only to consider the statement made by each general that his opponent was in the end obliged to withdraw. Gregg says: "Defeated at every point, the enemy withdrew to his left." "Heavy skirmishing was still maintained by the Third Pennsylvania Cavalry with the enemy, and was continued until nightfall." "The enemy retired his columns behind his artillery, and at dark withdrew from his former position;" and on this subject Stuart writes: "Gradually this hand-to-hand fighting involved the greater portion of the command, till the enemy was driven from the field, which was now raked by their artillery, posted about three-quarters of a mile off." "Our own artillery commanding the same ground, no more hand-to-hand fighting occurred, but the wounded were removed, and the prisoners (a large number) taken to the rear."

Stuart's artillery commanding the same ground as Gregg's, no more hand-to-hand fighting occurred; in other words, Stuart's forces were withdrawn from the attack, the attempt to carry Gregg's position having utterly failed. These words admit of no other construction. Stuart's was the attacking force. If Gregg had been driven from the field, why did not Stuart carry out his confessedly intended plan, and march to the rear of the Federal line of battle? The sentence which follows the statement that no more hand-to-hand fighting occurred, "but the wounded were removed and the prisoners taken to the rear," is a *quasi* confession that we were repulsed, but we succeeded in removing our prisoners and wounded. So that, even in these apparently opposite statements, we find sufficient in Stuart's report to prove the correctness of Gregg's.

The facts summed up, then, are these: Stuart, on the 3d of July, attempted to reach the rear of the Federal line of battle, but, encountering Gregg's command, after a stubborn fight, in which the first mounted charge of Stuart's troopers was partially successful, he was utterly and entirely defeated, and, under cover of night, retreated from his position before his successful antagonist.

A word as to one or two facts. Major McClellan states that the last charge in the cavalry battle at Gettysburg was made by Southern cavalry, and that by this charge his (Gregg's) division was swept behind the protection of his artillery, and that the field remained in the undisputed possession of Stuart, save that an artillery duel was maintained until night. In each of these statements Major McClellan has fallen into error. The last charge was not made by the Southern cavalry, unless it can be said that a repelling charge is not a charge. Every charge made by Stuart's cavalry on that day was met, and met successfully, by a counter-charge. Nor were Gregg's troops at any time on that day swept behind the protection of his artillery. The Seventh Michigan Regiment was driven about half way across the open field in which the charge of the First Virginia and the other troops mentioned in Stuart's report was made, but before it reached General Gregg's artillery the attacking column was in flight, pursued by the First Michigan and portions of the Third Pennsylvania and First New Jersey Cavalry.

The field did not remain in Stuart's possession. After the mounted charges had ceased, no part of Stuart's command occupied any portion of the field except the line of skirmishers, which was deployed a short distance in front of the crest mentioned in his report, and immediately after dark General Stuart withdrew his command. General Gregg occupied the field of the hand-to-hand fight and held possession of it during the night. General Custer, in his official report, writes: "We held possession of the field until dark, during which time we collected our dead and wounded." It was true, then, that "Stuart advanced not a pace beyond where he was met," and the victory remained with General Gregg.

CONFEDERATE NEGRO ENLISTMENTS.

BY EDWARD SPENCER.

No circumstances connected with the late war caused more surprise, perhaps, than the general conduct of the slave population of the South during the whole contest. This surprise was common to the people of both sections, for there were few persons at the North who did not expect, and at the South who did not fear, a servile insurrection as the Federal armies penetrated deeper into the Southern territory. The people of the South did not, of course, have any great opinion of the negroes' courage, but still they felt apprehensive about the women and children left at home, and fearful, too, in regard to neglected plantation work; and the *fact* of this apprehension is embodied in all the draft schemes and conscription laws of the Confederacy, which, both under the State government regimen, and later under the general conscription system, made specific provision for a certain line of exemptions, looking to the peace and good order of the plantations, and keeping the negroes at work. These exemptions included detailed officers and veterans, home guards, etc., and, even in the last and severest conscription law passed in the fall of 1864, one overseer was exempted "for each plantation containing over fifteen able-bodied male slaves."

On the other hand, a slave insurrection was counted on at the North as one factor in the war. It was deprecated, of course; it was not invited, but it was still looked for, and the Emancipation Proclamation was calculated upon as a means of inciting the negroes to strike for their freedom. Those who will examine the periodicals of the period—the *Atlantic Monthly*, for instance; the *Continental*

CONFEDERATE NEGRO ENLISTMENTS.537

Monthly, etc.—will find them teeming with historical instances written up of slaves who had so risen. The *Atlantic*, in particular, in urging the Emancipation Proclamation, took occasion to give, as arguments for it, detailed accounts of the revolt of Spartacus, of the Maroons, of Nat. Turner's outbreak, etc.; all showing the wish that was father to the thought. Butler speculated in this sort of business at Fortress Monroe and New Orleans, and Hunter tried it in South Carolina and Florida. Higginson's regiment at Beaufort was intended to be a nucleus for the negro rising which was looked for on the Carolina coast.

The negroes, however, refused to disturb the Confederates with any fire in the rear. They behaved in the most exemplary manner everywhere. Where the Federal armies settled down they came in in large numbers, and established their camps upon the fringes of the army, playing the parts of "intelligent contrabands" to perfection. They told miraculous stories, and brought in no end of "grape-vine" intelligence for the divertissement of the newspaper correspondents, and the *gobemouches*; but they were disgustingly apathetic on the subject of striking "blows for liberty." They had no fight in them, in fact, and, when they came into camp, had no idea of any other freedom than freedom from work and free rations. The best of the negroes, where they could, stayed at home and worked along as usual, and there was no general enlistment of the negroes until the substitute brokers began to buy them up, and put them in the army by wholesale.

There can be no doubt that the negroes behaved very well, and that the Confederate people had a lively and very grateful appreciation of the fact. There is evidence enough and to spare of this. I have before me a curious pamphlet, "Marginalia; or, Gleanings from an Army Note-book," by "Personne," army correspondent of the Charleston *Courier*, published at Columbia, S. C., in 1864, which abounds with instances and recitals of the good conduct of the negroes. Thus, "Personne" relates the story of Daniel, a slave of Lieutenant Bellinger, who was shot to pieces trying to take his master's sword to him, in the fort at Secessionville, during the assault on that post, and he says: "Such instances of genuine loyalty have their parallel nowhere so frequently as in the pages of Southern history, and gives a flat contradiction to all the partial and puritanical statements ever made by Mrs. Stowe and her tribe of worshiping abolitionists." "The fidelity of our negroes," this writer says, in another place, "has been as much a subject of gratification to us as of surprise to the enemy. It has been thought that every slave would gladly avail himself of an opportunity to regain his freedom; but the prophets have been disappointed."

General John B. Gordon, United States Senator from Georgia, who used to own several plantations and a great many slaves, in his testimony before the Ku-Klux Investigating Committee, in July, 1871, spoke in the strongest terms of the good conduct of the Southern negroes during and after the war. He said that "they have behaved so well since the war that the remark is not uncommon in Georgia, that no race, relieved from servitude under such circumstances as they were, would have behaved so well." As for their conduct during the war, when he was asked about that, General Gordon said:

Well, sir, I had occasion to refer just now to a little speech which I made at Montgomery, Alabama, where General Clanton also spoke. He and I both struck on that train of thought. I went so far as to say that the citizens of the South owed it to the negroes to educate them. One of the things which I mentioned, and which General Clanton also mentioned, was the behavior of the negroes during the war; the fact that when almost the entire white male population, old enough to bear arms, was in the army, and large plantations were left to be managed by the women and children, not a single insurrection had occcurred, not a life had been taken; and that, too, when the Federal armies were marching through the country with freedom, as it was understood, upon their banners. Scarcely an outrage occurred, on the part of the negroes, at that time. * * * The negroes were aware that the contest would decide whether they were to be slaves or freemen. I told my slaves of it at the beginning of the war. I think that the negroes generally understood that if the South should be whipped freedom would be the result.

The negroes, in fact, as General Gordon said, were happy because they were treated kindly and had few cares. They were attached to their masters, with whom they had been associated all their lives, being naturally an amiable, good-tempered race, with very strong local attachments, and very affectionate to their kinsmen and those they were used to look up to. They have an ardent clansense, and the master used to be revered as the head of the sept. This was the case everywhere, except on the large coast plantations, where the negroes seldom saw a white man, were brutalized, of low intelligence, speaking a language of their own, scarcely to be understood by the whites. These negroes, like those of Cuba, were only half naturalized and had many of their old barbarian African habits and instincts; but elsewhere the case was different. As General Gordon said:

In the upper part of the State, where I was raised, the negro children and the white children have been in the habit of playing together. My companions, when I was being raised, were the negro boys that my father owned. We played marbles, rode oxen, went fishing, and broke colts together; a part of my fun was to play with those colored boys. The negro girls—those who were raised about the house—

were raised very much as the white family was raised. They were raised in the family, and, of course, the intelligence of the family extended, in some measure, to the negroes.

These house servants considered themselves to "belong to de fam'ly," and no people in the world have such an acute aristocratic pride as the negroes. The good family slaves looked down with ineffable contempt upon "de pore white trash," and they do so still. A great part of the lordly airs which negro legislators have put on of late years proceeds from their contempt for the carpet-baggers, whom they consider as being of the "trash" species. Wade Hampton's old body-servant was senator from Columbia, South Carolina, and used to make Tim Hurley stand about, and treated Chamberlain, and Moses, and Scott with huge disdain; but he touches his hat to his old master to this day, and all the former slave negroes have the same sort of recognition for "de quality," under no matter what adverse circumstance, that the Irish peasantry have for their lineal descendants of the O'Brien's and the O'Shaughnessey's who used to rule over them with rods of iron.

Strong friendships and the utmost familiarity of personal relationship grew out of this life-long intercourse between the house servants and their masters; and a great many body-servants not only followed their masters to the field, and devoted themselves to their service in the tenderest way, but fought, bled, and died for them. There are some touching instances of this intercourse and this devotion which are worth relating. When General Joseph E. Johnston was at Jackson, at the Lamar House, in the full tide of a brilliant reception, an old negro woman, in a coarse sunbonnet, with a cotton umbrella under her arm, rapped at the door, and asked: "Is dis Mr. Johnston's room?" "Yes." "Mr. Joe Johnston's room?" "Yes." "I wants to see him, den;" and in marched the old lady, going up to the distinguished soldier, and laying her hand familiarly upon his epauleted shoulder. Johnston turned, a look of surprise and gladness overspread his face, he took both the bony, bird-claw hands warmly in his own, and exclaimed: "Why, Aunt Judy Paxton!" The old negress scanned his features with tears in her eyes, and at last said, in a querulous treble, made touching with undisguised emotion: "Mister Joe, you is gittin' old." Then, patting his hand, the old nurse turned half apologetically to the assemblage, and said: "Dis here's my own boy. Many's de time I's toted you in dese yere arms; didn't I, honey?" Such a scene would be strange elsewhere, but it was not so in the South. The artless sense of equality grew out of the strongest sort of affectionate regard.

General Gordon, in the testimony cited above, said:

The very kindliest relations exist between the old masters and their former servants. I could give, from my own personal knowledge, instances of the very tenderest expressions of kindness and enthusiastic demonstrations of love on the part of negroes for their old masters. In one case, a body-servant of mine came a long distance to see me. After having been captured by the Federal army in Georgia, and staying with them for months, he came back to me just after the surrender, and told me he preferred to serve me rather than have his freedom, if he must be separated from me, though he wanted his freedom. His wife was my wife's chambermaid. She wanted to go with me to Brunswick. She had been raised by my wife, and had been raised very much as my wife was. I had paid an enormous price for her husband after my marriage, so as to have him with his wife. I had been offered $2,500 for him, which I had refused to take. I would not have sold him at all, any more than I would have sold my brother. These two negroes were anxious to go with us to Brunswick, but I had but little money, and was unable to take them. On my return to that portion of Georgia, two years afterward, I walked from my father's house a mile before breakfast to their little cabin to see them. When I got to the door the woman was sitting at the breakfast-table. As I opened the door she was in the act of drinking coffee from a saucer. In her excitement at seeing me, she let the saucer fall upon the floor, sprang to me, gathered me in her arms, and sank at my feet, crying: "Massa John, I never knew who my friends were before."

These are two instances from the associations of two leading Confederates. Take another, from General Lee's life, to show the Caleb Balderstone sort of devotion with which these house servants used to guard their masters' interests. It is from "Personne's" pamphlet, and relates to the last year of the war, when provisions were scarce, and the General himself only had meat twice a week:

Having invited a number of gentlemen to dine with him, the commander-in-chief, in a fit of extravagance, ordered a sumptuous repast of cabbage and middling. The dinner was served, and, behold, a great pile of cabbage, and a bit of middling, about four inches long and two inches across. The guests, with commendable politeness, unanimously declined middling, and it remained in the dish untouched. Next day, General Lee, remembering the delicate tid-bit that had been so providentially preserved, ordered his servant to bring him "that middling." The man hesitated, scratched his head, and finally owned up: "De fac is, Marse Robert, dat dar middlin' was borrowed middlin'. We all didn't have nary a spec, so I done borrowed it, an' now I done paid it back to de man whar I got it from, sar."

This servant was a true Southern family darkey, with all the pride of his connections in him. He was like the waiter at the Southern hotel where the abolitionist lecturer put up, and who was so impassive and unresponsive to the enthusiast's praises of freedom and horror of slavery, that at last the latter cried: "Leave me! leave me! I cannot endure the spectacle of such obtuseness after such misfortune. Go! I will not be waited upon by one who is a slave indeed!" "Excuse me, master," said the negro, "I'd like werry much to 'commodate you, sar, but I'se 'sponsible for de spoons, sar." General Lee's servant was responsible, in his own opinion, for the good appearance of his master's table, and if he had not been able to secure the bacon, he would have suffered as many agonies as Louis XIV.'s grand valet did when the turbot did not come in time to be served at the king's banquet.

The devotion of this class of negroes, many of whom followed their masters to the field, was only exceeded by their pride in their families and place. John Robinson, a Savannah pilot, attached to a Nassau blockade-runner, was two or three times captured, but retained his loyalty through all, and always returned to his old master and his old master's family. His master was killed in the defense of Fort McAlister, and John was taken to Fort Lafayette, and kept prisoner for eight months, while every persuasion, and a hundred dollars a month wages, were offered him to enter the Federal service, but he continued staunch. In one of the battles near Petersburg, a slave in a Federal regiment saw his former young master on the field in danger. He threw down his musket, and ran to him and carried him into the Confederate ranks. There are repeated instances of negroes on the plantations concealing and saving their master's property at great personal hazard to themselves; burying cotton and plate, and guarding the caches faithfully. When the war broke out, John Campbell, the well-known horse-racer, went to Mobile, leaving his stables in Kentucky in charge of a slave. Four years later, when Campbell returned, a poor man, his negro had all the horses and their increase waiting for his master, and in the very best condition. There was nothing to prevent this faithful fellow from making away with all of Campbell's property.

This class of negroes in the South knew that the war would set them free, as General Gordon said, but they did not want much to be free. Not that they wanted to be slaves at all, but they looked down upon and despised the condition of the free negroes whom they saw around them, and they considered that the Federals, in waring upon their "families" were waring upon themselves. They got bravely over this sort of thing very shortly after the war ended, but they were sincere in the feeling during the war, and would have fought, nay, did fight sometimes, by the side of their masters. A good many of these servants who followed their masters afield, albeit not fond of bullets, are known to have now and then taken "hot shots" at the "Yankees." Lieutenant Shelton's man Jack, of the Thirteenth Arkansas, fell at his master's side at the battle of Belmont. When Jack was shot, Jack's son took his rifle and went to

the field to avenge his "daddy." Major White, of the Alabama
battalion that bore his name, had a negro servant who risked his life
to bear off his master's body from the field when he was shot down,
and after the funeral he took his master's horse and effects, and rode
home with them, over a thousand miles, to the old plantation. A
Florida negress illustrated the principle of "family" pride which is
characteristic of the race, in a quaint and touching way. Her young
masters, both lads, were conscripted and ordered to Pensacola. As
they were taking tearful leave of friends and home, the old "mammy"
said: "Now, young marsters, stop dis hyar cryin'; go and fight fer
yo' country like men, and mind, don't disgrace de family nor *me*
nuther."

I could accumulate columns of this sort of anecdotes, all well au-
thenticated, but what I have given will more than suffice. The Confederates found by experience that the negroes, as a rule, were faithful and well behaved, and they trusted them in some things a great
deal. This was especially the case with the slave owners. Between
the poor whites, however, and the negroes, there was no sort of
sympathy nor confidence, and this circumstance alone would have
prevented the Confederate Government from originally putting the
negroes in the field, if it had ever entertained such an idea. But,
indeed, no such idea was entertained. They were willing to use the
negroes for teamsters, cooks, etc., and did so use them to a considerable extent from the first. Later on, as men grew scarcer, it became
the custom to make requisitions upon communities for slaves to work
upon fortifications and upon government farms, in the salt-works,
powder factories, nitre bureaus, etc., but there was no thought of
putting them in the field until long after they had been extensively
enlisted in the Federal army, and the phrase, "the colored troops
fought bravely," had passed into a proverb.

In fact, the Confederates had no sort of opinion of the bravery
of the colored troops, and even at the last nothing but sheer necessity
drove them to think of the race as food for powder. In the Richmond *Examiner*, in 1863, at the time the colored troops began to be
sent to the field in the Federal forces, there was a very bumptious
burlesque of the negro soldiers' bill, the favorite measure of Thad.
Stevens. The editor said, in that high and mighty style which was
peculiar (happily) to this sheet alone:

Enlightened Europe may turn from the sickening horrors of a servile insurrection, invoked by the madmen at Washington, to a phase of this war, as it will be
waged next summer, which, when depicted with historical accuracy and physio-
logical fidelity, can scarcely fail to relieve its fears as to the future of the white race

at the South, and conduce, in no small degree, to the alleviation of any epigastric uneasiness that Exeter Hall may experience in regard to the corporeal welfare of the colored brethren. The fate of the negro, of the white population at the South, and of the Northern army, respectively, will be decided in a brief contest, which will occur about the middle of next June, and which we will describe as gravely and succinctly as possible. On the 1st of April, fifty thousand negroes, who have been previously drilled in various camps of instruction, will be debarked at Acquia creek. But it will require at least six weeks of incessant toil to perform this simple feat. It is at last accomplished. The skirmishers of the grand colored division are thrown out. They deploy.

The voice of an overseer calling hogs is heard in a distant field. They rally in the reserve. No rebels being visible, they are again thrown forward. They feel for the enemy, but he is not to be felt. They fire at nothing, fifty feet in the air, and hit it every time. The rebels being thus driven to their earthworks, the grand colored division advances at the *pas de charge*, singing a Methodist refrain, to storm the enemy's position, and to carry the crest at all hazards. Of a sudden, the artillery of A. P. Hill's command belches forth a hurricane of shell and shrapnell. There is a rising of wool, as of quills upon the fretful porcupine, under the caps of dusky brigadiers and sooty major generals; there is a simultaneous effusion of mellifluous perspiration from fifty thousand tarry hides; there is a display of ivory like fifty thousand flashes of lightning; fifty thousand pairs of charcoal knees are knocking together * * * at the self-same moment a scattering, as if all the blackbirds, crows, and buzzards in creation had taken wings at once. To a man the Northern army lies prostrate in the field, asphyxiated by the insufferable odor bequeathed to the atmosphere by the dead, departed host. For a like cause, the rebel army is in full retreat to Richmond. Solitary and alone, with his nose in his hand, A. P. Hill surveys the silent scene.

The *Examiner* to the contrary, notwithstanding, the negroes stood fire pretty well, and made tolerably good subsidiary troops in the Federal army—much better than ordinary militia—and they did most valuable work by enabling the veterans to be concentrated for important services. The Confederates found this out, and, after being made very angry at being confronted with their own slaves, and being shot down by them, they fell to thinking the matter over very seriously.

I cannot discover exactly when it was that the idea of enlisting negro soldiers in the Confederacy was first broached, but I find the Mobile *Register*, before the middle of October, 1864, claiming that "a year ago" it had referred to the important reserve power of resistance which the Confederacy would be able to call upon in the last extremity, in the persons of its slaves. The *Register* says the subject "is now actively discussed." It does not consider that the time has yet arrived for such a step, and, anyhow, it was too late in the season to undertake such a thing then. But the policy of the government ought to be settled in regard to the matter, and preparations made for the next campaign. And from the date of this article the matter came to be generally discussed, and there was a rapid revolution of public feeling on the subject. At first everybody was extremely hostile to such a movement, and the soldiers particularly. But three or four circumstances combined to make a rapid change in the public sentiment. In the first place, by an act of the Confederate Congress, approved February 17th, 1864, there were some thirty thousand or forty thousand slaves drafted into the army as cooks, teamsters, trainsmen and the like, and the soldiers found that they not only got along very well with Cuffee, but that he saved them no end of work and trouble, was handy, amiable, liked the service well enough, and was not without a spirit of adventure. Some of the negro teamsters did a little amateur fighting now and then, and they showed themselves very skilful in plundering a battle-field.

Slavery, too, was on its last legs as October rolled by. The enemy had possession of more than half the Confederate territory, and wherever they marched they set the negroes free. Slaves had lost their market value even in Richmond, where, when sugar was selling at from eight dollars and a half to eleven dollars and eighty-seven cents per pound, coffee at twelve dollars, tea at forty-two dollars, bicarbonate of soda at five dollars and thirty-seven cents, flour at three hundred and fifty dollars, and a china dinner and tea set brought two thousand four hundred and fifty dollars at auction, good, likely negroes brought only from four thousand five hundred dollars to six thousand dollars. (Richmond *Sentinel*, October 28th, 1864.) This, in gold rates, and estimating flour at six dollars per barrel, would make negroes only seventy-five dollars to one hundred dollars apiece, or about one-tenth their price at the beginning of the war. People saw from this heavy discount that slavery was doomed, and a good many patriotic planters were quite willing to sell their slaves to the Confederate Government, and take their chances in Confederate States bonds in preference to negroes. Another thing was that of the Confederate Congress that met at Richmond for the last time in the second week of November, 1864—(it adjourned *sine die* on the 17th of March, 1865)—more than half the members represented constituencies in which slavery was practically rubbed out by the war process. The Senators and Representatives of Missouri, Kentucky, Arkansas, Tennessee, Louisiana, Florida, and parts of Georgia, Alabama, and Mississippi, knew that their constituents' slaves were gone, and they had no particular reason for wishing to save the slaves of other sections yet uninvaded by the enemy.

Still, although the question began to be debated actively, and the army showed itself in favor of the movement, there was no concerted serious attempt to concentrate public opinion in regard to it until the latter part of October, 1864. Two events at that time suddenly waked the Confederates to the gravity of their situation. Sherman began his march to the sea, and the elections in Ohio, Indiana, and Pennsylvania showed the rebels that McClellan was certain to be defeated for the Presidency, and that Lincoln would give them four years more of war unless they surrendered. The Confederates hoped much from McClellan's election; they were sanguine that he would be elected, and their disappointment was proportionately great. The march of Sherman in the same way showed them what Grant had several times insisted upon, that the Confederacy was like an empty egg-shell—all its powers of resistance had been drained to keep the frontier line strong.

From this time forth, then, even the most sanguine began to lose all hope, and those who still believed in a successful resistance knew that it could only be made by a consecration of every possible resource of the country to that one object. Hence the idea of employing slaves as soldiers immediately began to take shape and proportion, and the agitation of it became active and unremitting. The people of Richmond had become acquainted with the negro in a semi-military capacity since the passage of the act of February 17th, 1864, "to increase the efficiency of the army by the employment of free negroes and slaves in certain capacities." Under that act there had not only been large enlistments of negroes for camp duties and cooks, teamsters, etc., but there were also heavy requisitions made upon the surrounding country for slaves to work upon the fortifications. These, when drafted, were organized into large gangs, and quartered in and around the city, under military discipline. In the early morning these gangs used to be marched through the city on their way to their work on the fortifications, shouldering their picks and shovels, and trotting along at a regulation step. They are fat and saucy and greasy, full of laugh and song, and they kept step instinctively as they sang their own versions of "Dixie" and "John Brown's Body," rapping, castanet-wise, upon the pavements with the wooden soles of their huge and shapeless canvas shoes. Many a Richmond mother, as she heard the bacon-colored gangs clatter by her door, thought of her own ragged, half-starved boy in the trenches at Petersburg, and said to herself: "If the cause demands *him* as food for powder, why not send out *these* for the Yankees to shoot at, also?"

Butler, at this very time, had ten thousand Virginia negroes at work cutting his Dutch Gap canal, about which the Richmond people gave themselves much needless excitement, since they might

35

have known that the more nearly the doughty General's works approached the point of completion (and of danger) the more it would be sure to flag. But the thought must have occurred to many at Richmond that, if Butler could employ these ten thousand negroes to cut a way *into* Richmond for him, what sort of paralysis was it that prevented the Confederate Government from equally employing ten thousand or fifty thousand negroes to keep him *out* of that city? A sure sign that this question had then begun to ferment actively in the public mind, may be got from the fact that at this time "the opposition" opened fire against the enlistment of negroes. The Holden party in North Carolina, and their Raleigh organ, the *Standard*, the ultra States' Rights party, represented by the Richmond *Examiner* and Charleston *Mercury*, by Wigfall and obstreperous Congressmen like him, and the pure obstructionists, like Henry S. Foote and Governor Brown, of Georgia, and, in a lesser degree, Alexander H. Stephens, began to murmur and denounce. If the Confederacy, they said, could not be saved except by such means as these, it was not worth saving. To which the natural reply of the administration party was that, if the Confederate people preferred to give up their liberties sooner than give up their slaves, the cause was practically hopeless. The enlistment party, in fact, as the opposition knew, contemplated a step further. They were willing, sooner than be subjugated, to abolish slavery entirely, and ask to be restored to the old colonial relationship to England, provided that country could not otherwise be induced to recognize the Confederacy. This, probably, was a *dernier resort*, which President Davis would have unflinchingly contemplated; but he had no sooner broached the subject in the Richmond *Sentinel* than the storm of indignation with which it was received showed him his mistake, and no more was said about it, except by the anti-enlistment party in the Confederate Congress, who made use of it in their steady antagonism to the administration policy.

It must be said, however, in justice to the Confederate people, that the social difficulties of the negro enlistment problem engaged their attention much more deeply than the probable monetary losses. An article on this subject in the *Sentinel* of November 2d, copied from the able Lynchburg *Republican*, put this side of the case very strongly. We cannot ask these negroes to fight for us, it in substance said, unless we give them their freedom; but that involves the freedom of their children and families also, and so we not only abolitionize the country, but convert it into a sort of free-negro paradise, with the bottom rail on top—for the negroes, if we succeed, will be the saviors of the country. "Instead of being a war for the freedom of the white man, it will degenerate into a war for the freedom and equality of the slaves." It would be better, the *Republican* argued, to accept Lincoln's than this sort of abolition.

Nevertheless, the die was cast. The army could not be recruited any more, owing to the apathty and discontent of the people, and General Lee, it is now known, said the cause was lost unless he was efficiently reinforced before the winter ended. The Confederate Congress met on Monday, November 7th, at noon, and as soon as it was organized the message of President Davis was received. In this paper, admirably written, with characteristic courage and directness he met and stated the question of the hour. Referring to the act of February 17th, of the previous Congress, which, he said, was less effective than it was expected to be, he remarked: "But my present purpose is to invite your consideration to the propriety of a radical modification in the theory of this law." The slave, he said, was to be viewed not only as property, but as a person under the law. His services to the State increased in value in proportion as he became a veteran. For this he should be rewarded, as well as his master. He would not advise anything further just now than the equitable determination of these relations. He was opposed, at present, to the general levy and arming of slaves as soldiers. "But should the alternative ever be presented of subjugation, or of the employment of the slave as a soldier, there seems no reason to doubt what then should be our decision." In the meantime, he would recommend the training of forty thousand negroes for duties under the act of February 17th. This message, in which the duty of the State to the slaves as persons was fairly, and fully, and ably stated, opened the whole question at once, and henceforth the history of negro enlistments is recorded in the proceedings of the Confederate Congress and the State Legislatures. The soldiers in the different camps, as soon as the question was agitated among them, gave it their hearty approval, and adopted resolutions to that effect. The poor fellows were so hard bested that they welcomed any measure which promised them a modicum of relief.

Hon. James A. Seddon, Secretary of War, in his report, supplemented Mr. Davis' message with some still stronger recommendations of his own. The slaves, he said, had even a stronger interest in the victory of the Confederates than the white people. The latter risked their political independence, but the former their very existence as a race. If the cruel enemies of the South should triumph, they would extinguish the negroes in a few years, as they had already extinguished the Indians. He recommended that the States which had absolute and exclusive control of the matter, should legislate at once with a view to the contingency of negro enlistments. On the next day, in the Confederate Congress, Senator G. A. Henry, of Tennessee, and Representative Wickham, of Virginia, introduced bills to extend and perfect the operations of the act of February 17th, 1864.

The opposition now began to take the field, alarmed at the progress which the matter had already made in public opinion. The Raleigh *Confederate*, in a dispassionate article, praises the proposed enlargement of the teamster enlistment, temporizes in regard to the constitutional and organic question, but opposes peremptorily the negro soldier enlistment programme. Governor Vance, of North Carolina, in his annual message to the Legislature of that State, took strong ground in opposition to the measure. The thing was totally inadmissible, he said. It was opposed to the theory of the Southern government, and was inexpedient and unwise beside. It may be remarked here, that there were, all along, in the South, two parties, and two sets of opinion in regard to the war, and the conduct of it—one party, of which Mr. Davis was the representative and leader, looking upon it as a social revolution and a struggle for existence; the other, represented by Mr. Stephens, Mr. Henry S. Foote, Mr. Vance, and many others, regarding it rather as a political movement. In the view of the former party, any means to promote the success of the cause which was so vital, were admissible; but the latter party were disposed to measure the means they employed for resistance by the rule of expediency. The former, as soon as the case grew to be desperate, wanted to arm the slaves, or resume colonial dependence; the latter, as soon as independence eluded their grasp, proposed negotiations, and wanted to " settle " the thing by peace congresses, or even by submission according to protocol. The distinction here made should be carefully noted, for the Confederacy was finally broken to pieces upon this rock. Mr. Davis carried his point of war at any price, and his opponents henceforth bent their united energies to paralyze his exertions. He was not the wisest of politicians, nor the best of generals; but his sincerity and intensity of purpose elevated him far above the half-hearted people around him as a promoter of vigorous, and, consequently, successful war. In spite of his patronage of Bragg and Hood, and his opinionativeness generally, it is tolerably certain that, if Davis had made himself dictator, he would have been able to carry on the war for still another year.

There had been already, some weeks before the meeting of the Confederate Congress, an important conference of the governors of the different States, at Augusta, Georgia, October 17th, at which the subject under consideration had been freely discussed, but without positive action. Governor Smith, of Virginia, in his message to the Virginia Legislature, December 7th, now took the ground that the time had come to put the slaves in the field, and to sacrifice slavery to the cause of independence. The slaveholders should take the initiative in this, in order that people might no longer say, as they had been saying, that this "was the rich man's war;" and Governor Smith gave plenty of other good reasons why the negroes should be made soldiers of. The *Sentinel* of the 10th quotes, with approval, the remarks of the St. Louis *Republican* upon the language attributed to Lincoln, that the war could not be carried on "according to Democratic arithmetic," "then, if the rebels put two hundred and fifty thousand slave negroes in the field, they cannot be conquered, according to Mr. Lincoln's arithmetic." Senator Hunter, of Virginia, who was constantly and throughout opposed to the policy of negro enlistments, introduced a bill into the Confederate Congress, on December 9th, to regulate impressments. On the same day, Governor Bonham, of South Carolina, sent his message to the Legislature of that State, in which he denied the authority of the Confederate Government to enlist slaves, as well as the expediency of such enlistments. The "reserved rights of States" played a big part in these last days of the Confederacy, when all who valued their persons or their property more than they did the "cause," were sedulous to contrive means to save them.

Events, public opinion, and the newspapers, meantime, moved much more swiftly than the Confederate Congress. The limits of the Confederacy were being narrowed continually by the Federal arms, and there were great and bitter dissensions at Richmond, and throughout what was left of the Confederacy. The politicians wrangled, the contractors robbed, the government was helpless, the soldiers starved. The columns of the *Sentinel*, for six weeks from December 13th, are doleful reading indeed. During this period, Congress approached the matter of negro enlistments in many ways, but never had the courage to grapple with it. There were bills to pay for slaves, to regulate impressments, etc., to create negro home guards, but the bull was never taken resolutely by the horns. But, in the meantime, the dissatisfaction grew, the pressure from the camps increased, the area of the Confederacy diminished, and with the appreciation of slavery as a money interest. On the 28th of January, 1865, the Confederate House, for the first time, went into secret session on the subject of negro enlistments, and there the discussions formally began. The proposition was, at first, to impress forty thousand negroes for menial service in the army. On the 30th, a proviso, offered by J. M. Leach, of North Carolina (one of the obstructionists), that none of the negroes so impressed should be put in the army, was voted down.

On February 2d, Gholson, of Virginia, in the House, and on the 4th, Orr, of South Carolina, in the Senate (both of them obstructionists), tried, but failed, to carry propositions to the effect that the enlistment policy was disheartening and demoralizing, and would divide the Confederacy. On the other hand, Conrad, of Louisiana, and Brown, of Mississippi, both introduced propositions which recited the contrary. In fact, as has been said before, the representatives of invaded States were generally for arming the negroes, those of States not overrun for the contrary policy. These propositions were duly referred, and I find that the subject was actively discussed in secret session of both houses on the 4th, 6th, 7th, and 8th. On the 9th, the Senate rejected Senator Brown's enlistment proposition. On the 11th of February there was a great public meeting in Richmond, at which Secretary Benjamin and Senator Henry both spoke in zealous and earnest advocacy of the enlistment programme, and on the 13th, there were two new bills introduced by Mr. Oldham, of Texas, and Mr. Barksdale, of Mississippi, looking to negro enlistments. Senator Oldham's bill was offered in the Senate, and was not heard of again. In the House, a motion to reject Barksdale's bill was defeated by a two-thirds vote. This bill provided for the enlistment of slaves by their masters, and did not reward them with their freedom for volunteering—in fact, there was no volunteering about it. They were to be sent to fight the Yankees as they had been sent to work on the defenses.

On the 15th, the subject of enlistments came up in the Virginia Legislature, which, on the 17th, adopted resolutions recommending the enlistment policy. It was not, however, until the 27th that this Legislature voted to instruct its Senators to vote for the measure in the Confederate Congress. The subject was ardently discussed in secret session of that Congress from the 17th to the 25th. In this interval, the soldiers from Mississippi, Virginia, South Carolina, Tennessee, and Texas, and elsewhere, declared in favor of the new policy, and a letter of General Lee's was published looking to the same end. In that letter the illustrious commander-in-chief said that he considered the measure " not only expedient but necessary." If the Confederates did not make use of the slaves the Federals would. The Confederacy was too weak in men to stand long the pressure of war waged in its present tremendous shape. The negroes had the physical powers and the habits of discipline to make good soldiers, and, with proper training, their efficiency would be unquestionable. They would make willing soldiers, provided emancipation was their reward.

In spite of this letter, however, the Senate defeated the measure again on the 25th, but on the 1st of March, Barksdale's resolution, materially amended, came up in the House and was passed. Wigfall, Hunter, Caperton, Miles, and other leaders opposed the enlistment policy savagely, but, still, when the bill of Barksdale finally came up in the Senate, Hunter and Caperton voted for it, even while speaking against it. The vote in the Senate on the final passage of the bill, March 7th, 1865, was as follows:

YEAS—Messrs. Brown, Burnett, Caperton, Henry, Hunter, Oldham, Semmes, Sims, and Watson—9.

NAYS—Messrs. Barnwell, Graham, Johnson (Ga.), Johnson (Mo.), Maxwell, Orr, Vest, and Wigfall—8.

Thus, the instructions of the Virginia Legislature, by compelling Hunter and Caperton to vote contrary to their opinions, carried the bill through.

This bill enacted that in order to secure additional forces to repel invasion, etc., the President be authorized to ask for and accept from slave owners the services of as many able-bodied slaves as he thinks expedient; the same to be organized by the commander-in-chief under instructions from the War Department, and to receive the same rations and compensation as other troops. If a sufficient number of troops cannot thus be secured, the President is authorized to conscript three hundred thousand men without regard to color. There is no provision for emancipation or for volunteering, except that the last section says:

That nothing in this act shall be construed to authorize a change in the relation which the said slaves shall bear toward their owners, except by the consent of the owners and of the States in which they may reside, and in pursuance of the laws thereof.

This measure was, of course, ineffective. It did not embody the views of Mr. Davis, nor of General Lee, nor of the Virginia Legislature. It was comparatively useless as a means to reinforce the army immediately, and this was the more singular, since it was now well known in Richmond that General Lee had told the Virginia Legislature that, unless he was reinforced he could not maintain the struggle any longer than the opening of the spring campaign. Nothing can reveal more forcibly the selfish narrow-mindedness and jealousy of the slave-holding interests than this bill.

Still, if there had been time to do it, Jefferson Davis would have, doubtless, conscripted the three hundred thousand negroes which the law empowered him to call for. But there was not time. The House concurred in the Senate amendments on the 9th, by a vote of thirty-nine to twenty-seven, and the bill was promptly approved on March 13th. On the 15th, the Adjutant General's office gave authority to Majors J. W. Pegram and T. B. Turner, to raise a company or companies of negro volunteers at Richmond, and muster them into the service. These volunteers were called for under the several acts of the Confederate Congress and the Legislature of Virginia, and every man was called upon to constitute himself a recruiting officer. The rendezvous was established at Smith's factory, Twenty-first street, between Main and Carey streets. But this call was only made on the 10th of March, and Richmond was evacuated on April 2d, while Lee's surrender took place on the 9th. The Confederate Congress adjourned *sine die* on the 17th, and the last issue of the Richmond *Sentinel*, my authority in these matters, is dated April 1st, when Sheridan had already forced Lee's lines. Mr. Lincoln, apparently, did not think much of the impressment and enlisting of slaves. He said, in a speech made at Washington on the 17th of March, that the negro could not stay at home and make bread and fight at the same time, and he did not care much which duty was allotted to him by the Confederates. "We must now soon see the bottom of the rebels' resources."

We hear not much more of the negro enlistment question. The papers urge the importance of dispatch, patience, discipline. The Twenty-first street recruiting office apparently got on well, and another office was opened successfully in Lynchburg. A portion of the recruits of Messrs. Pegram and Turner went into camp on the north side about the 27th of March. The Lynchburg papers published a circular of citizens of Roanoke county, pledging themselves to emancipate such of their negroes of the military age as would volunteer to enlist, and, on the 28th, the Adjutant General's office at Richmond published its regulations in regard to negro enlistments. The provisions were merely formal, and did not vary from the regulation orders except in one particular: the negroes, as enlisted, were to be enrolled only in companies, under the control of the inspector general, as the government did not contemplate at that time the formation of either regiments or brigades of negroes.

The Confederate negro soldiers never went into action. On March 30th, 31st, and April 1st, the *Sentinel* reports the enemy "massed in heavy force on our right," cavalry skrmishes at Dinwiddie Court-House, heavy fighting on our right, tremendous artillery firing, pertinacious assaults upon Gordon, a great battle with no particulars, and then—the curtain descends for good and all, and there is no more Southern Confederacy, much less enlistment of negro volunteers and conscripts to do battle for it.

Would they have fought for it? If enlisted six months earlier would they have been able to turn the tide of defeat? Who knows? Who can tell? People have before now both fought and voted to enslave themselves—people are doing the same thing every day. It is, perhaps, fortunate that the negroes were not enlisted in time to prolong the long agony of the Southern Confederacy.

HOW JEFFERSON DAVIS WAS OVERTAKEN.

BY MAJOR GENERAL JAMES HARRISON WILSON.

ON the first Sunday of April, 1865, while seated in St. Paul's Church, in Richmond, Jefferson Davis received a telegram from Lee, announcing the fall of Petersburg, the partial destruction of his army, and the immediate necessity for flight. Although he could not have been entirely unprepared for this intelligence, it appears that he did not receive it with self-possession or dignity; but with tremulous and nervous haste, like a weak man in the hour of misfortune, he left the house of worship and hurried home, where he and his personal staff and servants spent the rest of the day in packing their personal baggage. At nightfall everything was in readiness; even the gold then remaining in the Treasury, not exceeding in all forty thousand dollars, was packed among the baggage,* and

---

* In a recent article Mr. Reagan says: "If it is meant by this statement simply that the money in the Treasury (gold and all) was taken, with the archives of public property, away from Richmond by the proper department officers, the statement is correct; but if it is meant by this insidious form of statement to be understood that this, or any other public money, was taken from Richmond in Mr. Davis' baggage, then the statement is wholly untrue."

I quote from the historian of "The Lost Cause" again in full (the italics are mine): "He nervously prepared at his house his private baggage, and he never ventured in the streets until, under cover of the night, he got, unobserved, on the train that was to convey him from Richmond. *He did not forget the gold in the Treasury; that, amounting to less than forty thousand dollars, it had been proposed some days before, in Congress, to distribute as largesses to the discontented soldiers; but Mr. Davis had insisted upon reserving it for exigencies, and it was now secured in his baggage.* He did not forget his sword. That, a costly present from some of his admirers in

under cover of darkness the President of the Confederacy, accompanied by three members of his Cabinet—Breckenridge, Benjamin, and Reagan—drove rapidly to the train which had been prepared to carry them from Richmond. This train, it is said, was the one which had carried provisions to Amelia Court-House for Lee's hard-pressed and hungry army; and, having been ordered to Richmond, had taken those supplies to that place, where they were abandoned for a more ignoble freight.* As a matter of course, the starving rebel soldiers suffered, but Davis succeeded in reaching Danville in safety, where he rapidly recovered from the fright he had sustained, and astonished his followers by a proclamation as bombastic and empty as his fortunes were straitened and desperate.†

England, had been sent to the Richmond armory for some repairs; it was abandoned to the fire there. The last seen of this relic of the Southern Confederacy was a twisted and gnarled stem of steel, on private exhibition in a lager beer saloon in Richmond, garnished with a certificate that it was what remained of Jeff Davis' sword, and that the curiosity might be purchased for two hundred dollars. Mr. Davis was accompanied at the first stage of his flight by some of his personal staff and three members of his Cabinet—General Breckenridge, Secretary of War; Mr. Benjamin, Secretary of State, and Mr. Reagan, Postmaster General. His wife was in North Carolina." (Pages 508 and 509.)

Just what the historian means by this extract I leave Mr. Reagan and Mr. Davis to reconcile with the facts. The declaration is explicit that Mr. Davis had insisted in reserving it (the gold) "for exigencies, and it was now secured in his baggage."

* This statement rests upon newspaper report, which I have not time to verify.

† In support of the substantial accuracy of this narrative, I quote from the "Life of Jefferson Davis, with a Secret History of the Southern Confederacy, Gathered Behind the Scenes in Richmond," by Edward A. Pollard, author of "The Lost Cause," etc., an octavo volume bearing the imprint of the National Publishing Company, 1869:

"In the morning of the 2d of April, General Lee saw his line broken at three points, at each of which a whole Federal corps had attacked, and all day long the enemy was closing on the works immediately enveloping Petersburg. But the work, decisive of the war, was done in two hours. At eleven o'clock in the morning General Lee wrote a dispatch to President Davis, at Richmond, advising him that the army could not hold its position, and that preparations should be made to evacuate the Capital at night. * * * No sound of the battle—not an echo, not a breath—had yet reached the doomed city. It was a lovely Sabbath day, and Richmond basked in its beauty and enjoyed more than usual remission from the cares of the week. (Page 487.)

"Ladies dressed in old finery, in which the fashions of many years were mingled, were satisfied to make a display at St. Paul's about equal to the holiday wardrobes in better days of the negroes at the African Church. At the former church worshiped Mr. Davis. He now sat stiff and alone in 'the President's pew,'—where no one outside his family had ever dared to intrude since Mrs. Davis had ordered the sexton to remove two ladies who had ventured there, and who, on turning their faces to the admonition to leave, delivered before the whole congregation, had proved, to the dismay and well-deserved mortification of the President's wife, to be the daughters of General Lee. * * * In the midst of the services a man walked noisily into the church, and handed the President a slip of paper. Mr. Davis read the paper, rose and walked out of the church without agitation, but his face and manner evidently constrained." (Page 488.)

Then follows a dramatic description of the tumultuous scene which took place during the day and evening in Richmond :

"A scene never to be forgotten in the memories of Richmond. The night was hoarse with the roar of the great fight. But where, in this dramatic and tumultuous scene, was President Davis? When he had received news of Lee's defeat he had slunk from his pew in St. Paul's Church, and while the fountains of his government were being broken up, and the great final catastrophe had mounted the stage, the principal actor was wanting; he, the President, the leader, the historical hero, had never shown his face, had never spoken a word, was satisfied to prepare secretly a sumptuous private baggage, and to fly from Richmond—a low, unnoticed fugitive— under cover of the night. In such scenes a great leader is naturally sought for by the love and solicitude of his people; there are words of noble farewell to his countrymen; there are touching souvenirs of parting with his officers. But there were none of these in Mr. Davis' case. * * * He did not show himself to the public, as a great leader might be expected to do in such a supreme calamity; he attempted no inspiration, comfort, or advice; hid in his house, busy only with his private preparations, inquired of by no one, without any mark of public solicitude for him, without the least notice from popular sympathy or anxiety, the unhappy, degraded President of the Southern Confederacy never showed his face in the last catastrophe of his Capital until he stole on the cars that were to bear him to a place of safety, and fled from the doomed city, unmarked among the meanest of its fugitives. He left no word of tender or noble farewell for Richmond, and the last souvenir of his power was an order to burn the city that for four years had given him shelter, countenance, and hospitality. * * * There was no last council of conference. All that there was of deliberative assembly—all that remained of the once proud and loquacious government of Jefferson Davis—was to appoint the rendezvous and time for flight, the Cabinet members being instructed to meet the President at the Danville depot a little before midnight." (See pages 491 and 492; also, second paragraph on page 508.)

After instituting a comparison between Jefferson Davis and Rienzi, the last of the Roman tribunes, in which he says: "They failed alike, from the same ignorance of government, the same ill distribution of obstinacies and weakness, haughty refusals in one instance and mean compliance in another, the same repulse of counselors, the same paltry intrigues of the closet and boudoir, the same contempt of fortune, presuming upon its favors as natural rights or irrevocable gifts," Mr. Pollard goes on to add:

" Rienzi, at another time, attempted to escape from his capital in the disguise of a baker. Jefferson Davis' effort to escape was perhaps not less mean in its last resources. But Rienzi did what the chief of the Southern Confederacy did not do; and at the last he was unwilling to leave his capital without at least the dignity of an adieu; without some words addressed to the people; without something of invocation not to be omitted in any extremity of despair, or to be forgotten in any haste of personal alarm. We have seen that Jefferson Davis fled from Richmond, without a word of public explanation, with none of that benediction or encouragement which a great leader is expected to impart to his people in such a catastrophe. He escaped with the ignominy of an obscure, mean fugitive, if not positively in the character of

It is stated, upon what appears to be good authority*, that Davis had, many weeks before Lee's catastrophe, made "the most careful and exacting preparations for his escape, discussing the matter fully with his Cabinet, in profound secrecy; and deciding that in order to secure the escape of himself and his principal officers, the 'Shenandoah' should be ordered to cruise off the coast of Florida, to take the fugitives on board." These orders were sent to the rebel cruiser many days before Lee's lines were broken. It was thought that the party might make an easy and deliberate escape in the way agreed upon, as the communications with the Florida coast were at that time scarcely doubtful, and once on the swift sailing "Shenandoah," the most valuable remnant of the Anglo-Confederate navy, "they

---

a deserter. Some explanation has been offered of his singular neglect on this occasion of those whom, in his day of power, he was accustomed, after the affectation of a fond and paternal ruler, to call 'his people,' in the statement that the government at Richmond had no expectation of Lee's disaster, and was thus painfully hurried in its evacuation of the Capital." (Page 504.)

* Mr. Reagan asserts, in an article recently published, that he does not believe "that any such a subject was considered or discussed by Mr. Davis or any member of his Cabinet, at any time before or after the surrender of General Lee." Traversing this statement, and the one that "the government at Richmond had no expectation of Lee's disaster, and was thus painfully hurried in its evacuation of its capital," Mr. Pollard says, in the work from which I am quoting: "The statement is untrue, and the excuse is unavailing. The writer well knows, what has not heretofore been imparted to public curiosity, that Jefferson Davis had, many weeks before Lee's catastrophe, *made the most careful and exacting preparations for his escape.* The matter had been fully consulted with his Cabinet, in profound secrecy; and it had been agreed that, to secure the escape of the President and his principal officers, the "Shenandoah" should be ordered to cruise off the coast of Florida, to take the distinguished fugitives on board, who had selected the coast for their exit from the Confederacy, and their extrication from its falling fortunes. These orders had been sent to the Confederate cruiser many days before Lee's lines were broken. It was calculated that in the last resource of the surrender of Lee's army, and of the neutralization of other organized forces of the Confederacy, the President's party might make an easy and deliberate escape in the way agreed upon, as the communications with the Florida coast were then scarcely doubtful, and once on the "Shenandoah," a fast sailer, the most valuable remnant of the Confederate navy, they might soon obtain an asylum on a foreign shore. Other preparations were made for the flight; all the papers of the government were revised and marked for destruction, abandonment or preservation, according to their contents; and even Mr. Davis' private baggage was put in order for transportation. Of course, the public knew nothing of these preparations, and it did not even suspect them." (Pages 504, 505, 506, and 507.) I do not undertake to decide as to whether Mr. Pollard or Mr. Reagan is more worthy of belief. My aim is merely to give the authority upon which I make the statements in this narrative. The declarations of Mr. Pollard are sufficiently explicit to justify me in their quotation.

might soon obtain an asylum on a foreign shore." When Davis
and his companions left Richmond in pursuance of this plan, they
believed that Lee could avoid surrender only a short time longer.
A few days thereafter the news of this expected calamity reached
them, when they turned their faces again toward the South.*

---

* In reference to the incidents which followed upon Mr. Davis' flight from
Goldsboro', North Carolina, I again quote from the historian of "The Lost Cause:"

"The resumption of Mr. Davis' flight toward the South was in consequence of
what had taken place in his interview with Generals Johnston and Beauregard. It was
an interview of inevitable embarrassment and pain. The two generals were those
who had experienced most of the prejudice and injustice of the President; he had
always felt aversion for them, and it would have been an almost impossible excess
of Christian magnanimity if they had not returned something of resentment and
coldness to the man who, they believed, had arrogantly domineered over them, and
more than once sought their ruin. We have seen how unceremoniously and cruelly
Johnston had been hustled off the stage of Atlanta. True, he had now been restored
to command; but under circumstances which made it no concession to the public
and no favor to him, for he was restored only to the conduct of a campaign that was
already lost, and put in command of a broken and disorganized force that Sherman
had already driven through two States. When, some time before, public sentiment
was demanding his return to service, he wrote bitterly that he was quite sure that
if the authorities at Richmond restored him to command, they were resolved not to
act toward him in good faith and with proper support, but to put him in circumstances where defeat was inevitable, and thus confirm to the populace the military
judgment of the President. He had no reason to thank Mr. Davis for his present
command in the forests of North Carolina, where the President had now come to
him to ask little less than a miracle at his hands. As for General Beauregard, his
painful relations with Mr. Davis had been public gossip ever since the battle of
Manassas. There had been, too, a recently unpleasantness, fresh in the minds of
both, on account of General Beauregard having evacuated Charleston against the
orders of the President, although what idea the latter could have had, within the
limits of sanity, in attempting to hold this city after Sherman's army had flanked it,
is difficult to imagine.

"These three men were now to meet to consult of the condition of the country,
and the occasion invoked that they should rise above personal feelings in the circumstances of a great public sorrow and anxiety. There was obtained for the interview
a mean room on the second floor of a house owned by a Confederate officer. Mr.
Davis sat cold, dignified, evidently braced for an unpleasant task. He spoke in a
musing, absent way, and it was remarked that, while speaking, he never looked
toward either commander, his eyes being amused by a strip of paper which he was
twisting in his hands. His heart must have beat with a great anxiety, for he must
have known how much depended on these generals countenancing his plans of continuing the war; and yet he spoke as one who had merely resolved to state his case,
and who cared not to influence the decision one way or the other. It was as if he
had said openly to his generals: 'If you decide to continue the war, to keep your
armies in the field, well and good; but understand, it is no obligation conferred
upon me, and I shall regard it as no concession to me.' And yet his heart secretly
hung on their replies, and beneath his cold exterior the practised eye might have
seen the deep under-play of the nerve, the flutter of the suppressed emotion.

Breckenridge, the Secretary of War, was sent to confer with Johnston, but found him only in time to assist in drawing up the terms of his celebrated capitulation to Sherman. The intelligence of this event caused the rebel chieftain to renew his flight, but while hurrying onward, some fatuity induced him to change his plans and to

---

" The President spoke at length. General Johnston sat at as great a distance from him as the room allowed. He was, evidently, impatient; he knew what was coming; he had anticipated all that the President said before he had come into the room, and he listened as one oppressed with the fulness and readiness of reply. Yet, when the President stopped speaking, he remained profoundly silent. 'General Johnston,' Mr. Davis said, 'we should like to now hear your views.' It was a reply that came with a bluntness and defiance that brought a sudden color to the cheeks of the President. 'Sir,' blurted out General Johnston, 'my views are, that our people are tired of war, feel themselves whipped, and will not fight!' In these few words he had said all that was necessary; and he spoke them suddenly, without preface. But he continued to speak in short, decisive, jerky sentences, as if in haste to deliver his mind. He suggested that the enemy's military power and resources were now greater than they had ever been. What could the President hope to oppose to them in the present demoralized condition of the South? 'My men,' he .said, 'are, daily, deserting in large numbers, and are taking my artillery teams to aid their escape to their homes. Since Lee's defeat, they regard the war as at an end. If I march out of North Carolina her people will all leave my ranks. It will be the same as I proceed south through South Carolina and Georgia, and I shall expect to retain no man beyond the by-road or cow-path that leads to his house. My small force is melting away like snow before the sun, and I am hopeless of recruiting it. We may, perhaps, obtain terms which we ought to accept.' A silence ensued. It was broken by the President saying, in a low, even tone: 'What do you say, General Beauregard?' 'I concur in all General Johnston has said,' he replied. There was another pause in the conversation, when, presently, General Johnston, as if regretting the cruel plainness of his remarks, and thinking he had wounded enough the unhappy President, who was still twisting, abstractedly, the piece of paper in his hands, proceeded to suggest, at some length, the hope of getting favorable terms from the enemy. He thought it would be legitimate, and according with military usage for him to open a correspondence with General Sherman, to see how far the generals in the field might go in arranging terms of peace. Mr. Davis could not but be sensible of the wisdom of this suggestion, although he listened coldly to it, and it was very little of consolation for the destruction of such towering and grotesque hopes as he had brought into the interview. General Breckenridge, who had been present at the whole of the interview, now ventured to advise that General Johnston should, at once, and on the spot, address a letter to Sherman to prepare an interview. 'No,' replied General Johnston—probably anxious to show a mark of deference to the President, out of pity for the mortification already inflicted upon him—'let the President dictate the letter.' The letter, proposing a suspension of hostilities, was dictated by the President. And thus, Mr. Davis himself virtually subscribed the token of submission of the Confederate army, second in importance and numbers to that of Lee, yet unwilling to go further in the sequel and to write gracefully his entire submission to the inevitable.

"On the 16th of April, the President, his staff and Cabinet left Greensboro'. It was a slow travel, in ambulances and on horseback, and the dejection of the party

adopt the alternative of trying to push through the Southwest toward the region which he fondly believed to be yet under the domination of Forrest, Taylor, and Kirby Smith, and within which he hoped to revive the desperate fortunes of the rebellion. He confided his hopes to Breckenridge, and when he reached Abbeville, South Caro-

---

was visible enough. Mr. Davis was the first to rally from it. When he and his companions had left Richmond, it was in the belief of the majority that Lee could avoid surrender but a few days longer, and with the intention, as we have already said, of making their way to the Florida coast, and embarking there for a foreign land. The President had clung, at Danville, to the hope that Lee might effect a retreat to Southwestern Virginia, and he had remained there long enough to see that hope disappointed. Again, when he had sought General Johnston's demoralized and inconsiderable army, it had been from a feeble diversion of hope that it might not yield to the example of Lee's surrender, and that, under the inspiration of the presence and the direct command of the President, it might be induced to keep the field. That expectation had been brought to a painful end, and it appeared as if the President would be recommitted now to the original design of fleeing the Confederacy, and would now make an earnest effort to escape. But his mind was disordered and undecided. It was distressing to see how he hesitated between assured safety in flight from the country, and the possible hope that the cause of the Confederacy might not be beyond redemption. Anyhow, there were no signs yet that he was pursued by the enemy, and he had appeared to consider himself sure of ultimately making good his escape after he had once got out of sight of Richmond. He had shown great trepidation in getting out of the Capital, but in the leisure of a journey, unmolested by pursuit, and entertained by the fresh air and pleasing sights of spring, he had time to recover, to some extent, his self-possession, and to cast about for something to be saved from the wreck of his hopes.

"In the meditations of his journey through North Carolina, the fugitive President, although anxious for his personal safety, appears to have conceived the alternative of venturing to the Southwest, within reach of the forces of Taylor and Forrest, in the hope of reviving the fortunes of the Confederacy within a limited territory. He suggested the alternative to General Breckenridge, as they traveled together, after the news of Johnston's surrender, but received only an evasive reply, the latter not sharing his hopes, but unwilling to mortify them by a candid declaration of opinion. Mr. Davis was remarkable for a sanguine temperament, but it was that which we observe in weak characters, 'hoping against hope,' fickle, flaring, extravagant, rather than that practical energy which renews itself on disaster, and conquers fortune. The vision he had conjured up of a limited Confederacy around the mouths of the Mississippi might have looked plausible upon paper, but it was fatally defective in omitting the moral condition of the South. The unhappy President had not yet perceived that he had lost the faculty of encouraging others, that the Southern people were in despair, and that wherever he might go he would find their countenances averted, their hopes abandoned, and their thoughts already committed to submission. But he was to realize very shortly how morally deserted and practically helpless he was. His first discovery of it was at Abbeville, South Carolina, where occured one of the most pathetic scenes in history, over which the tenderness and charity of some of the actors have been disposed to draw the curtain, committing its sorrows to secrecy.

lina, he called a council of war to deliberate upon the plans which he had conceived for regenerating what had now become in fact "The Lost Cause." This council was composed of Generals Breckenridge, Bragg, and the commanders of the cavalry force which was then escorting him. All united that it was hopeless to struggle

---

"Mr. Davis reached Abbeville on the 1st of May. So far he had been accompanied by the fragments of five brigades, amounting in number to less than one thousand men, and reorganized into two battalions, at the front and in the rear of the long train which signaled his flight and foolishly obstructed his effort at escape. There were already painful evidences of the demoralization of the escort, and the story told almost at every mile, by stragglers from Johnston's command, was not calculated to inspire them. At Abbeville, Mr. Davis resolved upon a council of war. It was composed of the five brigade commanders, and General Braxton Bragg (for the year past the 'military adviser' of the President) was admitted to the last scene of the deliberations of the lost cause.

"In the council Mr. Davis spoke with more than his accustomed facility and earnestness, inspired by hope, but without volubility or extravagance. He made a statement of surpassing plausibility. The South, he declared, was suffering from a panic; it yet had resources to continue the war; it was for those who remained with arms in their hands to give an example to reanimate others; such an act of devotion, beside being the most sublime thing in history, might yet save the country, and erect again its declining resolution.

"'It is but necessary,' he said, 'that the brave men yet with me should renew their determination to continue the war; they will be a nucleus for rapid reinforcements and will raise the signal of reanimation for the whole country.' No one of the council answered him at length; the replies of the commanders were almost sunk to whispers; the scene was becoming painful, and it was at last agreed that each in his turn should announce his decision. Each answered slowly, reluctantly, in the negative. The only words added were that, though they considered the war hopeless, they would not disband their men until they had guarded the President to a place of safety. 'No,' exclaimed Mr. Davis, passionately, 'I will listen now to no proposition for my safety. I appeal to you for the cause of the country.' Again he urged the commanders to accept his views.

"'We were silent,' says General Basil Duke, one of the council, 'for we could not agree with him, and we respected him too much to reply.'

"Mr. Davis yet stood erect, raised his hands to his head, as if in pain, and suddenly exclaiming, 'All hope is gone!' added haughtily, 'I see that the friends of the South are prepared to consent to her degradation;' and then, sweeping the company with a proud and despairing glance, he attempted to pass from the room. But the blow was too much for his feeble organization. His face was white with anger and disappointment, and the mist of unshed tears was in his eyes—tears which pride struggled to keep back. The sentiment that all was lost went through his heart like the slow and measured thrust of a sword ; as the wound sunk into it it left him speechless; loose and tottering, he would have fallen to the floor, had not General Breckenridge ended the scene by leading him faltering from the room. In a dead and oppressive silence the deserted leader, the fallen chief, secured a decent retreat for agonies which tears only could relieve.

"It was the last council of the Confederacy. The hateful selfishness which originates in the attempt of each individual to extricate himself from a common

36

longer, but they added that they would not disband their men till they had guarded their chieftain to a place of safety.   This was the

---

misfortune soon broke out, no longer restrained by the presence of the President. The soldiers were discharged, but they clamored that they had no money to take them home.   What of the Treasury gold that remained was divided among them. So fearful were they of marauders that many buried their coin in the woods and in unfrequented places.   With the disbandment of the troops Mr. Benjamin suggested a separation of the Cabinet officers from the President, making an excuse that so large a party would advertise their flight and increase the chances of capture.   Mr. Davis was left to make his way to Georgia, Postmaster General Reagan continuing to journey with him, and General Breckenridge only to a point where he thought it convenient to leave for Florida.   There were also in the party two or three of his staff officers and a few straggling soldiers, who still kept up some show of an escort. Mrs. Davis had already preceded her husband to Georgia, and he now traveled slowly, and almost desolately, on horseback, having arranged that she should await him in the town of Washington.

"From this place the now hunted President was soon driven again on his journey by news of the occupation of Augusta.   He had also received news of the assassination of President Lincoln, and that event, he declared, confirmed his resolution not to leave the country.   He inferred from the newspapers that he was accused as an accomplice in the crime, and he remarked to one of his staff officers that he 'would prefer death to the dishonor of leaving the country under such an imputation.'   But with such a sentiment, it will occur to the reader that it would have been noble and decorous for Mr. Davis to have surrendered himself at the nearest Federal post and to have demanded a trial.   It would have placed him in a grand and winning attitude, one becoming a great man, one honorable to himself and the South, and redeeming him more than anything else in the eyes of the world. But, unfortunately, he accepted the base alternative of continuing his flight, *and that, too, with the artifice of a mean disguise.*

"On continuing his journey, accompanied by his wife, whom he had overtaken at Washington, it was determined that the President and his friends should thereafter travel as an emigrant party.   Mr. Reagan was still in his company.   General Breckenridge had left outside the town of Washington, taking with him forty-five Kentucky soldiers, a straggling remnant of Morgan's Brigade.   Ten mounted men had offered to escort Mrs. Davis, and although they had accepted their paroles, justly considered that they might protect a distressed lady from marauders.   All tokens of the President's importance, in dress and air, were left aside; a covered wagon, pack-mule, and cooking utensils, were provided at Washington; and it was designed that Mr. Davis, his wife, and his wife's sister, should pass as a simple country family, emigrating from Georgia, and having fallen in with straggling soldiers for their protection.   Mr. Davis' dignity was laid aside without much difficulty.   Carlisle said: 'A king in the midst of his body-guard, with all his trumpets, war-horses, and gilt standard-bearers, will look great, though he be little; but only some Roman Carus can give audience to satrap ambassadors while seated on the ground, with a woolen cap, and supping on boiled peas, like a common soldier.' Mr. Davis, in the dress of a country farmer, had none of these traces of imperialism which cling to those 'born to purple.'   His features, just and handsome, without being remarkable, were those which might command by assumed airs, or might be practiced to particular expressions, but scarcely those which could assert superiority without an effort and at a glance.   He incurred but little chance of detection in the dress he had assumed of an honest, well-to-do emigrant."

last council of the Confederacy. Davis, who had hitherto commanded with all the rigor of an autocrat, found himself powerless and deserted. From this day forth he was little better than a fugitive, for although his escort gave him and his wagon train nominal company and protection till he had reached the village of Washington, just within the northeastern boundary of Georgia, they had long since learned the hopelessness of further resistance, and now began to despair even of successful flight. A division of National cavalry, under Stoneman, and a brigade under Palmer, had already burst from the mountains of North Carolina, and were in hot pursuit; while rumors reached him of another mounted force, sweeping destructively through Alabama and Georgia, cutting off, by its wide extended march, the only route to the trans-Mississippi and the far Southwest.

In order that we may properly understand the difficulties which were now rapidly encompassing Davis, and which ultimately led to his capture, let us leave him at Little Washington and consider the movements of the force then marching through Alabama and Georgia. It consisted of three divisions of cavalry, each nearly five thousand strong, an aggregate of nearly fifteen thousand men, all splendidly mounted, armed, and equipped, and, what was better still, inspired by the belief that they were invincible. It will be remembered that after the capture of Selma, on April 2d (which took place at nightfall of the very Sunday that Davis fled from Richmond), and the passage of the victorious cavalry to the south side of the Alabama, their march was directed to the eastward by the way of Montgomery, Columbus, West Point, and Macon; while a detached brigade, under Croxton, moved rapidly in the same direction, by a more northern route, through Jasper, Talladega, and La Grange. The limits of this sketch forbid a detailed narrative of how these gallant troopers captured the last stronghold of the Confederacy, pausing in their march to raise the National flag over the first rebel capitol; how the astonished rebel ladies at the beautiful village of Tuskegee bedecked their horses with flowers as a reward for perfect discipline and good behavior; how they spared one printing press, claimed by a strong-mined woman, upon the condition that "she and her descendants, unto the fourth generation, should permit nothing but Bibles, Testaments, and school books to be printed upon it," and destroyed another, which had fled from them already through four States; or how two of Iowa's most gallant soldiers, Winslow and Noble, led by the intrepid General Upton, under the cover of darkness, broken only by the incessant flash of fifty-two cannons, carried the works which covered the bridges across the Chattahoochee river at Columbus. A thousand incidents of daring and hardihood and a thousand scenes of exciting incident might be described. The flash and roar of artillery, the terrible crash of the breech-loading carbines, the headlong charge and shout of armed men, the neighing of war-horses, the wild excitement of victory, the confusion of night fighting, the burning of military stores and store-houses, the building of bridges, the passage of rivers in the light of burning cotton bales and gin-houses, and last, though not least, the appealing faces of the colored people, who hailed the advancing Union cavalry with transports of delight, and whose eyes were blinded with tears as the hurrying squadrons passed into the darkness, not heeding their prayer to be led out of the land of bondage, all conspire to make this one of the most exciting campaigns of the entire war.

On the evening of the 11th day of April, while the cavalry corps was marching from Selma to Montgomery, an officer of the advance guard sent in copies of the Montgomery papers of the 6th and 7th, containing brief accounts of the operations of General Grant about Petersburg, and from which, making allowance for rebel suppressions, it was supposed the Army of the Potomac had gained a decisive victory. It was stated that Davis and the rebel government had already gone to Danville, but that their cause was not yet lost. On the 14th and 15th information was received confirmatory of Lee's defeat, and the evacuation of Richmond. It was also reported that Grant was pressing the rebel army back upon Lynchburg. From these facts, together with the many rumors from all quarters, indicative of unusual excitement among the rebels, there was little room to doubt that they had met with a great disaster in Virginia; but, as a matter of course, no definite or reliable information as to the extent of the disaster or the probable course that would be adopted by the rebel government could obtained. It was assumed, however, that the rebel leaders would either endeavor to concentrate the remnant of their forces in North Carolina, and make further head against our armies, or that they would disband and endeavor to save themselves by flight. In either case it was clearly our duty to close in upon them by the line upon which we were moving, with the greatest possible rapidity, so as to join in the final and decisive struggle, assist in sweeping up the fragments of the wreck, and capture such important persons as might seek safety in flight. Accordingly our march from Montgomery to Macon, a distance of two hundred and thirty-five miles, including the passage of the Chattahoochee and Flint rivers, and the capture of the two fortified towns of Columbus and West Point, was made in less than six days. In order to cover the widest possible front of operations, and to obtain such information in regard to hostile movements as might enable us to act advisedly, detachments were sent off to the right and left of the main column, scouting in all directions. At Macon, we were arrested by the armistice concluded between Generals Sherman and Johnston, though not till after the city had fallen into our possession.

During my conference with Generals Cobb and G. W. Smith, on the evening of the 20th of April, I received conclusive information in regard to Lee's surrender, and the course of events in Virginia. The commanding officer of our advanced guard, moving rapidly, had taken possession of this place, and after securing his prisoners, had confined the generals in a building occupied by them as headquarters. On my arrival, late at night, at the place where the leading officers were confined, General Cobb protested in the strongest manner against his capture, claiming the protection of the alleged armistice. For reasons not necessary to recapitulate here, I declined to entertain this protest, and decided to hold him and his command as prisoners of war; but remarked, "If an armistice is in force, there must be some reason for it, and I can imagine none which will justify it except the capture or destruction of Lee's army." This remark drawing out no reply, I asked squarely if Lee had surrendered. Cobb still declined to answer, whereupon I turned to G. W. Smith, a graduate of West Point, and formerly in the regular army, and repeated the question, remarking that my future course would depend materially upon his reply. Smith also hesitated, but seeing that it was wiser to be frank, he acknowledged that Lee's army had been defeated and compelled to surrender. I replied at once, "If that is the case, every man killed hereafter is a man murdered," adding, "I shall govern my command in accordance with this principle, and shall wait here a reasonable time for specific orders from General Sherman." General Cobb, in a subsequent conversation with me, remarked that the relations established at West Point seemed to be like those of Free Masonry, adding, "When you asked me if Lee had surrendered, I stood silent, and no consideration could have induced me to confirm your suspicions in reference to that matter; but when you turned to General Smith with the same question, he answered frankly and without hesitation, telling you the whole truth as clearly and without equivocation as if he had been under oath." It must be remembered, however, that Cobb was a politician and the other a soldier.

The situation of my command was peculiar. Originally organized as a corps under General Sherman, the commanding general of the Military Division of the Mississippi, and not having been transferred, it still formed a legitimate part of his command, wherever he might be. It will be remembered that General Sherman, with the main body of his army, was at that time in North Carolina, moving northward. Before leaving North Alabama, he had instructed me to report, with my entire corps, except Kilpatrick's Division, to Major General George H. Thomas, to assist in the operations against Hood.* It was the intention of General Sherman, however, as developed in frequent conversations with me while lying at Gaylesville, Alabama, in October, 1864, that as soon as Hood could be disposed of, and the cavalry could be reorganized and remounted, I should gather together every man and horse that could be made fit for service, and march through the richer parts of Alabama and Georgia, for the purpose of destroying the railroad communications and supplies of the rebels, and bringing my force into the theatre of operations, toward which all of our great armies were then moving. In the campaign terminating at Macon, I had actually started under the direct instructions of General Thomas, but with the "amplest latitude of an independent commander," transmitted through him from General Grant, the commander-in-chief. I found myself cut off from all communication with these generals, but liable to receive orders from either or all of them, and from the Secretary of War in addition. My paramount duty was clearly to take care of the public interests first, and to reconcile orders afterward, should they come in conflicting terms from different directions.

In anticipation of a final break up of the rebel forces, we had already determined to keep a sharp look out for Davis and the leading authorities. As soon as I became satisfied, by information received by telegraph, in a short time, from General Sherman, that he had actually concluded an armistice, and intended it to apply to my command, I felt bound to observe it, but only upon condition that the rebels should also comply with its provisions in equal good faith, or that I should not be ordered by higher authority to disregard it. One of its provisions was that neither party should make any change in the station of troops during the continuance of the armistice. My command, therefore, remained in camp, but was kept on the alert, ready to move in any direction. Having heard from citizens, however, that Davis, instead of observing the armistice, was making his way toward the South with an escort, I took possession of the railroads, and sent scouts in all directions, in order that I might receive timely notice of his movements. The armistice was declared null and void by the Secretary of War; but, at least one day before I had been advised of this, through General Thomas, I received from General Sherman a dispatch, in cipher, informing me of the formal termination of hostilities by the surrender of General Johnston, and all the forces under his command east of the Chatta-hoochee. This was on the 27th of April. Immediately afterward, I disposed of my troops for the purpose of taking possession of the important points in Georgia, and paroling the rebel prisoners, who might have to pass through them in order to reach their homes. I felt certain, from what I could learn, that Davis and his Cabinet would endeavor to escape to the west side of the Mississippi river, notwithstanding the armistice and capitulation; and, therefore, gave instructions to the different detachments of the corps to look out for and capture him, and all other persons of rank or authority with whom they might come in contact.

On the 28th of April, General Upton was ordered, with a detachment of his division, to proceed by rail to Augusta, while the rest of the division, under General Winslow, was ordered to march by the most direct route to Atlanta, a regiment under Colonel Eggleston having been sent by rail to that place immediately after the receipt of the telegram just mentioned from General Sherman. General E. M. McCook, with a detachment of seven hundred men, was directed to proceed by rail to Albany, Georgia, and march thence by the most direct route to Tallahassee, Florida, while General Croxton, with the remainder of this division, was held at Macon, with orders issued subsequently to watch the line of the Ocmulgee river from the mouth of Yellow creek to Macon. General Minty, commanding the Second Division—General Long having been wounded at Selma—was directed, about the same time, to send detachments to Cuthbert and Eufaula, and to watch the line of the Ocmulgee, from the right of the First Division to Abbeville, and as much of the Flint and Chattahoochee, to the rear, as practicable. The ostensible object of this disposition of troops was to secure prisoners and military stores, and to take possession of the important strategic points and lines of communication; but the different commanders were directed to keep a vigilant watch for Davis and other members of the rebel government.

The first direct information of Davis' movements reached me on the 23d of April, from a citizen, now a prominent lawyer and politician in Georgia, who had seen him at Charlotte, North Carolina, only three or four days before, and had learned that he was on his way, with a train and an escort of cavalry, to the South, intending, as was then understood, to go to the Trans-Mississippi Department.

This information was regarded as entirely trustworthy, and hence the officers in charge of the different detachments afterward sent out were directed to dispose of their commands so as to have all roads and crossings vigilantly watched. It was thought, at first, that Davis would call about him a select force, and endeavor to escape by marching to the westward through the hilly country of Northern Georgia. To prevent this, Colonel Eggleston was directed to watch the country in all directions from Atlanta. General A. J. Alexander, with the Second Brigade of Upton's Division, was directed by General Winslow to scout the country to the northward as far as Dalton, or until he should meet the troops under General Steedman operating in that region. Beginning his march from Macon, General Alexander, at his own request, was authorized to detach an officer and twenty picked men, disguised as rebel soldiers, for the purpose of obtaining definite information of Davis' movements. This party was placed under the command of Lieutenant Joseph O. Yoeman, First Ohio Cavalry, and at the time acting inspector of the brigade. Verbal instructions were also given to other brigade and division commanders to make similar detachments. General Croxton was directed to send a small party toward Talladega, by the route upon which he had marched from that place; while Colonel Eggleston was directed to send another party by rail to West Point. By these means it was believed that all considerable detachments of rebels would be apprehended, and that such information might be obtained as would enable us to secure the principal rebel leaders, if they should undertake to pass through the country under military escort.

It is, perhaps, proper to state, that in declaring the armistice of Sherman void, the Secretary of War had directed that my command should resume active operations and endeavor to arrest the fugitive rebel chiefs. He sent numerous telegrams urging the greatest possible exertions, but as we had already anticipated orders, and disposed of our forces to the best possible advantage, there was nothing left but to notify him of what we had done, and to assure him that unless Davis should undertake to escape as an individual fugitive, we had no doubt of securing him. After a rapid march toward the upper crossings of the Savannah river, in Northeastern Georgia, Yoeman with his detachment, looking as much like rebels as the rebels themselves, joined Davis' party escorted by five small brigades of cavalry, and continued with them several days, watching for an opportunity to seize and carry off the rebel chief; but this daring purpose was frustrated by the vigilance of the rebel escort. At

Washington, Georgia, the rebel authorities heard that Atlanta was occupied by our troops, and that they could not pass that point without a fight. They halted, and for a short time acted with irresolution in regard to their future course. The cavalry force which had remained true to Davis, probably numbering two thousand men, now became mutinous and declined to go any further. They were disbanded and partially paid off in coin which had been brought to that point in wagons. Lieutenant Yoeman lost sight of Davis at this time, but dividing his party into three or four detachments, sought again to obtain definite information of the fallen chieftain's movements, but for twenty-four hours was unsuccessful. Persevering in his efforts, however, he became convinced that Davis had relinquished his idea of going into Alabama, and would probably try to reach the Gulf or South Atlantic coast, and escape by sea. This was a correct conclusion, and, as has been shown, was the identical plan adopted before leaving Richmond. Relying upon his judgment, Yoeman sent couriers with this information to General Alexander, and by him it was duly transmitted to me at Macon. The same conclusion had already been forced upon me by information derived from various other sources. With railroad communication through most of Northern Georgia, and with a division of four thousand National cavalry operating about Atlanta, it would have been next to impossible for a party of fugitives, however small, to traverse that region by the ordinary roads; and from the nature of the case this must have been clear, even to Davis. After carefully considering all the circumstances, I, therefore, became convinced that he would either flee in disguise, unattended, or endeavor to work his way southward into Florida. With the view of frustrating this plan, I now directed all the crossings of the Ocmulgee river, from Atlanta to Hawkinsville, to be watched with renewed vigilance.

On the evening of May 6th, having received the intelligence sent in by Yoeman, I directed General Croxton to select the best regiment in his division and to send it under its best officer, with orders to march eastward, by the way of Jeffersonville, to Dublin, on the Oconee river, with the greatest possible speed, scouting the country well to the northward, and leaving detachments at the most important cross-roads, with instructions to keep a sharp look out for all detachments of rebels. By these means it was hoped that Davis' line of march would be intercepted and his movements discovered, in which event the commanding officer was instructed to follow it, wherever it might lead, until the fugitives should be overtaken and captured. General Croxton selected for this purpose the First Wisconsin Cavalry, commanded by Lieutenant Colonel Henry Harnden, an officer of age, experience, and resolution. During that day and the next, the conviction that Davis would try to escape into Florida became so strong, that I sent for General Minty, commanding the Second Division, and directed him also to select his best regiment, and order it to march without delay to the southeastward along the northern bank of the Ocmulgee river, watching all the crossings between Hawkinsville and the mouth of the Ohoopee river. In case of discovering the trail of the fugitives, they were directed to follow it to the Gulf coast, or till they should overtake and capture the party of whom they were in pursuit. General Minty selected his own regiment, the Fourth Michigan Cavalry, commanded by Lieutenant Colonel Pritchard, an excellent and spirited officer. In the meantime, General Upton, at Augusta, had sent me a dispatch advising me to offer a reward of one hundred thousand dollars for the capture of Davis, urging that the Secretary of War would approve my action, and that it would induce even the rebels to assist in making the capture. Not caring, however, to assume the responsibility of committing the government in this way, I authorized him to issue a proclamation offering a reward of one hundred thousand dollars to be paid out of such money as might be found in the possession of Davis or his party. This was done, and copies scattered throughout the country as early as the 6th of May.

As soon as it was known at Atlanta that Davis' cavalry escort had disbanded, General Alexander, with five hundred picked men and horses, of his command, crossed to the right or northern bank of the Chattahoochee river, occupied all the fords west of the Atlanta and Chattanooga Railroad, watched the passes of the Altoona mountains, and the main crossings of the Etowah river, and with various detachments of his small command patrolled the principal roads in that region day and night, until he received news of Davis' capture in another quarter. The final disposition of our forces may be described as follows: General Upton, with parts of two regiments, occupied Augusta, and kept a vigilant watch over the country in that vicinity, informing me by telegraph of everything important which came under his observation. General Winslow, with the larger part of Upton's Division, occupied Atlanta, and scouted the country in all directions from that place. General Alexander, with five hundred picked men, patrolled the country north of the Chattahoochee, while detachments occupied Griffin and Jonesboro', closely watching the crossing of the Ocmulgee, and scouting the country to the eastward. Colonel Eggleston, commanding the post of Atlanta, had also sent a detachment to West Point, to watch the Alabama line in that quarter. General Croxton, with the main body of the First Division, in reserve near Macon, had sent a detachment to the mountain region of Alabama, marching by the way of Carrolton to Talladega, another through Northeastern Georgia toward North Carolina, and was also engaged in watching the Ocmulgee from the right of Upton's Division to Macon, and in scouting the country to his front and rear. General Minty, commanding the Second Division, with the main body well in hand, also near Macon, was scouting the country to the southeast, watching the lower crossings of the Ocmulgee, and had small parties at all the important points on the Southwestern Railroad, and in Western and Southwestern Georgia. Detachments of the Seventh Pennsylvania Cavalry occupied Cuthbert, Eufaula, Columbus and Bainbridge, and kept a vigilant watch over the lower Flint and Chattahoochee, while General McCook, with a detachment of his division at Albany, and seven hundred men between there and Tallahassee, Florida, was scouting the country to the north and eastward. We also had rail and telegraphic communication from my headquarters at Macon with Atlanta, Augusta, West Point, Milledgeville, Albany and Eufaula, and, finally, Palmer, in hot haste, was approaching the line of the Savannah from South Carolina with one brigade. By inspecting the map for a moment it will be seen that our troops, amounting to fifteen thousand horsemen, were occupying a well defined and almost continuous line from Kingston, Georgia, to Tallahassee, Florida, with detachments and scouts well out in all directions to the front and rear. With vigilance on the part of the troops, it is difficult to perceive how Davis and his party could possibly have hoped to escape. From the time they were reported at Charlotte till their capture, we were kept informed of their general movements, and were enabled thereby to dispose of our forces in such a manner as to render the capture morally certain. Rumors came in from all directions, but by carefully weighing them the truth became sufficiently manifest to enable us to act with confidence. The rebels at that time had ceased to care for Davis, and, in the hope that he would prove to be an acceptable offering for their own sins, they seemed to be not unwilling that he should be caught.

In pursuance of his instructions, Lieutenant Colonel Harnden, with three officers and one hundred and fifty men of the First Wisconsin Cavalry, left Macon, Georgia, on the evening of May 6th, 1865, and marched rapidly during the whole night, by way of Jeffersonville, toward Dublin, on the Oconee river. At Jeffersonville, Colonel Harnden left one officer and thirty men, with orders to scout the country in all directions for reliable information in regard to the route which Davis had taken. With the remainder of his small command, he continued the march till the next evening, reaching Dublin at about seven o'clock. During the night and day he had sent out scouts and small parties on all the side roads, in the hope of finding the trail of the party for whom he was looking; but nothing of importance occurred until after he had bivouacked for the night. The white inhabitants of Dublin expressed entire ignorance and indifference in regard to the movement of important rebels, but were unusually profuse in their offers of hospitality to Colonel Harnden. This being a trait in Southern character which the Colonel had never seen manifested so decidedly before, its exhibition at that time and place aroused his suspicions, and they were strengthened by the unusual commotion among the colored people. He, therefore, declined all offers of hospitality, and bivouacked with his command in the outskirts of the village, taking precautionary measures to ascertain, if possible, what strange thing had happened in that vicinity. Although he displayed great tact and vigilance, he gained no valuable intelligence till about midnight, at which time he was aroused by a negro man, who had stolen secretly, at that late hour, to his camp, for the purpose of telling him that Davis, with his wife and family, had passed through Dublin that day, going south, on the river road. The negro reported that he had assisted the party in question to cross from the east to the west side of the river, that they had eight wagons with them, and that another party, without wagons, had gone southward on the other side of the Oconee river. His information seems to have been of the most explicit and circumstantial character. He had heard the lady called "Mrs. Davis," and a gentleman, riding a "spirited bay horse," spoken of as "President Davis," adding that "Mr. Davis" had not crossed the river at the regular ferry with the rest of the party, but had gone about three miles lower down, and crossed on a small flatboat, and rejoined the party with the wagons near the outskirts of the town, and that they had all gone toward the south together. This colored man had evidently made careful and discreet observation of all that took place, and told his story so circumstantially that Colonel Harnden could not help believing it. The ferryman was called up, and examined, but, either through stupidity or design, succeeded in withholding whatever he knew in regard to the case.

But, in view of the facts already elicited, after detailing Lieutenant Lane and sixty men to remain at Dublin, and to scout the country in all directions, particularly toward the sea-coast, Colonel Harnden and the rest of his party, not exceeding, in all, seventy-five men, took to horse, at an early hour in the morning, and began the pursuit of the party just mentioned. Five miles south of Dublin, he obtained information, from a woman of the country, living in a cabin by the roadside, which left him no room to doubt that he was on the track of Davis in person. He dispatched a messenger to inform General Croxton of his good fortune, and pushed rapidly in pursuit; but the courier lost his way, and did not succeed in reaching Macon till some time after the news of Davis' capture had been received. The trail on which the fugitives were traveling led southward through an almost trackless region of pine forests, intersected by swamps and sluggish streams, with here and there, at rare intervals, the cabin of a family of "poor white folks" or fugitive negroes, and, therefore, affording but little food for either man or beast. The rain began to fall toward noon, and, as there was no road entitled to the name, the tracks of the wagon wheels upon the sandy soil were soon obliterated; but, after a long search, a citizen was impressed, and compelled to act as guide till the trail was again discovered. The pursuit was continued with renewed vigor; but, as the wagon tracks were again lost in the swamps of Alligator creek, the pursuing party were again delayed till another unwilling citizen could be found to guide them to the path upon which the trail was again visible. Colonel Harnden reports this day to have been one of great toil to both men and horses, as they had marched forty miles through an almost unbroken forest, most of the time under a beating rain, or in the water up to their saddle girths. They bivouacked, after dark, on the borders of a dark and gloomy swamp, and sleeping on the ground, without tents, during the night, they were again drenched with rain.

Before daylight of the 9th, they renewed their march, their route leading almost southwest through swamp and wilderness to Brown's ferry, where they crossed to the south side of the Ocmulgee river. The bed of the river was too treacherous and its banks too steep to permit the crossing to be made by swimming, which would have been most expeditious, so the impatient colonel had to use the ferry-boat; and, in his hurry to ferry his command over rapidly, the boat was overloaded, and a plank near the bow sprung loose, causing the boat to leak badly. No means were at hand with which to make repairs, and hence lighter boat loads had to be carried. This prolonged the crossing nearly two hours. During this delay, Colonel

Harnden learned from the ferryman that the party he was pursuing had crossed about one o'clock that morning, and were only a few hours ahead of him on the road leading to Irwinsville. He also learned from the ferryman several facts apparently trivial in themselves, but which, taken with what he already knew, were strongly confirmatory of the belief that he was on the right track. At Abbeville, a village of three families, he halted to feed, and just as he was renewing his march he met the advance guard of the Fourth Michigan Cavalry, Lieutenant Colonel Pritchard commanding, moving southeasterly on the road from Hawkinsville. Ordering his detachment to continue its march, Colonel Harnden rode to meet Colonel Pritchard, and after recounting his orders, gave him such information in regard to Davis' movements as he had been able to gather. This was about three o'clock in the afternoon. After a conversation between these officers, the precise details of which are variously reported, they separated, Colonel Harnden to rejoin his command, already an hour or more in advance, and Colonel Pritchard continuing his march along the south side of the Ocmulgee. It will be remembered that Colonel Pritchard began his march from the vicinity of Macon, on the evening of May 7th, under verbal orders given him by General Minty, in pursuance of instructions from corps headquarters. His attention was particularly directed to the crossings of the Ocmulgee river, between Hawkinsville and Jacksonville, near the mouth of the Ohoopee, with the object of intercepting Davis and such other rebel chiefs as might be making their way out of the country by the roads in that region. He had, however, not gone more than three miles from Abbeville before he obtained from a negro man (perhaps the same one which Harnden had met previously) such additional information in regard to the party as convinced him that it was his duty to join in the pursuit. In this he was clearly right, and had he done otherwise would have been censurable for negligence and want of enterprise. Colonel Harnden having informed him that he had force enough to cope with Davis, Colonel Pritchard determined to march by a more circuitous route toward Irwinsville. Why he did not send a courier on the trail pursued by Colonel Harnden, to notify the latter of his newly-formed plan, has not been explained. This would probably have prevented the collision which afterward occurred between his regiment and that of Colonel Harnden, and would not have rendered the capture of Davis less certain. No reflection upon the conduct of Colonel Pritchard is intended by this remark, for it is believed that this omission was simply an oversight, which might have occurred to any confident and zealous officer in the heat and anxiety of the hour.

In carrying out the plan which he had adopted, Colonel Pritchard selected from his regiment seven officers and one hundred and twenty-eight men, his object being to get his very best troopers and fleetest horses, and at four o'clock began the pursuit, leaving the remainder of his regiment under command of Captain Hathaway, with orders to picket the river and scout the country in accordance with previous instructions. The route pursued by Colonel Pritchard led down the river southeasterly nearly twelve miles to a point opposite Wilcox's mill, and thence southwest for a distance of eighteen miles, through an unbroken forest to Irwinsville, the county seat of Irwin county. He reached the village at one A. M. of the 10th, and after causing great excitement among the women, by representing his command as the rear guard of Davis' party, he succeeded in restoring quiet, and learned that the party he was searching for had encamped that night at dusk about a mile and a half north of the village, on the Abbeville road. Having secured a negro guide, he turned the head of his column northward, and, after moving cautiously to within a half mile of the camp, halted his main body and dismounted twenty-five men under Lieutenant Purinton. This party was directed to move noiselessly through the woods to the north side of the camp, for the purpose of gaining a position in its rear, and preventing the possibility of escape; also, in the hope that it might possibly interpose itself between Davis and his escort. In case of discovery by the enemy Lieutenant Purinton was directed to begin the attack from wherever he might be, while Colonel Pritchard would charge upon the camp along the main road. Purinton having reached the point assigned him without giving an alarm, the attack was delayed till the first appearance of dawn, at which time Colonel Pritchard put his troops again in motion, and continued his march to within a few rods of the camp undiscovered. Having assured himself of his position, he dashed upon the camp without further delay, and in a few moments had secured its occupants and effects, and placed a guard of mounted men around the camp, with dismounted sentries at the tents and wagons. No resistance was offered, because the enemy, in fancied security, had posted no sentries, and were, therefore, taken in their beds completely by surprise.

Almost simultaneously with the dash of Colonel Pritchard and his detachment, but before the prisoners had been actually secured, sharp firing began in the direction of Abbeville, and only a short distance from the camp. This turned out to be an engagement between a party under Lieutenant Purinton and the detachment of the First Wisconsin Cavalry, under Colonel Harnden, who, it seems, had followed the rebel trail the night before till it was no longer distinguishable in the dark, had gone into camp only two or three miles behind the party he had been pursuing so long, and had renewed the pursuit in the morning as soon as he could see to march. Both Colonel Pritchard and Colonel Harnden were informed that Davis had been reported as having with him a well-armed body-guard, variously estimated at from ten to fifty picked men. Supposing from this that he had determined to sell his life dearly, they expected and were prepared for desperate resistance. The sergeant in command of Harnden's advanced guard had orders to move rapidly, and as soon as he discovered the enemy to wheel about and give notice to the colonel, following closely behind. The sergeant had not gone more than two miles when he was challenged by an unknown party, found across the road a short distance ahead ; obeying orders literally, he wheeled about without answering the challenge and notified Colonel Harnden, who at once pressed forward with his troopers divided into two detachments, one on the road and the other moving through the forest. In the collision which occurred the men of both regiments seemed inspired by the greatest courage and determination, but the Michigan men, being outnumbered, were pressed back rapidly. Owing to the darkness it was several minutes before either party discovered that they were fighting friends instead of the enemy. The discovery was finally made by the capture or surrender of one of the Michigan men. In this unfortunate affair two men of the Fourth Michigan were killed, and one officer wounded, while three men of the First Wisconsin were severely and several slightly wounded. It is difficult, under the circumstances as detailed, to perceive how this accident could have been avoided. Colonel Harnden certainly had no means of knowing and no reason to suspect that the party whom he found in his front were any other than the rebels he had been pursuing, while Colonel Pritchard claims, and no doubt justly, that he had cautioned Lieutenant Purinton particularly to keep a sharp look out for the First Wisconsin, which he knew would approach from that direction. The hurry with which the corps was subsequently mustered out of service, and the absence of the principal officers, prevented an investigation of the details of this affair, and the circumstances which led to it. At this late day nothing more can be said of them than what is contained in the official documents on file in the War Department, except that not the slightest blame was ever intended to be cast upon Colonel

Harnden, as seems to have been at one time assumed by the commission convened by the Secretary of War for the purpose of awarding the prize offered for the capture of Davis.

During the skirmish just described, the adjutant of the Fourth Michigan Cavalry, Lieutenant J. G. Dickinson, after having looked on the security of the rebel camp, and sent forward a number of the men who had straggled, was about to go to the front himself, when his attention was called, by one of his men, "to three persons dressed in female attire," who had, apparently, just left one of the large tents near by, and were moving toward the thick woods. He started at once toward them and called out "Halt!" but, not hearing him, or not caring to obey, they continued to move off. Just then they were confronted by three men, under direction of Corporal Munger, coming from the opposite direction. The corporal recognized one of the persons as Davis, advanced with carbine, and demanded his surrender. The three persons halted, and by the actions of the two who were afterward ascertained to be women, all doubt as to the identity of the third person was removed. The individuals thus arrested were found to be Miss Howell, Mrs. Davis, and Jefferson Davis. As they walked back to the tent, Lieutenant Dickinson observed that Davis' top boots were not entirely covered by his disguise, and that this fact led to his recognition by Corporal Munger.*

---

* The following account of Davis' capture is taken from Pollard's work, previously mentioned: "But the last device of the distinguished fugitive, the only one in which he had shown any ingenuity, and had confessed his real anxiety for escape, was in vain, and he was captured three days' journey from Washington. He had scarcely expected to fall in with any enemy north of the Chattahoochee river, the boundary of the 'Department of the Southwest,' and there he had designed to part with his wife, and to commit her to her journey to the 'Shenandoah.' He was overtaken by a small body of Federal cavalry, originally sent out to post a skirmish line through that part of Georgia reaching to Augusta, but now diverted to his pursuit. The wicked and absurd story that Mr. Davis was captured disguised in female attire is scarcely now credited. He was aroused in the early gray of the morning by a faithful negro servant (the same who has since attended his broken fortunes), who had been awakened by the sound of firing in the woods. The President had not laid off his clothes, and, in a moment, he had issued from the tent where he had been sleeping. The woods were filled with mounted troops, ill-defined in the mist of the breaking morning, and, noticing that they were deploying as if to surround the camp, he quickly imagined their character and design, and returned within the tent, either to alarm Mrs. Davis, or there to submit decently to capture. She besought him to escape, and, urging him to an opening in the tent, threw over his shoulders a shawl which he had been accustomed to wear. His horse, a fleet and spirited one, was tied to a tree at some distance. He was within a few steps of

Again calling attention to the fact that this extract is made from a work, the materials for which were "gathered behind the scenes in Richmond," I leave the reader to decide for himself how trustworthy this authority may be. I have no wish to do Mr. Davis, or his apologist, an injustice, and still less, if possible, to do violence to the facts of history.

It will be observed that even Mr. Pollard admits that Mrs. Davis besought her husband to escape, and "urging him to an opening in the tent, threw over his shoulders a shawl which he had been accustomed to wear."

The friends of Davis, immediately after his capture became known, strenuously denied that he was disguised as a woman, and many good people, particularly those of rebel proclivities, looked upon this denial as settling the question for good and all. It is, therefore, necessary to detail the proofs upon which this story rests, as well as to specify the exact articles of woman's apparel which constituted the disguise. It is stated by Lieutenant Dickinson, in writing, that the rebel chieftain was one of the three persons "dressed in woman's attire," and that he had "a black mantle wrapped about his head, through the top of which could have been seen locks of his hair." Captain G. W. Lawton, Fourth Michigan Cavalry, who published an account of the capture in the *Atlantic*

---

the animal that might have borne him out of danger, when a Federal soldier halted him and demanded to know if he was armed.

"In relating the encounter afterward, in his prison at Fortress Monroe, Mr. Davis reported himself as saying: 'If I were armed, you would not be living to ask the question.' If he did say so, it was a sorry bravado, and, as none of his captors appear to have recollected such words of defiance, we are permitted to hope that Mr. Davis' memory is at fault, and that he submitted to his fate really with more dignity than he claims for himself. While he was parleying with the soldier, Colonel Pritchard, commanding the body of cavalry, rode up, and, addressing him by name, demanded his surrender. Not one of his escort or companions came to his aid. He submitted, walked back to the tent, and, in the presence of his wife, asked Colonel Pritchard that she might continue her journey. The reply of the Colonel was that his orders were to arrest all the party. Mr. Davis rejoined with sarcasm: 'Then, sir, what has been said is true; your government does make war upon women!' These were the only words of displeasure or of bitterness in the dialogue of the capture. The unhappy prisoner, after these words, was coldly silent. Asking no questions of his fate, not intruded upon by any curiosity of his captors, conversing only with the faithful and devoted wife, from whom he was not yet divided, and whose whispers of affectionate solicitude, by his side, were all to lighten the journey, he rode moodily in the cavalcade back to Macon, where first he was to learn the extent of his misery, and to commence the dread career of the penalties he had accumulated by four long and bitter years of war." (Pages 513 to 524 inclusive.)

Monthly for September, 1865, asserts explicitly, upon the testimony of the officers present, that Davis, in addition to his full suit of Confederate gray, had on "a lady's waterproof (cloak), gathered at the waist, with a shawl drawn over the head, and carrying a tin pail." Colonel Pritchard says, in his official report, that he received from Mrs. Davis, on board the steamer Clyde, off Fortress Monroe, "a waterproof cloak or robe" of dark or almost black waterproof stuff which was worn by Davis as a disguise, and which was identified by the men who saw it on him at the time of the capture. He secured the "other part" of the disguise the next day. It consisted of a small black shawl, with a red border four or five inches deep, which was identified in a similar manner by Mrs. Davis and the soldiers. A convincing circumstance in this connection should be mentioned. Colonel Pritchard, in looking over the wrappings on board the steamer for the shawl in question, picked out one like it, but not the identical one, when little Jeff, a bright boy of seven or eight years, with the artlessness of childhood, said: "That isn't the shawl my papa had on when captured; this is the one," picking up another. Various partisans and friends of Davis still persist in denying that he was captured in the disguise of a woman; but in their efforts to explain away the story they have confirmed it in all its essential parts. Colonel Harrison, of his staff, in a newspaper article published shortly after the capture, admits that Mrs. Davis had thrown over him a "dressing gown."

Between the various explanations which have appeared from time to time, nearly all of the truth has been told, for Davis certainly had on both the shawl and waterproof, the former folded triangularly and pulled down over his hat, and the latter buttoned down in front and covering his entire person except the feet. In addition to this he carried a small tin pail and was accompanied by his wife and his wife's sister, one on each side, both of them claiming him as a female relative, and both trying to impose him upon the soldiers as such. The articles of the disguise are now in the keeping of the Adjutant General of the Army at Washington, and I am assured by him that they correspond in all respects to the description given of them. From the foregoing, it will be seen that Davis did not actually have on crinoline or petticoats, but there is no doubt whatever that he sought to avoid capture by assuming the dress of a woman, or that the ladies of the party endeavored to pass him off upon his captors as one of themselves. Many loyal men have declared that Davis should have been tried by drum-head court-martial and executed; but what new disgrace could the gallows inflict upon the man who hid himself under the garb of woman, when, if ever, he should have shown the courage of a hero?

Shortly after the recognition of Davis by his captors, Colonels Pritchard and Harnden rode up to where the group were standing. Davis, recognizing them as officers, asked which of them was in command. As these officers were lieutenant colonels of different regiments, belonging to different brigades of different divisions, and had, therefore, probably never before met, except casually, much less compared dates of commissions, they were somewhat taken aback at the question, and hesitated what answer to make. Whereupon Davis upbraided them with ignorance, reproached them with unchivalrous conduct in hunting down women and children, and finally declared, with the air and manners of a bravo, that they could not have caught him but for his desire to protect "his women and children." "How would you have prevented it, Mr. Davis?" said Colonel Pritchard. "Why, sir, I could have fought you, or eluded you." "As for fighting us," replied the Colonel, "we came prepared for that; it would have saved us some trouble, and, doubtless, you a good deal; but as for 'eluding us,' I don't think your garb is very well adapted to rapid locomotion." In addition to Davis and his family, Colonel Pritchard's detachment captured, at the same time, John H. Reagan, rebel Postmaster General, Colonel B. N. Harrison, private secretary, Colonels Lubbock, and Johnston, aides-de-camp to Davis, four inferior officers and thirteen private soldiers, besides Miss Howell, two waiting-maids, and several colored servants.

This brings us again to the question of Davis' disguise at the time of his capture, touching which I submit the following letter, written by J. G. Dickinson, late Adjutant Fourth Michigan Cavalry, to the Detroit *Tribune:*

I have read John H. Reagan's letter to Governor Porter, in the publication you exhibited to me. It contains severe criticisms upon published statements of General James H. Wilson, concerning the flight, capture, and disguise of Jefferson Davis. I remember Mr. Reagan, who was captured with Davis. I had the honor of being with General Pritchard, as Adjutant of the Fourth Michigan Cavalry, at the capture, and personally took part in the arrest of Davis, while he was attempting to escape, *disguised in female attire.* There has never been any doubt or denial from any authentic source, expressed or asserted, to my knowledge, respecting the disguise and attempted escape of Mr. Davis, until Mr. Reagan's letter appeared; and Mr. Reagan does not speak, regarding the disguise, upon his own knowledge. The facts were well known, and often repeated, in our camp, to interested inquirers, by those having personal knowledge of them.

The first report of the capture was made to Major Robert Burns, Assistant Adjutant General of General R. H. G. Minty's staff. I drew the report, immediately after our return to Macon, for Captain John C. Hathaway, commanding the regiment while Colonel Pritchard was absent in charge of the prisoners on the way to Washington. I made a full written statement of the facts for General Wilson, at the request of Major Van Antwerp, his aide-de-camp, and another statement to General John Robertson, Adjutant General of Michigan. The facts are beyond dispute respecting the female disguise. I know all about it, because I saw it, and, assisted by Corporal Munger, and others present, *arrested Jefferson Davis when he was in such female disguise.* Mr. Reagan did not then see him; but there were several Confederate officers present who did see the arrest, and made no effort to aid their chief.

The facts concerning the capture and the disguise are well remembered by those present, many of whom are now living in this State. The part I took in the immediate capture of Jefferson Davis I shall not soon forget. I think we acted with magnanimity and care toward the fallen chief of the Confederacy. He could have been detained at the spot where arrested, for the gaze of all his officers, family, and escort, but he was permitted to retire to his tent, and disrobe from his female disguise.

Jeff Davis, and all who were captured with him, well know that great kindness, and fair consideration, such as were due to a prisoner of his importance, were extended to him by every member of our command; and nothing was done or said, except what was necessary for his security and conduct. Though he called us vile names at first, I think he subsequently behaved himself.

Immediately upon the charge into the camp, Captain Charles T. Hudson, leading the advance guard, passed well through the camp, and our colonel following, swung round, enveloping the entire camp. In this movement, I met, in front of a small fly tent, Colonel Harrison, Davis' private secretary (as I afterward learned). I stopped, and made inquiry as to their force in camp, and, while he was replying, I heard some one calling me. I turned, and saw Private Andrew Bee, of L Company, who, pointing to three persons dressed in female apparel, at some distance, and moving away, called out to me, "Adjutant, there goes a man dressed in woman's clothes." I started at once after them, calling out "Halt!" repeatedly, and reaching them just as several troopers, in charge of Corporal Munger, dashed up, bringing their carbines ready for use. The fugitives halted; Mrs. Davis threw her arms around her husband's shoulders, and the lady close to him formed a shield, which was respected. I noticed several Confederate officers near; one, a tall fellow, was, apparently, very excited.

Davis had on a black dress, and, though it did not fit fairly at the neck, it covered his form to the boots; the boots betrayed his disguise. A black shawl covered his head and shoulders. His identity was confirmed by the removal of the shawl from his face. I promptly directed him to retire to his quarters, and ordered Corporal Munger to place the men with him, and keep careful guard.

I then started to report to Colonel Pritchard, but Mrs. Davis called to me and I dismounted a moment to hear her. She asked me what we were going to do with Mr. Davis, and whether she and the escort would be taken with him. I replied that Colonel Pritchard would see to the disposal of the party. She then made some other requests relative to the preservation of her baggage. I think Lieutenant Perry J. Davis, our quartermaster, then came up, and I mounted and left her with him.

I reported to Colonel Pritchard, as promptly as I could, the circumstances of the capture, and what I had done as to the guard. In the meantime, Davis had disrobed and come out, the guard retaining him in custody, and when Colonel Pritchard and staff approached, he called to him. I was near to him, but do not remember the exact language used, further than that Davis characterized our command as "a set of thieves and vandals, for attacking a train of women and children."

I know the colonel spoke quite sharply to him, but his exact language I will not attempt to state, as the colonel will answer for that. I know he had been informed of the disguise by me.

I have the names of several of the men of our regiment who were present at the capture, and I think Lieutenant James Vernor, of Detroit, has their address.

J. G. DICKINSON,

Late Adjutant Fourth Michigan Cavalry.

Through the kindness of Major Robert Burns, of Kalamazoo, Michigan, I am enabled also to quote the statements of Private Andrew Bee, Corporal George Munger, and William P. Stedman, and an extract from a letter of Captain Charles T. Hudson, all of the Fourth Michigan Cavalry, together with a letter from Major Burns himself, commenting upon these documents. It will be seen that there is a close agreement between all these parties (they actually made the capture), and their statements are conclusive as to the question of the disguise. It will be observed that none of them say anything whatever about petticoats, and that no officer has ever alleged that any such garment was used. The newspapers which published the first accounts are solely responsible for the very natural assumption that a man disguised in his wife's clothing would not forget the important item of the petticoat. The letters are as follows:

OCTOBER 19th, 1877.

On the morning of May 10th, 1865, I was one of the fourteen men under Lieutenant J. G. Dickinson who were dismounted by order of Lieutenant Colonel Pritchard, and directed to enter and guard the camp in which Jefferson Davis and party were supposed to be. I was the first man who entered it, and immediately went to the first of three tents standing on the right-hand side of the road, and raised the flap to enter it. Mrs. Davis, from the inside of the tent, requested me to go back, " as there were ladies in there who were not dressed." This I could see for myself, she being in her night-gown, barefooted and bareheaded. I stepped back to the outside and waited there a few minutes. Very soon two persons who looked like women, but who really were Jefferson Davis and his sister-in-law (Miss Howell), appeared from the tent, Miss Howell carrying a tin pail. In the meantime, the firing between the First Wisconsin and the Fourth Michigan could be heard, and the bullets were flying over the camp. Lieutenant Dickinson was walking up and down in front of the three tents, very much excited, with a white blanket over his arm, listening to the firing. Just as Miss Howell and Mr. Davis appeared he was approaching the first tent, from which they came, and *she* said to him: " Please, lieutenant, let me and my grandmother go to the brook to get ourselves washed." Dickinson immediately turned to me, and said: " Never mind them women folks, Andrew Bee; come here and guard them officers," referring to some rebel officers, among whom were Private Secretary Johnston (he, doubtless, meant Harrison) and General Reagan, who had just come out of the second tent. Just then a white servant girl came out of the first tent, Mrs. Davis remaining in to dress or attend the children, of whom there were three.

The three " women " (Mr. Davis, Miss Howell, and the servant girl) then started for the brook, Mr. Davis stooping over, as a very old woman would, so that his head was not on a level with Miss Howell's, but was lower. Mr. Davis had on a black morning gown, belted at the waist, and reaching to his ankles, a shawl over his head, beard, and shoulders, and a black cloth under the shawl, covering his forehead. They had got about six or eight rods from the tent when I, who had been watching them all the time, saw that the old woman had on boots. I at once said to Dickinson: "See! that is Jeff, himself! That is no woman! That is old Jeff Davis!" and started on the run after them. As I got up to them, I exclaimed: "Halt! Damn you, you can't get any further this time!" Mrs. Davis at that moment came running out of the tent, and when she reached Mr. Davis, she put her arms around his neck and said: "Guard! do not kill him!" At the same instant Corporal Munger, 'of Company C, mounted, came from another direction and headed Davis. I said to him: "Never mind, Munger, I will take care of that old gentleman myself." Lynch and Bullard were quite near at the time. Munger was the second man who saw and recognized Davis. Next to Munger was Lynch, who had been foraging around near the second tent, and who had already secured Mr. Davis' bay horse, with the pistol-holsters filled with gold coin.

The only portion of the face of Mr. Davis which could be seen, when he was disguised, were the eyes and the nose, he covering the moustache, mouth, and beard with the shawl, held closed with one hand. After Mr. Davis was halted, he did not attempt any further disguise, but soon returned to his tent.

ANDREW BEE.

PAW-PAW, October 15th, 1877.

Dear Sir :—Your letter, of September 28th, came to hand in due time, but I have neglected to answer it until now. You wanted a full statement of the capture of Jeff Davis, as I remembered it to be. It has been some time since the capture, but I will give you as full an account of the matter as I can. I don't know as I can give you the conversation of Davis, just as it was, but think I can give you the substance. It was between twelve and one o'clock on the morning of May 10th, 1865, and as soon as we got within a few rods of the camp the regiment was halted and a portion was dismounted, and advanced partly around the camp, and there waited for day; and, as soon as it commenced to get light, the dismounted men charged on the camp, and the mounted men followed after. I was among the mounted men, and as we came into camp I saw a horse that I thought was better than my own, and I stopped to exchange, Corporal George Munger stopping with me. I dismounted to change the saddle from my horse to the other. As I was about to buckle the girth, I saw what I supposed to be some women leaving camp, and spoke to Munger and told him they ought to be stopped, and he rode out and halted them. I followed after as soon as I could mount. When Munger overtook them, Mrs. Davis turned and said: "We are going to the spring after water." Munger told her she would have to go back, and at the same time rode around in front of them. Davis saw that he was caught, and threw off his shawl and waterproof. Mrs. Davis threw her arms around his neck and said: "Don't shoot him!" Davis said: "Let them shoot! I might as well die here as anywhere!" I think he asked if "there was a man among us." About this time Adjutant Dickinson and some others came up and took him in charge. In regard to what he had on, as near as I can recollect, it was a waterproof skirt, and a dark shawl over his head and shoulders. He was about twenty-five rods from camp when stopped. I was one of the guards that went to Fortress Monroe with Davis, and from there we were ordered to Washington, where a statement of the capture was made before the Secretary of War by George Munger, Crittenden, Andrew Bee, and myself. You will find that statement the same as this, or nearly so.

JAMES F. BULLARD.

DETROIT, December, 1873.

To the Editor of the Tribune :—Then, as daylight began to appear, the advance were sent to capture the camp. We rode into camp without starting a person until our men gave a yell that soon made a stir. I halted my horse near the largest tent. Some of the boys were about to go into it, but were stopped by the request of a woman inside, saying that there were undressed ladies there. Soon after a woman came to the door of the tent and asked the men who were near if the servants could not go out after some water. Consent was given, when there came out of the tent a colored woman and a tall person wearing a waterproof dress and a small shawl around the head, and carrying a tin pail on the arm. I was well satisfied that the tall person was Davis, but I was at the side of the tent and several of our men in front, and, as the servants left the tent in front, I supposed that Davis would be stopped by some of them. But such was not the case, for the two passed entirely by all of the men. Then I put my horse to a gallop to overtake them. At the same time I saw two mounted men riding toward the servants from the Louisville road. The two mounted men were Munger, of Company C, and the other I took for Tibbet, of E Company. Davis then halted and turned to go back to the tent.

WILLIAM P. STEDMAN,
Company B, Fourth Michigan Cavalry.

Captain Charles T. Hudson, Fourth Michigan Cavalry, writes to the Detroit *Tribune,* July 24th, 1875, as follows:

I was not the first to see our distinguished captive, nor did I see him in his disguise at all. Several claim that honor, and, I have no doubt, all speak the truth. On our way back to Macon, however, Mrs. Davis told me, and I will use her own words: "I put my waterproof cloak and shawl on Mr. Davis upon the impulse of the moment, not knowing, or having time to think, what else to do, in hopes he might make his escape in that disguise; and I only did what any true woman might have done under similar circumstances." This was told me by Mrs. Davis in the course of conversation on our way back to Macon while halting to feed and rest our horses, she being in the ambulance at the time. Therefore, although I did not see Mr. Davis in the disguise of a woman, I had Mrs. Davis' word that she did disguise him that he might make his escape. If further proof is wanting, let me add, that upon our arrival at Fortress Monroe with our prisoners, acting under orders of the Secretary of War, I was sent on board of the Clyde, then lying in Hampton Roads, to get the shawl (the waterproof having been obtained the day previous by Colonel Pritchard) worn by Davis at the time of his capture. Upon making known my business to Mrs. Davis, she and Mrs. Clement C. Clay, particularly the latter, flew into a towering rage, and Mrs. Clay, stamping her foot on the deck of the vessel, advised Mrs. Davis to "shed her blood before submitting to further outrage." After telling Mrs. Davis that my orders were imperative, and that she had better submit gracefully to my demands, she became somewhat pacified, and said *she* "had no other wrappings to protect *her* from the inclemency of the weather." I then told her I would go ashore and buy her a shawl, which I did, paying six dollars for it. Upon presenting it to her, she held it up, and, with scorn and contempt, turned to Mrs. Clay and exclaimed, "a common nigger's shawl." She then handed me two shawls very similar in appearance and told me to take my choice, adding that she did dress Mr. Davis in her attire and would not deny it, at the same time expressing great surprise that the Secretary of War should want her clothing to exhibit, as if she had not already been sufficiently humiliated.

The letter of Corporal Munger, directed to Colonel Burns, is as follows:

SCHOOLCRAFT, Michigan, October 29th, 1877.

*Dear Sir :—*Yours of the 20th, asking for a statement of my participation in the capture of Davis, is at hand. I have had a great many calls for a statement from almost every State in the Union. I just received one from the *Tribune* office last week. I thought I would not say anything about it. There has been a great deal said by different ones regarding the capture of Davis. They all seem to differ more or less. If I should make a statement it would not correspond with all. Colonel Pritchard's statement is as near right as any I have seen as regards Davis' disguise. Davis had on a lady's waterproof cloak or dress, and a red and black (or black and white) shawl, thrown over his head and shoulders over a suit of gray clothes, and a pair of cavalry boots. I don't know if Dickinson ordered Bee to let the woman pass or not, only what I heard the morning of the capture. I believe Bee was on guard at the tent. I did not see Dickinson until after Davis was taken back to the tent and had taken off his disguise. Dickinson might have halted Davis, but not in my hearing; he certainly did not stop. He was about four rods from the tent when I first saw him. Bullard and I were changing horses, as we used to do sometimes when we found better ones. Bullard had just thrown his saddle on his horse. I was just buckling my girth when I saw the three women, as I supposed them to be, who afterward proved to be Davis, Mrs. Davis, and Miss Howell. I said to Bullard, "Those women ought not to be allowed to go out of camp; you go and stop them." Bullard said, "You go; you have your saddle on." I mounted my horse, rode around in front of the party, and said to them, "Where are you going?" Mrs. Davis said, "With my old mother after some water." [Mrs. Davis had a pail on her arm.] I said, "What is she doing with those boots on?" When I saw his boots I cocked my gun and laid it across my saddle. Mrs. Davis put her hand over Davis' face and said, "Don't shoot; you may not admire Mr. Davis' principles, but he is a reverend man." That is all that was said there. As soon as Bullard buckled his saddle he rode up to where we were. He heard the most of this conversation. We went back to the tent with them. There Davis took off his disguise and said he thought our government more magnanimous than to be chasing up women and children. This is as near right as I could see it at the time.

GEORGE MUNGER.

The following letter from Colonel Burns explains itself:

KALAMAZOO, October 21st, 1877.

*My Dear General :—*Inclosed you will find some further memoranda in regard to the Davis disguise question. On Friday evening Bee came to my house and made and signed the statement, a copy of which I inclose. He had received a letter from the editor of the Detroit *Tribune* on the same subject, requesting that he should put his recollections of the matter into shape and send to him. Bee is a Norwegian, of very little or no education, and his accent and "patois" are so strong that it is hard work to understand him. There was no shaking him in any of the statements he made, but he insisted that each one was literally true. He was very positive as to the exact words used by Dickinson. Dickinson's English, undoubtedly, was better than Bee's memory. They agree in substance with my memoranda of the circumstances, and go to show that Dickinson was deceived in supposing they were all women.

As to the "morning gown" Mr. Davis had on, Bee says it was a long black gown, such as he has seen gentlemen wear in the South, with a belt on, and very long.

If Davis had come out of the tent erect, with that gown on, and no shawl, he would have thought nothing of the matter, having seen gentlemen in them before, though he had always supposed they had no coats on under them. He was very positive also as to the words used by Miss Howell, and as to the "form bowed down" of Davis. I understand that one of the points made by Davis' apologists, is that he was arrested the moment he stepped out of the tent. Bee explicitly denies that. I asked him how far Davis had got from the tent before he was halted, when he at first said "about twenty rods." Upon my request that he would be more definite he pointed out a building about one hundred and twenty-five feet from where we sat, and said: "Just about as far as that building." He insists that *he* was the first man to recognize Davis, and this because he suspected something wrong when the three moved away from the tent. The letter from Bullard was written to me at my request, and speaks for itself. He, too, gives Davis a good start, as does also Stedman. Stedman corroborates pretty closely Bee's story as to what occurred in front of the tent. These statements were made by "the boys" without any knowledge of what the other was saying or writing, and agree pretty well in the main. Bee says he does not recollect any such man as Stedman, though he may have been present. I did not ask him anything about Stedman until after he had finished and signed his "version." I have written to George Munger, corporal of C Company, and expect to get *his* story in a few days. Being somewhat interested in the question, I have, whenever I came across anything in the papers relating to it, been in the habit of cutting it out and pigeon-holing it. Among the others the following from the Raleigh (North Carolina) *News*, of August 20th (1877, I think, though I will not be certain as to the year), published by the other side. It was signed by James H. Jones, Davis' colored coachman: "It has been stated that Mr. Davis had on a hoopskirt, and was otherwise disguised as a woman. This is wholly false. He was dressed in his ordinary clothing, with cavalry boots drawn over his pants, a waterproof over his dress-coat, a shawl thrown over his shoulders, and on his head a broad-brim white or drab Texas hat. He had not an article of female wear about his person." The chief point of difference between Jones and the others appears to be the *location* of the shawl only.

I saw Colonel Pritchard at Allegan, on Friday morning, and he says that he, too, has received various letters on the subject, which he expects to answer, and will lean far toward the woman disguise side of the question. Various conversations he had with Mrs. Davis, he says, will substantiate the fact that she denied nothing.

Many thanks for your account in the WEEKLY TIMES of our great ride. It is very interesting.

Yours, very truly,

ROBERT BURNS.

MAJOR GENERAL J. H. WILSON, St. Louis.

After quoting the foregoing documents, which all candid readers will admit to be entirely conclusive on the question of the disguise, I have only to add that all the statements made by me herein, or elsewhere (not only in reference to this question but to the question of the behavior of Davis at the time of his capture), are based upon the written and verbal reports made by the officers and men immediately after the events to which they referred. This is especially true of the conversation which was held by Mr. Davis with Colonel Pritchard and Colonel Harnden.

As soon as breakfast could be prepared, Colonel Pritchard, preceded by Colonel Harnden, began his return march, with prisoners and wagons, for Macon, about one hundred and twenty miles to the northwest of Irwinsville. The next day, he met a courier, with copies of the President's proclamation, offering a reward of one hundred thousand dollars for the capture of Davis. This proclamation had been received and promulgated on the 9th, and hence the officers in the pursuit of Davis were in no way inspired by the promise which it contained. They performed their part from a higher sense of duty, and too much praise cannot be awarded to Colonels Pritchard and Harnden, or to the officers and men of their regiments who participated in the pursuit. Colonel Pritchard arrived at Macon on the afternoon of the 13th, and reported at once, with his prisoners, at corps headquarters. When the cavalcade reached the city, the streets were thronged by crowds of rebel citizens, but not one kind greeting was extended to the deserted chieftain or his party. A good dinner was prepared and given to them by my servants, and, after three or four hours' rest, they were sent, under strong escort, toward the North, by way of Atlanta, Augusta, and Savannah, arrangements for which had been already made, in pursuance of orders from Washington. Colonel Pritchard, with a detachment of his regiment, was directed to deliver his prisoner safely into the custody of the Secretary of War. I also placed in his charge the person of Clement C. Clay, Jr., for whose arrest a reward had been offered by the President. Mr. Clay surrendered himself at Macon, about the 11th of May, having informed me by telegraph, from Western Georgia, the day before, that he would start for my headquarters without delay. Alexander H. Stephens, Vice President of the Confederacy, was arrested by General Upton, at Crawfordsville, about the same time, and also placed in charge of Colonel Pritchard; but he and Davis were not brought into personal contact, both expressing the desire that they might be spared that pain. General Upton was charged with making the necessary arrangements for forwarding the prisoners and escort safely to Savannah, to the department of General Gilmore.

In order to cut off all hope of escape, an escort of twenty-five picked men were specially charged with the safety of Davis, while eight hundred men, divided between three trains of cars, one preceding and one following the one that Davis was on, were sent as far as Augusta, to thwart any attempt which might be made to rescue the distinguished prisoners. This was merely an excess of precaution; it is not known that a single man in the South desired, or would have dared, to undertake his release, although that region was thronged with thousands of rebel soldiers on their way home. No accident, or delay of any kind, occurred during the trip to Savannah, where a gunboat was already in waiting. The prisoners were taken on board at once, and delivered at Fortress Monroe, for safe keeping, on the 22d of May. My command had also arrested Mr. Mallory, the rebel Secretary of the Navy, Mr. Hill, Senator, and Joseph E. Brown, Governor of Georgia. Breckenridge and Toombs managed to escape, by traveling alone, and as rapidly as possible—the former having passed through Tallahassee, Florida, only a few hours before the arrival of General McCook at that place. Both of his sons were captured, and, after a few days' detention, were paroled.

When Davis arrived at Macon, he looked bronzed, but hardy and vigorous, and had entirely recovered his equanimity and easy bearing. After he had dined, I had an interview with him, lasting over an hour, during which he talked freely and pleasantly about a variety of subjects. He asked about the different professors at West Point, discussing their merits and peculiarities with spirit and good-humor, showing clearly that he had neither forgotten them nor his own experience as a cadet. Thence he was led to the discussion of his own generals. He spoke in the highest terms of Lee, declaring him to be the ablest, most courageous, and the most aggressive; in short, the most worthy of all his lieutenants. He condemned the generalship of Johnston, and charged him with timidity and insubordination. He ridiculed the pedantry of Beauregard, and deprecated the gallant rashness of Hood. On the other hand, he expressed his admiration for the surprising skill and persistency of Grant, the brilliancy of Sherman, and the solid qualities of Thomas. In the course of our conversation, he referred to Mr. Lincoln, and his untimely death, speaking of him in terms of respect and high personal regard. He seemed to regret particularly that Mr. Johnson had succeeded to the Presidency, adding that both he and the Southern people would find him much more implacable and vindictive than Mr. Lincoln. He remarked, in reference to the reward offered for his arrest, as an accomplice in the assassination, that, while he was surprised that such a charge should have been brought against him, he had no serious apprehension of trouble therefrom. In this connection, he said: "I doubt not, General, the Government of the United States will bring a much more serious charge against me than that, and one which it will give me much greater trouble to disprove"—evidently alluding to that of treason. Other subjects were mentioned, and during the conversation he sent for and introduced his little boy. His conduct throughout was dignified, and eminently self-possessed. He spoke with great precision, and with more than an ordinary degree of suavity, but, withal, producing upon me the impression that he was acting, and not unnaturally, a borrowed character. After learning the disposition that I was ordered to make of him, he said: "I suppose, as a matter of course, that Colonel Pritchard is to be my custodian hereafter as heretofore, and I desire to express my satisfaction at this, for," continued he, "it is my duty to say that Colonel Pritchard has treated me with marked courtesy and consideration. I have no fault to find with him, and hope you will tell him so. I should do so myself but for the fact that it might look like a prisoner's effort to make fair weather with his captors." He spoke particularly of the dignity and self-possession of Colonel Pritchard, and did not conceal a regret that he had not been so fortunate in his own conduct at the time of his capture.

The body of this article was prepared, from official documents and private memoranda, shortly after the end of the war, when the events referred to were fresh in my mind. In re-writing it now, I have striven to set down naught in malice, and am sure that my narrative has not been colored in the slightet degree by the fact that the principal persons whom it concerns were leaders of the "lost cause." I have gathered all the information that could be had, and, such as it is, I now submit it to the public as my contribution to the history of the last days of the Confederacy, feeling fully assured that it cannot be controverted in any essential particular.

THE BLACK HORSE CAVALRY.

BY COLONEL JOHN SCOTT.

THE Black Horse Cavalry was organized, or rather first set in line, by Captain D. H. Jones, United States Army, afterward a Confederate general, at Waterloo, on the Rappahannock river, in Fauquier county, Virginia, on the 18th of June, 1859, the anniversary of the battle of Waterloo. On that day, so auspicious for the liberties of mankind, did this command come into existence which was destined to act so distinguished and important a part in the prolonged effort to establish the independence of a Southern Republic. Already had the storm-cloud began to gather, the hurricane to lower in the distance, and the organization of the Black Horse Cavalry was the first step which was taken in Fauquier county to meet the prognosticated war. The first captain elected was John Scott, a planter, residing in the neighborhood of Warrenton, and the author of "The Lost Principle." Robert Randolph, a young lawyer of the Warrenton bar, was chosen first lieutenant; Charles H. Gordon, a planter, residing near Bealton, was elected second lieutenant. The non-commissioned officers were: William R. Smith, first sergeant, who was during the war elected a lieutenant of the command, and was afterward one of the most distinguished captains of Mosby's Partisan Battalion, but was killed, sword in hand, in a night attack on a Federal camp at Harper's Ferry; James H. Childs was elected second sergeant; Richard Lewis was elected third sergeant; Robert Mitchell was elected fourth sergeant. The corporals were: Wellington Millon, Madison Tyler, N. A. Clopton, and M. K. James. These were all young gentlemen of the first respectability, and were either themselves planters or

(590)

the sons of planters. The rank and file were composed of young men of the same social material with the officers. Among them were to be found James Keith, now well known as one of the ablest and most distinguished judges in Virginia, and William H. Payne, a leading member of the Virginia bar, who, during the war, rose to be a brigadier general in Stuart's cavalry division. Another, a young lawyer of brilliant promise, was Thomas Gordon Pollock, the son of the author of " The Exode," a sublime production, and on his mother's side was sprung from the heroic blood of the Lees. During the war he was transferred, with the rank of captain, to the staff of Brigadier General James L. Kemper, and fell in storming Cemetery Heights. When it was discovered, in the spring of 1860, that the law allowed a third lieutenant to the command, an election was held in the town of Warrenton to fill the vacant post. There were several candidates, but the captain requested the men to elect A. D. Payne, which was done; for at that early period he discerned in him those high military qualities which, in the field, he afterward displayed. He has survived the war, and is now a distinguished member of the Warrenton bar.

The first service which the command was ordered to perform was to report to Governor Henry A. Wise, at Charlestown, Virginia, at which point were being collected the volunteer companies of the State to insure the execution of John Brown and his associates. When the command reached Piedmont station, now Delaplane, on the Manassas Railroad, it fell in with the "Mountain Rangers," a cavalry company, which Captain Turner Ashby, afterward so brilliant a figure in the Confederate army, had recruited in Upper Fauquier. Together these companies marched by night, fording the deep and rapid Shenandoah, and reported at daylight the next morning to the Governor at Charlestown. A detachment of the Black Horse escorted the prisoners to the place of execution, while the rest of the command was employed in keeping clear the streets, for it was feared even at the last moment that an attempt would be made to rescue Brown. Upon the return of the command to Warrenton, the ladies of that patriotic town received them graciously, and gave in their honor a handsome ball. So early was the strong and lasting covenant made between the women and the soldiers of the South!

The John Brown war, as the people called it, gave an immense impulse to the secession sentiment of Virginia, and when South Carolina seceded and coercion was talked of, the captain of the Black Horse immediately tendered his command to Governor Pickens. This act proved to be in advance of the popular feeling, and many murmurs were excited; but it was ratified by the command at its next meeting.

About the time of the formation of the Southern Republic, at Montgomery, fearing that Virginia would not take part in the movement, the captain of the Black Horse relinquished his command, and was commissioned captain in the army of the Confederate States.

On the 16th of April, 1861, the day before the Ordinance of Secession was passed by Virginia, orders were received by Lieutenant Randolph, commanding the Black Horse Cavalry, and by Captain Ashby, to assemble their respective commands and proceed, without delay, to Harper's Ferry. The object of this expedition was to capture the stores and munitions of war collected at that place, so necessary to the Confederates in the struggle in which they were about to engage. Success depended upon secresy and dispatch, and every available means was employed to collect the commands. By ten o'clock at night the Black Horse had left their homes, not to return for four weary years—many of them never. With light hearts they marched, in happy ignorance of the future, until, when within a few miles of their destination, they heard the explosion of the arsenal. When this sound fell on their ears, they felt that they had been thwarted in the object of the expedition. But on their arrival things were found not so bad as apprehension had painted. The rifle works on the Shenandoah, it is true, were entirely destroyed, but the fire in the musket machine-shops had been arrested after about a third of the machinery had been wholly or partially destroyed. The building in which the manufactured arms were deposited contained over twenty thousand stand of Minnie rifles and rifled muskets, of which about seven thousand fell into the hands of the captors uninjured, and many others in a condition that admitted of repair. A large proportion of the hands employed were sent, with the uninjured machinery, to an armory established in North Carolina. The Black Horse Cavalry, after remaining several days on picket duty at Harper's Ferry, was ordered on similar service to Berlin bridge, which crosses the Potomac from the county of Loudon. It was while the command were at Harper's Ferry that Major Thomas J. Jackson, of the Virginia Military Institute, was ordered, by Governor Letcher, to take command, and the high reputation which he had won in the Mexican war inspired the volunteers with cheerfulness and confidence.

From Berlin bridge, the Black Horse was ordered back to Warrenton, where the vacant captaincy was filled by the election of

William H. Payne, heretofore, as before stated, a private in the command. This gentleman was, at that time, a member of the Warrenton bar, and had been, along with Captain B. H. Shackleford, a Secession candidate for the State Convention which cut the ties which bound the Commonwealth to the Federal body. His genius, gallantry, and recognized devotion to the Southern cause pointed him out for the vacant post. Captain Payne marched his command to the Fauquier Springs, where it was mustered into the Confederate service, and from that point conducted it to Manassas, where, together with a few other companies, it formed the nucleus of the Army of Northern Virginia, with which, through all vicissitudes, it remained until the final day of dissolution at Appomattox Court-House. At the time when a raid was made by Captain Tompkins, of the Federal army, on Fairfax Court-House, where the lamented Captain John Quincey Marr was killed, the Black Horse, at the request of their captain, were ordered to that point, from which they performed much arduous scouting duty, and became well known to the enemy. Upon the advance of General McDowell, the Black Horse rejoined the army at Manassas. On the 4th of July, in an attempt to ambuscade a detachment of the enemy, two members were killed and several wounded by the mistaken fire of a South Carolina regiment of infantry. In the memorable battle of the 21st of July, in which so absolute a victory was won by the Confederate arms, the Black Horse Cavalry distinguished itself in the pursuit of the flying enemy, and the next day were thanked by President Davis in a speech. Soon after the battle of Manassas, the Black Horse Cavalry was selected by General Joseph E. Johnston, commanding the army, to be his body-guard. In this capacity it received Prince Napoleon and his suite, consisting of Count Sartiges and others, upon their visit to the Confederate army, escorted them to the general's headquarters, and was, the next day, the escort at a review of the army at Centreville.

In the fall of 1861 the command was incorporated in the Fourth Virginia Cavalry, when Captain William H. Payne was promoted to be major of the regiment, and Lieutenant Robert Randolph succeeded to the captaincy, but was soon after detached to form the body-guard of General Earl Van Dorn, commanding a division at Manassas. When General Earl Van Dorn was assigned to an independent command in the further South, he made an unsuccessful application to be allowed to carry the Black Horse with him. In the spring of 1862 the command accompanied General Johnston to Yorktown, and on the march was employed as scouts in the rear, and as guides

38

to the brigade and division commanders, on account of their familiarity with the roads, water-courses, and points suitable for camping. When the army reached Culpepper county it was reported that the enemy, under General Sumner, had advanced as far as Warrenton Junction. General Stuart ordered a detail of ten of the Black Horse to change overcoats with the Governor's Guard, theirs being of a dark hue, and recrossing the Rappahannock to report the movements of the enemy. This detail did not rejoin the command until the march from Richmond to the Peninsula. The Fourth Virginia Cavalry was kept behind the earthworks, extending from Yorktown to James river, until General Johnston began to withdraw his forces. The regiment was then sent to Yorktown, and brought up the Confederate rear from that point of our lines. As soon as McClellan discovered that the rifle-pits in his front had been vacated, he pressed forward and overtook the Fourth Regiment about a mile and a half before it reached Fort Magruder. On this ground, the next day, the principal part of the battle of Williamsburg was fought—one of the best contested of the war, the number of troops on the Confederate side being taken into account. The Fourth halted and then slowly fell back, passing Fort Magruder. The Federals followed, and when they reached the edge of the woods, ran out Gibson's Battery to engage a Confederate battery in the fort. At the same time a company of the Richmond Howitzers, stationed on elevated ground on the opposite side of the road, also engaged the Federal battery, and a brisk cannonade was exchanged. General Johnston, who occupied a favorable position for observation, discovered that Gibson's Battery was worsted in the encounter and ordered the Fourth Virginia to charge. The regiment was already stripped for the fight, and passing Fort Magruder in a rapid charge, captured the Federal battery. Leaving a few men to take care of the capture, the regiment proceeded by that road into a dense wood, the land on either side of it being too miry for the operations of cavalry. At about two hundred yards after entering the woods, where the road made a sudden turn, the regiment ran upon a large body of opposing cavalry, when Colonel Wickham ordered it to fall back to the edge of the woods. In the execution of this movement Colonel Wickham was pierced by a sabre, and a color-bearer had his flag wrenched from his hands.

Colonel Wickham, being disabled from his wound, relinquished the command of the regiment to Major Payne. Toward nightfall the command was moved back to Williamsburg, and camped for the night. The next day the Fourth Virginia occupied in the line of battle the vacant space between Fort Magruder and the redoubt to its right. The Federal skirmishers advanced against this part of the line, and took position in some timber which had been cut down the past winter. They opened a destructive fire upon the regiment by which several were killed and wounded—among them Major Payne, very severely. He was conveyed to a hospital in Williamsburg, and fell into the enemy's hands when the Southern army withdrew. Finding that the cavalry could not cope upon terms of advantage with sharpshooters thus posted, the regiment was relieved by infantry and moved further to the right of the line of battle.

After the battle of Williamsburg the Confederate army continued its retreat on Richmond, the cavalry protecting the rear. The Black Horse participated in the dangers and hardships of this service, in performing which they were compelled to subsist on parched corn. Near Hanover Court-House, while on picket duty, the Black Horse assisted in checking the pursuit of General Branch's North Carolina troops by Fitz John Porter, who had overpowered and badly worsted them, and in this effort lost many men wounded and prisoners. The command took part in Stuart's raid around McClellan's army as it lay before Richmond, which was esteemed at the time a brilliant and hazardous feat, and participated in the fight at the old church in Hanover, where the gallant Captain Latane was killed.

The regiment to which the Black Horse was attached was now, for a time, camped near Hanover Court-House, and while here an interesting· incident took place. An English officer, who warmly sympathized with the Southern cause, presented, at Nassau, to a captain in the Confederate navy a rifle of beautiful workmanship, which he desired him, on his return to Richmond, "to present to the bravest man in the Confederate army." The naval officer, embarrassed by the scope of his commission, and not knowing, to be sure, where he should find the bravest soldier in the Southern army, thought he could best fulfil his commission by giving the rifle to Captain Robert Randolph, to be by him presented to the bravest man in the Black Horse Cavalry. But Captain Randolph was as much embarrassed in the execution of this commission as the naval captain had been, for how was it possible for any one to say in that command who was the bravest man? Robert Martin was the first sergeant, and in that capacity had displayed the highest qualities of a soldier, and had, in consequence, won the esteem and respect of both men and officers. Robert Martin, too, was foremost in every fight. He appeared to court danger for itself, and it seemed there was nothing he so little valued as life. To him, by general consent, therefore, the rifle was awarded as "the bravest of the brave."

About this time General Lee, having heard that Burnside had been moved by sea from North Carolina, and was at Fredericksburg, sent a brigade of cavalry, which embraced the Black Horse, to make a reconnoissance in that direction. The command saw active service and gained valuable information for the General, and on its return to Hanover Court-House, the battle of Cedar Mountain having been fought, it was ordered to join in the pursuit of Pope. The Fourth Regiment crossed the Rappahannock at Wallis' ford, and, marching through farms, regardless of roads, came into the main road from Culpepper Court-House to Fredericksburg, and turning to the right, attacked the cavalry protecting Pope's extreme left and drove it across the Rappahannock at Ellis' mill. Turning toward Brandy Station, on the Orange and Alexandria Railroad, the command found that General Lee, with Longstreet's Corps, had established his headquarters at Willis Madden's house. Continuing its march, it crossed the railroad and rejoined Stuart, who, with Jackson's Corps, pursued the enemy to the crossings of the Rappahannock at the railroad bridge and Beverly's ford. Thus were the two armies again confronting each other, but on opposite sides of the river. In this situation General Lee, with the ultimate purpose of forcing an action, marched his army by the left flank, and crossing the Hazel river into what is known as the Little Fork of Culpepper, grouped his whole army on the Upper Rappahannock, opposite the Fauquier Springs.

But Stuart's Cavalry, during this movement, had been detached from the army, and crossing the Rappahannock at Waterloo, the first drill-ground of the Black Horse, passed through Warrenton, and attacked, in the rear of Pope's army, Catlett's Station at midnight, thus striking his line of communication with his base of supply. This brilliant exploit resulted in the capture of Pope's headquarter wagons, the destruction of large army stores, and the capture of many prisoners.

Upon the return of the cavalry to the army, across the Rappahannock, the Black Horse was assigned to duty at the headquarters of Jackson, who was about to make his celebrated flank and rear movements on Pope's army, which culminated in the second battle of Manassas.

It had been the purpose of the Confederate commander, when he took position on the Upper Rappahannock, to cross his army at the Fauquier Springs, and occupying Lee's ridge and the adjacent highlands, to compel Pope to deliver battle at some point between Warrenton and Bealton. With this object in view he had crossed

Early's Brigade, of Ewell's Division, on what is known as the Sandy Ford dam, a point two miles below the Springs, to protect the men engaged in repairing the bridge at the Springs, over which the army was to pass. But this able plan was defeated by heavy rains, which fell the night before, and swelled the river to such an extent as to interrupt work on the bridge. This enforced delay enabled the Federal general to anticipate his opponent in the occupation of Lee's ridge, and secured to him the advantage of position which Lee had been maneuvring to obtain. Prompted by his military genius, Lee determined to cross the Rappahannock higher up, at Hinson's ford, and marching through Upper Fauquier to gain Pope's rear and compel him to engage battle on other ground than that on which the Federal army was so strongly posted. In pursuance of this plan, Jackson began his movement through the country above designated, until he struck Pope's line of communication at Bristow Station and Manassas Junction, as Stuart had before struck it at Catlett's Station. But the blow delivered by Jackson was a far more serious one; for, in order to regain his lost ground, the Federal commander was compelled to fight the second battle of Manassas. When Jackson struck the railroad at Bristow Station, where the sound of his cannon first apprised Pope of his whereabouts, he left General Ewell to guard the crossings of Broad run. He then moved down the railroad to Manassas, where he captured, in addition to several trains of cars, a large amount of army supplies, all of which were destroyed, except such as could be applied to immediate use. When this capture was first reported to the enemy, it was supposed to have been made by one of Stuart's raiding parties, and in consequence a New Jersey brigade of infantry, stationed below Manassas, was ordered up to retake the place. Possessed with this belief, the command marched to within a short distance of the fortifications, when it was found that it had to cope with Jackson's infantry, instead of Stuart's cavalry. The guns from the fortification opened upon the advancing Federals in front, while on their left flank they were assailed by Braxton's Battery. In this trying situation the brigade behaved in a soldierly manner, and marched from the field with ranks unbroken and colors flying. But when they reached the woods they broke when they were charged by a detachment of twenty of the Black Horse, commanded by Jackson in person, and many prisoners were taken.

Noiselessly and swiftly Jackson traversed the country between Hinson's ford and Bristow Station. With such caution was his march conducted, under the shelter of forest lands, by day, no camp-fires being allowed by night to indicate the presence of an army, that the enemy were kept in complete ignorance of the important movement. The perilous expedition, and the responsibility which attached to it, did not depress the General, but acted rather like an elixir upon him. His spirits rose high, and he relaxed much from his silent and austere mood. On the march he conversed freely with Lieutenant A. D. Payne, whose roused spirit kindled with his own at the approaching conflict, when a second time a great battle was to be fought on the border land of the hostile republics. The General used few words, but probed his subject to the bottom. His conversation was chiefly about the war, and he expressed himself freely about the merits of the officers of the Federal army, but with more reserve as to the Confederate officers. They were passing through the country of General Turner Ashby's nativity, and were at one time near the place of his birth and the scenes of his early life. Ashby, but a little before, and while attached to Jackson's army, had been killed, about the close of the magnificent campaign in the Valley. The career of the deceased officer had been brief, but as glorious as the morning star before it brightens into the perfect day. In a single sentence, Jackson photographed this peerless soldier, who has been so justly compared, for generosity and courage, to the immortal Black Prince. He said: "Ashby was born a soldier, and I feel his loss now. He was a man of intuitive military perception; his judgment was never surpassed."

At The Plains, a village on the Manassas Railroad, about four miles east of Salem, Lieutenant A. D. Payne, with thirty men, was sent back to guide and accompany General Lee, who was with Longstreet's Corps, while Captain Randolph, with the rest of the Black Horse command, remained with Jackson. The lieutenant retraced his steps, and reported to General Lee as he was crossing the Rappahannock at Hinson's mill. The troops were hurried on in the direction of Salem, the track over which Jackson had just passed, and encamped for the night between that point and Orlean. General Lee made his headquarters at Prospect Hill, the seat of the late Dr. Jaquelin A. Marshall, and was then the residence of his family. With his staff, the General found quarters in the house, but Lieutenant Payne and his men camped in the yard. By some unaccountable neglect, the main highway, leading past Prospect Hill from Orlean to Waterloo, and from thence to Warrenton, had not been picketed nor guarded, so that there was that night between the Confederate general and the Federal army, which lay scattered between Waterloo and Warrenton Junction, nothing but this open highway. In this exposed condition things remained for several hours, when it was discovered by Colonel Charles Marshall, the vigilant aide-de-camp of General Lee. About midnight, with consternation, he aroused Lieutenant Payne, and communicated the fact to him, and that the nearest brigade was a mile distant. With his whole force, all the roads in the direction of the enemy were picketed; but, fortunately, the enemy were not apprised of the General's exposed position, and the night passed without alarm. The next day, just before the head of the column arrived at Salem, information was brought to General Lee that a body of the enemy's cavalry were approaching that place. Lieutenant Payne, with his small detachment, was thrown forward to reconnoitre, for the rest of Stuart's cavalry were with Jackson. He dashed into the village, but was soon driven out by overwhelming numbers, and he endeavored, but without success, to entice them into an ambuscade prepared for them by General Longstreet. During the skirmishing which took place with the Federal cavalry, several prisoners were captured, from whom information was gained that Lieutenant Payne had struck Buford's Brigade of Federal cavalry, who, having captured some of Jackson's stragglers, had heard from them, for the first time, of his movement. The next day General Lee reached Thoroughfare gap, but did not succeed in forcing a passage through it till late in the evening. During the entire day he was uneasy for Jackson's safety, and, in the evening, requested Lieutenant Payne to send him a soldier who was acquainted with the passes of Bull Run mountains. The man was stripped of all the indicia of a soldier, and, dressed in the garb of a countryman, was mounted on a lame horse and a wagon saddle. Thus equipped, he was started with a dispatch for Jackson, concealed on his person, and was directed, at every hazard, and with all celerity, to deliver it.

Later, Lee directed Lieutenant Payne to make a reconnoissance to the rear of the force opposing him at Thoroughfare gap, and report without delay. Taking with him a party of five or six trusty men, the gallant officer made a detour to the right, and succeeded in reaching the turnpike, which connects Warrenton with Alexandria, near New Baltimore, about nine o'clock at night. From that point, he proceeded down the turnpike, and, mixing with the enemy, discovered that they were retiring rapidly toward Gainesville. This highly important information he quickly communicated to the Confederate general, at the residence of Colonel Robert Beverly. The next day, about noon, in advance of Longstreet's march, this detachment of the Black Horse opened communications with Jackson's Corps, near Groveton, a place on the Warrenton turnpike, below New Baltimore. As soon as the two corps of the Confederate army were again united, Lieutenant Payne, with his detachment, was ordered to report to his command. The Black Horse, thus consolidated, took part in the great battle of the 30th, the Second Manassas, in which General Pope was as disastrously defeated as McDowell had been on the same ground. In this engagement, many members of the Black Horse were fatally wounded, among them Erasmus Helm, Jr., than whom there was no braver soldier nor more charming gentleman.

The second battle of Manasses continued through three days, and was unsurpassed for severity by any fought during this bloody war. The effect of the heavy rain, which had prevented Lee from crossing his army at the Fauquier Springs, was now experienced in all its force; for Pope, in this prolonged struggle, was heavily reinforced from McClellan's army transported from Harrison's Landing, which could not have been done had the battle taken place in the vicinity of the Rappahannock according, as we have seen, to Lee's first design. The Federal army, having been routed from every position it had occupied in the battle, retreated into the strongly intrenched camp at Centreville, whose fortifications had been constructed by the combined skill of Johnston and Beauregard during the first winter of the war, and now a second time offered its shelter to a broken, defeated and demoralized Federal army. On Sunday morning, while the victorious army was recruiting its wearied virtue and binding up its wounds, Lee and Jackson, sitting on a fallen tree, were engaged in close consultation. Their horses were grazing at a short distance, when an alarm was given that the Federal cavalry were approaching. The two generals sprang for their horses, but failed to secure them, and in doing so Lee fell forward and so injured his hands as to be compelled to ride in an ambulance through the ensuing Maryland campaign with his hands bandaged and in a sling. At this critical moment two privates of the Black Horse tendered their horses and the officers were again mounted. But it proved to be a false alarm. At noon the Confederates began to march to Pope's rear, at Centreville, passing Sudley church and Cub run bridge, the object being again to interrupt Pope's communications, and compel a renewal of the conflict. When the Federal general discovered this movement he moved out of the ramparts at Centreville, and with disorganized masses recommenced his retreat toward the Potomac. From the crest of a high hill Jackson saw the retreating columns, and, at the same time, observed a detachment of the

Federal army as it was taking position behind the Independent and unfinished Manassas Railroad. This was evidently a force thrown out to protect the Federal retreat. Jackson immediately attacked it, but with an inadequate force, and the fight at Chantilly took place, which lasted until night. It is left to the future historian to inquire why the entire strength of the Confederate army was not employed against the retreating columns of the enemy. Perhaps it was because Fate had declared against the establishment of the Southern Republic, and it was by such means that her conclusions were to be wrought out.

Flushed by this victory, it was determined to cross the Potomac and carry the war into the enemy's country. If this military policy had been adopted as promptly after the first victory at Manassas, it is clear that the Confederate States would have been triumphant in the war. The sound policy of secession would then have been vindicated, and have marked the beginning of a great nation instead of being hawked at as a "perfidious bark built in the eclipse" that has wrecked the fortunes of a people.

The army marched for Edwards' ferry. Along the route there was manifested by the people the greatest curiosity and desire to see their great General—"Stonewall Jackson," as he had been baptized on the battle-field. Groups would be collected on the road, composed of all ages and both sexes, black and white crowded together. When Jackson would be pointed out to them they would send up a great shout, and the General, lifting his cap, would gallop away from the applause. In this connection an amusing incident occurred which created no little merriment, and exemplifies the liberties his soldiers would sometimes take with "Old Stonewall," as they called their darling. The Black Horse sent forward one of their members to ride as near to Jackson as military etiquette would allow. He was, by all odds, the ugliest fellow in the command; indeed, the Black Horse used to brag that he was the ugliest fellow in either army. When the next admiring crowd was passed, and they demanded to see the great captain, this soldier was pointed out to them. When they shouted and cheered he halted, and, with the utmost complaisance, received their compliments. Jackson, of course, had galloped on as usual. When the General, turning in his saddle, saw what was going on he was greatly amused, and the joke was repeated until the novelty wore off.

The Black Horse accompanied Jackson in his expedition to Williamsport, Martinsburg, and Harper's Ferry. At the latter place he employed the pen of Lieutenant A. D. Payne to copy his order of assault to be delivered to his officers—orders which were never acted on, as the place was surrendered before the assaulting columns began their work. The General remained at Harper's Ferry till a late hour of the night, disposing of the prisoners and the material of war which he had captured. He then started, escorted by Lieutenant Payne, with a detachment of twenty of his command, to reach Lee's headquarters at Sharpsburg, leaving his army to follow. At daybreak, a little out of the town, the party halted, and built a fire in a skirt of woods. Here Jackson slept while a party was sent to discover the position of Lee's headquarters. As soon as this fact was reported to him he joined the general commanding. The next day the battle of Sharpsburg was fought, during which the Black Horse acted as aides and couriers. In Jackson's report of this campaign he extols the conduct of this command, naming and complimenting its officers.

When the Confederate army recrossed the Potomac, General Stuart made strenuous efforts to have the Black Horse restored to the cavalry division. He wanted them to accompany his raid around McClellan's army at Harper's Ferry, where it lay gathering strength for another invasion of Virginia. But Jackson would not agree to Stuart's proposal. He said: "I know the Black Horse, and can employ the greater part of the command for staff duty." In this raid Stuart took with him fifteen squadrons of horse, composed of details from his regiments, one of which the writer of this commanded. The raiders crossed an obscure ford of the Potomac, above Harper's Ferry, General Wade Hampton, with a battery of horse artillery, being in the van, and camped that night at Chambersburg. The next day they passed through Emmettsburg on their return to the Potomac, and, marching all night, early the ensuing day reached White's ford of the Potomac, below Harper's Ferry, having thus made the circuit of the Federal army. But here Stuart encountered a formidable force of infantry and cavalry, stationed to oppose his passage of the river. Without hesitation, and with that undaunted courage which he showed on every battle-field, he drove the enemy before him, rapidly threw his command over the river, without so much as losing a horse-shoe, and marched off for the army headquarters as the artillery of the enemy was taking position on the heights he had just evacuated. As he passed their camps the infantry cheered him, a compliment they were always slow to pay the cavalry.

When McClellan crossed the river at Harper's Ferry, Lee was encamped at Winchester. Jackson then restored the Black Horse to its place in the cavalry division, for Stuart was ordered to throw himself in front of the advancing columns of McClellan, and delay his march until Lee could again interpose between the Federal army and Richmond. In obedience to this order, Stuart crossed the Blue Ridge into Loudon county, and heavily skirmished with the Federal advance through that county and Upper Fauquier. At Union, near the dividing line of the counties, he held his position so well that it was not until the evening of the second day that he was compelled to relinquish it. At Upperville, Markham, and Barbee's cross-roads, Stuart made stands until compelled to retreat by the pressure of numbers. In the meantime, Lee crossed the Blue Ridge, at Chester gap, and took position on the south bank of the Rappahannock. He was there informed that McClellan had been relieved, and Burnside promoted to the command of the Federal army, and that he had indicated his intention of marching toward Fredericksburg. Lee again put his army in motion, and posted it on the Spottsylvania Heights, at Fredericksburg, and confronted Burnside on the opposite side of the river. The Union army again suffered defeat, and again changed its general.

In the winter of 1863, while General Hooker was on the north bank of the Rappahannock, the Black Horse was detached from the Fourth Virginia Cavalry, and ordered to Lower Fauquier and Stafford county to report the enemy's movements to General Lee. During this time the command performed many brilliant exploits in its numerous encounters with the enemy, captured three hundred prisoners, and minutely reported Hooker's movements. Its services were handsomely acknowledged by General Lee and General Stuart in general orders.

An incident that occurred at this time illustrates the nature of this service. General Fitz Lee, with a brigade of cavalry, had crossed the Rappahannock, at Kelly's ford, and moving down the north bank of the river, had driven the enemy's pickets to within three miles of Falmouth. At Hartwood church he captured a number of prisoners, and detailing a guard of men, whose horses were in a weak and crippled condition, ordered Lieutenant A. D. Payne to take command and conduct them to the army, crossing at the United States ford. But he informed him that he would, in all probability, fall in with a company of Confederate cavalry which had been on picket. After proceeding about two miles, Lieutenant Payne came suddenly on a body of cavalry drawn up in the road, and discovered, after calling to know to which flag they belonged, that they were a squadron of the enemy. He immediately turned about, and, ordering the guard to shoot any prisoner who should attempt to escape, endeavored to return to Fitz Lee. Finding himself rapidly pursued, he turned off the main road, but soon encountered, drawn up in line, another force of Federal cavalry. He passed very near to them, and, much to his relief, succeeded in reaching his brigade. There he informed Major Morgan, of the First Virginia Cavalry, of the perils he had escaped, and directed him to the place where he would find the squadron he had last seen. Major Morgan at once, with an adequate force, repaired to the spot, finding the enemy occupying the same position, who at once surrendered. When Morgan returned with his prisoners, Lieutenant Payne inquired of their commander why he did not attempt to rescue the prisoners. The officer replied, "I was only waiting to surrender, for we were all too much excited to see that the greater part of your force were prisoners." Lieutenant Payne replied: "I was not quite that far gone; but if you had made an attack I should have been compelled to withdraw the guard and let the prisoners go."

When Fitz Lee returned to his position on the left flank of the army, Captain Randolph, again in command of the Black Horse, gave permission to ten or a dozen of the men to follow the march of the enemy toward Fredericksburg and pick up stragglers and horses. This they did for some distance, but finding neither men nor horses, the party returned. Two of them, however, "Old Blaze" and Joe Boteler, concluded to follow the hunt yet longer. A narrative of their adventures may prove interesting, and will at least show how such work may be done. Near the Stafford line they stopped at Mrs. H.'s and applied to have their canteens filled with brandy. This the old lady positively refused to do, saying: "You are in danger enough, without adding to it by drink." But she relented when they promised to bring her back "six Yankees."

And this is how they complied with their engagement. Between Spotted tavern and Hartwood church, the scouts charged with a yell a small party of the enemy and succeeded each in capturing a mounted cavalryman. These prisoners were disarmed and dismounted, and ordered to remain on the roadside until the captors should return. To induce them to do so, they were told that there was a force in the woods who would capture them if they attempted to escape. Depositing the arms and horses with a citizen, the scouts continued their ride in the same direction. Soon they came in sight of the rear guard of a cavalry force, and, taking advantage of a body of wood to conceal their numbers, charged with a shout. This hurried the retreat, and two of them, who had straggled, were taken prisoners. A little further on they met a soldier in blue, who proved to be an Irishman, and not suspecting an enemy, was easily added to their list of captures. Retracing their steps, they called for the horses and arms they had left, and, to their surprise, found their first capture waiting for them by the wayside. Remounting them on their own steeds, they met a little boy, who informed them that there were "three Yankee cavalrymen" at his uncle's, who lived a mile from the road. The horses were a temptation which the scouts could not resist, but the difficulty was how to dispose of their five prisoners while they went to secure them. Knowing two ladies zealous for the cause, they prevailed upon them to furnish a supper for the captured soldiers, but to delay in its preparation until their return. As fortune would have it, there were at the house two citizens who were charged with having taken the oath. The captured horses and arms having been secreted, with the exception of two carbines, these were loaded and given to the suspected citizens, and they were ordered to stand guard at the door. They were frankly told of the suspicion that attached to them, and that if they allowed the prisoners to escape they would be sent to Castle Thunder. The scouts followed their boy guide to his uncle's gate. One of them entered by the front door while his companion went around to the rear. As he entered the sitting-room on the first floor he found three Union soldiers. They sprang for their arms, which they had left in the hall, but the other scout coming to his companion's assistance, they were forced to surrender. One of them proved to be a courier of Colonel Kellogg, of the Eighteenth Pennsylvania, and had on his person valuable dispatches. The next step was to secure the horses, which having done, the Confederates returned with their additional prisoners and relieved the citizen guard. Supper over, the party started for the Confederate camp, but stopped at a house on the road, where the prisoners were allowed to sleep until daylight. Passing Mrs. H.'s, where they had been supplied with their brandy, they exhibited their eight prisoners, two more than they had promised to bring. As they entered camp with their captures, they were warmly congratulated by their comrades, and sent forward by Captain Randolph to General Stuart's headquarters. When told of the adventures of the scouts, the General expressed great satisfaction, but remarked it was the first time in his experience he had ever known whisky or brandy entitled to be put on the credit side of the sheet.

In the ensuing campaign of 1863, the Black Horse constituted a part of Stuart's cavalry division, and participated in the battle of

Chancellorsville, the severe fight at Brandy Station, and in all the movements conducted by Stuart to mask the movements of Lee's army in the Valley of Virginia as it was being marched for the invasion of Maryland and Pennsylvania. At Aldie, in the county of Loudon, the Black Horse, under command of Lieutenant A. D. Payne, covered itself with glory. The Southern cavalry had been pressing the pursuit from the direction of the Blue Ridge, during the day, and had brought the enemy to a stand at a point on the Middleburg road two miles from Aldie, and at an equal distance from that place on the Snickersville road, these two roads converging at Aldie. Colonel Mumford was in advance with the Fourth Regiment, the Black Horse being the leading squadron. He halted his command, and taking with him two pieces of artillery, he ordered Lieutenant A. D. Payne to follow with his command. He posted the artillery on a prominent point in the angle formed by the two roads, and commenced firing on the enemy who were advancing in large numbers on the Snickersville turnpike. To capture the guns placed in this exposed position the Federals sent forward a regiment of Massachusetts infantry. In this critical position of his guns, Colonel Munford ordered Lieutenant Payne, who had not with him more than thirty of his men, the rest being scattered as videttes, to charge the advancing column of cavalry, but never expecting, as he afterward said, to see one of them return alive. Lieutenant Payne formed his men in the turnpike in a column of fours, and down upon the enemy he rode with a loud cheer, the dust concealing the insignificant nature of his force. The regiment, thus deceived by the boldness and impetuosity of the attack, fired at random and was thrown into confusion. A number of prisoners were captured before they discovered their error, and returned to the attack. But the object of the cavalry charge had been attained and the guns were withdrawn in safety, and the timely arrival of the rest of the brigade saved the detachment from destruction.

When Stuart discovered Hooker's intention to cross the Potomac at Edwards' ferry, he left two brigades of cavalry posted between Lee and the Federal army to continue to perform outpost duty, while with the rest of his division he moved to the rear of the enemy's cavalry, and placed himself between the Federal army and Washington. This he effected, crossing the Bull Run mountain, and, after raiding through Prince William and Fairfax counties, recrossed the railroad at Burk's Station, where he found a large store of forage of great value to his tired animals. From this point he marched to the Potomac, at Seneca falls, where, as the fording was deep, the caissons were emptied and the bombshells carried over by cavalrymen in their hands. After capturing a canalboat laden with commissary stores, Stuart proceeded to Rockville, in the direction of Washington City. Here a large Union flag was flying, which he would not allow his men to pull down, saying he was not fighting the flag, but his real motive was that he wanted it as a decoy. From Rockville several regiments were sent in the direction of Washington, who captured the long wagon-train so often spoken of in connection with this campaign. It was drawn by more than an hundred mules, and seemed a rich prize; but it proved in the end a serious disadvantage, for it retarded the movements of the command, beside requiring a large detail of men. This raid produced great consternation among the enemy, and drew from Meade's army all his available cavalry to oppose it. But for this encumbrance Stuart could to better advantage have engaged the enemy, and destroyed, or, at least, interrupted the communications with Washington and Baltimore. At Westminster, eighteen miles west of Baltimore, the Fourth Virginia Regiment charged a regiment of Federal cavalry, driving a portion of it toward Baltimore, and the rest toward Frederick. From this point Stuart proceeded to Hanover, in Pennsylvania, where he engaged a large cavalry force under General Kilpatrick. In this fight the Second North Carolina Regiment was commanded by Lieutenant Colonel William H. Payne, formerly captain of the Black Horse. He bore himself with conspicuous gallantry, and was taken prisoner in a charge which he led, the regiment sustaining considerable loss in killed and wounded. The effort of Kilpatrick to detain Stuart was foiled by this fight, and he moved on to Carlisle barracks, which, with his artillery, he set on fire. From Carlisle the Southern cavalry marched to Gettysburg, and took position on Lee's left, near Huntersville. They took part in the battle on the memorable 3d of July, 1863, in which the Southern Confederacy received its death wound. Upon Meade's advance into Virginia, Lee retired to the south bank of the Rapidan, with headquarters at Orange Court-House, where he remained until October 11th. He then determined to assume the offensive.

With this intent he ordered General Fitz Lee, with whom the Black Horse was serving, to cross the Rapidan at Raccoon and Morton's fords, where he found himself face to face with Buford's cavalry division. In the fight which ensued, the Black Horse lost some of its bravest men, and the Fourth Virginia two of its most gallant officers. This spirited attack, combined with an attack by General Lomax's Brigade, compelled Buford's retreat to the direction of Stevensburg, closely pursued by Lomax. Captain Randolph, in command of the Black Horse, with some other men from the regiment, arrived at Stevensburg as the Third Virginia Cavalry had been repulsed. Being in line of battle he charged the Federals with great spirit, and drove them back on their dismounted line. Captain Randolph then ordered his men to fall back a few hundred yards in an open field, and there rallied them around their colors, under a heavy fire of the enemy. By this gallant conduct a large number of the Third Virginia, with their lieutenant colonel, were rescued. For this service General Fitz Lee complimented Captain Randolph in high terms, and said it was the most beautiful sight he had ever witnessed. This commendation was greatly valued by the command, but it had been dearly bought by the loss of many of its bravest members. General Fitz Lee continued the pursuit of Meade as far as Bull run, who, occasionally, turned upon his pursuers, and punished their audacity, as at Bristow Station. General R. E. Lee fell back to the Rappahannock, General Fitz Lee on the railroad, and Stuart, with Hampton's Division, on the turnpike, bringing up the rear. As soon as Fitz Lee crossed the river he sent two of the Black Horse back to watch the enemy's advance, and report his progress in rebuilding the railroad, but with permission to take any other men with them they might select. They crossed the river and recruited Sergeant Joseph Reid, of the Black Horse, a man remarkable even in that army and in that command for sagacity, calmness in the moment of danger, and a lion-like courage. Having collected much valuable information the party reported to General Fitz Lee, who ordered Sergeant Reid to take command of his scouts operating in Lower Fauquier, Prince William, and Stafford counties. So well did he perform this hazardous service, that he has left with the people of those localities many a thrilling tale of his daring and hairbreadth escapes. In consequence of information sent by Sergeant Reid, that the Federal army was moving toward the Rappahannock, furnished with eight days' cooked rations, and sixty rounds of ammunition, General Lee withdrew to the south side of the Rapidan. During this movement Meade advanced to Mine run, in Spottsylvania, where an undecided affair took place between the two armies, the Fourth Virginia Cavalry holding Roberson's ford on the Rapidan and repelling the efforts of the enemy's cavalry to effect a passage of the river at that point. From this point the Black Horse, with the exception of Sergeant Reid's party, were sent to Upper Fauquier and Loudon counties to observe and report the enemy's movements, on which duty they remained during the winter, at the close of which they were ordered to report to the regiment at Orange Court-

House. In the spring of 1864, before Grant, who now commanded the Union army, began his forward movement, General Sedgwick made a reconnoissance in force in the direction of Madison Court-House, and was met by A. P. Hill's Corps. In the collision which ensued Second Lieutenant Marshall James, one of the most gallant officers of the Black Horse, with a small detachment, greatly distinguished himself. In the latter part of April the cavalry corps marched to Fredericksburg and took position on the right of the Army of Northern Virginia. In May they broke camp to meet Grant's advance from Culpepper into the Wilderness by way of Germanna ford.

On the 4th and 5th of May were fought the battles of the Wilderness, after which Grant commenced upon Richmond his celebrated movement by his left flank. The Black Horse engaged in the desperate fighting which lasted for several days, in which the cavalry was employed to stem the torrent of Grant's advance until the infantry could be marched around to his front. During these engagements the Black Horse lost heavily in killed, wounded, and prisoners. Among the latter was a young Englishman by the name of Alston, who had crossed the sea to join this command. He was as gallant, in army phrase, as they make them, and true to the cause for which, he had staked his life. While in prison his friends in England sought to procure his release, and the Federal authorities were willing to set him at liberty upon condition of his returning home and taking no further part in the war. But Alston would not consent to be separated from his comrades. He was, in due course of time, exchanged, but died in Richmond before he could rejoin his command.

On Sunday, May 8th, the Southern cavalry were driven back to a position near Spottsylvania Court-House, where they formed a thin screen, behind which the infantry was concealed. The enemy advanced in full confidence of encountering only the force they had been driving, from cover to cover, since earliest dawn, but they were met by a murderous fire from a long line of battle, which sent some of them to the rear, but stretched most of them on the field. The day after the battle of Spottsylvania Court-House, Captain A. D. Payne ordered two of his chosen scouts to report for duty to the general commanding. They were directed to approach as near Chancellorsville as possible and report whether the troops that had been stationed at that point had been moved toward Spottsylvania Court-House, and to discover, if possible, at what point Grant was concentrating his army. The scouts, being entirely unacquainted

39

with the country, were sent to General Early, in the hope of obtaining a guide. But while Early could not furnish them a guide, he concerted with them signals, which, being communicated to the pickets, would enable them to re-enter his camp at any hour of the night, and himself conducted them through the lines of General Joe Davis' Brigade. Protected by the darkness, they soon found themselves in the midst of Grant's moving army, and made the discovery that the troops from Chancellorsville had been moved up to Spottsylvania Court-House, and that the centre of Grant's camp was south thirty degrees east from a particular house which had been marked on General Lee's diagram of the country, and furthermore that the Federals were throwing up earthworks. As soon as this information was communicated to General Lee, he turned to his map, and, drawing the line as the scout had reported, appeared greatly pleased. He said to the officers around him: "I am in the right position."

On the evening of the 9th, the cavalry followed Sheridan in his raid on Richmond, and had desperate fighting with his rear guard. On the 10th, the Black Horse, under command of Captain A. D. Payne, charged a party of the enemy and captured a number of prisoners. On the 11th, the Confederate cavalry, still in pursuit of Sheridan, renewed the fight at the Yellow tavern, near Richmond, in which General Stuart was mortally wounded. On the 12th, they engaged the head of Sheridan's column, at Meadow bridge, on the Chickahominy, but, overwhelmed by the weight of superior numbers, were compelled to withdraw. In the execution of this order, Lieutenant Colonel Randolph, a former captain of the Black Horse, was instantly killed. A braver and more beloved officer never perished on the field.

On Grant's arrival near Richmond, a desperate engagement occurred near Harris' shop, in which the Southern cavalry behaved with great gallantry, fighting for many hours as infantry, and for the greater part of the day resisted and obstructed the advance of Grant's whole army, until Lee had time to get his troops up from his line of battle and deliver the heavy blow which the next day he inflicted on the Federal army at the Second Cold Harbor. In this sanguinary engagement the Black Horse lost more than half the men taken into action.

Soon after, at Trevellyann's Station, General Hampton fought, perhaps, the bloodiest cavalry fight of the war, in which the Fourth Virginia Regiment behaved with conspicuous gallantry, sustaining again a heavy loss. Sheridan was now compelled to retire upon the main body, harassed by the Confederate cavalry, by whom he had been completely foiled in his attempt upon the communications leading to Richmond by way of the Virginia Central Railroad and James River canal. Returning to Lee's army, the Black Horse were occupied in arduous picket duty, and engaged in daily skirmishes, taking part, also, in the overthrow of Wilson's cavalry raiders.

In August, 1864, General Fitz Lee's cavalry division was sent to reinforce Early in the Valley, who had fallen back after his campaign against Washington. In the fight at Waynesborough the Black Horse was the leading squadron of the Fourth Regiment, and was especially complimented by General Early. After driving the enemy through the town, the Confederate cavalry halted on a hill in the western suburbs, when an officer in the Union service, Captain J. A. Bliss, faced his squadron, and, placing himself at its head, ordered a charge. But his men followed not their gallant leader. He, not looking to see, or, as it appeared, caring whether he was accompanied by his command, dashed alone into the midst of the Black Horse. No one fired at him, the men not wishing to kill so brave an officer. With his sabre he wounded several of the command, and some one knocked him from his horse, and might have killed him but for the interposition of Captain Henry Lee, a brother of Fitz Lee, who, observing the dismounted officer to make the Masonic sign, went to his assistance.

During this campaign, and after the affair just mentioned, George W. Martin and —— Campbell, of the Black Horse, with a member of the First Virginia Regiment, were returning from a scout late in the evening. It was raining, and the soldiers had their oilcloths thrown over their shoulders, which, in a great measure, concealed their uniform. On looking back, they saw three mounted men coming up behind them, whom they inferred were Union soldiers, as they were in the rear of Sheridan's forces. Drawing and cocking their pistols, they rode slowly, that they might be overtaken. The Federals—for such the party were—had had their suspicions aroused, and also prepared for the fight. As soon as they came alongside of them, the scouts wheeled and demanded a surrender, when they were fired upon by their opponents. They proved to be Lieutenant Meiggs, of Sheridan's staff, and two orderlies. Lieutenant Meiggs' shot passed through Martin's body, but he braced himself, returned the fire, and killed Meiggs. The other two scouts captured one of the orderlies. The other made his escape, and reported to Sheridan that his party had been bush-whacked, who, in retaliation, ordered the burning of every house in a radius of five miles. Joshua Martin was carried to the house of a farmer, where he was tenderly nursed until sufficiently recovered to return to his home in Fauquier. After the war closed, General Meiggs, believing that his son had been assassinated, sought to have Martin arrested and tried by a court-martial for murder; but when the facts, as above stated, were certified to him by Captain A. D. Payne, the matter was dropped, for Lieutenant Meiggs had been slain in open and legitimate war. George W. Martin is now at home, a prosperous agriculturist, and one of the most respected citizens in the community in which he resides.

In the month of December, the Black Horse was ordered into Hardy county, and performed hazardous but thankless service among the "Swamp Dragoons," as the disloyal element in that county named itself. They suffered severely from cold, but consumed large quantities of pork and apple brandy, in which, at that season, that inhospitable region abounds.

Returning from this duty, the command proceeded to Richmond, where it remained until the beginning of the final act in this stupendous tragedy. They fought side by side with their brethren of the cavalry at Five Forks, who never displayed a more indomitable spirit than in these closing scenes of the war. They were in the saddle day and night, marching and fighting without food, and without sleep, in the vain endeavor to protect the Confederate trains from the swarming hordes of the enemy's cavalry. At High bridge, the Black Horse shared, with their comrades of Fitz Lee's Division, the last rays of glory that fell on the Army of Northern Virginia, capturing an infantry brigade, and slaying its commander on the field. Near Farmville, the cavalry repulsed a division of Gregg's cavalry, which came upon them unawares, and nearly succeeded in capturing General Lee. But, instead, in this collision, General Gregg was taken prisoner. On April 9th, General Fitz Lee was ordered to hold the road from Appomattox Court-House to Lynchburg, which he did, in spite of repeated efforts by the enemy's cavalry to wrest it from him, until a flag, conveying the intelligence of a truce, compelled him to pause in his advance upon the enemy. Thus, sword in hand, the Black Horse, which had formed the nucleus of the Army of Northern Virginia, was found at the post of duty and of danger when that army of tattered uniforms and bright muskets surrendered to overwhelming numbers and resources. Of this army it might be said: "Vital in every part, it could only by annihilation die." The division of General Fitz Lee did not surrender until some time afterward; but, being cut off from the main body of the army, the Black Horse patiently awaited the approach of night, and, under its friendly cover, sought their various homes, which, four years before, they had left to fight for and protect. But the command was again collected at the Fauquier Springs, by order of Lieutenant Ficklin, Captain A. D. Payne being then a prisoner of war. They had resolved to repair to Johnston's standard, which was still, as they thought, flying in North Carolina. But the writer of this article repaired to their rendezvous, and informed Lieutenant Ficklin that General Johnston, too, had surrendered, and that the cause for which they had all fought had been lost. The Black Horse Cavalry was then disbanded, on the margin of the same river on which it had been organized, and but two miles lower down the stream.

The Black Horse Cavalry may now be found settled, for the most part, in their native seat, Lower Fauquier, as diligent in peace as they were courageous and faithful in war. But members of the command may be found scattered among the States, assiduous, in all the fields of enterprise, to catch the golden smiles of fortune. Of the Black Horse it may be said, as it was said of Cromwell's Ironsides, except that they tread the higher walks of life: "That, in every department of honest industry, the discharged warriors prospered beyond other men; that none were charged with theft or robbery; that none were heard to ask an alms; and that if a baker, a mason, or a wagoner attracted notice by his diligence or sobriety, he was, in all probability, one of Oliver's old soldiers."

DEATH OF GENERAL JOHN H. MORGAN.

BY H. V. REDFIELD.
[Second article.]

It is a singular fact that nearly two-thirds of the able-bodied white men of East Tennessee enlisted in the Federal army and fought the war through on the side of the Union. Singular, I say, because northward, in Kentucky, the Southern cause had more aid and encouragement than in East Tennessee; while Virginia, on the eastern boundary, was nearly unanimously Confederate, as well as Georgia and Alabama upon the southern border and Middle Tennessee upon the west. How is this to be accounted for? What strange freak made East Tennessee so loyal to the government, while upon all sides, North, East, South, and West, she was surrounded by the hosts in rebellion? That Kentucky was partially loyal, we can account for only because of her geographical position, making her more a Western than a Southern State; but here is East Tennessee, bordering upon the Cotton States, and allied to them by every interest, yet taking up arms for the Union with as much alacrity as though she bordered upon Lake Erie instead of the Cotton States. For illustration, take the two counties of Marion and Franklin, lying together, the former in the division of the State known as East Tennessee and the latter in Middle Tennessee, Marion bordering upon the Georgia and Alabama line and Franklin upon that of Alabama. The people of these two counties were identical in interest, and no argument could reach one that did not apply to the other. Yet, when the issue came these two counties stood as far apart as the poles. Marion voted for the Union until the last, when ballots were super-

(614)

ceded by bullets, while Franklin unanimously voted to take the State out of the Union. Indeed, at the June election, 1861, there was but one vote cast for the Union in that county! And so furious were the people in the cause that they held a sort of convention, passed a so-called ordinance of secession, and declared Franklin county out of the Union in advance of the State's action! The first regiment raised upon Tennessee soil was raised there—that of Colonel Peter Turney—which hurried off to Virginia, twelve hundred strong, before the State had formally "seceded." A capital command was this, going forth amid the huzzas and plaudits of the people, but never returning again as a regiment. A fragment came back—that was all. But in the adjacent county of Marion, how different was the feeling of the people! A majority were for the Union, and neither the firing upon Sumter or the President's proclamation could shake their allegiance to the old government. And when it came to the test and every able-bodied man had to go into one army or the other, a majority of the citizens of Marion made their way northward and entered the Federal ranks.

Although East Tennessee had a population of only about two hundred and fifty thousand, she put twenty-one cavalry regiments into the Union army and eight infantry regiments. Of this number twelve were organized as cavalry and the rest as mounted infantry, which is the same. In this there is no account taken of the Tennesseeans who enlisted in Kentucky, Ohio, Indiana, and Illinois regiments, of whom there were thousands. The policy of the government in mounting so large a proportion of the Tennessee troops was to get the benefit of their gallant horsemanship. Accustomed from early youth to horseback exercise they excelled in that branch of service. Some of the best cavalry in the service was from Tennessee. The Tennessee troops in the Union army are without a historian. There has been no extended narratives of their battles and exploits. And to this day it is not generally known in the North how great the aid the national cause received from the strong arms of the Tennessee Unionists. Had all the border slave States taken the course of East Tennessee, the war would not have lasted a year. But south of the Ohio and the Potomac there was no territory, not even Eastern Kentucky or Western Virginia, the population of which was as loyal to the government as that of East Tennessee. Virginia proper, lying eastward and northward of this section, was so true to the Confederacy that the whole State did not furnish five hundred white men to the Union army. Of course, in this estimate, I do not include what is known as Western Virginia, or any part of it. For the year ending May 1st, 1866, the records show that nearly fifteen thousand white Tennesseeans were mustered out of the Union army and eighty-five Virginians! Why this vast difference in sentiment in communities of the same blood, institutions, habits, customs, and interests?

A detail of the exploits of the Tennessee troops in the Union army would fill volumes; but so far from a single volume on the subject, there has never been anything like a connected narrative. The Tennessee troops were fighters, rather than writers, and they left little record of their transactions. It was Tennessee troops who finally routed the famous cavalry command of John H. Morgan and killed that daring raider. He vanquished armies, and captured more prisoners on single raids than his own men numbered; yet a strange fate decreed that he should meet his fate at the hands of Tennessee Unionists—the Thirteenth and Ninth Tennessee Cavalry regiments, aided by the Tenth Michigan. This brigade killed the great raider, and effectually broke up and scattered his command. In the garden of Mrs. Williams, in Greenville, Tennessee, a plain stone is set on the spot where Morgan fell. After his marvelous escape from the Ohio Penitentiary, he reorganized his command and entered Kentucky again. The expedition was unfortunate, and he returned to Virginia, and from thence operated in East Tennessee. He formed a plan to attack a brigade of Tennessee and Michigan troops at Bull's gap, above Knoxville. On the 3d of September he arrived in Greenville, his command camping near by, and a portion of his staff taking up their quarters at the residence of Mrs. Williams. This is the finest residence in Greenville—a large double brick house, not far from that of the late Andrew Johnson, but much larger and finer than any Johnson ever lived in, except the White House. It was built by Dr. Alexander Williams, who died a few years before the war, and, at the time of the tragedy, was occupied by his widow and a few members of the family. Mrs. Williams is now dead, but the house stands just as it did, and the surroundings are almost precisely the same as on that moist and gloomy September morning, in the year 1864, when the roof sheltered John H. Morgan the last night he spent on earth. I have passed the house dozens of times, but never without casting my eyes on the spot where the great cavalryman fell, and also at the point in the road where Private Andrew Campbell stood, whose unerring bullet pierced the heart of Morgan.

Morgan is accused of carelessness in posting himself and command, for the night, so near the enemy, and with so little precaution. The prime cause of the calamity to his command and death of himself was owing to the fact that he had ridden his troops very rapidly; they were worn out, and the pickets on the east side of the town fell asleep. Colonel Miller, who was posted near Bull's gap, did not know of the presence of Morgan in that part of the country until six P. M., September 3d. It is said that a woman brought him the news, and many pictures have been painted of her rapid horseback ride from Greenville to the gap; but upon a recent visit to Greenville, those having personal knowledge of the matter denied that there was "a woman in it." But, however this may be, when the news came, Colonel Miller and General Gilliam held a short consultation, and the command was ordered to be in readiness to move. At eleven o'clock that night, in the midst of a terrible thunder-storm, which fairly drenched the soldiers, the Thirteenth Tennessee moved out toward Greenville, by way of the Arnett road. At midnight they were followed by the rest of the command, making a total of about two thousand men, fifteen hundred of whom were Tennesseeans. The storm increased, the rain fell in torrents, the heavens fairly shook with rolling thunder, while there was no light other than the flashes of lightning. But the dark column of horsemen moved steadily on, and John Morgan slept his last sleep on earth. In so stormy and tempestuous a night he may have felt secure from intrusion, be the enemy ever so vigilant. Just before the first streak of dawn the advance swung around in rear of Morgan's command, captured the pickets who were asleep, and virtually got between Morgan and his soldiers. Sharp fighting ensued and great confusion. At the opportune moment Colonel Ingerton, commanding the Thirteenth Regiment, sent Companies I and G on a bold dash into town, in hopes of getting the great cavalry chieftain. It was not yet fairly daylight, and the Federals had all the advantage. These companies surrounded the Williams house, some of Company G occupying the street which leads from the depot to Main street. The first intimation Morgan had was from a servant, who rushed to his room, saying, "the Yankees are coming!" Morgan did not believe it, and prepared to go to sleep again. Again the news came, and with it was the accompaniment of musketry firing, which gave forth no uncertain sound. Looking out he was horrified to see the enemy around the house, and without waiting to fully dress he and Major Gassett, of his staff, rushed out into the garden, or back yard. Escape seeming to be cut off in that direction they ran into the cellar, where they remained a few moments. Feeling that death or capture awaited them there, and observing from the enemy's movements that their whereabouts was known, they ran out into the garden again, Gassett concealing himself in an outhouse and Morgan attempting to hide among the grape vines. His white shirt betrayed him as he crouched behind the vines and posts. Private Andrew Campbell saw him from the street, not over fifty yards distant, and fired, hitting Morgan plump in the breast, and killing him instantly. He never spoke. Morgan's friends claim that he was foully murdered, and that he had called out that he would surrender. Campbell says that he was trying to get away, and making no motion that looked like a surrender. The soldiers carried the body of Morgan to the street, threw it across a horse and rapidly returned to the main column, who were engaged with Morgan's command, which they routed. They captured two cannon, many wagons, and prisoners, and, in fact, virtually broke up Morgan's command. The forces engaged on the Union side were the Thirteenth Tennessee Cavalry, Colonel Miller; Ninth Tennessee Cavalry, Colonel Brownlow, and Tenth Michigan, Major Newell. So complete was the surprise and rout of Morgan's command that the Federal loss was but two killed and four wounded.

Morgan's body was carried on a horse about one mile, where it was laid by the roadside, and afterward turned over to some of Morgan's friends, who came for it with a flag of truce. The body was carried to Abington, Virginia, and buried, and soon after removed to Richmond. Whatever became of Campbell I do not know. He is marked on the muster rolls as having moved to Ohio. Immediately after the victory, he was promoted to second lieutenant in Company E, same regiment, by General Order No. 95, which states that the promotion is made as "a reward for his gallantry in the engagement at Greenville, Tennessee, on the 4th instant, and for his success in arresting, by an accurate shot, the flight of General John H. Morgan, one of our country's most prominent enemies."

THE MISTAKES OF GETTYSBURG.

BY GENERAL JAMES LONGSTREET.
[Second article.]

IN my first article I declared that the invasion of Pennsylvania was a movement that General Lee and his council agreed should be defensive in tactics, while, of course, it was offensive in strategy; that the campaign was conducted on this plan until we had left Chambersburg, when, owing to the absence of our cavalry, and our consequent ignorance of the enemy's whereabouts, we collided with them unexpectedly, and that General Lee had lost the matchless equipoise that usually characterized him, and, through excitement and the doubt that enveloped the enemy's movements, changed the whole plan of the campaign, and delivered a battle under ominous circumstances. I declared that the battle of the 2d was not lost through the tardiness of the First Corps, but through the failure of the troops ordered to co-operate to do so; that there was no order ever issued for a sunrise attack; that no such order could have been issued, and that the First Corps could not possibly have attacked at that time; that when it did attack its movement was weakened by the derangement of the directing brigade of support under General Wilcox, and was rendered hopeless by the failure of Ewell's Corps to co-operate, its line of battle having been broken through the advice of General Early, and that in this attack Hood's and McLaws' Divisions did the best fighting ever done on any field, and encountered and drove back virtually the whole of the Army of the Potomac. I held that the mistakes of the Gettysburg campaign were:

First, the change of the original plan of the campaign, which was to so maneuvre as to force the Federals to attack us; second, that if the plan was to have been changed at all it should have been done at Brandy Station, near Culpepper Court-House, when we could have caught Hooker in detail, and, probably, have crushed his army; third, that Stuart should never have been permitted to leave the main route of march, and thus send our army into the enemy's country without cavalry for reconnoissance or foraging purposes; fourth, that the crushing defeat inflicted on the advance of the Federal army in the casual encounter of the 1st, at Willoughby's run, should have been pushed to extremities, that occasion furnishing one of the few opportunities ever furnished for "pursuit pell-mell;" fifth, the army should have been carried around to Meade's right and rear on the night of the 1st, and placed between him and his capital, and thus forced him to attack us, as he certainly intended doing; sixth, when I attacked the enemy's left on the 2d, Ewell should have moved at once against his right, and Hill should have threatened his centre, and thus prevented a concentration of the whole Federal army at the point I was assaulting; seventh, on the morning of the 3d we should still have moved to the right, and maneuvred the Federals into attacking us; eighth, the assault by Pickett, on the 3d, should never have been made, as it could not have succeeded by any possible prodigy of courage or tactics, being absolutely a hope-less assault. These points I supported with the most particular proof. Not a single one of them has been controverted. The truth of a single fact, or the correctness of a single opinion laid down in that article, has not been disproved. Very few of them have been questioned—none of them overthrown.

The first point that demands attention is the number of forces on each side engaged in the Gettysburg campaign. In my first article I claimed that we had fifty-two thousand infantry, and the Federals ninety-five thousand men; stating, further, that those were the highest figures of our forces, and the lowest of theirs. General R. R. Dawes, in commenting on this estimate, disagrees with it quite widely. The main point that he makes is to quote from Swinton's "Army of the Potomac," the following paragraph (page 310): "The number of infantry present for duty in Lee's army on the 31st of May, 1863, was precisely sixty-eight thousand three hundred and fifty-two. I learn from General Longstreet that, when the three corps were concentrated at Chambersburg, the morning report showed sixty-seven thousand bayonets, or above seventy thousand of all arms." This statement is certainly explicit, but there are discrep-ancies on the face of it that should have warned a cautious and capable writer not to accept it: First, any one at all familiar with the history of the campaign, or even the leading points of it, must have known that the three corps of the army were never "concentrated at Chambersburg" at all; second, it is well known that any organization upon sixty-seven thousand bayonets would have involved an infantry force alone of "over seventy thousand," and thus have left no margin in the estimate that Mr. Swinton ascribes to me for the other arms of the service.

If General Dawes had followed Swinton's narrative closely, he must have discovered that (page 365) he says: "General Lee's aggregate force present for duty on the 31st of May, 1863, was sixty-eight thousand three hundred and fifty-two." These are the precise figures that he gives, on page 310, as the aggregate of the infantry alone. My information upon this subject was taken from General Lee's own lips. He estimated his force to be, including the detachments that would join him on the march, a trifle over seventy thousand. On the 30th of June, or the 1st of July, he estimated his infantry at fifty-two thousand bayonets. If Mr. Swinton received any information from me on the subject, he received this, for it was all that I had. Since I have read the report of the Adjutant General of the Army of Northern Virginia, lately published, I am inclined to believe that General Lee included in his estimate two brigades of Pickett's Division (Jenkins' and Corse's) which were left in Virginia, or some other detachments made during the march. If this surmise is correct, it would make the total figures considerably less than I gave them. I am certain the real strength of his army cannot go above the number given in my first article. As to the strength of General Meade's army, I take his own statement for that. In his evidence taken before the Committee on the Conduct of the War (page 337 of their report), he says: "My strength was a little under one hundred thousand—probably ninety-five thousand men." I used, in my narrative, the lowest figures that he gave. In printing the article, it is made to appear that Meade had ninety-five thousand infantry. It should have been ninety-five thousand men. This much as to the comparative strength of the two armies. It is the truth, and will stand as history that Meade's army was nearly double that of Lee.

In my first article, I claimed that my troops fought an extraordinary battle on the 2d. I asserted that my thirteen thousand men virtually charged against the whole Federal army, encountered nearly sixty-five thousand of the enemy, and broke line after line of fresh troops, until at length, after three hours' of the best fighting ever done, they found themselves, in a single line of battle, charging fifty thousand Federals, intrenched, massed on Cemetery Ridge. Then, when one-third of their number lay in their bloody track, dead or wounded, and they were exposed in front and flank to an overwhelming fire, and their supporting brigades had gone astray, and there was no sign of positive or strategic co-operation from their comrades, I ordered them to withdraw to the peach orchard that they had wrested from the Third Corps early in the engagement. This claim has been severely criticised. It can be established by the testimony of every honest and well-informed man who was in that battle. But I relied for my proof upon the official report of General Meade himself. He made this report, it will be remembered, thinking that the whole or greater part of Lee's army had charged his position in the afternoon of the 2d. He says:

> The Third Corps sustained the shock most heroically. Troops from the Second were sent by Major General Hancock to cover the right flank of the Third Corps, and soon after the assault commenced. * * * The Fifth Corps, most fortunately, arrived, and took position on the left of the Third. Major General Sykes, commanding, immediately sending a force to occupy Round Top Ridge, where a most furious contest was maintained, the enemy making desperate but unsuccessful attempts to secure it. Notwithstanding the stubborn resistance of the Third Corps, under Major General Birney (Major General Sickles having been wounded early in the action), superiority of number of corps of the enemy enabling him to outflank its advanced position, General Birney was compelled to fall back and re-form behind the line originally desired to be held. In the meantime, perceiving the great exertions of the enemy, the Sixth Corps (Major General Sedgwick) and part of the First Corps, to which I had assigned Major General Newton, particularly Lockwood's Maryland Brigade, together with detachments from the Second Corps, were brought up at different periods, and succeeded, together with the gallant resistance of the Fifth Corps, in checking, and finally repulsing, the assault of the enemy. * * * During the heavy assault upon our extreme left, portions of the Twelfth Corps were sent as reinforcements.

To make this specific and positive proof still more conclusive, I may add the testimony of General Meade given before the Committee on the Conduct of the War, in which he says (speaking of this battle of the 2d): "My extreme right flank was then held by a single brigade of the Twelfth Corps, commanded by General Green." Then the troops opposing my thirteen thousand men (two divisions of my corps) were as follows: Third Corps, eleven thousand eight hundred and ninety-eight; Fifth Corps, ten thousand one hundred and thirty-six; Sixth Corps, fifteen thousand four hundred and eight; Pennsylvania Reserves, four thousand five hundred; Lockwood's Maryland Brigade, two thousand five hundred; total, forty-four thousand four hundred and forty-two. The above figures are taken from the Congressional Report, page 428. To these figures must be added

the detachments from the other corps enumerated by General
Meade. As he is not minute in his statements, I have no accurate
data by which I can tell precisely what these "detachments" were.
As General Meade states, however, that he left but a single brigade
to guard his extreme right, and as he·had no use for troops elsewhere, it is reasonable to suppose that the other corps may have
sent as many as twenty thousand men, other than those enumerated
above. Indeed, this estimate is quite low, in all probability; because
General Meade believed, and his counselors all believed, as is shown
by their concurrent testimony, that the assault made by my handful
of heroes was really the onset of the whole of Lee's army. It is fair
to presume, then, that, under this belief, he massed everything that
he could get his hands on in front of the direct attack. He says as
much as this when he says he left "only a single brigade" on his
right. My former estimate, therefore, "that my thirteen thousand
men met sixty-five thousand men during the three hours' fighting
that afternoon," will not be abandoned until the report of General
Meade, and the figures of the Congressional Report, shall have been
overthrown; conceding, of course, to the technical demand of historical statement that the "detachments" of other corps sent forward
may not have been exactly twenty thousand men.

It has never been claimed that we met this immense force of
sixty-five thousand men at one time; nor has it been claimed that
each and every one of them burnt powder in our faces. But they
were drawn off from other parts of the field to meet us, and were
hurried to our front and massed there, meaning to do all the mischief
they could. If some of them did not shoot us, or stick us with their
bayonets, it was simply because they could not shoot through the
solid blocks of their own troops, or reach us with their bayonets over
the heads of their comrades. But they were in position and eager
for battle—ready to rush down upon us the moment the line next in
front of them was broken. The *morale* of their presence in reinforcing the position and threatening our flanks as we pressed on, was
about as effective as their actual bloody work could have been. As
to the accounts of the Cincinnati *Gazette* and the New York *World;*
they were not given as documents of historical record, but simply as
confirmatory of General Meade's statements, which are, of course,
historical. It was not too much to assume that the representatives
of these papers would know what Federal corps were actively
engaged in the battle of the 2d. They both confirmed the account
given by General Meade in the belief that the whole of the Confederate army was engaged in the assault, and in the statement that very

nearly the whole of the Federal army was engaged in repelling it. After a review, therefore, of the whole situation, and a careful reading of everything that has been published since the appearance of my first article, I am confirmed in the opinion then expressed that my troops did, on that afternoon, "the best three hours' fighting ever done by any troops on any field."

In my general narrative I did not give a detailed criticism or account of the tactical movements of the 2d for two reasons : First, my newspaper friends admonished me that my article had grown quite long, and that it was already clear enough to satisfy the most skeptical mind ; second, I thought that my allusions to time, cause, and effect would arrest the attention of those who had misconceived, and therefore misrepresented them, and that they would hasten to make proper explanation and corrections. I find their minds, however, so filled with prejudice and preconceived opinions, that it seems imperative I should explain the relations of our tactical moves on the 2d, and force a confession from even their reluctant mouths. Having demonstrated beyond cavil in my first article that General Lee never ordered a sunrise attack, that he never expected one, and that it was physically impossible to have made one, I shall now show that even if one had been made it could not have bettered the result that was achieved by the afternoon attack. It will be proved that the battle made by my men could not have been so improved, in plan or execution, as to have won the day. The only amendment that would have ensued, or even promised victory, was for Ewell to have marched in upon the enemy's right when it was guarded by a single brigade, run over their works and fall upon their rear while I engaged them in front, and while Hill lay in a threatening position in their centre. Had this co-operative movement been made the battle would, in all probability, have been ours. As it was, no disposition of the men under my charge, no change in the time, or method, or spirit of the assault, could have changed the result for the better.

Let us briefly review the situation on the morning of the 2d. During the night of the 1st, General Sickles rested with the Third Corps upon the ground lying between General Hancock's left and Round Top, General Geary's Division of the Twelfth Corps occupying part of the same line. General Meade had given General Sickles orders to occupy Round Top if it were practicable ; and in reply to his question as to what sort of position it was, General General Sickles had answered : "There is no position there." At the first signs of activity in our ranks on the 2d, General Sickles became apprehensive that we were about to attack him, and so reported to General Meade. As our move progressed, his apprehensions were confirmed, and being uneasy at the position in which his troops had been left, and certain that he was about to receive battle, he determined to seize the vantage ground in front of the peach orchard. Without awaiting for orders, he pushed forward and took the position desired. Meanwhile, the reports made to General Meade drew his attention to our part of the field, and finally he rode out just in time to see the battle open. It will be seen, therefore, that General Sickles' move, and all the movements of the Federal left, were simply sequents of mine. They would have followed my movements inevitably, no matter when they had been made. Had the attack been made earlier or later we should have seen the Federals move just as they did, and with the same results—except that if I had attacked earlier I should have had Geary's Division of the Twelfth Corps in my immediate front in addition to the Third Corps. This would certainly have been the effect of " a sunrise attack."

Colonel Taylor, in referring to the hour of my battle on the 2d, says: " Round Top, the key of their position, which was not occupied in the morning, was now held in force." The answer to this statement, direct and authoritative, is at hand. General Meade says, in Congressional Report, page 332: " Immediately upon the opening of the batteries (which began the battle) I sent several staff officers to hurry up the column under General Sykes of the Fifth Corps, then on its way, and which I expected would have reached there at that time. The column advanced rapidly, reached the ground in a short time, and General Sykes was fortunately enabled, by throwing a strong force upon Round Top mountain, where a most desperate and bloody struggle ensued, to drive the enemy from it, and secure our foothold upon that most important position." Even the Muses were invoked to speed this helter-skelter march toward the knob of ground now suddenly grown in importance.

> " On to the Round Top!" hailed Sykes to his men;
> " On to the Round Top!" echoed the glen.
> " On to the Round Top!"

In my former narrative I showed that General Meade did not appreciate the importance of this position until the battle had finally opened. He had ordered Sickles to occupy it "if practicable;" but it was not occupied in force when my battle opened, and was made strong as the fight progressed, as much by the fragments of the enemy's broken lines, that took shelter behind its boulders, as by any

40

definite plan to seize it. It is needless to say that the same thing
would have happened had the battle taken place either earlier or
later. The force stationed there when the battle opened had been
there all day, and was wholly inadequate to hold it; hence General
Meade's anxiety to hurry up additional troops after the battle had
opened, and his congratulation that Sykes, by throwing forward "a
strong force," was enabled to drive us from it and secure it to the
Federals. But why go further with these details? It is impossible
that any sane man should believe that two of my divisions, attacking
at any hour or in any manner, could have succeeded in dislodging
the Army of the Potomac. We had wrestled with it in too many
struggles, army against army, to prefer, in sincerity, any such claim.
From daylight until dark, not a single Confederate soldier, outside
of my two divisions and the three supporting brigades, was advanced
to battle, or made to even threaten battle. The work was left
entirely with my men. General Ewell dates his co-operative move
at dusk. General Meade says it was at eight o'clock. In any event
it was after my battle had closed, and too late to do any good.
Hence there seems to be no place for honesty in the speculation that
my command could have won the field by different battle. It is
equally out of sense to say that if my attack had been made "at
sunrise," Ewell would have given me the co-operation that he failed
to give in the afternoon when the attack really did come off. His
orders, given in the morning after it was decided that I should lead
the attack, were to remain in line of battle, ready to co-operate with
my attack whenever it should be made. If he was not ready in the
afternoon, it is folly to say that he would have been ready at sunrise.

My opinion of the cause of the failure of the battle of the 2d, as
given at the time, is very succinctly stated by Colonel Freemantle,
on page 138, of his "Three Months in the South." He says, quoting
me: "He said the mistake they made was in not concentrating the
army more and making the attack on the 2d with thirty thousand
men instead of fifteen thousand." * I doubt now if thirty thousand
men could have made a successful attack, if Colonel Taylor is correct
in his idea as to the manner in which General Lee would have fought
them. He says that General Lee ordered that the column should go
to the attack with its right flank exposed to the enveloping forces on
the Federal left. Under this disposition I do not think thirty
thousand men could have successfully made the attack. The battle

---

* It seems, from recent publications, that my column of attack on the 2d was
only about twelve thousand. It was given me as fifteen thousand men at the time.

should not have been made under the circumstances. We should have drawn everything up on the night of the 1st, and made a quick move by our right flank on the morning of the 2d, so as to seize the Emmettsburg road. Had we done this, we should either have been attacked—the very thing we had been hoping and mourning for—or we should have dislodged Meade from his position without striking a blow. If we had been attacked, we should have certainly repulsed it. Had Meade deserted his position without striking a blow in its defense, the moral effect in our favor would have been tremendous. To show that one of these results would certainly have followed, I quote a dispatch sent in cipher from General Meade to General Halleck just before my battle on the 2d. The dispatch reads: "If not attacked, and I can get any positive information of the enemy which will justify me in doing so, I will attack. If I find it hazardous to do so, and am satisfied that the enemy is endeavoring to move to my rear and interpose between me and Washington, I shall fall back on my supplies at Westminster." If, however, no decisive result had followed immediately upon the flank movement that should have been made on the night of the 1st, or the morning of the 2d, the thirteen days that elapsed between our first rencontre and our re-crossing of the Potomac would have surely given time and opportunity for different work and greater results than were had at Gettysburg.

It is conceded by almost, if not quite, all authority on the subject, that Pickett's charge, on the 3d, was almost hopeless. We had tested the enemy's position thoroughly on the day before, and with a much larger force than was given to Pickett. We had every reason to believe that the position was much stronger on the 3d than it was on the 2d. The troops that had fought with me the day before were in no condition to support Pickett, and, beside, they were confronted by a force that required their utmost attention. The men of Generals Pickett, Pettigrew, and Trimble, however, received and executed their orders with cool and desperate courage. When the utmost measure of sacrifice demanded by honor was full they fell back, and the contest was ended. The charge was disastrous, and had the Federal army been thrown right upon the heels of Pickett's retreating column, the results might have been much more serious.

In this connection it may be noted that the Federal line in front of these troops was not broken so much by direct assault as by crushing in the lines on their left. General Humphreys was forced to change front, partially, two or three times to meet threatened flank movements against him, and he was in that way drawn off from immediate connection with his right.   The skilful handling of these troops, commanded by General A. A. Humphreys, was noted at the time, and has been particularly noted since by General Humphries (of Mississippi).   At this late day the official relations of General Lee and myself are brought into question.   He is credited with having used uncomely remarks concerning me, in the presence of a number of subordinate officers, just on the eve of battle.   It is hardly possible that any one acquainted with General Lee's exalted character will accept such statements as true.   It is hardly possible that any general could have been so indiscreet as to have used such expressions under such circumstances.   There certainly never was, in the relations between General Lee and myself, anything to admit the possibility of his having used the expression attributed.   Our relations were affectionate, intimate, and tender during the whole war.   That his confidence in me was never shaken, there is the most abundant proof; but I cannot be tempted, even by direct misrepresentations, into a discussion of this subject.   I will advert to one point that will go to show the relations that existed between us.   It is an incident of the second battle of Manassas.

When the head of my column reached that field it was about twelve o'clock on the 29th.   As we approached the field we heard sounds of a heavy battle, which proved to be General Jackson very severely engaged with the enemy.   As my column deployed on the field, the enemy at once withdrew, in good order, however, and took up a strong position a little in the rear of where the heaviest fighting had been going on.   During the lull that succeeded, General Lee rode up to where I was and told me that he had determined to attack the position taken by the enemy, and indicated his purpose to have me open the fight.   My men were then arranged for battle, but I asked General Lee to withhold the order for attack until I had made a careful reconnoissance, and determined exactly how the troops had best be handled.   He consented, of course, to this, and I went forward to make the reconnoissance.   After a careful examination of the ground, I rode back to General Lee, and reported that the position was very strong and the prospects hardly such as to warrant the heavy sacrifice of life that a serious attack would involve.   General Lee was not satisfied, however, but seemed disposed to insist upon an attack.   He began to suggest moves by which an advantageous assault might be made.   Before the question was at all decided, a dispatch was received from General Stuart, giving us notice that a very strong column was moving up against my right. General Lee ordered me at once to reinforce that part of my line and be ready to repel the attack. I ordered the reinforcing column to the march and rode out rapidly in advance, that I might see precisely what was needed. The threatening column proved to be General Fitz John Porter's command. After seeing it, I reported back to General Lee that it was too light a column, in my opinion, to mean a real attack. This presumption was correct, and the advance soon halted and then withdrew.

General Lee then recalled the question of an immediate attack upon the main position of the Federals. I was thoroughly convinced that the position was too strong to be taken without very severe loss, and I suggested to General Lee that the attack be postponed, and that we make a forced reconnoissance just at nightfall, and that we could then prepare to attack at daylight, if it seemed advisable after thorough investigation to make the attack at all. He consented very readily to this, and I left him to prepare for the forced reconnoissance. The reconnoissance was successfully made at nightfall. During the night several of my brigadiers came in and they all agreed in reporting the position very strong. At about midnight Generals Hood and Evans, and possibly one or two others, came to my headquarters and made similar reports, expressing apprehensions as to the result of the attack. Everything developed by this closer reconnoissance went to confirm the impression made upon me by my reconnoissance during the day. I, therefore, determined not to make the attack, and ordered my troops back to the original line of battle.

The next day the Federals advanced against General Jackson in very heavy force. They soon made the battle so severe for him that he was obliged to call for reinforcements. At about three P. M., while the battle was raging fiercely, I was riding to my front, when I received a note from Generals Hood and Evans, asking me to ride to a part of the field where they were standing. I changed my course and hurried to the point indicated. I found them standing upon a high piece of ground, from which they had full view of the battle made against Jackson We could see the solid masses of the Federals forming for a charge against Jackson's weakening lines. They were gathered in immense force, and it seemed impossible that Jackson's thin lines could withstand the onset. The Federals moved forward steadily, surging on in solid blocks, headed directly for Jackson's lines. Just then a courier arrived in great haste with orders from General Lee for me to hurry to the assistance of Jackson. It was in the very crisis of the battle. I had very serious doubts about being able to reach General Jackson in time to be of any service to him. I had no doubt, however, that I could impede or paralyze the immense mass of men that was pressing steadily to his overthrow. We were standing on the flank of the advancing columns. They swept on at right angles to our line of vision. They were within easy artillery range, and I felt certain that a heavy enfilading fire poured unexpectedly into their charging columns would disconcert and check it. Instead of moving to reinforce Jackson therefore, I sent dispatches for batteries to hurry to where I was. In an exceedingly short time Captain Wiley's six-gun batteries came dashing up at full gallop, the horses covered with foam, and the men urging them forward. They were wheeled into position and directed against the moving flank of the enemy. The range was fair, and as the six guns flashed, the heavy shot went ploughing through the solid flank of the Federals, doing terrible damage.

The result was as anticipated. The line faltered for an instant, started again, hesitated, re-formed, and pressed forward, and then, as a rear broadside was poured into them, broke ranks and retired slowly, sullenly, and doggedly. General Jackson did not pursue, and the Federals halted after moving back a short distance, and arranged to re-form their ranks and renew the charge. As soon as they started, however, they were obliged to face against General Jackson. This exposed them, of course, to our enfilading fire. We now had several batteries in position, and as soon as the lines had taken shape and started on their second assault, we poured a perfect hail of balls into their flanks and scattered them again. Although discomfited, they were not broken, but retired with their slow, angry, sullen step. When they had gone beyond the fair range of our batteries they halted, and tried to form again for the third assault. I now determined to end the matter, feeling that I had an easy victory in my grasp. I, therefore, ordered every battery to be in readiness, and drew my men up for a charge, designing to throw them into the broken ranks of the enemy as soon as my artillery had dispersed them. The Federals moved forward once more. When they were fairly in range every gun was opened upon them, and before they had recovered from the stunning effect, I sprung every man that I had to the charge, and swept down upon them like an avalanche. The effect was simply magical. The enemy broke all to pieces. I pushed my men forward in a pell-mell pursuit, hoping to reach the main Federal lines at the same time with their retreating forces. We succeeded in this and drove the enemy back, pursuing them until fully ten o'clock at night. In the meanwhile, I received a note from General Lee. He had heard my guns, and at once supposed I had thought it best to relieve Jackson in a different manner from that indicated by his orders. He, therefore, wrote me that if I had "found anything better than reinforcing Jackson, to pursue it." I mention this incident simply to show the official relations that existed between General Lee and myself. As to our personal relations I present two letters throwing light upon that subject. One is from Colonel W. H. Taylor, Assistant Adjutant General, and the other is from General Lee himself:

HEADQUARTERS ARMY OF NORTHERN VIRGINIA,
April 26th, 1864.

My Dear General :—I have received your note of yesterday, and have consulted the General about reviewing your command. He directs me to say that he has written to the President to know if he can visit and review the army this week, and, until his reply is received, the General cannot say when he can visit you. He is anxious to see you, and it will give him much pleasure to meet you and your corps once more. He hopes soon to be able to do this, and I will give you due notice when he can come. I really am beside myself, General, with joy of having you back. It is like the reunion of a family.

Truly and respectfully yours,
W. H. TAYLOR, A. A. G.

To GENERAL LONGSTREET.

LEXINGTON, VA., March 9th, 1866.

My Dear General :—Your son Garland handed me, a few days since, your letter of the 15th of January, with the copies of your reports of operations in East Tennessee, the Wilderness, etc., and of some of my official letters to you. I hope you will be able to send me a report of your operations around Suffolk and Richmond previous to the evacuation of that city, and of any of my general orders which you may be able to collect. Can you not occupy your leisure time in preparing memoirs of the war. Every officer whose position and character would give weight to his statements, ought to do so. It is the only way in which we can hope that fragments of truth will reach posterity. Mrs. Longstreet will act as your amanuensis. I am very sorry that your arm improves so slowly. I trust that it will, eventually, be restored to you. You must present my kindest regards to Mrs. Longstreet. I hope your home in New Orleans will be happy, and that your life, which is dear to me, will be long and prosperous.

Most truly yours,
R. E. LEE.

There is one point to which I call especial attention. The friends of Colonel J. B. Walton, Chief of Artillery of the First Corps, think that in my first an inferential injustice was done to that gentleman. Colonel Walton was an officer of great worth, and at all times had the confidence of his commanding officers, and it is with pleasure that I correct what certainly was an unintentional derogation of his quality. It is true that in part of my first narrative there were sentences subject to the erroneous impression that Colonel Walton was not in full command of the artillery of the First Corps at the battle of Gettysburg. My orders, however, as well as my instructions, quoted in another part of the narrative, were addressed to Colonel J. B. Walton, as Chief of Artillery, and show conclusively that he was in command on that day. Colonel Alexander figured more prominently in the correspondence that passed between myself and the artillery, simply because I had consulted personally with Colonel Alexander on these points before the battle opened, and because he was most directly interested in the handling of the artillery massed at the peach orchard, and under cover of which Pickett was to make his charge. Colonel Walton was a brave and capable officer, and I regret that my narrative was so construed as to reflect upon his fair and spotless record.

There were two or three trifling inaccuracies in my first account of this battle which need correction: The scout, upon whose information the head of our column was turned to the right, reported at Chambersburg on the night of the 28th of June. It is printed the 29th. Several orders that I issued on the 1st of July, and so dated, appear under the date of the 18th. The real strength of Pickett's Division was four thousand five hundred bayonets. It was printed five thousand five hundred. In the paragraph where I stated that General Meade anticipated my attack of the 3d, and told General Hancock that he intended to throw the Fifth and Sixth Corps against its flanks when it was made, it is printed that he gave this information in the "evening," when, of course, it should have been "morning."

I have now done, for the present, with the campaign of Gettysburg. What I have written about it has been compelled from me by a desire on the one hand to have future historians properly informed upon the most important movement of the war, and a necessity on the other hand of correcting important mis-statements made ignorantly or maliciously concerning it. I have written nothing that was not supported by abundant proof, advanced no opinions not clearly justified by the facts. As disastrous as the results of that battle were, and as innocent as I was of bringing them upon my people, I accepted my share of the disaster without a murmur, and cheerfully bore the responsibility of it as long as there was a possibility of injuring the cause we were engaged in by a discussion of the points involved. I should probably have never written a line concerning the battle, had it not been for the attempt of the wordy soldiers to specifically fix upon me the whole burden of that battle—their rashness carrying them so far as to lead them to put false orders in the mouth of our great captain, and charge me with having broken them. To disprove these untrue assertions, and to give the world the truth concering the battle, then became what

I considered an imperative duty. I repeat that I regret most deeply that this discussion was not opened before the death of General Lee. If the charges so vehemently urged against me after his death had been preferred, or even suggested, in his lifetime, I do not believe they would have needed any reply from me. General Lee would have answered them himself, and have set history right. But, even as the matter is, I do not fear the verdict of history on Gettysburg. Time sets all things right. Error lives but a day—truth is eternal.

There is an incidental matter to which I shall refer in this connection. It is in regard to a statement made by Mr. Swinton. In his "Ultimo Suspiro," he gives the history of a meeting which he says took place on the 7th of April, 1865, between General Lee and his leading officers. He says that this meeting was a private council, and that the officers united in advising General Lee to surrender on that day—two days before the surrender took place at Appomattox. In describing that meeting, he does me the grave injustice of putting my name among the officers who gave General Lee this advice. The truth of the matter is, I never attended any such meeting. I had no time to have done so. I was kept incessantly busy in the field during the days preceding the surrender at Appomattox. All night long of the 1st we marched with Fields' Division from Richmond to Petersburg, reaching that point at early dawn on the 2d. I at once went to General Lee's headquarters. I found him in bed in his tent. While I was sitting upon the side of his couch, discussing my line of march and receiving my orders for the future—this involving a march on the Five Forks—a courier came in and announced that our line was being broken in front of the house in which General Lee had slept. I hurried to the front, and as fast as my troops came up they were thrown into action to check the advance of the Federals until night had come to cover our withdrawal. We fought all day, and at night again took up our march, and from that time forward until the surrender, we marched, and fought, and hungered, staggering through cold, and rain, and mud, to Appomattox—contesting every foot of the way, beset by overwhelming odds on all sides. It was one constant fight for days and days, the nights even giving us no rest. When at length the order came to surrender, on the 9th, I ordered my men to stack their arms, and surrendered four thousand bayonets of Fields' Division—the only troops that General Lee had left me. I also turned over to General Grant one thousand three hundred prisoners taken by the cavalry and by my troops while on the retreat. As to the conference of officers on the 7th, I never attended, and, of course, did not join in the advice it gave to General Lee. Mr. Swinton has been clearly misinformed upon this point.

THE FIRST CAVALRY.

BY CAPTAIN JAMES H. STEVENSON.

WHEN the war-cloud suddenly burst over Charleston harbor, in the early dawn of that memorable 12th of April, the loyal people of the North found the national existence threatened by armed and organized treason, without adequate preparation to meet the impending danger. It was supposed, however, that seventy-five thousand militia would be able to quell the insurrection in a very short time, and President Lincoln issued his proclamation calling out that number of men to serve for a period of three months. This levy was soon raised; but the people, having been thoroughly aroused to the danger which threatened the Union, continued to form regiment after regiment of volunteers, in anticipation of their services being needed. Some even began to organize companies for the cavalry arm of the service, but they were regarded as altogether visionary. The government threw cold water upon the cavalry movement, and plainly intimated that it could manage the rebels without that arm. Nothing discouraged, "Young America" persisted in sounding "Boots and Saddles," and many young men were found anxious to have a tilt with the "chivalry" on the "sacred soil" on horseback. Very soon, the government began to think that a regiment of volunteer cavalry might be of some service, and, accordingly, the following circular was issued:

WAR DEPARTMENT, WASHINGTON, May 1st, 1861.

TO THE GOVERNORS OF THE SEVERAL STATES, AND ALL WHOM IT MAY CONCERN:

I have authorized Colonel Carl Schurz to raise and organize a volunteer regiment of cavalry. For the purpose of rendering it as efficient as possible, he is

(634)

instructed to enlist principally such men as have served in the same arm before. The government will provide the regiment with arms, but cannot provide the horses and accoutrements. For these necessaries we rely upon the patriotism of the States and the citizens, and for this purpose I take the liberty of requesting you to afford Colonel Schurz your aid in the execution of this plan.

(Signed)   SIMON CAMERON,
Secretary of War.

On the 3d of May, Colonel Schurz passed through Philadelphia, when he heard of some gentlemen engaged in organizing a regiment of cavalry, and to these he made known his authority, and requested them to unite with him. These gentlemen thought the government would soon call for more cavalry, and, therefore, declined to join Colonel Schurz, except one of the lieutenants, named William H. Boyd, to whom Colonel Schurz gave authority to raise a company for his regiment. This was the first company of volunteer cavalry duly authorized to be raised for the war.

At that time, there was a troop composed of some of the best young men of Germantown and vicinity, all mounted, armed, and fully equipped for active service, undergoing a thorough course of drill at Chestnut Hill, under the instructions of James H. Stevenson, who had just returned from California, after serving a term of enlistment as sergeant in the First United States Dragoons. William Rotch Wister, Esq., was captain of the troop, and, on hearing of Colonel Schurz's authority, he visited Washington to try and have his men accepted as part of Schurz's regiment. On his return, the following note was received:

WAR DEPARTMENT, June 14th, 1861.

CAPTAIN WILLIAM ROTCH WISTER,
Philadelphia:

Dear Sir:—This department, I am instructed by the Secretary to say to you, will accept your light horse company, to be attached to the regiment of cavalry being formed to serve for three years, or during the war, if ready to be so mustered, and will, in that event, furnish the holsters, pistols, and swords, but not the uniforms, horses, or equipments.

Very respectfully,

(Signed)   J. P. SANDERSON,
Chief Clerk.

They felt very much elated at this; but there was still an obstacle in the way. The government would not muster in a man unless a fully organized company, with a minimum aggregate of seventy-nine men, were presented to the mustering officer. Captain Wister and his gay troop rode all over the country, among the farmers' sons, in quest of recruits; but all his efforts failed to raise the requisite number of men who were able and willing to find their own horses and equipments, notwithstanding that the government had offered to pay the troopers forty cents per day for their use and risk; with the proviso, however, that, in case the trooper lost his horse in any way, he must furnish another, or serve on foot. This proviso was the straw that broke the camel's back. After three months spent in drilling, and in unavailing efforts to fill up, Captain Wister's troop disbanded, on the 30th of June, and its members sought service in other commands.

In the meantime, Colonel Schurz had gone to New York, and had succeeded in raising four companies of Germans who had seen service in the cavalry of Europe. And here, also, he was joined by six companies of Americans, which had been organized in hopes of being accepted by the government. A company from Michigan also joined him, which, with Boyd's Philadelphia company, completed the regiment. About this time Colonel Schurz was appointed Minister to Spain, and some trouble was then experienced in getting a suitable commander. At last Major Andrew T. McReynolds, a Michigan lawyer, who had seen service in the cavalry in Mexico, was accepted by the government in lieu of Colonel Schurz, and things again looked favorable. No one knew how the men were to be mounted and equipped. The several States had made no efforts to comply with the request of the War Secretary; the men, with few exceptions, were unable to mount and equip themselves, and things had about come to a stand-still. It was even feared that the organization could not be kept together, as the men were not mustered into service. On the 10th of July the government came to its senses, and an order was issued requiring the proper departments to furnish horses and equipments to companies of volunteer cavalry when ready to be mustered into service; and on the 19th of July Captain Boyd's company was mustered in at Philadelphia by Major Ruff, the United States mustering officer. The company had appeared before him to be mustered in on the 16th, but were rejected because they lacked one man of the requisite number. The officers of the company were: Captain, William H. Boyd; First Lieutenant, William W. Hanson; and Second Lieutenant, James H. Stevenson (he who had been drilling Captain Wister's troops at Chestnut Hill). On the 22d of July, Boyd's company arrived at Washington, amid the excitement caused by the Union repulse at Bull run the previous day. That night they listened to horrifying tales of the sanguinary deeds performed by the "Black Horse Cavalry" on that disastrous field, but it only seemed to stimulate the boys with a desire to measure swords with horsemen so renowned.

They had not long to wait, for, on the 18th of August, not quite one month from the date of their muster into service, Boyd's company were sent on a scout toward Mount Vernon. While they were feeling their way through a large woods, in the vicinity of Pohick church, they suddenly came upon a squadron of the famous "Black Horse Cavalry" drawn up in line on a broad road ready to receive them. Captain Boyd placed himself at the head of his company, and at once commanded it to "charge!" The boys answered with a yell, and dashed upon the foe, who confidently expected to see them run at the very sight of such an array. So sudden and so unexpected was the onset, that the enemy had only time to fire one volley before the "blue jackets" were upon them, when, marvelous to relate, they broke and fled in confusion. Boyd's men pursued them several miles, putting two of them *hors du combat*, and then returned to Alexandria to report to General Franklin what they had done. The General was delighted, and at once notified General McClellan, who reviewed the company on the 22d of August, and complimented Captain Boyd and his officers and men for their gallant conduct. The charm was broken, and that company never afterward had any dread of the Confederate cavalry. In this charge, Captain Boyd lost one man killed, Jacob Erwin, who is now buried in the Odd Fellows' Cemetery, in Philadelphia. He was the first cavalryman killed in the rebellion, and this was the first charge made by volunteer cavalry. So much for Pennsylvania.

Boyd's company was then attached to General Franklin's head-quarters, and was the pet of the whole division commanded by that gallant soldier. When the regiment to which the company belonged was authorized to be raised, the government supposed it would not require any more volunteer cavalry, and that regiment was to be known as the First United States Volunteer Cavalry. But when it was determined to call out a large force of this arm, the government declined to have anything to do with volunteers, and this regiment found itself without a patron. At this juncture a controversy arose between Governor Morgan, of New York, and Governor Curtin, of Pennsylvania, as to the proprietorship of the regiment, which was decided in favor of New York, she having raised ten out of the twelve companies. We had been called the "Lincoln Cavalry" up to that time; but after that we were known as the First New York (Lincoln) Cavalry. Captain Boyd then made several efforts to get his company transferred to a Pennsylvania regiment, but without success. Governor Curtin had designated the company as the "Tenth Pennsylvania Cavalry" during the controversy with Governor Morgan, and Pennsylvania never had a regiment to fill the vacancy left for Boyd's men.

The company remained with General Franklin throughout the Peninsular campaign, rendering valuable services. By its bold conduct, and timely warning, it saved Franklin's right flank at Savage's Station; and, after hard service in the battle of White Oak Swamp, it covered the retreat, at midnight, to the James river. It rendered good service at Malvern Hill, and cleared the road of teams on the following day, so that the artillery and ambulances could pass. A company of Rush's Lancers took its place at General Franklin's headquarters, at Harrison's Landing, when ordered to proceed with the regiment to join Burnside at Fredericksburg. It marched with that officer to Antietam, and won laurels at Hyattstown, Maryland, just before that battle, and at Williamsport, at its close, where several of its members were wounded by grapeshot while charging upon a battery. In Western Virginia, it made its mark among Imboden's men, helping to capture the camp of that bold partisan on two different occasions. In the Shenandoah Valley, under Milroy, it performed many bold deeds, in company with the regiment, while fighting against Mosby, Gilmore, and Imboden. Here Captain Boyd was promoted to the rank of major, and Lieutenant Stevenson, who had been adjutant of the regiment and acting assistant adjutant general of the cavalry brigade, was promoted to be captain of Boyd's company.

Just then, General Lee slipped away from Hooker at Fredericksburg, *en route* for Gettysburg, and suddenly confronted Milroy at Winchester. The First New York Cavalry were at Berryville, and were compelled to retire before the advance of Rodes' Division, of Ewell's Corps. A brigade of rebel cavalry pursued and overtook them at the Opequan, but the First New York "cleaned them out" nicely, killing and wounding over fifty of them, and causing them to retire from the field. When Milroy found he was surrounded by Lee's army, he sent for a bold officer and fifty men to carry a dispatch to Martinsburg, and Major Boyd was detailed with his old company. They knew every cow-path in the Valley, and succeeded in flanking the rebel force then between Winchester and Martinsburg, and sent the first intelligence to Baltimore and Washington that Lee's army was at Winchester. That night, a dispatch arrived at Martinsburg for Milroy, and three men of Boyd's company volunteered to take it through. Their names were Oliver Lumphries, John V. Harvey, and George J. Pitman, all sergeants. After several hairbreadth escapes, they arrived in the beleaguered town at midnight, and Milroy called a council of war. It was determined to spike the guns, destroy the artillery ammunition, leave everything on wheels behind, and cut a way through the enemy's lines to Martinsburg or Harper's Ferry. The disaster of that day is too well known to require a recital of it here.

Major Boyd fought the advancing enemy at Martinsburg, while our wagon train, which had gone from Berryville to that place, got well under way, and then he followed it to Williamsport, Maryland. The enemy followed closely, and Boyd was compelled to fight and fall back, and then fight again, in order to save the train, which he succeeded in doing, and conducted it in safety to Harrisburg, Pennsylvania. Then he began a system of partisan warfare, dashing upon the enemy in front and on both flanks, causing them to think there was a large force in their front, and preventing them from doing much mischief that they otherwise would have done, and helped to save the State capital from the invaders. From the 15th of June, when they left Winchester, to the 15th of July, this company was never out of sight of the enemy, and seldom a day passed without their having a fight. They captured many prisoners, and a vast amount of property, beside saving untold thousands to the people of the Cumberland Valley. At Greencastle, Pennsylvania, the company attacked Jenkins' rebel brigade, and here they lost William H. Rihl, who was the first soldier killed in Pennsylvania during the war.

For his services in this, the Gettysburg campaign, Governor Curtin rewarded Major Boyd with the Colonelcy of the Twenty-first Pennsylvania Cavalry, and commissioned his able lieutenant, O. B. Knowles, a major in the same regiment. Lieutenant William H. Boyd and Sergeant E. Knowles were also transferred to the Twenty-first—the first as captain and the other as adjutant of the regiment. Captain Stevenson then took command of his company, and under him it won fresh laurels in the Shenandoah Valley after Gettysburg. It was with General Sigel in the battle of New Market, and was the last to leave the field. It led the advance, under General Hunter, upon Lynchburg, and greatly distinguished itself in the battle of Piedmont, and in the subsequent fighting during Hunter's retreat from Lynchburg over the Alleghanies into the Kanawha Valley. Again at Snicker's gap, Ashby's gap, and Winchester, under General Crook, this company played a conspicuous and noble part. And at Moorfield, under General Averill, it formed part of the gallant two hundred of the First New York (Lincoln) Cavalry, commanded by Captain Jones, that defeated McCausland's whole brigade, returning from the burning of Chambersburg, Pennsylvania. It served under Averill during the memorable advance of General Sheridan against General Early in the Shenandoah Valley, and took part in every battle during the campaign. In the battles of Opequan, Fisher's Hill, Brown's gap, and Wier's cave, the valiant conduct of this company attracted the attention of all who beheld it. And at the battle of Nineveh, when Capeheart's Brigade attacked and defeated Mc-Causland's Division, this company led in the charge.

When Sheridan set out from Winchester to join Grant, his way was obstructed by the rebels, under Rosser, at the bridge over North river, near Mount Crawford. The First New York Cavalry, under Lieutenant Colonel Battersby, was ordered to swim the river a mile above the bridge, and charge the rebels in flank; which they did in fine style—driving them out of their works, pursuing them about ten miles, capturing prisoners, guns, and wagons, and saving the bridge over Middle river. For this General Custer, to whose division they belonged, complimented them in person. Next day Custer advanced upon Waynesborough, where Early's forces were intrenched, and, after some severe fighting, charged the works, driving the enemy out, capturing nearly every man, and all the guns and material of war. The First New York Cavalry led the charge. Again at Dinwiddie Court-House and Five Forks, the regiment won fresh laurels under the eyes of Sheridan and Custer. At Sailor's creek the First New York (Lincoln) Cavalry led the charge over the enemy's works, capturing General Ewell and his staff and hundreds of prisoners, beside guns and battle-flags. At Appomattox Station they charged with Custer, in the darkness, and took hundreds of prisoners, many guns and wagons, beside four trains of stores, which were waiting for Lee's hungry army. And the next day they were dashing forward with Custer to attack the enemy, when they were stopped by news of the surrender of Lee.

When the regiment re-enlisted as veterans, in 1864, Captain Stevenson induced his men to be credited upon the quota of the Twentieth Ward of Philadelphia, notwithstanding the fact that New York offered much larger bounties to the men, and had offered the captain five hundred dollars to take his company to that State. On the arrival of Company C in Philadelphia, on veteran furlough, the Twentieth Ward Bounty Fund Committee gave them a hearty reception in the old North Baptist church, Eighth street, above Master street, upon which occasion the ladies of the ward presented the company with an elegant guidon, and Captain Stevenson was presented with a sword, sash, and belt. The company participated in sixty engagements with the enemy during their four years' of service, and the little guidon above mentioned, which is now in possession of Captain Stevenson, was completely riddled with bullets.

It may not be amiss to state that not only was the present Secretary of the Interior our first colonel, but that Charles B. Evarts, a son of the present Secretary of State, was a soldier in the regiment. This young man was at college, but reading in the New York papers of the daring and seemingly romantic deeds of the First New York (Lincoln) Cavalry, he ran away from school and enlisted in the regiment as a private soldier, his father being at the time in Europe. He served faithfully and with much credit during the severe campaign of 1864, and on our return from the Lynchburg raid he was commissioned a lieutenant by President Lincoln and assigned to duty as an aide on the staff of General William H. Seward, son of the then Secretary of State.

STONEWALL JACKSON AND HIS MEN.

BY MAJOR H. KYD DOUGLAS.

It was on the field of Manassas, a bright Sunday afternoon, the 21st of July, 1861. The armies of McDowell and Beauregard had been grappling with each other since early morning, and, in their mutual slaughter, took no note of the sacredness of the day, nor its brightness. In Washington General Scott was anxiously awaiting the result of his skilful plan of battle, and General Johnston had come down from the Valley of Virginia, in response to Beauregard's appeal—"If you will help me, now is the time." Hotly had the field been contested, and the hours passed slowly to men who had never tasted of battle before. Wavering had been the fortunes of the day, but it was evident the advantage was with the Federal army, and, before our brigade went into action, it seemed to us the day was lost. After changing position several times, without fighting, General Jackson learned that Bee was hard pressed, and he moved to his assistance, marching through the wounded and the stragglers, who were hurrying to the rear. It was then after two o'clock, and the General formed his brigade along the crest of the hill near the Henry House, the men lying down behind the brow of it, in support of the two pieces of artillery placed in position to play upon the advancing foe.

General Bee, his brigade being crushed and scattered, rode up to General Jackson, and, with the excitement and mortification of an untried but heroic soldier, reported that the enemy were beating him back.

(642)

"Very well, General, it can't be helped," replied Jackson.

"But how do you expect to stop them?"

"We'll give them the bayonet!" was the answer, briefly.

General Bee wheeled his horse, and galloped back to his command. As he did so, General Jackson said to Lieutenant Lee of his staff:

"Tell the colonel of this brigade, that the enemy are advancing; that when their heads are seen above the hill, let the whole line rise, move forward with a shout, and trust to the bayonet. *I am tired of this long range work.*"

In the storm which followed Bee's return to his command, he was soon on foot, his horse shot from under him. With the fury of despair he strode among his men, and tried to rally and to hold them against the torrent which beat upon them; and, finally, in a voice which rivaled the roar of battle, he cried out: "Oh, men, there are Jackson and his Virginians standing behind you like a *stone wall!*" Uttering these words of martial baptism, Bee fell dead upon the field, and left behind him a fame which will follow that of Jackson as a shadow.

It would be but the repetition of history to mention, at length, the movements of Jackson's Brigade that day. It was Bee who gave him the name of "Stonewall," but it was his own Virginians who made that name immortal. This brigade checked the victorious tide of battle, but to turn it back was no easy labor. Around the Henry House and its plateau the contest raged with renewed violence and vacillating success for an hour; and then Jackson led his men in their last bayonet charge, and pierced the enemy's centre. The timely arrival of Kirby Smith and Early upon their flank, finished the work, and defeat was turned into a rout. General Jackson will be forgiven for this sentence in a letter to a friend: "You will find, when my report shall be published, that the First Brigade was to our army what the Imperial Guard was to Napoleon; through the blessings of God it met the victorious enemy, and turned the fortunes of the day."

And who was Stonewall Jackson, and of what stock? Although he was of sterling and respectable parentage, it matters little, for, in historic fame, "he was his own ancestor." And it is well enough that Virginia, who gave to the war Robert Edward Lee, of old and aristocratic lineage, should furnish Jackson as the representative of her people. On the 21st of January, 1824, in Clarksburg, among the mountains of Western Virginia, was born this boy, the youngest of four children; and, with no view to his future fame, he was named Thomas Jonathan Jackson. It was a rugged, honest name, but is no cause of regret that it is now merged in the more rugged and euphonious one he afterward made for himself. No comet was seen at his birth, and there is little record of his boyhood, except that he was left an orphan when he was three years old, and, being penniless, had a hard time of it in his youth. But his father had been a lawyer, and he was taken care of by some of his relatives. At sixteen, he was appointed a constable, and two years afterward entered West Point as a cadet. He graduated in 1846, went to Mexico, and served as lieutenant in the battery of Magruder—"Prince John"—who afterward served under Jackson in Virginia. Jackson was twice breveted for gallantry, and returned from Mexico, at the age of twenty-four, with an enviable reputation and the rank of major. He served a while in Florida, but his health gave way, and he was compelled to quit the army. In 1851 he was appointed Professor in the Virginia Military Institute, at Lexington. He there married a daughter of Rev. George Junkin, D. D., who was President of what is now Washington and Lee University. Dr. Junkin was an earnest Union man, and, at the breaking out of the war, resigned his position, and went back to Pennsylvania; but it is said the loyalty of the old gentleman was not proof against the pride he felt in his famous son-in-law. Major Jackson's wife soon died. He then married a daughter of Rev. Dr. Morrison, another Presbyterian clergyman, of Charlotte, North Carolina. She now lives in Charlotte, with her only child, Julia, who was not six months old when her father died at Chancellorsville. In 1857 Major Jackson went to Europe. While in France, he rode on horseback, with some French officers, over the field of Waterloo. It is said he seemed perfectly familiar with the topography of the ground and the maneuvres of the two armies, and sharply criticised one of the Emperor's movements, by saying, "There's where Napoleon blundered.' Such presumption was unheard of since the time the young Corsican, in Italy, criticised the venerable Wurmser. But what seemed effrontery in Bonaparte was genius in Napoleon, and the name of Stonewall will save his criticism.

After his return from Europe, Jackson led a quiet and unobtrusive life at Lexington, less known than any other professor. His delicate health forbid much social enjoyment. I met him there in 1860, and once said to a classmate in the law school, who had been at the Institute:

"It seems to me, Terrill, I'd like to know Major Jackson better; there is something about him I can't make out."

"Nobody can; but it wouldn't pay," replied "Bath." "Old Jack's a character, genius, or just a little crazy, or something of that sort. He lives quietly, and don't meddle with people; but he is as systematic as a multiplication table, and as full of military as an arsenal. Stiff, you see, and never laughs, but kind-hearted as a woman; and, by Jupiter, he teaches a nigger Sunday-school. But, mind what I say, if this John Brown business leads to war, he'll be heard from."

Well, it did lead to war, and Jackson was heard from, and Colonel Terrill fell fighting under him.

I have referred to Major Jackson's ill-health. It took the form of dyspepsia, and once, during the war, he told me he had suffered with it for twenty years, and he knew of no misery which attacked a man as it did, physically, mentally, and morally, and was as likely to drive one to suicide. It produced in him that simplicity of diet which was as conspicuous as his simplicity of manners. He never was a hearty eater, but often ate of one or two things on the table plentifully, eating some things he did not like, and liking many things he did not eat. In the army, he rarely accepted an invitation to dinner, and when he did, it was generally to oblige his staff. He once said to me that he believed he was fonder of whisky and brandy than any man in his army; and yet he never tasted it. His discipline commenced with himself, and controlled his appetite as firmly as he did his troops.

In face and figure, Stonewall Jackson was not striking. Above the average height, with a frame angular, muscular, and fleshless, he was, in all his movements, from riding a horse to handling a pen, the most ungraceful man in the army. His expression was thoughtful, and generally clouded with an air of fatigue. His eye was small, blue, and in repose as gentle as a young girl's. With high, broad forehead, small, sharp nose, thin, pallid lips, deep set eyes, and dark, rusty beard, he was not a handsome man. His face in the drawing-room or tent, softened by his sweet smile, was as different from itself on the battle-field as a little lake in summer noon differs from the same lake when frozen. Walking or riding the General was ungainly; his main object was to go over the ground, without regard to the manner of his going. His favorite horse was as little like Pegasus as he was like Apollo; he rode boldly and well, but certainly not with grace and ease. He was not a man of style. General Lee, on horseback or off, was the handsomest man I ever saw. It was said of Wade Hampton, that he looked as knightly when mounted as if he had stepped out from an old canvas, horse and all. Breckenridge was a model of manly beauty, and Joe Johnston looked every inch a soldier. None of these things can be said of Jackson.

Akin to his dyspepsia, and perhaps as a consequence, was his ignorance of music. One morning, at Ashland, he startled a young lady from her propriety by gravely asking her if she had ever heard a new piece of music called " Dixie," and as gravely listening to her while she sang it. He had heard it a thousand times from the army bands, and yet it seemed new to him. Judged by the Shakespearean standard, who could be more " fit for treasons, stratagems, and spoils?" And yet there was one kind of music which always interested and delighted him. It was the " rebel yell" of his troops. To this grand chorus he never failed to respond. The difference between the regular " hurrah" of the Federal army, and the irregular, wild yell of the Confederates, was as marked as the difference in their uniforms. The rebel yell was a peculiar mixture of sounds, a kind of weird shout. Jackson was greeted with it whenever he made his appearance to the troops, on the march or in battle; and just as invariably he would seize his old gray cap from his head in acknowledgment, and his "little sorrel," knowing his habit, would break into a gallop and never halt until the shout had ceased. I remember one night, at tattoo, this cry broke forth in the camp of the Stonewall Brigade, and was taken up by brigades and divisions, until it rolled over field and wood throughout the whole corps. The General came hastily and bareheaded from his tent, and going up to a fence near by, he leaned upon it and listened in quiet to the rise, climax, and conclusion of that strange serenade, raising his head to catch the last sound, as it grew fainter, and until it died away like an echo along the mountains. Then turning toward his tent he muttered, in half soliloquy, " That was the sweetest music I ever heard."

General Jackson's troops and his enemy's believed he never slept; the fact is, he slept a great deal. Whenever he had nothing else to do, he went to sleep, especially in church. I remember during the invasion of Maryland, on Sunday night he rode three miles in an ambulance to attend church in Frederick, and then fell asleep as soon as the minister began to preach; his head fell upon his breast, and he never awoke until aroused by the organ and choir. He could sleep anywhere and in any position, sitting in his chair, under fire, or on horseback. On a night march toward Richmond, after the battles with McClellan, he was riding along with his drowsy staff, nodding and sleeping as he went. We passed by groups of men sitting along the roadside, and engaged in roasting new corn by fires made of fence-rails. One group took us for cavalrymen, with an inebriated captain, and one of the party, delighted at the sight of a man who had found whisky enough to be drunk, sprang up from the fire and, brandishing a roasting-ear in his hand, leaped down into the road, and seizing the General's horse, cried out: "I say, old fellow, where the devil did you get your liquor?" In an instant, as the General awoke, the fellow saw his mistake; and then bounding from the road he took the fence at a single leap, exclaiming: "Good God, it's old Jack!" and disappeared in the darkness. Yes, General Jackson slept a great deal, but he was never caught napping.

He gave to sleep many moments which other men would have given to conversation. He was essentially a silent man; not morose, but quiet. He smiled often, rarely laughed. He never told a joke, but did not discourage them in others, and if one struck his peculiar fancy, he would smile in mild approval. He did not live apart from his staff, but liked to have them about him, and they were nearly all very young men. Universally polite in manner, he encouraged the liveliest conversation among them, although he took little part in it. He was not a man of words; they seemed to embarrass him. When he had ideas he put them into action, not into language. His military dispatches were as brief as if studied, like the one he sent after the defeat of Milroy: "God blessed our arms with victory at McDowell yesterday." He never discussed his plans; indeed, he never told them. The next officer under him never knew his intention nor object. He never volunteered his opinion to his superior, nor asked advice of his subordinates. He was as self-reliant as he was silent, and believed "he walks with speed who walks alone." He was reticent to a fault. "If my coat knew what I intended to do, I'd take it off and throw it away," was one of his sayings. This reticence often led to embarrassment and complaint from the officer next in command, and might have led to disaster in case of his death; but he evidently thought it better to run that risk than the risk of having his plans discovered. He never called a council of war; when called into council by General Lee, with Longstreet and Stuart, and the Hills, he let the others do the talking. If he made suggestions he did it briefly, and never attempted to sustain them by argument. He advised the flank movement at Chancellorsville, which resulted in the defeat of Hooker and his own death; when it was vigorously opposed he did not defend it. General Lee adopted it, and, as at other times when a hazardous movement was to be undertaken, he ordered Jackson to execute it. I question whether he could have discussed his plans satisfactorily if he had desired, or persuaded any one of the wisdom of those unprecedented and eccentric movements of his, which violated all the rules of war, and always ended so brilliantly. His reticence, his mystery, were necessities of his nature, as much as the result of his unparalleled self-reliance; a self-reliance which can only be appreciated by those who know that the courage necessary to go through a battle is not to be compared with that necessary to inaugurate it. "Audacity, audacity, always audacity," was the motto of Danton. So thought Jackson, too. After the defeat of Banks at Winchester, and before he moved forward to Harper's Ferry, he knew that McDowell and Fremont were moving against his rear, and what their design was; and yet he marched boldly into the trap prepared for him, and then broke it into pieces and escaped. But as a soldier, he was guided by another principle which he once tersely expressed thus: "Mystery, mystery is the secret of success." This mystery was not an affectation; it was a policy, a conviction. He was compelled to take his staff and his general officers into his confidence, and when he did so he did it without reluctance or distrust. But they never attempted to force his confidence, and once he ordered one of his body-guard to be dismounted, and "put under arrest as a spy," for repeating to him an ill-timed question about the movements of a division.

His most popular virtue was swiftness of execution. With him action kept pace with design. He was the rapidest mover in the South, and, from the very outstart of the war, his old brigade and division were known as "Jackson's foot cavalry." "What sort of man is your Stonewall, anyway?" said one of Pope's men; "are his soldiers made of gutta-percha, or do they run on wheels?" And when the raid once began, or the battle had been joined, he never hesitated, and rarely changed his first plans. He sometimes went at his object with such apparent recklessness that he marched into battle by the flank, and commenced the fight with the first file of four. This kind of movement would not stand the test of military criticism, but it always succeeded. "The fate of a battle is the result of a moment, of a thought," said Napoleon. The deplorable weakness of indecision, which has wrecked so many military reputations, was unknown to Jackson. Golden opportunities lost have changed many a shout of victory into a cry of defeat, and from Carrick's ford to Gettysburg the track of war is lined with the graves of brave men who died while their generals were deliberating. In absolute freedom from this weakness, Stonewall Jackson deserves a place by the side of Napoleon, the Archduke Charles, and Frederick the Great.

General Jackson was never elated by victory, nor depressed by disaster. It might be said of him, as it was of Massena: "He was endowed with that extraordinary firmness and courage which seemed to increase in excess of danger. When conquered, he was as ready to fight again as if he had been conqueror." Always victorious, with one exception, General Jackson was not often called upon to illustrate this virtue. But at Strasburg, when he determined to wait for Winder, as Napoleon did for Ney in Russia, while Fremont and Shields were closing in on both flanks, and escape seemed almost impossible, his face was as pale and firm as marble, his thin lips shut, his brow thoughtful and hard; or at second Manassas, where his little corps struggled for hours and days against the army of Pope, and Longstreet did not come; when the sun seemed to stand still, and night would not fall, Jackson spoke not a word of hope nor fear. If he sought counsel of heaven, he asked none of man, and no man dared offer it. Such confidence and faith were contagious. His soldiers believed he could do anything he wished, and he believed they could do anything he commanded. "Jackson's men will follow him to the devil, and he knows it," said a Federal prisoner, and that was the philosophy of much of his success.

General Jackson was the wonder of the press. No officer, in either army, was the subject of so many newspaper paragraphs, and yet he knew nothing of it, for, as a rule, he never read the papers. No great man of this century has gone to his grave so marvelously ignorant of the wideness of his fame. Regulating his conduct with a view solely to his proper responsibility, he did not care what the world said of it, and never looked to see. At the beginning of the war, he used to glance over the papers to get at the news, but when he became the subject of their praise and speculations he stopped even that. The press, which proved a very Marlborough to some generals, had no effect on him. He had no war correspondents, and when in full command he permitted none in his army, if he knew it. He said he did not want his friends to know his movements, and certainly not his enemies. He wished no pen to write him into fame. It was said the press of the North gave Rosecrans his military reputation, and also took it away. They had no such chance at General Jackson. He made his own fame; but they have generously helped to make it world-wide and lasting.

But the press have done much to give the public a false impression of the religious side of Jackson'a character. He was a member of the Presbyterian Church, a strictly Christian, liberal gentleman. But he was neither bigot nor Pharisee. He held his own devotions in secret. He made no parade of his religion, nor pressed his creed upon any one. He was not Cromwellian in this regard; he believed other paths led to heaven just as surely as the one he was traveling. On his staff were the sons of clergymen of the Episcopal, Reformed and Presbyterian Churches, and some others who were very much in the dark as to their religious faith. The fact is, this Presbyterian elder, as he is sometimes called, became such by marriage. The first prayers said over him were those of his pious Methodist mother— although it appears in his youth he was not more pious than the average young man. When in Mexico, he was nearly persuaded to be a Romanist. He afterward was a member of the Episcopal Church, and, finally, settled down in the Presbyterian Church, to which his wife belonged. When the Louisiana Brigade applied for a chaplain, he recommended that a priest be sent them, because a large majority were Roman Catholics. His own devotedness was illustrated by the purity of his life, not by professions, and his faith and simplicity were well known to his troops. He often attended their services and prayer-meetings, night or day, and, kneeling in the midst of the same scarred veterans he had led in so many battles, he led them in prayer to the Lord of Hosts. When he was thus in camp, all noise was hushed. Dropping their cards, and all other amusements, old men and young gathered around him, standing and kneeling, with uncovered heads, in sacred silence. A thousand hands would have been raised to smite the impious wretch who dared to scoff when Stonewall Jackson prayed.

It is not practicable to attempt here any discussion of the campaigns of General Jackson. True, his career was very short. On May 2d, 1861, he took command at Harper's Ferry as colonel in the Virginia service. On May 2d, 1863, he fell at Chancellorsville as lieutenant general in the Confederate army. For these two years he monopolized the admiration of the continent; never blundered, never failed, and perished in the execution of his greatest achievement. No wonder his success bewilders criticism. Where in all history was great renown so quickly won?

It is an interesting study to follow the successive steps of Jackson's military career, and watch his development as occasion required. There is no more exciting page in the annals of modern warfare than his campaign of thirty days in the Shenandoah Valley. Its strategy, battles, and results, justify the tribute paid to it by Colonel Crozet, who served under Napoleon, and pronounced it "extra-Napoleonic." In Jackson's military life there was no dangerous precociousness. He never sought promotion, but never expressed a doubt of his ability to manage any command given him. He put forth no useless strength. What was in him we shall never know, for he went to the grave with the richness of the mine unexplored. He was equal to each new occasion as it arose, and in his movements there was no monotony, except in success. Had he survived Chancellorsville, a new field of trial awaited him. Whether it be true or not, as stated, that the order had been written assigning him to the command of the Army of Tennessee, it is more than probable he would have been sent to take command of that unfortunate army. Had he gone there, with the prestige he had gained and the hopes he would have inspired, who can say to what end the war would have been prolonged. Thus the shot which struck Jackson crippled both armies of the Confederacy, and from that day it tottered to its fall.

I can only refer to the resignation of General Jackson in January, 1862, by which the Confederacy nearly lost his services. This step was caused by the insubordination of General Loring, who now holds a command under the Khedive of Egypt. General Loring had served in Mexico as General Jackson's senior in rank, and he was impatient at being his subordinate in Virginia. Being ordered to Romney by General Jackson, after the "Bath trip," he prevailed on the War Department to countermand the order. General Jackson promptly resigned, and there was at once a storm. The army became excited, the people of the Valley indignant; Jackson was cool and immovable. The Governor of Virginia interposed, and the Secretary of War yielded. Loring was sent elsewhere, and Jackson resumed his command, and this was the last time the War Department ever undertook to interfere with his proper authority.

There are one or two incidents connected with the campaigns of General Jackson which press upon me for recognition. I ought not to omit to say a word in justice to the memory of Colonel Miles, who fell just before the surrender of Harper's Ferry to General Jackson, in September, 1862. Indignant and chagrined as the North justly was at the capitulation of eleven thousand troops, and the surrender of such immense stores, without a decent defense, it sought to make a holacaust of Colonel Miles, and charged him with both cowardice and treachery. That officer died with his face to the foe, and he should be a man of many scars who calls him a coward. Baser still was the charge of treachery, for baser would have been the crime. It was said he had communicated with General Jackson, and had surrendered according to their agreement. To make such a charge without proof, is like stoning the dead. Having been very closely associated with General Jackson in this movement, it is more than improbable that any serious communication could have passed between him and Colonel Miles without my knowledge; almost impossible it could have been held without the knowledge of some one of the staff. And yet no one at headquarters ever heard of it; no one in our army ever believed it. The ungrateful charge cannot be true. Colonel Miles was incompetent, but he was no traitor. He was too feeble for the responsibility which fell upon him, but he was too true to his commission to betray his army. The surrender of Harper's Ferry was a deep mortification to the North. If the charges were true, it ought to be greater.

Scarcely in the same connection, but as illustrative of the credulity of people during the war, I recall attention to the beautiful legend of Barbara Fritchie. There are few things among Whittier's poems more touching than this story of the war. It is as tender as the ballad of Maud Muller—and about as true. It seems like iconoclasm to break the poetic image which Mr. Whittier has carved, and if he had not thrown his chippings over Jackson's grave, I would not care to look beyond the beauty of his work. The facts are few. General Jackson's headquarters, in Maryland, were three miles short of Frederick, and, except when he passed through it to leave it, he went into the city but once—on Sunday night to church. On the morning he left, I rode with him through the town. He did not pass the house of Barbara Fritchie; nothing like the fiction of Mr. Whittier ever occurred, and Stonewall Jackson and that historic old lady never saw each other I understand Mr. Whittier has said that if the story, as he told it, is not true, it will go down to posterity as such, until it gets beyond the reach of correction. *Exegi monumentum*—pardonable loyalty, questionable ambition. It may be suggested with diffidence, that the name of Stonewall Jackson will live as long as that of Mr. Whittier and his poems, and history will teach the poet's children that the Army of Virginia did not make war upon flags when waved by old women.

The death of General Jackson was characteristic in its singularity. At night, when the battle had ended, just as he had achieved what he believed to be the most successful movement of his career, he, whom the enemy began to believe both invulnerable and invincible, fell at the hands of his own people. It is needless to repeat the painful story of his wounding and death. At first it was not believed his wounds were mortal, and the army thought, in the language of General Lee: " Jackson will not—he *cannot* die." But it was written. Pneumonia lent its fearful aid to the enemy, and on

Sunday afternoon he closed his eyes and smiled at his own spoken dream—"Let us cross over the river and rest under the shade of the trees." The dream thus spoken is yet unbroken; and his soul went out to heaven, uplifted by sighs and prayers, rising that hour from altar and cloister, all over the South, for his recovery.

On Friday, the 15th of May, 1863, his body was taken for burial to his home, in Lexington. He had not been there since he left it, two years before, at the beginning of the war. Only two years, and yet how like romance is the simple story of his growth in fame. And now he lies buried as he directed, "in the Valley of Virginia," and among the people he loved so well. It were better so. He could not have saved the South, and it was merciful that he should perish first. The tender memory he left behind him in the army, and the stern sense of duty he bequeathed his soldiers, will be told by this little incident, with which I close this unworthy sketch. The army of Lee was on its march to Gettysburg, and the commanding general had given strict orders for its discipline in Pennsylvania. An officer riding to camp from Chambersburg, late at night, was halted by the outposts. Having neither pass nor countersign, in his dilemma he bethought him of an old pass in his pocket-book, signed by General Jackson, whose recent death hung like a cloud over the army. He found it, handed it with confidence to the sentinel. The trusty fellow managed to read it by the light of a match, and as he did so he seemed to linger and hesitate over the signature. And then, as the light went out, he handed it back, and looking up toward the stars beyond, he said, sadly and firmly: "Captain, you can go to heaven on that paper, but you can't pass this post."

To Jackson's death this whole land has been speedy to do full justice. In this tribute there has been no North, no South. The one admired him greatly, the other loved him dearly. And coming from over the sea, it is said, an affectionate friend planted on his grave, at Lexington, a sprig of laurel brought from the grave of Napoleon. This was most fit; it was appropriate that the greatest general of the Old World should welcome to the tomb and immortality the most brilliant soldier of the New. From his grave, and from kindred others North and South, let us hope that the true spirit of reconstruction, in justice, prosperity, and peace, will come at last.

THE FAMOUS FIGHT AT CEDAR CREEK.

BY GENERAL A. B. NETTLETON.

WHEN, in 1864, with Grant and Meade and Sheridan in the East, and Sherman and Thomas in the West, the National army closed with the Confederate, it was in a struggle which all regarded as the final one. In June, after Grant with all his available force had besieged Richmond and Petersburg, Lee, feeling secure behind his fortifications, detached an army of twenty-five thousand picked troops under General Jubal A. Early, including the flower of his Virginia cavalry, to invade the North by way of the Shenandoah Valley, threaten Washington from the rear, and, if possible, compel Grant to retreat from the James, as McClellan had been forced to do two years before. Hunter's failure at Lynchburg, and his painful retreat through the wilderness of West Virginia, had left a virtually open road for Early's force to the boundary of Pennsylvania, if not to Washington, and this open road Early was not slow to travel. The defeat of the Union provisional force at Monocacy, the appearance of the rebel infantry before the western defenses of the National Capital on the 12th of July, and the subsequent burning of Chambersburg by Early's cavalry, under McCausland, had produced a very considerable civilian panic, attracted the anxious attention of the whole country, and convinced Grant, before Petersburg, that decisive measures were required in the neighborhood of the Potomac if he was to retain his grip on the rebel capital. Accordingly, two small-sized infantry corps (Wright's Sixth and Emory's Nineteenth) were dispatched to Washington *via* Fortress Monroe, and were soon followed by two divisions (the First and

Third) of the already famous cavalry corps of the Army of the Potomac. A new Middle Department was erected, and General P. H. Sheridan, as its commander, was given his first opportunity to earn his spurs in control of a separate army and an independent campaign.

By the middle of August, the armies of Sheridan and Early confronted each other in the Valley north of Winchester. Then ensued that brilliant campaign of the Shenandoah which, through a score of minor engagements, resulted in the thorough defeat of Early's army in the battle of Winchester, or the Opequan, on September 19th, followed on the 22d by its disastrous rout at Fisher's Hill, and its confused retreat beyond Staunton, where the pursuit was discontinued. At this time Sheridan and his whole victorious army considered the enemy in the Shenandoah Valley as thoroughly and permanently broken, dispirited and disposed of. The question asked about our camp-fires was: Where shall we be sent next? Our success in the Valley, coupled with Sherman's victories in the West, had lighted up the whole horizon and given the nation the first real glimpse of its final triumph and the coming of peace. But such troops as Sheridan could spare was needed before Richmond, and our army began falling back toward the Potomac, preparatory to such a transfer. During our return march the rear of our several columns was persistently harassed by a large force of surprisingly active cavalry, under General T. L. Rosser, who provokingly refused to consider himself or his command as *hors de combat.* Among many memories of hard service, those who were among Custer's troopers in the Valley will not soon forget their arduous task of protecting the rear of a victorious army against the onslaughts of the crushed enemy's horsemen!

After several days of this annoyance, and on the night of October 8th, near Fisher's Hill, Sheridan notified General Torbert, Chief of Cavalry, that he would halt the army there for twenty-four hours, and that on the following day he (Torbert) must face about, and "whip the enemy or get whipped himself." Rosser's saucy cavalry numbered about three thousand effectives, and was supported by some fifteen hundred infantry and two batteries, under Generals Lomax and Bradley Johnston. With Merritt's First Division deployed to the right of the Valley pike, and Custer's Third extending from Merritt's right westward, across the back road, toward the North mountain, the bugles sounded the advance early on the morning of the 9th. The two lines of battle met at Tom's creek, and one of the most spirited cavalry engagements of the war speedily ended in the capture of eleven Confederate cannon, being all the enemy's artillery save one piece, and a galloping pursuit of the defeated force continuing twenty miles beyond the battle-field. The army then, unmolested, resumed its northward march, and crossed to the north side of Cedar creek, where it faced about toward the hypothetical enemy, and went into camp, the centre of the infantry resting on the Valley pike. The Sixth Corps continued on to Front Royal, on its way to join Grant at Petersburg. The three cavalry divisions took their positions as follows: Merritt's on the left (east) of the infantry, picketing the line of the North fork Shenandoah river; Custer's on the right of the infantry, picketing a line five or six miles in length, and extending to the western boundary of the Valley; Powell's West Virginia Division in the vicinity of Front Royal, at the foot of the Blue Ridge, and connecting with Merritt's left.

On the 12th, our scouts reported that Early's reorganized infantry force had advanced to Fisher's Hill, their old Gibraltar, six miles south of our position at Cedar creek, which unexpected intelligence caused Sheridan to halt the Sixth Corps near Front Royal to await developments. At this juncture, Lieutenant General Grant recommended that a part of Sheridan's force should establish a strong position in the vicinity of Manassas gap, from which a fresh campaign against Gordonsville and Charlottesville could be executed. To this Sheridan demurred, and, on the 13th of October, he was summoned to Washington, by Secretary Stanton, for a conference about future operations. Having decided not to attack Early immediately in his strong position at Fisher's Hill, and having no apprehension of his taking the offensive, Sheridan started for Washington, on the 16th, and, in order to improve the time during his absence, he took the bulk of the cavalry force with him to Front Royal, designing to send it on a raid against the Virginia Central Railroad at Charlottesville. General H. G. Wright, as the senior officer, was left in command of the main army, which had been rejoined by the Sixth Corps. On arriving at Front Royal, on the evening of the 16th, Sheridan received the following dispatch from Wright:

HEADQUARTERS MIDDLE MILITARY DIVISION,
October 16th, 1864.

MAJOR GENERAL P. H. SHERIDAN,
Commanding Middle Military Division.

General:—I enclose you dispatch which explains itself (see copy following). If the enemy should be strongly reinforced by cavalry, he might, by turning our right, give us a great deal of trouble. I shall hold on here until the enemy's movements are developed, and shall only fear an attack on my right, which I shall make every preparation for guarding against and resisting.

Very respectfully, your obedient servant,

H. G. WRIGHT,
Major General Commanding.

[*Inclosure.*]

To LIEUTENANT GENERAL EARLY:

Be ready to move as soon as my forces join you, and we will crush Sheridan.

LONGSTREET,
Lieutenant General.

This dispatch, translated by our signal officers from the rebel signal flag on Three-Top mountain, whether genuine or a ruse, seemed to betoken activity of some sort on the part of the Confederates. Sheridan attached to it sufficient significance to induce him to abandon the raid on Charlottesville, and to order all the cavalry back to the army at Cedar creek, with the following message to General Wright, dated the evening of the 16th:

The cavalry is all ordered back to you; make your position strong. If Longstreet's dispatch is true, he is under the impression that we have largely detached. I will go over to Augur, and may get additional news. Close in Colonel Powell, who will be at this point [Front Royal]. If the enemy should make an advance, I know you will defeat him. Look well to your ground, and be well prepared. Get up everything that can be spared. I will bring up all I can, and will be up on Tuesday, if not sooner.

On the same night, after having thus provided for the safety of his army, Sheridan himself, escorted by the Second Ohio Cavalry from Custer's Division, passed on to Piedmont, east of the Blue Ridge, whence he took cars for Washington.

On the return of the cavalry to the army, instead of being placed in its former position, the divisions of Merritt and Custer, aggregating nearly eight thousand of the finest mounted troops in the world, were both ordered to the right of the infantry, where Wright anticipated attack, should any be made, while Powell's Division, instead of being "closed in," as directed in Sheridan's last message, was left in the neighborhood of Front Royal, near the eastern margin of the Valley—its attenuated line of pickets only connecting with the left of the infantry along the river front.

It was no longer a matter of indifference where the cavalry was placed. For the first time during the war the Federal cavalry was really raised to the dignity of a third arm of the service, and given its full share in the hard fighting, heavy losses, and great victories under the leadership and discipline of Sheridan. With their Spencer repeating-carbines, their expertness in transforming themselves

42

on occasion from troopers into foot soldiers, not unfrequently fighting rebel infantry behind breastworks—added to the celerity of movement and audacity of spirit, without which cavalry is well-nigh useless—Sheridan's mounted force was at once the eye and the right arm of his fighting column.

Cedar creek, flowing from the west and north, joins the North fork of the Shenandoah near Strasburg, on the Valley pike. About the same point the North fork turns sharply eastward toward the Blue Ridge, the two streams thus forming a partial line of defense nearly across the Valley. In the bend of the river rises the bold front of Massanutten mountain—the northern extremity of a subordinate range extending southward from this point parallel to the Blue Ridge, and dividing the Shenandoah Valley lengthwise. The Valley pike, the race-track of armies, and formerly one of the noblest highways of the continent, leads southward to Staunton and beyond, and northward through Winchester to the Potomac.

After the ceaseless activity, watchfulness and fighting of the Valley campaign, then considered at an end, our troops found the quiet of camp life a luxury to be appreciated. Arrears of sleep were to be made up, neglected correspondence revived, wardrobes renovated, and toilets attended to. Since the 10th of October this quiet of the main army had only been varied and amused by the invariable day-break skirmish between our pickets and the enemy's scouting parties; the usual grapevine telegrams, announcing the wholesale surrender of the Confederacy to Grant; the customary pleasantries at the expense of the hundred day troops, who were so eager to get to the front and smell powder before their term expired; the prevalent wicked offers to bet that "Old Jubal" was still on the retreat toward the Gulf, and the perennial grumbling about rations, with a corresponding alacrity in consuming them.

The 18th of October in the Shenandoah Valley was such a day as few have seen who have not spent an autumn in Virginia; crisp and bright and still in the morning; mellow and golden and still at noon; crimson and glorious and still at the sun setting; just blue enough in the distance to soften without obscuring the outline of the mountains, just hazy enough to render the atmosphere visible without limiting the range of sight. As evening closed above the Valley the soft pleadings of some homesick soldier's flute floated out through the quiet camp, while around a blazing camp-fire an impromptu glee club of Ohio boys lightened the hour and their own hearts by singing the songs of home. An unusually large letter mail arrived that evening, and was distributed to the men, which reminds me that the

First Connecticut Cavalry, belonging to Custer's Division, had a unique and pleasant manner of announcing the arrival of a mail; the regimental trumpeters, constituting a sort of a cornet band, would form in front of the colonel's tent and play "Home, Sweet Home," sometimes following that immediately with "The Girl I Left Behind Me."

The letters were all read and their contents discussed, the flute had ceased its complaining, the eight o'clock roll-call was over, taps had sounded, lights were out in the tents, cook-fires flickered low, the mists of the autumn night gathered gray and chill, the sentinels paced back and forth in front of the various headquarters, the camp was still—that many-headed monster, a great army, was asleep. Midnight came, and with it no sound but the tramp of the relief guard as the sergeant replaced the tired sentinels. One o'clock, and all was tranquil as a peace convention; two, three o'clock, and yet the soldiers slept. At four the silence was broken by sharp firing in the direction of our cavalry pickets, toward the western side of the Valley. The firing increased in volume, suggesting an attack in force by cavalry. General Custer (than whom, by the way, the wars of the century probably have not developed an abler leader of a cavalry division) quietly dispatched a regiment to support our outposts and awaited developments, which speedily came. Fifteen minutes later heavy skirmish firing was heard on the left of the infantry, two miles from where our cavalry division was encamped. The firing on our extreme right gradually died away and that in front of the infantry line rapidly increased, showing that the movement on our right had been a feint, while the real attack had now begun against the centre and left.

"Boots and saddles!" was blown from division, brigade, and regimental headquarters. The darkness rang with the blare of bugles and the shouts of officers hurrying the troopers from their dreams to their horses. The rattle of musketry in front of the infantry increased to heavy volleys, the volleys thickened into a continuous roar, and now, as day began to dawn, the deep bass of the artillery came in to complete the grand but terrible chorus of battle. The cavalry were speedily mounted and in line by regiments, awaiting orders. Awaiting orders! That is the time that tries the courage of the bravest. Once in the heat, and hurry, and inspiration of the battle, the average soldier forgets fear in the excitement of the hour; but to stand at a safe distance, though within easy sight and hearing of the conflict, ready, expectant, every nerve strung, awaiting the word of command to march into the hailstorm of death

—that is the crucial test. It is at such a time that all the mental struggle involved in a soldier's death is undergone, leaving nothing but the mere physical pang of sudden dying to complete the sacrifice.

"Custer's Division to the Centre!" was the laconic command from General Wright; and as the sun was rising, our four thousand troopers, with accompanying batteries, marched into the fight. As we came into full view of the field, the whole sickening truth flashed upon us—the infantry had been surprised in their beds by Early's reinforced army; our best artillery was already in the hands of the Confederates and turned against us; thousands of our men had been killed, wounded, or captured before they could even offer resistance; Sheridan's victorious and hitherto invincible army was routed and in disorderly retreat before a confident, yelling, and pursuing enemy. The roads were crowded with wagons and ambulances hurrying to the rear, while the fields were alive with wounded, stragglers, camp-followers, and disorganized troops, without officers, without arms, and without courage—all bent on being the first to carry the news of the disaster back to Winchester. A brave nucleus of the army, which had not shared in the surprise and the consequent demoralization, was fighting with determined pluck to prevent disaster from becoming disgrace. The timely arrival and the spirited onset of the cavalry soon checked the pursuit by the Confederates and gave time for our infantry to begin re-forming their lines; but the battle and the retreat continued. Two regiments of cavalry were speedily deployed across the country—well to the rear—for the purpose of checking the stampede and turing back the flying mob of panic-stricken infantrymen; but the attempt was fruitless and was soon abandoned. Our two divisions of cavalry deployed in heavy lines to the right and left of the Valley pike, and began their hot day's work against rebel infantry and artillery.

At nine o'clock a portion of the enemy's troops occupied, and were plainly seen plundering, the camps where the Sixth Corps had slept the night before; our left was being pressed with great vigor by a flanking force which seemed determined to reach the pike, and thus strike our wagon trains; General Wright had unquestionably resolved on a retreat to a new line near Winchester, and the best we hoped for was, that our mounted troops could so protect the retreat and retard the pursuit, as to prevent the annihilation of the broken army and the exposure of Washington. The universal thought and, in varying phrase, the spontaneous utterance was: "Oh for one hour of Sheridan." The unvarying success that had attended our leader in all his campaigns; the instinctive promptness with which he seemed to seize the key of every situation, however difficult; the amazing quickness and precision with which he formed new plans on the field, and his thunderbolt method of executing each design; his success in imparting to his infantry much of the mobility and dash of cavalry, and to his cavalry much of the coherency and steadiness of infantry—all these had combined, in spite of not a few unheroic personal traits, to give his army unbounded faith in his leadership and enthusiasm for the man. But Sheridan was twenty miles away, at Winchester, where he had arrived the day before from Washington. Meantime, the battle and the day wore on together. The sulphurous cloud that overhung the field, and the dense volumes of dust that rose behind the wheeling batteries and the charging troops, contrasted grimly with the sweet light of that perfect October day, as it could be seen beyond the limits of the battle-field. At noon, and for some time previously, the enemy was opposed only by Merritt's and Custer's cavalry and Getty's Division of infantry, with their accompanying batteries, while the main portion of the Sixth Corps was more than two miles to the right and rear of Getty, engaged in reorganizing, and the Nineteenth Corps was, in turn, to the right and rear of the Sixth.

At this juncture, those of us who were stationed near the Winchester pike heard, far to the rear of us, a faint cheer go up, as a hurrying horseman passed a group of wounded soldiers, and dashed down that historic road toward our line of battle. As he drew nearer, we could see that the coal black horse was flecked with foam, both horse and rider grimed with dust, and the dilated nostrils and laboring breath of the former told of a race both long and swift. A moment more and a deafening cheer broke from the troops in that part of the field, as they recognized in the coming horseman their longed-for Sheridan. Above the roar of musketry and artillery, that shout arose like a cry of victory. The news flashed from brigade to brigade, along our front, with telegraphic speed, and then, as Sheridan, cap in hand, dashed along the rear of the struggling line, thus confirming to all eyes the fact of his arrival, a continuous cheer burst from the whole army. Hope took the place of fear, courage the place of despondency, cheerfulness the place of gloom. The entire aspect of things seemed changed in a moment. Further retreat was not longer thought of. At all points to the rear stragglers could be seen by hundreds voluntarily rejoining their regiments, with such arms as they could hastily find—order seemed to have come spontaneously out of chaos, an army out of a rabble. [The cannonade of the early morning, when the battle opened, had been attributed by Sheridan, at Winchester, to a reconnoissance, which he knew had been ordered from our lines, and it was only when the head of the column of fugitive troops and baggage wagons was seen, between nine and ten o'clock A. M., approaching Winchester "with appalling rapidity," that a conception of the real situation dawned on the astounded general, and promptly started him on his now famous "ride" to the front.]

The enemy, believing the continued cheers announced the arrival of Federal reinforcements, became more cautious, and even, like ourselves, threw up temporary breastworks. Our commander instantly decided to hold the line we were then fighting on, and sent galloping orders to the Sixth and Nineteenth Corps to hasten up to our support before the enemy should attack. By two o'clock our lines were fully re-formed, the various infantry divisions, greatly strengthened by the return of stragglers, were in position, and the cavalry had been sent to the flanks—Custer to the right, and Merritt to the left. Everything now indicated that we should be able to hold our ground without further retreat. By this time Early, apparently satisfied that we had received no reinforcements, made a confident and persistent assault upon our lines—obviously determined to close the day with our final rout, and, returning the courtesy of thirty days before, send the remnant of Sheridan's army "whirling through Winchester." The attack was repulsed at every point. This defensive success under Sheridan's leadership perfectly restored the courage and spirit of the army. It had got over its panic, and was again ready for business.

Shortly after this attack and repulse, report came from the Front Royal pike, which was held by Powell's cavalry, that a strong column of rebel infantry was marching past our left, and toward Winchester—a report which, although proving erroneous, delayed the execution of Sheridan's quickly-formed intention to attack the enemy and save the day. At four P. M. the command was sent along the line to prepare for a general forward movement. Everything was soon ready; two hundred bugles sounded the advance; all our artillery opened on the enemy with shot and shell, and the long line of cavalry and infantry moved steadily forward across the open plain, under a heavy fire, toward the rebel position, with a coolness and order I never saw surpassed during four years' of service. To one who had seen the rout and panic, and loss of the morning, it seemed impossible that this was the same army. The enemy was evidently astonished at our taking the offensive, but met our attack with confident coolness, and then with determined fury. As soon as the

Confederate infantry was fully engaged with ours in the centre, the order was given for the cavalry divisions to charge both flanks of the enemy's line. The bugles sounded, the horses caught the spirit of the hour, and pressed forward with steady but resistless speed; seven thousand troopers, with drawn sabres, sent up a battle yell wild enough to wake the slain over whom we galloped, and we were in the midst of that grandest of martial movements—a genuine cavalry charge.

The effect was magical. The enemy's mounted troops first made a stout resistance, then scattered like sheep to the hills, and his infantry line, having both flanks turned back upon itself by our cavalry, and its centre crushed by a final magnificent charge of our infantry, broke in confusion, and started southward in confused retreat. Panic seized every part of the rebel force; infantry vied with artillery, and both with the wagon trains, in a harum-scarum race for the Cedar creek ford, and, as the sun went down, the army, which at daybreak had gained one of the most dramatic and over-whelming victories of the war, was a frantic rabble, decimated in numbers, and flying before the same army it had, twelve hours before, so completely surprised and routed. Our cavalry pressed the pursuit with a vehemence and success that astonished even the much-expecting Sheridan. Merritt on the left of the pike, and Custer on the right, met with no opposition from the scared and fugitive mob of mingled "horse, foot, and dragoons." The pike was blockaded for miles with cannon, caissons, ambulances, and baggage wagons, which our troopers easily captured, and turned backward toward our lines. The chase continued, with constant captures of prisoners and war material, until, near the foot of Fisher's Hill, the dense darkness enforced a truce between pursuers and pursued. Both infantry and cavalry returned to sleep in their camps of the night before, hungry and half dead with fatigue, but happy, and having about them, as trophies of the day's work, forty-five pieces of captured and recap-tured artillery, and a field full of wagons, ambulances, and prisoners of war. This ended the career of Early's army. As an army it never fought another battle—its commander never again attempted to redeem the Shenandoah Valley, nor to invade the North.

This free-hand sketch of an historical military episode, taken from the point of view of a participant with the Union cavalry, and making no pretensions to microscopic accuracy of detail, suggests one or two obvious commentaries:

FIRST. The skill, the courage, and the self-command with which the initial part of Early's movement of October 19th was planned and executed could not well be surpassed. To move a fully equipped army of infantry and artillery on a still night along the front of a powerful and presumably watchful enemy, twice ford a considerable stream, noiselessly capture or "relieve" the hostile pickets on the river bank, place a turning force on the enemy's flank, surprise the bulk of the hostile army in bed, and, after reducing it one-sixth in numbers, drive it in pell-mell retreat, shelled by its own artillery, requires, it need not be said, some of the very highest military qualities in both commander and troops. Whether the chief credit for the achievement is due to General Early, or to his subordinate, General Gordon, is a question of personal, rather than of public, interest.

SECOND. The negligence which could expose Sheridan's victorious army to the possibility of such a surprise, humiliation and rout, especially after the distinct warning of three days before, stands without explanation, and without excuse. Forty-one hundred men killed and wounded are a heavy price to pay for the failure to keep one's eyes open, and make a timely reconnoissance.

THIRD. Early's neglect to relentlessly press his advantage during the forenoon of the 19th, before Sheridan reached the field, and while there was in his immediate front, for much of the time, only one battered division of infantry and two divisions of cavalry, indicates that he was overcome with causeless timidity in the hour of his greatest triumph—an experience not uncommon to commanders whose persistent courage (not personal bravery) in the open field does not equal their genius for unusual strategic enterprises. Several of Early's most intelligent subordinates attribute the fatal delay to three things—their commander's willingness to let well enough alone; the profound respect of Early's army for Sheridan's cavalry, which had never been surprised, and never known defeat, and the impossibility of preserving discipline among the destitute Confederate soldiers so long as there was anything to plunder in the captured Federal camps. The last-named cause receives grim confirmation from the fact that, on repossessing the battle-field of the morning, we found that hundreds of the Union slain had been stripped to entire nudity—the writer having counted sixty-three instances of this in riding hurriedly across a single section of the plain.

FOURTH. Stripped of all poetic glosses, and analyzed after fourteen years of peace, when *nil admirari* seems to have become the motto of all, the result achieved by Sheridan's matchless generalship, after he reached his shattered army on the field of Cedar creek— as an illustration of the wonderful influence of one man over many, and an example of snatching a great victory from an appalling defeat—still stands without a parallel in history.

GENERAL STUART IN CAMP AND FIELD.

BY COLONEL JOHN ESTEN COOKE.

THE famous General "Jeb" Stuart was, perhaps, the most picturesque figure moving on the great arena of the late civil war. Young, gay, gallant; wearing a uniform brilliant with gold braid, golden spurs, and a hat looped up with a golden star and decorated with a black plume; going on marches at the head of his cavalry column with his banjo-player gayly thrumming behind him; leading his troops to battle with a camp song on his lips; here to-day and away to-morrow, raiding, fighting, laughing, dancing, and as famous for his gallantry toward women as for his reckless courage. Stuart was in every particular a singular and striking human being, drawing to himself the strongest public interest both as a man and a soldier. Of his military ability as a cavalry leader, General Sedgwick probably summed up the general opinion when he said: "Stuart is the best cavalryman ever foaled in North America." Of his courage, devotion, and many lovable traits, General Lee bore his testimony on his death, when he retired to his tent with the words: "I can scarcely think of him without weeping." Stuart thus made a very strong impression both on the people at large and on the eminent soldiers with whom he was associated, and a sketch of him ought to interest, if faithfully drawn. The writer of this paper believes it is in his power to present such a sketch, having enjoyed his personal friendship, and observed him during a large part of his career; and the aim will be to make the likeness presented as accurate as possible to the original.

Up to the outbreak of the war Stuart's life was scarcely marked by any incident of interest. He was a native of Patrick county,

Virginia, and came of a family of high social position and some distinction. Having graduated at West Point, he served for some years
as a lieutenant in the United States army, and when it was obvious
that Virginia would secede, he resigned his commission and came to
his native State, where he was put in command of the First Regiment of Cavalry, operating on the Upper Potomac. He had been
prominent, at this time, in only one scene attracting public attention.
This was in 1859, at Harper's Ferry, where he was directed by
General, then Colonel, R. E. Lee to summon John Brown to surrender. He recognized Brown, then passing as "Captain Smith,"
as soon as the engine-house door was half opened, as an old acquaintance in Kansas, and advised him to surrender, which Brown declined
doing, adding, "You know, lieutenant, we are not afraid of bullets,"
when Stuart stepped aside, and the attack and capture of the old
marauder followed.

In a sketch so limited as the present, it is impossible to more
than refer to the main points in Stuart's career as a soldier. From
the first, his cavalry operations were full of fire and vigor, and
General J. E. Johnston, under whom he served in the Valley, called
him "the indefatigable Stuart." He became famous for his gayety,
activity, and romantic exploits, and after fighting all day would dance
nearly all night at some hospitable house. He wore at this time his
blue United States army uniform, and a forage cap covered with a
white "havelock," resembling a chain helmet, which made his head
resemble that of a knight of the days of chivalry; and at the head
of his troopers, as they moved through the spring forests, he was a
romantic figure. When Johnston crossed the mountains, Stuart
covered the movement with very great skill, charged the Zouaves at
Manassas, held the outposts afterward toward Alexandria, and
brought up the rear when Johnston fell back to the Rapidan, subsequently taking a prominent part in the obstinate battles on the
Chickahominy. Just preceding these battles he made his remarkable march, with about fifteen hundred cavalry, entirely around
General McClellan's army, originating thus the system of cavalry
"raiding," which afterward proved so fatal to the South.

The ability and energy displayed in these movements gained
for him the commission of major general, and from that time, to his
death, he remained Chief of Cavalry of General Lee's army. When
the Confederate forces advanced northward in the summer of 1862,
Stuart's cavalry accompanied the column, and took part in all the
important operations of that year—on the Rapidan, the Rappahannock, the Second Manassas, Sharpsburg, and Fredericksburg. In

these bustling scenes Stuart acted with immense energy and enthusiasm, laying broad and deep his reputation as a cavalry officer. By incessant fighting, and an ardor and activity which seemed to pass all bounds, he had by this time won the full confidence of General Lee. His rank, in the estimation of General Jackson, was as high. This will be understood from what took place in May, 1863, at Chancellorsville. When Jackson was disabled, and Stuart assumed command, and sent to ascertain Jackson's views and wishes as to the attack on the next morning, the wounded commander replied: " Go back and tell General Stuart to act on his own judgment, and do what he thinks best. *I have implicit confidence in him!* "—an expression for which my authority was his brave Adjutant General, Colonel Pendleton, and which ought to be sufficient to make the reputation of any soldier. Stuart's attack with Jackson's Corps on the next morning fully justified this confidence. His employment of artillery in mass on the Federal left, went far to decide this critical action. At the battle of Fredericksburg, in the preceding December, the same masterly handling of his guns had protected Jackson's right toward the Massaponnax, which was the real key of the battle; and in these two great actions, as on the left at Sharpsburg, Stuart exhibited a genius for the management of artillery which would have delighted Napoleon. In the operations of 1863, culminating at Gettysburg, he was charged with misconception or disobedience of orders in separating himself from the main column, although he protested to me, with the utmost earnestness and feeling, that he had been guilty of neither. Then the hurried and adventurous scenes followed, when General Lee attempted, in October, 1863, to cut off General Meade at Manassas, when the cavalry was the only arm which effected anything, and General Kilpatrick was nearly crushed near Bucklands—the brief campaign of Mine Run—and the furious wrestle between Lee and Grant in the Wilderness, in May, 1864. When General Grant moved toward Spottsylvania Court-House, it was Stuart who, according to Northern historians, so obstructed the roads as to enable General Lee to interpose his army at this important point. Had this not been effected, Richmond, it would seem, must have fallen; Stuart thus having the melancholy glory of prolonging, for an additional year, the contest, ending only in April, 1865. His death speedily followed. General Sheridan turned against him his own system, organized on the Chickahominy, in June, 1862. The Federal horse pushed past Lee's army to surprise Richmond; Stuart followed in haste, with such small force of cavalry as he could collect on the instant. The collision took place at Yellow tavern, near Richmond, and in the engagement Stuart was mortally wounded, and, two or three days afterward, expired.

The death of the famous cavalryman produced a deep and painful sensation, in some degree akin to that produced by the death of Jackson. The Southern people, indeed, had become accustomed to couple together the three great names, Lee, Jackson, and Stuart, valuing each for his peculiar qualities. No comparison is intended to be made between these three distinguished soldiers; but it is interesting to notice how sharply contrasted they were in character, and how peculiarly each was fitted for the sphere in which he moved, and his special functions. Lee, the head and front of the struggle, was the born commander-in-chief, fitted for the conception of great campaigns, ever wide awake, a man of august dignity by nature, calm, suave, grave, taking good and evil fortune with the same imposing serenity; in person, one of the most noble and graceful men of his epoch, and the finest rider in the Southern army; in character, simple, pure, patient, binding to himself both the love and respect of men. Jackson was the infantry leader, the "right arm" to execute what Lee conceived; in person not graceful, in manner silent, reserved, and often abrupt; cautious in council, but rapid and terrible in execution, going to battle with muttered prayers on his lips, leaving all to Providence, but striking with all the power of his arm to do his own part, and in many ways resembling the Ironsides of Cromwell. Stuart, on the contrary, was the cavalier, essentially belonging to the class of men who followed the fortunes of Charles I.—ardent, impetuous, brimming over with the wine of life and youth, with the headlong courage of a high-spirited boy, fond of bright colors, of rippling flags, of martial music, and the clash of sabres; in all the warp and woof his character an embodiment of the best traits of the English cavaliers—not of their bad traits. Although his utter carelessness as to the impression he produced subjected him to many calumnies, it is here placed on record, by one who knew his private life thoroughly, and was with him day and night for years, that he was, in morals, among the purest of men—a faithful husband, absolutely without vices of any description, and, if not demonstrative in his religious views, an earnest and exemplary Christian. His love for his wife was deep and devoted; and on the death of his little daughter, Flora, he said to me, with tears in his eyes: "I shall never get over it."

When one day some person in my presence indulged in sneers at the expense of "preachers," supposing that the roystering young commander would echo them, Stuart said, coldly: "I regard the

Christian ministry as the noblest work in which any human being can engage." He never touched spirits in any form during his whole life, having promised his mother, he told me, that he would not; did not use tobacco even; never uttered anything approaching an oath, or touched cards, or indulged in any one of the vices supposed to be habitual with soldiers. In spite of all, however, those who hated or envied him, called him a drunkard and a libertine.

Stuart naturally attracted most attention in his military character, and I am satisfied that, as time passes on, and the circumstances of the late struggle are better known, his reputation as a soldier will steadily increase. His youth, gayety, and apparent thoughtlessness, his song-singing, his rattling banjo—all were against him in the estimation of grave people in black coats, who could not or would not believe that this "mere boy" was by birth a soldier—even a great one. Successful soldiership requires a peculiar organization, which is neither that of the statesman, the orator, the writer, and the thinker. What is demanded is the genius of the man born to lead, direct, and act—often on sudden emergency, and as though from instinct. Stuart was, by nature, intended to lead and command men. He took his place at the head of troops as by right, and his followers felt that he was entitled to lead them, without sharing in that unthinking admiration which he generally aroused. I had the conviction forced upon me, after observing him in his earliest campaigns, that he was a thorough soldier. He had the instinctive power of penetrating his enemy's design, an eye consummate in the choice of ground for fighting on, with cavalry, infantry, or artillery; and, while reckless, apparently, in attacking, knew well when he ought to retreat. The success of his retreats, indeed, from positions of the most hazardous character, will probably remain his greatest claim to good soldiership—at least they so impressed me while closely observing how they were accomplished on many occasions in Virginia, Maryland, and Pennsylvania.

His personal bearing on the field was peculiar. He was rarely excited by anything, though he exhibited all the ardor of a young soldier while actually fighting, and often crossed swords like a common *sabieur*. As frequently, however, he remained quiet, appearing to be indulging in reflection. In very dangerous and critical situations I have seen him throw his leg over the pommel of the saddle, drum upon his knee carelessly, and then give his orders so quietly that it was difficult to believe that it was "touch and go" whether he would extricate his command, or be cut to pieces. Any question of his personal fate obviously never entered his mind—a common trait, it may be said, with soldiers; but Stuart evidently possessed the additional merit of being able to *think* with entire calmness, while the air around him was full of bullets, and shells were bursting over and around him. In a cavalry charge, however, the *thinker* disappeared, and he became the *actor*. He went in front of his men, at a gallop, with immense joy, ardor and *elan*. His face glowed, he was full of laughter, and often roared out, in his gay, sonorous voice, some one of his favorite ballads. This eccentric habit attracted the attention of Jackson's men at Chancellorsville— men habituated to the gravity and prayers of their wounded leader. Stuart led Jackson's Corps against General Hooker's intrenchments, with drawn sabre and floating plume, singing "Old Joe Hooker, will you come out of the Wilderness!"

He had the genius to understand what an enemy ought to, and probably would do—in proof of which I remember that he said to me, in the winter of 1862: "The next battle will be near Chancellorsville," where it accordingly took place, nearly six months afterward; but he was as great as an executive officer as in council, if not greater. I am sure that he loved fighting in person, from the ardor of his blood, his high health, and natural excitability and impetuosity. He would certainly have made an excellent private, and told me, when there was some question of virtually superseding him, that, if they did so, he would enlist. The War Office might deprive him of his commission, he said, or force him to resign; but there was one thing they could not do—prevent him from going into the ranks with his sabre as a private of the Confederate States army, which, he added, he certainly should do. I am certain that he would have followed this course at once, and not in the least from any feeling of "spite." He produced upon me the impression of being more thoroughly and completely *devoted* to the cause in which he was fighting than any other person, without exception, with whom I was thrown during the war. His faith in the justice of the struggle was absolute, and he never, to my knowledge, had one moment's doubt as to the result of the war. His words and actions invariably indicated the most unswerving conviction that the South was fighting in the holiest of causes, and must achieve her independence. His duty, therefore, was plain. He would do his best, count his life as nothing, and stand or fall as heaven decreed. He said to me: "I never expect to come out of this war alive;" and though he was undoubtedly ambitious, immensely so even, and void of glory, he ought to have credit for the nobler motive—love of the cause, and devotion to it, even to the death.

The object of this sketch is chiefly to draw the likeness of General Stuart as he appeared in the familiar scenes of the camp; as this familiar phase of any human being is generally the most characteristic and suggestive; but the subject of his genius as a soldier ought not to be dropped without some reference to the estimate placed upon him by those best able to judge him truly. General Lee unquestionably regarded him as a cavalry commander of the first order of merit, and attached the very highest value to his co-operation in the campaign. The estimates of General Lee, either of friend or foe, were calm, impartial, and rarely, if ever, affected in the least degree by private feeling. Thus, he esteemed the late General Meade very highly as a soldier, declaring that he was the best officer of the Federal army, and had "given him more trouble than any of them." An estimate which he precisely reversed in the case of General Sheridan, whose ability as a cavalry officer he considered very small. His opinion of Stuart may be seen in his reports, but was plainest to those who observed, at close view, how much he counseled with and trusted to him. The cavalry, under their ardent young leader, were the eyes and ears of his army in every campaign; and although Lee would not officially censure Stuart, it seems plain that, right or wrong, he regarded the defeat at Gettysburg as in some measure due to the absence of Stuart, to whom he had always looked for prompt and reliable information of the movements of the enemy. Finally, when Stuart fell, in May, 1864, and Lee said that he could scarcely think of him without weeping, the acute grief of the great soldier for a man he had loved so much was certainly mingled with deep regret for the loss of the soldier whose services were so important to him in the critical condition of affairs at the moment.

In camp, in bivouac, on the march, and "off duty" everywhere, Stuart was a striking personage. Some human beings are only notable on great occasions, in imposing attitudes gotten up for the emergency, and once back in private, living their every day lives, are commonplace and uninteresting. This was far from being the case with Stuart. There was about the man a perennial interest as vivid with those who saw him, hour by hour, as with strangers glancing at him in his splendid uniform at the head of his column, or leading a charge. The ardor, mirth, and romance of the man in his public phase, were all natural, and as characteristic of him in private with friends and staff officers as on the field before the eyes of the world. He had an immensely strong physique, and unfailing animal spirits —loved song, laughter, jesting, rough practical jokes, and all the virile divertisements of camp. His surroundings were all in unison with his youthful love of movement, incident, and adventure. He rarely settled down, unless compelled to do so, in any formal head-quarters. "Here to-day and away to-morrow," might have been considered one of his maxims. Thus his quarters were, except in winter, the most impromptu affairs. A canvas "fly" stretched over a pole, the horses affixed to the boughs of the forest near, saddled and champering their bits, the red battle-flag rippling in the brilliant sunshine, couriers going and coming, the staff grouped around, wait-ing, booted and spurred, for the order to mount, which they knew might come at any moment, and from the canvas tent the song or laughter of Stuart busy at his desk, from which he would rise from time to time to come to the opening, yawn, throw a jest at some one, and then return to his work—such, in brief outline, were these first bivouacs of Stuart, who always moved in "light marching order," that is to say, with his blanket behind his saddle, and his hat, gloves, and sabre beside him; a true cavalier, ready at all moments to be up and away.

With his staff officers, Stuart was perfectly familiar, and more like a "big boy" among a group of small ones, than a general enthroned among subordinates. It was his delight to jest at the expense of each and all, and he was perfectly willing that they should jest at him in return. His humor was often rough, uncere-monious—that of the cavalryman; but he was not guilty of the smallness of becoming irritated if he was retorted on in kind. He seemed cordially to hate ceremony, and wholly ignored his rank in his military family, though at times he was exceedingly imperious. If on such occasions, however, he thought that he had wounded any one, he would speedily regret it, put his arm around the individual, laugh, and say, "Come, old fellow, get pleased. I never joke with any one unless I love them."

This was the boy speaking through the man's lips; indeed, there was a pervading spirit of boyishness about Stuart which made it impossible to be permanently angry with him, however rough his jest at one's expense. He was, in the interval of all this gayety, an exceedingly hard worker, and a very stern disciplinarian. One of his humorous orders to his inspector general was: "Cry aloud—spare not—show my people their transgressions!" And he never hesitated to compel obedience to his orders, and to throw the whole weight of his official displeasure against any officer of his command, however high his rank. With a very warm and kind heart, he had little of the softness of disposition which induces reluctance to punish.

neglect of duty. This latter trait is said to have, in some measure, characterized General Lee. It did not characterize Stuart. He was a very stern man where he had convinced himself that there was wilful opposition to his orders, or even a failure, from negligence, to comply with them. From this resulted a very excellent state of discipline, generally, and a wholesome indisposition to act in opposition to his known wishes, or brave his displeasure. He had none of the mock dignity of small men in command, and spoke and acted with entire naturalness. Often his utterances were full of rough humor. Having reported to him, on one occasion, that a force of Federal cavalry had crossed the Rappahannock below Fleetwood, and were drawn up on the southern bank, I received from him the order: " Well, tell Colonel Beale to *lick into 'em, and jam 'em right over the river.*" At Fredericksburg, in the evening, when one of his officers sent a courier to ask how the battle was going, his answer was: " Tell him Jackson has not advanced, but I have, and that I am going on, *crowding 'em with artillery.*" While conversing with him, one day, in regard to his hazardous expedition around General McClellan's army, on the Chickahominy, I said that, if attacked while crossing below, he would certainly have been obliged to surrender, when his reply was: " No, one other course was left—to die game !" In these straightforward and unceremonious utterances, Stuart expressed his character, that of the hard-fighting cavalryman, revealed as he worded it on another occasion—to " go through, or *die trying.*" Returning to him as he appeared in camp, it may be said that he was both a lovable and a provoking person—lovable from the genuine warmth of his character, and provoking from the apparent disregard of the feelings of those around him, or, at least, from his proneness to amuse himself at any and everybody's expense. When the humor seized him, he laughed at nearly everybody. General Lee he invariably spoke of, as he treated him, with profound respect; but he even made merry with so great a man as Jackson, or " Old Stonewall," as he affectionately styled him. The two distinguished men seemed to have a sincere friendship for each other, which always impressed me as a very singular circumstance indeed; but so it was. They were strongly contrasted in character and temperament, for Stuart was the most impulsive and Jackson the most reserved and reticent of men. But it was plain that a strong bond of mutual admiration and confidence united them. Jackson would visit Stuart, and hold long confidential conversations with him, listening to his views with evident attention; and Stuart exhibited, on the intelli-

43

gence of this great man's death, the strongest emotion. "It is a national calamity," he said, in a voice of the deepest feeling.

Our recollections of human beings generally attach to some particular locality with which we associate them, and the writer of these pages returns in memory, when thinking of Stuart, more especially to his quarters near Fredericksburg in the winter of 1862, which he humorously styled "Camp No Camp." Here, with his tent pitched under shelter of a pine thicket, and his horses picketed near—for he believed that exposure hardened them—with a slender little Whitworth gun posted like a graceful watch-dog in front, and surrounded by his mirthful young staff officers, Stuart passed the long months of the winter succeeding the hard battle. Jackson's quarters were at "Moss Neck," some miles down the river, and they exchanged visits often—Stuart making merry over all things, and not sparing even the grave and devout "Stonewall," whose eyes would twinkle at his companion's jests. Jesting, indeed, seemed to be a necessity of Stuart's nature. Mirth and humor burst forth from this strong nature as a flower bursts from its stalk. At "Camp No Camp" the days and nights were full of song and laughter. Stuart's delight was to have his banjo-player, Sweeney, in his tent; and even while busily engaged in his official correspondence, he loved to hear the gay rattle of the instrument, and the voice of Sweeney singing "J'ine the Cavalry," "Sweet Evelina," or some other favorite ditty. From time to time he would lay down his pen, throw one knee over the arm of his chair, and call his two dogs—two handsome young setters, which he had brought across the Rappahannock—or falling back, or utter some jest at the expense of his staff. As frequently he would join in the song, or volunteer one of his own—his favorite being "The Bugles Sang Truce," "The Dew is on the Blossom," and some comic ballads, of which the one beginning "My Wife's in Castle Thunder," was a fair specimen. These he roared out with immense glee, rising and gesticulating, slapping his staff officers on the back, and throwing back his head while he sang, and almost always ending in a burst of laughter.

These personal traits of an eminent man are recorded with the view of presenting him to the reader just as he appeared—precisely as a painter drawing his likeness would present his low, athletic figure, his heavy brown beard, his flowing mustache, his lofty forehead, finely-outlined nose, and blue eyes as penetrating and brilliant as an eagle's. This *personnel* of the man was a large part of him, so to speak. You could never dissociate the genius of the soldier from the appearance of the individual. If ever human being *looked* his character, it was Stuart, in his short fighting jacket, heavy with gold braid, his huge gauntlets, and boots reaching to the knees, his hat with its black feather, his sabre and pistol, his rattling spurs, and his gay, alert, off-hand bearing as of one ready to mount in an instant and take part in a "fight or frolic." Youth, high health, humor, courage—unthinking resolve, indeed, to "do or die"—were revealed in every trait and every movement of the individual. Here was plainly a powerful military machine with all the wheels in perfect order, and to be relied upon for any work, however arduous. One of his letters to me was signed, "Yours *to count on*," and this truthfully expressed the character of the man. General Lee knew well that Stuart would never allow indolence or procrastination to stand in the way of obedience to an order—that he was what the Duke of Wellington called a "two-o'clock-in-the-morning man," ready at any instant for any work; and it was this combination of a powerful physique, unfailing promptness, and military genius which made the services of the soldier so invaluable. In activity, energy, and acumen, Stuart was, I am convinced, the first cavalry leader of his epoch, and among the most remarkable of any epoch. When he fell, there were eminent men to take his place—leaders as devoted, hard fighting, and faithful—but no other could precisely fill the vacuum. With the death of Jackson and Stuart, in May, 1863, and May, 1864, something seemed wanting which could not be supplied. When these two men disappeared, the great conflict appeared gloomy and hopeless.

The familiar sketch here presented of this eminent man, has given the reader, I trust, a tolerably distinct conception of the character and appearance of the individual—the writer's aim having been to leave the record of events in the career of *the soldier* to the historian, paying chief attention to the characteristics of *the man*. The likeness is at least accurate as far as it goes, and has this merit, that it is based on intimate personal association with the personage whose portrait is traced. The traits of Stuart's character were as obvious as those of his personal appearance. All was on the surface. Foibles he had—a hasty temper, an imperious will, a thirst for glory, the love of appearance, and a susceptibility to flattery that all observed; but there his faults ended. To counterbalance these weaknesses, he was honest, true, devoted, generous, as brave as steel, and faithful to his principles and his religious profession. The controlling instinct, I believe, of his whole nature was to do his duty "up to the hilt"—to use one of his own phrases—and in the performance of this duty he disregarded all personal considerations. He fell defending the capital, in a desperate struggle, and came to his death by reckless exposure of himself—his only thought having been to accomplish his end. And as his life had been one of earnest devotion to the cause in which he believed, so his last hours were tranquil, his confidence in the mercy of Heaven unfailing. When he was asked how he felt, he said, "Easy, but willing to die, if God and my country think I have done my duty." His last words were: "I am going fast now; I am resigned. God's will be done." As he uttered these words he expired.

THE BATTLE OF SHILOH.

BY COLONEL WILLS DE HASS.

THE 6th of April, 1862, was a day fraught with momentous issues for the future of the American Republic. The evening of the 5th had witnessed the concentration of a great army, whose leaders had boastingly declared in the pride of their strength should, on the coming morn, overwhelm and destroy the army of the Union which lay encamped in conscious security around the wilderness church of Shiloh! At no period during our prolonged and sanguinary civil war was the Union more imperiled than on that eventful Saturday evening. The battle of Shiloh was the first decisive and, pre-eminently, the most important of the war. Defeat then would have been the greatest disaster that could have befallen the arms of the Union. The country can never know the full danger of that hour, and the pen of the historian can never portray the peril which hung over the Army of the Tennessee. Congress received the announcement of events then culminating in "profound silence," the official dispatch of victory declared it was "the hardest battle ever fought on this continent," the President proclaimed a day of fasting and prayer for the great deliverance by this and other achievements of our arms; but the peril of the army, the severity of the battle, and the magnitude of the victory will, perhaps, never be fully known or appreciated. General Grant says, in his report: "There was the most continuous firing of artillery and musketry ever heard on this continent kept up until nightfall;" and the Southern accounts describe it as the "most sanguinary battle in history, in proportion to the numbers engaged." We propose to give a succinct and

impartial recital of the principal facts and incidents, now passed into
history, of that great struggle for the Union. With a brief retrospect, I will pass to the consideration of my subject.

The fall and winter campaigns of 1861–62, had made manifest
that a decisive blow must be struck in the Southwest or the cause of
the Union materially suffer. The new department commanders—
General Buell in that of Ohio, and General Halleck in that of Missouri—united their energies, and the capture of those important
strongholds, Forts Donelson and Henry, rapidly followed. These
successes led on to other operations. With the opening spring it
was resolved to follow up the retreating armies of the Confederacy
and strike an effective blow in the neighborhood of Corinth, Mississippi, where it was known that the most formidable defenses were
in course of construction. In February, a new district was formed,
called West Tennessee, and by order of General Halleck, General
Grant was appointed to its command, with headquarters in the field.
The most strenuous exertions were made to organize a force of sufficient strength to meet and overcome, in connection with the army
of General Buell, the Confederate forces at Corinth. The Tennessee
expedition was ordered to rendezvous at Paducah, at the mouth of
the Tennessee river, and every available Western regiment was
hurried forward to join it. With how much haste this was done, I
may mention that my own regiment, which had already received
orders to join General Rosecrans in Western Virginia, had the order
countermanded and, without arms, were hurried forward to the
mouth of the Tennessee river. Steamers great and small were put
into requisition, and by the 10th of March, a fleet of formidable
strength was ready to ascend the Tennessee. About this time arose
a dilemma. General Grant, as alleged, on account of some dissatisfaction with the Donelson affair, was ordered to remain at Fort
Henry and to turn the command over to General Charles F. Smith,
an officer of the regular army, with few equals in or out of the
service. It was this officer to whom all agree in giving the honor
of saving the day at Donelson. The expedition steamed up the
Tennessee and reached the point known as Pittsburg Landing, two
hundred and twenty miles from Paducah, our (Sherman's) division
going into camp at Shiloh Church on the 18th and 19th of March.
Savannah, ten miles below, was selected as the headquarters of the
commanding general. The division of General Lew Wallace was
landed at Crump's, four miles above Savannah, and the other five
divisions of McClernand, Smith, Hurlbut, Sherman, and Prentiss,
disembarked at Pittsburg Landing, which consisted of a warehouse,

grocery, and one dwelling. It was a point whence roads led to Corinth, Purdy, and the settlements adjacent. It appeared to have been regarded as of some importance, in a military view, by the Confederates, for after the fall of Donelson they erected a battery on the high bluff overlooking the landing, and General Cheatham occupied Shiloh as a military camp.

The country is undulating table-land, the bluffs rising to the height of one hundred and fifty feet above the alluvial. Three principal streams and numerous tributaries cut the ground occupied by the army, while many deep ravines intersect, rendering it the worst possible battle-ground. The principal streams are Lick creek, which empties into the Tennessee above the landing; Owl creek, which rises near the source of Lick creek, flows southeast, encircling the battle-field, and falls into Snake creek, which empties into the Tennessee below the landing, or about three miles below Lick creek. The country at the period referred to was a primeval forest, except where occasional settlers had opened out into small farms. The Army of the Tennessee lay within the area indicated, extending three and a half miles from the river and nearly the same distance north and south. Much discussion has arisen as to whom belongs the credit of the great central movement, of which the Tennessee expedition was the initiation and Sherman's march the culmination; and in connection with this no little crimination and recrimination has been indulged by particular officers as to the military judgment displayed in landing the Army of the Tennessee on the *west* side of that river. The disposition of the army, neglect of proper fortifications and general want of precautionary measures, have been subjects of free discussion and condemnation. Whether just or not, can hereafter, perhaps, be better determined. General Sherman says the camp was chosen by General Smith, and by his orders he (Sherman and Hurlbut) took position. He further says: "I mention for future history that our right flank was well guarded by Owl and Snake creeks, our left by Lick creek, leaving us simply to guard our front. No stronger position was ever held by any army."—(*Record of court-martial, Memphis, Tennessee, August*, 1862.)

When the writer reached Shiloh (April 2d) he found the impression general that a great battle was imminent. Experienced officers believed that Beauregard and Johnston would strike Grant or the Army of the Tennessee before Buell could unite the Army of the Ohio. We found the army at Shiloh listless of danger, and in the worst possible condition of defense. The divisions were scattered over an extended space, with great intervals, and at one point a most dangerous gap. Not the semblance of a fortification could be seen. The entire front was in the most exposed condition. One or two sections of batteries at remote points, no scouts, no cavalry pickets, a very light infantry picket within one mile of camp, were all that stood between us and the dark forest then filling with the very flower of the Southern army. To my inexperienced judgment, all this appeared very strange, and I communicated these views to our brigade commander, who expressed himself in the same spirit, but remarked that he was powerless. One day's work in felling trees would have placed the camp in a tolerable state of defense. The men were actually sick from inaction and over-eating. A few hours' active exercise with the axe and shovel would have benefited their health, and might have saved their camp from destruction, with thousands of valuable lives. This would have produced a much better *morale* effect than the neglect which had been urged as the reason why the camp was not protected! It was surprising to see how speedily the same men cut down trees and erected works of defense on the approach to Corinth. A little of the vigilance then used would have saved life, property and reputation at Shiloh. That a grave military error was committed in disposing the army and neglecting the proper defenses at Shiloh, there can be no question. If General Smith erred in selecting the ground or disposing the troops, who was responsible when that officer lay prostrate on his death-bed?

General Halleck had, in general orders, directed the camp to be fortified, and supposed this had been done, for, in his first dispatch from St. Louis, announcing the battle, he says: "The enemy attacked our *works* at Pittsburg, Tennessee, yesterday, and were repulsed with heavy loss." We do not appear, however, as the censor, simply the historian, whose province, although not always pleasant, should be guided by the line of duty, truth, and justice. It shall be our endeavor to avoid partisan issues and confine this statement to plain, historical facts. Thursday, the 3d, being quite unwell, remained in my tent. On Friday, made and received few visits, and in afternoon witnessed the first "speck of war." A small detachment of the Fifth Ohio Cavalry, with a portion of the Seventieth Ohio Infantry, made a short reconnoissance and fell in with the advance of the Confederate army. We lost a few men; killed and captured half a dozen of the enemy. Of the wounded was an intelligent non-commissioned officer, who died during the night. This officer communicated information that the entire Confederate army had advanced from Corinth, and were to attack us on the following (Saturday) morning. This information, of such vital importance to our army, was disregarded, and we slumbered on the very verge of a volcano. "It was expected," says General Beauregard, "we should be able to reach the enemy's lines in time to attack them *early on the fifth instant*. In consequence, however, of the bad condition of the roads from late heavy rains, the army did not reach the immediate vicinity of the enemy until late on Saturday afternoon. It was then decided the attack should be made on the next morning at the earliest hour practicable." On Saturday morning an order was issued by General Sherman to cut a road from Owl creek, in front of the church, to an old cotton-field, three-fourths of a mile east of our camp. The creek was securely bridged, and the road cut of sufficient width to admit the passage of our army on its anticipated march to Corinth! About two o'clock P. M., Colonel Jesse Hildebrand, commanding Third Brigade, Sherman's Division, to which my regiment was attached, invited me to accompany Colonel Buckland, commanding Fourth Brigade, same division, Colonel Cockerel, Seventieth Ohio Volunteers, and one or two other officers, on a short reconnoissance. We had not advanced half a mile from camp when we were met by squads of the fatigue party sent out to cut the road, with the startling intelligence that the rebel cavalry were in considerable force in the wood immediately across the old cotton-field. Our pickets extended to the line of the field. We rode to a position commanding the wood referred to, and with a glass saw the enemy in considerable force. We afterward learned they were Forrest's cavalry, and their commander, riding a white horse, was plainly visible.

It was manifest their object was not to attack, but watch our movements, and prevent the advance of the reconnoitering parties. The officers (Hildebrand and Buckland) remained some time, then returned to camp to report the situation to General Sherman, and get their respective commands in readiness, as both anticipated an attack. Remaining under orders to watch the movements of the enemy, the afternoon wore away. Before leaving it was deemed expedient to strengthen the picket line with three additional companies, charging them not to advance, not to bring on an engagement, but watch closely all movements of the enemy during the night, and report promptly the approach of attack. That evening a free interchange of opinion took place at our tent, where General Sherman called while we were at tea. The full particulars, which have been hurriedly recited, were detailed. He was incredulous that an attack was meditated—believed they were only present to watch our movements; said news had been received that evening that Buell would join us in forty-eight hours, and then we would advance on Corinth.

General Sherman's positive manner of uttering his opinions had the effect to quiet the apprehensions of some of the officers present, but others were not satisfied. The principal officers of the Third and Fourth Brigades, and Fifth Ohio Cavalry, commanded by a son-in-law of the late President Harrison, were convinced that attack was at hand. Letters written that night by officers could be produced to show the feeling pervading the camp of the Seventy-seventh Ohio. Thus stood matters on that eventful Saturday night. Colonel Hildebrand and myself occupied the same tent; it stood adjacent the primitive little church which was destined to fill so important a page in our country's annals. Colonel Hildebrand, not feeling well, retired early, but I remained up late writing letters, and preparing for the morrow. The men were ordered to stack arms in front of their tents, prepared to advance or repel attack, and that if firing were heard during the night to remain quiet—await the long-roll or bugle-call. Every soldier in the regiment felt that a battle was imminent; in an hour the whole camp was asleep. How unconscious of danger lay the army of the Union that night! Outside of the immediate brigades named, few dreamed of danger; but their visions were of home and the loved ones who looked so fondly for their return; but, alas! how hopeless to thousands, who, that night, slept their last sleep on earth.

On our front—in the depth of the dark forest—how different the scene! At midnight, stepping from my tent, beneath the shadow of that quiet church, I listened for a premonition of the coming storm. But all was still save the measured tread of the sentinel, and the gentle whispers of the genial night breeze. No sound came from the distant wood; no camp-fires shed their lurid light against the walls of living green; no drum-beats or bugle-blasts were heard, for quietness reigned by imperious command throughout the rebel camps. Those who slept dreamed of booty and glory, for Beauregard had assured them that they should sleep in the enemy's camp to-morrow night, eat well-baked bread and meat, and drink real coffee. It is also alleged, of the same commander, that he declared he would water his horse on Sunday evening in the Tennessee, or another place where water is supposed not to be very abundant. He did not redeem either of the latter promises, but he did the first. Long before early dawn on that calm, Sabbath morn, the rebel army had breakfasted, and stripped for the bloody work before them. Their blankets, knapsacks, etc., were laid aside, their only incumbrance being their arms, haversacks, and canteens. The latter, it has been asserted, were filled with "powder and whisky," which, of course, is a popular delusion. Certain it is, however, they fought with the desperation of men inflamed with something more stirring than Yankee hatred and Southern patriotism. By three o'clock they were on the move. At daybreak General A. Sidney Johnston said to General Beauregard: "Can it be possible they are not aware of our presence?" "It can scarcely be possible," replied the latter; "they must be laying some plan to entrap us." General Johnston commanded, with Beauregard second in command. With us the latter was regarded as chief commander, as it was his army that lay at Corinth, and he it was whom we supposed we would have to fight.

General Johnston, after evacuating Nashville, moved his army with all possible dispatch to Corinth, declaring, as a recent biographer of this great military genius asserts, with almost the spirit of prophesy, that the decisive battle in the Southwest would be fought in the neighborhood of Shiloh church. This, the biographer asserts, was not sheer guessing, but the result of clear and close calculation. [General Hurlbut recently informed me that it has only been a few months since he learned, from a son of General Johnston, the real plan of the battle of Shiloh, as arranged by his father.] The united armies of Johnston and Beauregard numbered about fifty thousand men, and constituted the fighting material of the Confederate army, commanded by the most experienced officers—Johnston, Beauregard, Bragg, Hardee, Polk, Cheatham, Breckenridge—and a long list of subordinate commanders, presenting an array of names that ought to infuse confidence in any army. With their united forces it was "determined," says General Beauregard in his report, "to assume the offensive, and strike a sudden blow at the enemy in position under General Grant, on the west bank of the Tennessee, at Pittsburg, and in the direction of Savannah, *before he was reinforced by the enemy under General Buell, then known to be advancing via Columbia.* By a rapid and vigorous attack on General Grant, it was expected he would be beaten back into his transports on the river or captured," etc. The disposition of the forces of General Grant, who, on account of the continued illness of General Smith, and an explanation with General Halleck, was ordered, March 14th, to assume command of the Army of the Tennessee, were as follows: General Sherman occupied the extreme front at Shiloh church; Generals Prentiss and Hurlbut lay on the left; Generals McClernand and W. H. L. Wallace on the right and rear. The form of the encampment was a semi-circle with its greater arc on the left. Two roads led from the landing to Corinth, distant twenty miles—one by the way of the church, and the other through General Prentiss' camp, intersecting the road from Hamburg, seven miles further up the river. These troops, particularly the advance division under Sherman, were mostly fresh from the recruiting camps, and wholly unpracticed, even in the simplest company maneuvres. Many of the regiments were not supplied with arms until their departure up the Tennessee. This was the case with my own regiment. With such disadvantages we went into the great battle of Sunday.

At gray dawn, on the morning of the 6th, Lieutenant Burriss, of Captain Sisson's company, Seventy-seventh Ohio Volunteers—a regiment recruited from the border counties of Western Virginia and Ohio—came to brigade headquarters and communicated the intelligence that the enemy were gathering in great force. He was sent back with orders to Captain Sisson to maintain the picket line, but if attacked to retire in order, holding the enemy in check. We heard dropping shots over the whole of our immediate front and tolerably brisk firing on the left, in the direction of General Prentiss. As Colonel Hildebrand was not well, he was advised to remain quiet, and I would report the facts to General Sherman, whose headquarters were about four hundred yards to our rear. In a few minutes Captain Sisson reached camp, confirming all his lieutenant had communicated, and adding that the enemy swarmed in the old cotton-field already referred to; that he had watched them from the moment he discerned a man, and felt confident they were gathering for an attack. They had already commenced firing on our pickets, and believed, from the rapid firing on Prentiss' line, that he had been attacked in force. Captain Sisson returned to his command, and the writer went at once to General Sherman's headquarters. He was met at his tent. The facts related were communicated, and for some minutes we listened to the firing. The General appeared to be in doubt as to attack, but ordered the brigade into readiness for action.

Returning to regimental headquarters, the men were found promptly responding to the long-roll and preparing for action. Partaking of a hasty breakfast, they fell into line. The morning was bright, warm, and genial. Although early spring in that luxuriant Southern clime, nature had robed herself in a rich mantle of green; the woods were vocal with feathered songsters, and the air redolent of perfume from bud and wild flower. The swamp lily, with its brilliant petals, contrasted beautifully with the deep green foliage and spotless blossom of the American *cornus*. The scene was altogether lovely, save where man, by his unlicensed passions, was spreading death and desolation. It was now about half-past six o'clock. The fire on our front grew hotter and nearer. The regiment was in line. Colonel Hildebrand was pressed to join in a cup of coffee, remarking that it would better fit him for duty, when, in the very act of taking the coffee, a shot from the enemy's gun, *unlimbered in the road we cut the day before*, in full view of our camp, told us, as it crashed through the trees over our tent, that the battle had opened! Colonel Hildebrand said: "Colonel, aid me with the brigade; send the major with the regiment; ride at once to the Fifty-third and form them into line." The Fifty-third Ohio was alluded to, which constituted part of our brigade. Their camp was across a ravine to the left of the Fifty-seventh Ohio, and some distance from brigade headquarters. It was here where General Sherman rode early in the opening of the battle and lost his orderly —shot by his side—in the ravine near the camp of the Fifty-third. It may be here stated that Shiloh church stood on the brow of a sloping hill, at the base flowing Owl creek. To the left of the chapel were the camps of the Seventy-seventh and Fifty-seventh Ohio. The brigade headquarters were immediately to the right of the church. The wood had been cut for camp use from a considerable portion of the hillside fronting the church. Down this hill front, in the direction of Owl creek, the Fifty-seventh and Seventy-seventh Ohio were thrown, and also a portion of the Fourth Brigade. Taylor's battery had a good position to the right of the church, and was ordered to unlimber for action. The Fifty-third formed in their own camp, which was an old peach orchard. They were supported by Waterhouse's battery.

The hour was now about seven o'clock, and the battle opened with great fury. The enemy advanced to the attack of our forces by three distinct lines of battle. The first, according to General Beauregard's report, "extended from Owl creek on the left to Lick creek on the right, a distance of about three miles, supported by the third and the reserve." The first line was commanded by General Hardee, supported by General Bragg; the second line by Generals Bragg and Polk, and the third by General Breckenridge. These lines were separated from five to eight hundred yards. General Beauregard was on the left, General Johnston on the right. Standing in front of Shiloh chapel, looking down into the dark wood from which issued the deep roar of heavy cannon and the sharp rattle of musketry, scarcely a man was visible; but as the unclouded sun fell on their burnished arms the whole scene became lighted up, presenting a panorama most effective, and one which can never be forgotten by those who witnessed it. The lines closed steadily on us, the enemy moving forward at all points. Squadrons of cavalry had been thrown out on both wings to drive in the Union pickets. Hardee had deployed his forces in lines of brigades, with their batteries in the rear. Against these well-disciplined troops did our raw regiments contend. Onward came the surging masses, backward fell our lines; then rallying would, by a terrific fire, check the shouting legions in gray! Checked again and again, they still pressed forward. The keen eye of Hardee soon detected the wide gap between Sherman and Prentiss. This gap—more than a mile in width—General Sherman says was left to be occupied by part of Buell's troops. It almost proved to be an open highway to the flanks and rear of the Union lines. General Hurlbut has recently informed the writer that he was opposed to flanking movements which might jeopard his own command. Into this gap he pushed several brigades commanded by Gibson, Anderson, Pond, and others, and attempted to sweep round on Sherman's left. The camp of the Fifty-third Ohio having been gained and three of Waterhouse's guns captured, the line near Sherman's headquarters was enfiladed and driven back in confusion. McClernand promptly supported Sherman, but seeing the flanking movement of Hardee, I was ordered to hurry up reinforcements. Meeting an advancing column, I found on inquiry it was General Smith's Division, commanded by General W. H. L. Wallace, of Illinois. He was advised of the attempted flank movement, and requested to change his line of march in the direction indicated. That gallant officer adopted the suggestion, and ordered a brisk movement in the direction indicated. He soon fell mortally wounded.

Half an hour after we separated he engaged the enemy, and the most terrific firing heard during the day came from that quarter. The force encountered was Ruggles' Division of Bragg's Corps. He requested that a battery should be sent to him. Captain J. W. Powell, with great promptness, took position, and remained in command of his battery until his right arm was shot off. This gallant officer is the distinguished Major Powell, in charge of the geographical and geological survey of the Rocky mountain region. As a scientist he is doing good service, as he did as a soldier in the wilderness of Tennessee. He was a meritorious officer, and his success in the field of science has been great. It is hoped that Congress will give him ample means to carry out his enlarged views in the department to which he has been assigned. General Grant, it may be stated in explanation, his headquarters being at Savannah, did not reach the battle-ground before ten o'clock. He doubted for a time that it was an attack, but the continuous and heavy firing convinced him otherwise, and steam was ordered on his flag-vessel, the Tigress. Up to the hour named we were without a general commander. The fighting was irregular and miscellaneous. Each division commander had quite as much as he could do to attend to his own defenses or aid those in advance. The subordinate commanders felt that much depended on themselves, and the men realized the vital importance of doing their whole duty. As a distinguished clergyman said in his sermon on the Sabbath following the battle, the "fighting was done by *march*, not *brain!*" The army really did not know when it was whipped. A prominent Confederate officer afterward said: "You were thoroughly beaten on Sunday, but did not know it." This was literally true.

The battle went on hour by hour. The Union army was steadily beaten back at all points. The great leader of the Confederates had fallen, for Albert Sidney Johnston was as great a military genius as the country has produced. His death was caused by a Minnie ball severing the femoral artery at about half-past two o'clock. This was a most critical point. Breckenridge's reserves had been ordered up. Johnston said: "I will lead these Kentuckians and Tennesseeans into the fight," and, waving his sword, pressed forward to take a certain position, which they did gain—but their brave leader was gone! The death of Johnston caused a brief pause. Thirty minutes were probably consumed in Beauregard taking command, and these were precious moments for the Union army. It enabled our shattered ranks to close up and prepare for the next assault. It came. Beauregard, concentrating all his energies in the moment, exclaimed, as the brigades filed by him: "Forward, boys, and drive them into the Tennessee!" His purpose was to gain the river, capture our transports, and destroy our army. One or more deep ravines, with marshy approaches, intervened. These must be crossed. In the meantime some heavy siege guns, which lay on the hill at the landing, had been wheeled into position; a battery of Parrotts had also been prepared for action. A few trees were felled, some bales of hay and a few barrels filled with earth, afforded slight protection to the gunners. But there was a determined feeling in the army *not to be driven into the river*. An officer, now no more, who did valiant service on that bloody field, well expressed this feeling. When asked what he intended doing if pressed to the water, replied: "Give them these twelve shots and take the consequences." In addition to the siege guns and Parrotts, the two wooden gunboats, "Tyler" and

"Lexington," lay, one at the mouth of the principal ravine and the other a short distance below.

The Union army had been pressed back within half a mile of the Tennessee. A desperate and final struggle was now to be made. About four o'clock, after half an hour's comparative quiet, the deep-mouthed guns again opened; the roll of musketry was heard in continuous volleys, the wild tumult, the wierd shriek, the crashing timber, all bespoke the terrible conflict. The battle-ground has become fearfully contracted; the enemy's shell fall into the river and explode amid the transports! Another advance is ordered. The shattered brigades of Beauregard enter the ravine and close up on the contracted lines, protected by the siege guns. "Three different times," reports one of the commanders, "did we go into that 'valley of death,' and as often were we forced back." Another reports: "A murderous fire was poured into us from masked batteries of grape and canister and also from rifle-pits." General Bragg ordered General Chalmers to drive us into the river at all hazards. In vain did this brave Carolinian, who sacrificed his own life and a large portion of his command, attempt to do so. The concentrated fire of the Union army, aided by the formidable natural barriers, prevented the execution of Beauregard and Bragg's *humane* orders! Gradually the firing ceased. The Sabbath closed upon a scene which had no parallel on the Western Continent. The sun went down in a red halo, as if the very heavens blushed and prepared to weep at the enormity of man's violence. Night fell upon and spread its funereal pall over a field of blood where death held unrestrained carnival! Soon after dark the rain descended in torrents, and all through the dreary hours of that dismal night it rained unceasingly. The groans of the dying, and the solemn thunder of the gunboats came swelling at intervals high above the peltings of the pitiless storm.

General Beauregard redeemed his promise, and slept in the camp of the Union army that night. That officer, we have reason to believe, occupied our tent that Sabbath night. He says: "I established my headquarters at the church at Shiloh, *in the enemy's encampment*," etc. His dispatches were written on a *desk* in one of the Union tents. Our tent was the only one thus provided. These facts are mentioned as not of much historical importance, but simply as incidents of the day. It was known through all of Sunday that General Buell was hurrying on with all possible dispatch. That officer, with two of his corps commanders, Nelson and Crittenden, had reached General Grant's headquarters on the hill at the river by half-past four o'clock.   An hour after, portions of their commands had crossed, and were climbing the steep river banks to take part in the last desperate struggle of Sunday.   The appearance of Buell's advance, in the dark hours of that terrible Sabbath afternoon, was a spectacle the most inspiriting that despairing men ever looked upon.   As they filed across the broad bottoms of the Tennessee, with colors flying, and filling the vale with their shouts of encouragement, the most despairing felt that the day was not entirely lost. Language is inadequate to express the sublime emotions which spring from the presence of a succoring army.   What the "eagles of Dessaix were to Consular France, the banners of Buell were to the arms of the Union," as his gallant army surged onward to the red field of Shiloh!   General Sherman, at a recent interview, informed me that when Buell inquired the force and condition of the Army of Tennessee, and was answered—showing fifteen thousand men, with the division of Lew Wallace, not engaged on Sunday—and Buell assured him that the Army of the Ohio would be ready to co-operate in an offensive movement on Monday, it was then and there determined to make a determined advance early on the morrow.

Monday morning, at six o'clock, the combined forces of Grant and Buell moved against the enemy.   General Buell's fresh troops, with the division of Lew Wallace, not engaged on Sunday (*why*, may, perhaps, never be known), pressed the enemy at all points. Steadily the army of the Union regained our camps, and by noon a signal victory had been achieved.   Beauregard withdrew his forces in good order, and pursuit was not continued beyond Shiloh church. Tuesday, the 8th, General Sherman determined to pursue.   With two brigades from his own division, two from Buell's army (Generals Garfield and Wood), and two regiments of cavalry, he proceeded from Shiloh in the direction of Corinth.   At the distance of a little over a mile, we came upon the advance camp of the enemy, on Saturday night.   Everywhere along our line of march remains of the retreating army were noticed.   Fresh graves were all around; the dead, dying, and wounded lay in tents, old houses, and upon the ground.   We were marched to a point about four and a half miles from the church, when our videttes informed us the rebel cavalry were directly ahead, concealed in ravines, and behind a long row of tents.   General Sherman ordered skirmishers thrown out, deploying companies A and B of my own regiment, when orders were given to the Seventy-seventh to support skirmishers.   The regiment was led within fifty yards of the line of tents.   The ground was an old cotton-field, partly covered by fallen trees; hence the name of the engagement, "Fallen Tim-

44

ber." The field was skirted by heavy wood. Almost immediately
the enemy's skirmishers opened fire, and the writer realized that he
was an object of particular mark. A fierce yell filled the air, and
the rebel cavalry came up from ravine and behind tents as thick as
they could ride. I ordered the men to up and fire, which order had
scarcely been executed when the entire line was ridden down, the
men sabred and shot by a force ten times superior to our own. The
dash was one of the boldest of the war, and the loss sustained over
one-third of my command. The promptness of Colonel Hildebrand,
in ordering up the other regiments of his brigade, I think saved the
day, and the commanding general and staff from capture. An officer
of his staff (McCoy) was ridden down, and, as General Sherman
assured me, he narrowly escaped. I regard this statement due the
memory of a brave and meritorious officer.

The dead were buried on the spot; the wounded removed to
camp; the rebel camp destroyed, with a large amount of property,
and this was the last of the fighting at Shiloh. The losses sustained
by both armies exceeded the frightful number of twenty-five thousand men. Four years after the battle, a writer, visiting Shiloh and
Corinth, gave a hideous picture of the condition of things. He
stated that twelve thousand Confederate soldiers lay unburied on
the two fields! After the battle of Shiloh, General Grant ordered
the dead of both armies to be buried. The inhumation, however,
consisted of little more than a thin covering of earth, which the
heavy rains have long since washed off, and the remains of brave
men, who periled all for their country's sake, lie exposed to the
elements. This fact is disgraceful to the government and the
people, and should be remedied with the least possible delay.
Instead of squandering means over idle parades, it should be our
duty and pleasure to give the bleaching bones of our gallant dead
the rites of decent burial. Regarding this as fitting opportunity, it
is respectfully and earnestly suggested that Congress adopt some
measure for the preservation of the remains at Shiloh—that a
cemetery be established, and graves properly marked; also, that the
church at Shiloh be rebuilt as a national memorial!

As the church that *was at Shiloh* has passed into history, a brief
description may not be uninteresting. It was a small, unpretending
edifice, of hewn logs, and occupied the brow of a hill, with a commanding prospect. It was built in 1849–50 by Rev. Jacob J. Wolff,
a local minister of the Methodist Church. It was not a costly edifice;
no massive architrave was there; no stained windows or carved
lintels; but these were not essential to the simple-minded people

who worshiped in it, and who worshiped before they had a church in the grand old woods, which we know " were God's first temples." The church at Shiloh had two doors and one window, which was without glass. Of pulpit and seats none were visible, as the Confederate General Cheatham had removed them for camp use previous to our occupancy. Before the battle the flooring boards were being rapidly converted into coffins for Union soldiers. After the battle it was used as a hospital up to the time the army advanced on Corinth. A guard was placed over it so long as any portion of our camp was maintained; but no sooner had the guard been removed than the vandalism of curiosity-hunters utterly demolished the structure, and carried off the last remnant of a log.

Before closing I may be expected to answer one question: *Was the army at Shiloh surprised?* It has already been shown what was the condition of things on the 5th, and surely no one will say that the Third Brigade of Sherman's Division *was surprised.* The same may be said of the Fourth Brigade, and the principal officers of the Fifth Ohio Cavalry; but here exceptions cease. The whole of that army, with individual exceptions, in addition to those named, were surprised. There was a general feeling that an attack was imminent, but that it would come on Sunday morning, April 6th, few believed. As to where the responsibility and censure belong, is one of those open questions which may be difficult to settle. General Grant's biographer, Professor Coppe, discussing this point, says: "At the outset our troops were shamefully surprised." For want of these precautions (proper fortifications, etc.), continues the same biographer, " we were surprised, driven back from every point in three great movements of the enemy," etc. This is saying too much, and cannot be justified. Another point demands brief remark. How much had Buell to do with saving the honor of the nation at Shiloh? Certain facetious writers have asserted that "Providence, the gunboats, and Buell saved the day." In reply, we have to say that the first of these had much to do with the national honor, the second very little, and the third very considerable. But whether the day would have been lost without his timely co-operation; whether the Army of the Tennessee would have been able, as asserted by Sherman, to take the offensive on the morrow; whether the presence of Buell's fresh troops inspirited the shattered brigades of Grant, and dispirited those of Beauregard, are points to be well considered.

It is certainly in bad taste to charge the first day's operations at Shiloh a "Second Bull Run disaster," and that the commanding officers ought to have been "shot;" and it is alike to be condemned to deny credit to Buell's army for the gallant and timely aid afforded on Monday. Let justice be rendered where it belongs. Impartial history will accord to both armies their full credit. In my dispassionate judgment, no men could have done better than Grant's army did on Sunday. Veterans could not have withstood the solid lines and unbroken fire which girdled them throughout that long and terrible day. It is true there was disorder, and many brigades on the front, after hours of incessant fighting, did give way; but the men were not whipped—only disheartened. Some obloquy has been thrown on certain Ohio troops. This was both unjust and cruel. No men could have stood better against a wall of fire than those Western troops, fresh from the plough and the shop. The Confederate dead who lay over that field on Sunday night told how severe had been the fire, and dreadful the carnage, inflicted by the sturdy men of the West.

The charge that the officers were derelict is also unjust. That grave military errors were committed in the disposition of the camp, and the exercise of proper precaution, has been shown; but that they were remiss on the field is not true. General Grant, after reaching the field, was active, and his presence gave confidence. The division commanders were untiring in their efforts; General Sherman particularly distinguished himself, and by his presence and bravery greatly inspirited the men. McClernand, Hurlbut, and others did effective service. General Prentiss, who was captured with part of his division, contended bravely with an overpowering force before he succumbed. The brigade commanders displayed great courage, coolness and skill. The same may be said of regimental commanders, and down to the lowest non-commissioned officers.

If the army had not behaved well, where would it have been when darkness closed the scene? It has been assumed by those inimical to officers engaged at Shiloh, that the army was utterly demoralized and routed from any definite line. This is untenable. Sherman's line of battle was never wholly destroyed. Sixteen years have elapsed since that day of carnage and disaster. Quietness reigns over the field then crimson by the best blood of the nation, and peace has been proclaimed throughout the land. Shiloh rests in its primitive solitude. May its maimed and riven forests never more be stirred by the breath of war, nor its peaceful sleepers be disturbed by the tread of contending hosts. The great battleground of the war, let it be erected into a holy, hallowed cemetery, where the heart of the nation can offer homage to the memory of her brave sons who gave up their lives that the nation might survive.

THE CAREER OF GENERAL A. P. HILL.

BY HON. WILLIAM E. CAMERON.

THE numerous biographers of Lee and Jackson are, perhaps, responsible for the remarkable fact that no history of A. P. Hill has yet been given to the public. Any adequate life of the Confederate commander, or of his foremost lieutenant, so necessarily involves constant presentation of the deeds wrought by one no less lofty in character, steadfast in purpose, and terrible in battle than either, that we may not be surprised if the general public has thus far been satisfied with the frequent recurrence of his name and deeds in the pages of Dabney, Cooke, McCabe, Randolph, and others. But it is not just to one who, in any other association, would have been *facile princeps;* of whom it may truthfully be said that he was a determining factor in every important battle of the campaigns in the East, that his achievements should serve the one purpose of magnifying others, or that he should be seen only in the reflected light of stars of larger magnitude.

Measured by the standards which men apply to the claimants of mastership in war, Hill was not a great commander. Such have not come in troops, nor in triplets, upon any age or stage of the world; and the late American conflict, while prolific of good soldiers, and developing among a people inured to peace a wonderful aptitude for fighting, formed in this respect no exception to the experience of centuries. If that stern clash of antagonistic prejudices and contending interests produced, on either side, a genius family comparable to that of Frederick or of Marlborough, there was but one—and he fell before either friend, or foe, or fate, had found the limit of his

(693)

power. What he did will survive as rivaling the best exploits of the most renowned in arms, and Jackson stands among captains as Shelley among poets—enlarged by death into the perfection of promise. But he stands alone, so far as this country is concerned.

Nor would any judicious admirer of General Hill (and this paper is written from a standpoint of affectionate appreciation) institute any comparison between his qualities of leadership and those of General Lee. Their respective positions well suited and well describes their distinctive capacities. The one possessed all the characteristics of great military talent, and fell, by temperament alone, just short of genius; the other had some of those characteristics, pluck, endurance, executive ability, and magnetism in perfection; but some, as readiness of intuition and resource, were his in less degree; and some, as broadness of strategic vision, he lacked. But his tasks were no mere mechanic registrations of the will of another; nor was that sphere, in which he was great, contracted; nor was his success on many hazardous fields attained otherwise than by a longer exercise of that individual discretion without which no man can maneuvre men. If he had no part in ordering the movements of armies, he was laden always with a large share of the responsibility of making those movements successful; and if it was not his to create the plans of battle, it was often his, after those plans had been disarranged by adverse circumstances, or thwarted by the short-comings of others, so to wield the forces at his disposal as to turn the doubtful scale of battle. It was asked of Napoleon, at St. Helena, during a discussion of the merits of his marshals, whether Ney would have been equal to the command of an independent army. "I do not know," was the reply; "he could never be spared to make the experiment."

Ambrose Powell Hill was born in Culpepper county, Virginia, in the year 1825. The "American Encyclopedia" curtly says, in continuance of the life then begun, that he graduated at West Point in the class of 1847; served in Mexico; resigned in March, 1861, a commission as lieutenant in the United States Topographical Engineers; entered soon after the Confederate service. At the battle of Manassas he was colonel of the Thirteenth Virginia Infantry; was subsequently promoted to be a brigade, division, and corps commander, and was killed in front of Petersburg, on April 2d, 1865. And this is correct so far as it goes—there is no better way of not knowing a man than to gaze upon his bare skeleton.

When Hill reported to Richmond, in the spring of 1861, the authorities were in the full tide of experiment, both as to men and affairs. It is no wonder that there, as in Washington, the posts of honor and responsibility should, at first (with few exceptions), have fallen into the hands of a set of superannuated worthies, or that the early employment of those who were thereafter to be the leaders of their respective sides should seem ludicrously small, in the light of subsequent events. Jackson was given, in the outset, the humble position of major of engineers; Mahone was ordered to take charge of the quartermasters' supplies in Virginia. Hill was first created a lieutenant colonel, but, shortly afterward, was assigned, with full grade, to the Thirteenth Infantry, and was ordered to the Upper Potomac, where, under General Joseph E. Johnston, was forming the army that afterward turned the scale at Manassas. The campaign of that column was one of bloodless maneuvres, though Colonel Hill received honorable mention for the conduct of a small, but successful, expedition against the Federal advance at Romney. Nor in the engagement at Manassas, which shortly ensued, was anything developed but the gallantry of the troops, and of their commanders. It was only when the Southern army was confronted with McClellan's host on the Peninsula that opportunities for distinction were fairly offered to the capable and brave. Hill's bearing at the battle of Williamsburg, and the collisions that precluded settlement in the lines around Richmond, marked him for early promotion. On the 26th of February, 1862, he was appointed brigadier general, and assigned the First, Seventh, Eleventh, and Seventeenth regiments of Virginia infantry; and on May 25th he was commissioned major general, and placed in command of the brigades of J. R. Anderson, Gregg, Pender, Branch, Field, and Archer. Soon was his fitness for this perilous distinction to be tested.

It will not comport with the limits of this sketch to attempt anything resembling a report of the various engagements from which General Hill drew steady acquisitions of fame as a brilliant chief of division. That will only be accurately done when the history of the Army of Northern Virginia shall come to be written. But a partial exception must be made in regard to the initial steps of his career, betokening, as they did, the fiery energy and unconquerable endurance that ever afterward distinguished his course upon the field of battle. He strode across the threshold of war as though upon familiar ground, and in all the perilous crises of after days, though experience added to the thoroughness of his dispositions, and the celerity of his attack, his qualities of vigor and boldness, of cool determination, and unflinching obstinacy, never shone brighter than in the Seven Days' Fight around Richmond.

General Lee had just succeeded Johnston in command of the Confederate army; McClellan was gathering his strength for the long-promised spring upon Richmond; Stuart had swooped, with his bold troopers, from the Chickahominy to the James; Jackson was sweeping down from the Valley to add Blucher's vim to Wellington's attack upon the young Napoleon! It was the eve of the mighty conflict which for seven days surged and thundered around the Southern capital; and to the grand game, in which life, and death, and national existence were to be the stakes, there came, on either side, troops whose mettle was yet to be thoroughly tested, and officers to whom, with few exceptions, belonged, as yet, only the name of generals. In the fearful ordeal how many passed scathless through the storm of shot and shell, and yet went down, no more to rise? Reading over, now, the roster of both armies, one wonders what became of men who brought to those scenes such magnificent reputations, and who left them never more to protrude their over-estimated heads above the surface of events. Here was the first great winnowing field, and the guns were great threshing-machines, before which the chaff and the wheat were separated as though by magic. But from the pounding process came also forth the fair, round grain, that was henceforth to be the sustenance and reliance of Union and Confederacy.

Lee's plan of attack contemplated the turning of McClellan's right flank by Jackson's movement through Hanover. A. P. Hill was stationed on the left of the Confederate lines, fronting the Federal intrenchments at Mechanicsville, and was expected to await the uncovering of his front by Jackson and D. H. Hill, and then to cross the Chickahominy and sweep to the right, down that wing of McClellan's army which rested on the north side of the river. The morning of the 26th of June was fixed as the time when the flanking column should arrive upon the field, but General Jackson was delayed by ignorance of the country and the inefficiency of his guides, and only came in sight of the enemy's position at a late hour in the afternoon. Then he found the bridge across Tattopottamoy creek destroyed, and was forced, while repairing it, to content himself with an artillery fire upon the Federal camps. But at the sound of this cannonading Hill sent his front brigades into action, captured with a dash the works in front of Mechanicsville, swept over and down the river, carrying all before him until the fortifications on Beaver Dam creek barred further progress and night fell upon his impatient energy. At early dawn a new assault was made and sustained with great gallantry but unsupported for two hours, at the end of which,

General Jackson having crossed above, a general charge dislodged the enemy and completed the success which Hill had so brilliantly inaugurated. The bridges of Beaver Dam having been restored, Jackson, reinforced by the division of D. H. Hill, took a large swing to the left to turn the next stronghold of the enemy between Gaines' mill and new Cold Harbor, while A. P. Hill, supported by Longstreet, moved by the north bank of the Chickahominy to take that position in front.

This direct march brought the Confederates about noon on the 27th within sight of the now desperate foe. A range of hills behind Ponhite creek, and covering New Bridge, which was the remaining communication between McClellan's divided forces, had been fortified in the most elaborate manner. Three lines of infantry in rifle-pits occupied the rising slope, and the ridge was crowned with field-pieces so posted as to sweep every approach. The assault must be made through an opening four hundred yards in width, and the natural difficulties were increased by abattis along the whole extent of the line, while the advancing columns were exposed to a sweeping fire from the heavy batteries on the south side of the Chickahominy. Desperate seemed the attempt, but Hill formed his columns and prepared again to bear the brunt of battle. At two o'clock Jackson, who should before now have appeared in rear and flank of Cold Harbor, was still missing. Again such trivial cause as the bad hearing of a courier had destroyed the success of a grand combination and given the enemy time and notice. Every moment seemed an hour while standing on the brink of that desperate venture and listening in vain for the guns that should tell of Jackson's arrival. At last General Lee decides that time is even more important than co-operation, and Hill's brave division is again launched forth alone to contend with half of McClellan's army. Sent in with admirable vigor, the troops pass the abattis, leap the ravine, rush over the intermediate lines upon the slope, and scramble breathless into the very mouths of the guns that crown the ridge.

For two mortal hours of agony this fearful work continues. Again and again these superb troops clamber up and dash themselves against the sides of this artificial Gibraltar, and each time they recoil with shattered ranks from the determined fire of the enemy. "Hill's single division fought," says General Lee, "with the impetuous courage for which that officer and his troops are distinguished." Still the incessant shower of missiles from the forts on the eminence, still the crash and bustle of the enfilading batteries across the stream. The slaughter has been terrific; some of Hill's brigades were broken; and at four o'clock, though Longstreet had thrown his fine division in upon the right, and Hood's Texans and Law's Mississippians were surpassing heroism in their magnificent disregard of death, the fortune of the day remained with McClellan. But Hill re-formed his shattered lines and still fought on close under the frowning brow of the hostile intrenchments. And now, through the swampy woodland to the left rings a cheer and the rattle of musketry. It passes like wine through the veins of the men of whom one bloody morning has made veterans. Jackson, with defiant energy, had rectified the blunders of his guides, and is on the field. Now the obstinate foe is beset on every side. But even yet victory wavers in the balance. The Federals make stout resistance even to the impetuous legions, fresh and used to triumph, of Jackson and the elder Hill. It is almost dusk, and yet the tenacity of the assailed is more than equal to the desperate courage of their assailants. At last comes the supreme moment. Jackson sweeps, in one of his resistless moods, upon the rear; Hill puts forth one last imperious effort for the centre, and on the right Wood and Law make up their minds to win. They all succeed. The Federals pour madly back across the river. Now, if a Jackson, or Hill, or Longstreet were on the thither flank, McClellan would be in deadly toils! But on the Confederate right sloth, if not timidity, prevailed. McClellan, floundering through the White Oak swamp, on the one road which offered him passage to the James, was not intercepted. Again Hill and Longstreet come upon his rear and lock with him in deadly combat at Frazier's farm; but the clutch that should be upon his throat is wanting. At Malvern hill he is forced to time and do battle again; but the grand scheme of envelopment has failed.

Hill's was now a household name throughout the South, and the army christened his command "The Light Division," and lavished upon it unselfish praise. But no time was given to the younger commander nor his men to rest upon these laurels. Already, while McClellan was gathering up the bruised fragments of his grand army at Berkeley, the Federal Government, not dismayed by disaster, was organizing a new movement upon Richmond. From the Army of the Mississippi, where he had won, in easy circumstances, some incipient reputation, General John Pope was called to measure swords with Lee. The remains of the armies sent into the Valley originally under Fremont, Banks, Shields, and McDowell, were moved forward upon Culpepper Court-House with the design of seizing upon Gordonsville. This force of sixty thousand men, preceded by the boastful declarations of their leader, advanced without interruption until a point eight miles south of Culpepper was reached. There it encountered General Jackson, who had been dispatched with Ewell's and Hill's divisions, and his own under Ganeral Taliaferro, to resist this new combination; and on the 9th of August the battle of Cedar run was fought, resulting in a decisive repulse to the Federal van-guard of twenty-eight thousand men under General Banks. About the same time General Lee detected the transfer of McClellan's forces from the Lower James to the Potomac, and at once set the remainder of his army in motion for the Rappahannock—hoping to overwhelm Pope while the bulk of his reinforcements were yet *en route*. Leaving McLaws, D. H. Hill, and Walker in front of Richmond, General Lee joined Jackson with the divisions of Longstreet, Jones, Hood, and R. H. Anderson on the 19th of August, and on the same day Pope, in the meantime strengthened by Reno's corps, of Burnside's army, commenced a full retreat for the north branch of the Rappahannock. Jackson, Hill, and Ewell were at once started in eager pursuit, striking for the upper fords of the Rappahannock, in order to pass upon the flank of the enemy, and having for an objective point Manassas Junction. Longstreet, in the meantime, occupied Pope's attention at the fords along the river, delaying him with threatening demonstrations to gain time for Jackson's establishment well in his rear. The march of the latter, for the first four days, was a continual skirmish. At Warrenton Springs, the enemy were found in force, and it was found necessary to amuse him there while a still larger detour to the left should be made. On the 25th, Longstreet occupied the ford at that point, and Jackson, now free from embarrassment, moved swiftly northward, crossed the Bull Run mountains at Thoroughfare gap, and, on the night of the 26th, effected the capture of Manassas Junction, with Trimble's Brigade of Stuart's cavalry. He was now, with three divisions, directly across the path of Pope to Washington, and was destined through the two following days to sustain, unaided, the onsets of a vast army. First, on the 27th, the attack fell upon Ewell, who had been left at Bristow Station. Finding from the constant pouring in of fresh troops that the whole Federal army was upon him, that officer skilfully withdrew to Manassas. That night Jackson formed his little army across Pope's line of advance, his left on Bull run, his right resting on Thoroughfare gap, through which Longstreet's march was anxiously expected. This position was full of peril, and the masses of the enemy were now hastening up to increase its imminence. McClellan's corps were now arriving upon the ground, and unless Longstreet should soon appear, the game would grow desperate. But nobly did Hill, Ewell, and Talia-ferro respond to the demands of their chief. First on one and then the other the unequal battle fell. Taliaferro and Ewell were wounded while gallantly encouraging their jaded troops to fresh efforts. Hill attacked with great spirit the head of the enemy's column, which was seeking to interpose between the Confederates and Alexandria.

The night of the 28th found both armies resolute in their posi-tions. The next morning Pope was ready to overwhelm Jackson. At ten o'clock his batteries opened on the right and the final strug-gle seemed to be at hand. But now Longstreet's columns, urged on by tales of Jackson's need, begin to file through Thoroughfare gap, and soon the Confederate right was strengthened with these brigades. And now once more Hill and his light division were to fill the place of glory. At two o'clock the enemy moved in masses upon the railroad embankments forming Jackson's left, and here Hill waged, against overwhelming odds, the fiercest contest of that fierce cam-paign. The Federals fought with persistent gallantry. Six times they pushed with superhuman courage up to the very face of the fire. Once they broke over a cut in the railway, found a gap in the line and fought, hand-to-hand, with their opponents. It was a battle of giants. For seven hours the combat lasted, and not until every round of ammunition had been exhausted, and night was gathering about the scene of slaughter, did Hill yield his position to the troops of Ewell—sent to relieve his exhausted brigades. In the final engagement of the 30th of August, again the heat and burden of the day fell upon the Confederate left, and though on one occasion, late in the day, the reserves of the army (Anderson's Division) were ordered up to reinforce that portion of the line, ere they came into action, the obstinate valor of Hill, Early, and Trimble had repulsed the enemy, and Anderson was sent to the right to take front in Longstreet's attack. That night Pope hurried—dismayed and un-done—into the fortifications on the Potomac. A new chapter in the war was about to be written in letters of blood.

The Sharpsburg campaign was now opened by the advance of Jackson into Maryland. Later, when that officer recrossed into Virginia, to effect the capture of Martinsburg and Harper's Ferry, A. P. Hill was still in the front of the advance. In the attack on the latter place his division made the assault, and were the first to enter the town. After the surrender Hill was left to dispose of the prisoners and captured stores, while Jackson hastened back to Sharps-burg, where Lee, with Longstreet and D. H. Hill, was beset by

McClellan's entire army. He arrived, not a moment too soon, to find his chief in perilous straits. It was the morning of the 16th of September. General Lee had drawn up Longstreet's and D. H. Hill's Divisions, both much reduced by the recent desperate contests at South mountain, on a range of eminences overhanging Antietam creek. In his front six full corps of Federal troops. Jackson, with seven thousand men, formed the left of Hill, and Walker—coming down from Harper's Ferry—prolonged the right of Longstreet. During this evening the Federals crossed the Antietam creek, and made a heavy onslaught upon the Confederate left centre, under General Hood, but were repulsed. The real work was not to be until the morrow. At dawn, on the 27th, McClellan opened his batteries upon the Confederate left, and, just at sunrise, poured Hooker's, Mansfield's, and Sumner's Corps upon Jackson's thin line. For several hours Jackson sustained this attack, but at length his men were pressed back, and Early and Hood were left alone to maintain that flank of the army. At this critical juncture General McLaws came on the field, and, aided by General Walker, who had been hurriedly withdrawn from the right, succeeded in re-establishing affairs, and pushing the enemy back to his original position. In the meantime, the centre was also heavily pressed, and D. H. Hill was fully employed in guarding his front from a series of impetuous and well-sustained assaults. At four o'clock in the afternoon McClellan, releasing his efforts on the left and centre, moved in large force against the right of Longstreet's position, where a bridge over the Antietam was defended by two small regiments under General Toombs. For a time, so stoutly fought the Confederates, the issue of this movement seemed doubtful, but after repulsing several sharp attacks Toombs' line was forced back, and the Federals swarmed across the creek, threatening to accomplish a complete victory. The enemy, turning to the right, had broken through Jones' Division, captured a battery, and were sweeping on with wild enthusiasm.

But at the moment of crisis brought also the means of meeting it. Opportunely, as if summoned by the lamp of Aladdin, now came in full swing across the fields Hill and his "light division." Called from Harper's Ferry to save the day, eighteen miles the gallant fellows had marched under the burning sun since morning, and now they marched as though fresh from bivouac. Throwing his batteries to the front, and opening a rapid fire upon the deploying masses of the enemy, Hill grasped the situation at a glance, and made, without halting, his dispositions. The Federal column, sweeping obliquely upon Jones' right, had exposed its own flank; Toombs, who had rallied his regiments, was ordered to fall upon it, while

Hill hurled Archer's fine brigade full in the face of the advancing foe; Gregg's and Branch's Brigades were thrown in with a like swift fierceness; and before these combined onsets the Federals first wavered, and then gave way. And Hill swept on, triumphant from the first, regaining the lost batteries, regaining the lost ground, never halting until the enemy were forced back across the Antietam, the bridge re-occupied, and the day saved; for with this charge of Hill and his two thousand, as terrible as any ever delivered by the Old Guard, with Ney for a leader, and under the eye of Napoleon, ended McClellan's efforts to break Lee's lines at Sharpsburg. On the retreat from Maryland, Hill brought up the rear, and at Shepherds-town inflicted upon the enemy, in repulse of a night attack made upon Pendleton's artillery, such fearful loss as effectually put an end to pursuit. In the battle of Fredericksburg, Hill held the right of the Confederate position, and was hotly engaged; and at Chancel-lorsville, where he was wounded, about the same time that Jackson fell, his record as a major general closes.

In May, 1863, General Lee formed three *corps d'armee*, from the troops then composing the army of Northern Virginia, assigning to the command of each a lieutenant general. Under Longstreet was the First Corps, composed of the divisions of McLaws, Pickett, and Hood; the Second, under Ewell, comprised the divisions of Early, Rodes, and Johnson; while to Hill was given the Third, with R. H. Anderson, Heth, and Pender as major generals. The commands of the last two were formed from Hill's own light division, with the addition to Pender of Pettigrew's Brigade, and to Heth of the Mississippi regiments, newly brigaded, under Joseph R. Davis. To this larger field Hill brought, unimpaired, the qualities which had distinguished him as a division commander; his promotion came at the suggestion of Lee, who had long since taken his measure, and ascertained his worth; and the troops had learned to repose absolute confidence in his leadership. Henceforth his place was to be at the right hand of the great commander, now bereft of the aid of Jackson. In the dark days that followed, casualty and the necessities of war called Longstreet and Ewell away from Lee, but Hill was ever at his side. Nor was the constancy of this trusted lieutenant ever shaken, or his high courage ever broken. Fate and death overtook this gallant soul at last; but fear or doubt never.

At Gettysburg, with Heth and Pender, he opened the engagement, winning a decided victory over the corps of Reynolds and Howard, and capturing the town. In the retreat, his columns again were in the rear. At the Wilderness, with Heth and Wilcox, he kept back for hours the combined forces of Getty, Birney, Mott,

Gibbon, and Barlow, inflicting upon them terrible loss, and maintaining his position against repeated assaults in front and flank until night put an end to the deadly contest, and until time had been gained for the march of Longstreet and Anderson to the rescue. Throughout the ceaseless warfare that attended the shifting of Grant's army to the banks of the James, Hill was always to the fore, and always gave a good account of himself and his men. At Petersburg, throughout the so-called siege, he held the right, or marching, flank of the army, and was constantly engaged. It was his strong hand that sent the Federal columns so often staggering back from their movements against Lee's communications. It was Hill's Corps that rolled Warren's line up like a scroll on the Weldon Railroad. It was Hill, with Heth and Wilcox, who overcame that bold Captain Hancock at Reams' Station. It was Hill who, with Mahone's Division, sent Hancock and Warren reeling for support from Hatcher's run. Everywhere and always, Hill was in the post of danger and won glory. Steadfast, alert, valiant, he never put his harness off, and always wore it well.

Through that last winter Hill's face and form became familiar sights to the troops. He was constantly on the lines, riding with firm, graceful seat, looking every inch a soldier. Like General Lee, he was rarely much attended. One staff officer and a single courier formed his usual escort, and often he made the rounds alone. Of ordinary height, his figure was slight but athletic, his carriage erect, and his dress plainly neat. His expression was grave but gentle, his manner so courteous as almost to lack decision, but was contradicted by a rigidity about the mouth and chin, and bright, flashing eyes that even in repose told another tale. In moments of excitement he never lost self-control nor composure of demeanor, but his glance was as sharp as an eagle's, and his voice could take a metallic ring. Of all the Confederate leaders, he was the most genial and lovable in disposition. In all his career he never advanced a claim, or maintained a rivalry. The soul of honor and of generosity, he was ever engaged in representing the merits of others; if he ever displayed a symptom of insubordination, it was when the government failed or delayed to recognize the services of some soldier to whom he thought promotion due. When news came of his death, there was not a man in the corps who did not feel that he had lost a friend.

On the 2d of April, 1865, Grant made an advance upon the right-centre of the lines in front of Petersburg; and, breaking through in heavy force, thr w back upon the right the larger portion of the two divisions of Hill's Corps, then occupying the trenches. General Hill, whose headquarters were in the suburbs of the city, was thus cut off from his command. Mounting rapidly, he set out, accompanied by a single courier, to break through the pickets of the enemy, and rejoin his scattered troops. Dissuasion was attempted, but he repelled it, and dashed off at full speed. General Ord, in the meanwhile, had thrown forces in the direction of the river, and Hill, spinning across the path of these, came suddenly upon a group of sharpshooters. Their summons to surrender was met by a charge toward them; the next moment the fatal shot was fired, and dead on the outposts fell A. P. Hill.

No history of him has yet been written; no stone marks his resting-place in Hollywood Cemetery. If the memories of war are to be perpetuated, not forgotten should he be—that Virginia soldier who never lost a post that duty gave him to defend, and who never failed to crown an attack—if not with success—with the blood-red crown of terrible endeavor. In what has been here written there is but the faintest outline of his brilliant campaigns. From Richmond to Chancellorsville, Hill's "Light Division" was either in the van as charging column, or came later into action as the well-chosen forlorn hope. At Sharpsburg, in the gathering dusk of a doubtful field— when the left wing was barely standing, the centre hardly resistant, the right already overwhelmed—with his worn and his numerically weak, but invincible column, Hill struck the exultant enemy, swept the debatable ground, gave courage to a despirited army by his ever advancing musketry, and saved, what bid fair to be, a day of decisive defeat. Follow him to the Potomac, thence to Rappahannock, to the Wilderness, throughout the wasting and wonderful struggle from the Mattaponi to Petersburg—the record of battles won, of positions saved, of guns and prisoners captured, gives Hill an emphatic claim to a soldier's fame. His death illustrates the character of his soldiership. Not as some of his equals in rank did his fidelity fall under the certainty of disaster; but manfully and well, in the very hour of defeat, he gave himself a sacrifice to one of the few remaining chances of saving the army.

The dead leaders, upon whom the world has lavished honors, leaned upon Hill as strong men upon a staff, and were not disappointed. And it is memorable and remarkable that Lee and Jackson—the magnet and meteor of the Confederacy—should, in their dying moments, have given their last earthly thoughts, their last coherent utterances, to this brave soldier and steadfast patriot. In the paroxysm of death, General Lee called on Hill "to move forward;" and, when Jackson was crossing the river to seek the shade of the trees, his last words were: "Tell A. P. Hill to prepare for action."

THE WAR'S CARNIVAL OF FRAUD.

BY COLONEL HENRY S. OLCOTT.

MINE is the most repulsive task that any one of the writers of this series of Annals will have assigned to him. All the others have their stories to tell of the clang of arms, the marshaling of armies, the thrilling episodes of personal danger and suffering, the political vicissitudes of the mighty struggle. To me comes the duty of showing the corruption that festered beneath the surface. The eye kindles, the pulse leaps, the imagination fires with their narratives of martial deeds; but what I shall say will make writer and reader alike deplore the baseness of human nature, which most displays itself in times of national calamity. Gladly would I leave my tale untold, and suffer the official record of my experience to lie in the archives of the government undisturbed, like a loathsome corpse in a dishonored grave. But a history of the Rebellion which should not embrace this chapter would be no history worthy of the name; and so, as no one can serve as my substitute, I comply with the editor's request.

I passed at the front the first year of the war, joining the Burnside expedition at Annapolis, participating at the capture of Roanoke Island, the battle of Newbern, the siege and capture of Fort Macon, the battles on the Rappahannock during Pope's retreat, and other military operations. Exposure to malaria finally disabled me with fever, and I was obliged to return home from Washington, where my horse stood ready saddled for a start the next morning with General Burnside to join Hooker with our Ninth Corps. I recovered after two months, and, while convalescent, was first

45   (705)

intrusted with the responsible duties which occupied my whole attention subsequently until the close of the war, and for some nine months longer.

By this time, November, 1862, the government had expended many millions of dollars, and the little army of twenty thousand men that we had when Sumter was fired upon had been increased to hundreds of thousands. The initial Confederate act of war not only forced upon us the gigantic work of transforming an industrial people into soldiers, but of arming and equipping them as well. This was the harder task of the two. Men there were by the hundred thousand, ready to take the field; but, to uniform them, cloth had to be woven, leather tanned, shoes, clothing, and caps manufactured. The canvas to shelter them had to be converted from the growing crop into fabrics. To arm them the warehouses and armories of Europe, as well as of this country, had to be ransacked. All considerations of business caution had to be subordinated to the imperious necessity for haste. If it was the golden hour of patriotism, so was it equally that of greed, and, as money was poured by the million, by the frugal, into the lap of the government, so was there a yellow Pactolus diverted by myriad streamlets into the pockets of scoundrels and robbers—official and otherwise. The public necessity was their opportunity, and they made use of it.

The rush of men to the front left the War Office no time to be nice over details; so that, as the volume of administrative business overflowed the bureau machinery for its supervision, things were, in a measure, suffered to take their course. An unhealthy tone pervaded everything; speculation was the rule—conservatism the exception. We floated, on a sea of paper, into a fool's paradise. Contractors, bloated with the profits on shoddy, rode in emblazoned carriages, which, a little while before, they would have been glad to drive as hirelings; and vulgar faces and grimy fingers were made more vulgar and coarse with the glare of great diamonds. Intrigue held the key to the kitchen-stairs of the White House, shaped legislation, sat cheek by jowl with Congressmen, and seduced commissioned officers from the strict path of duty. Our sailors were sent to sea in ships built of green timber, which were fitted with engines good only for the junkshop, and greased with "sperm" oil derived from mossbunkers and the fat of dead horses. For one pound of necessary metals, one yard of fabric, one gallon of liquid, the price of two was paid. Our soldiers were given guns that would not shoot, powder that would only half explode, shoes of which the soles were filled with shavings, hats that dissolved often in a month's showers, and clothing made of old cloth, ground up and fabricated over again.

In the navy yards there was a system of corrupt bargains between the public servants and contractors, under which goods of inferior quality and short of quantity were accepted as of the lawful standard and count; public property was purloined and carried off in open daylight; scores of superfluous men were quartered on the pay rolls by politicians; navy agents colluded with ring contractors to buy of them all supplies at highest market rates on an agreement for a fifteen per cent. commission, and clerks in the yards, for a consideration, would slip the pay requisitions of these ring thieves from the bottom to the top of the pile that awaited the official certificate of approval, so that they might draw their money at once, to the prejudice of honest dealers. There was no such thing as the taking of a general account of stock—not even a keeping of the accounts by double entry. The old regular officers in charge of bureaus, high toned and unsuspicious, were flattered into a fatal sense of security by subordinates bound body and soul to thieves.

In the military arsenals, the same rottenness prevailed. Here and there were to be found public servants without a moral ulcer within their breasts. But such were annoyed and hampered in the execution of duty, overridden, too, often by positive orders from superiors to receive supplies not up to army standard, and, when too obstinate, were removed to posts less desirable. The army standards were themselves debased under the plea of an exigency. In the lettings of contracts, a fair competition was frustrated by the transparent conspiracy of bidders, who would put in absurdly low proposals under fictitious names, and then bid themselves at the highest price that, from surreptitious information received, they knew would throw out honest competitors and secure them the contract. Their profits were calculated to come out of the delivery of inferior articles of skimped measure to government inspectors, with whom they had an understanding. Presents of horses, carriages, jewelry, wines, cigars, and friendly help toward promotion, though passing under a politer name than bribery, effected the same results as though they had not. Every artifice that rascally ingenuity could devise, and clever men and women carry out, was resorted to to procure the brigadier's stars or the colonel's eagles for ambitious incompetents. The sacredest secrets of our government were sold to the enemy; loud-mouthed hypocrites trafficked across the lines; the very medicines for the sick were adulterated, and dishonest gains were made

ANNALS OF THE WAR.

out of the transportation of the wounded. Nay, so vile was the
scramble for money, so debasing its influence, that our dead heroes
were followed into the very grave by the plundering contractor, who
cheated in the coffin that was to hold the sacred dust, and amassed
fortunes by supplying rotten head-stones in defiance of accepted
stipulations. What shall we call this wretched episode of national
history but a Carnival of Fraud? This was the Augean stable to
cleanse which the broom of authority was placed in my hands.

Of all this I knew nothing in November, 1862, when Secretary
Stanton first applied, through the United States Marshal at New
York, for my services. There had been much talk and a good many
wholesome truths told by the Democratic papers, but my experience
had been in the field, and, besides, it was not the likely thing for
Democratic papers to be seen about the camps in North Carolina.
Of one or two specific cases of fraud, the members of the Burnside expedition had been forced to have a very accurate knowledge. We lay in Hatteras Inlet a whole month, waiting upon
McClellan's movements in Virginia, so as to co-operate with him.
Of water we had a sufficient supply, but the contractor had put it
in cheap barrels, that had contained kerosene oil, and our stomachs
turned against it. When the order came to move upon Roanoke
Island, we attempted to cross the "swash," the great shoal that lies
between the ocean beach and Albemarle Sound, but scarcely a vessel
could be dragged through the channel, even by two powerful tugs,
until it had been emptied of everything portable; the agents, instructed to hire vessels of a certain draught only, had accepted others
that drew two or three feet more of water at exorbitant rates—some,
if I remember aright, at one thousand dollars per day! Conversing
with Burnside as the vessel we were on stuck fast half way over the
swash, I offered to send an account of this infamy to the Northern
press and denounce the responsible parties by name. But he protested, saying that as he would reap the credit of success, so he ought
to take the blame of failure. It was his fault and none other that
such vessels had been taken, and as commander of the expedition it
was *his* business to have seen that the agents did *their* duty. The
man's character, at least as I have always known it, is expressed in
that sentiment.

The occasion of my employment was the giving of a Delmonico
dinner by a German Israelite to a distinguished company of guests.
The host was one Solomon Kohnstamm, who had accumulated a
fortune of over a quarter of a million in the importing business at
New York, and enjoyed the reputation of a giver of good dinners

THE WAR'S CARNIVAL OF FRAUD.

and a jolly sort of fellow in general. In an evil hour he took to discounting the vouchers of recruiting officers, cheated, was suspected, in danger of arrest, and as a grand *coup* of diplomacy had spread the feast in question and bidden to it every civil and military official in the New York district who, under any contingency, might have a hand in arresting or prosecuting him criminally. I will spare the blushes of men now, as then prominently before the public eye, by not mentioning the names of Kohnstamm's guests. His frauds had come under the surveillance of the United States Marshal, and the circumstances of the dinner alarmed the authorities, who saw through the trick and feared the ends of justice might be defeated. I was, as I have said, convalescent at this time, and getting ready to return to the front at a very early date, when I received a notification that my services to examine the papers in this case of Kohnstamm were required. The Marshal told me that I would be free to leave for the army within a fortnight at farthest, and that the amount of fraud was supposed to be within twenty-five thousand dollars; in place of which my service was continued more than three years. The frauds of Kohnstamm turned out to be some three hundred thousand dollars, and the little local examination of a single case grew into a general inspection of arsenals and navy yards as connected with the equipment and clothing of the land and naval forces.

The vouchers discounted by Kohnstamm were the bills of landlords for the lodging and board of recruits for volunteer regiments prior to their muster into the United States service. They were certified by the ranking officer of the regiment and by the company officer engaged in the recruiting. After muster the men were duly taken on the regimental rolls, and the quartermaster was then legally empowered to issue to them tents, rations, and clothing. These necessary costs of organization were at first defrayed either out of the Union Defense Committee's fund or advanced by the officers of regiments and their friends out of their private means.

Kohnstamm's crime consisted in his procuring from landlords—generally German saloon-keepers—their signatures to blank vouchers, which he would have filled up by his clerks for, say, one or two thousand dollars each, and then either get unprincipled commissioned officers to append their certificates for an agreed price, or, cheaper still, forge them. By this device he drew over three hundred thousand dollars from the "Mustering and Disbursing Office" in New York, of which sum the greater proportion was in due time ascertained by me to be fraud. The examination of all these accounts was a work of time and laborious and patient research, as may be imagined. It was also necessary to proceed with the greatest prudence, for only a few days after my taking the papers in hand Secretary Stanton, acting, as soon became evident, upon erroneous reports, caused the offender to be arrested and lodged in Fort Lafayette. Kohnstamm was a Democrat, except, of course, in business matters, and a rich importer of thirty years' standing; had plenty of money, spent it liberally, and had but just given his grand dinner at Delmonico's. No wonder, then, that his arrest should have excited a bitter feeling against the War Department in the minds of people who knew nothing whatever of his offenses. There was a Democratic Governor at Albany, a Democratic Mayor at New York, a Democratic District Attorney, and Democrats on the grand jury. It came to my ears that the Secretary of War, the United States Marshal, and myself, were to be indicted for resisting the writ of *habeas corpus* under the alleged unconstitutional act of Congress suspending the same. It was an emergency demanding a bold course; so with the consent of the department, I went myself before the grand jury with my papers, and offered to answer any questions that might be asked of me. The result was a vote of commendation for what had been done, and all danger of indictment was removed. I pursued the same course with Governor Seymour and the District Attorney with equally satisfactory results, and then the trump card was played of giving the facts to the press, which was only too willing to publish them, and never subsequently, to my recollection, interfered with my official labors.

This adroit and epicurean criminal employed the best counsel at our bar, and enjoyed all the immunity from annoyance, after his release from Fort Lafayette, that one so circumstanced could expect. But that there were thorns in his bed of roses is beyond a doubt. In due time, he was held in one hundred and fifty thousand dollars bail in a civil suit, and, after a three weeks' session with me, the grand jury, under the lead of the late James W. Beekman, brought in forty-eight bills of indictment against him. Failing to get the required security, he lay two months in the House of Detention, after which his bail was reduced, and he was liberated from confinement. I found so many obstacles to getting him to trial that, finally, the Secretary caused a resolution of inquiry to be introduced in the Senate by Mr. Wilson, which settled the business. The case was peremptorily moved on, and that venerated jurist, Judge Samuel Nelson, turned a deaf ear to the excuses of counsel, and ordered the District Attorney to open for the prosecution. Out of the forty-eight indictments one had to be selected on the spur of the moment, and the court would only permit us to introduce testimony about seven others, to show the *scienter*, or guilty knowledge. Accordingly, eight cases of palpable forgery were designated, the trial proceeded (May 17th, 1864), and, on the 21st, the jury, after deliberating only twenty minutes, brought in a verdict of guilty. The court promptly sentenced him to ten years' imprisonment, at hard labor, at Sing Sing, and the rich Kohnstamm made his exit from the busy scene of his tradings and his triumphs.

So unexpected, but so welcome, was this result to the Scretary of War that, upon receiving the news, he telegraphed back a characteristic message, which, as I recall it, was as follows:

WAR DEPARTMENT, May 21st, 1864.

COLONEL H. S. OLCOTT, New York:

I heartily congratulate you upon the result of to-day's trial. It is as important to the government as the winning of a battle.

EDWIN M. STANTON,
Secretary of War.

Since I have anticipated events somewhat, to give a connected history of the Kohnstamm case, it may as well be said here that the civil suit was duly prosecuted to a successful issue, and a large sum of money paid over to the Treasury by the trustees of the felon's estate. As a farce after the tragedy, naturally followed his pardon by President Johnson, after two years' imprisonment, upon the petition of the usual string of wealthy and influential New Yorkers, who so often give their signatures to papers of this kind without proper consideration.

In December, 1862, being in Washington, the Assistant Secretary of War handed me, for examination, a claim for above three thousand dollars, which had been collected by one D'Utassy, colonel of the Garibaldi Guard, a New York volunteer regiment, upon his affidavit that it was correct. I found it to be a total fraud, the very signatures upon the sub-vouchers being forged. The delinquent was court-martialed, convicted, and sentenced to the penitentiary. The inquiry into this and the Kohnstamm cases developed such an astonishing condition of moral obliquity among contractors and regimental officers that the Secretary of War took prompt measures to bring the guilty to punishment. Several commissioned officers were dismissed the service, and a number, among them two officers of the regular army, were handed over to the civil authorities for prosecution. The Adjutant General also availed of my help, sending me claims filed for payment, that I might report my opinion of their validity; and various practical suggestions from me, for the reformation of abuses in local bureau management, were favorably received and acted upon. By the time that six months had elapsed, I had examined some two hundred witnesses, taken two thousand folios of testimony, and all idea of my being relieved from this unwelcome, though necessary, duty had been abandoned. The department threw upon me more and more responsibility, but, it must be confessed, accompanying it with a more than ample discretionary authority, thus affording me the highest proofs of the Secretary's satisfaction, and stimulating me to deserve its continuance. At the date of my second semi-annual report to the War Department, I had, in the preceding six months, made inspections in ten States; taken testimony in twenty-four cities and towns, beside camps and military posts; examined, with assistance, eight hundred and seventeen witnesses, written five hundred and fifty-three letters, and traveled over nineteen thousand miles.

With a department behind him whose chiefs approved his course, it was no very difficult affair for a non-partisan officer to effect reforms by the display of impartial severity. Old standards had been departed from; they had to be re-established. The old statutes of peace times were inadequate to meet new exigencies; new ones had to be enacted. Politicians had saddled their dishonest parasites upon the country; it was for us to convict these of their crimes, and warn their patrons to nominate no more such. And so it happened that, throughout the entire term of my Commissionership of the War Department, every reasonable suggestion that experience, in my particular department, warranted my making in the direction of reform, was unhesitatingly adopted by Mr. Stanton, and the successive Assistant Secretaries with whom I had the honor and pleasure to be brought into relation—Messrs. P. H. Watson, C. A. Dana, and Thomas T. Eckert. These suggestions covered the passage of laws by Congress, the reformation of standards for army-supply contracts, the suspension of contractors' vouchers and certificates, new regulations for the procurement of supplies, new methods of inspection, transportation, and chartering, the transfer and removal of influential officers, and other particulars which it is not necessary to specify.

At the East and North the army frauds were principally in manufactured articles; at the West and Southwest in animals, forage and transportation. I had comparatively little to do with the Ordnance Bureau, and will, therefore, leave the curious reader to glean from the papers of the day, and the records of Congress, a comprehensive idea of the swindling, greater or less, that the necessities of our government obliged it to submit to. But of the Quartermaster's Department I am as competent, perhaps, as any one else to speak. On the 5th of August, 1863, I received an order to inspect the Quartermaster and Commissary Departments of the Military Department of the Ohio, which included the States of Ohio, Indiana, and Kentucky. Major General Burnside was in command, with headquarters at Cincinnati. Upon reporting there my first care was to cause to be prepared by the chief quartermaster a complete list of all contracts awarded within a certain period, with the names of the bidders at each letting. With this as a guide it was a simple matter to learn what fraud had been practiced, for I had only to direct my orderlies to serve a summons upon each disappointed bidder to report at headquarters and testify, when the whole chicanery was invariably exposed. The regular dealers and responsible merchants were always to be found among this class, and, when satisfied the War Department was really in earnest, and would throw the market open to fair competition, they would tell the honest truth. Thus I discovered within forty-eight hours that by a corrupt conspiracy between a government purchasing agent, an inspector, a Cincinnati contractor, and an Indianapolis horse dealer, and Republican politician, the United States had been systematically robbed of one million dollars in the purchase of horses and mules, at the Cincinnati corral, during the preceding year. My duties were greatly lightened by the prompt and efficient co-operation of the Department Adjutant General, and Judge Advocate—Captain W. P. Anderson, and Major Henry L. Burnett.

At Louisville frauds alike shameful had been perpetrated in the purchase of animals, while one Black—a captain and assistant quartermaster, who boasted much of his influence with Secretary Stanton, and whom I especially gratified that official by bringing before a court-martial—had not only connived at the fraudulent adulteration of grain by his contractors, but absolutely stood by to see it done, and handled a shovel himself. This unconscionable rascal in uniform was convicted of the crime, and sentenced to "be dismissed the service of the United States, with loss of all pay and allowances due or to become due; to pay a fine of ten thousand dollars; and to be imprisoned at such place as the commanding general shall designate for the period of two years."

The delinquent horse, mule, hay, grain, and other contractors in the Department of the Ohio were thoroughly punished by fines and imprisonment, and thenceforward the government was enabled to obtain supplies at fair prices, and of good quality. This result, it should be noticed, was, in a peculiar degree, owing to the ability, zeal, and industry of Judge Advocate Burnett, whose services were appropriately recognized by the Secretary, by promoting him successively to colonel and brigadier general.

Many will recollect the great interest that was felt, in the year 1863, in the matter of the chartering of steam and other vessels at Fortress Monroe, in consequence of the discovery that a certain very influential Republican Senator of the United States had accepted a fee of three thousand dollars from the harbor master of that military post, while lying under charges in the Old Capitol Prison. There had been some very acrimonious passages between the Senator and Secretary Stanton, the former peremptorily demanding the prisoner's unconditional release (without mentioning the fact of the fee), the latter refusing. As a compromise it was finally agreed that I should be ordered to Fortress Monroe to prepare the case for speedy trial, and the necessary instructions were sent me from the department. I found plenty of fraud, but more to lay at the doors of others who had chartered vessels at the North, than at that of the prisoner. Enough, however, of probable cause was connected with him to induce his being tried before a military commission, over which Brigadier General Isaac I. Wister, of Philadelphia, presided, and his conviction followed.

In my "Third Semi-Annual Report to the War Department," in reporting this case, I used this language:

Evidence was elicited tending to show that the abuses of which the commission complained extend over the whole seaboard. The government has been in the habit of paying ruinous prices for the charter of vessels, some of which have been perfectly unseaworthy. The precious lives of officers and men, and public property to the value of millions of dollars, have been intrusted to rotten steamboat hulks, and greedy speculators and middlemen have been paid for their use prices of the most extortionate nature.

I have referred above to the loyal support constantly given me by Secretary Stanton. One instance will suffice by way of example. The Provost Marshal on Major General Schenck's staff, at Baltimore, had been guilty of scandalous conduct, which was at last brought to the Secretary's notice by a brigadier general of volunteers, who preferred formal charges. Through the Judge Advocate General I received the Secretary's order to investigate the charges and recommend what action should be taken. The result was the officer's arrest, confinement in the Old Capitol, his subsequent trial by court-martial, conviction of theft and perjury, and his sentence to the Albany Penitentiary, where he served out his term, if my memory is not at fault. The commanding influence of General Schenck in Congress, and the persistent interference of the Congressional delegation from the culprit's native State, gave Mr. Stanton much trouble. He was beset with petitions, remonstrances and personal appeals, but to no purpose. At last the Governor of the State came himself to Washington, and, in company with its Senators and Representatives, proceeded to the War Department and vainly coaxed the iron-willed chief to relent. "When you can show me that Colonel Olcott has furnished me with false testimony, or exceeded the limits of justice in his recommendations, then I will release your man and put mine in his place," was his reply. Thus baffled, one testy Congressman lost his temper and used a more peremptory tone, whereupon Mr. Stanton, rising and giving way to his wrath, threatened to put the member in the Old Capitol if he said another word, and the stormy interview was abruptly terminated. I have the story from the lips of the Assistant Secretary of War, who was present.

In the case of a contractor for transporting wounded soldiers through the city of New York, it was found that the government had been defrauded in both transportation and the cooked rations supplied, but on each of a pile of uncollected vouchers found in his desk when he was arrested by the general commanding, was the official certificate of the medical director that "this account is correct and just, and that the services were rendered by my order, and that they were necessary for the public service." Comparison of them with the medical director's own books showed at a glance the fraud. For instance, on May 30th, 1863, a charge was made by the contractor "for nursing and subsisting three hundred and fifty men from the steamer Cosmopolitan and delivering them at David's Island." But the hospital books in the office of the medical director, who certified to the correctness of the account, showed that on that day only ninety-seven men arrived at the island! The scamp was found guilty before a court-martial, after several hundred witnesses had been examined, and was sent to the penitentiary for a term of ten years. A radical reform in this branch of service was, of course, the most substantial fruit of the department's investigation.

The responsible officers of the War Department were all overworked. From the Secretary down there was no exception. Each crowded at least three years' proper work into one year, and some of us four or five. It was all I could do, though working night and day, Sundays and all, and with one, two, and at times three and four stenographers to help me, to keep ahead of my work. Again and again I urged the organization of a special bureau to have charge of the execution of the acts of Congress against fraud and malfeasance, and in a measure combine the duties and powers of the Judge Advocate and Inspector General. For this was what my own office had grown into, and there was more work than a dozen officers could thoroughly accomplish. "It is a curious anomaly," I said, in one of my reports to the department, "that a government disbursing one billion of dollars annually, has no organized system for the prevention and punishment of frauds, its effects in this direction having been entirely spasmodic and irregular. I am firmly convinced that a bill containing provisions calculated to remedy this evil would meet with the cordial support of the whole people, without regard to political party." What was true in 1864 is equally so in 1878, and to-day the creation of a respectable and responsible inspection bureau, clothed with large discretionary powers, would, in the hands of an honorable and courageous commissioned officer, do incalculable good.

While Philadelphia set a bright example of patriotic devotion during the war, and poured out her resources in unstinted measure for her country's salvation, yet it is true that vast frauds were perpetrated in that city. These extended to tents and other canvas goods, clothing, shoes, and stores of various kinds. In the two years preceding my inspection of the Schuylkill Arsenal the disbursements of the quartermaster had exceeded two hundred million dollars, and at that time were running on at the rate of from seventy million dollars to eighty million dollars annually. To inquire into so vast a business I was obliged to take it up by divisions; so, as nearly as practicable, I took testimony and inspected, *seriatim,* canvas goods (including tents, paulins, wagon-covers, knapsacks, and haversacks), leather and manufactures of leather, cloth, and clothing, and miscellaneous articles. The same old results ensued; inspectors, contractors, manufacturers, and middlemen, were arrested, commissioned officers displaced; trials were followed by convictions, fines, and assessed damages; new inspectors were appointed, new standards established, and abuses were reformed. The close of the war found me with this work only half completed, and so some great culprits, military and civilian, escaped the just punishment of their offenses, to figure as noisy politicians and be looked up to as successful men of affairs! The archives of the War Department have many an ugly secret smothered in its pigeon-holes, and, heaven knows! it will not be myself who will disturb them; there is stench enough in the air without this carrion.

I was unfortunate enough (or fortunate, as some might have it, though I did not see it in that light) to have so commended myself to the Secretary of the Navy by my work for the War Department that, February 6th, 1864, he applied to Secretary Stanton for my detail to him for temporary service. Receiving my orders, I reported to Mr. Welles a few days later; and, on the 16th, was officially commissioned as "Special Commissioner of the Navy Department." Mr. Welles had some suspicion that there were abuses in his navy yards needing correction, but no very definite information. A contractor, named Henry D. Stover, had been convicted by court-martial of an attempt to defraud the government in some trifling matter of sheet copper, and I was ordered to visit and confer with him in Fort Lafayette. I found him uncommunicative and evasive, and soon departed. Upon reflection, I concluded that the better course was to take the sworn testimony of our most responsible business men, who would assuredly lay bare existing abuses, if any existed. I first summoned Mr. William E. Dodge, Jr., and then, upon his recommendation, other dealers in metals. As Mr. Dodge's affidavit presents, in a condensed form, the facts about the system of navy contracts that flourished everywhere, it will be instructive to present extracts in this connection:

Our facilities, says he, for supplying metals to the government are almost unlimited. We have not, in one instance which I can now recall, furnished or sold anything to the Navy Department; but, according to the usages of the trade, have sold through brokers to a comparatively limited extent. We have not been able to transact business with the department without sacrificing self-respect! We have made several attempts to trade with the department in a fair, liberal spirit, without caring to realize any profit, except barely enough to cover expenses. We have never bid, except in reply to telegrams received from the Navy Department direct, and have been invariably underbid by parties without standing or respectability among merchants. In fact, so satisfied were we that our offers, however liberal they might be, would not result in business, that we finally were obliged to decline to enter the list against the set of disreputable characters, who seemed to have secured the favor of the department! It is a matter of personal knowledge with us that the leading houses of New York entertain the same views. It is also generally understood that some of our best houses, dealing in metals which have a fixed value like gold or silver, and which are liable to all the fluctuations incident to the times, have been obliged to wait three or four, five, or even six months for their money; while other houses, of no standing or reputation, have got their money for immense sales within two or three days!

With such a start, the sequel was not difficult to foresee. Before two days had passed the whole villainy was exposed. Within ten days General Dix, under orders of the Secretary of War, acting at the instance of Secretary Welles, had arrested every member of this infamous ring of contractors and middlemen, and turned over their books and papers to me for examination. I employed additional clerks, had ledgers, invoice, letter, requisition, check and deposit books analyzed, and one of the great sensations of the day was the reading to the United States Senate by Mr. Grimes, of Iowa, of a tabulated exhibit of Stover's profits on oil contracts during one year. Without having bought a gallon of "best winter strained sperm oil," such as his contracts called for (and despite his taking the same at one dollar per gallon, when the market price stood at two dollars), he had realized a profit of one hundred and seventeen thousand dollars on the year's transactions! What he had supplied to the Brooklyn yard was horse fat, menhaden, and other stinking fish oils, etc. The inspectors who passed it, and the engineers who used it, can best explain why it happened.

Regular dealers, as Mr. Dodge tells us, in oil, in sheet copper, in block and plate tin, spelter, timber, machinery, boiler felting, clothing, and every description of naval supplies, were crowded out of competition by these dishonest middlemen, and a general demoralization of public officials prevailed. My experience in the War Department made me wary about beginning a campaign against such a rich and formidable ring of contractors as I immediately discovered to exist, without full assurance of the support of the department. This came in the shape of the following letter:

NAVY DEPARTMENT,
WASHINGTON, February 18th, 1864.

Sir:—Your letter of the 17th instant is received. Unless otherwise directed, from information which you shall obtain, you can pursue the course deemed most advisable from your experience. The department has no political object in these inquiries. The Secretary has directed me to carry forward this matter in conjunction with yourself, and I have never been in political life. You may rest assured, and such information may be given to witnesses, that the guilty will be exposed and punished without regard to influence or position.

Very respectfully, your obedient servant,
[Signed]   G. V. FOX,
Assistant Secretary of the Navy.

To COLONEL H. S. OLCOTT, Special Commissioner, Navy Department.

No one could ask more. In fact, no subordinate ever had a more honorable, untiring, prompt or patriotic superior than I found, for the next year and a half, in Assistant Secretary Fox. An attempt was made at one time to make political capital out of an alleged expression of his in a letter to me, that a certain naval court-martial "was organized to convict." The only thing Mr. Fox ever said (in response to my particular request that the court to try these New

York cases should be composed of none but high-toned and fearless officers, without any political bias or aspiration) was, that I need not fear but that the guilty would be convicted, and punished if proven guilty. His official letter of February 18th, now first published, shows the whole attitude of the Navy Department toward this question of abuses and toward myself.

Senator Hale, of New Hampshire, from his place in the Senate openly charged Mr. Fox with having instructed me to inquire into his business relations, and of having made use of the expression above referred to; but in a document communicated to the Senate by Secretary Welles, in compliance with a resolution, Mr. Fox thus emphatically put his foot upon the falsehood. Addressing the Secretary of the Navy, he says:

> In obedience to your orders to cause to be investigated the alleged fraudulent transactions of all persons amenable to this department, the services of Colonel H. S. Olcott were temporarily obtained. This officer is attached to the War Department, is familiar with such investigations, and enjoys in an eminent degree the confidence of that department. * * * The allegation that I had said to him that the Navy Department had organized courts to convict, is not true. I said something like that of the recent law, passed by Congress, requiring contractors to be tried by court-martial.

I will not burden with details the present historical retrospect. Suffice it to say that the same gang of scamps supplied the Washington, Philadelphia, and New York Navy Yards. Their programme was simple, but effectual. Under the regulations, a contractor who had faithfully complied with the terms of a contract, was entitled to the first consideration of the navy agent (the purchaser of supplies in the open market at each naval station, the paying officer through whom all money passed to contractors) when extra supplies had to be obtained in open market. The ring thief had only to collude, in each transaction, with three men to have everything as he could desire: 1. The master-workman, upon whose recommendation the Navy Department's annual estimates of the supplies that would be needed in that shop are based. 2. The inspector, who must pass upon the goods delivered, and was officially supposed to reject such articles as were scant in measure or weight, or inferior in quality. 3. The navy agent, dispenser of patronage, golden fountain of riches. Other minor potential obstructionists had, of course, to be disposed of; but a little money, a good deal of soft talk, unlimited liquor, and, occasionally, some pressure from superiors, went a long way. Thus, practically, the master-workman would estimate for not above ten per cent. of the supplies he was morally certain would be required in his shop; the inspectors would see sperm oil in horse fat, two whole boxes of tin plates in the two halves of one box that had been sawed in two and fitted with an extra side each, pure "Banca" or "Lamb and Flag" tin in ingots of an equal mixture of tin and lead; and the benevolent navy agent, on a "divy" of fifteen per cent., would order of his pal the other ninety per cent. at open market prices, and throw in all additional orders that fortune might put it in his way to give out! And this was what I found in New York. The contractors were all convicted; arrests and removals were plentiful in the Brooklyn yard; Navy Agent Henderson was, December, 1864, indicted eight times by the grand jury, gave bail in thirty-two thousand dollars, was tried *and escaped because the government could not prove whether it was H. D. Stover or his book-keeper who had paid him (Henderson) the fifteen per cent. commission in the transaction, which was the subject of the indictment we had elected to try.* We proved the general agreement, the payments in gross of fifteen per cent. on all Stovers' open purchase orders, the deposit of the money in Henderson's bank, and its deduction each time from Stover's. But the Secretary had confidingly accepted Stover as State's witness, and was cheated when the pinch came! The other seven indictments were not tried. One experiment with such witnesses was enough.

Things were bad enough at New York, but, if anything, worse at Philadelphia. Discovery was brought about by an honest dealer, named Barstow, sending to the Navy Department, for examination, four cases of thirty-two ounce sheathing copper, that he had bought, in good faith, of a responsible firm, but which was of the kind rolled at the Washington Navy Yard. The copper was easily traced back to one Harris, keeper of a sailors' boarding-house, and a man of bad repute at the time. He was arrested by General Cadwallader, for account of the Secretary of the Navy, and lodged in Fort Mifflin. A political striker named Anthony Hale—"Tony" Hale—employed as a boss carter in the yard, was next arrested, and then one thing brought on another until, before I was through, thirty-one prisoners were in military custody. The arrests were effected by Mr. Benjamin Franklin, chief of detective police, whose services the Mayor placed at my disposal. A more untiring and faithful officer I never encountered than Mr. Franklin. Besides the man Harris, the prisoners were the Naval Constructor, first assistant engineer, timber inspector, master plumber, caulker, joiner, blacksmith, laborer and painter, the clerk of the yard, his chief clerk and check clerk, three clerks of the storekeeper, the master caulker's clerk, a quarterman laborer, a quarterman joiner, two quartermen plumbers, four receivers of stolen property, six contractors, and one purser's steward. A pretty lot of patriots and Republicans, indeed!

A few days of confinement in military prison brought on a contagion of repentance, confession and supplication. My time was taken up in hearing revelations of their rascalities from the cowardly culprits, whose friends, ignorant of what was going on, were besieging my offices with petitions for their release, and making my feelings cheerful with threats of personal violence conveyed by anonymous letters. The press overran with sensational articles, which I was too busy to read, and Congressmen became interested to a degree in the affairs of my commission. But it is only fair to say that not one newspaper thundered against the "arbitrary arrests" of the government; all united in expressing the hope that offenders might be brought to punishment. Nor did the Congressmen intercede or throw any impediments in my way.

Large recoveries of stolen copper, pitch, rosin, and other public property were made. Some fifteen hundred barrels of naval stores had been carted out of the yard by Hale in broad daylight, and, to say nothing of copper bath-tubs, brass filings, and other smaller things, the thieves had removed a steam engine bodily, and sold it to a junk dealer. Some sixty thousand and odd dollars in money and property were placed in my hands as restitutions, and by me turned over to the commandant of the yard. As usual, there were trials, convictions, and pardons, and the several cases presented features of comedy, tragedy, or farce, as it happened. There lies before me now, in a file of old documents, the certified memorandum of property given up by a poor young clerk who had been ruined by the richest of the New York gang of contractors—one Charles W. Scofield. This young man had a wife lying dangerously ill; she needed delicacies which his poverty denied her, when the contractor came, as the victim said to me, "like an angel out of heaven," and presented him with fifty dollars as an act of "pure friendship." No favors were asked at the time except that he would look after the contractor's goods, and see that they were duly inspected. But soon afterward something was asked—that short deliveries of goods might not be noticed, nor too close an inspection of them made. · In return for which service (which he was assured was rendered at every other yard) the clerk should receive half the contractor's profits on the overcharges. The sick wife's needs settled the matter, and the clerk turned up at last in prison. His contrition being sincere, the Secretary permitted him to make restitution, and be released from confine-

46

ment. He gave into my keeping nearly four thousand dollars in United States bonds, and was released on his parole. I found employment for him, and, at last accounts, he was living an honest life. Scofield was tried by court-martial, convicted, and sentenced to be imprisoned and pay a fine of twenty thousand dollars.

There were abuses in the Kittery, Boston, and Portsmouth yards also; but I need not go into particulars, since it would but be to repeat the same disgusting tale of treason, perjury, conspiracy, theft, and greed. The Secretary, no less than Mr. Fox and myself, was weary of these arrests; and, after taking some months to turn it over in his mind, Mr. Welles at last approved a plan I presented him, at the instance of Mr. J. P. Veeder, my chief assistant in the naval investigations, for the thorough reorganization of the affairs of the navy yards. My argument was that a system of book-keeping that was adequate to the wants of a vast commercial business like that of the house of A. T. Stewart & Co., or H. B. Claflin & Co., was good enough for a navy yard, where each ship was a customer, each master workman the head clerk of a department, the paymasters cashiers, the Navy Department principal creditor, and the Secretary of the Treasury book-keeper-in-chief. I proposed that we should begin with the taking of an account of stock, create the new office of chief accountant, open invoice-books like those of merchants, and not only devise a self-maintaining system of checks of one bureau upon another, and both upon the navy agent, but have a page for each transaction, where its complete history, from beginning to end, should be seen at a glance. Such unheard-of innovations upon naval routine could not, of course, be lightly approved; but at last the order came, and I was given the Boston yard to try the experiment in. I hired a competent book-keeper, had a suitable set of books made under Mr. Veeder's directions, overrode all opposition of officers and clerks, and, at the expiration of the first quarter, handed the Secretary the first trustworthy balance-sheet of a navy yard that had ever been seen. The credit for it is all due to my assistants.

The result was so satisfactory that the department ordered the new system applied to all the yards on the Atlantic seaboard, which was done—Philadelphia following next after Boston, and then New York and the others. Thus the primary object of all our labors was, apparently, effected in the bringing about of a reformation, of which individual arrests were but painful incidents. I was more than glad when, the war having closed, my resignation of the special commissionership of the Navy Department was finally accepted, after a delay of some months in considering the question. I was permitted to suggest the new office of Inspector of the Navy Department, and Mr. Veeder was appointed to the berth. But that amiable and non-combative old gentleman was soon forced, by the powerful influences arrayed against him, to retire, and since that time, as I learn, the old routine has, in a large degree, been re-established. Contractors and employes whom I convicted have been restored to favor, and a series of scandals is now being investigated by the present Congress.

My temporary detail to the Navy Department had not at all relieved me of my War Department duties. Quite the contrary; it seemed as though the more I had to do in the former field of labor the greater were the calls upon me in the latter. A sub-committee of the Committee on the Conduct of the War, visiting my New York offices one day, found the desks, chairs, and floor covered with the business papers of the navy ring, a dozen clerks assorting and analyzing them, and I taking depositions about army frauds in an adjoining room. They had come there to investigate my doings, at the instance of complaining contractors; but a half hour's observation amply sufficed, and they returned to Washington, and reported that if I asked for the whole power of Congress I ought to have it, for at least two departments of the government were rotten with fraud.

My narrative, as may readily be conceived from what has been given above, might be indefinitely extended. But I have not the heart to expatiate longer upon this chapter of national infamy. It is my deliberate conviction, based upon the inspection of many bureaus, and the examination of some thousands of witnesses, in every walk of life, that at least twenty, if not twenty-five, per cent. of the entire expenditures of the government during the Rebellion, were tainted with fraud. That is to say, that over seven hundred million dollars were paid to public robbers, or worse than wasted, through improvident methods. If the loss of the money were the only thing to be deplored, it would be, comparatively, a trifling affair; for this country has boundless resources, and unprecedented recuperative capacities. But every dollar of this ill-spent treasure contributed toward a demoralization of the people, and the sapping of ancient virtues. Let any one who surveys the present condition of public morals dare deny that we have made long strides toward the overthrow of the Republic since 1861.

STONEWALL JACKSON'S VALLEY CAMPAIGN.

BY COLONEL WILLIAM ALLAN.

AFTER the disastrous termination of Braddock's campaign against Fort Duquesne, in the summer of 1756, Colonel George Washington, to whom was intrusted the duty of protecting the Allegheny frontier of Virginia from the French and Indians, established himself at Winchester, in the lower Shenandoah Valley, as the point from which he could best protect the district assigned to him. Here he subsequently built Fort Loudoun, and made it the base of his operations. A grass-grown mound, marking the site of one of the bastions of the old fort, and Loudoun street, the name of the principal thoroughfare of the town, remain, to recall an important chapter in colonial history. It was this old town that Major General T. J. Jackson entered on the evening of November 4th, 1861, as commander of the "Valley District," and established his headquarters within musket shot of Fort Loudoun. He had been made major general on October 7th, for his services at the first battle of Manassas, and was now assigned to this important command because of the expectations formed from his capacity, as well as from the fact of his acquaintance with the country. His district embraced the territory bounded north by the Potomac, east by the Blue Ridge, and west by the Alleghenies. Born and reared in Western Virginia, and filled with a patriot's devotion to the land of his birth, he had manifested a strong desire to be employed in the operations in that region, and had cherished the ambition of freeing his former home from hostile domination. The Confederates, during the summer, had in that region been unsuccessful. General Robert Garnett had been forced to retreat by General McClellan, and had then met defeat and death at Carrick's ford, on Cheat river, July 13th. This gave the Federals the control of the greater part of Virginia, west of the Alleghenies, and the subsequent efforts of Generals Floyd and Wise, and still later, of General Lee, availed only to prevent further encroachments of the enemy—not to regain the lost territory.

When, therefore, General Jackson assumed command of the Valley of Virginia, the enemy had possession of all the State north of the Great Kanawha, and west of the Alleghenies, and had pushed their outposts into that mountain region itself, and in some cases eastward of the main range. Thus General Kelly had captured Romney, the county-seat of Hampshire county, forty miles west of Winchester, and now occupied it with a force of five thousand men. This movement gave the Federals control of the fertile valley of the south branch of the Potomac. Another, though much smaller force, occupied Bath, the county-seat of Morgan county, forty miles due north of Winchester, while the north bank of the Potomac was everywhere guarded by Union troops. The Baltimore and Ohio Railroad was open and available for the supply of the Federal troops from Baltimore to Harper's Ferry, and again from a point opposite (Hancock) westward. The section of about forty miles from Harper's Ferry to Hancock, lying for the most part some distance within the Virginia border, had been interrupted and rendered useless by the Confederates, but this gap was now supplied by the Chesapeake and Ohio Canal, which was open all the way from Cumberland, Maryland, to Georgetown, in the District of Columbia. The plan of operations that Jackson had conceived for regaining West Virginia was to move along the Baltimore Railroad and the turnpikes parallel to it, and thus enter West Virginia at the northeastern end. In this way he could turn the left flank of the enemy's forces, place himself on their communications and force them to evacuate, or fight under circumstances of his own selection. Having seen how his predecessors had been hampered, in trying to operate from Staunton westward, by the difficult and inaccessible nature of the country, composed almost entirely of mountains destitute of supplies, and penetrated by nothing but indifferent wagon roads, he was anxious to try a mode of approach, which, if more exposed to the enemy, had the advantage of being easier, by lying through a much more populous and cultivated region, of affording to some extent the use of a railroad for supplies, and which would soon place him in the midst of some of the most fertile parts of West Virginia. In order to carry out this scheme, he asked for his old brigade, which had been left at Manassas, and that all the forces operating along the line of the Alleghenies, southwest of Winchester, and lately commanded by General Lee, should be concentrated under his command. This would have given him fifteen thousand or sixteen thousand men, the least force with which he thought it possible to undertake so bold an enterprise.

His wishes were complied with in part. His own brigade was promptly sent to him, and one of the brigades of Loring's troops (General Loring had succeeded General Lee) reached him early in December. Subsequently two more brigades, under General Loring himself, were added, but all these troops only increased the small force of three thousand State militia, which he had assembled in the district itself, to about eleven thousand men. The greater part of General Loring's force did not arrive at Winchester until Christmas, thus preventing any important movements during November and December. But, meantime, Jackson was not idle. He spent the time in organizing, equipping, and drilling the militia and the scattered cavalry commands, which he consolidated into a regiment under Colonel Ashby, and sent expeditions against the Chesapeake and Ohio Canal, by breaking which he annoyed the enemy, and interrupted an important line of communication. By the last week in December, all the troops that the War Department thought it judicious to spare him had arrived, and, though the season was far advanced, he determined at once to assume the offensive. The winter had so far been mild, the roads were in excellent condition, and though his force was not large enough for the recovery of West Virginia, important advantages seemed within reach. The forces and positions of the enemy opposed to Jackson at the beginning of 1862 were as follows: General Banks, commanding the Fifth Corps of McClellan's army, with headquarters at Frederick, Md., had sixteen thousand effective men, the greater part of whom were in winter quarters, near that city, while the remainder guarded the Potomac from Harper's Ferry to Williamsport; General Rosecrans, still holding command of the Department of West Virginia, had twenty-two thousand men scattered over that region, but was concentrating them on the Baltimore and Ohio Railroad. He says, in his testimony (see Report of Committee on the Conduct of the War, 1865, Volume III.):

On the 6th of December, satisfied that the condition of the roads over the Alleghenies into Western Virginia, as well as the scarcity of the subsistence and horse feed, would preclude any serious operations of the enemy against us until the opening of the spring, I began quietly and secretly to assemble all the spare troops of the department in the neighborhood of the Baltimore and Ohio Railroad, under cover of about five thousand men I had posted at Romney, with the design of obtaining General McClellan's permission to take nearly all these troops and suddenly seize, fortify and hold Winchester, whereby I should at once more effectually cover the northeastern and central parts of Western Virginia, and at the same time threaten the left of the enemy's position at Manassas, compel him to lengthen his line of defense in front of the Army of the Potomac, and throw it farther south.

This plan of Rosecrans was foiled by Jackson's movement.

On the 1st of January, 1862, the latter left Winchester at the head of about ten thousand men, and moved toward Bath, in Morgan county. The fine weather of the preceding month changed on the very first night of the expedition, and a terrible storm of sleet and snow and cold set in, which, for the next three weeks, subjected the troops to the severest hardships, and finally forced their commander to suspend his forward movement. At first the troops marched cheerfully on in spite of cold and sleet. Bath was evacuated, but General Lander, who, within a day or two had superseded Rosecrans, hurried reinforcements to Hancock in time to prevent Jackson from crossing the Potomac. Jackson, having made a demonstration against Hancock, did what damage was possible to the Baltimore and Ohio Railroad, and placed himself between Lander, at Hancock, and Kelly, at Romney, moved toward the latter place as fast as the icy roads would permit. Kelly did not await his approach but hastily retired, and, on January 14th, Jackson entered Romney. Here, though the weather and roads grew worse, the Confederate leader had no intention of stopping. He arrived at Cumberland and preparations were at once began for a movement on New Creek (now called Keyser), but when the orders to march were given the murmuring and discontent among his troops, especially among those which had recently come under his command, reached such a pitch that he reluctantly abandoned the enterprise, and determined to go into winter quarters. Leaving Loring and his troops at Romney, he returned with his old brigade to Winchester and disposed his cavalry and militia commands so as to protect the whole border of the district.

This expedition, though it had cleared his district of the foe, and effectually broke up the all plans of the enemy for a winter campaign against Winchester, was disappointing to Jackson as well as to the public. Though believing that results had been obtained which outweighed all the suffering and loss, he was conscious that winter and the lack of cordial support had prevented the accomplishment of far more important ends. But this did not lower his self-reliance or diminish his clear-sightedness. The discontent among the troops left at Romney resulted, on the 31st of January, in an order from the Secretary of War, sent without consultation, to withdraw Loring from that place. Jackson obeyed the order, and at once resigned, on the ground that such interference, by the department at Richmond, with the details of military affairs in the field, could only lead to disaster. After explanations, and upon the urgent request of Governor Letcher and General J. E. Johnston, he withdrew the resignation. Subsequently there was no desire on anybody's part to interfere with him. For the next month Jackson remained quietly at Winchester. General Loring and all his troops that were not Virginians were ordered elsewhere, and in order to induce re-enlistments, furloughs were freely granted. The Confederate force was in this way reduced to about four thousand men, exclusive of militia.

With the 1st of March opened the great campaign of 1862, in Virginia, in which Jackson was to bear so prominent a part. In other sections of the Confederacy fortune favored the Federal cause, and the Union armies were on the full tide of success. On the 8th of February Roanoke Island fell, on the 16th Fort Donelson, on the 26th Nashville, and on the 27th the evacuation of Columbus (Kentucky) was begun. These successes made the Federal administration impatient to push forward operations in Virginia. At the urgent representation of General McClellan, President Lincoln had yielded his favorite plan of campaign—an advance against the Confederate lines at Manassas—and had reluctantly consented to the transfer of the Army of the Potomac to Fort Monroe, and its advance thence on Richmond. Before he would allow McClellan, however, to begin the transfer, the Potomac river, below Washington, must be cleared of Confederate batteries, the Baltimore and Ohio Railroad must be recovered and protected, and all the approaches to Washington must be made secure. To fulfil a part of these conditions, Banks' and Lander's commands were ordered forward, and on February 24th General Banks occupied Harper's Ferry. Soon after McClellan began the movements on his other wing that were preparatory to an attack on the Confederate batteries along the Lower Potomac. These indications of activity announced to General Johnston that the time had come for carrying out his plan—already determined upon—of retreating behind the Rappahannock. On the 7th of March he began the withdrawal of his army, and by the 11th all the infantry and artillery east of the Blue ridge had reached the new position.

Jackson, meanwhile, remained at Winchester, watching closely the advance of Banks, and doing what was possible to impede it. General Johnston thus describes the duty assigned to him:

After it had become evident that the Valley was to be invaded by an army too strong to be encountered by Jackson's Division, that officer was instructed to endeavor to employ the invaders in the Valley, but without exposing himself to the danger of defeat, by keeping so near the enemy as to prevent him from making any considerable detachment to reinforce McClellan, but not so near that he might be compelled to fight.

At this time Jackson's entire force did not amount to four thousand men, exclusive of the remnants of the militia brigades, which were not employed any more in active service. It consisted of the five regiments of his old brigade, now under Garnet, of three regiments and one battalion under Burks, and of two regiments under Fulkerson. He had also five batteries and Ashby's regiment of cavalry. General Banks had his own division, under Williams, and Shields' (late Lander's troops) Division, now incorporated in his corps. Two brigades of Sedgwick's were also with him when he crossed the Potomac. On the 1st of April the strength of Banks' corps, embracing Shields, is given by General McClellan at twenty-three thousand three hundred and thirty-nine, including three thousand six hundred and fifty-two cavalry, and *excluding* two thousand one hundred railroad guards. If Sedgwick's Brigades continued with him in his advance on Winchester his entire force was over twenty-five thousand. Jackson sent his stores, baggage and sick to the rear, but continued to hold his position at Winchester to the last moment.

Banks occupied Charlestown on the 26th of February, but only reached Stephenson's, four miles north of Winchester, on March 7th. Here Jackson drew up his little force in line of battle to meet him, but the Federals withdrew without attacking. The activity of Ashby, and the boldness with which Jackson maintained his position, impressed his adversary with greatly exaggerated notions of his strength. Banks advanced in a cautious and wary manner, refusing to attack, but pushing forward his left wing so as to threaten Jackson's flank and rear. By the 11th of March, the movement had gone so far that it was not longer safe for the Confederates to hold Winchester. Jackson remained under arms all day waiting an attack in front, but none was made, and late in the afternoon he ordered trains and troops into camp near the south end of the town. By some mistake the trains went on six miles further, and the troops had to follow. Jackson called a council of his chief officers—the first and last time, it is to be believed, that he ever summoned a council of war—to meet after dark in Winchester, and proposed to them a night attack upon Banks. His proposition was not approved, and he learned then for the first time that the troops were already six miles from Winchester and ten from the enemy. The plan was now evidently impracticable, and he withdrew from the town, which was occupied by the Federals on the next day (March 12th). The Confederates continued to retreat slowly to Woodstock, Mount Jackson (forty miles in rear of Winchester), and Shields' Division was thrown forward in pursuit to Strasburg on the 17th.

The retirement of Jackson, and the unopposed occupation of the Lower Valley by Banks, relieved General McClellan of all fears in that direction, and induced him, in pursuance of President Lincoln's requirement that Manassas Junction and the approaches to Washington from that direction be securely held, to send the following instructions to Banks, on March 16th:

Sir :—You will post your command in the vicinity of Manassas, intrench yourself strongly and throw cavalry pickets out to the front. Your first care will be the rebuilding of the railway from Washington to Manassas, and to Strasburg, in order to open your communications to the Valley of the Shenandoah. As soon as the Manassas Gap Railway is in running order, intrench a brigade of infantry, say four regiments, with two batteries, at or near the point where the railway crosses the Shenandoah. Something like two regiments of cavalry should be left in that vicinity to occupy Winchester, and thoroughly scour the country south of the railway and up the Shenandoah Valley. * * * Occupy by grand guards Warrenton Junction and Warrenton itself. * * * Some more advanced point on the Orange and Alexandria Railroad. * * *

In compliance with these instructions, Shields' Division was recalled from Strasburg, and Williams' Division began its movement toward Manassas on the 20th of March.

On the evening of the 21st, Ashby reported that the enemy had evacuated Strasburg. Jackson, divining that this meant a withdrawal toward Washington, at once ordered pursuit with all his available force. The whole of his little army reached Strasburg on the afternoon of the 22d, the greater part after a march of twenty-two miles. Meantime Ashby was following close behind the retreating enemy, and late in the afternoon of the 22d, as Jackson was entering Strasburg, Ashby was attacking the Federal pickets, one mile south of Winchester. After the skirmish, Ashby camped for the night at Kernstown, three miles south of Winchester. General Shields, who commanded the troops Ashby had attacked, and who was himself wounded in the skirmish, had displayed but a small part of his force; and this fact, combined with information gotten from within the Federal lines, misled the Confederates. The last of Williams' Division, of Banks' Corps, had left on the morning of the 22d for Manassas, but Shields' Division of three brigades still remained. The reports brought out led Ashby to believe that all but one brigade had gone, and that it expected to leave for Harper's Ferry the next day. This information, transmitted to Jackson, caused the latter to push on with all haste the next morning. At daylight he sent three companies of infantry to reinforce Ashby, and followed with his whole force. He reached Kernstown at two P. M., after a march of fourteen miles. General Shields had made his dispositions to meet attack, by advancing Kimball's Brigade of four regiments and Daum's Artillery to the vicinity of Kernstown. Sullivan's Brigade of four regiments was posted in rear of Kimball, and Tyler's Brigade of five regiments, with Broadhead's cavalry, was held in reserve. Ashby kept up an active skirmish with the advance of Shields' force during the forenoon.

But, though thus making ready, the Federal generals did not expect an attack in earnest. Shields says he had the country, in front and flank, carefully reconnoitred during the forenoon on the 23d of March, and the officers in charge reported "no indications of any hostile force except that of Ashby." Shields continues:

> I communicated this information to Major General Banks, who was then with me, and, after consulting together, we both concluded that Jackson could not be tempted to hazard himself so far away from his main support. Having both come to this conclusion, General Banks took his departure for Washington (being already under orders to that effect). The officers of his staff, however, remained behind, intending to leave for Centreville in the afternoon.

When Jackson reached Kernstown, his troops were very weary. Three-fourths of them had marched thirty-six miles since the preceding morning. He, therefore, gave directions for bivouacking, and says:

> Though it was very desirable to prevent the enemy from leaving the Valley, yet I deemed it best not to attack until morning. But, subsequently ascertaining that the Federals had a position from which our forces could be seen, I concluded that it would be dangerous to postpone the attack until the next day, as reinforcements might be brought up during the night.

Jackson, therefore, led his men to the attack. His plan was to gain the ridge upon which the Federal right flank rested, turn that flank, and get command of the road from Kernstown to Winchester, in the enemy's rear. He gained the top of the ridge, but Shields was able to hold him in check until Tyler's Brigade and other troops could be hurried to that flank, when Jackson, in turn, became the attacked party. For three hours of this Sunday afternoon the sanguinary and stubborn contest continued. The left half of the Confederate line was perpendicular to the ridge; the right half, which was mainly composed of artillery, ran along the ridge to the rear, and was thus at right angles to the other part. The brunt of the Federal attack was borne by the centre, near the angle presented by that part of the line. Fulkerson's Brigade, holding the extreme Confederate left, firmly maintained his position, but the centre was thinned and worn out by the persistent Federal attacks, until General Garnett, whose brigade was there, deeming it impossible to hold his position longer, ordered a retreat. This, of course, caused the retreat of the whole, which was effected with the loss of two disabled guns, and from two to three hundred prisoners.

Jackson's whole force at this time consisted of three thousand and eighty-seven infantry, of which two thousand seven hundred and forty-two were engaged in the battle of Kernstown; of twenty-seven guns, of which eighteen were engaged, and of two hundred and ninety cavalry. General Shields states his force at seven thousand, of all arms. The total Confederate loss was nearly seven hundred. The Federal is put by General Shields at less than six hundred.

Weary and dispirited was the little army which had marched fourteen miles in the morning to attack a force more than double its own, and which had for three hours wrestled for victory in so vigorous a fashion as to astonish and deceive the enemy. Baffled and overpowered, it slowly retraced its path for six miles more, and sank to rest. In the fence corners, under the trees, and around the wagons the soldiers threw themselves down, many too weary to eat, and forgot, in profound slumber, the trials, dangers, and disappointments of the day. Jackson shared the open air bivouac with his men, and found the rest that nature demanded on some fence rails in a corner of the road. Next morning he crossed to the south side of Cedar creek, and gradually retired before the advancing enemy once more to Mount Jackson.

The bold attack of Jackson at Kernstown, though unsuccessful, led to many important results. Its first effect was the recall of the Federal troops then marching from the Valley toward Manassas. General Shields says:

Though the battle had been won, still I could not have believed that Jackson would have hazarded a decisive engagement so far from the main body without expecting reinforcements. So, to be prepared for such a contingency, I set to work during the night (after the battle) to bring together all the troops within my reach. I sent an express after Williams' Division, requesting the rear brigade, about twenty miles distant, to march all night, and join me in the morning. I swept the forts and routes in my rear of about all their guards, hurrying them forward by forced marches, to be with me at daylight. * * * General Banks, hearing of our engagement on his way to Washington, halted at Harper's Ferry, and with remarkable promptitude and sagacity ordered back Williams' whole division, so that my express found the rear brigade already *en route* to join us. The General himself returned forthwith, and after making me a hasty visit, assumed command of the forces in pursuit of the enemy. This pursuit was kept up until they reached Woodstock.

Thus the design of McClellan to post Banks' Corps at Centreville (see letter of March 16th) became impracticable, and that body of over twenty thousand troops was thought necessary to guard against the further movements of Jackson's two thousand, and the imaginary reinforcements with which they supplied him. This battle, too, no doubt decided the question of the detachment of Blenker's Division of ten thousand men from McClellan, and its transfer to Fremont, recently placed in command of the Mountain Department, which embraced West Virginia. While *en route* from Alexandria to join Fremont, Blenker's Division was to report to Banks, and remain with him as long as he thought any attack from Jackson impending. A few days later the sensitiveness of the Federal Government to the danger of Washington, excited anew by Jackson's movements, led to the detachment of McDowell's Corps. McClellan had left over seventy thousand men for the defense of Washington and its approaches, and yet, after Kernstown, President Lincoln felt so insecure that, on April 3d, he countermanded the order for the embarkation of McDowell's Corps, and detained it in front of Washington, and so deprived McClellan of the finest body of troops in his army. Thus Jackson's bold dash had effected the object of General Johnston in leaving him in the Valley, in a way far more secure than either of them could have expected.

The next month was to Jackson one of comparative inaction. Having slowly retreated to the south bank of the Shenandoah, near Mount Jackson, he spent the next few weeks in resting and recruiting his forces. The militia of the adjoining counties had already been called to the field, but this resource was superseded on the 10th of April by the passage of the Conscription Act. The time for reorganizing the regiments was near at hand. New officers were to be elected. The ranks were filling up under the impetus given to volunteering by the conscription bill. The weather during the first half of April was very raw and cold, and during the whole month was exceedingly rainy. All these causes rendered quiet very acceptable to the Confederates. Nor was the enemy in haste to disturb them. Banks was, on April 4th, placed in independent command of the Department of the Shenandoah, and McDowell of the country between the Blue ridge and the Rappahannock, while Fremont was in command from the Alleghenies westward. These were all made independent of McClellan, and of each other. General Banks followed Jackson but slowly. He reached Woodstock on April 1st, and having pushed back Ashby's cavalry to Edinburg, five miles beyond, he attempted no further serious advance until the 17th. He then moved forward in force and Jackson retired to Harrisonburg, where he turned at right angles to the left, and crossing the main fork of the Shenandoah at Conrad's store, took up his position at the western base of the Blue ridge mountains, in Swift Run gap. This camp the Confederates reached on the 20th of April, and here they remained through ten days more of rain and mud.

Meantime, the advance of McClellan up the Peninsula had begun in earnest. General J. E. Johnston had transferred the mass of his army to the front of Richmond, and had taken command there in person. Ewell's Division alone remained on the Rappahannock to watch the enemy there, and to aid Jackson in case of need. This division was now near Gordonsville, and a good road from that point through Swift Run gap placed it within easy reach of Jackson. The latter, conscious of his inability with five or six thousand men (his force had nearly doubled since Kernstown by the return of furloughed men and by new enlistments) to resist in the open country the advance of Banks, had availed himself of the nature of the country to take a position where he could be attacked only at great disadvantage, and yet might threaten the flank or rear of the advancing column if it attempted to pass him. The main Shenandoah river covered his front—a stream not easily fordable at any time, and now swollen by the spring rains. The spurs of the mountains, as they run out toward this river, afford almost impregnable positions for defense, his flank could only be turned by toilsome, exposed marches, while good roads led from his rear to General Ewell. Thus, secure in his position, Jackson at the same time more effectually prevented the further advance of the Federal column than if he had remained in its front. For he held the bridge over the Shenandoah and was but a day's march from Harrisonburg, and should Banks venture to move forward toward Staunton, he was ready to hurl the Confederate forces against his enemy's flank and rear. General Banks, at Harrisonburg, was in the midst of a hostile country, and already one hundred miles from the Potomac, at Harper's Ferry, with which a long line of wagon communication had to be maintained. To push on to Staunton, with Jackson on his flank or rear, was virtually to sacrifice his present line of communication with no practicable substitute in view; to attack the Confederates on the slopes of the mountains, with even a greatly superior force, was to risk defeat.

On the 28th of April, Jackson applied to General Lee, then acting as commander-in-chief under President Davis, for a reinforcement of five thousand men, which addition to his force he deemed necessary to justify him in marching out and attacking Banks. Next day he was informed that no troops could be spared to him beyond the commands of Ewell and of Edward Johnson, the latter of whom was seven miles west of Staunton, at West View, with one brigade. Jackson at once decided upon his plan of campaign, and the very next day began to put it in execution. This campaign, so successful and brilliant in its results, and now so renowned, shows in its conception the strong points of Jackson's military genius, his clear, vigorous grasp of the situation, his decision, his energy, his grand audacity. It recalls the Italian campaign of 1796, when Napoleon astonished, baffled and defeated the armies of Beaulieu, Wurmser, and Alvinzy in succession. Jackson was now, with about six or seven thousand men, at the base of the Blue ridge, some thirty miles northeast of Staunton. Ewell, with an equal force, was in the vicinity of Gordonsville, twenty-five miles in his rear, and east of the mountains. Edward Johnson was seven miles west of Staunton with three thousand five hundred men. Such was the Confederate position. On the other hand, Banks, with the main body of his forces, of about twenty thousand men, occupied Harrisonburg, twelve or fifteen miles in Jackson's front. Schenck and Milroy, commanding Fremont's advance of six thousand men, were in front of Edward Johnson, their pickets already east of the Shenandoah mountain and on the Harrisonburg and Warm Spring turnpike. Fremont was preparing to join them from the Baltimore and Ohio Railroad with ten thousand men—making the total of Fremont's force some fifteen thousand men. McDowell, with thirty thousand men, had drawn away from the Upper Rappahannock, and was concentrating at Fredericksburg. This movement of McDowell had released Ewell and left him free to aid Jackson, who, with a force of about sixteen thousand men (including Ewell and Edward Johnson), had on his hands the thirty-five thousand under Banks and Fremont. The Warm Springs turnpike afforded Banks a ready mode of uniting with Milroy and Schenck, in which case Staunton would be any easy capture. Fremont was already preparing to move in that direction. Jackson determined to anticipate such a movement, if possible, by uniting his own force to that of Johnson, and falling upon Milroy while Ewell kept Banks in check. Then he would join Ewell and with all his strength attack Banks.

To accomplish this, Ewell was ordered to cross the mountain and occupy the position Jackson had held for ten days at Swift Run gap—thus keeping up the menace on Banks' flank. As Ewell approached, Jackson left camp on the 30th of April, and marched up the east bank of the Shenandoah to Port Republic. No participant in that march can ever forget the incessant rain, the fearful mud, the frequent quicksands which made progress so slow and toilsome. More than two days were consumed in going fifteen miles. Meantime, Ashby was demonstrating against the enemy and keeping Jackson's line close, to prevent information from getting through. At Port Republic, the army turned short to the left, left the Shenandoah Valley altogether, crossed Brown's gap in the Blue ridge, and marched to Mechanic's River Station, on the Virginia Central Railroad; thence, by road and rail, it was rapidly moved to Staunton, and by the evening of May 5th it had all reached that point. The movement by this devious route mystified friends as well as foes. One day is given to rest, and on the next Jackson hurries forward, unites Johnson's troops with his own, drives in the Federal pickets and foraging parties, and camps twenty-five miles from Staunton. On the morrow (May 8th) he pushes on to McDowell, seizes Sittlington's hill, which commands the town and camp of the enemy, and makes his dispositions to seize the road in the rear of the enemy during the night. But Milroy and Schenck have united, and seeing their position untenable, make a fierce attack in the afternoon to retake the hill and cover their retreat. For three or four hours a bloody struggle takes place on the brow of Sittlington's hill. The Federals, though inflicting severe loss, are repulsed at every point, and at nightfall quietly withdraw. They light their camp-fires and, in the darkness, evacuate the town. They retreat twenty-four miles to Franklin, in Pendleton county, where they meet Fremont, advancing with the main body of his forces. Jackson follows to this point; has found it impossible to attack the retreating foe to advantage, and now deems it unadvisable to attempt anything further in this difficult country with his ten thousand men against Fremont's fourteen thousand or fifteen thousand. Screening his movements from Fremont with cavalry, he turns back (May 13th), marches rapidly to within seventeen miles of Staunton, then turns toward Harrisonburg, and dispatches General Ewell that he is on his way to attack Banks with their united forces.

Meantime, important changes have taken place in the disposition of the Federal troops in the Valley. McClellan is calling for more troops and complaining that McDowell is withheld. The latter, having gathered Abercrombie's and other scattered commands from the country in front of Washington into a new division, to replace those sent to McClellan, now lies at Fredericksburg, impatient to take part in the movement on Richmond. Banks, hearing of Ewell's arrival in the Valley, fears an attack from him and Jackson combined, and retires from Harrisonburg to New Market. Jackson's inaction for some weeks, and now his movement to West Virginia, reassures the Federal administration, and Shields, with more than half of Banks' force, is detached at New Market, and ordered to Fredericksburg to swell McDowell's Corps to over forty thousand men. Banks is left with only some seven thousand men, and falls back to Strasburg, where he fortifies. He assumes a defensive attitude to hold the Lower Valley and to cover the Baltimore and Ohio Railroad. These movements of the enemy had nearly disarranged Jackson's plans. Upon the march of Shields toward Fredericksburg, General J. E. Johnston, commanding in chief in Virginia, thought it time to recall Ewell to meet the new danger thus threatened, and the orders reached Ewell while Jackson was yet one day's march short of Harrisonburg. After conference with Ewell, Jackson took the responsibility of detaining him until the condition of affairs could be represented to General Johnston, and, meantime, they united in a vigorous pursuit of Banks.

Ashby has followed close on Banks' heels, and now occupies his outposts with constant skirmishing, while he completely screens Jackson. The latter, having marched rapidly to New Market, as if about to follow the foe to Strasburg, to attack him there, suddenly changes his route, crosses the Massanutten mountains to Luray, where Ewell joins him, and pours down the narrow Page Valley, by forced marches, to Front Royal. This place is about one hundred and twenty miles (by Jackson's route) from Franklin, and the Confederates reached it on May 23d, ten days after leaving Franklin. This village (Front Royal) is held by about one thousand men under Colonel Kenly, of the First Maryland (Federal) regiment, who has in charge the large stores there gathered, and the important railroad bridges on the Shenandoah. This force also covers the flank and rear of Banks' position at Strasburg. Kenly is taken by surprise, makes what resistance he can; is forced across the bridges he vainly attempts to destroy, and flies toward Winchester. Jackson, too impatient to wait for his tried infantry, places himself at the head of a few companies of cavalry and pushes after the foe. He overtakes, attacks, and disperses Kenly's force, and in a few moments four-fifths

47

of it are killed, wounded or prisoners. Exhausted nature can do no more. Weary and foot-sore, the soldiers lie down to rest.

General Banks, amazed at this irruption, by which his flank is turned and his communications threatened, begins, during the night, a precipitate retreat to Winchester. Jackson anticipates this, and presses on, the next morning, to Middletown, a village between Strasburg and Winchester, to find the road still filled with Federal trains and troops. Capturing and scattering these in every direction, he follows on after the main body, which has already passed him toward Winchester. He overhauls them in the afternoon, pushes Banks' rear guard before him all night, and, having given but one hour to rest, at daylight, on the 25th of May, reaches Winchester, to find the Federal forces drawn up across the approaches to the town from the south and southeast. The main part of Banks' army occupies the ridge on which the battle of Kernstown had been fought, but at a point two miles further north, while another part held the Front Royal road, on which Ewell, with a part of his division, was advancing. A vigorous attack is at once made by the Confederates, which, for a short time, is bravely resisted; but the Federal lines begin to yield, and seeing himself about to be overwhelmed, Banks retreats through Winchester. Jackson presses closely, and the Federals emerge from the town a mass of disordered fugitives, making their way, with all speed, toward the Potomac. The Confederate infantry followed for several miles, capturing a large number of prisoners, and had the cavalry been as efficient, but few of Banks' troops would have escaped. Banks halts on the north side of the Potomac, and Jackson allows his exhausted men to rest at Winchester. Thorough and glorious was Jackson's victory. In forty-eight hours the enemy had been driven between fifty and sixty miles, from Front Royal and Strasburg, to the Potomac, with the loss of more than one-third of his entire strength. His army had crossed the latter river a disorganized mass. Hundreds of wagons had been abandoned or burned. Two pieces of artillery, and an immense quantity of quartermaster, commissary, medical, and ordnance stores had fallen into the hands of the victor. Some twenty-three hundred prisoners were taken to the rear when Jackson fell back, beside seven hundred and fifty wounded and sick paroled, and left in the hospitals at Winchester and Strasburg, making a total of about three thousand and fifty.

A day is given, according to Jackson's custom, to religious services and thanksgiving, and another to rest, and on the third he is again moving toward Harper's Ferry, in order, by the most energetic diversion possible, to draw away troops from Richmond. How well he effected this, a glance at the Federal movements will show. As above stated, the quiet that succeeded Kernstown, the advance of Banks far into the Valley, and the movement of Jackson to West Virginia had calmed the apprehensions of the Federal administration, for the time, in regard to Washington, and the urgent requests of McClellan and McDowell, that the latter's corps should be sent forward from Fredericksburg toward Richmond, were listened to. Shields was detached from Banks, and sent to McDowell, and, on May 17th, the latter was ordered to prepare to move down the Fredericksburg Railroad, to unite with McClellan before Richmond. On Friday, May 23d, the very day of Jackson's attack at Front Royal, President Lincoln and Secretary Stanton went to Fredericksburg to confer with General McDowell, found that Shields had already reached that point, and determined, after consultation, that the advance should begin on the following Monday (May 26th). McClellan was informed of the contemplated movement, and instructed to assume command of McDowell's Corps when it joined him. This fine body of troops, moving from the north against the Confederate capital, would have seized all the roads entering the city from that direction, and would have increased McClellan's available force by from forty to fifty per cent. There was strong reason to expect that this combined movement would effect the downfall of Richmond.

The Federal President returned to Washington on the night of the 23d to await the result. He there received the first news of Jackson's operations at Front Royal the preceding afternoon. The first dispatches indicated only an unimportant raid, and McDowell was directed by telegraph to leave his "least effective" brigade at Fredericksburg, in addition to the forces agreed upon for the occupation of that town. Later, on the 24th, the news from Banks became more alarming, and General McDowell was dispatched that:

General Fremont has been ordered by telegraph to move from Franklin on Harrisonburg, to relieve General Banks, and capture or destroy Jackson and Ewell's forces. You are instructed, laying aside, for the present, the movement on Richmond, to put twenty thousand men in motion at once for the Shenandoah, moving on the line, or in advance of the line, of the Manassas Gap Railroad. Your object will be to capture the forces of Jackson and Ewell, either in co-operation with General Fremont, or, in case want of supplies or of transportation interferes with his movements, it is believed that the force with which you move will be sufficient to accomplish the object alone. * * *

The following was sent to General McClellan at four P. M. on May 24th:

In consequence of General Banks' critical position, I have been compelled to suspend General McDowell's movements to join you. The enemy are making a desperate push on Harper's Ferry, and we are trying to throw Fremont's force, and part of McDowell's, in their rear.

A. LINCOLN.

Next day the news from Banks seems to have greatly increased the excitement in Washington. The following telegrams were sent to General McClellan (May 25th) by President Lincoln :

The enemy is moving north in sufficient force to drive Banks before him, in precisely what force we cannot tell. He is also threatening Leesburg and Geary, on the Manassas Gap Railroad, from both north and south, in precisely what force we cannot tell. I think the movement is a general and concerted one, such as could not be if he was acting upon the purpose of a very desperate defense of Richmond. I think the time is near when you must either attack Richmond or give up the job and come to the defense of Washington. Let me hear from you immediately.

A later one reads :

Your dispatch received. Banks was at Strasburg with about six thousand men, Shields having been taken from him to swell a column for McDowell to aid you at Richmond, and the rest of the force scattered at various places. On the 23d, a rebel force of seven to ten thousand men fell upon one regiment and two companies guarding the bridge at Front Royal, destroying it entirely, crossed the Shenandoah, and, on the 24th (yesterday), pushed to get north of Banks on the road to Winchester. Banks ran a race with them, beating them into Winchester yesterday evening. This morning a battle ensued between the two forces, in which Banks was beaten back into full retreat toward Martinsburg, and probably is broken up into a total rout. Geary, on the Manassas Gap Railroad, just now reports that Jackson is now near Front Royal, with ten thousand, following up and supporting, as I understand, the force now pursuing Banks; also, that another force of ten thousand is near Orleans, following on in the same direction. Stripped bare as we are here, it will be all we can do to prevent them crossing the Potomac at Harper's Ferry or above. We have about twenty thousand of McDowell's force moving back to the vicinity of Front Royal, and Fremont, who was at Franklin, is moving to Harrisonburg. Both of these movements are intended to get in the enemy's rear. One more of McDowell's brigades is ordered through here to Harper's Ferry. The rest of his forces remain, for the present, at Fredericksburg. We are sending such regiments, in dribs, from here and Baltimore as we can spare, to Harper's Ferry, supplying their places, in some sort, by calling in the militia from the adjacent States. We also have eighteen cannon on the road to Harper's Ferry, of which arm there is not a single one yet at that point. This is now our situation. If McDowell's force was now beyond our reach, we should be utterly helpless. Apprehensions of something like this, and no unwillingness to sustain you, has always been my reason for withholding McDowell's force from you. Please understand this and do the best you can with the forces you have.

The exaggeration of this dispatch shows the panic produced. Jackson had no troops at Orleans, or anywhere east of the ridge (except a little cavalry), and his entire force, which was all with him, was about fifteen thousand or sixteen thousand. This dispatch shows, however, that Jackson was, for the time, not only occupying all the troops in and around Washington, together with Fremont's forces, but was completely neutralizing the forty thousand under McDowell, and thus disconcerting McClellan's plans.

But if the skill, celerity, and daring of Jackson are illustrated in his movement against Banks, these qualities shine out far more brilliantly in his retreat from the Potomac, and in his battles at Port Republic. He moved to Harper's Ferry on the 28th of May, and spent the 29th in making demonstrations against the force that had been rapidly gathered there, but which was too strongly posted to be attacked in front. Time did not allow a crossing of the river and an investment of the place. The large bodies of troops which the Federal administration was hastening from every direction to overwhelm him, were already closing in. McDowell, with twenty thousand men, was hurrying toward Front Royal and Strasburg, and Fremont, now awake to the fact that his enemy had pushed him back into the mountains, and then slipped away to destroy his colleague, was moving with his fourteen thousand or fifteen thousand men toward Strasburg. General Saxton had seven thousand Federal troops at Harper's Ferry, and Banks was taking breath with the remnants of his command (some three thousand or four thousand men) at Williamsport, Maryland. Thus, over forty thousand men were gathering to crush Jackson, whose strength was now not over fifteen thousand. On the morning of May 30th he began his retreat by ordering all his troops, except Winder's Brigade and the cavalry, to fall back to Winchester. Nor was he an hour too soon, for before he reached that town McDowell's advance had poured over the Blue ridge, driven out the small guard left at Front Royal, and captured the village.

The condition of affairs when Jackson reached Winchester, on the evening of May 30th, was as follows: The Federals were in possession of Front Royal, which is but twelve miles from Strasburg, while Winchester is eighteen. Fremont was at Wardensville, distant twenty miles from Strasburg, and had telegraphed President Lincoln that he would enter the latter place by five P. M. the next day. The mass of Jackson's forces had marched twenty-five miles to reach Winchester, and his rear guard, under Winder (after skirmishing with the enemy at Harper's Ferry for part of the day), had camped at Halltown, which is over forty miles distant from Strasburg. The next day (Saturday, May 31st) witnessed a race for Strasburg, which was in Jackson's direct line of retreat, but it was

very different in character from the race of the preceding Saturday.
Orders were issued for everything in the Confederate camp to move
early in the morning. The two thousand three hundred Federal
prisoners were first sent forward, guarded by the Twenty-first Virginia Regiment; next the long trains, including many captured
wagons loaded with stores; then followed the whole of the army
except the rear guard, under Winder.

Jackson reached Strasburg on Saturday afternoon without molestation and encamped, thus placing himself directly between the
two armies that were hastening to attack him. Here he remained
for twenty-four hours, holding his two opponents apart until Winder
could come up, and the last of the long train could be sent to the
rear. Winder, with the Stonewall Brigade, had marched thirty-five
miles on Saturday, and by Sunday noon had rejoined the main body.
Meantime, Shields and McDowell had been bewildered at Front
Royal by the celerity of Jackson's movements, and had spent Saturday in moving out first toward Winchester and then on other roads,
and finally in doing nothing. Fremont had stopped five miles short
of Strasburg, on Saturday night, and on Sunday was held in check
by Ashby, supported by part of Ewell's Division. On Sunday
McDowell, despairing of "heading off" Jackson, sent his cavalry to
unite with Fremont, at Strasburg, in pursuing the Confederates, and
dispatched Shields' Division up the Luray Valley, with the sanguine
hope that the latter might, by moving on the longer and worse road,
get in the rear of Jackson, who, with a day's start, was moving on
the shorter and better. On Friday morning Jackson was in front of
Harper's Ferry, fifty miles in advance of Strasburg; Fremont was
at Moorefield, thirty-eight miles from Strasburg, with his advance
ten miles on the way to the latter place; Shields was not more than
twenty miles from Strasburg (for his advance entered Front Royal,
which is but twelve miles distant, before midday on Friday), while
McDowell was following with another divison within supporting
distance. Yet by Sunday night Jackson had marched a distance of
between fifty and sixty miles, though encumbered with prisoners
and captured stores, had reached Strasburg before either of his
adversaries, and passed between their armies, while he held Fremont
at bay by a show of force, and blinded and bewildered McDowell by
the rapidity of his movements.

Now followed five days of masterly retreat. The failure of
McDowell to attack him at Strasburg caused Jackson to suspect the
movement of his forces up the Page or Luray Valley. McDowell
himself did not go beyond Front Royal, but sent Shields' Division to

follow Jackson. The road up the Page Valley runs along the east side of the main Shenandoah river, which was then impassible except at the bridges. Of these there were but three in the whole length of the Page Valley, two opposite New Market, but a few miles apart, and a third at Conrad's store, opposite Harrisonburg. Jackson promptly burned the first two, and thus left Shields entirely unable to harass his flank or impede his march. Having thus disposed of one of the pursuing armies, he fell back before Fremont by moderate stages, intrusting the protection of his rear to the indefatigable Ashby. As Fremont approached Harrisonburg, on the 6th of June, Jackson left it. Instead of taking the road via Conrad's store to Swift Run gap, as he had done when retreating before Banks, in April, he now took the road to Port Republic, where the branches of the main Shenandoah unite. He next sent a party to burn the bridge at Conrad's store, which afforded the last chance of a union of his adversaries short of Port Republic. The bridge at the latter place, together with a ford on the south, near the smaller of the tributaries which there form the Shenandoah, gave him the means of crossing from one side to the other, which, by the destruction of the other bridges, he had denied to his enemies.

And now came the crowning act of his compaign. When his enemies were already closing in on his rear with overwhelming force he had, with wonderful celerity, passed in safety between them. He had continued his retreat until they were now drawn one hundred miles from the Potomac. A large fraction of his pursuers had given up the chase, and were off his hands. Banks had only come as far as Winchester. Saxton, from Harper's Ferry, had only followed the rear guard under Winder for part of one day, and then went into camp "exhausted," as he states. McDowell, with two divisions, had remained at Front Royal when Shields moved toward Luray, the latter officer undertaking, with one of his divisions, to "clean out the Valley." Hence Jackson had now but Fremont's forces, about equal to his own in number, pressing on his rear, while Shields was making his toilsome way up the Page Valley, and was a day or two behind. By laying hold of the bridges he had placed an impassable barrier between his two pursuers, and now he occupied the point where their two routes converged. No further to the rear would the Shenandoah serve as a barrier to their junction, for south of Port Republic its headwaters are easily fordable. Here, too, was Brown's gap near at hand, an easily defended pass in the Blue ridge, and affording a good road out of the Valley in case of need. In this position Jackson determined to stand and fight his enemies in detail.

On Friday the footsore and weary Confederates went into camp at different points along the five miles of road that intervened between Port Royal and Cross Keys, the latter a point half way between the former village and Martinsburg. The skirmish on that day, in which Fremont's cavalry was severely punished, is memorable because in it fell Turner Ashby, the generous, the chivalric, the high-toned knight—who, as commander of his horse, had so faithfully and gloriously contributed to Jackson's achievements. The next day was given to rest, and sorrow for the loss of Ashby replaced all other feelings for the time. But brief the time for sorrow. War gives much space to the grand emotions that lead to heroic doing or heroic bearing, but is niggardly in its allowance to the softer feelings of sadness and grief. As Ashby is borne away to his burial, all thoughts turn (once more) to the impending strife. Fremont was advancing. He had been emboldened by the retreat of the Confederates, and failing to comprehend the object of Jackson's movements, pushed on to seize the prey which he deemed to be now within his grasp. His troops were all up by Saturday night, and his dispositions were made for attack on Sunday morning, June 8th. But, though Fremont was thus close at hand, while Shields, detained by bad roads with his main body, was yet twelve or fifteen miles off on the east side of the river, yet the opening of the battle on Sunday, June 8th, was made by a dash of Shields' cavalry, under Colonel Carroll, into Port Republic. They had been sent on a day's march in advance, and meeting but a small force of Confederate cavalry, had driven them pell-mell into Port Republic, dashed across South river after them, seized and, for a few minutes, held the bridge over the larger stream. Jackson had just passed through the village as they entered it. Riding rapidly to the nearest infantry regiment north of the bridge, he put himself at the head of it, quickly retook the bridge, captured two cannon, and drove these adventurous horsemen back. They retired two or three miles with their infantry supports, and, as the bluffs on the west side of the river commanded the roads along the east side, a battery or two kept them inactive for the remainder of the day. It was at this time that Shields, from Luray, was dispatching Fremont as follows:

June 8th—9.30 A. M.

I write by your scout. I think by this time there will be twelve pieces of artillery opposite Jackson's train at Port Republic, if he has taken that route. Some cavalry and artillery have pushed on to Waynesboro to burn the bridge. I hope to have two brigades at Port Republic to-day. I follow myself with two other brigades from this place. If the enemy changes direction you will please keep me advised. If he attempts to force a passage, as my force is not large there yet, I hope you will thunder down on his rear. Please send back information from time to time. I think Jackson is caught this time.

Yours, sincerely,
JAMES SHIELDS.

Meanwhile, Fremont had marshaled his brigades, and was pressing on in brilliant array to "thunder down" on his adversary's rear. To General Ewell and his division had Jackson assigned the duty of meeting the foe. His other troops were in the rear, and nearer Port Royal, to watch movements there and to assist General Ewell if necessary. Ewell was drawn up on a wooded ridge near Cross Keys, with an open meadow and rivulet in front. On a parallel ridge beyond the rivulet Fremont took position. The latter first moved forward his left, composed of Blenker's Germans, to the attack. They were met by General Trimble, one of Ewell's brigadier's, with three regiments of his brigade. He coolly withheld his fire until the Germans were close upon him. Then a few deadly volleys and the attack is broken, and the Federal left wing bloodily and decisively repulsed. That sturdy old soldier, General Trimble, having been reinforced, presses forward, dislodges the batteries in position in his front, and threatens the overthrow of Fremont's left wing. While this last is not accomplished, the handling Blenker has received is so rough as completely to paralyze the remainder of Fremont's operations. The attack on centre and right become little more than artillery combats, and by the middle of the afternoon Fremont withdraws his whole line. Ewell's force was about six thousand and his loss two hundred and eighty-seven; Fremont's force twice as great and his loss over six hundred and fifty.

About the time of Fremont's repulse, General Tyler, with one of Shields' infantry brigades, reached the position near Lewistown, to where Colonel Carroll and his cavalry had retired in the morning. But so strong was the position held by the Confederate batteries on the west bank of the river, that Tyler felt it impossible to make any diversion in favor of Fremont, and with his force of three thousand men remained idle.

Jackson, emboldened by the inactivity of Shields' advance, and the easy repulse of Fremont, conceived the audacious design of attacking his two opponents in succession the next day, with the hope of overwhelming them separately. For this purpose he directed that during the night a temporary bridge, composed simply of planks, laid upon the running gear of wagons, should be constructed over the South river, at Port Republic, and ordered Winder to move his brigade at dawn across both rivers and against Shields. Ewell was directed to leave Trimble's Brigade and part of Patton's to hold Fremont in check, and to move at an early hour to Port Royal to follow Winder. Taliaferro's Brigade was left in charge of the batteries along the river, and to protect Trimble's retreat if necessary. The force left in Fremont's front was directed to make all the show possible, and to delay the Federal advance to the extent of its power. The Confederate commander proposed, in case of an easy victory over Shields in the morning, to return to the Harrisonburg side of the river and attack Fremont in the afternoon. In case, however, of delay, and a vigorous advance on Fremont's part, Trimble was to retire by the bridge into Port Republic and burn it, to prevent his antagonist from following.

Jackson urged forward in person the construction of the foot bridge and the slow passage of his troops over the imperfect structure. When Winder's and Taylor's Brigades had crossed he would wait no longer, but moved forward toward the enemy, and when he found him, ordered Winder to attack. The Federal General Tyler had posted his force strongly on a line perpendicular to the river, his left especially in a commanding position and protected by dense woods. Winder attacked with vigor, but soon found the Federal position too strong to be carried by his brigade of twelve hundred men. Taylor went to his assistance, but met with a stubborn resistance and varying success. Winder was forced back until other troops came up and enabled him once more to go forward. Jackson, finding the resistance of the enemy so much more stubborn than he had expected, and that his first attack had failed, determined to concentrate his whole force and give up all intention of recrossing the river. He, therefore, sent orders to Trimble and Taliaferro to leave Fremont's front, move over the bridge, burn it, and join the main body of the army as speedily as possible. This was done. Before his rear guard had arrived, however, a renewed attack in overwhelming force on Tyler had carried his position, captured his battery, and compelled him to retreat in more or less disorder. The pursuit continued for eight miles; four hundred and fifty prisoners and six guns were captured, and two hundred and seventy-five wounded paroled in the hospitals near the field. I have seen no official statement of the Federal loss, but the above was, of course, the greater part of it. Jackson's total loss was eight hundred and seventy-six.

Fremont had advanced cautiously against Trimble in the forenoon, and had followed as the latter withdrew and burnt the bridge. By this last act Fremont was compelled to remain an inactive spectator of the defeat of Tyler. General Fremont thus describes the scene when he reached the river:

The battle which had taken place upon the further bank of the river was wholly at an end. A single brigade, in fact, two, sent forward by General Shields had been simply cut to pieces. Colonel Carroll had failed to burn the bridge. Jackson, hastening across, had fallen upon the inferior force, and the result was before us. Of the bridge nothing remained but the charred and smoking timbers. Beyond, at the edge of the woods, a body of the enemy's troops was in position, and a baggage train was disppearing in a pass among the hills. Parties gathering the dead and wounded, together with a line of prisoners awaiting the movement of the rebel force near by, was all, in respect to troops, of either side now to be seen.

Thus the day ended with the complete defeat of the two brigades under Tyler. Gallant and determined had been their resistance, and Jackson's impetuosity had made his victory more difficult than it otherwise would have been. In sending in Winder's Brigade before its supports arrived, he had hurled this body of troops against more than twice their number. Taylor next attacked, but the repulse of Winder enabled the Federal commander to concentrate his forces against Taylor, and drive him from the battery he had taken. It was then that Jackson renewed the attack with the combined forces of three brigades, and speedily forced the enemy from the field. The Confederate trains had been moved in the course of the day across South river toward Brown's gap, and during the afternoon and night the Confederates returned from the battle-field and pursuit, to camp at the foot of this mountain pass. It was midnight before some of them lay down in the rain to rest. This double victory ended the pursuit of Jackson. Fremont, on the next morning, began to retreat, and retired sixty miles to Strasburg. Shields, so soon as his broken brigades rejoined him, retreated to Front Royal, and was there transferred to Manassas.

The battles of Cross Keys and Port Republic closed the Valley campaign of 1862. Just three months had passed since Jackson, with about four thousand troops badly armed and equipped, had fallen back from Winchester before the advance of Banks, with twenty-five thousand men. So feeble seemed his force, and so powerless for offense, that when it had been pushed forty miles to the rear, Banks began to send his force toward Manassas to execute his part of "covering the Federal capital" in McClellan's great campaign. While a large part of the Federal troops is on the march out of the Valley, and their commander is himself *en route* from Winchester to Washington, Jackson, hastening from his resting place, by a forced march, appears most unexpectedly at Kernstown, and hurls his little army with incredible force and fury against the part of Banks' army which is yet behind. He is mistaken as to the number of the enemy. Three thousand men, worn by a forced march, are not able to defeat the seven thousand of Shields. After a fierce struggle he suffers a severe repulse, but he makes such an impression as to cause the recall of a strong force from McClellan to protect Washington. The Federal administration cannot believe that he has attacked Shields with a handful men.

Falling back before his pursuers, he leaves the main road at Harrisonburg and crossing over to Swift Run gap, he takes a position in which he cannot be readily attacked, and which yet enables him so to threaten the flank of his opponent as to effectually check his further progress. Here he gains ten days' time for the reorganization of his regiments, the time of service of most of which expired in April; and here, too, the return of furloughed men, and the accessions of volunteers, doubles his numbers. Finding that no more troops could be obtained besides those of Ewell and Edward Johnson, he leaves the former to hold Banks in check while he makes a rapid and circuitous march to General Edward Johnson's position, near Staunton. Uniting Johnson's force with his own, he appears suddenly in front of Milroy, at McDowell, only eight days after having left Swift Run gap. He has marched one hundred miles and crossed the Blue ridge twice in this time, and now repulses Milroy and Schenck, and follows them up to Franklin. Then, finding Fremont within supporting distance, he, on May 14th, begins to retrace his steps, marching through Harrisonburg, New Market, Luray, Ewell joining him on the road, and swelling his force to sixteen thousand men, and, on May 23d, unexpectedly appears at Front Royal (distant by his route nearly one hundred and twenty miles from Franklin), and surprises and completely overwhelms the force Banks has stationed there. Next day he strikes with damaging effect at Banks' retreating column, between Strasburg and Winchester, and follows him up all night. At dawn he attacks him on the heights of Winchester, forces him from his position, and drives him in confusion and dismay to the Potomac, with the loss of immense stores and a large number of prisoners. Resting but two days, he marches to Harper's Ferry, threatens an invasion of Maryland, and spreads such alarm as to paralyze the movement of McDowell's four thousand men at Fredericksburg, and to cause the concentration of half of this force, together with Fremont's command, on his rear. The militia of the adjoining States is called out; troops are hurried to Harper's Ferry in his front; more than forty thousand troops are hastening, under the most urgent telegrams, to close in around him. Keeping up his demonstrations until the last moment, until, indeed, the head of McDowell's column was but twelve or fourteen miles from his line of retreat, at a point nearly fifty miles in his rear, he, by a forced march of a day and a half, traverses this distance of fifty miles, and places himself at

Strasburg. Here he keeps Fremont at bay until his long train of prisoners and captured stores has passed through in safety, and his rear guard closed up. Then he falls back before Fremont, while by burning successively the bridges over the main fork of the Shenandoah, he destroys all co-operation between his pursuers. Having retreated as far as necessary, he turns off from Harrisonburg to Port Republic, seizes the only bridge left south of Front Royal over the Shenandoah, and takes a position which enables him to fight his adversaries in succession, while they cannot succor each other. Fremont first attacks, and is severely repulsed, and next morning Jackson, withdrawing suddenly from his front, and destroying the bridge to prevent his following, attacks the advance brigades of Shields, and completely defeats them, driving them eight or ten miles from the battle-field.

A week of rest, and Jackson, having disposed of his various enemies, and effected the permanent withdrawal of McDowell's Corps from the forces operating against Richmond, is again on the march, and while Banks, Fremont and McDowell are disposing their broken or baffled forces to cover Washington, is hastening to aid in the great series of battles which, during the last days of June and the early ones of July, resulted in the defeat of McClellan's army and the relief of the Confederate capital.

I have thus tried to give you, fellow soldiers of the Army of Northern Virginia, an outline of one of the most brilliant pages of our history. Time has not permitted me to dwell on the great deeds which crowded those few months, or to characterize, in fitting terms of panegyric, the mighty actors in them. I have attempted nothing beyond a simple and carefully accurate statement of the facts. This may help to clear away from one campaign the dust and mould which already gathers over the memories of the great struggle. It may do more. It may, by touching the electric chord of association, transport us for the time into the presence of the majestic dead, and of the mighty drama, the acting of which was like another and higher life, and the contemplation of which should tend to strengthen, elevate, ennoble. It is wise in our day—it is wise always—to recur to a time when patriotism was a passion; when devotion to great principles dwarfed all considerations other than those of truth and right; when duty was felt to be the sublimest word in our language; when sacrifice outweighed selfishness; when human virtue was equal to human calamity. Among the heroes of that time Jackson holds a high place—a worthy member of a worthy band—aye, of a band than which no land in any age can point to a worthier.

MORGAN'S INDIANA AND OHIO RAID.

BY COLONEL J. E. M'GOWAN.

THIS writing was suggested by the perusal of a sketch of the Morgan raid of 1863, by General Basil W. Duke, printed in the WEEKLY TIMES of April 7th, 1877. I have followed the thread of his narrative, when necessary to the continuity of my story, accepting, without question, his account of what his own forces did, and adding to its value by corroborating it when I could. I have corrected, where their historical importance seemed to demand it, his errors as to the numbers and movements of the forces which followed and captured Morgan's command. The summer of 1863 opened on a favorable outlook for the Federal forces in the departments south of the Ohio. They had been recruited from the "six hundred thousand more" who went afield in August and September, 1862. The new levies had been weeded of worthless material by a severe winter's work—guarding lines of communication, or facing the enemy under Grant, Burnside, or Rosecrans. Stone River, though a "drawn battle," resulted in a considerable balance to the credit of the "invader," who held the field, fortified it and kept his lines open by rail and wagon train to the Ohio river. These armies were, in short, on the 1st of June, 1863, strong in numbers, in vigorous health, full of confidence, thoroughly disciplined and splendidly equipped. Grant's Army of the Tennessee, and the Army of the Cumberland, had been reorganized into corps, and had become well used to that system. The scattered troops in Kentucky were being placed on the same basis by Burnside, who commanded the Department of the Ohio, with headquarters at Cincinnati. On the 10th of

June it was announced in general orders that the army of occupation in Kentucky had been consolidated, for active service, into the Twenty-third Army Corps, under command of Major General George L. Hartsuff. This corps numbered, of all arms, about twenty-four thousand men.

The army headquarters at Washington had planned to move these three forces as near simultaneously as possible, and by pressing the enemy heavily on all sides at once, prevent him from dividing any one of his defensive forces to reinforce another. Grant was already pushing Pemberton into his forts at Vicksburg. Burnside and Rosecrans were to move on parallel lines, the first toward Knoxville, the second toward Chattanooga. It was a most favorable moment to strike directly into the heart of the Confederacy. Bragg had weakened himself to strengthen Johnston in his vain endeavor first to prevent, and then to raise the siege of Vicksburg. Burnside and his troops concentrated near the Tennessee line. His cavalry was thrown well forward. He waited the signal from Murfreesboro to move southward in concert with Rosecrans. Buckner held East Tennessee feebly. It was one of those supreme opportunities that occur in all great wars, which, if siezed in a strong hand and wielded with vigor, can be so improved as to end the strife in one heavy, short, and sharp campaign. A competent military critic, looking at the situation from to-day, would probably conclude that, had these three armies been controlled by one master of right qualities, he would have brought the campaign to a glorious end by autumn, and brushed the Confederacy out of Tennessee, North Georgia, Alabama, and Mississippi, if indeed he had not so weakened it that the whole structure would have tumbled into ruin before the dawn of 1864. But we had no such man at the head of Southwestern military affairs. They were in the hands of three commanders, entirely independent of each other, and probably jealous of each other. These chiefs had no very high opinion of General Halleck, the nominal commander-in-chief at army headquarters, and this last sentiment of the generals was indulged in by all ranks in their several armies. It was a different task to disconcert plans made by or for the heads of armies thus situated from that which would have been necessary to break the back of one of Grant's campaigns a year later. He had ample authority, and the rugged will to enforce his orders. But speculate as we may about "what might have been," history will record the fact that the nicely fixed plan for a grand co-operative campaign of the three armies mentioned was completely balked, that one of them came to grief and well-nigh to destruction at Chickamauga, while another was bottled up in a half-starved state, and that Grant's forces alone achieved anything but disaster until they were placed under one head the following November. For this fortunate escape of the Confederacy from a stunning blow, that government was indebted, first, to the divided councils of their enemies, and, second, to General John H. Morgan's dash, enterprise, and courage.

About the middle of June, Morgan appeared in the Cumberland river valley, on the south bank, at the head of a picked division of cavalry and a battery, aggregating about two thousand five hundred men. He maneuvred, or rather marched along the river, up and down, now approaching the stream, and now disappearing in some back valley. The last week in June he kept out of sight of the river, and was so profoundly quiet that the Federal commanders, who had been watching him closely for ten days, concluded he had returned to Bragg's main column near Tullahoma. They were sure, then, that their first surmise, that he had come into the valley to recruit his stock on its fine pastures, was correct. All vigilance north of the river was slackened. Videttes along the bank were recalled and sent to their several commands. The cavalry, under Hobson and Woolford, was permitted to scatter about the country, the better to enable men and horses to be fed. The force nearest the river was at Tompkinsville, twenty miles from Burksville, the county town of Cumberland County, Kentucky, a few miles south of which Morgan lay, holding his command very still and watching a chance to make a crossing. He waited until the 2d of July. The river had been swollen of late by heavy rains. It was out of its banks, a broad, swift, muddy torrent, over which the Confederate chieftain put his command on rafts made of log canoes, overlaid with fence rails. It was one of the boldest undertakings of the war, and the skill with which it was executed was equaled by the pluck which conceived and carried it through. When Morgan had nearly finished his crossing, one of Hobson's regiments, by mere accident, ambled within reach of his strong outposts, a mile from the ferry, which provoked a lively skirmish, the Federals being soundly whipped. And now, when the raiders were at full speed on their northward journey, our commanders began to have an inkling that these fellows had come into the valley of the Cumberland for something else than grass.

On the evening of the 3d, the rebels struck Woolford, with the First Kentucky Cavalry, and scattered him to the right and left near the village of Columbia. On the 4th, they made an unsuccessful attempt to capture Colonel O. M. Moore, of the Twenty-fifth Michigan Infantry, and a small garrison of his regiment at Green river bridge. After losing more than one-fifth as many men as Moore had with him, Morgan called off his assaulting column and rode round the bridge, fording the stream below. On the 5th, the raiders took Lebanon by assault. The post was defended by the Twenty-first Kentucky Infantry, Colonel Hanson, who made a gallant resistance. In the final assault on this post, a younger brother of the Confederate general was killed. He was a favorite with his elder kinsman, who, in his wild wrath at the boy's death, for once forgot what was due to prisoners of war, and soiled his record by wreaking a mean revenge on the officers he had captured. He ordered Colonel Hanson and his officers to be "double-quicked" in front of a squadron of cavalry with drawn sabres six miles north of Lebanon to a village, where he directed them to be paroled. This brutal order was brutally executed. It is due Morgan's memory to say that the order was given under peculiar excitement, and that, though I served two years with troops which came in contact with him a score of times, the one just related is the only instance of Morgan's abuse of prisoners which ever came to my ears in such form as to justify belief in its truthfulness. On the evening of the 6th, the raiders crosssed the Louisville and Nashville Railway, near Shepherdsville, north of Lebanon Junction. They stopped a passenger train, went through the passengers and mails in free-and-easy style, and then having passed the last fortified post on their route northward, pushed for the Ohio. The force sent in advance to seize boats with which to cross into Indiana, secured two large steamers on the morning of the 8th, and when Morgan reached Brandenburg at noon these transports awaited him.

Meantime, the whole of Burnside's army had been recalled from its line in the south of Kentucky, and had been pushed rapidly toward the northern border. Every available trooper was put in pursuit. General H. M. Judah, commandant Third Division, Twenty-third Army Corps, heard of Morgan's crossing of the Cumberland in his tent, at Glasgow, late on the night of the 2d. With his staff and a small escort he hastily rode to within a few miles of Burksville that night. Judah and Hobson held a short council; the scattered cavalry was speedily concentrated, and Hobson took command of that portion which made the chase direct astern, and he gathered into his command all the loose cavalry on his route. Judah, with the Fifth Indiana, the Fourteenth Illinois, the Eleventh Kentucky, a section of Henshaw's Illinois Battery and a section of three-inch Rodmans, manned by troopers of the Fifth Indiana, set out on

48

an interior line of the arc on which Morgan moved. And though his force was delayed almost an entire day in effecting a crossing of Green river, which was swollen by late rains, it reached Elizabethtown, on the Louisville and Nashville Railroad, on the evening of the 7th—the day before Morgan got to Brandenburg. From Elizabethtown Judah marched west to Litchfield, a village on the "old Hartford" road, the only practicable route of escape for raiders if they failed to make a crossing at Brandenburg.

There is plenty of internal and external evidence to show that Burnside intended that Morgan should cross the river and run through Southern Indiana and Southern Ohio. The Federal general's plan had been all thrown away by the necessity to pursue the raiders, and protect his supplies and communications; and he very naturally might conclude that the best compensation for this sacrifice was to give the "Knights of the Golden Circle" of Indiana, and the Vallandighammers of Ohio, a touch of the quality of their Southern friends. To one who was in a position to know pretty well what was afoot at headquarters, it looked very much as if Burnside was first intent on inducing the Confederates to visit the Northern States, and, second, that, failing in this, he would not let them return South without a fight with forces sufficient to whip and break in pieces, if not capture, the command. All the Federal dispositions were, apparently, made with these two objects in view, and the troops and gunboats acted precisely as if they were carrying out the programme. It was, also, regarded that his invasion of the North rendered his capture morally certain.

I am of opinion that either orders were issued to the troops and gunboats not to prevent Morgan from entering Indiana, or that the commanders of both the naval and land forces manifested gross carelessness and want of enterprise at that point in the pursuit, neither of which characterized their operations at any other time from the 3d of July, when the chase began, to the 26th, when it closed. I think it is clear, from Duke's account of the crossing at Brandenburg, that the master of the gunboat "Elk" offered the rebels very "judicious" resistance. Duke says: "A single well-aimed shot from her would have sent either of the boats to the bottom, and caused the loss of every man on board." But it does not look as if Lieutenant Fitch, who commanded her, cared to do more than annoy and delay, withal hindering, Morgan's enterprise in beginning a campaign "on Yankee soil," thus giving Hobson and Judah advantages in the pursuit which rendered the final capture of the rebels more certain. But, whatever may have been the orders to the gunboats, I know that General Judah, on whose staff I was serving as provost marshal, could have reached Brandenburg nearly, if not quite, as soon as Morgan did. I am pretty clear that the Confederates, what with the "Elk" and her consort on the river, and fifteen hundred troopers and four field-pieces on land, to oppose them, would have had a very lively time in initiating their visit to the people of Southern Indiana. And whether or not, as Duke says, the gunboat "could have become mistress of the situation if well and boldly handled," she and her mate, had they been supplemented by our forces of "horse marines" on land, could, with such aid, have scattered the raiders in flying fragments, if the attack had been made when the crossing was partially done, or forced a precipitate retreat by striking before the ferrying begun. During the whole day in which Morgan was crossing the Ohio, Judah lay within six hours' march of him to the south. Whatever Burnside's intentions were in the premises, Morgan succeeded, during twelve hours of intense anxiety and hard work, in placing his force on the Indiana shore; and probably desiring to imitate, as near as he could with the appliances at hand, another celebrated invader, at midnight of the 8th the two large steamers which he used were set on fire, and, with full head of steam on, were sent down the stream. By this lurid light, seemingly kindled to wantonly intensify the wrath and increase the exertions of his foes, the invader began his perilous march on Northern ground.

On the morning of the 9th, Judah marched his force, with haste, back to Elizabethtown, where men and horses were loaded on trains and carried to Louisville. There the cars were exchanged for steamboats, and our column was all at the Cincinnati wharf on the morning of the 14th. We were fitted out with a fleet of steamers, and, leisurely waiting until Morgan passed the city, we started up the river, under orders to keep as near abreast of the enemy as practicable, and not to land until we were certain of reaching Buffington ford about the same time the raiders did. We steamed slowly up the Ohio, sending boats ashore from the headquarters' steamer every few hours to get reports of scouts and citizens on the movements and whereabouts of Morgan. We landed at Portsmouth on the evening of the 16th, and had some trouble in convincing the loyal people of that town that they ought, in consideration of liberal compensation in cash, to furnish us a sufficient train to carry our extra baggage and ammunition. A little coaxing, emphasized in special cases by resolute-looking fellows with drawn sabres, was successful. At nightfall I drove up in front of the shabby old hotel, for the general's inspection, a dozen wagons. With vigilant guarding, we kept them a couple of days, and found them a tolerably efficient transportation force, though the men, mostly owners of the teams and wagons they managed, were ten times as great cowards as the average army mule-driver—a statement some old soldiers will be inclined to question, as they will hardly believe in greater cowardice than that displayed by the noble corps of patriots referred to. We struck out over the knobs that night, in a northeasterly direction, in order to reach the old Pomeroy stage road in the morning at Portland, on the Sciota Valley Railroad, by the time Morgan should cross the road at Jackson, a few miles further north. We reached Portland at sunrise. Smoke was rising over Jackson, and we were not long in ascertaining that it proceeded from the depot, which some foolish vandals of Morgan's had fired, thus revealing his whereabouts to his pursuers more accurately than they could otherwise have ascertained it.

And now began, on the morning of July 17th, the most exciting part of this exciting expedition. The rebels knew we were neck and neck with them. They knew Hobson was pursuing them in the rear with the eagerness of a bloodhound. They knew their only chance of escape lay in reaching the fords some time in advance of both pursuers. They had the advantage of distance on Judah—the road they traveled being several miles shorter than his, which followed the bends of the river.

From the morning of the 17th, on to the final encounter, we were constantly within reach of and feeling Morgan's right flank and rear. John O'Neil, since of Fenian and Canadian border fame, then a lieutenant in the Fifth Indiana Cavalry, was intrusted with the task of harassing the raiders, and keeping the Federal commander informed of all the enemy's movements. O'Neil was an ideal Irish dragoon, impetuous, brave, prudent. He did some as effective scouting and skirmishing with his command of fifty picked men along the bluffs of the Ohio on the two last days of the great raid, as any officer did during the war. As the raiders advanced they were, beside being harassed by O'Neil, harried by citizen militia, who felled trees across the road to halt the column, and that done poured in deadly volleys from rifles and shot-guns from secure perches on the steep hillsides. The Confederate officers and men said the resistance and annoyance by militia on their march of over three hundred miles of northern territory was nowhere so stubborn and effective as on the last day, from near Pomeroy to their last encampment on the Ohio, between Buffington and Blennerhasset shoals, though a good deal in this line, attributed to the militia by Duke, was the work of O'Neil and his fifty troopers. In the rear of Pomeroy, O'Neil made a particularly spirited onset upon the Confederates, in which he was aided by a small squad of soldiers who were home on furlough, and happening to hear of Morgan's movements, armed with such weapons as were at hand, and went out to give him some trouble. In this affair several Confederates were wounded, as we learned next day, and at least two were killed.

We learned, while resting and feeding at Pomeroy, Saturday evening, that late rains in the mountains of Pennsylvania had swelled the Ohio, and rendered the fords at Blennerhasset and Buffington uncertain, and, for any but a person who knew them intimately, dangerous. The Confederates learned this, to their dismay, late that night or early next morning. They had a party of men inspecting the fords all night, and they reported that an attempt to cross would be attended with great hazard. Morgan seemed to agree with this conclusion for he went into camp late on the night of the 18th, about a mile and a half above Buffington, and as soon as they could see he set some men to work calking some old flatboats found near the island. Some of his men tried Blennerhasset, and failed to get across. Then a party was sent to dislodge a battery planted by some militia so as to command Buffington. They found the little redoubt deserted, and the guns were discovered at the foot of the river bank where the prudent garrison pitched them before retreating. Then a squadron tried Buffington ford, and several were drowned. Their guide, a former drover, who lived near by and was impressed into the service, told me the same day that he purposely misled the Confederates into a deep eddy. He said seventeen, with their horses, perished. Then a strong picket line, with a considerable reserve in support, the whole dismounted, was so stationed as to cover the ford, and the Confederates awaited results.

While the rebels were making ineffectual attempts to cross the river, Judah's column was marching in inky darkness from Pomeroy to Buffington. The road is as crooked as a ram's horn, and has innumerable roads and lanes leading from it at all sorts of appreciable and inappreciable angles. Those who made that march will not likely forget it while memory lasts them. At each of the by-roads it was necessary to station a sentry from the advance—Major Lyle's Battalion of the Fifth Indiana—the sentry being instructed to point the right road to the head of the column when it came up. Generally these sentries, two minutes after the officer gave them their orders, were fast asleep. Their horses would walk away in search of something to graze or browse. The officer at the head of the command, thus left to his own judgment, several times took the wrong road. The moment the men were halted the majority of them would lean forward on their horses' necks and fall dead asleep. The task of rousing them, turning about the artillery which was twice involved in these blunders, and getting back on the right track was not a pleasant one, especially when the troops were jammed into a lane barely wide enough to hold them, and the high fences on either hand reinforced by impenetrable hedges of briars and underbrush. An officer who could get from the foot to the head of such a solid column of stupid somnolency without blaspheming, must be a man of rare self-control. I remember to have had my boots, a new and stylish pair, ruined, and my spurs dragged off in such a tedious expedition, and when my work was accomplished I had worn out my sword, and trampled a half-dozen poor fellows half to death, whose tumble from their horses was not enough to wake them from their deep slumbers, and whom it was impossible for one to see at a few feet distant, so dense was the darkness. Finally the general, with a volley of profanity by way of special emphasis, ordered Lyle to place three men at every by-road, and to order those who remained awake to take those who fell asleep under guard to headquarters, where they were to be punished by some infliction just short of decapitation. But despite mishaps and delays we arrived, as day was dawning, Sunday morning, July 19th, on the top of a high bluff, a mile and a half from Buffington ford, the road ahead of us leading directly to that point. A dense fog hung over the river and its shores, which was all that prevented the hostile forces from having a full view of each other. The bottom of the river where our road crossed it is fully a mile wide, and tapers almost to a point a mile and a half above, where the road by which the rebels reached their position passes close to the water's edge, and under a steep, high bluff. The Confederates were stretched out along a range of low hills, their left resting near and so as to cover a retreat through this narrow passage. Our position was not more than three-fourths of a mile from Morgan's right, with some broken and low woods between.

The command had halted, the staff and escort were dismounted and waiting to hear from O'Neil, who was, as we supposed, feeling his way along the river bank in the fog, he having taken a road which lay close to the bank on the last ten miles of the march. While thus loitering and maledicting the fog, a staff officer approached, having in charge a colored man who was terribly frightened. He said he had just got away from the rebels. He told us where they were, when they got there, how their force were disposed, where their wagon train lay, what they had been about during the night. The general at once began a raking cross-examination of the frightened creature, and, as a natural consequence, the witness stumbled. At once he was called a liar, and his story set down as sheer romance and the result of fright. The general refused to listen further to the man's story, and declared the whole of it improbable, as he was certain Morgan must be near Blennerhasset, several miles above. Staff officers interposed in vain with the plea that the fellow's story was sustained by every reasonable probability. We were silenced with the sneering dictum that niggers were natural liars, and that no sane officer would believe one unless he knew of his own knowledge that the story was true. Some of us may have thought that General Judah should have known the truth of the man's story, but military discipline forbade us putting such thoughts into words. We were not long to remain ignorant of our enemy's whereabouts. Lieutenant Armstrong, of the Fourteenth Illinois Cavalry, was sent for. The general directed him to proceed with his company—forty-five men—toward the river. The lieutenant was not ordered to load his pieces, nor given the slightest hint to be prepared for a sudden meeting with the enemy. Behind Armstrong's company rode the general and staff, and behind them, and close upon their heels, was Captain Henshaw with a piece of artillery. The road, after we descended the hills, was a narrow lane bordered on each hand by wheat fields, in which the grain was standing in shocks. The fences, which were high, were not let down; no kind of precaution was taken against a surprise, though the fog was so dense the men could barely see from head to foot of the small company, and the advance, where it had moved the regulation distance ahead of the company, was lost to view in the white gloom. To round up and make complete in all its parts this splendid exhibition of tactical skill, our main body was left lying about loose and too far from the river to support us in any sudden emergency at that point, where one was likely to arise.

We had approached within six hundred yards of the ford when a gust of air, hot as the breath of an oven, come down the valley; the fog lifted with nearly as great celerity as a stage curtain can be run up. Our party had no time to "take in the beautiful scenery disclosed to our view," mostly because a strong skirmish line in gray jackets, on foot, and not more than a hundred yards to our left and front, was made visible to our eyes by the sudden letting in of sunlight on that particular spot. The fellows were not long in making themselves heard and felt. On the instant the two parties discovered each other, our force received a rattling volley from a hundred carbines. The effect of this on a trap in a narrow line, moving by the flank in fours, carbines carelessly dangling, may be imagined by those who have "been there." The first effect was a recoil; and when the rebels, reinforced by their reserves, dropped their carbines after the first shot and charged us on a run, firing their pistols and yelling like devils, the recoil degenerated into a scrambling, rushing, tumbling panic. The postillions on the lead horses of Henshaw's gun were killed by the first shot. The team to the gun and limber chest was hopelessly entangled in a moment, forming an ugly barricade in the lane behind the staff, escort, and Armstrong's company. It was a comical panic—as seen from a later hour, when our nerves and wrath had settled and cooled—to those of the staff who had persisted in saying to the general that we were going into a trap. We enjoyed seeing him "getting out," as he lay on the opposite side of his horse's neck from the direction in which the leaden compliments were coming —that is, we enjoyed looking back upon this scene and laughing at it. While it was being enacted, we were looking out each for himself, and striving to get out of what we considered a disgraceful dilemma.

The result of this short interview with the enemy was not calculated to flatter our vanity. We, the general included, had learned that it was not safe to disregard all precautions dictated by the rules of war and common sense and prudence, when we had such men as Morgan, Duke, and Johnson for enemies, however jaded and toilworn they and their men might be. We lost a half-dozen men killed and wounded. Captain R. C. Kise, Assistant Adjutant General, and Captain Henshaw, were captured; Lieutenant Fred W. Price, of the staff, was wounded, and our gun was carried off by the rebel skirmishers. And beside, and worse than all, we had made ourselves utterly ridiculous and lost immensely on our stock of pride and self-respect. By the time this affair, which did not occupy more than twenty minutes, was over, the fog had entirely disappeared, and Morgan's lines were within easy view of our forces on the hill.

"Business" was now the order. The Fifth Indiana, Colonel Butler, was ordered to move down the road from which all had just been stampeded. Throwing out a strong line of skirmishers, dismounted, the regiment advanced briskly, forming a line as soon as the ground would permit. The Fourteenth Illinois followed close in the rear as a reserve. The Eleventh Kentucky made a detour to the right, and swung around to form on Butler's right. When this movement was well under way, I heard, as I rode in advance of the left of the Fifth, a rattling skirmish fire, and looking in the direction of the river, I saw O'Neil, at the head of his company, dashing over fences and ditches, and driving the enemy's guard from the ford pell-mell. The sight was inspiriting in the extreme. The entire line, which was by this time fully formed, dashed ahead and drove the enemy's advance back to his main force. In this dash two of Morgan's guns were captured and the one his men had taken from us was recaptured. Our four pieces were in position, and in less than five minutes after the first shot was fired we were engaging the enemy all along his line, and our guns were pouring into his left and centre a storm of case shot at a range of less than a half mile. We steadily pressed upon the rebels, crowding them back toward the point where the river road runs over a narrow strip and close to the bluff. A small force could hold that pass against a much larger one. We hoped Hobson was on the river road above, and that he, or the gunboat "Elk," which was steaming up the stream and pitching schrapnel into the Confederates, would be able to head them off and turn them back upon us. The fight was spirited and lasted about one hour. The enemy was nearly out of ammunition. No men could have behaved better than they did in their circumstances.

About 9.30 Hobson's battery opened on the Confederate rear-guard beyond the hills, and then the break began. Morgan, at the head of a portion of his command, rode through the narrow pass near the river, and made his way to Blennerhasset shoal. He crossed the river, being well mounted, and several men followed him. He had not more than reached the Virginia shore whon the "Elk" rounded a bend in the river and opened on those who were trying to follow their leader. Morgan rode back to the Ohio side under fire of the boat's bow gun and rejoined his comrades. On that Sunday forenoon about one thousand of the raiders were captured, with the entire wagon train and a battery of four 10-pounder Parrott guns. That train was probably the most unique collection of vehicles ever assembled for the transport of military supplies and baggage. It contained every sort of four-wheeled concern; old, lumbering omnibuses, a monstrous two-story pedler's wagon, a dozen or more hackney coaches used as ambulances, a number of barouches, top buggies and open buggies, and several ordinary express wagons and farm wagons. And the loads most of them contained were as little suggestive of military service as the wagons. If there was ever a thing in the dry goods, grocery, drug, confectionery, or fancy goods line not to be found in those carriages, my memory failed to suggest the missing article when I passed the train under an official inspection. Boots and shoes for men and women and children were everywhere. One barouche, in which a citizen who had been impressed as a guide, told me Morgan rode all night and all the day before, had a pair of ladies' fine kid boots suspended by their tiny silk lacings from one of the posts which supported the top. The field where was the first rebel line of battle, and the ground just in rear of it, showed equally with the train the ability of Morgan's command as "foragers." The camp was on a series of low ridges, and the battle-field was thickly studed with shocks of wheat, and both were literally strewn with every imaginable article of men's and women's wear. I was with the skirmish line which first advanced into this field, where the enemy had lightened themselves by abandoning most of their plunder, and well remember a tall trooper's unsoldierly performance in running his sabre through a bolt of calico which some Confederate had pitched into a wheat shock, and then cantering ahead with the line, while the gaudy-colored print streamed along the ground and flapped over obstacles many yards in his rear. A good many of our men's homes lay along the rebel line of march in Indiana and Ohio, and the sights I have described did not impress them with a solemn belief that the citizens of the Confederacy were the only people who had a right to apply the epithet "vandal" to their enemies.

The troops which captured a fraction of Morgan's command at Buffington, were those which had pursued him from Kentucky. As there had been no company reports possible from the 3d of July, it is not possible to more than approximate the number Judah and Hobson commanded that day. The two never had more than five thousand with them at any point of the chase. To estimate their losses by sickness and other causes, during those seventeen days, would be putting it within the truth. Their joint forces were about double Morgan's in this final struggle, not more. When Morgan returned to the hostile Ohio shore he gathered a few hundred of his men about him, hoping, probably, to make them a reorganizing nucleus for his little army. He struck out toward the interior, making a considerable detour to avoid Hobson's lines. But if he expected to be reinforced by the balance of his command, he was disappointed. Those he left behind were entirely surrounded, and out of ammunition. The fords were in the hands of the Federal forces, and all hope of final escape was gone. The officers wisely surrendered and made an end of their hardships. Morgan continued his flight until he was literally run down, as a fox is run down by hounds, and captured near Salinesville, a village in the southern part of Columbiana county, on the 26th. The force which pursued him from Buffington was a semi-brigade under Colonel B. H. Bristow, of the Eighth Kentucky Cavalry, an officer noted for his indomitable grip, and regarded as the most relentless and persistent pursuer in all our forces. He did not, as Duke says, "surround" Morgan, in the usual accepted meaning of that term among soldiers. He rode onto him—tread off his tail and rear, as it were—and finally rode over and through him, scattered his men right and left, and, turning about, faced the flying raiders and forced them to halt and succomb.

Thus ended the boldest, the only really successful raid of the war on either side. The capture and destruction of Morgan's command were trifling losses to the Confederacy compared to advantages it gained by his operations. He destroyed no supplies; hardly touched, let alone injured, our lines of communication; captured nothing of any moment to him or anybody, save some forage, food, a miscellaneous collection of merchandise, and a comical wagon train. But he delayed the invasion of East Tennessee three months. He thus broke the plan of co-operation, and delayed Rosecrans at Murfreesboro, giving Bragg time to get back the men he had loaned Johnston. Instead of a strong joint movement, Burnside and Rosecrans found all they could attend to as each approached his objective. The latter was so late in pressing his enemy into decisive action that that enemy had time to obtain reinforcements from Lee and Chattanooga; and instead of being a base from which the Federal army dictated terms to a quarter of the Confederate territory, came near being that army's' coffin. Had Morgan been readily beaten back from Kentucky in a crippled condition, Burnside would have met Rosecrans at Chattanooga by the 20th of July; the battle of Chickamauga would not have been fought; the war would have been abbreviated, how much?

General Duke treats Judah and Burnside as separate, independent commanders. He says: "Burnside was "—in June, 1863—"concentrating in Kentucky a force for the invasion of Tennessee, variously estimated at from twenty to more than thirty thousand men." Further on, he says: "It was estimated that on the Kentucky and Tennessee border there were at least ten or twelve thousand Federal troops under command of General Judah—five thousand of which were excellent cavalry." Again: "Bragg's chief object was to delay Judah *and* Burnside—the latter especially—to retard *their* advance and junction with Rosecrans," etc. Very little research would have enabled the general to present the real relation between these officers, and the truth, as to the troops they commanded, is surely not difficult to come at. Judah was a subordinate

of Burnside's, being lowest in rank of all the brigadiers in the
department. He commanded a division in the Twenty-third Army
Corps, which corps and "Burnside's force" for active field duty
were at that time identical. He was not only a subordinate, but out
of favor at headquarters, and was given a meaner and less important
part to play in the pursuit of Morgan than any officer of his rank.
In the invasion of East Tennessee, which began some time after the
destruction of Morgan's force, General Judah was denied any post—
being sent into retirement by Burnside on account of what his
superiors considered his blunders on the Morgan campaign. The
"ten or twelve thousand troops on the Tennessee border under
Judah" consisted solely of his dvision, made up of three brigades—
two of infantry and one of cavalry, and two batteries. He had less
than six thousand men for duty when Morgan crossed the Cumberland. General Duke says:

> At Pomeroy, where we approached the river again, a large force of regular
> troops appeared, but, although our passage by the place was one sharp, continuous
> skirmish, we prevented them from gaining a position that would have forced us
> into decisive combat. * * * General Morgan knew that he would be attacked
> on the following day. He at once, and correctly, conjectured that the troops which
> had been at Pomeroy were a portion of the infantry which had been sent from
> Kentucky to intercept us, and that they had been brought by the river from Cin-
> cinnati to Pomeroy.

Judah's command arrived at Pomeroy about the middle of the
afternoon of that day. There was not an infantry soldier in the
town from the time we got there until we left. We went into the
town slightly ahead of Morgan's advance. By order of the general,
I purchased forage for our horses of Hon. V. B. Horton. The
command lay and rested and fed until nearly night. The "sharp,
continuous skirmish," mentioned by Duke, was with O'Neil's squad
of fifty men and a few soldiers, not more than a score, who happened
to be home on furlough. I was with O'Neil a part of the evening,
and am not surprised that General Duke thought, at the time, that
he was "a host," for he certainly made the most possible, both of
show and noise, out of his limited force. But I am surprised that
the general should set down such an error of fact as veritable
history. It is not to be wondered at that General Morgan should
have fallen into the error of "conjecturing" that a large infantry
force had been sent by river from Cincinnati to intercept him, first
at Pomeroy, and, failing there, higher up; but General Morgan's
historian should not set down "conjectures" unless they are borne
out by the facts. Morgan's men were so worn down that they could

not do very effective scouting, hence his information as to our forces and movements was limited, and, it also seems, erroneous.

General Duke's error regarding the number and character of our forces at Pomeroy on the 18th, is duplicated in some particulars, and thrown into the shade in others, by his curious account of the affair near Buffington ford on the 19th. Telling what happened after our advance was stampeded, the General says: "The Federal infantry, eight or ten thousand strong, instantly deployed and advanced, flanked by three regiments of cavalry. Two pieces of our battery were taken at the first onset. * * * Upon the level and unsheltered surface of this river bottom we were exposed to a tremendous direct and cross-fire from twelve or thirteen thousand small-arms, and fifteen pieces of artillery." I was in the whole affair, from first to last, only ceasing my active work in the field when night came on, and I was ordered to find guards for a large number of prisoners. I was in the little tilt which resulted in capturing two of the Confederate, and recapturing our cannon. I was from end to end, and through and through Judah's lines all that forenoon, and fell in with Hobson's forces about one P. M. If there was a single infantry soldier engaged I failed to see him. I was utterly unable to procure an infantry guard for my prisoners that night—though "by order of the general commanding" I had plenary power—and I had to put my jaded cavalry provost guard on duty. The next day I had to put up with a squad of Cincinnati militia—who arrived on the 20th—as guards for a large party of Confederate officers. They turned out to be a first-rate set of men for the duty, being all ex-soldiers who had been discharged on account of wounds and sickness. We had four pieces of artillery. The gunboat "Elk" carried five, three of which she could bring to bear on the enemy's lines. Neither we nor the "Elk" fired a cannon after Hobson attacked. All of that infantry and several of these cannon were in General Duke's eye. None of our regular infantry came above Cincinnati, and the few militia who found their way so far as Buffington arrived the day after the fight and capture.

General Duke puts the force at Green river bridge—which his forces failed to capture—at six hundred. There were just one hundred and sixty men reported for duty to Colonel Moore that morning by his post adjutant. They were behind a hastily-constructed, but strong, parapet, in front of which they had made an ugly abattis, by cutting down trees. Artillery could not be brought to bear on Moore's position, and Colonel Johnson, who was ordered by Morgan to take it by storm, could only charge in a narrow front through several hundred yards of the abattis on horseback, as to dismount and lay siege would take too much time. After a few foolhardy attempts, and the loss of thirty or more men killed, the Confederates left Moore to celebrate the balance of the 4th of July in more peaceful style. It may be humiliating to Morgan's chief officers to admit that a paltry squad repulsed repeatedly, with heavy loss, their crack brigade; but history is not a record of the historian's feelings, nor is it such incidents as glory a party, or faction, or people. It is a cold-blooded truth, and the whole truth, or of no value. With the exceptions here noted, General Duke's account of the raid is a very correct one. He is particularly felicitous in pointing out the success of Morgan's strategy at and previous to his crossing the Cumberland. Had he been in our camps, and an habitue of our headquarters, he could not have more effectually set forth the completeness of the deception of our generals as to the movements and intentions of their enemy. And this capacity to deal in facts, and this ability to correctly conjecture what passes in the mind of an enemy with only his minor acts for a basis, makes blundering inexcusable in matters which are either of record or easily verified as to all their details by living witnesses.

Colonel R. A. Alston, chief of Morgan's staff, was captured on the evening of the 5th of July, on the road from Lebanon to Bardstown, together with an escort of twenty men, by Lieutenant Ladd, of the Ninth Michigan Cavalry, and seven men. Alston and his escort were riding some distance in Morgan's rear. Ladd, who was scouting, came upon them just after dark. He concealed himself in the bushes at the roadside, and, by various devices, completely fooled the Confederates as to the size of his force until he had them disarmed. Alston, who was a brave officer, was terribly chagrined, but, on his word of honor, he took his men to Lexington, the nearest military post, and surrendered the next day.

Major Dan McCook, paymaster, a gentleman probably sixty-five years old, but hale and much younger in appearance, accompanied General Judah from Cincinnati as a "volunteer aid." Major McCook was the father of the celebrated family of generals and colonels, the two most noted of whom were Major General A. McDowell McCook and Brigadier General Robert L. McCook. Robert was killed in the fall of 1862, in Southern Tennessee, while riding ahead of his command in an ambulance. He was quite ill at the time, had turned the active direction of the march over to the senior colonel, and was riding in advance to keep out of the dust and noise of the column. Under these circumstances his ambulance was attacked by a scouting party under a Captain Gurley, of the Confederate cavalry. He refused to surrender; a fight ensued, and General McCook was killed. It was charged and believed among our forces that Gurley was a "bushwhacker" after the pattern of Champ Ferguson and Gatewood. The old gentleman had heard that the slayer of his son was with Morgan, and his object in accompanying the pursuing column was to find and punish him for the deed, and he had no doubt of succeeding in his undertaking. He was constantly pushing himself into the most dangerous places. He was with our skirmishers back of Pomeroy, on the 18th, and gave the officers a good deal of trouble to keep him from uselessly exposing himself to danger, and, at the same time, betraying the weakness of our line to the enemy.

On the morning of the 19th, the Major insisted on going with the vidette in front of Lieutenant Armstrong's company. I advised him not to go, and other officers pointed out to him the fact that he did not know Gurley, and that no one in our command had any personal knowledge of him. At a bright rill of water, which runs through a dent in the river-bottom, a mile from Buffington ford, the staff halted to let their horses drink, and give the advance party time to ride ahead. When the vidette rode up the bank of the creek the old Major joined it, his eye flashing and his cheeks flushed with excitement. In return of our remonstrances, he swept a mock salute, and dashed out of sight into the fog, his fine sorrel charger seeming to partake of the spirit of his master. The little party he was with rode almost into the Confederate skirmish line before either saw the other. He and one soldier of the vidette were killed at the first fire. Major McCook's body was pierced by three balls. His horse, watch, and Henry rifle fell into the hands of the enemy.

I should, probably, add here that Captain Gurley was captured with others of Morgan's forces; that he was taken to Nashville, tried by military commission for the murder of General McCook; that he admitted the killing by his men; that he proved himself a regularly commissioned officer of the Confederate Government; that the court which tried him decided that the killing was a legitimate act of war; that the decision was confirmed by President Lincoln, and that Gurley then became an ordinary prisoner of war, and was exchanged with the others.

On board the steamer that carried General Judah and staff from Buffington to Cincinnati were one hundred and thirteen Confederate officers. Among these was one whom I have cause to remember, though his name has faded from my memory. How or where he got them I never cared to inquire, but he was dressed in a dainty, neat-fitting suit of black broadcloth, with silk tie and patent-leather boots to match. His face was fitted up with a rather thin aquiline nose, a firm mouth, kept resolutely closed, and a pair of keen black eyes. Under his hat was a symmetrical head, adorned with a heavy suit of black, slightly curly, hair. He wore a full beard, which was long, black, and very curly. He was decidedly a "sharp"-appearing fellow, and, withal, not bad-looking, and of both these facts he seemed to have full knowledge. Something in his bearing told us he intended to give us the slip, and all watched him intently. When the boat neared Cincinnati, a patrol was sent below with orders to clear the main deck of prisoners—sending them above. This done, guards were stationed on the stairs, with orders not to allow any one to pass up or down except by permission of the officer of the day. We landed at the foot of Broadway, and there was a great crowd on the wharf. My handsome captain had, somehow, eluded the guard sent to clear the main deck. He took advantage of the commotion among the mob on shore to step down the stage-plank while some of our officers were mounting their horses. He said to the officer in charge of the guard, which was standing with ranks open to receive the prisoners, that he was an officer of the boat. Naturally, he was believed. Slipping through the rank on his right, he mingled with the crowd at once, and made his way to and round the railway offices on the corner of Front and Broadway. He entered the first barber's shop he came to, had his hair trimmed close, his beard cut down to an inch in length, and shaved into a "Burnside"— a fashionable cut among the "nobs" at that time. This done, he stepped into a clothing store, secured a wide-brimmed straw and a long linen duster, ordering his silk tile to be sent to the Spencer House, whither he repaired, and, secure in his disguise, drank and chatted with our officers until evening, when he took the mail boat for Louisville. At Louisville he "had a good time," after which he left, mounted on a fresh horse, for Bragg's army. Whether he ever reached his destination or not I do not know. I gather all the facts related in this incident, after he left the boat, from a letter the captain had printed in the Louisville papers on the eve of leaving on his southward journey. He wound up with a graceful tender of thanks to Captain D. W. H. Day, and others of the staff, for their kind treatment; regretted that he had to leave us in unceremonious style; was sorry we could not have made the "grand round" of Louisville with him; but, really, his engagements called him South, and we must excuse him—we must, indeed. We read his good-natured banter with a laugh, and said he deserved his good luck.

My knowledge of Hobson's movements is limited, but it was not a very eventful ride his command had. In fact, they never once touched the enemy until after Judah attacked him at Buffington, and then the stern-chasers did their whole duty, not only taking most of the raiders captured round Buffington, but following those who got off with Morgan, and, finally, making a clean sweep of the fleeing remnant. The endurance displayed by that part of Morgan's command which was last captured, and by their captors, has few precedents in modern warfare. They were in the saddle almost day and night for twenty-four days, and no one, except those who have experience of it, knows how terribly wearing such work and such nervous straining is.

THE BURNING OF CHAMBERSBURG.

BY GENERAL JOHN M'CAUSLAND.

THE wanton destruction of the private property of citizens of Virginia, by the orders of General Hunter, a Federal commander, may be considered as one of the strongest reasons for the retaliation, by Early's order, upon the city of Chambersburg. Andrew Hunter lived in the county of Jefferson, near Harper's Ferry, and was a relative of General Hunter; A. R. Boteler and E. J. Lee also lived in the same vicinity. No reasons that I have ever heard have been given for the burning of their houses. Governor Letcher's property was in Lexington, Virginia; the Military Institute was near Lexington, also. I do not think that any better reasons can be given for the destruction of these properties than could have been given if General Hunter had destroyed every house, barn, or other building, that was standing and in good order, upon his line of march from Staunton to Lynchburg. The property of J. T. Anderson was in the county of Botetourt, and located near the banks of James river, at Buchanan. Mrs. Anderson and a lady relative were the only occupants at the time. I destroyed the bridge across James river to retard Hunter in his march upon Lynchburg, and it detained him with his army for two days, during which time he occupied this house as his headquarters. He promised the ladies protection, and after his departure, an officer and some soldiers returned with a written order from him to destroy everything about the premises. A few days afterward, as General Hunter was passing another Virginia mansion, a lady asked him why he destroyed the magnificent home of Colonel Anderson. He replied, "that Virginia women were worse traitors than their husbands, and he would burn the houses over their heads to make them personally and immediately experience some punishment for their treason;" and on another occasion said to a lady, that he would "humble the Virginia women before he left the State." I could enumerate many other acts of actual destruction, and threats and acts of wanton violence on the part of Hunter, all of which went to make up public sentiment that prevailed at the time in Virginia, and which required the military authorities to take some steps to prevent their recurrence in future, besides stopping the useless destruction that was then going on. But what I have given is considered sufficient to explain the reasons why the city of Chambersburg, in Pennsylvania, was destroyed.

It may be considered as indispensable to give the location of the forces composing the Union and Confederate armies during the latter part of the month of July, 1864, in order to properly under-stand the raid that was made into the State of Pennsylvania, and which resulted in the destruction of Chambersburg. Hunter's army (Union) was scattered along the northern bank of the Potomac river, in Maryland, from near Hancock to Harper's Ferry, the main body being near the latter place. Early's army (Confederate) was located on the opposite side of the same river with its main body near Mar-tinsburg. Each army had its cavalry on the flanks. My command was on the left of Early's army, and I think that Averill's cavalry was located opposite to me—at least a portion of it was there. When I speak of cavalry, in the course of this sketch, I am aware that the term is not properly applied; and, as far as the Confederate troops which I commanded were concerned, they were badly armed, badly mounted, and worse equipped—in fact, they were mostly mounted militia. The men would have made good soldiers if there had been time to discipline them, and arms and equipments to have furnished them. The horses were nearly all worn out, and there was no supply to draw others from. We attempted to get horses in Pennsylvania, but found them removed from the line of march, and we had no time to look for them elsewhere.

In July, 1864, the cavalry brigade which I commanded was encamped near the Potomac river, in the county of Berkeley, West Virginia. It made the advance post of the army under General Early, that was guarding the approaches into Virginia through the Shenandoah Valley. On the 28th of July, I received an order from General Early to cross the Potomac with my brigade and one under General Bradley T. Johnston, and proceed to the city of Chambers-burg, and after capturing it to deliver, to the proper authorities, a proclamation which he had issued, calling upon them to furnish me with one hundred thousand dollars in gold, or five hundred thousand dollars in greenbacks, and in case the money was not furnished I was ordered to burn the city and return to Virginia. The proclamation also stated that this course had been adopted in retaliation for the destruction of property in Virginia, by the orders of General Hunter, and specified that the houses of Andrew Hunter, A. R. Boteler, E. J. Lee, Governor Letcher, J. T. Anderson, the Virginia Military Institute, and others in Virginia, had been burned by the orders of General D. Hunter, a Federal commander, and that the money demanded from Chambersburg was to be paid to these parties as a compensation for their property. It appears that the policy of General Early had been adopted upon proper reflection; that his orders were distinct and final, and that what was done on this occasion by my command was not the result of inconsiderate action or want of proper authority, as was alleged by many parties at the North, both at the time and since the close of the war.

On the 29th of July, the two cavalry brigades that were to make the dash into Pennsylvania, by turning the right of Hunter's army, were assembled at or near Hammond's mill, in Berkeley county, West Virginia. During the night the Federal pickets on the northern side of the Potomac were captured, and the troops crossed just at daylight on the morning of the 30th, and moved out and formed the line of march on the National road. Major Gilmer drove the Federal cavalry from the small village of Clear Spring, and pushed on toward Hagerstown to create the impression that the rest of the troops were following. At Clear Spring we left the National road and turned north on the Mercersburg road. We reached Mercersburg about dark, and stopped to feed our horses, and to give time for the stragglers to come up. After this stop the march was continued all night, notwithstanding the opposition made at every available point by a regiment of Federal cavalry. Major Sweeney, with his cavalry battalion, kept the roads clear, and we reached Chambersburg at daylight on the 31st. The approach to the town was defended only by one piece of artillery and some irregular troops that were soon driven off, and the advance of our force took possession of the town. The main part of the two brigades was formed in line on the high ground overlooking the town. I at once went into the place with my staff, and requested some of the citizens to inform the city authorities that I wanted to see them. I also sent my staff through the town to find out where the proper officials were, and inform them that I had a proclamation for their consideration. Not one could be found. I then directed the proclamation to be read to many of the citizens that were near me, and requested them to hunt up their officers, informing them I would wait until they could either find them, or by consultation among themselves determine what they would do. Finally, I informed them that I would wait six hours, and if they would comply with the requisition their town would be safe; and in case they did not it would be destroyed in accordance with my orders from General Early. After a few hours of delay many citizens came to me—some were willing to pay the money, others were not. I urged them to comply with such reasons as occurred to me at the time, and told them plainly what they might expect. I showed to my own officers the written instructions of General Early, and before a single house was destroyed both the citizens and the Confederate officers that were present fully understood why it was done, and by whose orders. After waiting until the expiration of the six hours, and finding that the proclamation would not be complied with, the destruction of the town was begun by firing the most central blocks first, and after the inhabitants had been removed from them. Thus the town was destroyed, and the inhabitants driven to the hills and fields adjacent thereto. No lives were lost by the citizens, and only one soldier was killed, and he was killed after the troops left the vicinity of the place. About noon the troops were re-formed on the high ground overlooking the town, where the most of them had been posted in the early morning, and the return to the Potomac was begun shortly afterward. We encamped at McConnelsburg that night, and reached the river the next day, at or near Hancock, Maryland.

In confirmation of what I have written Major Gilmer says in his book, "Four Years in the Saddle," page 210: "He showed me General Early s order." General Early, in his "Memoir," page 57, says: "A written demand was sent to the municipal authorities, and they were informed what would be the result of a failure or refusal to comply with it." On page 59 he says: "On the 30th of July, McCausland reached Chambersburg, and made the demand as directed, reading to such of the authorities as presented themselves the paper sent by me." Colonel W. E. Peters, who commanded one of the regiments in Johnston's Brigade, when the burning commenced came and asked me if the burning was being done by my orders. I showed him the order of General Early, and he was satisfied, and proceeded to carry out the order as was being done by other regiments of his brigade. In this expedition the troops passed through more than one hundred miles of hostile territory, executed all orders that were issued with promptness and regularity, and never have I heard of any complaints of acts unauthorized by their superior officers. I think that these facts will show that this entire expedition was planned and executed in accordance with the orders of superior officers of competent authority to order it, and, moreover, that it was an act of retaliation perfectly justified by the circumstances, and was at all times kept clearly within the rule governing civilized warfare.

Vattel in his " Law of Nations," lays down the following rule, and it may not be inappropriate to quote it in order that many persons, who may read what is said about the destruction of Chambersburg, may have the opinion of a standard authority upon such proceedings :

A civil war breaks the bonds of society and governments, or at least suspends their force and effect. It produces in the nation two independent parties who consider each other as enemies, and acknowledge no common judge. Those two parties, therefore, must necessarily be considered as thenceforward constituting, at least for a time, two separate bodies, two distinct societies. Though one of the parties may have been to blame in breaking the unity of the State, and resisting the lawful authority, they are not the less divided in fact. Besides, who shall judge them? Who shall pronounce on which side the right or the wrong lies? On earth they have no common superior. They stand, therefore, in precisely the same predicament as two nations who engage in a contest, and being unable to come to an agreement, have recourse to arms. This being the case, it is evident that the common laws of war—those maxims of humanity, moderation and honor commonly observed—ought to be observed by both parties in every civil war. For the same reasons which render the observance of those maxims a matter of obligation between State and State, it becomes equally and even more necessary in the unhappy circumstances of the two incensed parties lacerating their common country. Should the sovereign conceive he has a right to hang up his prisoners as rebels, the opposite party will make refusals; or, to destroy their country, they will retaliate. The Duke of Alva made it a practice to condemn to death every prisoner he took from the Confederates in the Netherlands. They, on their part, retaliated, and at length compelled him to respect the law of nations and the rules of war in his conduct toward them.

The above the rule and example of nations, and applying it to this case, I think that any one can understand it.

THE BALTIMORE RIOTS.

BY FREDERIC EMORY.

The Baltimore riots of April 18th and 19th, 1861, and the disorders which followed them were, next to the conflict at Fort Sumter, the most exciting and significant of the events which preceded the general outbreak of hostilities between the North and the South. President Lincoln and his Cabinet were seriously inconvenienced, the North was aroused, the leaders of the new Confederacy were led to entertain hopes of valuable assistance from the Border States, and a formidable obstacle was interposed to the active prosecution of those military measures which the government at Washington had decided upon. The attack upon the Massachusetts troops was, in another sense, one of the most remarkable events of the civil war; for, unlike similar disturbances elsewhere, it was largely participated in by the friends of order and the enemies of secession. Parodoxical as the statement may appear, the riots of April, 1861, were the work mainly of the strong Union element in Baltimore. The sentiment of the best men of the city was overwhelmingly opposed to secession; but, on the other hand, it was just as strenuously opposed to coercion. The people of Baltimore loved the old flag; but they loved their brethren of the South, also; and, when it was proposed to whip them back into the Union, even the most ultra anti-secessionists were roused into angry opposition to the passage of Northern troops southward.

It is easy to prove by actual occurrences in this city at the time that the feeling here was, as I have said, overwhelmingly against secession. On the 10th of January, 1861, in answer to a call published in the newspapers, a mass meeting was held at the Maryland Institute for the adoption of measures favorable to the perpetuation of the Union of the States. This. meeting was one of the largest and most enthusiastic which had ever been held in the city. Every available spot was occupied, and the officers and speakers comprised some of the best citizens of Baltimore, among them Reverdy Johnson, Governor Bradford, and Judge Pearre. Subsequently, another mass meeting was held of citizens in favor of restoring the constitutional union of the States, in which the Hon. R. M. McLane, Mr. S. Teackle Wallis, Hon. Joshua Vansant, Dr. A. C. Robinson, and other well-known Southern sympathizers took an active part. Even as late as April 12th, when the siege of Fort Sumter had begun, and only one week before the riot, two men were assaulted and mobbed, one on Baltimore, the other on South street, *for wearing a Southern cockade.* On Sunday, April 14th, five days only before the riot, a secession flag was displayed from the mast of the Fanny Crenshaw lying at Chase's wharf, but was hauled down by a party of men from the city, who boarded the vessel. The flag was run up again, however, but the vessel had to be placed under the protection of the police authorities. These facts go to show, in the almost utter absence of manifestations to the contrary, that Baltimore was not at that time a secessionist city; and, had the subsequent policy of the government been one of conciliation, instead of coercion, it is doubtful whether serious trouble would have resulted.

Notwithstanding the strong Union feeling which prevailed in Baltimore, there was a decided under-current of sympathy for the South. This was to be expected. Baltimore has always been a Southern city in feeling, customs, and associations. The population is largely made up of immigrants from Virginia and North Carolina, while the rural population of Maryland, particularly of the lower counties, is Southern in methods of life, sympathies, social habits, amusements, as that of any of the Southern States. ' The slave-holding element, too, were excited over the prospective loss of their slaves. Still, there were very few who were disposed to go the length of opposition to the General Government, and those few were overawed and held in check by the strong anti-secession element. The secession element, however, was aggressive, sometimes boisterous, and never failed to take advantage of any accident or mistake which was calculated to inflame the passions of the more moderate men. They were unintentionally assisted in their schemes by President Lincoln himself, whose secret passage through Baltimore was undoubtedly the result of a misconception. When they were informed that the President had slipped through the city *incognito*, citizens of all shades of opinion resented it as an undeserved reflection upon the city. The act at once suggested the thought that the government regarded the city of Baltimore with suspicion and hostility, and did more than anything else to create a bad feeling toward the administration. Arrangements were made by the city authorities for the reception and entertainment of President Lincoln in this city, and, it is safe to say, that Mr. Lincoln might have passed through Baltimore without fear of molestation.

It is a mistake to suppose that the riot was an outburst of the rougher classes, or, as some have alleged, simply a rebel demonstration. On the contrary, the rioters were composed of three distinct elements, two of which were distinctly respectable, while the third, a very small one by the way, was composed of young men and boys—some of them roughs, but many of them respectable in their connections—who were attracted to the scene by the noise and excitement. The first and most influential class—the class, in fact, without whose encouragement and assistance the disturbance would have been almost impossible—was composed of sober, intelligent men, many of them Union sympathizers, who were knocked clear off their balance by the announcement that Northern troops were marching on the city. This class had hitherto restrained the most aggressive of the Southern sympathizers; but, having always been opposed to coercion, were infuriated by the announcement that the Northern troops were actually invading "the sacred soil of Maryland." The second class was composed of more advanced Southern sympathizers, together with the few extremists who were openly in favor of coercion. Of this class the most prominent were the late Judge T. Parkin Scott, then prominent at the bar, and William Byrne, the famous politician and gambler. Byrne was the recognized head of that class which advocated armed resistance to the passage of the troops from the first, and, with his companions, did inconceivable damage by loud talk and bravado. He was, at the time, the most influential man in Baltimore with that large class of hot-headed young men, ward politicians, gamblers, "floaters," idlers, etc., who are to be found in every large city. A man of good address and strong sense, kind and liberal, he carried with him a large clientele of adventurous spirits. Mr. Scott represented the soberer, but not less aggressive, wing of the extremist faction.

One of the most curious features of the riot was the attitude of the city and State governments. The city government was largely composed of ardent Southern men, but, at the same time, men who were sober and clear-headed enough to see that a collision between the Federal authorities and the citizens of Baltimore could not but result in the most disastrous consequences. The Mayor of Baltimore, at the time, was George William Brown, now Chief Judge of the Supreme Bench of that city, a person of determined courage and impartial judgment. The Marshal of Police was George P. Kane, a man of inflexible honesty and singleness of purpose and great determination. To these two men must be ascribed the highest honor for their strenuous efforts, in the great part successful, to prevent further bloodshed after the first attack at the Pratt street bridge. Had they been notified in time of the coming of the troops, it is probable that the riot might have been prevented altogether. It has frequently been asserted at the North that the city authorities were in league with the mob; but, after a diligent search, I think I may say, with perfect truth, that Mayor Brown and the Chief of Police, notwithstanding their strong Southern sympathies, did everything in their power to prevent bloodshed.

The Governor of Maryland, Thomas H. Hicks, was a Union man, although he had been elected as a Pro-slavery Know-Nothing. His loyalty was suspected at Washington, but he lent no countenance whatever to the proposed resistance to the "Federal invasion." After the event, Governor Hicks was the first man, however, to suggest the armed resistance which he afterward deprecated with so much honor; and, in this connection, I cannot forbear printing the following curious document written by him:

STATE OF MARYLAND, EXECUTIVE CHAMBER,
ANNAPOLIS, November 9th, 1860.

HON. E. H. WEBSTER.

My Dear Sir:—I have pleasure in acknowledging receipt of your favor introducing a very clever gentleman to my acquaintance (though a Democrat). I regret to say that, at this time, we have no arms on hand to distribute, but assure you that, at the earliest possible moment, your company shall have arms; they have complied with all required of them on their part. We have some delay in consequence of contracts with Georgia and Alabama ahead of us, and we expect, at an early day, an additional supply, and of the first received your people shall be furnished. Will they be good men to send out to kill Lincoln and his men? If not, suppose the arms would be better sent South. How does late election sit with you? 'Tis too bad. Harford nothing to reproach herself for.

Your obedient servant,

THOMAS H. HICKS.

The writer became conspicuously "loyal" before spring!

On the 18th of April, a dispatch was received in Baltimore from Harrisburg, Pennsylvania, announcing that the Northern Central

Railroad had been requested to furnish accommodations for the transportation of a number of troops through Baltimore. When the news became generally known, large crowds assembled on the street, and intense excitement reigned. About nine o'clock A. M. a meeting of the military organization known as the Maryland National Volunteers was held under the presidency of Mr. T. Parkin Scott, and inflammatory speeches were made. At two o'clock two trains, containing twenty-one cars, which had left Harrisburg at ten minutes after eight o'clock that morning, arrived in Baltimore. There were six companies of troops—two of United States Artillery from St. Paul, commanded by Major Pemberton, two from Pottsville, Pennsylvania, one from Reading, Pennsylvania, and one from Lewistown, Pennsylvania, the latter known as the Logan Guards. A large and excited crowd had assembled at the depot and, previous to the arrival of the troops, occupied itself in singing "Dixie's Land" and noisily cheering for the Confederacy. As the troops disembarked, they were pushed and hustled by the crowd, but no one was seriously hurt. Finally the line of march was taken up for Mount Clare station, where the troops were to re-embark for Washington.

The troops were accompanied through the streets by the crowd, which guyed and hissed them, all the while cheering for the Southern Confederacy and "Jeff" Davis, and groaning for "Abe" Lincoln. The troops behaved remarkably well, none of the men showing any signs of annoyance beyond an occasional angry look or exclamation. The city police accompanied them and succeeded in holding the crowd in check. When the troops arrived at Mount Clare, however, the crowd became more aggressive. The troops were subjected to numberless indignities, such as being spit upon, taunted, hustled, etc.; the mob all the while indulging in wild curses, groans, and yells, with threats such as these: "Let the police go and we'll lick you!" "Wait till you see Jeff Davis!" "We'll see you before long!" "You'll never get back to Pennsylvania!" etc. Several of the more adventurous rioters caught some of the soldiers by the coat tails and jerked them about, while others taunted individuals in the ranks about their appearance, awkwardness, etc. It was a severe trial for the Pennsylvania volunteers, but they passed through the ordeal with commendable nerve and courage.

As the train was leaving the station, a stone was thrown, by some one in the mob, into one of the cars, and, with a wild yell, the mob rushed after the slowly receding train. They were checked, however, by the city police, who behaved admirably throughout.

Later that afternoon, a disturbance occurred in the central part of the city, and a crowd of some two thousand people assembled, but were dispersed by the police after several persons had been slightly hurt. The same evening, an immense assemblage of people gathered in front of Taylor's building, on Fayette street, where a State's Rights' Convention of Marylanders was being held.

Baltimore was now at fever heat of excitement. Business was entirely suspended and the male population of the city turned out *en masse*. The streets were crowded all day, and until a late hour that night Baltimore, or Market street as it was then called, was thronged by a surging mob, which was thickest at the newspaper offices and other centres of information. The Union sympathizers had disappeared, and the city seemed to be a unit in opposition to the passage of Northern troops through Baltimore. The staidest and soberest citizens were infected by it. Men who all along had been opposed to secession, now openly advocated armed resistance, and it was declared, over and over again, in the most public manner, that no Northern troops should be permitted to enter Baltimore, or, if they did enter, to leave the city alive. The mob, however, was still under the control of the city authorities—that is to say, the Mayor and Marshal of Police retained, in spite of the open threats and great excitement, sufficient power to prevent any outbreak of violence. Unfortunately, however, the authorities at Washington attempted a maneuvre similar to that by which Mr. Lincoln was got through Baltimore. Finding that the feeling in Baltimore had become intense, and suspecting the city authorities of collusion with the mob, the government directed the officer in command of the troops *en route* for Baltimore to proceed to that city, from Philadelphia, without notice to the authorities of Baltimore, and to get through as quickly as he could. This was a most unfortunate order, for there is little doubt that had Mayor Brown been notified of the expected arrival of the troops, he could have provided for their efficient protection by the police. The Mayor and Chief of Police were not only *not* notified, but were kept in the dark as to the movements of the troops—so that when the troops reached the President street depot, they were completely taken by surprise. President Lincoln and his advisers are not to be blamed for not taking the Baltimore authorities into their confidence, for it was exceedingly difficult, in those days, to tell whom to trust and whom not to trust. It is to be regretted, however, that in this case the President was over-cautious, for I am pursuaded that, had the police of Baltimore been notified in time, the loss of life might have been avoided.

Early on the morning of April 19th, 1861, a train of thirty-five cars left the Broad and Washington avenue depot, Philadelphia, having on board twelve hundred troops from Boston, Lowell, and Acton, Massachusetts, and known as the Sixth Massachusetts Regiment, under the command of Colonel Edward F. Jones, a gallant soldier and courteous gentleman; and a regiment, one thousand strong, from Philadelphia, under the command of Colonel William F. Small. Nothing was known in Baltimore of their departure from Philadelphia, but about eleven o'clock it became noised abroad that a large force of Federal soldiers had arrived at President street depot. This depot is in the southeastern portion of the city, and is connected with the Baltimore and Ohio depot, which is situated in the southwestern section, by a line of rail along Pratt street—a leading thoroughfare—and some minor streets. It was necessary for the troops, on disembarking at President street depot, either to march to the Baltimore and Ohio depot or to be drawn thither in the cars by horses. The news of the arrival of the troops spread like wildfire, and in a comparatively short time an immense crowd gathered on Pratt street, with the intention of preventing the passage of the troops. While waiting for the appearance of the soldiers the crowd kept itself up to the requisite pitch of indignation and enthusiasm by "groaning" for Lincoln, Hicks, and the Federal Government, and by cheering Jefferson Davis and the Southern Confederacy. The first intimation had by the city authorities that the troops were about to enter the city was received by Mayor Brown about ten o'clock. Mr. Brown at once repaired to the office of the Police Commissioners, but found that the Marshal of Police had already gone to Camden station, where he had concentrated his men by request of the railroad authorities. The Mayor at once followed him to Camden station, and on arriving there found him posted with his men prepared to put down any attack. Unfortunately the mob had gathered not at Camden station but on Pratt street, at a point a short distance west of the depot where the troops were disembarking. Pratt street is a narrow thoroughfare, and easily capable of defense. The strategical position of the mob was excellent as they proceeded to fortify it.

About half-past eleven o'clock a car drawn by horses was seen approaching, and was greeted by the mob with cheers for the South. The car, and eight others which followed, were, however, permitted to pass without any molestation, except the usual taunts and gibes at the occupants. A trivial accident, which happened to the tenth car, let loose all the elements of disorder in the mob, and precipitated the fatal conflict. As this car neared Commerce street the brake was accidentally thrown out of gear, and the car stopped. The crowd took advantage of the mishap at once, and began to attack the occupants with stones. Windows were broken, and a few of the soldiers were hurt, but not seriously. Finally the driver of the car became frightened, lost his head, and, having attached his team to the other end of the car, started to haul it back to the depot. The mob followed the car, stoning it all the while, but the driver having urged the horses to a run, succeeded in distancing them. A large portion of the mob, however, followed it into the depot.

The section of the mob which remained at the bridge on Pratt street then, under the advice of their leaders, many of whom, as I have said, were well known citizens of Baltimore, began to build a barricade, Paris fashion. They commenced by digging up the paving stones and the railroad track for a distance of some fifty yards. The stones were piled up with the iron rails, the bridges over the gutters were torn up, and eight large anchors which were found on the wharf near by were placed on the barricade. A car loaded with sand attempted to pass, but was seized by the rioters, who backed it up to the barricade, and emptied the sand on the pile of stones and anchors. A large number of negroes were working on the wharves at the time. These were ordered to quit work, which they did with alacrity, and were directed by the rioters to assist them on the barricade. They complied and, as Colonel J. Thomas Scharf, in his "Chronicles of Baltimore" relates, "worked away with a will for Massa Jeff Davis and de Souf." At this stage of the proceedings Mayor Brown, who had hurried from Camden Station, arrived on the scene. What followed is best given in Mayor Brown's own words:

"On arriving at the head of Smith's wharf," he says in his official report, " I found that anchors had been piled on the track to obstruct it, and Sergeant McComas and a few policemen, who were with him, were not allowed by the mob to remove the obstructions. I at once ordered the anchors to be removed, and my authority was not resisted."

This, in my judgment, is signal proof that had the passage of the troops been intrusted to the city authorities, it might have been effected in safety, as the Mayor had the confidence of even the extreme secessionists. In the meantime, the commander of the Massachusetts troops, finding that the cars would not be permitted to pass through, decided to disembark his men and force a passage on foot through the mob. When this determination was announced, some confederates of the Pratt street rioters at once communicated the news to them. It was also rumored that the troops had decided to go by a different route to Camden station. A portion of the rioters at once started to head them off, while the main body maintained its position on Pratt street. A·large crowd assembled at the depot during the disembarkation of the troops, and here several exciting, but not very sanguinary, encounters occurred between Unionists and secessionists in the crowd. As the troops descended from the cars they were hooted, jeered, and twitted. They succeeded, however, in forcing their way to the footway, which extends for several hundred yards along the outer edge of the depot, where they formed in double file and awaited the orders of their officers.

At this point a man appeared bearing a Confederate flag at the head of about one hundred rioters. His appearance was the signal for wild cheering. A rush for the flag was made by several Northern sympathizers in the crowd, and the flag-staff was broken. One of these men was caught by the flag-bearer who, with his companions, throttled, and would have killed him, but for the interference of the police, who succeeded in bearing him away. The shreds of the flag were caught up and tied to the flag-staff. On being raised again they were saluted with an outburst of cheering. The men surrounding the flag then began to taunt the troops, and declared that they would be forced to march behind it to the Camden depot. Colonel Jones gave the order to march, and the troops started. The men surrounding the flag, however, planted themselves directly in front of the soldiers and refused to yield an inch. The troops wheeled about, but found themselves surrounded on all sides, and were unable to move in any direction. Several of the soldiers were hustled away from their comrades, and would have been roughly used by the crowd but for the police, who succeeded, with great difficulty, in rescuing them. The troops again endeavored to force a passage, and this time, with the assistance of the police, they succeeded. As they started, however, the Confederate flag was borne to the front, and they were compelled to march for several squares behind this flag. Too much praise cannot be given to the commander or men for their admirable self-control during this trying episode.

The presence of the Confederate flag was the immediate cause of the sanguinary street fight and loss of life which followed. Several Northern sympathizers in the mob, exasperated at the triumph of the flag-bearer and his friends, made another dash for the flag, but were defeated and pursued. Some of them took refuge in the ranks of the soldiers. This exasperated the citizens against the soldiers, and a savage attack upon the latter was made with stones and other missiles. One of the soldiers, William Patch, was struck in the back with a large paving-stone, and fell to the ground. His musket was seized, and the poor wretch was brutally beaten by the rioters before the police could rescue him. When Patch was seen to fall Colonel Jones gave the order "double quick" to his men, and the whole column started off on a run, ducking and dipping to avoid the stones. At this the crowd set up a yell of derision and started after them full tilt. Two soldiers were knocked down, while running, but managed to make their escape—one of them with the assistance of the police,

While the foregoing events were transpiring in and near President street depot, an immense concourse of people had gathered at the barricade. When the troops appeared in full run a great shout was raised, and the head of the column was greeted with a shower of paving-stones. The troops faltered, and finally, in the face of a second shower of stones, came to a dead halt. The patience of their commander was at last exhausted. He cried out in a voice, which was heard even above the yells of the mob, "Fire!" The soldiers leveled their pieces and the mob seemed to pause, as if to take breath. The soldiers fired. A young man, named F. X. Ward, now a well-known lawyer of this city, fell pierced by a ball. A hoarse yell of fear and rage went up from the mob, but it did not give way. The troops fired again and again, and the crowd wavering, they rushed upon them with fixed bayonets and forced a passage over the barricade. A scene of bloody confusion followed. As the troops retreated, firing, the rioters rushed upon them only to be repulsed by the line of bayonets. Some of the rioters fought like madmen. Finally, the mob, exasperated by their failure to prevent the passage of the troops, made a desperate rush upon them, and one young man, who was in the front rank of the rioters, was forced close upon the soldiery. One of the soldiers raised his gun, took deliberate aim at the rioter and fired. The cap exploded, but the gun failed to go off. The rioter rushed forward, seized the gun, wrested it by an almost superhuman effort from the soldier's grasp, and plunged the bayonet through the man's shoulder. During the firing a number of the rioters fell, killed and wounded. At the intersection of Charles and Pratt streets, Andrew Robbins, a soldier from Stoneham, Massachusetts, was shot in the neck by a rioter. He was carried into a drug store near by, and was protected from the mob. At Howard street a strong force of rioters from Camden station met the troops and refused to yield. The soldiers fired again and the mob gave way. The soldiers again started at the double quick and reached Camden station without further trouble. Thirteen cars were drawn out, and the soldiers left the depot amid the hisses and groans of the multitude. One of the most remarkable features of the riot was the persistency and courage with which the mob hung on to the troops, in spite of the continued firing. Another remarkable feature was the extraordinary coolness and forbearance of the troops.

Mayor Brown, during the progress of the riot, did one of the bravest things on record, and his conduct is remembered and frequently quoted in Baltimore to-day as a conspicuous example of unselfish devotion and courage. After ordering the removal of the anchors at the barricade, the Mayor made his way to Pratt street bridge, where he saw the troops approaching. He ran at once to the head of the column, the people crying as he passed: "Here comes the Mayor!" The Mayor shook hands with the officers in command, saying as he did so: "I am the Mayor of Baltimore." He then placed himself by Colonel Jones' side, and marched with him for several squares, begging, warning, and commanding the citizens not to offer any violence. In the excited state of feeling at the time, the Mayor's conduct was as plucky as anything I have ever read or heard of. His presence, doubtless, saved a great deal of bloodshed. When the Mayor left the head of the column, Marshal Kane, with fifty policemen with drawn revolvers, rushed to the rear of the column, formed a line across the street, and succeeded in keeping back the mob. This was one of the most exciting episodes of the riot.

The list of the killed and wounded was as follows: Soldiers killed—Addison O. Whitney, a young mechanic, of Lowell, Massachusetts; Luther C. Ladd, another young mechanic, also from Lowell; Charles A. Taylor, decorative painter, from Boston, and Sumner H. Needham, a plasterer from the same city—4. A number of soldiers were wounded. The citizens killed were: Robert W. Davis, Philip S. Miles, John McCann, John McMahon, William R. Clark, James Carr, Francis Maloney, Sebastian Gill, William Maloney, William Reed, Michael Murphy, Patrick Griffith—12. Wounded—Frank X. Ward, —— Coney, James Myers, and a boy whose name was not ascertained—4. The fact that more of the troops were not killed is to be ascribed to the fact that the citizens had no arms except paving-stones. Many more of the citizens were wounded beside those whose names were returned, and, perhaps, some more were killed. The lower classes generally concealed their injuries.

The death of Mr. Robert W. Davis was one of the most tragic incidents of the day. Mr. Davis was a member of the firm of Paynter, Davis & Co., dry goods dealers, on Baltimore street, and one of the most prominent citizens of Baltimore. Early on the

50

morning of the riot he went out on the line of the Baltimore and Ohio Railroad, a short distance from the city, for the purpose of looking at some land which he thought of purchasing. He was standing near the railroad track with some friends, among whom was Mr. Thomas W. Hall, Jr., a prominent journalist and lawyer of this city, and who is now City Solicitor of Baltimore. Mr. Davis was not aware that there had been a riot in the city, and as a car containing the troops came by, he incautiously shook his fist at them in mock defiance. A soldier in the car, however, mistaking the gesture for one of real hostility and, probably, thrown off his balance by the fearful occurrences of the day, raised his gun and fired. The unfortunate man, who had been laughing and chatting with his friends a moment before, fell into their arms. Mr. Hall asked him if he was hurt. "I am killed," was all he said. When the news of Mr. Davis' death reached the city, it added fuel to the flames.

Marshal Kane's three hundred and fifty policemen were almost powerless in the face of the mob, which meanwhile had broken into all the gun stores in town, and had completely gutted them. During the afternoon, Governor Hicks issued an order for the assembling of the State troops, and by five o'clock quite a number had reported for duty. In the meantime, however (about half-past two), news reached the rioters that the renowned Seventh Regiment from New York was expected. An immense mob at once repaired to the depot and surrounded some volunteers from Philadelphia, who were found to have arrived there. The windows of the cars were smashed with paving-stones, and a number of the Philadelphians injured, but none of them seriously. Marshal Kane, accompanied by Colonel C. C. Egerton, a personal friend and well-known as an officer, and one of the militia organizations, appeared on the scene and succeeded in appeasing, for a time, the passions of the mob by announcing that it had been decided that the troops should return to Philadelphia. The mob, believing that the Marshal would act toward them in good faith, withdrew. Later, however, it was rumored that the command was about to force a passage through the city, and with a howl of disappointment, the rioters again repaired to the depot. This time they could not be reasoned with. Rushing pell-mell upon the train, they riddled it with stones. Some twenty of the volunteers were badly injured about the head and body by being struck with heavy stones. The soldiers were, with considerable difficulty, removed to some freight cars near at hand, where they were better protected from the mob. Over one hundred of the soldiers were separated from their comrades during the transfer, but were rescued by the police, who took them to the Eastern station-house for safety. A short time after the freight train was backed out of the depot and, finally, the soldiers returned to Philadelphia, rather than attempt to force a passage through the streets of Baltimore. The mob was thus victorious, and all that night, and for several days after, the riotous element was practically in control of the city.

It is difficult to overestimate the strength and depth of the popular indignation excited by the riot at the North For days after the outbreak the newspapers teemed with bitter denunciation of the Baltimoreans, whose opposition to the passage of the troops was generally set down to "pure cussedness," and all-prevailing sympathy with secession. After the years which have rolled by this is seen to be a narrow and partisan view of the occurrence. The people of the North had good reason, however, to think that henceforth Baltimore must be regarded as one of the enemy, for the attack upon the Northern troops was one of the bloodiest and most vindictive outbursts of popular feeling on record. It confirmed all that had been said of the Baltimoreans, and lent a decided color of reason to the President's secret passage through the city.

After the departure of the Northern troops, the police department was informed that a freight car was at the depot containing a large quantity of arms and ammunition, which had been left there by the Massachusetts troops. General James M. Anderson at once repaired to the depot, and with a large force of policemen took possession of the car. Subsequently the arms and accoutrements were removed and appropriated by the city authorities, who used them in arming the citizens and militia for the protection of the city.

On the afternoon of the riot a meeting of citizens was held in Monument Square, at which the Governor, the Mayor, and a number of prominent citizens made addresses, counseling moderation. The indignation of the populace, however, was so great that the efforts at pacification met with little encouragement. Seeing that the temper of the people was even angrier and more excited than before, the authorities decided to request the President to prevent, if he could, the further passage of troops through the town. Accordingly, the following letter was dispatched to the President:

MAYOR'S OFFICE, BALTIMORE, April 19th, 1861.

Sir:—This will be presented to you by the Hon. H. Lennox Bond, George W. Dobbin, and John C. Brune, Esqs., who will proceed to Washington by an express train, at my request, in order to explain fully the fearful condition of affairs in this city. The people are exasperated to the highest degree by the presence of troops, and the citizens are universally decided in the opinion that no more should be ordered to come. The authorities of the city did their best to-day to protect both strangers and citizens, and to prevent a collision, but in vain; and but for their great efforts a fearful slaughter would have occurred. Under these circumstances it is my solemn duty to inform you that it is not possible for more soldiers to pass through Baltimore unless they fight their way at every step. I, therefore, hope and trust, and most earnestly request, that no more troops be permitted or ordered by the government to pass through the city. If they should attempt it, the responsibility for the bloodshed will not rest upon me.

With great respect, your obedient servant,

GEORGE WM. BROWN,
Mayor.

To His Excellency, ABRAHAM LINCOLN, President United States.

It is easy, from the foregoing, to obtain an idea of the actual state of affairs in Baltimore at the time, for Mayor Brown, to my own knowledge, is thoroughly dispassionate, and, of all men, one of the least likely to over-state a case. The response to this letter was conveyed through a dispatch from the committee sent to Washington by the Mayor, as follows:

WASHINGTON, April 20th, 1861.

To MAYOR BROWN, Baltimore:

We have seen the President and General Scott. We have from the former a letter to the Mayor and Governor, declaring that no troops shall be brought through Baltimore if, in a military point of view, and without interruption from opposition, they can be marched around Baltimore.

H. L. BOND,
J. C. BRUNE,
G. W. DOBBIN.

This response of Mr. Lincoln was very unsatisfactory to the people of Baltimore, although it is difficult to see, looking back upon it from this point of time, how Mr. Lincoln could have unreservedly promised that no troops should pass through Baltimore. It was of the highest importance that easy and rapid communication should be maintained with the North, and that the troops should be forwarded as rapidly as possible. It was simply asking the government to cut off its right hand to request that it should not continue the transportation of troops through Baltimore. The people of this city, however, were not concerned about the inconvenience which it might cause the government. They were agreed on one point, viz., that the passage of troops through Baltimore should not be permitted under any consideration.

In response to the general sentiment, Mayor Brown, on Saturday morning, issued the following:

MAYOR'S OFFICE, BALTIMORE, April 20th, 1861.

All the citizens having arms suitable for the defense of the city, and which they are willing to contribute for the purpose, are requested to deposit them at the office of the Marshal of Police.

GEORGE WM. BROWN,
Mayor.

The promptness and heartiness with which this call was responded to, showed the depth of the popular feeling on the subject. At nine o'clock on the morning after the riot, the City Council met and appropriated half a million dollars for the defense of the city. The directors of the banks also met on the same morning and volunteered to lend the city half a million dollars at once. From this fact alone it may be seen that the feeling was not confined to a clique or even a small majority of the citizens. Almost every respectable citizen, whatever his political convictions, shared in the earnest opposition to any further encroachment upon the soil of Maryland from the North. Early that morning the Confederate flag had been displayed from Taylor's building, the rendezvous of the Maryland Guard, and had been greeted with vociferous cheers. The city was given over to excitement throughout the day. There was a rumor of a projected raid upon Fort McHenry, several miles below the city, where a number of troops were quartered, but a strong military force was sent out by the civil authorities and the attack was prevented. The populace was further excited by the arrival of companies of militia rom the counties, who came to defend the city against the Northern myrmidons. About half-past two o'clock that afternoon the mob broke into a public hall belonging to the German Turners, who were supposed to be Northern in their sympathies. The furniture was destroyed and a large quantity of liquor which was found there was appropriated by the crowd. A recruiting office was opened at the City Hall, under the nose of the Mayor, and large numbers of persons enrolled themselves for the defense of the city. As the men were enrolled, they were formed into companies of forty each. They selected their own officers, and joined what regiments they pleased.

There is little doubt that the formation of this military force prevented untold violence and bloodshed. In the first place, it gave the hungry, roving mob something to do, and thus distracted it for the time being. In the second place, it brought the element of disorder under a responsible head, and gave the city authorities an opportunity to recover themselves and to reassert their authority. Had the mob been left to itself, there is no telling what might have happened. As it was, the city, for many days, was in imminent danger, and it was only by *seeming* to co-operate with the riotous elements that the Mayor and his subordinates were enabled to prevent pillage and destruction.

Partly as a sop to the multitude, and partly to prevent the possibility of any immediate recurrence of the disturbance, it was decided by the authorities of the city and State to order the destruction of the bridges on the Philadelphia road. Accordingly, on Saturday night, a detachment of militia, assisted by citizen volunteers, set fire to several railroad bridges on the line of the Philadelphia, Wilmington and Baltimore Railroad and the Northern Central Railroad, and thus effectually prevented any further passage of troops. Early on Sunday morning, the news reached the city that a large force of military were encamped at Ashland, on the Northern Central Railroad, about fifteen miles from Baltimore, and that this force would advance and take possession of the city during the day. The most intense excitement ensued. The congregations left the churches *en masse*, and in a comparatively short time the streets were thronged with excited men. Had the troops actually attempted to enter Baltimore, an immense loss of life must have resulted, for the riotous elements were inflamed to the point of desperation. The relatives and friends of the men who had been killed the day before were particularly anxious to "get at" the troops, and the bare announcement to the citizens that twelve Baltimoreans had been killed, enraged them beyond measure. Fortunately, however, the troops were ordered to return to Harrisburg, and the danger, for the time being, was averted.

For days after this occurrence Baltimore was the centre of warlike preparations. It was, in fact, an armed camp. Nearly every citizen capable of bearing arms presented himself for enrolment, and in a short space of time there were not less than twenty thousand men under arms. There were not enough muskets, of course, for this large force and, accordingly, the men were provided with pikes until muskets could be obtained. I haved seen in a Northern city two of these pikes exhibited as a curiosity. The person in charge of them— an ordinarily intelligent man by the way—informed me that they were Marshal Kane's pikes, and that they had been used against the Massachusetts and Pennsylvania volunteers on the memorable 19th of April. The absurdity of the declaration will appear when it is stated—first, that Marshal Kane armed the mob simply in order to make it believe that the authorities were in sympathy with it, and prevent untold mischief; second, that Marshal Kane knew that so long as the mob was kept busy drilling, it could, to a certain extent, be held in control; third, that the idea of the authorities was that, by pacifying the mob, a few days could be obtained, and it might thus be possible to take such steps as would effectually prevent any recurrence of the trouble; fourth, that Marshal Kane's pikes were never used against the Northern soldiers at all.

From the 19th of April until the 13th of May, Baltimore was practically a Confederate town—a wedge of disaffection between the North and the South. President Lincoln and his Cabinet were greatly annoyed by this fire in the rear, and it was decided that the city must be reduced to submission as soon as possible. The President and his advisers wisely concluded, however, to allow things to remain as they were until the excited passions of the multitude had subsided. After the retreat of the volunteer troops from Ashland, the city was placed under patrol, guard-houses were established, and every precaution was taken to prevent a surprise. Colonel Isaac R. Trimble, who afterward became a general in the Confederate service, was placed in command of the ununiformed volunteers, and took possession of the Northern Central Railroad depot, where a regular camp was established. A curious feature of the preparations for defense was the tender, on the part of several hundred colored men, of their services "against the Yankees!" The Mayor thanked them for the offer, and informed them that their services would be called for if required.

Colonel Huger, of the regular army, afterward general under Lee, who had been for some time in command of the arsenal at Pikesville, a village near Baltimore, was in the city during all these troublous times, and, being a prime, social favorite of the young men about town, was approached for advice and assistance. The old colonel, who was decidedly Southern in his sympathies, and, in fact, went South shortly afterward, did a great deal to avert serious trouble. He was a splendid old fellow—a high liver, witty, good-humored, and a fine old-school officer. It was he who suggested the arming and drilling of the mob as the best means of keeping them employed and out of trouble. He was full of sadness, however, at the prospect before him, and when some of the young swells came to him bubbling over with indignation and sectional fervor, he would cry out: "Ah, boys, you'll get enough of this before you're through!"

In this connection, General Huger said to the city authorities: "If we don't give these fellows plenty to do, gentlemen, they will give us plenty to do!" And he was right. Baltimore had, at that time, one of the worst elements with which any city was ever afflicted. There was a certain class of men which lived and fattened on disorder. For a number of years the city had been the prey of brutal ruffians, who controlled the elections, and conducted themselves exactly as they pleased. You have probably heard of the "Plug-Uglies" and "Rip-Raps" of Baltimore." Well, these men had been cowed by the election of a reform administration; but the same spirit animated them still which had animated them before, when they openly beat, stabbed, and prodded with awls every citizen who attempted to vote according to his own mind. When the 19th of April disorder broke out, this element began to show its head again—profiting by the excitement and confusion to commit excesses. It was of the first importance that these people should be kept out of mischief, and all substantial citizens, whatever their political convictions, were agreed that the only way of keeping them quiet was to organize them into companies, put them under the drillmaster, and, as General Huger suggested, "give them plenty to do." To the government, however, this action of the city authorities seemed to be a deliberate note of defiance, and was, probably, the main cause of the bad blood and suspicion which afterward were found to exist.

This state of things continued for nearly a month, and no enemy having appeared, the rebellious elements began to tire of playing soldier, and, as had been expected, began to disintegrate. In a few days more the "roughs" were completely under control, a great many having gone off to Harper's Ferry to join General J. E. Johnston's army there, and the city authorities had resumed their legitimate influence. The arms which had been distributed among the rioters were buried, in order to prevent the wholesale stealing which was found to be going on, and also to prevent them from falling into the hands of irresponsible parties. These arms were afterward recovered by General Butler, who pretended, with an immense flourish of trumpets, that their concealment was part of a rebel plot to get possession of the city. This performance was of a piece with several others of the doughty warrior's feats. The people of Baltimore were very much excited against Butler, for his conduct here was marked by the same bravado, the same overbearing "loyalty," the same disingenuousness, which characterized his "military" career throughout the war. While he was encamped at the Relay House, seven miles from Baltimore, he set afloat the most absurd stories—one of them alleging that rebel sympathizers had poisoned the water in the neighborhood, and another that the Baltimore rebels had attempted to poison his men with strychnine. One of his soldiers, who was suddenly taken ill, was declared to have been poisoned, but on examination, made by a physician sent by the authorities of Baltimore city to investigate this particular case, it was found that the man was a person of intemperate habits, that he had been very imprudent in his diet, and that the symptoms were not such as ordinarily accompany poisoning by strychnia. Butler

also ordered the arrest of a number of persons for seditious utterances, and actually issued a proclamation "concerning one Spencer,"
who had been heard to express disloyal sentiments, and warning
others not to imitate his example. The General seems to have stood
in considerable awe of the Baltimore mob, although, at this time, the
civil authorities had regained full control of affairs. The following
letter from his aide, as late as May 11th, shows that an attack at the
Relay House, even then, was feared:

CAMP AT RELAY, Saturday, P. M.
To MAYOR BROWN:

Sir:—I represent General Butler at this camp during his absence at Annapolis.
I have received intimations, from many sources, that an attack on us by the Baltimore roughs is intended to-night. About four P. M. to-day these rumors were confirmed by a gentleman from Baltimore, who gave his name and residence in Monument street. He said he heard positively that on Saturday night the attack would
take place by more than a thousand men, every one "sworn to kill a man" before
he returned; a portion were Knights of the Golden Circle. I wish you to guard
every avenue of your city, and prevent these men from leaving town. They are
coming in wagons, on horses, and on foot, we are informed. We are also told that
a considerable force is approaching from the west, probably Point of Rocks, to attack
on that side, and co-operate with the Baltimore mob, with whom they have constant
communication. Mr. Clark, whom I have already sent to you, will tell something
about it. It may be all a sham, but the evidence is very cumulative, and from
several sources.

EDWARD G. PARKER,
Aide-de-Camp.

It *was* all a sham. The attack existed only in the fertile
imaginations of General Butler's informants. Quiet had for some
days been completely restored in Baltimore. A number of the
prominent agitators had gone South, and the riotous element—what
there was left of it—was without leaders. On the night of the 13th
of May, General Butler, with a strong force of volunteers, moved
from the Relay House to Federal hill—an elevation commanding
the harbor of Baltimore—and took possession.

The civil authority was, of course, deposed; the administration
of affairs was handed over to the military, and for several weeks
General Butler reigned supreme. Subsequently, he was removed
to new fields of activity, and was succeeded in turn by Generals
Dix, Wool, and Wallace. The only trouble which the government
had, subsequently, in Baltimore, was with the women—they did not
yield as soon as the men. A number of the most obstreperous were
imprisoned; fortifications, barracks, and hospitals were erected, and
Baltimore, for the remainder of the war, was practically a Federal
town.

THE CAPTURE OF MASON AND SLIDELL.

BY R. M. HUNTER.

On the 8th of November, 1861, the capture of John Slidell and J. M. Mason, the commissioners of the Southern Confederacy to England and France, was effected. It was the first considerable feat of the Federal navy, and, two weeks afterward, when the United States steamer "San Jacinto" landed her prisoners in Boston, the daring action of Captain Wilkes became the prevailing topic of the day, and superseded in interest the questions that grew out of Forts Henry and Donelson, and the battles and the strategic movements of our army on land. The writer was an eye-witness of the seizure and release of the British steamer Trent, and the capture of Slidell and Mason, and their secretaries, George Eustis aud J. E. McFarland. I have never seen, even in the official reports of Captain Wilkes and his officers, an account that does justice to the facts in all their relations, although it is the generally admitted fact that, at the time, there was less exaggeration in the publications of the Northern papers than in the English prints. The foreign publications were the letters of the officers of the Trent, Captain Moir, commanding, his purser, and Commander Williams, of the Royal Navy Reserve, who chanced to be a fellow-passenger of the voyaging emissaries. In Captain Moir's report to Lord Palmerston, the *Premier*, he says that Captain Wilkes sent an order (which he did not) to him to bring his ship close under the guns of the American sloop-of-war. These matters of detail, however, are, perhaps, not essential, only inasmuch as the truth thereof may put in its proper light the conduct of the officers of the "San Jacinto."

The "San Jacinto" had cruised during the fall months on the west coast of Africa, bearing a roving commission, and keeping a bright lookout for the privateer "Sumter." The cruise had not resulted in anything of practical benefit, either in the way of prize-money to the crew or service to the government, and the 1st of October beheld her steering for the Spanish Main, with her crew and officers in fine spirits and eager for adventure. Touching at Cienfuegos, news was received that Mason and Slidell had passed out of Charleston in the blockade-runner Theodora, and had reached

Havana. This was on the 23d of October, and orders were at once given to coal ship. The order was executed with dispatch, and on the 26th of the same month the "San Jacinto" was again in blue water shaping a course for Havana. I am afraid that the honor of suggesting the capture of Mason and Slidell must be awarded to our boatswain, J. P. Grace. On the evening of October 27th, this officer, while pacing the lee side of the quarter-deck with another warrant officer, said, in a tone which we distinctly heard in the wardroom, that the two chaps themselves ought to be overhauled wherever they might be, and the ship that did it would get honor that would compensate for the absence of prize-money won during the past four months. Two days afterward we passed under the frowning guns of Moro Castle and anchored in Havana harbor. No person except the officers were permitted ashore, and it was required that they should not appear in uniform. It was street talk at the time that Mason and Slidell had made the hardest part of their journey when they passed through the blockading squadron off Charleston, and the opinion prevailed that they were safe from interference from the United States. All but Captain Wilkes accepted this view of the case, and he retained his views within himself. Having frequent occasion to visit his cabin I saw that he was deeply engaged in the perusal of international law books, from which he was taking copious notes. On November 1st, Lieutenant J. A. Greer, navigating officer, brought word to the ship that Mason and Slidell, with their secretaries and families, were booked for England by the steamer Trent to St. Thomas, and thence by the regular West India packet to Southampton. The next day we went to sea, touching at Key West on the 3d. On the 4th we returned to the Cuban coast, and cruising along the northern shore awaited further information as to the movements of the Confederate representatives from Consul General Schufeldt. It was not received, and orders were given to bear away to the narrow channel of old Bahama, through which the Trent must necessarily pass on her way to St. Thomas. The point selected could not have been chosen to better advantage. Between the coral keys the distance across the channel was but fifteen miles, and no ship could pass without being seen by our topsail-yard lookout. Early on the morning of the 8th the ship was cleard for action.

If the Trent had left Havana on the 17th, she was due at the point where we were waiting on the 8th. The distance was but two hundred and forty miles, and the wind, blowing a full sail breeze from the southwest, should place the Trent under our guns by noon. The calculations were made with exactness, for at twenty

minutes to twelve o'clock the lookout aloft sang out "Sail ho!"
Lieutenant K. Randolph Breese, who had the deck, hailed the lookout, and asked for her direction. "Off the port bow, sir," came
back the reply. The "San Jacinto" was then heading north, and
presently the black smoke of a steamer was descried from our decks.
When the crew was piped to dinner, the mess-cloths were deserted,
and nearly everybody remained on deck, watching the smoke, until
out of the base of the ascending blackness came the spars, presently
the hull and full shape, of the steamship Trent. Until that moment,
probably, no one on board of the ship knew what the object of our
waiting was; but as soon as the Trent hove in sight, and her identity
was decided, there was no doubt of our mission. Then Captain
Wilkes called Lieutenant Fairfax into the cabin, and gave him his
instructions, of which the following is a copy:

UNITED STATES STEAMER "SAN JACINTO,"
AT SEA, November 8th, 1861.

Sir :—You will have the second and third cutters of this ship fully manned
and armed, and be in all respects prepared to board the steamer Trent, now hove-to
under our guns.

On boarding her, you will demand the papers of the steamer, her clearance
from Havana, with the list of passengers and crew.

Should Mr. Mason, Mr. Slidell, Mr. Eustis, and Mr. McFarland be on board,
you will make them prisoners, and send them on board this ship immediately, and
take possession of the Trent as a prize.

I do not deem it will be necessary to use force; that the prisoners will have
the good sense to avoid any necessity for using it; but if they should, they must
be made to understand that it is their own fault. *They must be brought on board.*
All trunks, cases, packages, and bags belonging to them you will take possession of,
and send on board the ship. Any dispatches found on the persons of the prisoners,
or in possession of those on board the steamer, will be taken possession of also,
examined, and retained if necessary.

I have understood that the families of these gentlemen may be with them.
If so, I beg you will offer them, in my name, a passage in this ship to the United
States, and that all the attention and comforts we can command are tendered them,
and will be placed at their service.

In the event of their acceptance, should there be anything which the captain
of the steamer can spare to increase the comforts, in the way of necessaries or
stores, of which a war vessel is deficient, you will please to procure them. The
amount will be paid by the paymaster.

Lieutenant James A. Greer will take charge of the third cutter, which accom-
panies you, and assist you in these duties. I trust that all those under your
command, in executing this important and delicate duty, will conduct themselves
with all the delicacy and kindness which become the character of our naval service.

I am, very respectfully, your obedient servant,

CHARLES WILKES, Captain.

LIEUTENANT D. M. FAIRFAX, U. S. N., Executive Officer "San Jacinto."

The officers detailed to go in the boats with Lieutenant Fairfax received their instructions, and Captain Wilkes walked forward to the mainmast, and gave the order "Beat to quarters." It was fifteen minutes after one o'clock when the boats were called away, Mr. Fairfax in the second cutter, and Lieutenant Greer commanding the third cutter. Before the boats were shoved off, the Trent had steamed well up toward the "San Jacinto," and was in mid-channel, when the gun on the topgallant forecastle, loaded with a round-shot, was fired in a line across the bows. Immediately the red cross of St. George went fluttering to her peak, but she kept on her course. "Put a shell in that gun," called out Captain Wilkes, "and let it go across her bows, so she may not mistake our intention this time." The shell exploded about one hundred fathoms ahead of the steamer, and immediately her engines stopped, and she rounded-to within two hundred feet of the man-of-war, and under the muzzles of our broadside, that would have sunk her at the word "Fire!" There was much confusion on the mail steamer, and the passengers could be seen running about the decks in the greatest state of excitement. As our men were going into their boats, Captain Moir, of the Trent, hailed us. "What do you mean," shouted he, "by stopping my ship? and why do you do it with shotted guns, contrary to usage?" Lieutenant Breese sang out, in reply: "We are going to send a boat on board of you. Lay-to."

At this instant the order to shove off was given to our boats, and the second and third cutters went dancing over the blue waves toward the Trent. Lieutenant Greer pulled up to the port gangway, and Mr. Fairfax went to the starboard side, and boarded the ship alone. The first officer met him as he came up the side, and asked what he wanted. "Are you the master of this ship, sir?"

"No, sir; first officer."

"I would like to see the captain;" and Captain Moir, at this instant, walked out of his cabin, and coming forward said, in angry tones: "How dare you come on board of my ship? What right have you here? This is an outrage the flag there (pointing to the red cross aloft) will make you pay for."

Lieutenant Fairfax bowed, and said: "I have instructions to effect the arrest of Messrs. Mason and Slidell, and their secretaries, Messrs. Eustis and McFarland. I have information that they are on board, and I would like to see your passenger list."

"For a damned impertinent, outrageous puppy, give me, or don't give me, a Yankee. You go back to your ship, young man, and tell her skipper that you couldn't accomplish your mission, because we wouldn't let ye. I deny your right of search. D'ye understand that?"

"I am sorry," quietly returned the officer, "to say I shall use force to carry out my orders, and, thanking you, sir, for your advice, I decline to return to the ship in any such a way as you propose."

The passengers, some forty or fifty in number, had gathered aft around the officer, and the crew also stood about. As Captain Moir made his assertion regarding the right of search the passengers applauded, and a young lady, whom I afterward learned was Miss Slidell, sprang on to a companion-way skylight, and said: "Quite right, captain; very right!"

Lieutenant Fairfax then came to the side of the ship to summon the boat crews, but the tones of the discussion had been highly pitched, and his call had a response before he made it. The blue jackets, twenty in number, and the marines, of whom there were ten, the former with cutlasses and pistols, and the marines with muskets and bayonets, sprung aft at once. A detachment was ordered to the lower deck, and the rest of the men formed in a line across the main deck, cutting off communication from abaft the main-mast to the forecastle. During this movement there appeared on the deck an officer, with a parrot-like voice, wearing the uniform of the Royal navy. Strutting up to Lieutenant Fairfax, he said: "I am the Queen's representative, sir, and I protest against this unwarrantable action under Her Majesty's flag, and on the deck of a British ship." The lieutenant paid no attention to this speech, delivered with great pomposity of manner, but turned to Captain Moir, and said: "You see I have force enough to carry out my orders;" and at this juncture Mr. Slidell and Mr. Mason came out of the cabin and stood in the crowd. Amid cries of "Piracy!" "Did you ever hear of such an outrage?" "They would not have dared to do it had there been an English man-of-war in sight!" Mr. Slidell stepped forward, and said: "Do you wish to see me?" and Mason, just beside him, echoed "to see me?" Mr. Fairfax vainly tried to induce them to accompany him to the "San Jacinto," and as they positively refused to go, he said: "Gentlemen, you may as well prepare to go at once, peaceably if you want to, but by force if necessary, for in twenty minutes you shall be on board that ship." The excitement was intense, and cries of "Shame!" from the passengers, in shrill crescendo, mingled with the stern tones of the boarding officers, as they ordered the men on guard at different points of the ship. In three minutes, Mason and Slidell, having the while stood hesitating before the cabin, turned and walked into their state-rooms. Mr.

Fairfax followed, and here he encountered an obstacle in the person of Miss Slidell who, filling the doorway, said: "Mr. Fairfax, I met you as a gentleman in Havana on Thursday. You outrage our hospitality by this proceeding, and I swear to heaven you shall not go into this cabin to my father." At this there was more excitement, and the passengers clustered in little groups, and spoke in loud tones. From where I stood I saw Mrs. Slidell approach the door and beg Mr. Fairfax to go away. He replied: "Madam, my orders are imperative. I shall obey them;" and just then Mr. Slidell began a most ungraceful movement out of the window of his cabin, which opened into a small gangway.

It was evident that Mr. Slidell was scared, perhaps excited is a better word, for his fingers twitched nervously, and for a minute or two he was unable to speak. Then Mr. Mason came out of his cabin, and Lieutenant Fairfax asked him if he was ready to go on board the "San Jacinto." Mason was cooler and more collected than his confrere, and replied with moderation in his tone: "No, sir; I decline to go with you." Fairfax, turning to his own officers, said: "Gentlemen, lay your hands on Mr. Mason," which we accordingly did. Mr. Mason then said: "I yield to force." Whereupon Commander Williams shouted: "Under protest, Mr. Mason, under protest." "Yes," said Mr. Mason, in the same tone as before, "precisely, under protest," and then walked down the companion ladder to the boat. Meanwhile, Mr. Slidell had recovered his equanimity to an extent which enabled him to say: "I will never go on board that ship." Mr. Fairfax took him by the collar, Engineer Houston and Boatswain Grace taking each one of his arms, marched him to the gangway; Miss Slidell in the meantime being in the enjoyment of an aggravated attack of hysterics. Other lady passengers were similarly occupied, while the gentlemen on board the ship had retreated in sullen silence to the taffrail, where they scowled defiance at the boarding party. There is no doubt in my mind that, had the Trent been an armed ship, she would have manifested a resistance of no small energy. The spirit prevailing on her decks may, without any stretch of truth, be called warlike. Captain Williams, Royal navy, who was in charge of the Central American and Mexican mails, now came out of his cabin, and passing to Mr. Charles B. Dahlgren, master's mate, handed him an unfolded paper, which Mr. Dahlgren declined to receive. Lieutenant Fairfax was on the lower deck, and Captain Williams, finding no officer who would accept the note, finally shoved it in his pocket; subsequently, it fluttered to the deck, and a marine stationed inside the cabin door secured it, and after reading handed it to me. I presented it to Captain Wilkes, but after a consultation we agreed that as the letter had no signature, and the manner in which it reached us was unofficial, that we would consider it as never having been written. Among my papers I found this redoubtable letter recently, and the following is an exact copy thereof:

> In this ship I am the representative of Her Majesty's Government, and I call upon the officers of the ship and passengers generally to mark my words, when, in the name of the British Government, and in distinct language, I denounce this an illegal act; an act in violation of international law; an act, indeed, of wanton piracy, which, had we the means of defense, you would not dare to attempt.

Mr. Eustis, one of the secretaries, was more violent than either of the principals, and made a demonstration in the direction of striking Lieutenant Greer with his fist. He passed into the boat *sans ceremonie*. McFarland had previously taken his seat alongside of Mr. Slidell in the stern-sheets of the boat. Our object having been accomplished, we bade the Trent good-bye, first bringing the personal effects of the prisoners to the "San Jacinto," and we were soon headed north, our mission in Bahama channel being *au fait accompli*.

We arrived at Port Royal too late to take part in the attack. Having been ordered home, on the 18th of November we steamed into the Narrows, where we were met by a steam tug, on board of which was the United States Marshal, with orders to proceed to Boston and deliver our prisoners at Fort Warren. We did not anchor until the 21st, and the cruise of the "San Jacinto" ended when we deposited the Confederate diplomats in the casements of that prison.

On the 3d of December, on the motion of Congressman Odell, Slidell and Mason were ordered into close confinement, in return for the treatment that Colonels Wood and Corcoran had received in Southern prisons. It was some time before the diplomatic correspondence that ensued between England, France, and the United States was made public. The United States agreed to release the prisoners, but declined to apologize to the English flag for an alleged offense where none was intended. Mason and Slidell joined their families in London in January, 1862, and their further actions passes out of the ken of the writer.

INDEX.

A

Abbeville, South Carolina, 560, 561, 567, 574, 575
Abbeville road, 575
Abercrombie's Brigade, 737
Abington, Virginia, 618
Abolitionists, 225, 227
Act of 1807, 220
Act of 1795, 220
Acton, Police Commissioner, 289, 296, 298, 300
Acton, Massachusetts, 781
Adairsville, Georgia, 333
Adams, James H., 320
Adams, Colonel John, 367
Adjutant General of the Army, 579, 711, 713
Adjutant General of the Cavalry, 134, 393, 527
Africa, 183, 794
African Church, 555
Agent of Exchange, 38, 40, 42, 45, 50, 51, 53, 57, 58, 186, 188
Aiken's Landing, Virginia, 34
Alabama, state of, 54, 70, 123, 152, 184, 185, 186, 189, 192, 411, 519, 542, 544, 563, 566, 569, 571, 614, 751, 778
Alabama (blockade runner), 30
Alabama River, 70
Albany, Georgia, 567, 571
Albany, New York, 287, 710
Albany *Evening Journal*, 405
Albany Penitentiary, 714
Albatross, U.S.S., 112
Albemarle Sound, 708
Aldie, Virginia, 146, 375, 377, 394, 451, 468, 481, 606
Alexander, Lt. Col. Andrew J., 139, 528, 568, 569, 570, 632
Alexander, General Edward P., 429, 430, 431, 441
Alexandria, Virginia, 27, 77, 80, 374, 403, 449, 599, 637, 666, 700, 733
Alger, Colonel Russell A., 475

"All Quiet Along the Potomac To-Night," 123
Allan, Colonel William, 724
Allatoona, Georgia, 334
Allegan, Michigan, 586
Allegheny Mountains, 225, 639, 724, 725, 726, 733
Alleghany Mountain Pass, 85
Alligator Creek, 573
Alston, Lt. Col. R. A., 54, 609, 766
Altoona Mountains, 570
Alvinzy, Baron Joseph, 735
Amelia Court-House, Virginia, 149, 339, 555
American Bible Society, 363
American Encyclopedia, 694
Ames, General Adelbert, 138, 140, 144, 233, 238, 239, 448
Amherst County, Virginia, 175
Amity Street, NYC, 291, 297
Anderson, General, 90
Anderson, Mrs. J. T., 770
Anderson, General James M., 787
Anderson, Colonel John T., 179, 770, 772
Anderson, General Joseph R., 179
Anderson, General Richard H., 196, 309, 313, 314, 420, 428, 429, 433, 435, 439, 495, 498, 699, 700, 703
Anderson, General Robert, 320, 321, 322, 323, 324, 325, 326, 327, 328, 329, 514
Anderson, Captain W. P., 713
Anderson's Battery, 85
Anderson's Brigade, 686, 695
Anderson's Crossroads, 368
Anderson's Division, 488, 493, 498, 700, 702
Andersonville, Ga., 45, 48, 49, 510
Andrew, Governor Albion, 231, 407, 412
Annals of The War, The, i, ii, iii, iv, 528
Annapolis, Maryland, 49, 230, 406, 408, 409, 412, 704, 793
Antietam, battle of, 384, 638
Antietam Creek, 456, 701, 702

Fort McAllister, 541
Fort McHenry, 789
Fort Mifflin, 720
Fort Morgan, 68
Fort Moultrie, 102, 107, 108, 109, 319,
320, 321, 322, 327, 514
Fort Pemberton, 111
Fort Richmond, 292, 293, 294, 295
Fort Schuyler, 292
Fort Stedman, 282
Fort Sumter, 17, 95, 96, 97, 99, 101,
102, 104, 107, 109, 163, 165, 319,
320, 321, 322, 323, 324, 325, 326,
327, 328, 406, 513, 514, 522, 523,
524, 525, 526, 615, 706, 775, 776
Fort Wagner, 96, 98, 99, 101, 102, 103,
104, 106, 110
Fort Warren, 43, 518, 800
Fortress Monroe, 23, 24, 26, 29, 30, 39,
43, 46, 53, 57, 68, 80, 126, 231, 233,
234, 354, 537, 578, 579, 583, 584,
588, 654, 714, 728
Forty-Eighth Virginia Infantry, 88
Forty-Fifth Street, (New York City),
290
Forty-Fourth Street, (New York City),
291
Forty-Seventh St., (New York City),
288
Forty-Sixth St., (New York City), 288,
289, 290, 299
Forty-Third St., (New York City), 291
forty-two pounders, 514, 525
"Fountain Rock," 181
Four Years in the Saddle, 773
Fourteenth Alabama Infantry, 335
Fourteenth Army Corps, 334
Fourteenth Illinois Cavalry, 753, 759,
760
Fourteenth St., (New York City), 297
Fourth Army Corps, 334
Fourth Avenue, (New York City), 300
Fourth Brigade, 681, 682, 685, 691
Fourth Michigan Cavalry, 570, 574,
576, 577, 578, 580, 582, 584
Fourth of July, 65, 247, 287, 293, 316,
350, 456, 529, 531, 593, 766
Fourth Pennsylvania Cavalry, 471
Fourth Virginia Brigade, 195
Fourth Virginia Cavalry, 393, 395, 396,
400, 593, 594, 596, 603, 606, 607,
608, 610, 611
Fourth West Virginia Cavalry, 187
Fowler, Robert, 407

Fox, Assistant Navy Secretary Gustavus
V., 23, 24, 26, 325, 718, 719, 722
France, 120, 164, 166, 227, 457, 644,
689, 794, 800
Franklin, Chief Benjamin, 720
Franklin, Captain Walter S., 292, 294,
299
Franklin, Major General William B.,
72, 79, 637, 638
Franklin, Virginia, 736, 737, 739, 748
Franklin County, Tennessee, 614, 615
Frazier's Farm, 698
Frederick, Maryland, 62, 146, 207, 318,
378, 409, 419, 439, 447, 451, 452,
453, 455, 607, 646, 652, 726
Frederick the Great, 459, 648, 693
Fredericksburg, Virginia, 137, 201, 203,
205, 206, 305, 391, 417, 418, 421,
433, 447, 448, 457, 487, 488, 596,
603, 604, 609, 638, 674, 702, 735,
737, 739, 740, 748
Fredericksburg, battle of, 61, 194, 213,
257, 390, 415, 638, 666, 667, 673
Fredericksburg Railroad, 739
Free Masonry, 565, 611
Freemantle, Colonel, 206, 432, 440, 626
Frémont, General John C., 169, 648,
649, 698, 733, 735, 736, 739, 740,
741, 742, 743, 744, 745, 746, 747,
748, 749
French, General William H., 259, 317,
318
French's Division, 258, 259
Fritchie, Barbara, 652
Froissart, Jean, 69
Front St., (Cincinnati), 768
Front Royal, Virginia, 306, 656, 657,
737, 738, 739, 740, 741, 742, 743,
747, 748, 749
Front Royal Pike, 662, 663, 738
Frothingham, Lt. Colonel, 297
Fry, Colonel, 359
Fulkerson's Brigade, 729, 732
Fulkerson's Virginia Regiment, 85, 729

G

Gaines' Mill, Virginia, 198, 202, 697
Gainesville, Alabama, 119
Gainesville, Virginia, 599
Galaxy, 521
Gardner, General Franklin, 115
Garfield, General James A., 689
Garibaldi Guard, 711
Garnett, Muscoe R. H., 222

683, 686, 688, 689, 690, 691, 692,
703, 750, 751, 752
Grant's army, 416, 465, 610, 692, 703
Gray, Colonel, 475
Great Kanawha River, 725
Greble, Edward, 233
Greeley, Horace, 203, 299, 302, 409
Green, Dr., 56
Green River, 247, 753, 754, 765
Green's Brigade, 112
Green's house, 400
Greenbrier County, Virginia, 176, 177
Greenbrier River, 85, 86, 91, 94
Greencastle, Pennsylvania, 639
Greene, General Nathanael, 138
Greene, General George, 213, 622
Greensboro, North Carolina, 152, 559
Greeneville, Tennessee, 616, 617, 618
Greenwood, Pennsylvania, 420
Greer, Lieutenant James A., 795, 796,
797, 800
Gregg, General David McM., 134, 141,
142, 143, 372, 374, 375, 376, 393,
394, 395, 397, 398, 402, 403, 448,
449, 450, 451, 468, 469, 470, 471,
473, 474, 475, 476, 478, 480, 481,
483, 484, 527, 528, 529, 532, 533,
534, 535, 612
Gregg, General John I., 112, 215, 377,
378, 471
Gregg's Brigade, 377, 378, 475, 478,
527, 695, 702
Gregg's Cavalry, 138, 469, 470, 488,
489, 527, 612
Gregg's Division, 135, 375, 376, 377,
378, 399, 400, 456, 469, 471, 534
Gregory, Edward S., 111
Grenada, Mississippi, 465
Griffin, General Charles, 489, 490
Griffin, Georgia, 570
Griffin's Division, 489, 490, 494
Griffith, Mississippi, 182
Griffith, Patrick, 785
Grimes, Senator James W., 718
Griswold, John A., 21, 22
Groveton, Virginia, 600
Gulf Coast, 229, 569, 570, 658
Gurley, Captain, 767

H
Hagerstown, Maryland, 394, 419, 772
"Hail Columbia," 69
Haines, Bluff, 112, 115
Hale, Anthony "Tony," 720, 721

Hale, Senator John Parker, 719
Hall, Lieutenant Robert M., 322
Hall, Thomas W. Jr., 786
Halleck, Gen. Henry W., 76, 318, 463,
627, 678, 680, 683, 751
Halltown, Virginia, 741
Hamburg, Tennessee, 684
Hamilton, Captain, 522, 523
Hamilton, Ohio, 45, 251, 252
Hamilton and Dayton Railroad, 251
Hamilton Easter & Co., 512
Hamilton's Crossing, 489
Hamlet, 459
Hammond's Mill, West Virginia, 772
Hampden-Sidney College, 194
Hampshire County, Virginia, 725
Hampton, Lieutenant Colonel Frank,
400
Hampton, General Wade, 135, 354,
355, 393, 394, 396, 399, 400, 401,
481, 482, 483, 530, 531, 539, 602,
610, 645
Hampton's Brigade, 394, 395, 399, 401,
402, 473, 474, 475, 478, 530
Hampton's "Cattle Raid," 394
Hampton's Division, 608
Hampton Roads, Virginia, 20, 21, 22,
23, 24, 26, 29, 230, 231, 232, 233,
234, 239, 523, 584
Hancock, General Winfield Scott, 65,
208, 210, 211, 212, 214, 259, 277,
427, 436, 454, 488, 491, 494, 495,
497, 498, 622, 624, 632, 703, 727
Hancock, Maryland, 771, 773
Hancock, Virginia, 725
Haner, Private George, 201
Hankinson's Ferry, 112, 128
Hanover, Pennsylvania, 607
Hanover Court House, Virginia, 595,
596, 696
Hanover Junction, Virginia, 378, 453,
471, 493, 607
Hanover Road, 476
Hanson, Lt. Col. Charles H., 54, 753
Hanson, Lieutenant William H., 636
Hard Times, Louisiana, 112
Hardee, General William J., 335, 683,
685, 686
Hardee's Corps, 333, 338
Hardie, General James A., 207
Hardy County, Virginia, 612
Harlem, New York, 303
Harman, Colonel, 398